California
Real Estate
Principles

10.1 Edition

Brady · Estes · McKenzie

OnCourse Learning

California Real Estate Principles, 10.1 Edition

**Mary Ellen Brady, Edwin Estes, Jr.,
and Dennis J. McKenzie**

Vice President, Real Estate Product Management: Eric Solecki

Executive Editor: Sara Glassmeyer

Project Manager: Arlin Kauffman,
LEAP Publishing Services

Product Specialist: Abby Franklin

Education Manager: Sherry Steele

Art and Cover Composition: Chris Dailey

Cover Image: © olivierpieri

For product information and technology assistance, contact us at
OnCourse Learning and Sales Support, 1-855-733-7239.
For permission to use material from this text or product.

Library of Congress Control Number: 2014960057
ISBN-13: 978-1-62980-179-7
ISBN-10: 1-62980-179-8

OnCourse Learning
3100 Cumberland Blvd, Suite 1450
Atlanta, GA 30339
USA

Visit us at **www.oncoursepublishing.com**

Printed in the United States of America
1 2 3 4 5 6 7 18 17 16

California Real Estate Principles

BRIEF CONTENTS

CONTENTS

INTRODUCTION

While students reading this text for the first time will not notice the changes in this edition, instructors who have taught from previous editions of this text will notice a number of changes. Our chapter covering: *A Career in Real Estate*, has been moved to the front of the book. As fellow real estate professors, we have noticed a number of questions from our students at Cerritos and Mt. San Antonio Colleges on the licensing process early during the semester. Rather than divert time away from the lesson at hand, we thought better to cover the licensing process at the beginning of the text.

You will also notice that there is no chapter devoted solely to mathematics. Over the past several years, we have noticed the Bureau of Real Estate placing a lesser emphasis on mathematics, with many of our former students reporting only one or even no math questions on the State Exam. Reflecting the Bureau's practice, we have moved the math material to the Appendix which still allows instructors and students to study mathematics. Replacing the mathematics chapter is a chapter devoted to disclosures. In our previous textbook, disclosures and contracts shared a chapter. However, realizing that about half of the questions on the Real Estate Exam are devoted to agency, contracts and disclosures, we felt disclosures and contracts deserved their own separate chapters; we hope you agree.

We thought it important that the subjects of agency, disclosures and contracts be sequential in the text, since there is considerable overlap on this topics. This required a certain amount of chapter reorganization. We understand this may be a little uncomfortable at first for instructors who have adopted earlier editions, but we hope you agree this edition to be superior.

We invite your comments on the 10th Edition and are always looking to improve this textbook. Your suggestions are welcome and we invited you to contact us through our publisher.

PREFACE

The revision of this California Real Estate Principles text was a collaborative effort. The authors worked in conjunction with real estate agents and attorneys as well as a number of instructors from both community colleges and real estate schools. The most up-to-date information was researched and applied so students will be able to utilize their knowledge from this book for the California Bureau of Real Estate (CalBRE) state license examination.

This informative text will assist the student in preparing for the California real estate state examination using the various practice test questions contained within this book.

NEW TO THIS EDITION

This edition has been updated to reflect the latest legislative changes. Examples, Student Learning Outcomes, and Reviewing Your Understanding questions have been updated throughout. We have reorganized the order and materials for this textbook to keep up with changes in the real estate profession and the California Real Estate State Sales and Brokers' examinations. One change that will jump out for many instructors is that we do not have a chapter devoted to mathematics. The reason for this is that the California Bureau of Real Estate has drastically reduced the number of math questions on the state exam. The math material that some authors include in a separate chapter has been reallocated to those chapters that pertain to the corresponding substantive chapters. Calculations involving interest will be found in the finance chapter, and those involving valuating properties will be found in the appraisal chapter. We think this will be easier for students to learn the material and provide instructors with a more fluid instruction process. For further information on the licensing process beyond what is covered in this text, please access the California Bureau of Real Estate (CalBRE) website at http://www.bre.ca.gov/. More specifically, changes include:

Chapter 1: A Career in Real Estate and the California Bureau of Real Estate License Examination Requirements

Added new requirements regarding experience and education for a broker's license. Added breakdown of courses required for continuing education for broker and salesperson. Updated changes to the CalBRE Summary. Updated statistics regarding number of real estate licensees. Updated CE information.

Chapter 2: Introduction to Real Estate

Clarified the difference between the terms real property and real estate.

Chapter 3: Real Estate Agency

Clarified agency creation. Clarified the establishment of real estate agencies.

Chapter 4: Real Estate Disclosures

Separated disclosures discussion from the Contracts chapter to create a new chapter. Expanded discussion of Seller's disclosure obligations. Expanded explanation of the Transfer Disclosure Statement

Agents' disclosure obligations. Expanded explanation of the Agents Visual Inspection Disclosure Statement. Created a discussion of Supplemental Statutory Disclosures: Lead Based Paint, Stigmatized Properties, Military Ordinances, Industrial Uses, Controlled Substances, Water Heater Bracing, Smoke Alarms and Carbon Monoxide Detectors. Explained Natural Hazard Disclosure Statement.

Chapter 5: Real Estate Contracts

Expanded discussion of the various listing agreements. Fully explained the terms of the CAR Purchase Agreement. Explained the difference between a single and multiple counter offer.

Chapter 6: Legal Descriptions, Methods of Acquiring Title, and Deeds

Clarified the elements of intestate succession. Elaborated on Freehold estates. Clarified same sex marriages and registered domestic partners.

Chapter 7: Encumbrances, Liens, and Homesteads

Clarified the creation of easements.

Chapter 8: Introduction to Real Estate Finance

Added reference to 1003 form in Appendix. Added information to loan analysis. Added lender's reasons for using ARMs. Added the Equal Opportunity Act is a federal law. Added the Real Property Loan Law applies to California properties. Loan terms to the chapter.

Chapter 9: Lenders

Part I: Real Estate Lenders

Changed write-offs to charge-offs. Added examples of REITs. Moved qualify for a REIT from Credit Unions paragraph to REIT paragraph.

Part II: FHA, VA, and Cal-Vet Loans and the Secondary Mortgage Market

Explained the reason for MIP. Updated information on MIP up-front fees. Updated dates for loan amounts for FHA loans. Region to region has been changed to county to county. Updated dates and eligibility regarding VA loans. Provided additional information regarding who is eligible for Cal-Vet loans. Updated information for thirty-year, fixed-rate conventional loan program. Added information regarding the Secondary Mortgage Market Financial Crisis.

Chapter 10: Real Estate Appraisal

Changed name of Office of Real Estate Appraisers (OREA) to Bureau of Real Estate Appraisers (BREA) throughout chapter. Basic appraisal categories of licensing/certification and education updated to reflect changes as of January 1, 2015. Expanded information related to Professional Designations. Explained in more detail the Home Valuation Code of Conduct (HVCC). Appraisal Methods is to be Appraisal Reports. 2014/2015 revisions of USPAP now included under Appraisal Reports with an explanation of those reports.

Chapter 11: The Role of Escrow and Title Insurance Companies

Identified "Civil Code" as "California Civil Code Section 1057." Updated Regulations of Escrow Holders. Department of Corporations is now Department of Business Oversight as of July 2013. Added information regarding services performed by escrow company. Under Escrow and RESPA added a "Mortgage Service Disclosure Statement" to be included with the other documents required to be furnished to borrower. Under Escrows Summarized added an explanation regarding attorneys handling escrows. Proration section from former chapter 6 added to this chapter. Documentary Transfer Tax section from chapter 6 added to this chapter. Under Nonrecurring Closing Costs Usually Paid by the Buyer changed "cost of appraisal from $350 or more" to "$350–450 or more."

Chapter 14: Taxation

Updated dates under "Real Property Tax Dates." Updated "Exemptions for Senior Citizens." Changed 3 1/3 to 3.33 under "Special Withholding Rules for Foreign and Out-of-State Sellers. Under "Gift Taxes" added new updates as of January 2014.

Appendix A: The State Exam

Updated examination weightings as of September 2015. Updated locations for examinations offered in electronic format. "Notification of Exam Results" for salesperson and broker examinees updated. Broker experience/education requirements updated. Updated directions regarding taking the Real Estate Principles practice exam.

Appendix B: Math

Math has been moved out of the main text to the appendix, so students have a single place to look for all formulas and real estate math.

Global Changes: Vocabulary and terms surrounding real estate principles have grown with the alphabet soup of the new regulations. While the principles language can at first seem complicated, as you progress through the chapters, you will find that the text makes them easier to understand. The glossary will add to your understanding and is a great asset when you need to check the meaning of a word or term.

Each chapter in the book is self-contained, allowing instructors to adapt the book to various course formats. Instructors and students alike will appreciate the practical application and multiple-choice questions—both designed for testing, learning, and review of the material covered in each chapter.

SUPPLEMENTS

Instructors who adopt this textbook receive access to an instructor's manual written by the authors. Each chapter is supported with chapter objectives, a suggested lesson plan, a 10-question review quiz of the previous chapter, and a 30-question chapter quiz and test for checking student understanding of the material. The manual also provides three exams: an exam covering Chapters 1 through 5, Chapters 6 through 10, and Chapters 11 through 15 that consists of 100 four-part multiple-choice questions; the final exam covers the entire book and includes 100 four-part multiple-choice questions, including answers.

Classroom PowerPoint® presentation slides also support each chapter by outlining learning objectives, emphasizing key concepts, and highlighting real-world applications to help further engage learners and generate classroom discussion. These instructional support materials are available online only to adopters from the text companion site www.oncoursepublishing.com.

This text may also be integrated with the *Instructor Guide* and *Student Study Guide* published by the California Community College Real Estate Education Center.

ACKNOWLEDGMENTS

Any book, in its final form, is the result of the time and talents of many individuals. While we cannot acknowledge all of the contributors, we are grateful for their review of information, their insights, and their suggestions—all of which have enhanced this edition. We hope that we have successfully included the information that they so generously provided.

We would also like to express our appreciation to those who served as reviewers and who provided insightful comments and valuable suggestions: Shad Jefferies, *San Diego Mesa College*; Timothy R. Durfield, *Citrus College*; Mary Ann Zamel, *Mt. San Antonio College*; Jill Carter, *West Los Angeles College*; Ray Solis, *Mira Costa College*; and Joan Brunswick, *Laney College*.

ABOUT THE AUTHORS

Mary Ellen Brady has been a successful California real estate broker and real estate salesperson for over twenty years. She is the owner of her own real estate company in addition to being the Real Estate Department chair and teaching at Cerritos College.

In 1993, 1996, and 1997, Ms. Brady was named the REALTOR® of the Year by the Downey Association of REALTORS®. She was President of the Women's Council of REALTORS® in 1997 and President of the Downey Association of REALTORS® in 1998. She has functioned as president and chair for many prestigious boards throughout the years. She received the impressive Norm Woest Award for her contributions to real estate education from the California Real Estate Educator's Association in 2007.

In addition to obtaining her Graduate REALTOR® Institute (GRI) designation, Mary Ellen has also acquired her e-PRO, NAHREP Certified Professional, and Senior Real Estate Specialist (SRES) designations. She has participated in negotiation and mediation training in association with the Pepperdine University School of Law, Straus Institute for Dispute Resolution.

Edwin Estes received his Bachelor of Arts degree from the University of Southern California and his Juris Doctorate degree from the Pepperdine University School of Law. A real estate licensee since 1976, he received his California broker's license in 1984 and has been a member of the California State Bar since 1983. Since that time, he has been active in real estate brokerage management, counseling, development, and investment brokerage. He is a former arbitrator for the American Arbitration Association and has served as a judge pro tem for the California Superior Court.

Professor Estes has been teaching Graduate REALTOR® Institute (GRI) classes as a master instructor for the California Association of REALTORS® since 1991; in addition to obtaining the real estate designations of Certified Commercial Investment Member (CCIM), Certified Real Estate Brokerage Manager (CRB), Graduate REALTORS Institute (GRI), Accredited Buyer Representative (ABR),

Accredited Buyer Representative Manager (ABRM), e-PRO, and Senior Real Estate Specialist (SRES), he is also an accomplished community college instructor, and serves as the Real Estate Program Coordinator for Mt. San Antonio College.

Mary Ellen Brady
Edwin Estes Jr., Esq.

DEDICATION

Dennis McKenzie was the original author of this textbook. Born on April 22, 1940, Dennis passed away on June 13, 2008. Holding two Masters Degrees (MBA and MA) in Business and Economics from Humboldt State University, Dennis was a gifted author and lecturer who will be long remembered for his contributions to the real estate profession. He began his teaching career at the College of the Redwoods in 1970 and retired from teaching in 2008. In addition to teaching seminars at the University of Southern California, Dennis taught real estate continuing education statewide in California as well as authoring numerous books on the subject of real estate, finance and economics. Dennis was the recipient of the Teacher of the Year Award from the California Real Estate Educators' Association as well as an educational consultant to the California Bureau (then Department) of Real Estate. This updated and revised textbook is devoted to Dennis McKenzie and the co-authors will forever remember his contributions to the real estate profession.

A career in real estate can be an exciting opportunity for certain people. The various job opportunities within the real estate industry may offer greater potential for movement and advancement than other areas of employment. Real estate is a people-oriented industry. Real estate professionals help or assist customers and clients to achieve their housing financial and investment goals. Thus, a career in real estate can lead to a wide range of employment activities from the entry-level position of sales agent to the role of the real estate broker/owner. However, there are pitfalls to consider! Not everyone can succeed in real estate. It is not to be viewed as a get-rich-quick industry. Success requires dedication and hard work.

STUDENT LEARNING OUTCOMES

At the conclusion of this chapter, you will be able to do the following:

- Describe the major career choices in the real estate industry.
- List the requirements for becoming a licensed real estate salesperson or broker.
- Examine personal questions to consider before becoming a real estate agent.
- Explain special issues for real estate licensees who wish to sell business opportunities.

A CAREER IN REAL ESTATE AND THE CALIFORNIA BUREAU OF REAL ESTATE LICENSE EXAMINATION REQUIREMENTS

1.1 STRUCTURE OF THE REAL ESTATE INDUSTRY

Although this chapter focuses on the rules for obtaining a real estate license, anyone interested in a career in real estate should recognize the diversity of the industry. In addition to acting as an agent for the buying and selling of properties, a person seeking a career in real estate could pursue many other activities. Real estate-oriented people are needed in the areas of construction, financing, escrow, appraising, property management, land development, and other related specialties. Each of these areas offers opportunities for well-trained people. Some of these specialties require a real estate license, whereas others require a different license or no license at all.

Real Estate Agents

The potential as a real estate sales agent is unlimited. A variety of opportunities exist as a result of the growing U.S. population and the continued expansion of the nation's economy. As a consequence, real estate agents are needed to assist people who wish to buy, sell, or develop real estate.

A real estate salesperson's license qualifies him or her to work for a real estate broker as a real estate agent. Although a new licensee may be considered an expert in the eyes of the public and the law, most new agents soon realize that additional training and education are necessary in order to satisfy the public's expectations.

As a salesperson gains experience, he or she may entertain the idea of becoming a real estate broker. Brokers can own and operate a business. A real estate salesperson cannot solely operate a real estate firm; he or she must be affiliated with a broker. Additionally, in all cases salespeople may only receive payment from their broker.

A real estate brokerage company may handle all kinds of properties, or it may specialize in just residential, commercial, industrial, farm, or vacant land sales. Some real estate brokers may choose to become consultants and work on a fee-per-hour basis rather than be paid a sales commission.

Although the field of real estate is complex, anyone interested in a career has boundless opportunities for personal satisfaction as well as the potential to earn an above-average income. Anyone who plans to enter the field of real estate must remember that experience, education, integrity, and resourcefulness are the key characteristics that the public expects to see in real estate agents.

However, success will not be easy. Real estate is a competitive business, and the failure and turnover rates for new licensees are very high. Several reasons for failure are discussed in detail later in this chapter.

Real Estate Trade Associations

People who choose real estate as a career quickly become aware of real estate trade associations. The largest is the **National Association of REALTORS® (NAR)**, which is identified by the symbol REALTOR®. The National Association of REALTORS® owns the nationally recognized designation REALTOR®. Only members of the National Association of REALTORS® can use the term REALTOR®. In California, the unauthorized use of the term REALTOR® constitutes a violation of California Bureau of Real Estate (CalBRE) regulations.

The National Association of REALTORS® is broken down into state associations, each of which provides services to its state members. The **California Association of REALTORS® (CAR)** is the state-affiliated group that provides services for California members. The major objectives of the California Association of REALTORS®, as set forth in its constitution, are as follows:

1. To unite its members
2. To promote high standards
3. To safeguard the land-buying public
4. To foster legislation for the benefit and protection of real estate
5. To cooperate in the economic growth and development of the state

The California Association of REALTORS® is, in turn, divided into numerous local groups called the Association of REALTORS® or Boards of REALTORS®. Local associations are usually broken down by cities or counties.

The main thrust of **REALTOR®** trade groups is to provide information and education for their members and to pursue political agendas that are favorable to real estate ownership. This is achieved using publications, seminars, state-national-international conventions, videos, CDs, online information, and various training sessions. Additional advantages of association membership include the substantial savings on insurance and other health benefits through group rates.

Another national real estate organization is the National Association of Real Estate Brokers. This trade association was formed in 1947 and consists of predominantly African-American real estate brokers whose members are called **REALTISTS®**. This organization has several state chapters and local boards throughout the United States.

A REALTIST® must be a member of both a local board and the national organization. REALTISTS® are working for better housing for the communities they serve on national and international bases. In many cases, individuals are both REALTORS® and REALTISTS® by virtue of voluntary dual membership.

Professional Designations and Code of Ethics

If an agent wishes to specialize in a particular aspect of real estate, trade associations provide advanced training that can lead to certified designations. Once earned, these professional designations allow designees to enjoy a national recognition and usually earn a higher income.

Virtually all trade associations have a code of ethics for their members. Violation of the code of ethics could lead to grounds for dismissal from the group and the loss of membership benefits.

Other Real Estate Employment

In addition to sales jobs, real estate-trained salaried positions may be available as a loan officer, an appraiser, an escrow officer, or a title officer. These salaried jobs are with financial institutions, appraisal companies, escrow companies, title companies, and some government agencies. Real estate developers and contractors frequently hire salaried personnel with a real estate background.

Additional opportunities for real estate students may exist in local, state, and federal governments. These include a variety of occupational levels, such as right-of-way agents, appraisers, leasing negotiators, planners, and Housing and Urban Development (HUD) housing program staff.

1.2 LICENSE REQUIREMENTS AND COMPETITION

Real Estate Salespersons

The current requirements to become a real estate salesperson are as follows:

1. Must be at least 18 years of age and provide proof of legal presence.
2. Conviction of a crime that is a felony or that involves moral turpitude may result in the denial of a license.

3. All sales license applicants must complete three college level courses prescribed by the California Bureau of Real Estate (CalBRE): Real Estate Principles, Real Estate Practice, and a third class approved by CalBRE, such as Real Estate Finance, Real Estate Appraisal, Legal Aspects of Real Estate, Real Estate Economics, Business Law, Accounting, or another real estate-related course approved by the Real Estate Commissioner before being allowed to take the real estate sales license examination. These courses can be taken at an accredited college or through a CalBRE-approved vocational school.

4. Must be able to pass the state examination consisting of 150 multiple-choice questions within a three and fifteen minute time period. A passing score is 105 or more correct answers, which represents 70 percent and up. The salesperson's examination is given as needed at designated locations in California, usually Oakland, Los Angeles, San Diego, Sacramento, and Fresno. The examination is difficult; a failure rate of 50 percent or more is common.

5. Upon completion of the examination, one must submit the required license fee on an approved application form along with a set of classifiable fingerprints. Applicants who fail may apply immediately to retake the exam.

Real Estate Brokers

Current requirements to become a real estate broker are as follows:

1. Must be at least 18 years of age and provide proof of legal presence.

2. Conviction of a crime that is a felony or that involves moral turpitude may result in the denial of a license.

3. Must complete at least eight approved real estate courses.
   The following five courses must be taken:

   a. Real Estate Practice

   b. Legal Aspects of Real Estate

   c. Real Estate Finance

   d. Real Estate Appraisal

   e. Real Estate Economics or Accounting

   Any three of the following courses must also be taken, for a total of eight courses, or another approved advanced real estate course:

   a. Real Estate Office Administration

   b. Escrow

   c. Mortgage Loan Brokering

   d. Real Estate Computer Applications

    e. Common Interest Development

    f. Real Estate Principles

    g. Property Management

    h. Business Law

       The courses must be taken through an accredited college or at a private vocational school approved by the real estate commissioner.

4. Must complete the experience requirements that consist of two years' full-time experience, within the last five years, as a real estate salesperson or its equivalent. *Equivalent* is experience in an allied field such as title, escrow, or finance. Equivalence can, in some cases, include education in lieu of experience, such as an accredited college degree, in real estate as a major or minor. This may be verified by submitting a copy of the degree earned.

5. Must pass the state examination consisting of 200 multiple-choice questions within five hours with a score of 150 or more correct answers, which represents a score of 75 percent or better. The test for the broker's license is more difficult than the salesperson's examination, and the failure rate is frequently high, averaging approximately 50 percent.

6. Must complete the license application and pay the proper fee.

7. The broker's examination is given monthly (or more often depending on demand) at the locations mentioned earlier for the sales examination.

    Real estate licensees are allowed to sell business opportunities as well as real estate. See Section 1.4 of this chapter for details regarding business opportunities.

State Examination

For a detailed explanation of the state real estate examination and official CalBRE instructions, see Appendix A. Also, a complete 150-question practice examination, including answers, in a format similar to the sales examination, is presented for your review in Appendix A.

Continuing Education Requirements

Real Estate Sales License

During a new real estate sales licensee's first four years, he or she must take the following five separate three-hour CalBRE-approved courses for a total of 15 hours of continuing education.

1. Ethics
2. Agency
3. Fair Housing
4. Trust Fund Handling
5. Risk Management

Once a real estate sales licensee completes the first renewal, any subsequent sales license renewal will require 45 hours of CalBRE-approved continuing education, with 18 hours mandated to be in Consumer Protection. After the first renewal of a sales license, an eight-hour combined survey course covering update issues on ethics, agency, fair housing, trust fund handling, and risk management can be taken. The remaining hours beyond the combined survey course can be CalBRE-approved continuing education courses of the sales licensee's choosing as long as said courses do not exceed the current CalBRE allotment of consumer service courses. See the CalBRE website at www.bre.ca.gov for the current allotment.

Real Estate Broker's License

During a new real estate broker licensee's first four years, he or she must take 45 hours of CalBRE-approved continuing education, which must include these six separate three-hour CalBRE-approved courses for a total of 18 hours of the required 45 hours, with 18 hours mandated in Consumer Protection:

1. Ethics
2. Agency
3. Fair Housing
4. Trust Fund Handling
5. Risk Management
6. Management & Supervision

The remaining 27 hours for a total of 45 hours can be CalBRE-approved continuing education courses of the broker's choosing so long as said courses do not exceed the current CalBRE allotment of consumer service courses. See the CalBRE website at www.bre.ca.gov for the current allotment.

Once a real estate broker licensee completes his or her first renewal, any subsequent broker license renewal will require 45 hours of CalBRE-approved continuing education. After the first renewal of a broker's license, an eight-hour combined survey course covering update issues on ethics, agency, fair housing, trust fund handling, risk management, and management & supervision can be taken. The remaining hours beyond the combined survey course can be CalBRE-approved continuing education courses of the licensee's choosing so long as said courses do not exceed the current CalBRE allotment of consumer service courses. See the CalBRE website at www.bre.ca.gov for the current allotment.

The CalBRE

The mission of the California Bureau of Real Estate (CalBRE) is to safeguard and promote the public interests in real estate matters through licensure, regulation, education, and enforcement. Here are some key points.

1. The California **real estate commissioner** is appointed by the governor and serves as the chief executive of the CalBRE.

2. The commissioner administers the Real Estate Law and issues regulations that have the force of law and become part of the California Administrative Procedures Code.

3. The commissioner and members of the bureau screen applicants for licenses and investigate complaints against licensees. After a proper hearing, if a licensee has violated a law or regulation, the commissioner can restrict, suspend, or revoke a real estate license.
   Restricted license: allows licensee to continue to work, but under limited conditions
   Suspended license: a temporary loss of license
   Revoked license: a loss of license
   Once a real estate broker's license is suspended or revoked, any salesperson working under said broker's license must cease working for that broker. Any commissions earned by the salesperson prior to the date of the broker's suspension or revocation are allowed to be paid to the salesperson.

4. A real estate license is required when a person performs a real estate act for another for compensation. The compensation may be in the form of a commission, a fee, a salary, or anything of value. The following exceptions do not need a real estate license:
   a. Principal handling his or her own affairs
   b. Attorney in fact acting under a power of attorney
   c. Appraiser (needs special license not issued by the CalBRE, but rather issued by the Office of Real Estate Appraisers)
   d. Attorney at law (lawyer) while performing duties as an attorney (if the attorney charges a fee as a broker, a real estate license is required)

    e. Trustee selling under a deed of trust

    f. Residential on-site property manager (a full-service off-site property manager must have a real estate license)

5. As of January 2009, the fine for an unlicensed person who receives an illegal commission is up to $20,000 and a maximum of six months in jail for an individual and up to $60,000 for a corporation. The fine for paying a commission to an unlicensed person is $100.

6. Fictitious business names: A licensed broker, corporation, or partnership may operate under a fictitious name (DBA, or *Doing Business As*) if the name is approved by the commissioner.

7. A corporate real estate license requires an officer to be licensed as a broker. A partnership real estate license requires one partner to be licensed as a broker. A real estate salesperson and a broker can form a real estate brokerage partnership.

8. Prepaid rental-listing license: A special license issued for a two-year period that allows a licensee to collect a fee for supplying a prospective tenant with a list of available rentals. This does not allow the licensee to negotiate rental contracts or perform any other real estate activity. Real estate brokers can collect a prepaid fee without a special license if done at their regular place of business.

How Real Estate Agents Earn Income

The majority of real estate professionals earn their income solely from commissions on sales or leases. This means if the broker or salesperson does not sell or lease a property, there is no income. In addition, once a purchase contract is created it takes from 45 to 60 days to close escrow. Real estate professionals must have a number of sales always in the pipeline to maintain a monthly income.

Salespersons in California are required to work under a broker. The brokerage firm will either charge a percentage of the commission, a desk fee each month, or a combination. Additionally, the sales person must withhold his or her own income taxes from any fees earned. A commission of $10,000 with a brokerage fee of 40% leaves the salesperson $6,000 to pay taxes, health insurance, and other business and personal costs. Additionally, all commissions are negotiable fees and vary from each transaction. This means those who make a living from real estate sales must have a good strategy in place to succeed.

How About a Part-Time Real Estate Job?

Many potential licensees hope to work part time until their sales volume supports full-time employment. In some cases, brokers do hire part-time salespeople with the expectation that they will eventually become full-time agents. Brokers agree that a great amount of time and resources go into training a part-time salesperson. Many brokers want new salespeople to commit to becoming full-time agents in the future. The part-time agent is usually not as successful as fully committed salespeople.

Working Hours and Fringe Benefits

The person who decides to enter real estate on a full-time basis initially faces the prospect of long hours, including evenings and weekends. Evenings and weekends are the only hours some prospective buyers and sellers have free to discuss their real estate needs.

In addition, the fringe benefits that often come with other jobs may not exist. For example, paid vacations, insurance benefits, or retirement funds are not common in the real estate business. If a real estate salesperson wants these items, he or she usually must pay for them out of his or her own earnings. If fringe benefits are of overriding concern, a prospective salesperson should explore these areas of question prior to joining a particular firm.

Realistic Picture

Real estate sales and related activities can offer unlimited opportunities for motivated individuals. Perseverance and hard work, coupled with good training and additional educational coursework, can help a person become financially independent and provide a valuable service for the public. Real estate is not a get-rich-quick business; it takes work and a willingness to be helpful and understanding.

1.3 PERSONAL PREPARATION TO ENTER THE REAL ESTATE INDUSTRY

Some people enter real estate sales with unrealistic expectations for earnings that do not materialize, which results in a negative employment experience. If possible, a prospective licensee should meet with a real estate instructor or career counselor and an experienced real estate broker and discuss what it takes to succeed in the local real estate market. Some community colleges offer an internship program, where students work in a local real estate office while taking real estate courses.

Personal Checklist

1. If at all possible, an interest inventory test, such as the Strong Inventory Test, should be taken. These tests indicate a person's interests and what vocations are suited to these interests. These tests are available at most local community colleges. Call the college's registrar, student services office, or assessment center for information.

2. If the local college has a career center, check with a counselor to verify which real estate courses are required. A call to a CalBRE-approved private vocational school can provide the same information. Many are listed in the telephone book or online. Be sure to discuss (or research online) the cost for textbooks, registration fees, matriculation requirements, and class hours, as well as the total scope of real estate course offerings.

3. Once the arrangements for a course of study have been established, it is a good idea to check the local real estate employment market. The executive officers of local real estate associations and boards can give indications of the sales activities in the local area. These indicators might include a list of the number of real estate salespeople, listings and sales activities, and average dollar volume of business. The real estate sections of many local newspapers also publish these statistics.

4. Select an area where you might like to work, and survey the real estate offices within this territory. Visit several offices and take a look around. Although a brief look does not indicate the success of a real estate company, it does give some important first impressions.

5. Check local newspaper real estate advertisements to determine which real estate offices are working which neighborhoods.

6. Try to narrow the real estate office choices to one to five offices, and attempt to identify the personnel within these offices. If possible, make an appointment with an employed salesperson to discuss the activities within each office. This can provide valuable facts concerning management, number of employees, rapport, and so on. Many times, the decision to attempt to join a firm is made at this time.

7. Once the selection process is narrowed, an appointment should be made for an interview with the owner-broker or the personnel manager.

    To assure a more informative interview, write down some specific questions to ask. The list should include questions regarding the existing number of salespeople, support personnel, training programs, commission splits, advertising and listing policies, employee-independent contractor arrangements, commission ratios once certain sales quotas have been reached, personal costs for office expenses, and fringe benefits (if any).

This suggested list of questions does not imply that the applicant is to interview management. However, not asking enough questions can lead to regret later. A well-conducted interview usually brings out information that is useful for both the applicant and the real estate company.

Questions to Ask Yourself Before You Enter the Real Estate Business

1. Why am I leaving my current employment? Are my reasons valid and logical, or are they emotional?

2. How many sales per month will I need in order to generate enough commission dollars to equal my present salary? (This projection should include money set aside for income taxes and insurance.)

3. What arrangements will be made for annual vacations and holidays?

4. What about the fringe benefits—health, life, and dental packages? How will these be paid for?

5. Will I need to work on weekends and during evening hours? If so, will this be continuous? If not, how long will it last? How will this affect my lifestyle? My family?

6. Do I have the stamina and energy it takes to be in sales?

7. Are my personality traits such that I will be continually charged and challenged? Will I be able to take the peaks and valleys of real estate sales?

8. Am I financially prepared to begin a career in real estate sales? Do I have the money to carry myself and my family for a period of time before sales start to materialize? In addition, the prospective salesperson should recognize that there are continuing out-of-pocket expenses such as the following:

   a. Local board, state, and national professional fees.

   b. The cost to drive and maintain a suitable automobile for use in transporting clients to and from properties. (This includes repair costs, additional gasoline, and comprehensive insurance coverage.)

   c. Incidental daily costs that arise in connection with food services for clients, such as coffee, luncheons, and dinners.

    d. Monthly office costs—copier fees, listing materials, and electronic keys for properties.

    e. Those pertaining to personal appearance, which requires business attire, personal grooming, and the uniform required by certain franchise offices.

9. How will my family or my other relationships cope with the change? Do they support my decision?

This list of questions is not intended to be a negative overview of real estate sales, but rather a serious review of what must be considered for a successful and professional entrance into the real estate field.

Ending Note

The real estate business provides an opportunity for a personally challenging and financially rewarding career, but it is not "easy for the taking." With dedication and hard work, you can become a successful real estate salesperson, earn a substantial income, and create opportunities for personal investments.

1.4 SELLING BUSINESS OPPORTUNITIES

A real estate license allows an agent to sell business opportunities. A business opportunity is defined as the sale or lease of a business, including stock, trade fixtures, trade name, and goodwill. This involves the sale of personal property, and all the rules of personal property apply.

The essential elements of the sale of a business opportunity include the following:

1. A bill of sale is the written instrument that passes title to personal property.

2. The financial statements needed when a business is sold are as follows:

    a. *Balance Sheet:* Shows the financial position of the business as of a given date

    Assets: Things of value owned by the business

    Liabilities: Unpaid debts and expenses of the business

    Net Worth: Owners' equity, the difference between the assets and liabilities

    b. *Profit and Loss Statement:* Shows the profit and loss of the business during a specific time period.

Gross Income   (Revenue from sales)

– Expenses   (Cost of goods and expenses)

Net Income   (Profit)

3. Bulk Sales Rules apply when a business is sold that involves inventory. A *bulk transfer* is defined as the transfer of a major portion of inventory other than a sale to customers. The transferee (buyer) must give public notice 12 business days before the transfer takes place. The notice requires recording a Notice of Intent to Sell Bulk and publishing it in a newspaper of general circulation. The purpose of this notice is to let creditors of the seller file a claim if trade credit is still owed on the inventory. If the buyer and seller do not comply with the bulk sale law, the sale is valid between them, but is void against the creditors who can then attach the inventory.

4. Other terms and definitions include the following:
   a. *Goodwill:* Expectation of continued public patronage.
   b. *Turnover:* Number of times the inventory is sold per year.
   c. *Sales and Use Tax:* A tax on the sale of personal property.
   d. *Alcoholic Beverage Control Act (ABC):* Rules involving the sale of a liquor license. One of these rules states that the person must be of good moral character. If a new license is issued by the state, the initial fees are relatively modest. But once a license is issued, because the number of liquor licenses is limited by population, a free market develops and the price for a liquor license can skyrocket.

Chapter Summary

Real estate offers many avenues for employment. In addition to sales, opportunities exist in the fields of real estate appraisal, finance, escrow, title insurance, construction, and development. Real estate trade associations, such as the National Association of REALTORS®, the National Association of Real Estate Brokers, and the California Association of REALTORS®, provide valuable services to their members and the public.

Real estate licensees are regulated by the California Bureau of Real Estate (CalBRE). The CalBRE is headed by the real estate commissioner, who is appointed by the governor.

The basic requirements to become a real estate salesperson are being 18 years of age or older, being a legal U.S. resident, completing approved courses in real estate principles, real estate practice, and one other CalBRE broker-level course, passing the 150-question state examination with a score of 70 percent or better, completing an application along with a set of classifiable fingerprints, and paying all fees. A real estate salesperson must work for a broker.

The basic requirements to become a real estate broker are being 18 years of age or older, being a legal U.S. resident, completing eight approved real estate courses, having two years' experience as a real estate salesperson or its equivalent, passing a 200-question state examination with a score of 75 percent or better, completing an application, and paying all fees. A real estate broker's license is good for four years. A real estate broker is allowed to operate his or her own real estate office and to hire real estate salespeople.

To renew a real estate sales or broker's license, a person must complete 45 hours of CalBRE-approved continuing education classes.

Within the first 45-hour renewal period, a licensee must take five separate three-hour courses in ethics, agency, fair housing, trust fund handling, and risk management. A broker licensee must complete an additional 3-hour course in management and supervision for the total 45 hours.

Prior to entering the real estate business, a person should conduct a serious self-appraisal. The real estate business offers many opportunities for self-motivated people, but it is not a get-rich-quick business.

Important Terms and Concepts

business opportunity

California Association
    of REALTORS® (CAR)

National Association of REALTORS®
    (NAR)

real estate commissioner

REALTIST®

REALTOR®

Practical Application

1. As a California real estate salesperson licensee, what are the educational requirements for renewal of your real estate license during the first four years?

2. After being a full-time California real estate broker for two years, what are the educational requirements for renewal of your real estate license?

3. What is meant by the term *bulk sale*?

Reviewing Your Understanding

1. Members of the National Association of Real Estate Brokers are called:
   a. REALTORS®
   b. REALTISTS®
   c. MAI
   d. RECI

2. A real estate broker's license enables a person to handle the sale of:
   a. registered mobile homes.
   b. business opportunities.
   c. trust deeds.
   d. all of these.

3. A statement that shows the financial position of a business as of a certain date is called:
   a. a profit and loss statement.
   b. Schedule E.
   c. a balance sheet.
   d. Schedule C.

4. A candidate for the real estate broker's examination must:
   a. be 21 years or older.
   b. have completed eight college-level real estate courses.
   c. have at least four years' experience as a real estate salesperson.
   d. be a resident of California.

5. Commission rates for real estate agents are established by:
   a. the real estate commissioner.
   b. local boards of real estate.
   c. multiple listing organizations.
   d. negotiations.

6. A passing score on the real estate salesperson's examination is:
   a. 50 percent.
   b. 70 percent.
   c. 75 percent.
   d. 80 percent.

7. The Real Estate Commissioner's Regulations apply to:
   a. REALTORS® only.
   b. REALISTS® only.
   c. real estate brokers only.
   d. all California real estate licensees.

8. The fine for an unlicensed person who receives an illegal commission is up to:
   a. $100.
   b. $1,000.
   c. $20,000.
   d. $50,000.

9. In California, the majority of the laws that regulate the real estate industry originate from:
   a. Commissioner's Code of Ethics.
   b. the property code
   c. the Treaty of Guadalupe Hidalgo.
   d. the Business and Professions Code.

10. The trade name REALTIST® designates a member of the:
    a National Association of REALTORS®.
    b. Consolidated Brokers of America.
    c. National Association of Real Estate Professionals.
    d. National Association of Real Estate Brokers.

11. The real estate commissioner has the right to issue regulations for the interpretation of Real Estate Law.

    a These regulations must be approved by the California Association of REALTORS®.

    b. These regulations have the same force and effect as Real Estate Law.

    c. These regulations become part of the California Administrative Code.

    d. Both b and c are correct.

12. To obtain a real estate sales license, an applicant must pass approved college-level courses in:

    a. business ethics.

    b. psychology.

    c. real estate principles, practice, and one other CalBRE-approved course.

    d. sales skills.

13. The California Association of REALTORS® is a professional real estate organization. The major purposes of this association include:

    a. promotion of high standards among members.

    b. safeguarding the real estate-buying public.

    c. fostering of legislation for the benefit and protection of California real estate.

    d. all of the above.

14. The maximum time allowed an applicant to take the salesperson's examination is:

    a. five hours.

    b. one and one-half hours.

    c. three hours and 15 minutes.

    d. as long as the applicant wishes to take.

15. If an applicant fails an examination, he or she:

    a. may not apply for a re-examination at any time.

    b. must wait a reasonable time after failure notice to apply.

    c. may apply for a re-examination immediately after notification of failure.

    d. is limited as to the number of times that an examination may be taken.

16. Which of the following is correct in regard to licensee continuing education after the first renewal period?

    a. Brokers must take 45 hours and salespeople must take 18 hours.

    b. Salespeople need 30 hours.

    c. Salespeople must take 45 hours and brokers must take 18 hours.

    d. Both brokers and salespeople need 45 hours.

17. Required real estate courses may be taken at which of the following institutions?

    a. Accredited community colleges

    b. Accredited California universities

    c. Commission approved vocational schools.

    d. All of the above

18. To become licensed to sell real estate in California, an applicant must do all of the following EXCEPT:

    a. be at least 18 years old.

    b. complete 3 college level real estate courses.

    c. pass the state license exam.

    d. have at least 2 years full time experience in real estate.

19. Which of the following needs a real estate license?

   a. A person selling their own home

   b. A person managing their own rental

   c. A full-service property manager

   d. None of the above

20. A passing score on the real estate broker's examination is:

   a. 55 percent.

   b. 60 percent.

   c. 70 percent.

   d. 75 percent.

STUDENT LEARNING OUTCOMES

This chapter stresses the historical, legal, civic, and economic importance of real estate. It also highlights the characteristics of and differences between real and personal property and their effect on today's real estate market. At the conclusion of this chapter, you will be able to do the following:

- Trace the history of real estate property ownership in California.
- Explain the term *bundle of rights* and list each of those rights.
- List the four-part definition of *real property*. Distinguish the difference between real and personal property.
- List the five legal tests of a fixture and explain their meanings.

INTRODUCTION TO REAL ESTATE

2.1 PRESENT AND HISTORICAL IMPORTANCE OF REAL ESTATE

The real estate profession touches the lives of more people than any other single investment. Moreover, real estate represents a significant portion of wealth and contributes to a substantial amount of commerce in the United States.

Impressive Statistics

Of the almost 2.5 billion acres of land in the United States, over 100 million acres are in California. (See the Special Interest Topic on page 23.) According to the U.S. Census Bureau, the population in California is over 37 million, with a projected increase of millions more in the next decades. These statistics are important to help people to become aware of the significance of real estate in their lives.

Historical Importance of Real Estate

California has perhaps the most interesting history of any state in the Union. The historical story of California can be told in terms of the use and occupancy of its land.

The earliest inhabitants of California were the Native Americans. Although they frequently led a nomadic existence, they were still governed by tribal rights to the land they occupied, including hunting, fishing, and gathering. The Native Americans respected and cherished the land because they recognized that their survival was based on products derived from the land.

Spanish Rule

In 1513, a Spanish explorer by the name of Vasco Núñez de Balboa first sighted the Pacific Ocean and claimed it for the king and queen of Spain. Many other Spanish explorers followed in the ensuing years. The years 1542 to 1822 were known as the period of exploration, discovery, and colonization.

The Spanish colonizers established forts, called *presidios*, in selected areas along the California coast to protect against invaders. Communities and agricultural towns known as *pueblos* appeared throughout the state to supply food for colonizers. During this period, the land was under Spanish domination. All land was held in the name of the king and queen of Spain, and private activities were governed by Spanish law. Spain did not recognize the ownership rights of Native Americans.

During the Spanish occupation of California, missionaries strived to spread Christianity among the natives by establishing a string of 21 missions ranging from San Diego to Sonoma, north of San Francisco.

Mexican Rule in California

In April 1822, Mexico, then a territory of Spain, established its independence and, in the process, took over the territory of California. During the Mexican reign, colonization of the territory of California continued to expand. Large Mexican land grants, called *ranchos*, were created and given to private citizens. Much of this rancho land was converted to agricultural use.

Under Mexican rule, colonization was encouraged, and land grants made extensive private ownership a reality for the first time in California's history.

American Rule in California

American settlers coming from the east were confronted by Mexican authorities, and these tensions led to the Mexican-American War in 1846. In 1848, the Treaty of Guadalupe Hidalgo ended the war with Mexico, and California became a territory of the United States.

California achieved full statehood on September 9, 1850, and from that time on, the population rapidly increased, aided by the gold rush in the Sacramento Valley. The new California legislature adopted

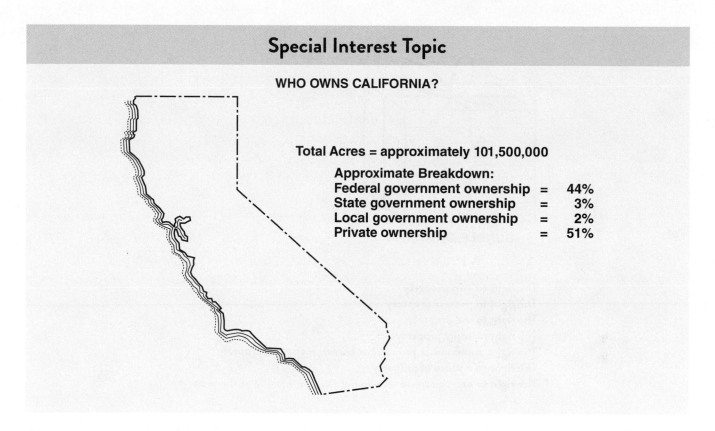

Special Interest Topic

WHO OWNS CALIFORNIA?

Total Acres = approximately 101,500,000

Approximate Breakdown:

Federal government ownership	=	44%
State government ownership	=	3%
Local government ownership	=	2%
Private ownership	=	51%

a land ownership recording system, which recognized and protected some, but not all, of the early Mexican land grants.

2.2 PROPERTY RIGHTS

As you launch your study of real estate, it is important to differentiate between real property in a physical sense, such as land and buildings, and real property in the legal sense, such as property rights. The law defines *property* as "that which is the subject of ownership." The law explains ownership as essentially "the right of one or more persons to possess and to use the thing which is owned, to the exclusion of others." In a legal sense, then, the word *property* does not refer exclusively to the physical thing owned. The law is also concerned with the rights and the interests the owner has in the thing he or she owns. Real estate may refer to property, but it also refers to the real estate profession. When discussing elements of property rights and ownership, it is probably best to use the term *real property*.

What kind of rights does an individual have as an owner of real property? The law designates the rights that accompany ownership as the **bundle of rights**.

These rights include the following:

BUNDLE OF RIGHTS

The right to own property
The right to possess property
The right to use property
The right to enjoy property
The right to encumber property or borrow money on property
The right to dispose of property
The right to exclude those who do not share ownership of the property

Although owners of real estate have a bundle of rights, they also have certain responsibilities to other persons regarding the use they can make of their property. Their rights are not absolute or unlimited. Ownership rights are subject to government control to promote public health, safety, and welfare. Zoning, building codes, and antidiscrimination laws are all examples of government control of property rights.

2.3 REAL PROPERTY VERSUS PERSONAL PROPERTY

To better understand laws and regulations relating to the acquisition and transfer of real property, a person needs to distinguish between real and personal property.

The law states that anything that is not real property is personal property. Likewise, any property that is not personal property is real property. To fully understand this concept, you need to understand what is meant by real property.

Real property consists of the following:

1. Land
2. That which is affixed to the land
3. That which is appurtenant or incidental to the land
4. That which is immovable by law

DEFINITION OF REAL ESTATE

Land

Affixed to land

Appurtenant to land

Immovable by law

Land

Land is the solid material of the earth, such as soil, rock, or other substances. It can be in the form of mountains, valleys, swamps, or any other kind of terrain. The technical definition of *land* includes the following:

1. Surface of the land
2. Airspace above the land
3. Materials and substances beneath the surface to the center of the earth

Surface of the Land

The surface of the land is defined as the space on the surface of the earth upon which people live. This includes *lateral support*, which is support from adjoining land, and *subjacent support*, which is support from underlying strata.

Airspace

Airspace (air rights) is more difficult to define. Modern theories based on air travel generally agree that an owner of real property owns a reasonable amount of airspace above his or her land, with the remainder being a public highway. Moreover, landowners have the right to prevent a use of airspace that would interfere with their use and quiet enjoyment of the land. However, the issue of what constitutes a *reasonable amount* is currently determined by the courts on a case-by-case basis whenever a lawsuit arises between disputing parties. With the advent of air travel, that which was considered air space and thus real property was reduced. Originally, it was thought that a property owner controlled the air space up to the heavens!

Minerals in the Ground

Solid minerals contained in the land—such as coal, iron ore, gold, or silver—are real property until they are taken from the ground, at which time they become personal property. A landowner who deeds the land to another conveys the minerals contained in the land, unless the mineral rights are reserved or have already been sold to some other party. When mineral rights have been reserved by the former owner or conveyed to another person, the owner of the mineral rights has an implied easement to enter upon the surface of the property to extract the minerals. Oil and gas are special classes of minerals and are governed by the *rule of capture,* also known as the *law of capture*; because of their shifting nature, they are not considered capable of absolute or exclusive ownership until reduced to capture or possession. However, the right to drill for oil and gas rests with the surface landowner or with the owner of the mineral rights if those rights belong to someone other than the surface landowner. Once oil and minerals are brought to the surface, they are considered personal property.

Water Rights

A working knowledge of the water rights of a property owner should include an understanding of the following issues:

1. Underground water rights
2. Riparian water rights
3. Right of appropriation

Underground Water

Underground or percolating water is water that is not confined to a well, a defined channel, or a water bed. In California, the landowner has neither ownership of specific underground water nor absolute ownership of waters running across or bordering property, such as a lake or a stream. Under the Concept of Reasonable Use, the landowner may take, in common with other owners, only his or her share of underground (percolating) waters for beneficial use. In a dispute, California regulatory agencies and the courts determine a *reasonable use*.

Riparian Rights

Owners of land that borders on a river or another flowing water course enjoy certain benefits regarding use of the water, under a concept known as riparian rights. Although these landowners have no absolute ownership of the waters, each owner has a personal right, along with other landowners, to use such waters in a "reasonable manner." Basically, each owner has a right to an amount of water in proportion to the amount of land owned that borders the water course and in light of the needs of all interested parties.

Right of Appropriation

The right of appropriation is that right given to the state to give permission to a nonriparian owner to take water from a river or lake.

Affixed to the Land

The second component of the definition of real property is "that which is affixed to the land," or anything regarded as a permanent part of the land. This includes:

1. Things permanently resting on the land, such as buildings.
2. Things permanently attached to a building, such as fixtures.
3. Things attached to the land by roots, such as trees and shrubs.

Natural trees, shrubs, and vines that are rooted in the ground are generally considered to be part of the land. In other words, natural vegetation is real property until severed or gathered, at which time it becomes personal property. On the other hand, farm produce and annual growing crops that are the result of labor are considered to be goods and are governed by laws of personal property. Growing vegetable crops are sometimes referred to as emblements.

Appurtenant to the Land

The third component of the definition of real property is "that which is appurtenant or incidental to the land." That which is appurtenant to the land is anything that, by right, is used by the land for its benefit and "goes with the land." Examples include the following:

1. Easements, such as the rights of way over adjoining lands, or passages for light, air, or heat from or across the land of another. (Easements are discussed in detail in a subsequent chapter.)

2. Stock in a mutual water company. A mutual water company is a nonprofit organization that is created to provide water to property owners within a specific district. Usually, each share is considered to be appurtenant to a specific piece of real property and cannot be sold separately. In other words, the stock is considered real property and transfers with the property.

Immovable by Law

Real property is also defined as any property that is immovable by law. For example, a property owner of land that contains Native American artifacts may be prohibited from disturbing them. When the law declares that an item of personal property is required to stay with the land, that item then becomes real property.

Personal Property

As was indicated previously, anything that is not real property is personal property. Personal property is movable, whereas real property is considered to be immovable. Other names for personal property are *chattels*. Examples of personal property include bonds, money, contracts, furniture, automobiles, and mortgages.

Other distinctions that might be made between real and personal property include these:

1. Contracts involving the sale of real property must be in writing and signed by the person whose title is being transferred. In the sale of some personal property, the transaction may not need to be in writing if the price is low enough. However, prudence suggests that all personal property sales contracts should be in writing to avoid misunderstandings. The contracts themselves are personal property even though the contracts might refer to the sale of real property.

2. Personal property, when sold, is usually transferred by use of a written bill of sale. Real property is transferred by delivery of a written a *deed*.

The Status of Property Can Change

Real property can become personal property, and personal property can become real property. For example, trees growing in a forest are considered real property. When the trees are cut and transported to

CHANGING CHARACTER OF PROPERTY

a sawmill, where they are made into boards, they become personal property. When the boards are used in the construction of a building, they change back to real property. If the building eventually outlives its usefulness and is torn down, the salvaged lumber becomes personal property once again.

2.4 FIXTURES

Fixtures are items that were originally personal property but are now attached to the land in such a manner as to be considered part of the land itself, thus becoming real property. Depending on the specific circumstances, certain items of personal property may become so integrated with the land that they are considered to be part of the real property and, consequently, belong to the current owner of the real estate.

The concept of fixtures can become a touchy question when land is bought or sold or when a tenant makes improvements on the property. If a legal dispute arises, the court must make a decision as to whether the property in question is a fixture and must remain with the real property or whether the item is still personal property and can be removed and taken by the seller or the tenant. If allowed to be taken, the seller and/or tenant must repair all damage caused by the removal.

Tests of a Fixture

To help determine whether an item is a fixture, which makes it real property, or is not a fixture, which makes it personal property, the

MEMORY TOOL
FIVE TESTS OF A FIXTURE "MARIA"

Method of
   attachment
Adaptability
Relationship
Intention
Agreement

courts have established the five **tests of a fixture**, which are method of attachment, adaptability, relationship of parties, intention of parties, and agreement between parties.

1. The courts are concerned with the *method* by which the property is incorporated into or attached to the land and its consequent degree of permanence. In other words, is the property nailed, cemented, welded, or bolted down? Or is it simply leaning against the building or hanging on the wall?

2. The courts are concerned with the *adaptability* to ordinary use of the attached personal property. In other words, is the item in question customized, or can it easily be used in some other building? Wall-to-wall carpeting is considered a fixture because it was cut for a room of a particular size and shape and the carpet is attached to a tack strip that is nailed to the floor, whereas a standard 9 × 12 rug is personal property because it is readily movable from house to house. Customized draperies or fireplace screens may also become fixtures.

3. The courts are concerned with the *relationship* between the person who adds the article and the party with whom he or she may be transacting business. In other words, is the dispute between a landlord and a tenant, a buyer and a seller, or a borrower and a lender? In a dispute between a landlord and a tenant, the courts tend to favor the tenant; between a buyer and a seller, the courts tend to favor the buyer; and between a borrower and a lender, the courts lean toward the lender.

4. The *intention* of the person attaching the personal property to the land is a very important issue. Intention is indicated by action or agreement of the parties, whether it be expressed or merely implied. If intention can be proved, the courts consider this the most important test.

5. The courts also look to the existence of any *agreements between the parties* regarding the item in question. In other words, has a right to the property in question been established by the signing of an agreement? Is the item mentioned in the real estate listing or purchase contract?

Take Proper Precautions

Many times problems arise between buyers and sellers regarding fixtures. Therefore, it is in the best interest of all parties to spell out clearly in the purchase contract the intentions of the seller and buyer regarding the items of personal property or fixtures and whether or not they will remain with the property. The purchase contract should state whether the washer and dryer, stove, or other questionable items are remaining with the property or if the seller reserves the right to remove these items after the sale.

Exception to the Fixture Rule

For every good rule, there is often an exception. In the case of fixtures, certain items remain personal property after they have been affixed to real property. Articles of personal property that a business tenant has attached to real property because of their need to be used in a trade or business are called trade fixtures. Examples are shelving, counters, or cash registers used by a business but not sold as merchandise to customers.

These trade fixtures are viewed as the personal property of the business tenant, and the tenant has the right to remove these items. The tenant must repair any damage caused by the removal. However, a residential tenant in a house or an apartment might install room dividers or different light fixtures. These fixtures may or may not be viewed as the personal property of the tenant. As noted earlier, the courts tend to favor the tenant. In many cases, these fixtures may be removed by the tenant, provided the premises are not damaged in the process of removal. However, the right to remove is not absolute; it depends on the circumstances in each case.

Chapter Summary

California's colorful history is closely tied to the concept of land ownership. A study of the early inhabitants of the state gives a better understanding of the foundation upon which real estate laws and regulations have been built.

Ownership of real property includes certain property rights called the *bundle of rights*. The bundle of rights includes the right to own, possess, use, enjoy, encumber, dispose of, and exclude.

Real property is defined as (1) land; (2) that which is appurtenant to the land, such as easements or stock in a mutual water company; (3) that which is affixed to the land, known as *fixtures*; and (4) that which is immovable by law.

The status of property can change. Real property can become personal property, and personal property can be changed to real property. In determining the status of real versus personal property, the courts have developed five tests to determine whether an item is a fixture. These tests are method of attachment, adaptability, relationship of the parties, intention of the parties to the transaction, and the existence of an agreement between the parties involved (the MARIA memory tool).

Important Terms and Concepts

appurtenant

bundle of rights

emblements

fixtures

right of appropriation

riparian rights

tests of a fixture

trade fixtures

Treaty of Guadalupe Hidalgo

Practical Application

1. A listing broker, while completing the walkthrough on her new listing, has found the following items: a large, attached, antique mirror in the entry; built-in bookshelves and media sound system in the family room; and freestanding washer, dryer, refrigerator, electric stove, and propane grill on the back deck. Which items are fixtures that will convey with the property?

2. After the close of the sale, the seller of a home removes an 8′ × 10′ metal prefab storage shed from the property. The buyer states that the shed is real property and should stay on the property as part of the sale. Who is right? How could this problem have been avoided?

3. How do trade fixtures differ from regular fixtures?

Reviewing Your Understanding

1. Which group of explorers and colonizers set up presidios and pueblos in the early days of California?

    a. Mexican

    b. British

    c. Spanish

    d. Native American

2. Which of the following is not considered to be part of the bundle of rights? The right to:

    a. own property.

    b. pay taxes.

    c. enjoy.

    d. encumber.

3. Which of the following is considered *land* and, therefore, is real estate?
   a. Oil deposits beneath the surface
   b. Harvested crops
   c. Trade fixtures
   d. Reasonable airspace above the land

4. The right of the owner of land bordering on a river to use the river water in a reasonable manner is called:
   a. appropriation rights.
   b. take-out rights.
   c. riparian rights.
   d. subjacent privileges.

5. Wall-to-wall carpeting in a single-family dwelling is usually considered to be:
   a. a fixture.
   b. a chattel.
   c. removable.
   d. separate property.

6. Which of the following is considered appurtenant to the land and upon sale or other transfer stays with the land and is not taken by the former owner?
   a. Stock in a mutual water company
   b. Trade fixtures
   c. An easement
   d. Both a and c

7. All other things being equal, in a dispute between a buyer and a seller over a fixture, the courts tend to favor:
   a. the seller.
   b. the buyer.
   c. the one with the most money.
   d. neither party.

8. In what year was California granted statehood?
   a. 1821
   b. 1846
   c. 1848
   d. 1850

9. The main feature of personal property is:
   a. its title is transferred by a deed.
   b. its immobility.
   c. its value is always less than that of real property.
   d. its mobility.

10. Which two terms do not belong together?
    a. Bundle of rights—use and enjoyment
    b. Real property—land
    c. Reasonable use—water rights
    d. Personal property—easement

11. Ownership of water rights to flowing water such as river are known as:
    a. underground water rights.
    b. appropriation rights.
    c. riparian rights.
    d. fixtures.

12. Unless otherwise noted, mineral rights:
    a. transfer with the land.
    b. are the personal property of the owner.
    c. are always reserved by the former owner.
    d. never carry an implied right to enter the land for extraction.

13. Freestanding items like washers, dryers, refrigerators, and stoves are considered to be:
    a. real property.
    b. personal property.
    c. fixtures.
    d. emblements.

14. The right of the state to give permission to a nonriparian owner to take water from a river or lake is called a:
    a. riparian right.
    b. possessor right.
    c. percolating right.
    d. right of appropriation.

15. Which mineral is not considered capable of absolute or exclusive ownership until reduced to possession?
    a. Gold
    b. Oil
    c. Iron
    d. Silver

16. *Chattel* is also known as:
    a. fixtures.
    b. real estate.
    c. personal property.
    d. real property.

17. Which of the following is not considered a test of a fixture?
    a. Relationship of the parties
    b. Method of financing
    c. Intention of the parties
    d. Method of attachment

18. Personal property that is attached to the land in such a manner that it becomes part of the real property is called a(n):
    a. fixture.
    b. chattel.
    c. trade fixture.
    d. emblement.

19. Arnold and Sally are tenants in an apartment. They permanently build shelves into the wall of the kitchen without permission from the terms of the landlord and outside the terms of their lease. When they move, the shelves will probably be considered:
    a. trade fixtures.
    b. personal property.
    c. appurtenances.
    d. real property.

20. Garcia leases a retail store and operates a jewelry business. When she moves, her business machines and shelves will probably be considered:
    a. trade fixtures.
    b. real property.
    c. appurtenances.
    d. separate property.

STUDENT LEARNING OUTCOMES

In recent years, the laws regarding a real estate agent's duties have changed drastically. This chapter defines the term *agency*, discusses the creation of agencies, and analyzes the duties and responsibilities of real estate agents. At the conclusion of this chapter, you will be able to do the following:

- Define agency and list the three ways in which agencies are created.
- Discuss the fiduciary relationship that exists between a principal and a real estate agent.
- Explain the difference between single agency and dual agency.
- List and give examples of several real estate agency violations.
- List and give examples of six ways in which real estate agencies are terminated.

REAL ESTATE AGENCY

3.1 AGENCY

The California Civil Code defines *agency* as "the representation of another person called a principal, by an agent, in dealings with third persons." An agent, therefore, is empowered to represent a principal in negotiating with a third party for the principal's benefit. Agencies are not required by law. However, because of the complexity of business and for convenience, principals frequently prefer to have experts represent them in transactions. Common examples of agents include travel agents, insurance agents, and real estate agents. There are two broad categories of agency. The first category is called general agency; the second is called special agency. A general agent is one who has broad powers to act on behalf of the principal. A special agent has limited or well-defined powers, frequently confined to a single transaction. Most real estate agencies are special in nature, with powers normally limited to the sale of a specific property. (See Figure 3.1.)

Employer-Employee and Independent Contractor Distinctions

A real estate agency differs from an employer-employee relationship; it also differs from an independent contractor relationship. An employer-employee relationship exists when an individual is hired by another to

FIGURE 3.1

Source: © 2015 OnCourse Learning

perform certain services under the strict supervision of the employer. The degree of direct control over the individual hired is important in determining whether that individual is an employee or independent contractor.

For example, assume Santos hired Brown to perform office work. Santos requires that Brown work from 9:00 A.M. to 5:00 P.M. Monday through Friday. Santos carefully supervises the method in which Brown performs work duties. Further, Santos provides fringe benefits and deducts money from Brown's paycheck each week for income taxes and Social Security. Under these circumstances, Brown is clearly an employee and an employer-employee relationship exists. An independent contractor relationship exists when an individual is hired to accomplish results and little or no supervision is required. Assume Santos hires West Company to perform janitorial services for an office. Santos pays West Company a fixed amount of money per month and does not supervise West Company. West Company is free to clean the office at a self-determined pace and at the company's own time schedule, provided it is after business hours. Further, Santos does not provide fringe benefits and does not take deductions for Social Security or income taxes out of West Company's pay. West Company, under these circumstances, is probably an independent contractor and not an employee.

A real estate agency differs from an employer-employee relationship and an independent contractor relationship. Whereas an employee works for an employer and is under the control of the employer for all work activities, a real estate agent's activities are not under the complete control of a principal. For example, most sellers do not tell a real estate broker when to open the real estate office, when to take a lunch hour, or when to return home!

A real estate agency is also different from an independent contractor relationship in that the agent is not free to do anything to achieve a sale. An agent must respect the lawful instructions of the principal. For example, a seller engages a real estate agent to find a buyer under certain lawful terms and conditions that the agent must follow to receive a commission.

A further distinction exists within a real estate brokerage. Due to the independent nature of the relationship between real estate salesperson and broker, an independent contractor relationship is usually recognized for income tax–reporting purposes. But because the real estate law requires the broker to supervise the activities of his or her salespeople, the real estate commissioner regards the relationship between a broker and his or her salespeople to be like that of an employer and employee.

Creation of Real Estate Agencies

Agencies are created in three ways: by agreement, by ratification, and by estoppel. (See Figure 3.2.)

By far, the greatest number of real estate agencies are created by agreement. The principal (usually the seller) appoints a real estate agent in writing, or by their mutual actions. The authorization to sell (listing agreement) is the document most frequently used to appoint real estate agents. The authorization to sell specifies the powers delegated to the agent, the terms and conditions of the proposed sale of the property, and the circumstances under which a brokerage commission is earned, as well as the brokerage amount. As will be outlined in Chapter 5, there are different types of listing agreements—each with different powers of agency.

The second method of creating an agency is by *ratification*. Under this concept, no agency is currently in existence; however, a series of events then occurs that creates an agency relationship. In other words, an unauthorized agent performs a service on your behalf of which you are unaware. Upon learning of the service, which turns out to be beneficial, you accept the responsibility for the agent's act. As an example, assume Chang, a real estate broker, approaches Johnson with an offer from a buyer to buy Johnson's store when Johnson had not previously considered selling the store. Johnson likes the price and terms and decides it would be advantageous to sell the property. By accepting the offer and agreeing to pay a commission, Johnson has created an agency with broker Chang. In essence, Johnson ratified broker Chang's unauthorized actions by accepting the buyer's offer.

The third method of creating an agency is by *estoppel*. In an estoppel situation, an individual knowingly allows another person to perform tasks beneficial to that individual. Later, the individual determines that the person did not act properly and decides to pursue legal recourse

FIGURE 3.2

CREATION OF REAL ESTATE AGENCIES

By Ratification
(approve unauthorized act)

By Agreement
(in writing)

By Estoppel
(mislead an innocent person)

Source: © 2015 OnCourse Learning

but may be prevented from doing so because there was no legal duty to care for that individual. For example, say Dang was selling his own home. Agent Jones offered Dang a price that was clearly below market value, but Dang was not aware of the market value of his property. During the transaction, Jones assisted Dang with the paperwork but never formally became Dang's agent. After the close of escrow, Dang discovers he underpriced his property and wants to sue Jones. Dang would only be able to recover from Jones if he could prove Jones had a duty to care for him. Such a duty exists between an agent and his or her principal, which you will learn is a fiduciary duty. In order to recover from Jones, Dang would have to show that Dang relied on the efforts of Jones and that Jones in fact performed the actions of an agent. This legal theory is called *agency by estoppel*.

Actual Versus Ostensible Agent

Sometimes on the state real estate examination and in agency discussions, this question comes up: What is the difference between an actual agent and an ostensible agent? Answer: An actual agent is directly appointed by a principal where the agent is granted certain powers to act on behalf of the principal. An ostensible agency exists when an agents purports to be the representative of a principal but has not been authorized to act on behalf of the principal and knowingly allows innocent third parties to believe that the unauthorized person is the principal's agent. Typically, the principal is not liable for the actions of the unauthorized agent. However, once the principal does become aware of the agent's actions and does not object, the principal can be liable by ratification.

Fiduciary Relationship

When a real estate brokerage is appointed as an agent, by the principal (seller) to represent the seller in negotiations with a buyer, a *fiduciary relationship* is created. This fiduciary relationship is one of loyalty, obedience, and confidentiality, and it obligates the agent to act in the principal's best interest. This relationship is probably the agent's most important duty. An agent cannot act in a manner that is detrimental to this fiduciary relationship. The agent (1) cannot profit from the agency without the consent of the principal, (2) must obey all lawful instructions of the principal, and (3) must keep all information told to the agent by the principal confidential unless instructed to disclose or such disclosure is required by law. The listing contract belongs to the brokerage firm and if the salesperson leaves the contract remains with the brokerage.

Seller's Agency

The majority of real estate agencies are created when a seller (principal) appoints a real estate broker (a **seller's agent**) to find a buyer for the seller's property. The agency relationship is between the seller and the broker, not between the broker and the buyer. Therefore, a real estate broker is legally bound to do the very best for the seller, which includes trying to get the best price and terms for the property.

Although the real estate broker may not be the buyer's agent, the broker owes a degree of good faith to the buyer. The agent must be honest and truthful and disclose any known defects in the property. Above all else, an agent must not misrepresent the property to a prospective buyer.

Buyer's Agency

Likewise, a buyer may appoint a real estate broker to be the **buyer's agent** to find property for the buyer. Under these circumstances, the buyer's broker is bound to reveal this fact to the seller. With a buyer's broker agency, the fiduciary relationship is between the buyer and the real estate broker, not between the seller and the buyer's broker.

Single Versus Dual Agency

When a real estate broker acts as an agent to only the seller or only the buyer, this is called a **single agency**. A real estate broker may represent both the buyer and seller in the same transaction, but only with the knowledge and consent of both parties. This is called **dual agency**. (*Note:* Two real estate licensees working for the same broker will be a dual agency if one licensee has the buyer and the other has the seller because it is the broker who determines the agency relationship.) Although common, dual agencies are considered by many attorneys as a conflict of interest with the potential for lawsuits. Real estate agents often carry errors-and-omissions insurance to help protect against this problem.

Agency Disclosure Requirements

California law requires all real estate agents to disclose in writing to the buyer and the seller whether the real estate broker is the agent of the seller, the buyer, or both. The buyer and the seller must sign a disclosure form explaining the real estate agency status. The agency disclosure must be done before the seller signs the listing contract and before the buyer signs the purchase contract. The disclosure and confirmation process is completed in three steps: disclosure, election, and confirmation.

Step 1: The real estate agent **discloses** or presents the choice of being the agent for only the seller, for only the buyer, or for both.

Step 2: The seller and/or buyer **elect** the type of representation; single or dual.

Step 3: The agent, seller, and buyer confirm the agency relationship and sign the required form. (See Figure 3.3.)

How the agency disclosure is made is a bit confusing. California Civil Code 2079.14 requires the listing agent to disclose only to the seller and the selling agent to disclose to *both* the seller and the buyer, unless one agent represents both seller and buyer, in which case a single disclosure is made to the seller and the buyer. It is important to remember that agency relationships are determined by the broker, not the individual salesperson or agent who is working for a brokerage company. When the law speaks of an *agent*, it is referring to all licensees working for a single real estate brokerage company.

Subagents and Cooperating Agents

If the seller gives permission in the listing agreement, a real estate agent can assign some of his or her duties to other licensed agents. These other agents are called *subagents*. The same fiduciary relationship exists between the subagent and the principal as exists between the listing agent and the principal. Subagents are required to try to get the best price and terms for the seller even if the subagent is from another office and has independently found a buyer. Prior to the mandated disclosure of agency relationships (pre 1990), most transactions contained subagency, where both agents represented the seller and no one represented the buyer. After agency relationships were required to be disclosed and buyers insisted upon representation, most MLS rules were changed to allow for buyer representation and subagency was virtually eliminated.

Due to the conflict and possible liability issues raised by subagency, most real estate agents feel uncomfortable acting as subagents and prefer instead to be viewed as *cooperating agents* who attempt to find a buyer for the other broker's listing and then to act as the agent of the buyer, not the subagent of the seller.

Buyer Agency

From a legal perspective, there is less risk to agents if they remain in single agency. Multiple Listing Service rules have been changed to allow compensation from the seller or the listing agent to the selling or cooperating agent regardless of the agency relationship. Now,

FIGURE 3.3 Disclosure Regarding Real Estate Agency Relationship

CALIFORNIA
ASSOCIATION
OF REALTORS ®

DISCLOSURE REGARDING
REAL ESTATE AGENCY RELATIONSHIP
(As required by the Civil Code)
(C.A.R. Form AD, Revised 12/14)

❑ (If checked) This form is being provided in connection with a transaction for a leasehold interest exceeding one year as per Civil Code section 2079.13(k) and (l).

When you enter into a discussion with a real estate agent regarding a real estate transaction, you should from the outset understand what type of agency relationship or representation you wish to have with the agent in the transaction.

SELLER'S AGENT
A Seller's agent under a listing agreement with the Seller acts as the agent for the Seller only. A Seller's agent or a subagent of that agent has the following affirmative obligations:
To the Seller: A Fiduciary duty of utmost care, integrity, honesty and loyalty in dealings with the Seller.
To the Buyer and the Seller:
   (a) Diligent exercise of reasonable skill and care in performance of the agent's duties.
   (b) A duty of honest and fair dealing and good faith.
   (c) A duty to disclose all facts known to the agent materially affecting the value or desirability of the property that are not known to, or within the diligent attention and observation of, the parties. An agent is not obligated to reveal to either party any confidential information obtained from the other party that does not involve the affirmative duties set forth above.

BUYER'S AGENT
A selling agent can, with a Buyer's consent, agree to act as agent for the Buyer only. In these situations, the agent is not the Seller's agent, even if by agreement the agent may receive compensation for services rendered, either in full or in part from the Seller. An agent acting only for a Buyer has the following affirmative obligations:
To the Buyer: A fiduciary duty of utmost care, integrity, honesty and loyalty in dealings with the Buyer.
To the Buyer and the Seller:
   (a) Diligent exercise of reasonable skill and care in performance of the agent's duties.
   (b) A duty of honest and fair dealing and good faith.
   (c) A duty to disclose all facts known to the agent materially affecting the value or desirability of the property that are not known to, or within the diligent attention and observation of, the parties.
An agent is not obligated to reveal to either party any confidential information obtained from the other party that does not involve the affirmative duties set forth above.

AGENT REPRESENTING BOTH SELLER AND BUYER
A real estate agent, either acting directly or through one or more associate licensees, can legally be the agent of both the Seller and the Buyer in a transaction, but only with the knowledge and consent of both the Seller and the Buyer.
In a dual agency situation, the agent has the following affirmative obligations to both the Seller and the Buyer:
   (a) A fiduciary duty of utmost care, integrity, honesty and loyalty in the dealings with either the Seller or the Buyer.
   (b) Other duties to the Seller and the Buyer as stated above in their respective sections.
In representing both Seller and Buyer, the agent may not, without the express permission of the respective party, disclose to the other party that the
Seller will accept a price less than the listing price or that the Buyer will pay a price greater than the price offered.
The above duties of the agent in a real estate transaction do not relieve a Seller or Buyer from the responsibility to protect his or her own interests. You should carefully read all agreements to assure that they adequately express your understanding of the transaction. A real estate agent is a person qualified to advise about real estate. If legal or tax advice is desired, consult a competent professional.
Throughout your real property transaction you may receive more than one disclosure form, depending upon the number of agents assisting in the transaction. The law requires each agent with whom you have more than a casual relationship to present you with this disclosure form. You should read its contents each time it is presented to you, considering the relationship between you and the real estate agent in your specific transaction. **This disclosure form includes the provisions of Sections 2079.13 to 2079.24, inclusive, of the Civil Code set forth on page 2. Read it carefully. I/WE ACKNOWLEDGE RECEIPT OF A COPY OF THIS DISCLOSURE AND THE PORTIONS OF THE CIVIL CODE PRINTED ON THE BACK (OR A SEPARATE PAGE).**

Buyer/Seller/Landlord/Tenant _____ Date _____

Buyer/Seller/Landlord/Tenant _____ Date _____

Agent _____ DRE Lic. # _____
                Real Estate Broker (Firm)
By _____ DRE Lic. # _____ Date _____
       (Salesperson or Broker-Associate)

Agency Disclosure Compliance (Civil Code §2079.14):
• When the listing brokerage company also represents Buyer/Tenant: The Listing Agent shall have one AD form signed by Seller/Landlord and a different AD form signed by Buyer/Tenant.
• When Seller/Landlord and Buyer/Tenant are represented by different brokerage companies: (i) the Listing Agent shall have one AD form signed by Seller/Landlord and (ii) the Buyer's/Tenant's Agent shall have one AD form signed by Buyer/Tenant and either that same or a different AD form presented to Seller/Landlord for signature prior to presentation of the offer. If the same form is used, Seller may sign here:

_____ _____ _____ _____
Seller/Landlord   Date   Seller/Landlord   Date

EQUAL HOUSING OPPORTUNITY

Reviewed by _____ Date _____

AD REVISED 12/14 (PAGE 1 OF 2) Print Date

DISCLOSURE REGARDING REAL ESTATE AGENCY RELATIONSHIP (AD PAGE 1 OF 2)

FIGURE 3.3 (Continued)

CIVIL CODE SECTIONS 2079.24 (2079.16 APPEARS ON THE FRONT)

2079.13 As used in Sections 2079.14 to 2079.24, inclusive, the following terms have the following meanings: **(a)** "Agent" means a person acting under provisions of Title 9 (commencing with Section 2295) in a real property transaction, and includes a person who is licensed as a real estate broker under Chapter 3 (commencing with Section 10130) of Part 1 of Division 4 of the Business and Professions Code, and under whose license a listing is executed or an offer to purchase is obtained. **(b)** "Associate licensee" means a person who is licensed as a real estate broker or salesperson under Chapter 3 (commencing with Section 10130) of Part 1 of Division 4 of the Business and Professions Code and who is either licensed under a broker or has entered into a written contract with a broker to act as the broker's agent in connection with acts requiring a real estate license and to function under the broker's supervision in the capacity of an associate licensee. The agent in the real property transaction bears responsibility for his or her associate licensees who perform as agents of the agent. When an associate licensee owes a duty to any principal, or to any buyer or seller who is not a principal, in a real property transaction, that duty is equivalent to the duty owed to that party by the broker for whom the associate licensee functions. **(c)** "Buyer" means a transferee in a real property transaction, and includes a person who executes an offer to purchase real property from a seller through an agent, or who seeks the services of an agent in more than a casual, transitory, or preliminary manner, with the object of entering into a real property transaction. "Buyer" includes vendee or lessee. **(d)** "Commercial real property" means all real property in the state, except single-family residential real property, dwelling units made subject to Chapter 2 (commencing with Section 1940) of Title 5, mobilehomes, as defined in Section 798.3, or recreational vehicles, as defined in Section 799.29. **(e)** "Dual agent" means an agent acting, either directly or through an associate licensee, as agent for both the seller and the buyer in a real property transaction. **(f)** "Listing agreement" means a contract between an owner of real property and an agent, by which the agent has been authorized to sell the real property or to find or obtain a buyer. **(g)** "Listing agent" means a person who has obtained a listing of real property to act as an agent for compensation. **(h)** "Listing price" is the amount expressed in dollars specified in the listing for which the seller is willing to sell the real property through the listing agent. **(i)** "Offering price" is the amount expressed in dollars specified in an offer to purchase for which the buyer is willing to buy the real property. **(j)** "Offer to purchase" means a written contract executed by a buyer acting through a selling agent that becomes the contract for the sale of the real property upon acceptance by the seller. **(k)** "Real property" means any estate specified by subdivision (1) or (2) of Section 761 in property that constitutes or is improved with one to four dwelling units, any commercial real property, any leasehold in these types of property exceeding one year's duration, and mobilehomes, when offered for sale or sold through an agent pursuant to the authority contained in Section 10131.6 of the Business and Professions Code. **(l)** "Real property transaction" means a transaction for the sale of real property in which an agent is employed by one or more of the principals to act in that transaction, and includes a listing or an offer to purchase. **(m)** "Sell," "sale," or "sold" refers to a transaction for the transfer of real property from the seller to the buyer, and includes exchanges of real property between the seller and buyer, transactions for the creation of a real property sales contract within the meaning of Section 2985, and transactions for the creation of a leasehold exceeding one year's duration. **(n)** "Seller" means the transferor in a real property transaction, and includes an owner who lists real property with an agent, whether or not a transfer results, or who receives an offer to purchase real property of which he or she is the owner from an agent on behalf of another. "Seller" includes both a vendor and a lessor. **(o)** "Selling agent" means a listing agent who acts alone, or an agent who acts in cooperation with a listing agent, and who sells or finds and obtains a buyer for the real property, or an agent who locates property for a buyer or who finds a buyer for a property for which no listing exists and presents an offer to purchase to the seller. **(p)** "Subagent" means a person to whom an agent delegates agency powers as provided in Article 5 (commencing with Section 2349) of Chapter 1 of Title 9. However, "subagent" does not include an associate licensee who is acting under the supervision of an agent in a real property transaction.

2079.14 Listing agents and selling agents shall provide the seller and buyer in a real property transaction with a copy of the disclosure form specified in Section 2079.16, and, except as provided in subdivision (c), shall obtain a signed acknowledgement of receipt from that seller or buyer, except as provided in this section or Section 2079.15, as follows: **(a)** The listing agent, if any, shall provide the disclosure form to the seller prior to entering into the listing agreement. **(b)** The selling agent shall provide the disclosure form to the seller as soon as practicable prior to presenting the seller with an offer to purchase, unless the selling agent previously provided the seller with a copy of the disclosure form pursuant to subdivision (a). **(c)** Where the selling agent does not deal on a face-to-face basis with the seller, the disclosure form prepared by the selling agent may be furnished to the seller (and acknowledgement of receipt obtained for the selling agent from the seller) by the listing agent, or the selling agent may deliver the disclosure form by certified mail addressed to the seller at his or her last known address, in which case no signed acknowledgement of receipt is required. **(d)** The selling agent shall provide the disclosure form to the buyer as soon as practicable prior to execution of the buyer's offer to purchase, except that if the offer to purchase is not prepared by the selling agent, the selling agent shall present the disclosure form to the buyer not later than the next business day after the selling agent receives the offer to purchase from the buyer.

2079.15 In any circumstance in which the seller or buyer refuses to sign an acknowledgement of receipt pursuant to Section 2079.14, the agent, or an associate licensee acting for an agent, shall set forth, sign, and date a written declaration of the facts of the refusal.

2079.16 Reproduced on Page 1 of this AD form.

2079.17(a) As soon as practicable, the selling agent shall disclose to the buyer and seller whether the selling agent is acting in the real property transaction exclusively as the buyer's agent, exclusively as the seller's agent, or as a dual agent representing both the buyer and the seller. This relationship shall be confirmed in the contract to purchase and sell real property or in a separate writing executed or acknowledged by the seller, the buyer, and the selling agent prior to or coincident with execution of that contract by the buyer and the seller, respectively. **(b)** As soon as practicable, the listing agent shall disclose to the seller whether the listing agent is acting in the real property transaction exclusively as the seller's agent, or as a dual agent representing both the buyer and seller. This relationship shall be confirmed in the contract to purchase and sell real property or in a separate writing executed or acknowledged by the seller and the listing agent prior to or coincident with the execution of that contract by the seller.

(c) The confirmation required by subdivisions (a) and (b) shall be in the following form.

_____(DO NOT COMPLETE. SAMPLE ONLY)_____ is the agent of (check one): ❑ the seller exclusively; or ❑ both the buyer and seller.
(Name of Listing Agent)

_____(DO NOT COMPLETE. SAMPLE ONLY)_____ is the agent of (check one): ❑ the buyer exclusively; or ❑ the seller exclusively; or
(Name of Selling Agent if not the same as the Listing Agent)   ❑ both the buyer and seller.

(d) The disclosures and confirmation required by this section shall be in addition to the disclosure required by Section 2079.14.

2079.18 No selling agent in a real property transaction may act as an agent for the buyer only, when the selling agent is also acting as the listing agent in the transaction.

2079.19 The payment of compensation or the obligation to pay compensation to an agent by the seller or buyer is not necessarily determinative of a particular agency relationship between an agent and the seller or buyer. A listing agent and a selling agent may agree to share any compensation or commission paid, or any right to any compensation or commission for which an obligation arises as the result of a real estate transaction, and the terms of any such agreement shall not necessarily be determinative of a particular relationship.

2079.20 Nothing in this article prevents an agent from selecting, as a condition of the agent's employment, a specific form of agency relationship not specifically prohibited by this article if the requirements of Section 2079.14 and Section 2079.17 are complied with.

2079.21 A dual agent shall not disclose to the buyer that the seller is willing to sell the property at a price less than the listing price, without the express written consent of the seller. A dual agent shall not disclose to the seller that the buyer is willing to pay a price greater than the offering price, without the express written consent of the buyer. This section does not alter in any way the duty or responsibility of a dual agent to any principal with respect to confidential information other than price.

2079.22 Nothing in this article precludes a listing agent from also being a selling agent, and the combination of these functions in one agent does not, of itself, make that agent a dual agent.

2079.23 A contract between the principal and agent may be modified or altered to change the agency relationship at any time before the performance of the act which is the object of the agency with the written consent of the parties to the agency relationship.

2079.24 Nothing in this article shall be construed to either diminish the duty of disclosure owed buyers and sellers by agents and their associate licensees, subagents, and employees or to relieve agents and their associate licensees, subagents, and employees from liability for their conduct in connection with acts governed by this article or for any breach of a fiduciary duty or a duty of disclosure.

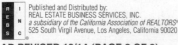

Published and Distributed by:
REAL ESTATE BUSINESS SERVICES, INC.
a subsidiary of the California Association of REALTORS®
525 South Virgil Avenue, Los Angeles, California 90020

Reviewed by _____ Date _____

EQUAL HOUSING OPPORTUNITY

AD REVISED 12/14 (PAGE 2 OF 2)

DISCLOSURE REGARDING REAL ESTATE AGENCY RELATIONSHIP (AD PAGE 2 OF 2)

Source: Reprinted with permission of California Association of REALTORS®.

agents may represent buyers in single agency while still receiving compensation from the seller or the listing agent. This practice of an agent representing only buyers is known as *buyer agency*, and some companies have developed a business model of only representing buyers and refusing to take listings from sellers.

Buyer's agents, wishing to better serve their clients, may now enter into formal written buyer representation agreements with their buyers. These agreements, similar in concept to a listing agreement between a seller's agent and a seller, require the buyer to pay a commission to his or her agent if the agent is not being compensated from the listing agent or the seller. This allows buyer's agents more freedom to provide better service to their buyers. Buyer's agents, under a buyer representation agreement, may now negotiate with "For Sale by Owner" properties and owners of unlisted properties without concern about being paid. If the seller is not willing to pay a commission to the agent, the buyer representation agreement provides that the buyer will pay the commission.

3.2 SOME AGENCY VIOLATIONS

There are over 400,000 real estate licensees in California. The percentage of licensees who violate agency laws is very small. Of those who are disciplined, most have committed violations unintentionally or through ignorance. Through education, examination, and on-the-job training, real estate licensees learn their duties and responsibilities and, therefore, reduce the possibility of agency violations. The following, from the Bureau of Real Estate (CalBRE) Reference Book (available to download at www.bre.ca.gov/), are examples of types of agency violations. The appropriate sections of the Real Estate Law are cited as a reference.

> **Trust fund–handling problems**. Section 10145. Number one on the CalBRE's list of violations are issues dealing with trust funds. Trust funds are defined as money or other items of value that an agent receives on behalf of a principal in the course of a real estate transaction that requires a license. General trust fund rules are outlined in the next section, but the point stressed here is that the most common agency violation is the failure to handle trust funds in an appropriate manner, as outlined by law and CalBRE regulations.

> **Misrepresentation**. Section 10176(a). Many complaints received by the real estate commissioner allege misrepresentation on the part of the broker or salesperson. This includes not only what was said but also the failure of a broker or salesperson to disclose a material fact about the property. Can a real estate agent

legally withhold information about a defect in the property? No. Failure to disclose is a type of misrepresentation!

False promise. Section 10176(b). A false promise and a misrepresentation are not the same thing. A misrepresentation is a false statement of fact. A false promise is a false statement about what the promiser is going to do in the future. To prove false promise, the injured party must show that the promise was impossible to perform and that the person making the promise knew it to be impossible. An example might be "Buy this home and it will double in value in six weeks!"

Commingling and conversion. Section 10176(e). Commingling takes place when a broker has mixed the funds of his or her principal with the broker's own money. Conversion is not the same thing as commingling. Conversion is misappropriating and using the client's money. This is a crime that carries a jail sentence.

Definite termination date. Section 10176(f). This section of the law requires a specified termination date for all exclusive contracts between a real estate agent and a principal relating to transactions for which a real estate license is required. What a definite termination date is has been the subject of a number of lawsuits. Generally, if a definite date is specified in the contract or if a definite period of time is indicated, the requirement is satisfied. However, if it cannot be determined from the exclusive listing contract when the listing is to expire, then the real estate agent may be in violation of the law.

Secret profit. Section 10176(g). Secret profit cases usually arise when the broker, who already has a higher offer from another buyer, makes a low offer, usually through a "dummy" purchaser. The difference is the secret profit. This is sometimes referred to as *divided agency;* agents must always disclose any self-interest they might have in a transaction and obtain their principal's consent. Many attorneys contend that an agent is guilty of secret profit or divided agency if the real estate agent derives any profit other than the agreed commission without disclosing the nature of the profits to the principal.

Other possible violations include dishonest dealing, obtaining a license by fraud, false advertising, conviction of crime, negligence, misuse of a trade name, and inducement of panic selling.

Trust Funds

A broker is required to keep an official record of all deposits that pass through his or her real estate business. This account must be kept using acceptable accounting procedures and is subject to audit by the California real estate commissioner.

Although not required by law, many real estate brokers open a trust fund account at a financial institution where all monies received on behalf of clients and customers can be deposited for safekeeping. Withdrawals can be made only by the broker or other authorized persons. The broker cannot put his or her personal funds in this trust fund account, with the exception of up to $200 to cover bank service fees.

If a broker receives a deposit from a prospective buyer *who does not instruct that the deposit be held uncashed*, the broker must, within three business days, do one of the following:

1. Give the deposit to the principal (the seller).
2. Put the deposit in escrow.
3. Put the deposit in a trust fund account.

If the broker fails to do one of these three things within three business days, the broker could be found guilty of commingling.

If asked by the prospective buyer to hold the deposit pending the seller's acceptance of the offer, then upon acceptance, the broker must, within three business days, do one of the three actions mentioned above.

Basic Rules of Entries

Trust fund records must be kept in chronological sequence in a CalBRE-approved columnar form or by a method deemed an acceptable accounting practice. If the funds *are not deposited* into a broker's trust fund bank account, the items must be entered in a trust fund logbook outlining what happened to the funds. If the funds are deposited into a broker's trust fund bank account, another entry must be made in another account in the name of the beneficiary of the funds. This is called a *double-entry accounting system*.

The bank account must be reconciled monthly with the bank statement, and the bank account must be reconciled monthly with each separate beneficiary. The broker's trust fund account must be kept in an institution insured by a government agency. If a CalBRE audit of a broker's trust fund finds a violation, the broker must bear the cost of the audit and, depending on the violation, the broker may lose his or her real estate license.

A more detailed explanation of trust fund requirements can be found in the required three-hour CalBRE continuing education course, Trust Fund Handling.

Recovery Fund

The state of California has a program whereby the public can recover money when there are certain uncollectable court judgments obtained against a real estate licensee on the basis of fraud, misrepresentation, deceit, or conversion of trust funds in a transaction. Called the recovery fund, this program is financed using a portion of real estate licensing fees. The maximum amount of money a person can receive from the fund is currently limited to $50,000 per individual claim, up to a $250,000 maximum for multiple claims against any one real estate licensee.

Responsibilities of Principals to Agents and Buyers

Agency is a two-way street. Real estate agents owe certain duties and responsibilities to principals; principals, in turn, owe certain responsibilities to agents. A principal must tell the real estate agent of any known defects in the property so the agent can properly disclose the defects to a prospective buyer. If the seller knows of a property defect and fails to tell the real estate agent, the seller can be held legally accountable. In short, a seller should not withhold pertinent information or distort facts about the property. In California, sellers of one to four residential units are required to complete and hand to the buyer, prior to the sale, a complete written disclosure regarding the property known as a Transfer Disclosure Statement which is discussed in Chapter 4.

Sellers usually enter into a contract (listing agreement) to have an agent sell their property. These contracts should be honored, and commissions should be paid when the property is sold. Sellers should not deal directly with prospective purchasers procured by the agent to evade the payment of a commission.

"As Is" Sale

Under the current version of the California Association of REAL-TORS® Purchase Agreement, properties are sold in their present (as is) condition. However, California laws and regulations require that the buyer be fully informed as to the condition of the property, including any known defects, before the buyer becomes bound by a purchase contract. If the buyer is fully informed and still wishes to proceed with the sale, then an "as is" transaction is permissible. *Caveat emptor*, the Latin phrase meaning "let the buyer beware," is no longer a defense in court in a real estate transaction. If a seller withholds material facts about the property, such as structural defects known to the seller, the seller can be sued by the buyer.

3.3 REGULATION OF BROKERS AND SALESPEOPLE

Real Estate Broker Versus Salesperson

Although brokers and salespersons are licensed by the CalBRE, a salesperson's license is valid only when he or she is working for a real estate broker. It is through this association with the real estate broker that a salesperson also becomes an agent. Therefore, only a real estate broker can contract directly with a principal. A real estate salesperson must use the broker's name when signing a listing agreement with a seller. (Requirements to become a licensed real estate agent are discussed in detail in Chapter 1.)

Considered an employee of the broker by the CalBRE for supervision purposes, a real estate salesperson is usually (as mentioned above) considered an independent contractor with the broker for other purposes such as income tax withholding, Social Security, and so on. The broker must supervise the real estate activities of all salespersons under the broker's jurisdiction. In other matters, however, the broker usually treats the salesperson as an independent contractor and does not require the salesperson to be at work at certain hours. The salesperson is responsible for final results, not the method used to attain the results.

By law, real estate salespersons are required to have a written employment contract with their broker. Commission details between the broker and salesperson should also be in writing. A real estate salesperson can receive compensation only from his or her broker. When escrow is closed, the escrow company usually sends the entire commission to the employing broker, who in turn writes a separate check to the salesperson for his or her share.

Violation of agency law by a real estate salesperson may subject the salesperson to disciplinary action and may also be a cause for disciplinary action against the employing broker who by law is responsible for certain acts of the salesperson. (See Figure 3.4.)

Regulation of Real Estate Agents

Real estate agents are regulated by government agencies and professional trade associations. The California real estate commissioner, using the employees of the CalBRE, is empowered to enforce the real estate law and to issue regulations that are enforced in the same manner as law. (See Chapter 1 for details regarding the real estate commissioner's regulation of licensees.)

FIGURE 3.4 Independent Contractor Agreement Form ICA

CALIFORNIA
ASSOCIATION
OF REALTORS®

INDEPENDENT CONTRACTOR AGREEMENT
(Between Broker and Associate-Licensee)
(C.A.R. Form ICA, Revised 11/13)

This Agreement, dated _____, is made between _____
_____ ("Broker")
and _____ ("Associate-Licensee").
In consideration of the covenants and representations contained in this Agreement, Broker and Associate-Licensee agree as follows:

1. **BROKER:** Broker represents that Broker is duly licensed as a real estate broker by the State of California,
☐ doing business as _____ (firm name), ☐ a sole proprietorship, ☐ a partnership, or
☐ a corporation. Broker is a member of the _____
Association(s) of REALTORS®, and a subscriber to the _____ Multiple
Listing Service(s). Broker shall keep Broker's license current during the term of this Agreement.

2. **ASSOCIATE-LICENSEE:** Associate-Licensee represents that: **(i)** he/she is duly licensed by the State of California as a ☐ real estate broker, ☐ real estate salesperson, and **(ii)** he/she has not used any other names within the past five years, except _____.
Associate-Licensee shall keep his/her license current during the term of this Agreement, including satisfying all applicable continuing education and provisional license requirements.

3. **INDEPENDENT CONTRACTOR RELATIONSHIP:**
   A. Broker and Associate-Licensee intend that, to the maximum extent permissible by law: **(i)** This Agreement does not constitute an employment agreement by either party; **(ii)** Broker and Associate-Licensee are independent contracting parties with respect to all services rendered under this Agreement; and **(iii)** This Agreement shall not be construed as a partnership.
   B. Broker shall not: **(i)** restrict Associate-Licensee's activities to particular geographical areas, or **(ii)** dictate Associate-Licensee's activities with regard to hours, leads, open houses, opportunity or floor time, production, prospects, sales meetings, schedule, inventory, time off, vacation, or similar activities, except to the extent required by law.
   C. Associate-Licensee shall not be required to accept an assignment by Broker to service any particular current or prospective listing or parties.
   D. Except as required by law: **(i)** Associate-Licensee retains sole and absolute discretion and judgment in the methods, techniques, and procedures to be used in soliciting and obtaining listings, sales, exchanges, leases, rentals, or other transactions, and in carrying out Associate-Licensee's selling and soliciting activities; **(ii)** Associate-Licensee is under the control of Broker as to the results of Associate-Licensee's work only, and not as to the means by which those results are accomplished; **(iii)** Associate-Licensee has no authority to bind Broker by any promise or representation; and **(iv)** Broker shall not be liable for any obligation or liability incurred by Associate-Licensee.
   E. Associate-Licensee's only remuneration shall be the compensation specified in paragraph 8.
   F. Associate-Licensee who only performs as a real estate sales agent, shall not be treated as an employee for state and federal tax purposes. However, an Associate-Licensee who performs loan activity shall be treated as an employee for state and federal tax purposes unless the activity satisfies the legal requirements to establish an independent contractor relationship.
   G. The fact the Broker may carry workers' compensation insurance for Broker's own benefit and for the mutual benefit of Broker and licensees associated with Broker, including Associate-Licensee, shall not create an inference of employment. (Workers' Compensation Advisory: Even though a Real Estate sales person may be treated as independent contractors for tax and other purposes, the California Labor and Workforce Development Agency considers them to be employees for workers' compensation purposes. According to that Agency: **(i)** Broker must obtain workers' compensation insurance for a Real Estate sales person and **(ii)** Broker, not a Real Estate sales person, must bear the cost of workers' compensation insurance. Penalties for failure to carry workers' compensation include, among others, the issuance of stop-work orders and fines of up to $1,000 per agent, not to exceed $100,000 per company.)

4. **LICENSED ACTIVITY:**
   A. All listings of property, and all agreements, acts or actions for performance of licensed acts, which are taken or performed in connection with this Agreement, shall be taken and performed in the name of Broker. Associate-Licensee agrees to and does hereby contribute all right and title to such listings to Broker for the benefit and use of Broker, Associate-Licensee, and other licensees associated with Broker.
   B. Broker shall make available to Associate-Licensee, equally with other licensees associated with Broker, all current listings in Broker's office, except any listing which Broker may choose to place in the exclusive servicing of Associate-Licensee or one or more other specific licensees associated with Broker.

Broker's Initials (_____)(_____)   Associate-Licensee's Initials (_____)(_____)

EQUAL HOUSING OPPORTUNITY

ICA REVISED 11/13 (PAGE 1 OF 4)

Reviewed by _____ Date _____

FIGURE 3.4 (Continued)

C. Associate-Licensee shall provide and pay for all professional licenses, supplies, services, and other items required in connection with Associate-Licensee's activities under this Agreement, or any listing or transaction, without reimbursement from Broker except as required by law.

D. Associate-Licensee shall work diligently and with his/her best efforts to: **(i)** sell, exchange, lease, or rent properties listed with Broker or other cooperating Brokers; **(ii)** solicit additional listings, clients, and customers; and **(iii)** otherwise promote the business of serving the public in real estate transactions to the end that Broker and Associate-Licensee may derive the greatest benefit possible, in accordance with law.

E. Associate-Licensee shall not commit any unlawful act under federal, state or local law or regulation while conducting licensed activity. Associate-Licensee shall at all times be familiar, and comply, with all applicable federal, state and local laws, including, but not limited to, anti-discrimination laws and restrictions against the giving or accepting a fee, or other thing of value, for the referral of business to title companies, escrow companies, home inspection companies, pest control companies and other settlement service providers pursuant to the California Business and Professions Code and the Real Estate Settlement Procedures Acts (RESPA).

F. Broker shall make available for Associate-Licensee's use, along with other licensees associated with Broker, the facilities of the real estate office operated by Broker at _____ and the facilities of any other office locations made available by Broker pursuant to this Agreement.

G. PROHIBITED ACTIVITIES: Associate-Licensee agrees not to engage in any of the following Real Estate licensed activities without the express written consent of Broker:

☐ Property Management; ☐ Loan Brokerage ☐ Business Brokerage; ☐ _____

☐ _____

However, if Associate-Licensee has a Real Estate Broker's License, Associate-Licensee may nonetheless engage in the following prohibited activity(ies) only: _____ provided that (1) such prohibited activities are not done under the Broker's License, (2) no facilities of Broker (including but not limited to phones, fax, computers, and office space) are used for any such prohibited activities, (3) Associate-Licensee shall not use any marketing, solicitation or contact information that include Broker's name (including business cards) for such prohibited activities, (4) Associate-Licensee informs any actual or intended Principal for whom Associate-Licensee performs or intends to perform such prohibited activities the name of the broker under whose license the prohibited activities are performed, and (5) if Associate-Licensee is performing other permitted licensed activity for that Principal under Broker's license, then Associate-Licensee shall inform any actual or intended Principal for whom the prohibited activities are performed that the prohibited activities are not performed under Broker's license.

5. PROPRIETARY INFORMATION AND FILES:

A. All files and documents pertaining to listings, leads and transactions are the property of Broker and shall be delivered to Broker by Associate-Licensee immediately upon request or termination of this Agreement.

B. Associate-Licensee acknowledges that Broker's method of conducting business is a protected trade secret.

C. Associate-Licensee shall not use to his/her own advantage, or the advantage of any other person, business, or entity, except as specifically agreed in writing, either during Associate-Licensee's association with Broker, or thereafter, any information gained for or from the business, or files of Broker.

6. SUPERVISION: Associate-Licensee, within 24 hours (or ☐ _____) after preparing, signing, or receiving same, shall submit to Broker, or Broker's designated licensee: **(i)** all documents which may have a material effect upon the rights and duties of principals in a transaction; **(ii)** any documents or other items connected with a transaction pursuant to this Agreement in the possession of or available to Associate-Licensee; and **(iii)** all documents associated with any real estate transaction in which Associate-Licensee is a principal.

7. TRUST FUNDS: All trust funds shall be handled in compliance with the Business and Professions Code, and other applicable laws.

8. COMPENSATION:

A. TO BROKER: Compensation shall be charged to parties who enter into listing or other agreements for services requiring a real estate license:

☐ as shown in "Exhibit A" attached, which is incorporated as a part of this Agreement by reference, or

☐ as follows:_____

_____

Any deviation which is not approved in writing in advance by Broker, shall be: (1) deducted from Associate-Licensee's compensation, if lower than the amount or rate approved above; and, (2) subject to Broker approval, if higher than the amount approved above. Any permanent change in commission schedule shall be disseminated by Broker to Associate-Licensee.

B. TO ASSOCIATE-LICENSEE: Associate-Licensee shall receive a share of compensation actually collected by Broker, on listings or other agreements for services requiring a real estate license, which are solicited and obtained by Associate-Licensee, and on transactions of which Associate-Licensee's activities are the procuring cause, as follows:

☐ as shown in "Exhibit B" attached, which is incorporated as a part of this Agreement by reference, or

☐ other: _____

_____

Broker's Initials (_____)(_____)   Associate-Licensee's Initials (_____)(_____)

ICA REVISED 11/13 (PAGE 2 OF 4)

Reviewed by _____ Date _____

FIGURE 3.4 (Continued)

C. PARTNERS, TEAMS, AND AGREEMENTS WITH OTHER ASSOCIATE-LICENSEES IN OFFICE: If Associate-Licensee and one or more other Associate-Licensees affiliated with Broker participate on the same side (either listing or selling) of a transaction, the commission allocated to their combined activities shall be divided by Broker and paid to them according to their written agreement. Broker shall have the right to withhold total compensation if there is a dispute between associate-licensees, or if there is no written agreement, or if no written agreement has been provided to Broker.

D. EXPENSES AND OFFSETS: If Broker elects to advance funds to pay expenses or liabilities of Associate-Licensee, or for an advance payment of, or draw upon, future compensation, Broker may deduct the full amount advanced from compensation payable to Associate-Licensee on any transaction without notice. If Associate-Licensee's compensation is subject to a lien, garnishment or other restriction on payment, Broker shall charge Associate-Licensee a fee for complying with such restriction.

E. PAYMENT: (i) All compensation collected by Broker and due to Associate-Licensee shall be paid to Associate-Licensee, after deduction of expenses and offsets, immediately or as soon thereafter as practicable, except as otherwise provided in this Agreement, or a separate written agreement between Broker and Associate-Licensee. **(ii)** Compensation shall not be paid to Associate-Licensee until both the transaction and file are complete. **(iii)** Broker is under no obligation to pursue collection of compensation from any person or entity responsible for payment. Associate-Licensee does not have the independent right to pursue collection of compensation for activities which require a real estate license which were done in the name of Broker. **(iv)** Expenses which are incurred in the attempt to collect compensation shall be paid by Broker and Associate-Licensee in the same proportion as set forth for the division of compensation (paragraph 8(B)). **(v)** If there is a known or pending claim against Broker or Associate-Licensee on transactions for which Associate-Licensee has not yet been paid, Broker may withhold from compensation due Associate-Licensee on that transaction amounts for which Associate-Licensee could be responsible under paragraph 14, until such claim is resolved. **(vi)** Associate-Licensee shall not be entitled to any advance payment from Broker upon future compensation.

F. UPON OR AFTER TERMINATION: If this Agreement is terminated while Associate-Licensee has listings or pending transactions that require further work normally rendered by Associate-Licensee, Broker shall make arrangements with another associate-licensee to perform the required work, or Broker shall perform the work him/herself. The licensee performing the work shall be reasonably compensated for completing work on those listings or transactions, and such reasonable compensation shall be deducted from Associate-Licensee's share of compensation. Except for such offset, Associate-Licensee shall receive the compensation due as specified above.

9. TERMINATION OF RELATIONSHIP: Broker or Associate-Licensee may terminate their relationship under this Agreement at any time, with or without cause. After termination, Associate-Licensee shall not solicit: **(i)** prospective or existing clients or customers based upon company- generated leads obtained during the time Associate-Licensee was affiliated with Broker; **(ii)** any principal with existing contractual obligations to Broker; or **(iii)** any principal with a contractual transactional obligation for which Broker is entitled to be compensated. Even after termination, this Agreement shall govern all disputes and claims between Broker and Associate-Licensee connected with their relationship under this Agreement, including obligations and liabilities arising from existing and completed listings, transactions, and services.

10. DISPUTE RESOLUTION:
Broker and Associate-Licensee agree to mediate all disputes and claims between them arising from or connected in any way with this Agreement before resorting to court action. If any dispute or claim is not resolved through mediation, or otherwise, instead of resolving the matter in court, Broker and Associate-Licensee may mutually agree to submit the dispute to arbitration at, and pursuant to the rules and bylaws of, the Association of REALTORS® to which both parties belong.

11. AUTOMOBILE: Associate-Licensee shall maintain automobile insurance coverage for liability and property damage in the following amounts $_____/$_____. Broker shall be named as an additional insured party on Associate-Licensee's policies. A copy of the endorsement showing Broker as an additional insured shall be provided to Broker.

12. PERSONAL ASSISTANTS: Associate-Licensee may make use of a personal assistant, provided the following requirements are satisfied. Associate-Licensee shall have a written agreement with the personal assistant which establishes the terms and responsibilities of the parties to the employment agreement, including, but not limited to, compensation, supervision and compliance with applicable law. The agreement shall be subject to Broker's review and approval. Unless otherwise agreed, if the personal assistant has a real estate license, that license must be provided to the Broker. Both Associate-Licensee and personal assistant must sign any agreement that Broker has established for such purposes.

13. OFFICE POLICY MANUAL: If Broker's office policy manual, now or as modified in the future, conflicts with or differs from the terms of this Agreement, the terms of the office policy manual shall govern the relationship between Broker and Associate-Licensee.

Broker's Initials (_____)(_____)   Associate-Licensee's Initials (_____)(_____)

ICA REVISED 11/13 (PAGE 3 OF 4)

Reviewed by _____ Date _____

EQUAL HOUSING OPPORTUNITY

INDEPENDENT CONTRACTOR AGREEMENT (ICA PAGE 3 OF 4)

FIGURE 3.4 (Continued)

14. **INDEMNITY AND HOLD HARMLESS; NOTICE OF CLAIMS:**
    A. Regarding any action taken or omitted by Associate-Licensee, or others working through, or on behalf of Associate-Licensee in connection with services rendered or to be rendered pursuant to this Agreement or Real Estate licensed activity prohibited by this agreement: **(i)** Associate-Licensee agrees to indemnify, defend and hold Broker harmless from all claims, disputes, litigation, judgments, awards, costs and attorney's fees, arising therefrom and **(ii)** Associate-Licensee shall immediately notify Broker if Associate-Licensee is served with or becomes aware of a lawsuit or claim regarding any such action.
    B. Any such claims or costs payable pursuant to this Agreement, are due as follows:
       ☐ Paid in full by Associate-Licensee, who hereby agrees to indemnify and hold harmless Broker for all such sums, or
       ☐ In the same ratio as the compensation split as it existed at the time the compensation was earned by Associate-Licensee ☐ Other: _____
       Payment from Associate-Licensee is due at the time Broker makes such payment and can be offset from any compensation due Associate-Licensee as above. Broker retains the authority to settle claims or disputes, whether or not Associate-Licensee consents to such settlement.

15. **ADDITIONAL PROVISIONS:** _____
    _____

16. **DEFINITIONS:** As used in this Agreement, the following terms have the meanings indicated:
    A. "Listing" means an agreement with a property owner or other party to locate a buyer, exchange party, lessee, or other party to a transaction involving real property, a mobile home, or other property or transaction which may be brokered by a real estate licensee, or an agreement with a party to locate or negotiate for any such property or transaction.
    B. "Compensation" means compensation for acts requiring a real estate license, regardless of whether calculated as a percentage of transaction price, flat fee, hourly rate, or in any other manner.
    C. "Transaction" means a sale, exchange, lease, or rental of real property, a business opportunity, or a manufactured home, which may lawfully be brokered by a real estate licensee.

17. **ATTORNEY FEES:** In any action, proceeding, or arbitration between Broker and Associate-Licensee arising from or related to this Agreement, the prevailing Broker or Associate-Licensee shall be entitled to reasonable attorney fees and costs.

18. **ENTIRE AGREEMENT:** All prior agreements between the parties concerning their relationship as Broker and Associate-Licensee are incorporated in this Agreement, which constitutes the entire contract. Its terms are intended by the parties as a final and complete expression of their agreement with respect to its subject matter, and may not be contradicted by evidence of any prior agreement or contemporaneous oral agreement. This Agreement may not be amended, modified, altered, or changed except by a further agreement in writing executed by Broker and Associate-Licensee.

Broker:

_____
(Brokerage firm name)

By _____
Its Broker/Office manager (circle one)

_____
(Print name)

_____
(Address)

_____
(City, State, Zip)

_____
(Telephone)   (Fax)

Associate-Licensee:

_____
(Signature)

_____
(Print name)

_____
(Address)

_____
(City, State, Zip)

_____
(Telephone)   (Fax)

Published and Distributed by:
REAL ESTATE BUSINESS SERVICES, INC.
a subsidiary of the California Association of REALTORS®
525 South Virgil Avenue, Los Angeles, California 90020

ICA REVISED 11/13 (PAGE 4 OF 4)

Reviewed by _____ Date _____

EQUAL HOUSING OPPORTUNITY

INDEPENDENT CONTRACTOR AGREEMENT (ICA PAGE 4 OF 4)

Source: Reprinted with permission of California Association of REALTORS®.

Special Interest Topic

Piece of the Pie

"I want a real estate license so I can get a share of the commission when I buy and sell my own properties." Some people do not wish to become real estate agents to serve the public, but want a license to deal on their own account. Is this a good idea? The answer is not clear-cut—it depends!

When a licensee buys and sells real estate as a principal, regulations require the licensee to disclose to the opposite party that he or she has a real estate license. Sometimes sellers and/or buyers refuse to deal with licensees as principals for fear that the licensee will take advantage of them. In some cases, the seller allows the buyer-licensee a portion of the commission. However, in some instances, the seller absolutely refuses to allow the listing broker to share the commission with a buyer-licensee.

Working Out-of-State Properties

Problem: A California broker wants to list or sell a property in another state where the California agent is not licensed.

Solution: Real estate professionals must be licensed in the state the property they are selling is located. If not then the solution is to refer the sale to a broker licensed in that state and receive a referral fee.

Commissioner's Former Code of Ethics

At one time, the California real estate commissioner established, by regulations, a code of ethics and professional conduct that applied to all real estate licensees. The code of ethics listed examples of unethical behavior by real estate licensees and required that licensees refrain from such behavior. In addition, the code of ethics outlined positive steps real estate licensees could take to improve the public's image of a real estate agent. In 1997, a regulation repealed the code in an effort to reduce the number of regulations over the real estate business. However, many topics regarding violations in the former code of ethics are still illegal in other code sections under California law.

Filing Complaints

If a person wishes to file a complaint about a real estate agent, they must send a written complaint to the real estate commissioner.

The commissioner then assigns the complaint to a deputy for investigation. Statements about the incident are taken from witnesses and the licensee. In addition, the real estate agent's records and accounts may be audited. An informal conference may be called to allow the investigating deputy to determine the seriousness of the complaint. If a violation of the law has occurred, a formal hearing is called and the agent's license may be suspended or revoked. Every year, the commissioner receives several thousand complaints about real estate licensees, but after an investigation, most are dismissed as not being in violation of real estate law or regulations.

Trade Associations

There are several national, state, and local professional real estate trade associations, such as the National Association of REALTORS® and the National Association of Real Estate Brokers. The role of trade associations is presented in detail in Chapter 1. Real estate trade associations have membership rules and codes of ethics to help monitor the activities of their members. This indirectly works as a form of self-regulation. Members who violate the real estate trade association rules of conduct can be suspended from membership and, in the process, lose many benefits.

3.4 TERMINATION OF A REAL ESTATE AGENCY

There are six basic ways to terminate a real estate agency. (See Figure 3.5.)

1. Termination by *completion of the agency agreement.* The agent fulfills his or her responsibilities by securing a buyer who is ready, willing, and able to buy the property on the exact terms of the listing or on other terms agreeable to the seller. When this occurs, the agent is eligible for the commission and is normally paid at close of escrow.

2. Termination by *expiration of time.* If an agent fails to find a ready, willing, and able buyer by the termination date of the listing, the agency is terminated. Most listings contain a clause, however, that

FIGURE 3.5

Source: © 2015 OnCourse Learning

allows the agent to give the seller a list of prospects to whom the agent has shown the property during the term of the listing. If any of these prospects buys the property directly from the seller or through another broker during the designated protection period after the listing expires, the agent is entitled to a commission. In a buyer's agency, the exact same issues apply, except the word *buyer* is substituted for *seller*.

3. Termination by *death of the principal or death of the agent*. An agency is automatically terminated if the principal or the agent dies during the term of the listing. One exception is if the principal dies after a purchase agreement is signed, in which case the agent is entitled to the commission. The sale is usually binding on the heirs of the decedent.

4. Termination by *destruction of the property*. If a major catastrophe such as an earthquake or a fire occurs, causing damage to the property, the agency is terminated.

5. Termination by *mutual consent*. The principals and the agent can mutually agree to terminate the agency.

6. Termination by *unilateral action of the agent or the principal*.

Either party can terminate the agency unilaterally. However, the party that cancels the agency may be liable for damages. If a principal cancels the agency, the agent is usually entitled to the full commission or, at a minimum, to reimbursement for expenses and time spent.

Chapter Summary

An agency relationship is created when a principal appoints an agent to represent the principal in dealings with third parties. A real estate agency is usually created when a seller appoints a real estate broker to find a buyer for the seller's property. There are two broad categories of agency: general agency and special agency. Real estate agents are usually special agents. When a real estate broker represents only the seller or only the buyer, it is called a single agency. If the broker represents both the buyer and seller, it is called a dual agency. A real estate agency differs from an employer-employee relationship and an independent contractor relationship.

Agencies are created in three ways: by agreement, by ratification, and by estoppel. Most real estate agencies are created by written agreement. A fiduciary relationship is established when a real estate agent is appointed by the principal. This relationship is one of binding trust and loyalty and obligates the real estate agent to act in the principal's best interest.

The agent, nonetheless, owes the opposite party a full disclosure of all known defects. A real estate agent must be honest and truthful and must not misrepresent the sale. Agency violations may include trust fund–handling problems, misrepresentation, false promise, commingling, definite termination date, and secret profit. A principal should advise a real estate agent of any known defects to the property. A seller should not withhold information from the real estate agent or buyer. A seller can be held liable for distortion of facts about the property.

A real estate broker can contract directly with a principal, whereas a salesperson cannot. Only through the real estate salesperson's association with a broker does the salesperson become an agent. Salespersons must have a written employment contract with a broker and can receive compensation only from the employing broker.

Real estate agents are regulated by the CalBRE and by professional trade associations if they are members of those organizations.

Agencies are terminated by completion of the agency agreement, by expiration of time, by death of the principal or agent, by destruction of the property, by mutual consent, and by unilateral termination by the agent or the principal.

Important Terms and Concepts

agent	misrepresentation
buyer's agent	principal
commingling	recovery fund
conversion	secret profit
dual agency	seller's agent
false promise	single agency
fiduciary	special agency
general agency	trust fund
independent contractor	

Practical Applications

1. Real estate salesperson Ames from Vista Realty is the agent for the sale of the Alvarez home at 123 Main Street, Somewhere, CA. Salesperson Jones also works for Vista Realty and brings in an offer on the Alvarez home from Buyer Patel. Explain the agency relationship between Alvarez, Vista Realty, and Patel.

2. A real estate salesperson from Acme Properties shows a potential buyer a home listed with Lake Realty. While showing the home,

the Acme agent mentions that based on the information supplied by Lake Realty, the home is 2,100 square feet and the lot is one-half acre. In fact, the home is 2,000 square feet and the lot is only one-quarter acre. Which real estate company is guilty of misrepresentation? How should the salesperson from Acme Properties have handled the situation?

3. Excellent Realty has a signed contract to act as the exclusive agent for the seller of a condo (priced at $375,000) for a period of 90 days. Within 60 days, a buyer is found who makes an offer of $360,000. Prior to accepting the offer, the seller dies. The heirs then cancel the agreement with Excellent Realty. Excellent Realty contends that it is entitled to a commission based on the $360,000 offer. The heirs deny that they must pay the commission. Who is right and why?

Reviewing Your Understanding

1. A real estate agency exists between the:
   a. seller and buyer.
   b. broker and principal.
   c. borrower and lender.
   d. landlord and tenant.

2. A fiduciary relationship is best described as:
   a. ethics and honesty.
   b. ethics and trust.
   c. trust and confidence.
   d. loyalty and confidentiality.

3. A real estate salesperson is a(n):
   a. direct agent.
   b. agent by virtue of his or her contract with a broker.
   c. employee of the seller.
   d. employee of the buyer.

4. The use of cooperating agents is illegal under California law.
   a. True
   b. False

5. A real estate agency can be created by all of the following, EXCEPT:
   a. ratification.
   b. agreement.
   c. estoppel.
   d. doctrine of realty determination.

6. All of the following are methods of terminating a real estate agency, except for:
   a. estoppel.
   b. mutual consent.
   c. completion of agency.
   d. expiration of time.

7. A home seller must inform his or her real estate agent when the seller is aware of:
   a. termite infestation discovered earlier.
   b. a leaky roof.
   c. an inoperative fireplace.
   d. all of the above.

8. All of the following are true, EXCEPT:
   a. real estate salespersons and brokers are required to be licensed.
   b. a real estate broker, not the salesperson, is appointed by the principal to be the agent.
   c. dual agency does not require written conformation from the buyer and seller.
   d. dual agency means the real estate broker represents both the buyer and seller.

9. A listing agent owes the buyer:
   a. the duty to see that the property is sold at the lowest possible price.
   b. a disclosure of known defects.
   c. a fiduciary relationship.
   d. the right to know the seller's lowest acceptance price.

10. An independent contractor would expect which of the following from her broker?
    a. A vacation schedule
    b. Paid medical insurance
    c. A regular schedule for work
    d. To be responsible for her own withholding taxes

11. If a real estate salesperson decides to work for a new broker, the existing listings obtained by the salesperson belong to whom?
    a. The salesperson
    b. The former broker
    c. The new broker
    d. The seller, who can automatically cancel the listing

12. Unless instructed to hold the check uncashed, a buyer's deposit must be placed with the appropriated party or account within how many business days?
    a. Three
    b. Five
    c. Seven
    d. Nine

13. Ms. Lightdeer showed a property to Mr. and Mrs. Chu without having an agency agreement with the owner. Later, the owner accepted the offer to purchase, which was submitted by Ms. Lightdeer on behalf of Mr. and Mrs. Chu. The owner consented to Ms. Lightdeer's unauthorized acts. Under these circumstances, an agency could be created by:
    a. fiduciary.
    b. estoppel.
    c. ratification.
    d. assumption.

14. The maximum amount per individual claim against the Bureau of Real Estate Recovery Fund is:
    a. $10,000.
    b. $20,000.
    c. $50,000.
    d. $100,000.

15. A real estate broker who has been appointed in writing to be a property owner's agent to find a buyer under a specified set of terms is best described as a:
    a. general, ostensible agent.
    b. general, actual agent.
    c. special, actual agent.
    d. special, ostensible agent.

16. A real estate agent mistakenly states that the portable dishwasher is included in the sales price of the home. This agent is guilty of:
    a. false promise.
    b. misrepresentation.
    c. divided agency.
    d. secret profit.

17. When a real estate agent mixes his or her personal funds with that of a principal, the agent is guilty of:
    a. commingling.
    b. conversion.
    c. trust funding.
    d. embezzlement.

18. In today's real estate market, when a real estate agent uses agents from other real estate companies to help find a buyer, the other agents are called:
    a. principals.
    b. listing agents.
    c. cooperating agents.
    d. finder agents.

19. A salesperson has a signed listing agreement that has gone under contract. The buyer's inspection report, which was sent to the broker and salesperson, shows a number of items that the seller's disclosure did not mention. The buyer terminates the contract. In this case all of the following are true EXCEPT:
    a. the buyer's earnest money will be returned in full.
    b. the salesperson is due a commission.
    c. the seller, broker, and salesperson will now have to disclose the items the buyer found.
    d. the broker can restart efforts to sell the home.

20. All of the following are true, EXCEPT:
    a. all real estate brokers are required to establish reasonable procedures to supervise the activities of salespersons transacting business under the name of the broker.
    b. "as is" home sales are allowed in California if proper disclosures are given.
    c. by law, real estate salespersons are required to have a written contract with their employing broker.
    d. a majority of real estate complaints against agents are valid enough to warrant disciplinary action by the real estate commissioner.

21. A real estate broker is allowed to keep _____ of his or her money in a trust fund to handle bank service charges.
    a. $200
    b. $300
    c. $400
    d. $500

22. The top producing salesperson Jane, at ABC Realty has become a broker and decided to open her own office. She currently has 10 listings with ABC Realty. What will happen to these listings when Jane opens her new office?
    a. Jane will have to leave the listings but will be paid a full commission when they close.
    b. Jane may take her listings since they belong to her.
    c. Jane will have to leave the listings with ABC since they belong to the brokerage.
    d. Jane is required to pay ABC Realty a fee to take the listings to her new firm.

23. Which of the following might be considered an example of secret profit and a violation of the law?
    a. Seller sells for 50 percent more than he or she paid for the property.
    b. Buyer believes the property is worth more than the asking price.
    c. Broker receives a referral fee from a title company without telling the principals in the sales transaction.
    d. Broker earns a commission after showing the property to only one buyer, who then purchases within one week.

24. Under a buyer's agency, the fiduciary relationship is between the broker and the:
    a. seller.
    b. buyer's broker.
    c. buyer.
    d. seller and buyer.

25. When a California real estate broker sells a property in another state where the California agent is not licensed, the use of a licensed broker in the other state does not allow the California broker to share in the commission.
    a. True
    b. False

STUDENT LEARNING OUTCOMES

In recent years, real estate agents have had to be more diligent in seeing that items which could have an adverse effect on a property's value are disclosed to a buyer. In fact, most lawsuits against real estate agents involve the failure to disclose a material fact about a property. At the conclusion of this chapter, you will be able to do the following:

- Give four examples of a material fact to be disclosed about a property.
- Identify when a Transfer Disclosure Statement must be used in a real estate transaction.
- Recognize an agent's statutory duty to inspect and report on a residential property.
- Determine which disclosures must be used in a single-family residence real estate transaction.
- List three of the ramifications of failing to disclose a material fact in a real estate transaction.

A frequently heard mantra from real estate attorneys and brokers is: Disclose, Disclose, Disclose! Most lawsuits against sellers and real estate agents stem from a failure to disclose the condition of a property. Real estate agents must educate both sellers and buyers on what disclosures have to be made in a real estate transaction and what the law imposes on both sellers and buyers as it relates to the disclosure of defects in a property. The old rule of "caveat emptor" or "buyer beware" is no longer followed in California. Likewise, buyers need to understand that no property is perfect.

REAL ESTATE DISCLOSURES

4.1 STATUTORY DISCLOSURES

Agency

Previously in Chapter 3, you learned about the requirement of an agent to disclose agency and confirm the election of the principal as to the type of agency (single or dual) that will take place in the transaction. Agency must be disclosed and confirmed in all single-family (one to four residential units) transactions.

Material Facts

Sellers are required to disclose all material facts concerning the property they are selling. A material fact can be defined as something that affects the value of the property. Commonly, this would include items such as roof leaks, broken appliances, and a hole in a wall. But other items not so apparent could also constitute a material fact affecting the value of the property, including, but not limited to: a neighbor's barking dog, traffic caused by an elementary school in the area, or noise from a neighborhood park. If an item affects the value of the property and is not readily noticeable to the buyer, it must be disclosed. Since it is hard to say what a court would determine as being readily noticeable to a buyer, it is best to disclose anything that might affect the value or desirability of the property. Sellers should ask themselves: "If I were purchasing this property, would I want to know …?"

Real Estate Transfer Disclosure Statement

In California, sellers of one to four residential units must furnish buyers with a completed Transfer Disclosure Statement (TDS). This disclosure statement details various facts about the property—needed repairs, the condition of appliances, improvements added with or without building permits, the existence of any known harmful substances, and so on.

The details noted are based upon an inspection conducted by the listing agent involved in the sale and upon statements made by the seller. This TDS must be provided even if the transaction is an "as is" sale. The responsibility for providing this disclosure rests with the real estate agents. If no agent is involved, the seller must still provide the statement. The Transfer Disclosure Statement must be signed by the buyers, the sellers, and all real estate agents involved in the transaction. Ideally, the TDS should be given to the buyers before they sign the purchase contract. If the TDS is personally given after the purchase contract is signed, the buyer has a three-day right to cancel the sale. If the TDS is mailed to the buyer, then the buyer has five days in which to rescind. The current CAR Residential Purchase Agreement provides a buyer a five-day recession period following a late disclosure by the seller. It is important to note that while the parties could agree by contract to reduce or eliminate the five-day recession period stated in the contact, they cannot reduce the amount of time allowed in the statute. So the buyer will always have at least three days to rescind following a late delivery of the TDS.

The TDS is separated into four parts. Part I is used by the seller to disclose any previous inspections or reports on the property. Typically, these additional reports are attached as addenda to the TDS. Part II is divided into three subparagraphs. Paragraph II. A asks the seller to identify any items that the property contains, and then at the end, whether any of those items contained are not in proper working order. It is important to point out that the seller is not required to repair any item unless the seller agrees to do so in the purchase agreement. Additionally, the seller is not required to inspect their own property to determine if any of the items are not in proper working order. The seller is to simply state, to the best of their knowledge, what items are present in the property and whether they know if the items are not in proper working order. Paragraph II. B asks if the property has any structural problems and a series of boxes are listed for the seller to check. If any of these boxes are checked, then the seller must describe what the defect is in the space provided at the bottom of the paragraph. Paragraph II. C is a series of questions for the seller to answer as either yes or no. If the seller answers yes to any of these questions, then the seller must further explain why that question was answered in the affirmative at the bottom of the page.

Paragraph III may be used for the listing agent to report what material facts they are aware of, following a discussion with the seller and conducting a reasonably diligent visual inspection of the accessible areas of the property.

Paragraph IV may be used for the selling agent to report what material facts they are aware of, after conducting a reasonably diligent visual inspection of the accessible areas of the property.

Certain sellers are not required to complete a TDS (but are still required to disclose any material facts known to them about the property). These sellers include lenders who have foreclosed on or have taken the property back with a deed in lieu of foreclosure, estates in probate or under a testamentary trust, trustees under an irrevocable trust, trustees conducting judicial foreclosures, nonjudicial foreclosures under a deed of trust, bankruptcies, conservatorships, and guardianships. Sellers that are not required to complete a TDS can be divided into two categories: lenders selling foreclosures and court-supervised sales.

See Chapter 5 for an example of a Real Estate Transfer Disclosure Statement.

Residential Environmental and Earthquake Hazards Disclosures

The buyer is given a booklet entitled "Environmental Hazard and Earthquake Guide," and the buyer and seller sign a disclosure form addressing various earthquake issues, including a braced water heater, a bolted-down foundation, unreinforced masonry, and other building construction items. The booklet also discusses hazardous wastes, asbestos, formaldehyde, lead paint, mold, and radon gas. Some of these items will be discussed further in this chapter.

Death

Deaths that occurred on a property may or may not affect the value of the property. If the death occurred more than three years ago, the statute of limitations on disclosure has run out so the death no longer has to be reported. For deaths which have occurred within the last three years, the seller would need to disclose the death if it affects the value of the property. Some legal authorities do not consider a death by natural causes to be a material fact (since everyone dies). However, deaths from homicides, particularly murder and in many cases suicide, probably should be disclosed. Frequently, agents and sellers are asked to make a judgment call and some agents take the position to disclose all deaths, regardless of the cause, that occurred in the last three years. When it comes to disclosure of material fact, it is probably best to err on the side of caution; when in doubt, it is best to disclose.

One cautionary note on the disclosure of a death: unless it is a homicide or suicide, it is probably best not to disclose the cause of death. The disclosure of a death due to AIDS for example, is illegal and could create a cause of action against the agent of discrimination! Chronic diseases, such as AIDS, cancer, Parkinson's, etc., are considered to be disabilities and thus protected under the 1988 Amendments to the Federal Fair Housing Act and the Unruh Civil Rights Law. If you find that an occupant died from a disease within the last three years and feel the need to report the death, then you should do just that: report the death, but not the cause.

Stigmatized Properties

While the statute of limitations does not require an agent to disclose a death that occurred more than three years ago, other events could cause the property to become stigmatized and affect its value. A property that was the scene of a historical event or used in a popular television program [people still visit the house shown in the television series *The Brady Bunch* and *The Beverly Hillbillies* (which is located in Bel Air, not Beverly Hills)]. A house reputed to be haunted in the community or a property that was home to an infamous celebrity may be considered stigmatized and thus suffer a loss in value. Agents need to keep in mind that if an event causes a loss in value to the property, that fact needs to be disclosed to the buyer.

Lead-Based Paint

Lead is a heavy, malleable metal that can cause illness, mental retardation, and even death if ingested. Children can be very susceptible to the effects of lead if they ingest it at a young age. Infants and young children have been known to eat peeling paint chips which can cause development problems. When sanding or stripping lead-based paint from walls, adults can suffer from lead-based paint poisoning should it become airborne and be inhaled.

Under federal law buyers and tenants of properties constructed prior to 1978 must be given a lead-based paint notice prior to purchasing or renting a residential property. Agents should understand that a property constructed prior to 1978 may or may not contain lead-based paint. Because of California's strict environmental laws, it is quite possible that homes built in the early 1970s and 1960s may not contain lead-based paint. Nevertheless, since real estate licensees are not qualified to determine whether or not a house contains lead-based paint, they must make sure that all buyers and tenants of properties constructed prior to 1978 receive a lead-based paint notice. Moreover, if a homeowner hires a contractor to disturb more than six square feet of wall in a pre-1978-constructed house, that contractor must be certified, test for the presence of lead paint, and follow strict lead-based paint contamination procedures in dealing with any lead debris.

Methamphetamine and Other Illegally Controlled Substances

The manufacture of controlled substances can be a nightmare for landlords and property managers. Methamphetamine production especially can create soil contamination of the property. If a seller is aware of the manufacture of controlled substances on their property, it must be disclosed to the buyer prior to the transfer of the property.

Industrial Use Zone

Residential properties adjacent to an area that allows for manufacturing, commercial, or airport uses must be disclosed to buyers prior to the transfer of the property. Should the industrial use create a nuisance to the property being transferred, the existence of the nuisance must also be disclosed.

Ordinance Locations

Properties within a one-mile radius of any federal or state ordinance location must be disclosed to buyers prior to the transfer. Generally, this involves areas that were used for military training purposes that may contain potentially explosive munitions. Children have been known to explore such areas and discover unexploded ordinance or shells with tragic results. When moved, the shells can detonate and cause loss of limb or death to those handling them.

Condominium or Planned Unit Developments

Properties located in an area subject to a home or property owner's association need to be disclosed to potential buyers. California Civil Code §4525 requires sellers of condominiums and planned unit developments to provide copies of financial statements and contact information for the owner's association. This information is included in the California Association of REALTORS® Purchase Agreement.

Natural Hazard Disclosure Statement

Sellers are required to issue a disclosure report called a Natural Hazard Disclosure (NHD) Statement regarding possible natural hazards. The report must answer the following questions.

1. Is the property in a special flood area? This typically concerns areas within the 100-year flood plain or in an alluvium area where flash floods could cause property damage.

2. Is the property in an area of potential flooding or an inundation area? This is an area which could receive water damage if a water-retaining dam were to fail.

3. Is the property in a very high fire severity area? This is an area that is prone to high fire danger. Typically, these areas have large brush or chaparral concentrations; a wild land forest fire risk area. Some areas of California are not covered by a municipal, county fire department or a fire protection district. While the California Department of Forestry (Cal Fire) will attempt to put out fires on public lands, it is not required to do so. Moreover, Cal Fire typically does not employ equipment to extinguish structure fires like fire engines that carry water.

4. Is the property in an earthquake fault zone? This is an area within a quarter mile of an earthquake fault.

5. Is the property in a seismic hazard zone? This is an area prone to landslides or soil liquefaction.

Sellers who are exempt from providing a Transfer Disclosure Statement are also exempt from providing a NHD report if they are not within such a zone. Unfortunately, a seller will only know if they are in a zone if they check the state maps identifying these zones. Since these maps are not available to the general public, all sellers are advised to purchase an NHD report from a commercial provider.

An NHD report also discloses whether the property is located in an area subject to a Mello-Roos Community District and/or a 1915 Bond Act assessment. Both of these assessments are used for public property improvements such as schools, parks, roads, lighting, and sidewalks. More on these fees will be discussed in the taxation chapter.

California law requires that the potential existence of gas and hazardous liquid transmission pipelines be disclosed to buyers. This information can be found in the current CAR Purchase Agreement. Whether or not those pipelines exist is not known to the agents so typically a NHD report will make this disclosure as well.

Property Tax Reassessment

A notice of supplemental tax bill must be given to all buyers of residential properties. Under Proposition 13, properties are reassessed upon transfer. This reassessment can cause a dramatic increase in property taxes to a new buyer from what the seller was paying. Typically, the buyer will receive their first property tax bill based on the seller's old assessment. A supplemental tax bill will be sent to the buyer a few months later, which can come as a shock to the unsuspecting buyer.

The *Notice of Your Supplemental Tax Bill* is designed to alert the buyer about the coming supplemental bill.

Formaldehyde

Formaldehyde is a preservative most known for preserving animals in biology and anatomy classes. It was also used in the 1970s as an insulation material. Formaldehyde foam was sometimes pumped into exterior walls through holes bored near the ceiling joists. Once inside the airspace between the drywall and the exterior wall between the studs, the foam hardened and created an insulating barrier. Unfortunately, the curing process could take years. During the curing, formaldehyde gas sometimes escaped into the house. Inhaling formaldehyde gas can create health problems. As a result, this process is no longer used. However, a seller who is aware that this process was done on their property must disclose it to a potential buyer.

Water Heater Bracing, Carbon Monoxide Detectors, and Smoke Alarms

Sellers are required to disclose whether a property is compliant with water heater bracing and whether it has carbon monoxide detectors and operating smoke alarms. State law requires that all water heaters are either braced or anchored so they do not fall over during an earthquake. A falling water heater can cause severe burning if the scalding water is released. A fallen gas water heater can cause a gas line rupture, which can lead to a fire or an explosion.

Carbon monoxide is an odorless, colorless gas that is toxic to humans and animals. It is generated by the burning of fossil fuels. Residential properties are required to have a carbon monoxide detector and the disclosure of such can be found in the Transfer Disclosure Statement. Sellers who are exempt from providing a TDS must provide a separate disclosure. Homes that do not contain a fossil fuel source are exempt from this disclosure; for example, an all-electric home (no gas appliances or heaters) without a fireplace or an attached garage (since automobiles are typically fossil fueled) may be exempt. Since carbon monoxide is heavier than air, carbon monoxide detectors are usually found plugged into an electrical outlet close to the floor of a property. They can typically be purchased at local hardware stores. All California properties are required to have at least one smoke alarm; how many smoke alarms a property has may depend on the building code that was in effect at the time the house was constructed. The current building code requires smoke alarms on each floor and in every sleeping area. Older houses may only have a single smoke alarm located outside of the sleeping areas (bedrooms). The agent's job is to make sure the property has at least one smoke alarm outside of the sleeping areas; it is the seller's responsibility to make sure their house is in compliance with the law.

The current Transfer Disclosure Statement contains the necessary language for the mandated disclosures for water heater bracing, carbon monoxide detectors, and smoke alarms. For sellers who are exempt from a Transfer Disclosure Statement, a separate Water Heater Bracing, Carbon Monoxide, and Smoke Alarm Disclosure must be made. Probate sales are exempt from smoke alarm and carbon monoxide disclosures, but such properties must contain a smoke alarm and carbon monoxide detector. Local ordinances may have increased requirements beyond state law as well.

Mold

Mold is an organism that grows where there is a food source and water. Typically, it is found in humid, warm, dark conditions in a property. While many people are not particularly sensitive to the effects of mold, it can be debilitating to some people and, if ignored, can cause significant damage to a structure. While minor cases may be described as "mildew," an agent should not ignore or make light of a potential mold infestation. Like any other defect, it is important for an agent to make sure that any evidence or suspicion of mold is disclosed to the buyer or tenant of a property. While mold may be visible as a gray or greenish darkened area, it may also be invisible because it is hidden by a cabinet or encased in a wall. Sometimes a musty smell in confined areas will alert an agent to the potential of mold. Since only an environmental engineer or specialist in mold inspection can make a determination if mold exists (which may require the taking of air samples as well as collecting scrapings of the darkened areas and submitting them to a laboratory for testing), agents should never make a conclusion that mold exists or recommend a specific remediation for mold infestation; that is the responsibly of the environmental engineer! If an agent suspects mold due to seeing darkened areas or detecting a musty odor, they should disclose to the buyer their suspicions and recommend the buyer determine the source.

Radon Gas

Radon is a colorless, odorless radioactive gas that can be released from rock beneath the ground. Radon is frequently found in areas where large amounts of granite rock are located (which is not to be confused with decomposed granite, frequently found in landscaping). As the rock decays, radon gas can be released and will then rise through the soil into the air. Structures, including residential homes, can trap the released gas within the living space of the property.

Radon is relatively easy to test for and to mitigate. Real estate professionals should recommend homes be tested for the presence of the gas as part of the buyers inspection. Mitigation includes using fans to move the gas from the trapped area to above the home where it can dissipate without causing harm. Kits are available for homeowners to test for radon gas. If a homebuyer is concerned about radon gas, it is best to hire an environmental engineer to test for its presence. Some homeowners have been known to set self-testing kits outside, which reduces a radon gas reading. For the test to be accurate, the measuring kit must remain inside the house.

Megan's Law

A buyer is given notice that an online data bank is available to screen the nearby area for registered sex offenders. This disclosure is included in the California Association of REALTORS® Residential Purchase Agreement. Agents should not go to the Megan's Law website with their buyers since the database may not be accurate and may not include the names of offenders who have recently moved into the neighborhood, particularly if the offenders have not reregistered with law enforcement. Of course, it will not include the names of any offenders who are unknown to law enforcement because they have not been caught. Agents should direct any questions buyers may have regarding the website and the information it contains to local law enforcement. More information can be found at the Megan's Law website. See http://www.meganslaw.ca.gov.

Seller Financing Addendum and Disclosure Statement

If a sale involves a *seller carry loan,* then a statement clearly outlining all the financing terms and conditions must be signed by the buyer, seller, and real estate agent, if any. This statement must be signed before the buyer signs the promissory note and other critical loan papers. The Seller Financing Addendum is added to the offer (Residential Purchase Agreement) by the buyer to the seller. The seller will then consider the terms of both the offer and the proposed terms of the seller carry back note contained in the Seller Financing Addendum. If the seller accepts the offer, the Seller Financing Addendum becomes part of the contract between the buyer and seller.

Agent Visual Inspection Disclosure

Under California Civil Code §1102, the agents involved in a transaction are required to make a diligent visual inspection of accessible areas and disclose to the buyer any item that could be a material fact. As discussed earlier regarding the Transfer Disclosure Statement, an agent may record the results of their inspection on the TDS form. Interestingly, the Civil Code does not mandate any particular form for the agent to make their disclosure. They may type a narrative discussion on their office letterhead and provide that as their disclosure. Since most lawsuits against real estate agents are from a failure of an agent to disclose a material fact, the California Association of REALTORS® recommends the use of the Agent Visual Inspection Disclosure form (AVID). The AVID is a three-page form for agents to disclose their inspection findings.

The first page of the AVID is devoted to what is not included in an agent's visual inspection. Agents frequently get into trouble by trying to over disclose facts of a property. This seems hard for many students to understand, since they are told the more disclosure the better. But problems, and liability, can be created when an agent goes beyond their duty of care and delves into areas they do not understand. The standard of care is a reasonably competent and diligent visual inspection of accessible areas of the property. Reasonably competent means to enter every habitable room, to spend time looking around to see if there is any evidence of a problem. This also known as looking for a "red flag" or something that indicates a problem. A stain on a ceiling would be a red flag of water intrusion from the roof. A door that does not close easily is a red flag of some structural issue. An uneven floor would be a red flag of a potential crack in the slab. But agents are cautioned to limit their investigation to a visual inspection. Agents are not to lift up carpets or move furniture and should never attempt to operate appliances. Turning on a garbage disposal will only result in two results: a noise or no noise. All a noise will tell you is that the garbage disposal makes a noise; you do not know if the appliance will chew up an apple or a carrot! Finally, the inspection is of accessible areas. Agents are not to climb on the roof, into the attic, or under the house. It is important for the agent to conduct an inspection, but not to go beyond what is expected of a licensee.

The first page of the AVID states what the agent will inspect, but more importantly, it tells the buyer what the agent will not inspect. The agent will not climb on the roof or into the attic; they will not test appliances or look under carpets, behind wall hangings, or up the chimney; they will not climb hillsides or look behind bushes; they will not measure the square footage, research the existence of permits, or research public records. The AVID also states that the buyer is recommended to hire an appropriate professional to make further inspections of the property that go beyond the agent's visual inspection.

The second page of the AVID contains a list of rooms or areas of the property for the agent to record any red flags discovered in those rooms. It is not a place for the agent to give flowery descriptions of the property. Statements like "looks good" or "nice condition" may be interpreted by a jury to mean a warranty on the condition of the property and lead to liability against the agent!

The third page of the AVID provides additional room for the agent to complete their report as well as comment on the condition of the exterior of the property. It will be signed by the agent making the inspection (both agents in the transaction should complete their own AVID independently of each other). The form is then signed by both the seller and the buyer in the transaction as well as each agent representing the parties.

The above list includes many major, but not all, material facts and disclosures that should be given to a buyer in a 1- to 4-unit residential real estate transaction. Individual cases and circumstances will vary. For additional information about what other disclosures might be required in a particular sales transaction, salespeople or broker associates should consult their employing broker and consult other qualified experts, as well as obtain appropriate legal advice if needed.

Chapter Summary

A material fact is defined as a condition, item, or fact that might affect the value of a property. Sellers are required to disclose any fact or condition that might affect the value of the property. The days of caveat emptor or buyer beware are long gone. The seller's disclosure begins with the Transfer Disclosure Statement. While some sellers are exempt from the TDS [e.g., lenders selling foreclosed properties or those sales under court supervision (probate, bankruptcy, etc.)], most sellers are required to complete a TDS. Failure to do so constitutes a violation of Civil Code §1102.

Real estate agents must disclose any material fact that they know or should have known about the property. "Should have known" is defined as what could be discovered following a reasonably competent diligent visual inspection of accessible areas of the property. While agents are not supposed to test appliances, access hidden areas, or research governmental records, they are expected to enter every habitable room, walk around the property, and look for red flags that indicate a material fact. While agents are not required to use a specific form to disclose the results of their investigation, most agents will use the third page of the TDS form or the Agent's Visual Inspection Disclosure (AVID) form. The AVID form is the preferred disclosure vehicle because of the increased space in which to make disclosures and the boiler plate language on the first page which clearly explains to a buyer what the agent is not expected to inspect.

The seller and agent can use a variety of forms to make additional disclosures which may be required by statute. The California Association of REALTORS® provides hundreds of forms to its members both online and at the local Association of REALTORS® store. All real estate licensees are expected to know which form needs to be used for which disclosure in a transaction and when the disclosure is expected to be made.

Important Terms and Concepts

accessible areas
Agent's Visual Inspection Disclosure form (AVID)
carbon monoxide
controlled substance
flood
formaldehyde
inundation
lead-based paint
material fact
methamphetamine

mold
Natural Hazard Disclosure (NHD) Statement
radon
reasonably competent
red flag
smoke alarm
soil liquefaction
Transfer Disclosure Statement (TDS)
visual inspection

Practical Application

1. On a listing appointment, an agent notices that although the walls of an older house are smudged and in need of painting, the ceilings appear to be freshly painted and the house smells of fresh paint. When the agent arrived at the house, she noticed the shingles on the roof were worn and weathered. Do the freshly painted ceilings constitute a "red flag"?

2. An agent is aware that an old Victorian home that has been on the market for a long time has a reputation for being haunted. A buyer is very interested in Victorian homes and was overheard

saying that he does not believe in ghosts or supernatural occurrences. Based on the fact that the buyer does not believe in ghosts, does the agent have a legal duty to inform the buyer that the home has a reputation for being haunted?

3. When on a listing presentation, an agent learns that the seller's gay son died in the front bedroom eight months ago due to complications from the AIDS virus. Knowing a buyer might be concerned about the cause of death, what if any disclosure should be made in this case?

Reviewing Your Understanding

1. All residential properties must have a lead-based paint disclosure if they were built prior to:
   a. 1980.
   b. 1978.
   c. 1975.
   d. 1985.

2. Which seller is exempt from completing a Transfer Disclosure Statement?
   a. An investor who never lived in the property
   b. A seller who purchased the property three years ago under a probate
   c. A lender selling a property which they previously foreclosed upon
   d. A seller who inherited a property 10 years ago

3. Under state law, a buyer who personally receives a Transfer Disclosure Statement form to a buyer in escrow may cancel the agreement within:
   a. 3 days.
   b. 5 days.
   c. 10 days.
   d. 17 days.

4. Which is not part of an agent's inspection duties?
   a. Inspecting the roof from the driveway
   b. Turning on the garbage disposal to see if it works
   c. Walking into every room of the house
   d. Looking in the garage

5. The *Notice of Your Supplemental Tax Bill* is designed to:
   a. protect the seller from increased property taxes.
   b. give the buyer notice of the supplemental property tax bill.
   c. the agent from having to pay too much income tax.
   d. define how property taxes will be paid.

6. A Natural Hazard Disclosure Statement is typically prepared by:
   a. the seller.
   b. the seller's agent.
   c. the buyer's agent.
   d. a commercial company.

7. A Natural Hazard Disclosure Statement would not cover:
   a. earthquake faults.
   b. soil erosion.
   c. severe fire area.
   d. inundation zones.

8. The person primarily responsible for disclosing problems with the property is the:
   a. listing broker.
   b. selling broker.
   c. seller.
   d. buyer.

9. A seller is not required to:
   a. inspect their own property.
   b. disclose material facts affecting the property.
   c. complete a Transfer Disclosure Statement.
   d. make the property available to the buyer to inspect.

10. Methamphetamine manufacture by a previous occupant poses a danger to buyers because:
    a. they may become addicted to the drug.
    b. the property might have a bad reputation from being occupied by drug users.
    c. there could be soil contamination.
    d. drugs are bad and should be avoided.

11. All of the following would require the listing agent disclose to a buyer EXCEPT:
    a. the home may have structural issues.
    b. the seller died of AIDS on the property.
    c. the seller has mentioned past termite issues.
    d. the property may need a new roof.

12. Sellers who have never lived in a residential property would be well advised to:
    a. hire a professional property inspector to investigate the property.
    b. complete a Transfer Disclosure Statement to the best of their ability.
    c. refuse to complete a Transfer Disclosure Statement since they are not familiar with the property.
    d. ask the agent to complete the Transfer Disclosure Statement for them.

13. An agent completing a visual inspection would not be expected to:
    a. look at the roof for damage.
    b. inspect each accessible area inside and out of the property.
    c. check ceilings for evidence of leaking from the roof.
    d. move furniture to see if there are any hidden issues.

14. Radon gas is:
    a. odorous.
    b. not dangerous.
    c. bluish in color.
    d. hazardous to humans.

15. An agent who suspects a seller is not disclosing a material fact should:
    a. do nothing since they have no actual knowledge of the fact.
    b. confront the seller with their concerns and disclose what they know to the buyer.
    c. tell the buyer's agent what they suspect.
    d. make a note to themselves in the transaction file.

16. Water heaters are required to be braced out of concerns for:
    a. small children climbing on them.
    b. threat of falling over during an earthquake.
    c. maintaining the water temperature.
    d. keeping the water at a proper level.

17. The proper term for the device that will alert the occupants of a property to the danger of smoke and fire is:
    a. smoke alarm.
    b. fire alarm.
    c. Carbon Monoxide detector.
    d. fire detector.

18. The listing agent's duty under the Transfer Disclosure Statement is a little different than that of the selling agent in that the listing agent:
    a. has a greater duty to inspect.
    b. must make an inquiry to the seller.
    c. must inspect after the selling agent conducts his inspection.
    d. must follow the seller's instructions when asked not to disclose an item.

19. Upon discovering that a seller recently painted the interior of a room, an agent should:
    a. complement the seller on their good taste.
    b. note this fact in their inspection as the paint might cover a red flag.
    c. suggest the seller raise the price because of the property improvement.
    d. say nothing since any buyer could see the room was recently painted.

20. All of the following could be considered to be a red flag EXCEPT:
    a. the seller died of HIV/AIDS.
    b. doors that don't close properly.
    c. floors that slope.
    d. windows that don't shut easily.

STUDENT LEARNING OUTCOMES

This chapter presents the legal requirements for an enforceable real estate contract. It includes a definition of a contract, outlines the essential elements of a valid contract, and discusses how contracts are terminated. Two important real estate contracts, the authorization to sell (listing agreement) and the purchase agreement (deposit receipt), are discussed. Copies of these and other contracts used in a typical residential sale are presented in the chapter appendix. At the conclusion of this chapter, you will be able to do the following:

- Define contracts and list the legal requirements for an enforceable contract.
- Describe how contracts are terminated or discharged.
- List seven provisions that should be part of a real estate contract.
- Explain the purpose of an authorization to sell (listing agreement) and discuss the various types of listing agreements.
- Discuss the essential elements of a purchase agreement.
- Discuss the purpose of an option contract.
- Explain the use of a counteroffer form.

REAL ESTATE CONTRACTS

5.1 LEGAL REQUIREMENTS FOR ENFORCEABLE CONTRACTS

A **contract** is generally defined as an agreement between two or more persons, consisting of a promise or mutual promises to perform or not to perform certain acts. If the contract is executed under proper conditions, the law enforces the contract and requires the parties to abide by the terms or incur damages. A **unilateral contract** is created by only one party extending a promise without a reciprocal promise by another party. An example is a reward. If you lose your wallet and offer $100 for its return, this is a unilateral contract because you promise to pay $100 in exchange for an act (find and return your wallet).

However, most real estate contracts are **bilateral contracts** in nature, in which a promise from one person is made in exchange for a promise from another person. For example, in a listing agreement a seller promises to compensate the broker to achieve the purpose of the agreement. The broker in turn promises to use due diligence in attempting to find a ready, willing, and able buyer for the property under terms that are acceptable to the seller.

A contract may be created by expression or by implication. An **expressed contract** is one wherein the parties have agreed to perform an act or acts verbally or under a written agreement. An **implied contract** is one wherein the parties have not formally agreed verbally or through a written agreement to perform an act. Instead, they agree to perform by their actions rather than by their words.

For example, say you reach agreement with a contractor to build a fence around your home and you mutually agree to a style, a size, costs, and a starting date. Under these circumstances, you have probably created an expressed contract. On the other hand, assume you had talked to the contractor about the fence but your discussions were inconclusive and no promises were made. The next day, the contractor

FIGURE 5.1

TYPES OF CONTRACTS

UNILATERAL	**=**	**PROMISE FOR AN ACT**
BILATERAL	**=**	**PROMISE FOR A PROMISE**
EXPRESSED	**=**	**VERBAL OR WRITTEN**
IMPLIED	**=**	**CREATED BY ACTIONS**
EXECUTORY	**=**	**SOME ACTION NEEDED**
EXECUTED	**=**	**COMPLETED CONTRACT**

Most real estate agreements are expressed bilateral contracts.

Source: © 2015 OnCourse Learning

appears on your property with a load of materials and begins building the fence. If you do not stop the contractor and the fence is built, an implied contract may be established.

A contract can also be labeled as an executed contract or an executory contract. In an executed contract, all parties have performed and fulfilled their obligations. An executory contract means that some act of the contract remains to be completed by one or more of the parties. A real estate purchase agreement, discussed later in this chapter, is a good example of an executory contract. Once the offer is accepted it becomes an executory bilateral contract in which the seller promises to sell and the buyer promises to buy. The contract is not completed until all the buyer's contingencies and due diligence duties are completed and escrow is closed. The purchase agreement then becomes a completed or executed contract. (See Figure 5.1.)

Legal Effects of Contracts

Once a contract is created, what are the prospects that the agreement will stand up in court in the event of a dispute? Here are four important legal terms regarding contracts:

1. *Valid.* A valid contract is one that is binding and enforceable in a court of law. It has all the essential elements required to be valid.

2. *Void.* A void contract is an agreement that the courts will not consider a contract; in other words, the contract has no legal effect.

An example is a contract by a minor (someone under 18 years of age) to purchase a home. A minor may acquire real property through a will or by a gift. However, a minor may not buy or sell real property except through a court-appointed person acting on the minor's behalf. An exception is a category of minor called an *emancipated minor*. Examples of emancipated minors are those minors who are married or serving in the military or whose parents have been relieved of legal responsibility for their minor's actions. Emancipated minors can legally contract for real property.

3. *Voidable*. A voidable contract exists where one of the parties (the injured party) has the option of proceeding with the contract or calling it off. Examples include contracts entered into because of duress (force), menace (threat of force), undue influence (pushed by a person with excess power), or fraud (misrepresentation).

4. *Unenforceable*. An unenforceable contract appears to be valid but cannot be sued upon. An example is an oral agreement for the sale of real property by an agent for a commission. A California law called the statute of frauds requires that certain contracts, including real estate contracts, must be in writing to be enforceable. (See Figure 5.2.)

FIGURE 5.2

LEGAL EFFECTS OF CONTRACTS

✓ **VALID**
 binding and enforceable

✓ **VOID**
 no legal effect, no contract

✓ **VOIDABLE**
 one party can cancel due to fraud, duress, or undue influence, but the other side cannot cancel

✓ **UNENFORCEABLE**
 appears valid, but cannot be enforced in court

Source: © 2015 OnCourse Learning

Essential Elements of a Real Estate Contract

The five essential elements for an enforceable real estate contract are (1) parties capable of contracting; (2) mutual consent; (3) lawful object; (4) a sufficient consideration; and (5) according to the statute of frauds, it must be in writing. (See Figure 5.3.)

Parties Capable of Contracting

For a contract to be valid, there must be at least two or more parties with the legal capacity to contract. As a general rule, anyone is capable of contracting. However, there are some exceptions. A minor is incapable of contracting for real property unless the minor is emancipated. Persons who are declared incompetent by the courts cannot contract. Like minors, however, incompetents can acquire title to real property by gift or by will. Certain classifications of convicts are considered incapable of contracting. On the other hand, foreigners can buy and sell real property, although there are certain state and federal withholding regulations when selling real property. Partnerships and corporations are regarded as artificial beings and can also hold and dispose of real property.

Mutual Consent

The parties to a contract must mutually agree to be bound by the terms of the contract. This is exemplified by an offer by one party and an acceptance by the other. The offer must be definite and certain in its terms. A typical example is where a buyer makes an offer to purchase real estate under certain terms and conditions. The seller then accepts the offer, and the acceptance is communicated either in person, by mail, by fax, or electronically to the buyer. This offer and acceptance constitute mutual consent.

Lawful Object

A contract must have a lawful object. An object refers to what is required to be done or not to be done. A contract is void if there is a single object

FIGURE 5.3

Source: © 2015 OnCourse Learning

and that one object is unlawful or impossible to perform. A contract for a gambling debt in California or a contract to commit a crime is not a lawful object. Therefore, the contracts would not be valid.

Sufficient Consideration

Consideration is defined as "a benefit conferred or agreed to be conferred on the person making the promise or on any other person or a detriment suffered or agreed to be suffered." Consideration can be as simple as the return of one promise for another promise. The consideration must have some value. In many cases, the consideration is money, but it need not be. It must be something of value in exchange for something of value and is termed a "valuable" consideration. For example, love and affection might be considered "valuable" or "good" consideration on a gift deed. If there is a dispute as to what constitutes "sufficient" consideration, the parties to the contract may need to bring a court action to clarify the issue.

The Statute of Frauds

According to the *statute of frauds* in the California Civil Code, a real estate contract must be in writing to be enforceable in court. Similarly, any change from the original contract must also be in writing and dated and initialed by the parties involved. The purpose of the law is to prevent perjury, forgery, and dishonest conduct on the part of unscrupulous people in proving the existence and terms of certain important types of contracts. The so-called parol evidence rule applies. This rule states that oral evidence may not be used to modify a written contract that appears to be complete. Oral evidence is allowed to prove fraud or other illegal aspects of a written contract. Practically speaking, a written contract is simply a good way to help eliminate ambiguities and misunderstandings that might arise at a later date.

The California Civil Code requires that the following contracts must be in writing to be enforceable:

1. An agreement that, by its terms, is not to be performed within a year from the making thereof.
2. A special promise to answer for the debt, default, or miscarriage of another, except in the cases provided for in Civil Code Section 2794.
3. An agreement made on consideration of marriage other than a mutual promise to marry.
4. An agreement to lease real estate for more than one year or for the sale of real property or of an interest therein. A lease for one year or less need not be in writing to be valid.

5. An agreement authorizing or employing an agent, broker, or any other person to purchase or sell real estate or to lease real estate for a period longer than one year or to procure, introduce, or find a purchaser or seller of real estate or a lessee or lessor of real estate where such lease is for a period longer than one year, for compensation or a commission.

6. An agreement that, by its terms, is not to be performed during the lifetime of the promisor or an agreement to devise or to bequeath any property or to make any provision for any reason by will.

7. An agreement by a purchaser of real property to pay an indebtedness secured by a mortgage or deed of trust on the property purchased, unless assumption of said indebtedness by the purchaser is specifically provided for in the conveyance of such property.

8. In single-family residential transactions, an agreement to pay a real estate agent a commission. Such agreements not only have to be in writing, but there must also be a disclaimer that commissions are not set by law and are negotiable between the agent and the principal (typically the seller). This negotiation disclosure must be in 10-point bold type or in red ink. Since printers and photocopiers do not always have colored ink, most residential listing agreements use 10-point bold type for this disclosure.

Any contract that does not comply with the preceding is not void, but is unenforceable.

Discharge of Contracts

Contracts can be discharged in a number of ways. **Full performance** is the normal situation, wherein the parties accomplish what they set out to do in the contract. At the other extreme is a *breach* of the contract, which means that at least one of the parties did not fulfill its part of the agreement. In the case of a breach, the injured party has a number of legal remedies available.

Three common remedies are to (1) liquidate damages, (2) *sue for specific performance,* or (3) sue for damages. Liquidated damages allows the seller to keep the buyer's earnest money if the buyer is in breach. Specific performance allows the seller or buyer to sue the party in default to complete the contract and buy or sell the property. When you sue for damages, you are attempting to receive monetary compensation for the damage because the other party will not complete the contract.

Statute of Limitations

To initiate a lawsuit, the **statute of limitations** states that you must begin the lawsuit within a legally prescribed time period. If you fail to initiate the lawsuit within the time period outlined in the statute of limitations, you may have no remedy in the courts and your rights to sue are said to have "outlawed." Four real estate examples of statute of limitation periods are as follows:

1. Three years to bring action for removal of encroachments.
2. Four years to bring action on a written contract.
3. Five years to bring action for recovery of title to property.
4. Ninety days after filing a mechanic's lien, the mechanic must bring a court foreclosure to enforce the lien.

Sometimes, even though the issue is within the statute of limitations, certain rights may be set aside using the Doctrine of Laches. This doc- trine states that if an unreasonable delay in bringing an action results in an unfair situation for a defendant, the extent of the lawsuit might be limited.

Other ways to discharge a contract include the following:

1. Part performance
2. Substantial performance
3. Impossibility of performance
4. Agreement between the parties
5. Release
6. Operation of law
7. Acceptance of a breach of contract

Provisions in Contracts

The following basic provisions should be part of a real estate contract:

1. The date of the agreement
2. The names and addresses of the parties to the contract
3. A description of the property
4. The consideration
5. Reference to the creation of new mortgages or deeds of trust, if any, and the terms thereof; also, the terms and conditions of existing mortgages, if any
6. Any other provisions that may be required or requested by either of the parties
7. The date and place for closing the contract

In the real world, most real estate contracts are preprinted forms that cover the current legal requirements per California law.

Real Estate Licensees Should not Practice Law

A real estate agent is not licensed to practice law. Therefore, a real estate agent should not create a contract from a blank sheet of paper. Current practice allows a real estate agent only to fill in blanks on a preprinted real estate form.

On some occasions, a discrepancy occurs between a preprinted clause in a contract and a handwritten clause. The usual rule is that the handwritten clause supersedes the preprinted clause.

5.2 AUTHORIZATION TO SELL

Commonly referred to as the *listing agreement,* the contract to sell is one of the most common contracts found in a real estate transaction. A listing agreement to sell is the formal contract wherein the owner of the property (the seller) will act in good faith to accomplish the sale of the property under certain stipulated conditions. The listing agreement creates a contract between a real estate broker and the seller.

As noted in the previous chapter, the listing agreement to sell also establishes an agency relationship between the broker and the principal. This agency is referred to as a fiduciary relationship.

A listing agreement is a bilateral contract in that there is an exchange of promises. The seller promises to cooperate with the agent in making the property available to prospective buyers and, should an acceptable offer be presented, to pay the agent a commission on the sale of the listed property. The broker promises to use diligence in attempting to procure a purchaser. Both the seller and agent may make additional promises regarding the terms of the listing agreement. Thus, there is a promise for a promise—the required ingredient for a bilateral contract.

Different Types of Authorization to Sell

There are essentially four different types of listing agreements: (1) open listing, (2) exclusive agency listing, (3) exclusive authorization and right-to-sell listing, and (4) net listing.

All of these should be in writing, and real estate regulations require that all parties must be given copies at the time of signature. (See Figure 5.4.)

FIGURE 5.4

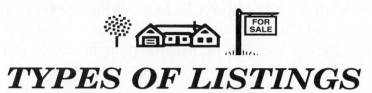

TYPES OF LISTINGS

Open
Exclusive Agency
Exclusive Right to Sell
Net

Source: © 2015 OnCourse Learning

Open Listing

The **open listing** can be given simultaneously to more than one agent. Only one commission is payable, and it is paid to the agent who first procures an offer acceptable to the seller. Even the owner can sell the property to his or her own prospective buyer without paying a commission to any agent. For these reasons, most agents are generally reluctant to spend their time on this type of listing arrangement.

Prior to the Multiple Listing Service, most listings were taken as open; a seller would enter into open listing with all real estate brokers in a town or community, but would only owe a commission to the agent who presented an acceptable offer. This successful agent was referred to as the procuring cause of the sale.

Exclusive Agency Listing

In an **exclusive agency listing,** one broker is named in the contract. The named broker may cooperate with other brokers and agree to share his or her commission with them if they bring in a buyer. The seller reserves the right to sell the property him- or herself to prospects he or she finds without paying a commission. Since the seller may avoid paying a commission if they are able to show that they were the one who procured the buyer, agents and sellers frequently find themselves in disputes under an exclusive agency listing over who found the buyer. In a real sense, under an exclusive agency listing, the seller and broker are in competition with each other to find a buyer. This is not a desirable position for an agent to be in with their fiduciary. An exclusive agency listing must have a definite termination date.

Exclusive Authorization and Right-to-Sell Listing

The **exclusive authorization and right-to-sell listing** is the most common form of listing used in the real estate business. The broker is entitled to a commission no matter who sells the property, including the owner, during a specific time period. Because the broker can expect compensation (assuming the property is reasonably salable), the broker is willing to spend considerable time attempting to find a buyer. The broker is also more likely to spend money to advertise and promote the property.

If authorized by the seller, the listing broker may cooperate with other brokers, who help the listing agent find a buyer and agree to split the commission. An exclusive authorization and right-to-sell listing, like the exclusive agency listing, must contain a definite termination date. If a real estate agent accepts any exclusive listing without a definite termination date, he or she is in violation of the real estate law.

California Association of REALTORS® (CAR) Residential Listing Agreement (Exclusive Authorization and Right to Sell)

The most common listing form in California, the CAR Exclusive Right to Sell (version November 2013), is now summarized by paragraph (see the appendix of this chapter for an example of an Exclusive Authorization and Right-to-Sell listing form):

1. The agreement is clearly labeled as an exclusive right to sell, the listing agreement which identifies the parties, the listing period, and the location of the property.
2. Those items of real property that the seller is removing and those items of personal property that the seller is willing to leave behind are identified. Agents need to remember to repeat these items in the purchase agreement (see paragraph 8 of the CAR Residential Purchase Agreement (RPA-CA) below.
3. The listing price and any additional terms such as whether the seller will sell to an FHA or VA buyer are listed here.
4. The amount of compensation to the listing broker and how much will be shared with the cooperating agent are listed here. The

parties may also provide for a transaction coordinator fee and additional fees to be paid by the seller. The Safety Clause (paragraph 4.a.2.) allows for the agent to receive a commission if the seller sells the property after the listing expiration to a buyer identified by the agent within three days of the expiration of the listing. The parties may also exclude other brokers and buyers from this agreement.

5. The listing requires the agent to submit this listing to the Multiple Listing Service (MLS) within 48 hours. The parties can agree to exclude the listing from the MLS or from the Internet. However, by doing so, the seller is warned that this will limit the number of buyers who may see the property and could cause the seller to receive less for the property. Agents who do not submit their listings to the MLS are suspect of self-dealing, meaning they may have held the listing back from the MLS in hopes of finding the buyer themselves and be entitled to receive both sides of the transaction or a double commission.

6. The seller represents to the agent that they are not aware of any condition affecting the transfer or sale of the property without a full disclosure to the agent.

7. The listing agreement is a bilateral contract in that the seller and agent are exchanging promises. The agent is agreeing to use due diligence in seeking a buyer and the seller is agreeing to cooperate with the agent in their efforts to sell the property.

8. The seller agrees to allow the agent to accept an earnest money deposit from a buyer looking to purchase the property.

9. Both parties acknowledge agency relationships previously disclosed by the agent and agency relationships (dual or single) will be confirmed at the time the purchase agreement is presented.

10. The seller agrees that the broker will not be responsible for damage to or theft of the property, will carry insurance, and will lock up valuables.

11. Since the property will be marketed through photographs and on the Internet, the seller is aware that this could lead to a loss of privacy and understands the potential risks.

12. The seller agrees to allow the agent to install a lockbox or key safe to hold a key to the property. Today's lockboxes are very sophisticated and can record the date, time, and agent identification of those accessing the lockbox.

13. The seller allows a "for sale" sign to be installed on the property.

14. Both parties agree to follow fair housing laws.

15. Attorney's fees will be recoverable by the prevailing party if the party seeking fees agrees to mediation prior to filing a lawsuit of request for arbitration.

16. Parties may add additional terms not stated in the listing contract.

17. The agent taking this listing may have it canceled by their manager or broker within five days. Typically, this is only done if the agent makes a mistake in preparing the listing agreement. *Note:* The listing is a contract between the seller and the broker, not the salesperson or broker associate who actually takes the listing from the seller.

18. Should the seller transfer the property to an alter ego (a trust, for example), the listing is still valid.

19. While mediation is a required part of the agreement (failure to attempt to first mediate a dispute could cause the party to forfeit their right to attorney's fees), arbitration must be separately agreed to by both parties initialing the paragraph.

20. This listing represents the entire agreement between the parties and there is no other agreement.

21. Seller states that they are the true owner of the property and are entitled to sell it.

Net Listing

Under a **net listing**, the seller stipulates a set sum of money that the seller wants regardless of the final sale price of the property. For example, assume that a seller of a home states that he or she wants to net $62,000 cash from the sale after paying off a $325,000 existing loan and $4,000 in escrow, title, and other seller closing costs. The broker is free to sell the property for any price as long as the price covers the seller's net, loan payoff, and $4,000 in closing costs.

Assume the broker finds a buyer who will pay $425,000 for the property. The broker would then earn a commission of $34,000, computed as follows:

$$
\begin{array}{r}
\$425,000 \text{ Sales price} \\
- 325,000 \text{ Seller's existing loan balance} \\
- 4,000 \text{ Seller's closing} \\
- 62,000 \text{ Seller's net} \\
\hline
\$\ 34,000 \text{ Broker's commission}
\end{array}
$$

The commission would then represent 8 percent of the sales price: $34,000 commission ÷ $425,000 sales price = 8% commission rate

Due to past abuses by some real estate agents, California law requires that the broker must notify the seller of the size of the broker's commission and obtain the seller's approval before the net sale can close. The idea is that if the seller feels the broker misled the seller regarding the size of the seller's potential net, the seller will have a chance to halt the sale. If the real estate broker fails to comply with this presale disclosure, the seller may later institute a lawsuit against the broker and the broker's license may be revoked or suspended by the California real estate commissioner. It should be noted that the real estate commissioner (and virtually all real estate brokers) does not favor taking net listings. A net listing may be taken on an open, exclusive agency, or exclusive authorization and a right-to-sell basis.

Multiple Listing Service

The **Multiple Listing Service (MLS)** is a listing service usually controlled by a group of brokers who are affiliated with a real estate association. Listings are placed on the MLS, and that information is then disseminated to all members of the MLS. Some limited information about the listed property is also released to the public via numerous websites. The seller gets significantly greater market exposure through this type of service, given that most MLS systems have hundreds, even thousands, of members. Through the use of computers, this kind of quick mass exposure gives the seller a better chance of receiving the best possible price and terms.

The exclusive authorization and right-to-sell listing contract is widely used when submitting or inputting a listing on the MLS. Under the terms of the MLS, the listing broker controls the listing and agrees to split the commission in some manner with the cooperating agents. A property can be submitted to the MLS only if the agent has the prior written permission of the seller.

5.3 THE REAL PROPERTY PURCHASE AGREEMENT

The California Association of REALTORS Residential Purchase Agreement (RPA-CA), is a contract between the buyer and seller that outlines the terms for the purchase of real property. It also acts as a receipt for the buyer's deposit toward the purchase of the property. In addition, the purchase agreement spells out the details regarding the payment of the broker's commission and frequently sets up the guidelines for the escrow instructions.

The Offer and Acceptance

The prospective buyer stipulates the price and terms of the offer, and the offer is then put on the purchase contract form. By regulation, all offers received by the broker must be presented to the seller. If the seller accepts the offer, communication of acceptance must be delivered back to the buyer or authorized third party (usually the buyer's agent) either in person, by mail, by fax, or electronically. At that time, there is a binding executory contract because offer, acceptance, and notification of the acceptance have occurred. At any time prior to receiving communication that the seller has accepted the offer, the buyer can withdraw the offer and not be liable on the contract.

The broker must now show that he or she has reasonably supervised the transaction. Signed copies of the offer and the acceptance must be left with all parties at the time they sign. Then a final completed copy with all signatures must be given to all parties.

Rejection of the Offer

If the terms of the offer are unacceptable, the seller can reject the offer outright. The legal effect of this is that no contract exists because there has been no acceptance. The buyer, however, may make another offer which will reject the original offer. More on the counteroffer will be given following the discussion of the purchase agreement.

The Purchase Agreement

While a number of purchase agreements may be used in residential real estate, the most widely used is published by the California Association of REALTORS® (CAR). The CAR Purchase Agreement (dated November 2014) or RPA-CA is included in the appendix of this chapter and will be briefly explained below.

Prior to acceptance, the RPA-CA is an offer to the seller from the buyer. In Paragraph 1, the buyer identifies him- or herself, the property, the purchase price, and the escrow period. In Paragraph 2, agency relationships are confirmed between the buyer and seller. The selling agent, writing the offer for the buyer, will know if the seller is represented by another agent or is listed in the same office. Prior to writing the offer, the selling agent will have the buyer elect the correct representation (single or dual) and complete the confirmation paragraph.

Financing terms are stated in Paragraph 3, including whether the buyer will take the earnest money deposit to escrow or has given the deposit to the selling agent. Most buyers will rely on a loan, the terms of which will be stated in subparagraph D. It is important that agents drafting the offer make sure the columns add up to the correct purchase price in subparagraph G. The balance of Paragraph 3 provides for the verification of the down payment, closing costs, and buyer's qualification to obtain financing. The offer's pre-printed terms provide the buyer 21 days to obtain loan approval. The buyer agrees to use good faith in obtaining financing, and the representations made by the buyer regarding the type of loan they are seeking are made in good faith. For example, if a buyer states that he or she is making a 20 percent down payment, changing to a 96.5 percent FHA loan would be a breach of good faith. While not recommended (since most sellers are not interested in taking their property off the market for a buyer who cannot yet perform), Paragraph 4 allows the buyer to make the offer contingent on the sale of his or her property. Frequently, the buyer will want to add terms to the offer, which can be made through addenda and/or advisories under Paragraph 5 or written in the space provided in Paragraph 6.

Buyers will frequently ask the seller to pay for inspection reports and/or to obtain proof the property is in a certain condition. These documents can be requested by identification in Paragraph 7. The party responsible to the cost will also be stated. This is true for the expenses of escrow and title insurance as well.

As was discussed in Chapter 2, personal property will be removed by the seller and all real property will be transferred to the buyer. However, the parties are free to agree to change what will remain or be removed in Paragraph 8. Typically, possession to the property will be made on or before 6:00 P.M. on the date of recordation of the deed, but this too can be changed in Paragraph 9. If a tenant is to remain in possession, that fact needs to be clearly stated in this paragraph.

In Chapter 4, a number of statutory disclosures were discussed which may have to be disclosed to the buyer. Many of these are reiterated in Paragraph 10: Natural Hazards, Lead-Based Paint, Transfer Disclosure Statement, Mello-Roos Community Facilities Act. These include illegal controlled substances, industrial uses, military ordinances nearby, withholding taxes, and the Megan's Law database. Since the disclosure of a database containing sexual offenders in an area is required in all transactions, the disclosure of the Megan's Law website is made in the purchase agreement: www.meganslaw.ca.gov. Agents are reminded not to access this site with their clients since it may not be current and/or accurate and to refer any questions on sexual offenders in the area to local law enforcement. Under Paragraph 11, the property is to be transferred in its present condition (sometime referred to "as is"). However, agents and the parties need to understand that despite transferring the property "as is," the seller is required to disclose all material facts (those items which could affect the value of the property). This does not relieve the buyer from conducting an investigation of the property which is disclosed in Paragraph 12. Agents may not advise the buyer how to take title to the property (which will be discussed in Chapter 6). The buyer is advised to discuss the legal and tax ramifications of taking title in Paragraph 13.

As mentioned above, the seller is required to disclose all material facts, and Paragraph 14 gives the seller 7 seven days from acceptance to do this. The buyer has 17 days from acceptance to investigate and inspect the property. This investigation period will continue until the buyer releases the inspection contingency; however, the seller may give a notice to perform two days prior to the buyer's inspection period concludes. If after receiving the notice to perform from the seller, the buyer does not release the inspection contingency, the seller may cancel the transaction. Under Paragraph 15, the buyer also has the opportunity to make a final walk through the property five days prior to closing, to verify the property is in the same condition as it was when the purchase agreement was made. Should the buyer request the seller repair an item and the seller agree, such repair will be done prior to the final walkthrough under Paragraph 16. Escrow will typically prorate taxes and other items split between the buyer and seller as provided for under Paragraph 17. Although the agents are not parties to this agreement, they are referenced in Paragraph 18 and escrow's duties and responsibilities are stated in Paragraph 20. Should a party be signing on behalf of another entity like a trust or corporation, an addendum will be added stating that capacity under Paragraph 19.

Breach is the nonperformance by a party legally obligated to perform. Paragraph 21 not only defines breach, but it also allows the parties to designate the buyer's deposit as liquated damages in case of a breach. In other words, should the buyer fail to perform after releasing all contingencies (like financing and inspection), then the seller may keep the buyer's deposit. This should not be confused with a nonrefundable deposit; in most cases, a nonrefundable deposit is not allowed in a residential purchase agreement. As an effort to avoid litigation, the parties are required to mediate any disputes prior to initiating litigation or arbitration. Failure by a party to attempt to mediate a dispute could cause that party to forfeit their ability to collect attorney's fees if they are successful in their action against the other party per Paragraph 25 in the contract. Arbitration is an alternative to litigation where an arbitrator will decide the dispute as opposed to a judge or jury. Since a party is giving up a constitutional right by going with arbitration, both parties must initial the arbitration paragraph for it to be included in Paragraph 22. Likewise, the parties must initial the liquated damages paragraph for it to be included. Since mediation is not an optional paragraph, it is required regardless if either section of Paragraph 21 is initialed.

Other provisions such as clarifying the selection of services providers, reporting the sale to the Multiple Listing Service, allowing attorney's fees to the prevailing party, prohibiting assignment of the contract without permission, affirmation of fair housing laws, affirmation that this is a complete agreement between the parties, definitions, time limit to accept the offer, and who may receive communication of acceptance are all stated in Paragraphs 23–32. It is important to remember that the contract will not be created until the offer's acceptance is personally communicated back to the buyer or their agent if the agent's name is written in Paragraph 31. Some contracts follow the mailbox rule, which means if an acceptance is made by the seller and is mailed back to the buyer, an acceptance is communicated the moment the envelope is place in the mailbox. The Real Estate Purchase Agreement does not follow the mailbox rule: all acceptances must be personally received by the buyer.

COUNTEROFFERS

If the seller believes that the offer is basically a good one but there should be a change in price or terms, the seller can make a counteroffer to the buyer. Most agents will recommend the seller respond to all offers with a counteroffer. A **counteroffer** by the seller automatically does away with the buyer's original offer and, in effect, is merely an offer made by the seller to the buyer. As such, the legal requirements for withdrawal or acceptance and communication of acceptance exist in reverse order. If the buyer accepts the changes, that fact must be indicated in writing, and communication of acceptance of the counteroffer must be delivered back to the seller. At any point prior to the communication of acceptance of the counteroffer, the seller may withdraw the counteroffer. In a seller's market (where there are more buyers than sellers), a seller may receive more than one offer at a time; this is referred to as a *multiple offer situation*. While most offers are responded to with a single counteroffer, some form publishers (including the California Association of REALTORS®) offer a multiple counteroffer form. On such a form, the seller will respond to more than one offer at the same time, with the same or different terms. The seller will sign the multiple counteroffer form. The buyer(s) will accept, reject, or in some cases even counter back at a higher price knowing that there is a competing buyer against them. When the multiple counteroffer(s) is returned to the seller, signed by the buyer(s), the seller will have to accept the best multiple counteroffer with a countersignature. Despite two or more buyers accepting the multiple counteroffer from the seller, no agreement will exist until the seller signs a second time. It would be unethical (which could lead to disciplinary charges against the listing agent) for a listing agent to reply to a single buyer's offer with the multiple counteroffer form. The use of the multiple counteroffer form signifies to the buyer(s) that there is at least one other buyer with an offer on the property.

See the appendix of this chapter for an example of the California Association of REALTORS(R) Residential Purchase Agreement (RPA-CA) Counteroffer and Multiple Counteroffer.

OPTIONS

An **option** is a contract between the owner of a property (the optionor) and a potential purchaser (an optionee). Under an option, the optionor gives to the optionee the right to purchase real estate under a set of terms and conditions within a designated time period. To be binding, the optionee must pay consideration (an option fee) to the optionor.

Here is the key point: The optionee is not required to exercise the option (purchase the property). The optionee has the choice of buying or not buying. If the optionee decides to buy, the owner must sell under the terms of the option. If the optionee decides not to buy, the optionor (owner) keeps the option fee.

Sometimes a combination of lease and option is used, by which a person leases the property for a certain time and then has the option to purchase the property when the lease expires. The use of lease or option agreements usually increases during "tight" markets when sellers have a difficult time finding buyers. The seller attempts to entice someone to purchase by allowing the person(s) to rent for a while, then buy later—a sort of try-before-you-buy situation.

Broker Supervision and Recordkeeping

A broker is required to exercise reasonable supervision over the activities of his or her salespeople. Reasonable supervision includes the establishment of policies, rules, procedures, and systems to review, oversee, inspect, and manage the activities that require a real estate license.

A real estate broker is required to keep copies of all listings, deposit receipts, canceled checks, trust funds, and any other documents in connection with any sale transaction for at least three years. Forms pertaining to acting as a mortgage broker must be kept for four years. As noted in Chapter 4, a broker must also maintain current trust fund records.

5.4 SAMPLE CONTRACTS

The appendix of this chapter includes samples of contracts and forms typically used in a simple real estate residential sale. The forms are copyrighted by the California Association of REALTORS® and are reprinted with permission by the California Association of REALTORS®. Endorsement is not implied.

The forms are as follows:

1. Residential Listing Agreement (Exclusive Authorization and Right to Sell)
2. Seller's Advisory
3. California Residential Purchase Agreement and Joint Escrow Instructions
4. Real Estate Transfer Disclosure Statement
5. Buyer's Inspection Advisory

Real estate contracts and forms are subject to change as new laws and/or regulations are enacted. A situation may occur in a real estate transaction that would require a specialized, as opposed to standard, form. All parties should seek legal and other advice from qualified professionals.

Chapter Summary

A contract is an agreement between two or more persons, consisting of a promise or mutual promises to do or not to do certain acts. In a unilateral contract, a promise is made by one party in exchange for an act by another party. In a bilateral contract, one party exchanges promises with another party. Contracts may be created by expression or implication. Contracts can be valid, void, voidable, and unenforceable.

There are five essential elements of a real estate contract: (1) parties capable of contracting; (2) mutual consent; (3) a lawful object; (4) sufficient consideration; and (5) according to the statute of frauds, the contract must be in writing. An executed contract is one that has been completed or fulfilled. An executory contract is one that remains to be fulfilled.

Full performance discharges or terminates a contract. Contracts can also be terminated by expiration of time and mutual consent, in addition to other technical means. A breach of contract means that at least one of the parties did not fulfill its part of the agreement. The three most common remedies for a breach are liquidated damages, or to sue for specific performance or damages. If liquidated damages is used the deposit maybe no more than 3% of the purchase price for buyer occupancy. Beyond the prescribed period, a person's rights are said to have outlawed.

A real estate contract should contain the date of the agreement, the names and addresses of the parties, a description of the property, the consideration, the mortgage terms, the date and place of closing the contract, and any other provisions required or requested by the parties. A listing agreement is the contract between the principal, usually the seller, and the real estate broker. Types of listings include the open, exclusive agency, exclusive authorization and right-to-sell, and net listing. The Multiple Listing Service is an organization whereby member brokers agree to pool listings and share information and commissions.

The purchase agreement is the contract between the buyer and seller. To be binding, certain requirements must be met. Common real estate forms are provided in this chapter. For one- to four-unit residential properties, various disclosure statements must be presented to the buyer before the close of the sale.

Important Terms and Concepts

bilateral contract	implied contract
contract	Multiple Listing Service (MLS)
counteroffer	net listing
deposit receipt	open listing
exclusive agency listing	option
exclusive authorization and	statute of frauds
right-to-sell listing	statute of limitations
executed contract	unenforceable
executory contract	unilateral contract
expressed contract	valid
fiduciary relationship	void
full performance	voidable

Practical Application

1. Sara Hennings, age 17, joins the Army and then signs a lease agreement and moves into an apartment near the base. Using correct contract language, describe in complete detail Sara's contract, beginning with words such as *unilateral, bilateral, expressed, implied, executed, executory, valid, void, voidable,* and *unenforceable.*

2. Homeowner Vargas signed a 180-day exclusive right-to-sell listing with Sunrise Realty. After 90 days, Vargas unilaterally canceled the listing and gave it to Ambrosini Properties, who 10 days later brought in a full-price offer. The sale closed and a full commission was paid to Ambrosini Properties. Later, Sunrise Realty filed a lawsuit for another full commission. What are the legal issues?

3. A buyer makes an offer on a property and includes the liquidated damages clause in the contract. Thirty-five days after acceptance, the buyer gets "cold feet" and does not want to purchase the property. The buyer has not released any contingencies and gives no reason for canceling the agreement. The seller, upset at the buyer's refusal to complete the contract, demands to keep the deposit as liquidated damages. Is the deposit refundable?

Reviewing Your Understanding

1. All of the following are covered by the statute of frauds, except for:
   a. the payment of an agent's commission.
   b. a two-year lease.
   c. an agreement not to be performed within the lifetime of the promisor.
   d. a six-month tenancy.

2. Which of the following is not considered an essential element of a real estate contract?
   a. Consent of the parties
   b. lawful object
   c. Consideration
   d. Parol evidence

3. Contracts may be discharged by:
   a. impossibility of performance.
   b. agreement of the parties.
   c. both a and b.
   d. none of the above.

4. The most common form of listing agreement found in California is a(n):
   a. open listing.
   b. exclusive authorization and right-to-sell listing.
   c. net listing.
   d. exclusive agency listing.

5. By law, which of the following listings must have a definite termination date?
   a. Open listing
   b. Exclusive agency
   c. Exclusive authorization and right-to-sell listing
   d. Both b and c

6. Of the following listings, which stipulates that the agent will be paid no matter who sells the property?
   a. Exclusive right-to-sell listing
   b. Exclusive agency
   c. Net listing
   d. Open listing

7. An exclusive listing is:
   a. a unilateral contract.
   b. a bilateral contract.
   c. both a and b.
   d. none of the above.

8. A deposit receipt is:
   a. a receipt for the buyer's deposit.
   b. a real estate purchase contract when properly executed.
   c. a common term for the purchase contract.
   d. all of the above.

9. Which of the following statements is true if, during the escrow process but prior to closing the sale, a fire destroys the home being sold?
   a. The buyer must complete the purchase.
   b. The buyer need not complete the purchase, but the seller retains the deposit.
   c. The buyer need not complete the purchase and is entitled to the deposit back.
   d. The buyer must complete the purchase for the land, not the remains of the building.

10. After signing a deposit receipt, the seller decides not to sell. The buyer can do all of the following, except:
    a. cancel the agreement and get a refund of any deposit.
    b. sue for specific performance.
    c. sue on criminal grounds.
    d. sue for money damages.

11. A contract that still needs some action by one or more of the parties is:
    a. executory.
    b. executed.
    c. valid.
    d. voidable.

12. Within the prescribed time period, an inexcusable delay might limit a lawsuit according to the:
    a. statute of frauds.
    b. statute of limitations.
    c. Doctrine of Laches.
    d. Stoppel of Contracts.

13. Which best describes a voidable contract?

    a. Valid and enforceable

    b. Valid on its face, but for some reason cannot be sued upon

    c. Valid on its face until the injured party voids the contract

    d. Void on its face until enforceable

14. A 17-year-old divorced man wishes to sell his separate real property. A real estate broker legally:

    a. can accept the listing.

    b. cannot accept the listing until the owner is 18 years old.

    c. can accept the listing only if the owner has a legal guardian.

    d. cannot accept the listing unless the owner's parents consent.

15. Agency relationships are typically confirmed:

    a. on a separate agency confirmation form.

    b. in Paragraph 2 of the purchase agreement.

    c. verbally between the buyer and seller.

    d. in writing between the two agents.

16. The liquidated damages clause:

    a. creates a nonrefundable deposit.

    b. is always limited to 2 percent of the purchase price.

    c. allows the seller to keep the buyer's deposit if the buyer breaches the contract.

    d. is not enforceable.

17. Megan's Law is concerned with which issue?

    a. The location of registered sex offenders

    b. The possibility of mold and its required disclosure

    c. The issue of AIDS and/or death in the home

    d. The hazards of earthquakes and unbraced water heaters

18. Prior to signing a listing agreement, the seller asks the real estate agent: "What is the commission rate in our area?" According to regulations and the California Association of REALTORS® Residential Listing Agreement in the appendix of this chapter, the correct answer is:

    a. 6 percent.

    b. all commission rates are negotiable.

    c. 7 percent according to the association of REALTORS®.

    d. 10 percent according to the Bureau of Real Estate.

19. A contract that can be canceled by one party due to fraud, misrepresentation, or duress is known as what type of contract?

    a. Valid

    b. Void

    c. Voidable

    d. Unenforceable

20. Under the purchase agreement, mediation:
    a. is a requirement under the contract.
    b. must be initialed by both parties to be included.
    c. is voluntary between the parties.
    d. does not apply to buyers who do not intend to live on the property.

21. Under the preprinted language of the California Residential Purchase Agreement (RPA-CA) the amount of time the seller has to accept the offer from the buyer is:
    a. 24 hours
    b. 3 days
    c. 5 days
    d. none, the agent must include an acceptance date

22. According to the residential listing agreement in the appendix of this chapter, the listing broker is entitled to the commission if the property is sold during the listing period by:
    a. the seller.
    b. the listing broker.
    c. the cooperating broker, if any.
    d. any of the above.

23. A buyer and seller sign a valid California Residential Purchase Agreement and Joint Escrow Instructions contract as outlined in the appendix of this chapter. Per the terms of the contract, any statutory and lead disclosures cannot be waived by the mutual agreement of the buyer and the seller.
    a. True
    b. False

24. The time frame from which a party must perform or act under the California Residential Purchase Agreement (RPA-CA) is from:
    a. the date of acceptance
    b. the date on the first page of the contract
    c. the date of opening of escrow
    d. the date of closing of escrow

25. Seller's acceptance to the purchase agreement (shown in the appendix of this chapter):
    a. follows the mailbox rule.
    b. may be done within five days of the date of the offer.
    c. must be personally received by the buyer.
    d. may be done during escrow.

SAMPLE FORMS

The appendix of this chapter includes samples of contracts and forms typically used in a simple real estate residential sale. The forms are copyrighted by the California Association of REALTORS® and are reprinted with permission by the California Association of REALTORS®. Endorsement is not implied.

The forms are as follows:

1. Residential Listing Agreement (Exclusive Authorization and Right to Sell) (Figure 5.5)
2. Seller's Advisory (Figure 5.6)
3. California Residential Purchase Agreement and Joint Escrow Instructions (Figure 5.7)
4. Real Estate Transfer Disclosure Statement (Figure 5.8)
5. Buyer's Inspection Advisory (Figure 5.9)

Real estate contracts and forms are subject to change as new laws and/or regulations are enacted. Situations may occur in a real estate transaction that require specialized, as opposed to standard, contract forms. All parties should seek legal and other advice from qualified professionals.

FIGURE 5.5

CALIFORNIA
ASSOCIATION
OF REALTORS®

RESIDENTIAL LISTING AGREEMENT
(Exclusive Authorization and Right to Sell)
(C.A.R. Form RLA, Revised 11/13)

1. **EXCLUSIVE RIGHT TO SELL:** _____ ("Seller")
   hereby employs and grants _____ ("Broker")
   beginning (date) _____ and ending at 11:59 P.M. on (date) _____ ("Listing Period")
   the exclusive and irrevocable right to sell or exchange the real property in the City of _____,
   County of _____, Assessor's Parcel No. _____,
   California, described as: _____ ("Property").

2. **ITEMS EXCLUDED AND INCLUDED:** Unless otherwise specified in a real estate purchase agreement, all fixtures and fittings that are attached to the Property are included, and personal property items are excluded, from the purchase price.
   ADDITIONAL ITEMS EXCLUDED: _____.
   ADDITIONAL ITEMS INCLUDED: _____.
   Seller intends that the above items be excluded or included in offering the Property for sale, but understands that: (i) the purchase agreement supersedes any intention expressed above and will ultimately determine which items are excluded and included in the sale; and (ii) Broker is not responsible for and does not guarantee that the above exclusions and/or inclusions will be in the purchase agreement.

3. **LISTING PRICE AND TERMS:**
   A. The listing price shall be: _____
   _____ Dollars ($ _____).
   B. Additional Terms: _____
   _____.

4. **COMPENSATION TO BROKER:**
   Notice: The amount or rate of real estate commissions is not fixed by law. They are set by each Broker individually and may be negotiable between Seller and Broker (real estate commissions include all compensation and fees to Broker).
   A. Seller agrees to pay to Broker as compensation for services irrespective of agency relationship(s), either ☐ _____ percent of the listing price (or if a purchase agreement is entered into, of the purchase price), or ☐ $ _____,
   AND _____, as follows:
   (1) If during the Listing Period, or any extension, Broker, cooperating broker, Seller or any other person procures a ready, willing, and able buyer(s) whose offer to purchase the Property on any price and terms is accepted by Seller, provided the Buyer completes the transaction or is prevented from doing so by Seller. (Broker is entitled to compensation whether any escrow resulting from such offer closes during or after the expiration of the Listing Period, or any extension.)
   OR (2) If within _____ calendar days (a) after the end of the Listing Period or any extension; or (b) after any cancellation of this Agreement, unless otherwise agreed, Seller enters into a contract to sell, convey, lease or otherwise transfer the Property to anyone ("Prospective Buyer") or that person's related entity: (i) who physically entered and was shown the Property during the Listing Period or any extension by Broker or a cooperating broker; or (ii) for whom Broker or any cooperating broker submitted to Seller a signed, written offer to acquire, lease, exchange or obtain an option on the Property. Seller, however, shall have no obligation to Broker under paragraph 4A(2) unless, not later than 3 calendar days after the end of the Listing Period or any extension or cancellation, Broker has given Seller a written notice of the names of such Prospective Buyers.
   OR (3) If, without Broker's prior written consent, the Property is withdrawn from sale, conveyed, leased, rented, otherwise transferred, or made unmarketable by a voluntary act of Seller during the Listing Period, or any extension.
   B. If completion of the sale is prevented by a party to the transaction other than Seller, then compensation due under paragraph 4A shall be payable only if and when Seller collects damages by suit, arbitration, settlement or otherwise, and then in an amount equal to the lesser of one-half of the damages recovered or the above compensation, after first deducting title and escrow expenses and the expenses of collection, if any.
   C. In addition, Seller agrees to pay Broker: _____.
   D. Seller has been advised of Broker's policy regarding cooperation with, and the amount of compensation offered to, other brokers.
   (1) Broker is authorized to cooperate with and compensate brokers participating through the multiple listing service(s) ("MLS") by offering to MLS brokers out of Broker's compensation specified in 4A, either ☐ _____ percent of the purchase price, or ☐ $_____.
   (2) Broker is authorized to cooperate with and compensate brokers operating outside the MLS as per Broker's policy.
   E. Seller hereby irrevocably assigns to Broker the above compensation from Seller's funds and proceeds in escrow. Broker may submit this Agreement, as instructions to compensate Broker pursuant to paragraph 4A, to any escrow regarding the Property involving Seller and a buyer, Prospective Buyer or other transferee.
   F. **(1)** Seller represents that Seller has not previously entered into a listing agreement with another broker regarding the Property, unless specified as follows: _____.
   (2) Seller warrants that Seller has no obligation to pay compensation to any other broker regarding the Property unless the Property is transferred to any of the following individuals or entities: _____
   _____.
   (3) If the Property is sold to anyone listed above during the time Seller is obligated to compensate another broker: (i) Broker is

Seller's Initials (_____)(_____)

Reviewed by _____ Date _____

EQUAL HOUSING
OPPORTUNITY

FIGURE 5.5 (Continued)

Property Address:_____ Date:_____

not entitled to compensation under this Agreement; and (ii) Broker is not obligated to represent Seller in such transaction.

5. MULTIPLE LISTING SERVICE:

A. Broker is a participant/subscriber to _____ Multiple Listing Service (MLS) and possibly others. Unless otherwise instructed in writing the Property will be listed with the MLS(s) specified above. That MLS is (or if checked ☐ is not) the primary MLS for the geographic area of the Property. All terms of the transaction, including sales price and financing, if applicable, (i) will be provided to the MLS in which the property is listed for publication, dissemination and use by persons and entities on terms approved by the MLS and (ii) may be provided to the MLS even if the Property is not listed with the MLS.

BENEFITS OF USING THE MLS; IMPACT OF OPTING OUT OF THE MLS; PRESENTING ALL OFFERS

WHAT IS AN MLS? The MLS is a database of properties for sale that is available and disseminated to and accessible by all other real estate agents who are participants or subscribers to the MLS. Property information submitted to the MLS describes the price, terms and conditions under which the Seller's property is offered for sale (including but not limited to the listing broker's offer of compensation to other brokers). It is likely that a significant number of real estate practitioners in any given area are participants or subscribers to the MLS. The MLS may also be part of a reciprocal agreement to which other multiple listing services belong. Real estate agents belonging to other multiple listing services that have reciprocal agreements with the MLS also have access to the information submitted to the MLS. The MLS may further transmit the MLS database to Internet sites that post property listings online.

EXPOSURE TO BUYERS THROUGH MLS: Listing property with an MLS exposes a seller's property to all real estate agents and brokers (and their potential buyer clients) who are participants or subscribers to the MLS or a reciprocating MLS.

CLOSED/PRIVATE LISTING CLUBS OR GROUPS: Closed or private listing clubs or groups are not the same as the MLS. The MLS referred to above is accessible to all eligible real estate licensees and provides broad exposure for a listed property. Private or closed listing clubs or groups of licensees may have been formed outside the MLS. Private or closed listing clubs or groups are accessible to a more limited number of licensees and generally offer less exposure for listed property. Whether listing property through a closed, private network - and excluding it from the MLS - is advantageous or disadvantageous to a seller, and why, should be discussed with the agent taking the Seller's listing.

NOT LISTING PROPERTY IN A LOCAL MLS: If the Property is listed in an MLS which does not cover the geographic area where the Property is located then real estate agents and brokers working that territory, and Buyers they represent looking for property in the neighborhood, may not be aware the Property is for sale.

OPTING OUT OF MLS: If Seller elects to exclude the Property from the MLS, Seller understands and acknowledges that: (a) real estate agents and brokers from other real estate offices, and their buyer clients, who have access to that MLS may not be aware that Seller's Property is offered for sale; (b) Information about Seller's Property will not be transmitted to various real estate Internet sites that are used by the public to search for property listings; (c) real estate agents, brokers and members of the public may be unaware of the terms and conditions under which Seller is marketing the Property.

REDUCTION IN EXPOSURE: Any reduction in exposure of the Property may lower the number of offers and negatively impact the sales price.

PRESENTING ALL OFFERS: Seller understands that Broker must present all offers received for Seller's Property unless Seller gives Broker written instructions to the contrary.

| Seller's Initials (   ) (   ) | Broker's Initials (   ) (   ) |

B. MLS rules generally provide that residential real property and vacant lot listings be submitted to the MLS within 2 days or some other period of time after all necessary signatures have been obtained on the listing agreement. Broker will not have to submit this listing to the MLS if, within that time, Broker submits to the MLS a form signed by Seller (C.A.R. Form SELM or the local equivalent form).

C. MLS rules allow MLS data to be made available by the MLS to additional Internet sites unless Broker gives the MLS instructions to the contrary. Seller acknowledges that for any of the below opt-out instructions to be effective, Seller must make them on a separate instruction to Broker signed by Seller (C.A.R. Form SELI or the local equivalent form). Specific information that can be excluded from the Internet as permitted by (or in accordance with) the MLS is as follows:

(1) Property Availability: Seller can instruct Broker to have the MLS not display the Property on the Internet.

(2) Property Address: Seller can instruct Broker to have the MLS not display the Property address on the Internet.

Seller understands that the above opt-outs would mean consumers searching for listings on the Internet may not see the Property or Property's address in response to their search.

(3) Feature Opt-Outs: Seller can instruct Broker to advise the MLS that Seller does not want visitors to MLS Participant or Subscriber Websites or Electronic Displays that display the Property listing to have the features below. Seller understands (i) that these opt-outs apply only to Websites or Electronic Displays of MLS Participants and Subscribers who are real estate broker and agent members of the MLS; (ii) that other Internet sites may or may not have the features set forth herein; and (iii) that neither Broker nor the MLS may have the ability to control or block such features on other Internet sites.

(a) Comments And Reviews: The ability to write comments or reviews about the Property on those sites; or the ability to link to another site containing such comments or reviews if the link is in immediate conjunction with the Property.

RLA REVISED 11/13 (PAGE 2 OF 5)

Seller's Initials (_____)(_____)

| Reviewed by _____ Date _____ |

RESIDENTIAL LISTING AGREEMENT - EXCLUSIVE (RLA PAGE 2 OF 5)

FIGURE 5.5 (Continued)

Property Address:_____ Date:_____

(b) Automated Estimate Of Value: The ability to create an automated estimate of value or to link to another site containing such an estimate of value if the link is in immediate conjunction with the Property.

6. **SELLER REPRESENTATIONS:** Seller represents that, unless otherwise specified in writing, Seller is unaware of: (i) any Notice of Default recorded against the Property; (ii) any delinquent amounts due under any loan secured by, or other obligation affecting, the Property; (iii) any bankruptcy, insolvency or similar proceeding affecting the Property; (iv) any litigation, arbitration, administrative action, government investigation or other pending or threatened action that affects or may affect the Property or Seller's ability to transfer it; and (v) any current, pending or proposed special assessments affecting the Property. Seller shall promptly notify Broker in writing if Seller becomes aware of any of these items during the Listing Period or any extension thereof.

7. **BROKER'S AND SELLER'S DUTIES:** (a) Broker agrees to exercise reasonable effort and due diligence to achieve the purposes of this Agreement. Unless Seller gives Broker written instructions to the contrary, Broker is authorized to (i) order reports and disclosures as necessary, (ii) advertise and market the Property by any method and in any medium selected by Broker, including MLS and the Internet, and, to the extent permitted by these media, control the dissemination of the information submitted to any medium; and (iii) disclose to any real estate licensee making an inquiry the receipt of any offers on the Property and the offering price of such offers. (b) Seller agrees to consider offers presented by Broker, and to act in good faith to accomplish the sale of the Property by, among other things, making the Property available for showing at reasonable times and, subject to paragraph 4F, referring to Broker all inquiries of any party interested in the Property. Seller is responsible for determining at what price to list and sell the Property. Seller further agrees to indemnify, defend and hold Broker harmless from all claims, disputes, litigation, judgments attorney fees and costs arising from any incorrect information supplied by Seller, or from any material facts that Seller knows but fails to disclose.

8. **DEPOSIT:** Broker is authorized to accept and hold on Seller's behalf any deposits to be applied toward the purchase price.

9. **AGENCY RELATIONSHIPS:**
   A. Disclosure: If the Property includes residential property with one-to-four dwelling units, Seller shall receive a "Disclosure Regarding Agency Relationships" (C.A.R. Form AD) prior to entering into this Agreement.
   B. Seller Representation: Broker shall represent Seller in any resulting transaction, except as specified in paragraph 4F.
   C. Possible Dual Agency With Buyer: Depending upon the circumstances, it may be necessary or appropriate for Broker to act as an agent for both Seller and buyer, exchange party, or one or more additional parties ("Buyer"). Broker shall, as soon as practicable, disclose to Seller any election to act as a dual agent representing both Seller and Buyer. If a Buyer is procured directly by Broker or an associate-licensee in Broker's firm, Seller hereby consents to Broker acting as a dual agent for Seller and Buyer. In the event of an exchange, Seller hereby consents to Broker collecting compensation from additional parties for services rendered, provided there is disclosure to all parties of such agency and compensation. Seller understands and agrees that: (i) Broker, without the prior written consent of Seller, will not disclose to Buyer that Seller is willing to sell the Property at a price less than the listing price; (ii) Broker, without the prior written consent of Buyer, will not disclose to Seller that Buyer is willing to pay a price greater than the offered price; and (iii) except for (i) and (ii) above, a dual agent is obligated to disclose known facts materially affecting the value or desirability of the Property to both parties.
   D. Other Sellers: Seller understands that Broker may have or obtain listings on other properties, and that potential buyers may consider, make offers on, or purchase through Broker, property the same as or similar to Seller's Property. Seller consents to Broker's representation of sellers and buyers of other properties before, during and after the end of this Agreement.
   E. Confirmation: If the Property includes residential property with one-to-four dwelling units, Broker shall confirm the agency relationship described above, or as modified, in writing, prior to or concurrent with Seller's execution of a purchase agreement.

10. **SECURITY AND INSURANCE:** Broker is not responsible for loss of or damage to personal or real property, or person, whether attributable to use of a keysafe/lockbox, a showing of the Property, or otherwise. Third parties, including, but not limited to, appraisers, inspectors, brokers and prospective buyers, may have access to, and take videos and photographs of, the interior of the Property. Seller agrees: (i) to take reasonable precautions to safeguard and protect valuables that might be accessible during showings of the Property; and (ii) to obtain insurance to protect against these risks. Broker does not maintain insurance to protect Seller.

11. **PHOTOGRAPHS AND INTERNET ADVERTISING:**
    A. In order to effectively market the Property for sale it is often necessary to provide photographs, virtual tours and other media to buyers. Seller agrees (or ☐ if checked, does not agree) that Broker may photograph or otherwise electronically capture images of the exterior and interior of the Property ("Images") for static and/or virtual tours of the Property by buyers and others on Broker's website, the MLS, and other marketing sites. Seller acknowledges that once Images are placed on the Internet neither Broker nor Seller has control over who can view such Images and what use viewers may make of the Images, or how long such Images may remain available on the Internet. Seller further agrees that such Images are the property of Broker and that Broker may use such Images for advertisement of Broker's business in the future.
    B. Seller acknowledges that prospective buyers and/or other persons coming onto the property may take photographs, videos or other images of the property. Seller understands that Broker does not have the ability to control or block the taking and use of Images by any such persons. (If checked) ☐ Seller instructs Broker to publish in the MLS that taking of Images is limited to those persons preparing Appraisal or Inspection reports. Seller acknowledges that unauthorized persons may take images who do not have access to or have not read any limiting instruction in the MLS or who take images regardless of any limiting instruction in the MLS. Once Images are taken and/or put into electronic display on the Internet or otherwise, neither Broker nor Seller has control over who views such Images nor what use viewers may make of the Images.

12. **KEYSAFE/LOCKBOX:** A keysafe/lockbox is designed to hold a key to the Property to permit access to the Property by Broker, cooperating brokers, MLS participants, their authorized licensees and representatives, authorized inspectors, and accompanied prospective buyers. Broker, cooperating brokers, MLS and Associations/Boards of REALTORS® are not insurers against injury, theft, loss, vandalism or damage attributed to the use of a keysafe/lockbox. Seller does (or if checked ☐ does not) authorize Broker to install a keysafe/lockbox. If Seller does not occupy the Property, Seller shall be responsible for obtaining occupant(s)' written permission for use of a keysafe/lockbox (C.A.R. Form KLA).

RLA REVISED 11/13 (PAGE 3 OF 5)

Seller's Initials (_____)(_____)

Reviewed by _____ Date _____

FIGURE 5.5 (Continued)

Property Address: _____ Date: _____

13. SIGN: Seller does (or if checked ☐ does not) authorize Broker to install a FOR SALE/SOLD sign on the Property.

14. EQUAL HOUSING OPPORTUNITY: The Property is offered in compliance with federal, state and local anti-discrimination laws.

15. ATTORNEY FEES: In any action, proceeding or arbitration between Seller and Broker regarding the obligation to pay compensation under this Agreement, the prevailing Seller or Broker shall be entitled to reasonable attorney fees and costs from the non-prevailing Seller or Broker, except as provided in paragraph 19A.

16. ADDITIONAL TERMS: ☐ REO Advisory Listing (C.A.R. Form REOL) ☐ Short Sale Information and Advisory (C.A.R. Form SSIA)

_____

_____

_____

_____

_____

_____

17. MANAGEMENT APPROVAL: If an associate-licensee in Broker's office (salesperson or broker-associate) enters into this Agreement on Broker's behalf, and Broker or Manager does not approve of its terms, Broker or Manager has the right to cancel this Agreement, in writing, within **5 Days** After its execution.

18. SUCCESSORS AND ASSIGNS: This Agreement shall be binding upon Seller and Seller's successors and assigns.

19. DISPUTE RESOLUTION:

   A. MEDIATION: Seller and Broker agree to mediate any dispute or claim arising between them regarding the obligation to pay compensation under this Agreement, before resorting to arbitration or court action. Mediation fees, if any, shall be divided equally among the parties involved. If, for any dispute or claim to which this paragraph applies, any party (i) commences an action without first attempting to resolve the matter through mediation, or (ii) before commencement of an action, refuses to mediate after a request has been made, then that party shall not be entitled to recover attorney fees, even if they would otherwise be available to that party in any such action. THIS MEDIATION PROVISION APPLIES WHETHER OR NOT THE ARBITRATION PROVISION IS INITIALED. **Exclusions from this mediation agreement are specified in paragraph 19C.**

   B. ARBITRATION OF DISPUTES:
   Seller and Broker agree that any dispute or claim in Law or equity arising between them regarding the obligation to pay compensation under this Agreement, which is not settled through mediation, shall be decided by neutral, binding arbitration. The arbitrator shall be a retired judge or justice, or an attorney with at least 5 years of residential real estate Law experience, unless the parties mutually agree to a different arbitrator. The parties shall have the right to discovery in accordance with Code of Civil Procedure §1283.05. In all other respects, the arbitration shall be conducted in accordance with Title 9 of Part 3 of the Code of Civil Procedure. Judgment upon the award of the arbitrator(s) may be entered into any court having jurisdiction. Enforcement of this agreement to arbitrate shall be governed by the Federal Arbitration Act. Exclusions from this arbitration agreement are specified in paragraph 19C.
   "NOTICE: BY INITIALING IN THE SPACE BELOW YOU ARE AGREEING TO HAVE ANY DISPUTE ARISING OUT OF THE MATTERS INCLUDED IN THE 'ARBITRATION OF DISPUTES' PROVISION DECIDED BY NEUTRAL ARBITRATION AS PROVIDED BY CALIFORNIA LAW AND YOU ARE GIVING UP ANY RIGHTS YOU MIGHT POSSESS TO HAVE THE DISPUTE LITIGATED IN A COURT OR JURY TRIAL. BY INITIALING IN THE SPACE BELOW YOU ARE GIVING UP YOUR JUDICIAL RIGHTS TO DISCOVERY AND APPEAL, UNLESS THOSE RIGHTS ARE SPECIFICALLY INCLUDED IN THE 'ARBITRATION OF DISPUTES' PROVISION. IF YOU REFUSE TO SUBMIT TO ARBITRATION AFTER AGREEING TO THIS PROVISION, YOU MAY BE COMPELLED TO ARBITRATE UNDER THE AUTHORITY OF THE CALIFORNIA CODE OF CIVIL PROCEDURE. YOUR AGREEMENT TO THIS ARBITRATION PROVISION IS VOLUNTARY."
   "WE HAVE READ AND UNDERSTAND THE FOREGOING AND AGREE TO SUBMIT DISPUTES ARISING OUT OF THE MATTERS INCLUDED IN THE 'ARBITRATION OF DISPUTES' PROVISION TO NEUTRAL ARBITRATION."

   | Seller's Initials _____ / _____ | Broker's Initials _____ / _____ |

   C. ADDITIONAL MEDIATION AND ARBITRATION TERMS: The following matters shall be excluded from mediation and arbitration: (i) a judicial or non-judicial foreclosure or other action or proceeding to enforce a deed of trust, mortgage or installment land sale contract as defined in Civil Code §2985; (ii) an unlawful detainer action; (iii) the filing or enforcement of a mechanic's lien; and (iv) any matter that is within the jurisdiction of a probate, small claims or bankruptcy court. The filing of a court action to enable the recording of a notice of pending action, for order of attachment, receivership, injunction, or other provisional remedies, shall not constitute a waiver or violation of the mediation and arbitration provisions.

Seller's Initials (_____)(_____)

| Reviewed by _____ Date _____ |

EQUAL HOUSING OPPORTUNITY

RESIDENTIAL LISTING AGREEMENT - EXCLUSIVE (RLA PAGE 4 OF 5)

FIGURE 5.5 (Continued)

Property Address:_____ Date:_____

20. **ENTIRE AGREEMENT:** All prior discussions, negotiations and agreements between the parties concerning the subject matter of this Agreement are superseded by this Agreement, which constitutes the entire contract and a complete and exclusive expression of their agreement, and may not be contradicted by evidence of any prior agreement or contemporaneous oral agreement. If any provision of this Agreement is held to be ineffective or invalid, the remaining provisions will nevertheless be given full force and effect. This Agreement and any supplement, addendum or modification, including any photocopy or facsimile, may be executed in counterparts.

21. **OWNERSHIP, TITLE AND AUTHORITY:** Seller warrants that: (i) Seller is the owner of the Property; (ii) no other persons or entities have title to the Property; and (iii) Seller has the authority to both execute this Agreement and sell the Property. Exceptions to ownership, title and authority are as follows: _____
_____.

By signing below, Seller acknowledges that Seller has read, understands, received a copy of and agrees to the terms of this Agreement.

Seller_____ Date _____
Address _____City _____ State _____ Zip _____
Telephone _____ Fax _____ Email _____

Seller _____ Date _____
Address _____City _____ State _____ Zip _____
Telephone _____ Fax _____ Email _____

Real Estate Broker (Firm) _____ Cal BRE Lic.# _____
By (Agent) _____Cal BRE Lic.# _____ Date _____
Address _____City _____ State _____ Zip _____
Telephone _____ Fax _____ Email _____

Published and Distributed by:
REAL ESTATE BUSINESS SERVICES, INC.
a subsidiary of the California Association of
REALTORS®

Reviewed by _____ Date _____

EQUAL HOUSING OPPORTUNITY

RLA REVISED 11/13 (PAGE 5 OF 5)

RESIDENTIAL LISTING AGREEMENT - EXCLUSIVE (RLA PAGE 5 OF 5)

FIGURE 5.6

CALIFORNIA
ASSOCIATION
OF REALTORS®

SELLER'S ADVISORY
(C.A.R. Form SA, Revised 11/13)

Property Address: _____ ("Property")

1. **INTRODUCTION:** Selling property in California is a process that involves many steps. From start to finish, it could take anywhere from a few weeks to many months, depending upon the condition of your Property, local market conditions and other factors. You have already taken an important first step by listing your Property for sale with a licensed real estate broker. Your broker will help guide you through the process and may refer you to other professionals, as needed. This advisory addresses many things you may need to think about and do as you market your Property. Some of these things are requirements imposed upon you, either by law or by the listing or sale contract. Others are simply practical matters that may arise during the process. Please read this document carefully and, if you have any questions, ask your broker or appropriate legal or tax advisor for help.

2. **DISCLOSURES:**

   A. **General Disclosure Duties:** You must affirmatively disclose to the buyer, in writing, any and all known facts that materially affect the value or desirability of your Property. You must disclose these facts whether or not asked about such matters by the buyer, any broker, or anyone else. This duty to disclose applies even if the buyer agrees to purchase your Property in its present condition without requiring you to make any repairs. If you do not know what or how to disclose, you should consult a real estate attorney in California of your choosing. Broker cannot advise you on the legal sufficiency of any disclosures you make. If the Property you are selling is a residence with one to four units except for certain subdivisions, your broker also has a duty to conduct a reasonably competent and diligent visual inspection of the accessible areas and to disclose to a buyer all adverse material facts that the inspection reveals. If your broker discovers something that could indicate a problem, your broker must advise the buyer.

   B. **Statutory Duties** (For one-to-four Residential Units):

      (1) You must timely prepare and deliver to the buyer, among other things, a Real Estate Transfer Disclosure Statement ("TDS"), and a Natural Hazard Disclosure Statement ("NHD"). You have a legal obligation to honestly and completely fill out the TDS form in its entirety. (Many local entities or organizations have their own supplement to the TDS that you may also be asked to complete.) The NHD is a statement indicating whether your Property is in certain designated flood, fire or earthquake/seismic hazard zones. Third-party professional companies can help you with this task.

      (2) Depending upon the age and type of construction of your Property, you may also be required to provide and, in certain cases you can receive limited legal protection by providing, the buyer with booklets entitled "The Homeowner's Guide to Earthquake Safety," "The Commercial Property Owner's Guide to Earthquake Safety," "Protect Your Family From Lead in Your Home," and "Environmental Hazards: A Guide For Homeowners and Buyers." Some of these booklets may be packaged together for your convenience. The earthquake guides ask you to answer specific questions about your Property's structure and preparedness for an earthquake. If you are required to supply the booklet about lead, you will also be required to disclose to the buyer any known lead-based paint and lead-based paint hazards on a separate form. The environmental hazards guide informs the buyer of common environmental hazards that may be found in properties.

      (3) If you know that your property is: (i) located within one mile of a former military ordnance location; or (ii) in or affected by a zone or district allowing manufacturing, commercial or airport use, you must disclose this to the buyer. You are also required to make a good faith effort to obtain and deliver to the buyer a disclosure notice from the appropriate local agency(ies) about any special tax levied on your Property pursuant to the Mello-Roos Community Facilities Act, the Improvement Bond Act of 1915, and a notice concerning the contractual assessment provided by section 5898.24 of the Streets And Highways Code (collectively, "Special Tax Disclosures").

      (4) If the TDS, NHD, or lead, military ordnance, commercial zone or Special Tax Disclosures are provided to a buyer after you accept that buyer's offer, the buyer will have 3 days after delivery (or 5 days if mailed) to terminate the offer, which is why it is extremely important to complete these disclosures as soon as possible. There are certain exemptions from these statutory requirements; however, if you have actual knowledge of any of these items, you may still be required to make a disclosure as the items can be considered material facts.

   C. **Death and Other Disclosures:** Many buyers consider death on real property to be a material fact in the purchase of property. In some situations, it is advisable to disclose that a death occurred or the manner of death; however, California Civil Code Section 1710.2 provides that you have no disclosure duty "where the death has occurred more than three years prior to the date the transferee offers to purchase, lease, or rent the real property, or [regardless of the date of occurrence] that an occupant of that property was afflicted with, or died from, Human T-Lymphotropic Virus Type III/Lymphadenopathy-Associated Virus." This law does not "immunize an owner or his or her agent from making an intentional misrepresentation in response to a direct inquiry from a transferee or a prospective transferee of real property, concerning deaths on the real property."

   D. **Condominiums and Other Common Interest Subdivisions:** If the Property is a condominium, townhouse, or other property in a common interest subdivision, you must provide to the buyer copies of the governing documents, the most recent financial statements distributed, and other documents required by law or contract. If you do not have a current version of these documents, you can request them from the management of your homeowners' association. To avoid delays, you are encouraged to obtain these documents as soon as possible, even if you have not yet entered into a purchase agreement to sell your Property.

Seller's Initials (_____)(_____)

Reviewed by _____ Date _____

EQUAL HOUSING
OPPORTUNITY

SA REVISED 11/13 (PAGE 1 OF 2) Print Date

SELLER'S ADVISORY (SA PAGE 1 OF 2)

FIGURE 5.6 (Continued)

Property Address:_____ Date:_____

3. **CONTRACT TERMS AND LEGAL REQUIREMENTS:**
   A. **Contract Terms and Conditions:** A buyer may request, as part of the contract for the sale of your Property, that you pay for repairs to the Property and other items. Your decision on whether or not to comply with a buyer's requests may affect your ability to sell your Property at a specified price.
   B. **Withholding Taxes:** Under federal and California tax laws, a buyer is required to withhold a portion of the purchase price from your sale proceeds for tax purposes unless you sign an affidavit of non-foreign status and California residency, or some other exemption applies and is documented.
   C. **Prohibition Against Discrimination:** Discriminatory conduct in the sale of real property against individuals belonging to legally protected classes is a violation of the law.
   D. **Government Retrofit Standards:** Unless exempt, you must comply with government retrofit standards, including, but not limited to, installing operable smoke detectors, bracing water heaters, and providing the buyer with corresponding written statements of compliance. Some city and county governments may impose additional retrofit standards, including, but not limited to, installing low-flow toilets and showerheads, gas shut-off valves, tempered glass, and barriers around swimming pools and spas. You should consult with the appropriate governmental agencies, inspectors, and other professionals to determine the retrofit standards for your Property, the extent to which your Property complies with such standards, and the costs, if any, of compliance.
   E. **EPA's LEAD-BASED PAINT RENOVATION, REPAIR AND PAINTING RULE:** The new rule requires that contractors and maintenance professionals working in pre-1978 housing, child care facilities, and schools with lead-based paint be certified; that their employees be trained; and that they follow protective work practice standards. The rule applies to renovation, repair, or painting activities affecting more than six square feet of lead-based paint in a room or more than 20 square feet of lead-based paint on the exterior. Enforcement of the rule begins October 1, 2010. See the EPA website at www.epa.gov/lead for more information.
   F. **Legal, Tax and Other Implications:** Selling your Property may have legal, tax, insurance, title or other implications. You should consult an appropriate professional for advice on these matters.
4. **MARKETING CONSIDERATIONS:**
   A. **Pre-Sale Considerations:** You should consider doing what you can to prepare your Property for sale, such as correcting any defects or other problems. Many people are not aware of defects in or problems with their own Property. One way to make yourself aware is to obtain professional home inspections prior to sale, both generally, and for wood destroying pests and organisms, such as termites. By doing this, you then have an opportunity to make repairs before your Property is offered for sale, which may enhance its marketability. Keep in mind, however, that any problems revealed by such inspection reports or repairs that have been made, whether or not disclosed in a report, should be disclosed to the buyer (see "Disclosures" in paragraph 2 above). This is true even if the buyer gets his/her own inspections covering the same area. Obtaining inspection reports may also assist you during contract negotiations with the buyer. For example, if a pest control report has both a primary and secondary recommendation for clearance, you may want to specify in the purchase agreement those recommendations, if any, for which you are going to pay.
   B. **Post-Sale Protections:** It is often helpful to provide the buyer with, among other things, a home protection/warranty plan for the Property. These plans will generally cover problems, not deemed to be pre-existing, that occur after your sale is completed. In the event something does go wrong after the sale, and it is covered by the plan, the buyer may be able to resolve the concern by contacting the home protection company.
   C. **Safety Precautions:** Advertising and marketing your Property for sale, including, but not limited to, holding open houses, placing a keysafe/lockbox, erecting FOR SALE signs, and disseminating photographs, video tapes, and virtual tours of the premises, may jeopardize your personal safety and that of your Property. You are strongly encouraged to maintain insurance, and to take any and all possible precautions and safeguards to protect yourself, other occupants, visitors, your Property, and your belongings, including cash, jewelry, drugs, firearms and other valuables located on the Property, against injury, theft, loss, vandalism, damage, and other harm.
   D. **Expenses:** You are advised that you, not the Broker, are responsible for the fees and costs, if any, to comply with your duties and obligations to the buyer of your Property.
5. **OTHER ITEMS:**_____
   _____
   _____

Seller has read and understands this Advisory. By signing below, Seller acknowledges receipt of a copy of this document.

Seller _____ Date _____

Print Name _____

Seller _____ Date _____

Print Name _____

Real Estate Broker _____ By _____ Date _____
                                                              (Agent)

Address _____ City _____ State _____ Zip _____

Telephone _____ Fax _____ E-mail _____

Reviewed by _____ Date _____

SA REVISED 11/13 (PAGE 2 of 2)

SELLER'S ADVISORY (SA PAGE 2 OF 2)

FIGURE 5.7

CALIFORNIA
ASSOCIATION
OF REALTORS®

CALIFORNIA
RESIDENTIAL PURCHASE AGREEMENT
AND JOINT ESCROW INSTRUCTIONS
(C.A.R. Form RPA-CA, Revised 11/14)

Date Prepared: _____

1. OFFER:
   A. THIS IS AN OFFER FROM _____ ("Buyer").
   B. THE REAL PROPERTY to be acquired is _____, situated
     in_____ (City),_____ County, California,
     _____(Zip Code), Assessor's Parcel No. _____ ("Property").
   C. THE PURCHASE PRICE offered is _____
     _____ Dollars $ _____.
   D. CLOSE OF ESCROW shall occur on _____ (date)(or _____ **Days** After Acceptance).
   E. Buyer and Seller are referred to herein as the "Parties." Brokers are not Parties to this Agreement.

2. AGENCY:
   A. DISCLOSURE: The Parties each acknowledge receipt of a ☑"Disclosure Regarding Real Estate Agency Relationships" (C.A.R.
     Form AD).
   B. CONFIRMATION: The following agency relationships are hereby confirmed for this transaction:
     Listing Agent _____ (Print Firm Name) is the agent of (check one):
     ☐ the Seller exclusively; or ☐ both the Buyer and Seller.
     Selling Agent _____ (Print Firm Name) (if not the same as the
     Listing Agent) is the agent of (check one): ☐ the Buyer exclusively; or ☐ the Seller exclusively; or ☐ both the Buyer and Seller.
   C. POTENTIALLY COMPETING BUYERS AND SELLERS: The Parties each acknowledge receipt of a ☑"Possible Representation
     of More than One Buyer or Seller - Disclosure and Consent" (C.A.R. Form PRBS).

3. FINANCE TERMS: Buyer represents that funds will be good when deposited with Escrow Holder.
   A. INITIAL DEPOSIT: Deposit shall be in the amount of ....$ _____
     (1) Buyer Direct Deposit: Buyer shall deliver deposit directly to Escrow Holder by electronic funds
     transfer, ☐ cashier's check, ☐ personal check, ☐ other _____within 3 business days
     after Acceptance (or _____);
     OR (2) ☐ **Buyer Deposit with Agent:** Buyer has given the deposit by personal check (or _____)
     to the agent submitting the offer (or to _____), made payable to
     _____. The deposit shall be held uncashed until Acceptance and then deposited
     with Escrow Holder within **3** business days after Acceptance (or _____).
     Deposit checks given to agent shall be an original signed check and not a copy.
     (Note: Initial and increased deposits checks received by agent shall be recorded in Broker's trust fund log.)
   B. INCREASED DEPOSIT: Buyer shall deposit with Escrow Holder an increased deposit in the amount of ....$ _____
     within ____ **Days** After Acceptance (or _____).
     If the Parties agree to liquidated damages in this Agreement, they also agree to incorporate the increased
     deposit into the liquidated damages amount in a separate liquidated damages clause (C.A.R. Form RID)
     at the time the increased deposit is delivered to Escrow Holder.
   C. ☐ **ALL CASH OFFER:** No loan is needed to purchase the Property. Written verification of sufficient funds
     to close this transaction IS ATTACHED to this offer or ☐ Buyer shall, within **3 (or _____) Days** After
     Acceptance, Deliver to Seller such verification.
   D. LOAN(S):
     (1) FIRST LOAN: in the amount of ....$ _____
     This loan will be conventional financing or ☐ FHA, ☐ VA, ☐ Seller financing (C.A.R. Form SFA),
     ☐ assumed financing (C.A.R. Form AFA), ☐ Other _____. This loan shall be at a fixed
     rate not to exceed _____% or, ☐ an adjustable rate loan with initial rate not to exceed _____%.
     Regardless of the type of loan, Buyer shall pay points not to exceed _____% of the loan amount.
     (2) ☐ **SECOND LOAN** in the amount of ....$ _____
     This loan will be conventional financing or ☐ Seller financing (C.A.R. Form SFA), ☐ assumed
     financing (C.A.R. Form AFA), ☐ Other _____. This loan shall be at a fixed rate not to
     exceed _____% or, ☐ an adjustable rate loan with initial rate not to exceed _____%. Regardless of
     the type of loan, Buyer shall pay points not to exceed _____% of the loan amount.
     (3) FHA/VA: For any FHA or VA loan specified in 3D(1), Buyer has **17 (or ___) Days** After Acceptance
     to Deliver to Seller written notice (C.A.R. Form FVA) of any lender-required repairs or costs that
     Buyer requests Seller to pay for or otherwise correct. Seller has no obligation to pay or satisfy lender
     requirements unless agreed in writing. A FHA/VA amendatory clause (C.A.R. Form FVAC) shall be a
     part of this transaction.
   E. ADDITIONAL FINANCING TERMS: _____
     _____
   F. BALANCE OF DOWN PAYMENT OR PURCHASE PRICE in the amount of..............................$ _____
     to be deposited with Escrow Holder pursuant to Escrow Holder instructions.
   G. PURCHASE PRICE (TOTAL): ....$ _____

Buyer's Initials (_____)(_____)   Seller's Initials (_____)(_____)

© 1991-2014, California Association of REALTORS®, Inc.

RPA-CA REVISED 11/14 (PAGE 1 OF 10) Print Date

EQUAL HOUSING
OPPORTUNITY

CALIFORNIA RESIDENTIAL PURCHASE AGREEMENT (RPA-CA PAGE 1 OF 10)

FIGURE 5.7 (Continued)

Property Address: _____   Date: _____

H. **VERIFICATION OF DOWN PAYMENT AND CLOSING COSTS:** Buyer (or Buyer's lender or loan broker pursuant to paragraph 3J(1)) shall, within **3 (or ___) Days** After Acceptance, Deliver to Seller written verification of Buyer's down payment and closing costs. (☐ Verification attached.)

I. **APPRAISAL CONTINGENCY AND REMOVAL:** This Agreement is (or ☐ is NOT) contingent upon a written appraisal of the Property by a licensed or certified appraiser at no less than the purchase price. Buyer shall, as specified in paragraph 14B(3), in writing, remove the appraisal contingency or cancel this Agreement within **17 (or ___) Days** After Acceptance.

J. **LOAN TERMS:**
(1) LOAN APPLICATIONS: Within **3 (or ___) Days** After Acceptance, Buyer shall Deliver to Seller a letter from Buyer's lender or loan broker stating that, based on a review of Buyer's written application and credit report, Buyer is prequalified or preapproved for any NEW loan specified in paragraph 3D. If any loan specified in paragraph 3D is an adjustable rate loan, the prequalification or preapproval letter shall be based on the qualifying rate, not the initial loan rate. (☐ Letter attached.)
(2) LOAN CONTINGENCY: Buyer shall act diligently and in good faith to obtain the designated loan(s). Buyer's qualification for the loan(s) specified above **is a contingency** of this Agreement unless otherwise agreed in writing. If there is no appraisal contingency or the appraisal contingency has been waived or removed, then failure of the Property to appraise at the purchase price does not entitle Buyer to exercise the cancellation right pursuant to the loan contingency if Buyer is otherwise qualified for the specified loan. Buyer's contractual obligations regarding deposit, balance of down payment and closing costs **are not contingencies** of this Agreement.
(3) LOAN CONTINGENCY REMOVAL:
Within **21 (or ___) Days** After Acceptance, Buyer shall, as specified in paragraph 14, in writing, remove the loan contingency or cancel this Agreement. If there is an appraisal contingency, removal of the loan contingency shall not be deemed removal of the appraisal contingency.
(4) ☐ NO LOAN CONTINGENCY: Obtaining any loan specified above is NOT a contingency of this Agreement. If Buyer does not obtain the loan and as a result does not purchase the Property, Seller may be entitled to Buyer's deposit or other legal remedies.
(5) LENDER LIMITS ON BUYER CREDITS: Any credit to Buyer, from any source, for closing or other costs that is agreed to by the Parties ("Contractual Credit") shall be disclosed to Buyer's lender. If the total credit allowed by Buyer's lender ("Lender Allowable Credit") is less than the Contractual Credit, then (i) the Contractual Credit shall be reduced to the Lender Allowable Credit, and (ii) in the absence of a separate written agreement between the Parties, there shall be no automatic adjustment to the purchase price to make up for the difference between the Contractual Credit and the Lender Allowable Credit.

K. **BUYER STATED FINANCING:** Seller is relying on Buyer's representation of the type of financing specified (including but not limited to, as applicable, all cash, amount of down payment, or contingent or non-contingent loan). Seller has agreed to a specific closing date, purchase price and to sell to Buyer in reliance on Buyer's covenant concerning financing. Buyer shall pursue the financing specified in this Agreement. Seller has no obligation to cooperate with Buyer's efforts to obtain any financing other than that specified in the Agreement and the availability of any such alternate financing does not excuse Buyer from the obligation to purchase the Property and close escrow as specified in this Agreement.

4. **SALE OF BUYER'S PROPERTY:**
   A. This Agreement and Buyer's ability to obtain financing are NOT contingent upon the sale of any property owned by Buyer.
   OR B. ☐ This Agreement and Buyer's ability to obtain financing are contingent upon the sale of property owned by Buyer as specified in the attached addendum (C.A.R. Form COP).

5. **ADDENDA AND ADVISORIES:**
   A. ADDENDA: ☐ Addendum # _____ (C.A.R. Form ADM)
      ☐ Back Up Offer Addendum (C.A.R. Form BUO)   ☐ Court Confirmation Addendum (C.A.R. Form CCA)
      ☐ Septic, Well and Property Monument Addendum (C.A.R. Form SWPI)
      ☐ Short Sale Addendum (C.A.R. Form SSA)   ☐ Other _____

   B. BUYER AND SELLER ADVISORIES: ☑ Buyer's Inspection Advisory (C.A.R. Form BIA)
      ☐ Probate Advisory (C.A.R. Form PAK)   ☐ Statewide Buyer and Seller Advisory (C.A.R. Form SBSA)
      ☐ Trust Advisory (C.A.R. Form TA)   ☐ REO Advisory (C.A.R. Form REO)
      ☐ Short Sale Information and Advisory (C.A.R. Form SSIA)   ☐ Other _____

6. **OTHER TERMS:** _____
   _____
   _____
   _____

7. **ALLOCATION OF COSTS**
   A. **INSPECTIONS, REPORTS AND CERTIFICATES:** Unless otherwise agreed in writing, this paragraph only determines who is to pay for the inspection, test, certificate or service ("Report") mentioned; it **does not determine who is to pay for any work recommended or identified in the Report.**
   (1) ☐ Buyer ☐ Seller shall pay for a natural hazard zone disclosure report, including tax ☐ environmental ☐ Other: _____
       _____ prepared by _____.
   (2) ☐ Buyer ☐ Seller shall pay for the following Report _____
       prepared by_____.
   (3) ☐ Buyer ☐ Seller shall pay for the following Report _____
       prepared by _____.

Buyer's Initials (_____)(_____)   Seller's Initials (_____)(_____)

RPA-CA REVISED 11/14 (PAGE 2 OF 10) Print Date

CALIFORNIA RESIDENTIAL PURCHASE AGREEMENT (RPA-CA PAGE 2 OF 10)

FIGURE 5.7 (Continued)

Property Address: _____ Date: _____

 B. GOVERNMENT REQUIREMENTS AND RETROFIT:

  (1) ☐ Buyer ☐ Seller shall pay for smoke alarm and carbon monoxide device installation and water heater bracing, if required by Law. Prior to Close Of Escrow ("COE"), Seller shall provide Buyer written statement(s) of compliance in accordance with state and local Law, unless Seller is exempt.

  (2) (i) ☐ Buyer ☐ Seller shall pay the cost of compliance with any other minimum mandatory government inspections and reports if required as a condition of closing escrow under any Law.

   (ii) ☐ Buyer ☐ Seller shall pay the cost of compliance with any other minimum mandatory government retrofit standards required as a condition of closing escrow under any Law, whether the work is required to be completed before or after COE.

   (iii) Buyer shall be provided, within the time specified in paragraph 14A, a copy of any required government conducted or point-of-sale inspection report prepared pursuant to this Agreement or in anticipation of this sale of the Property.

 C. ESCROW AND TITLE:

  (1) (a) ☐ Buyer ☐ Seller shall pay escrow fee _____.

   (b) Escrow Holder shall be _____.

   (c) The Parties shall, within **5 (or ___) Days** After receipt, sign and return Escrow Holder's general provisions.

  (2) (a) ☐ Buyer ☐ Seller shall pay for **owner's** title insurance policy specified in paragraph 13E _____.

   (b) Owner's title policy to be issued by _____.

   (Buyer shall pay for any title insurance policy insuring Buyer's **lender**, unless otherwise agreed in writing.)

 D. OTHER COSTS:

  (1) ☐ Buyer ☐ Seller shall pay County transfer tax or fee _____.

  (2) ☐ Buyer ☐ Seller shall pay City transfer tax or fee _____.

  (3) ☐ Buyer ☐ Seller shall pay Homeowners' Association ("HOA") transfer fee _____.

  (4) Seller shall pay HOA fees for preparing documents required to be delivered by Civil Code §4525.

  (5) ☐ Buyer ☐ Seller shall pay HOA fees for preparing all documents other than those required by Civil Code §4525.

  (6) ☐ Buyer ☐ Seller shall pay for any private transfer fee _____.

  (7) ☐ Buyer ☐ Seller shall pay for _____.

  (8) ☐ Buyer ☐ Seller shall pay for _____.

  (9) ☐ Buyer ☐ Seller shall pay for the cost, not to exceed $ _____, of a standard (or ☐ upgraded) one-year home warranty plan, issued by _____, with the following optional coverages: ☐ Air Conditioner ☐ Pool/Spa ☐ Other: _____.

   Buyer is informed that home warranty plans have many optional coverages in addition to those listed above. Buyer is advised to investigate these coverages to determine those that may be suitable for Buyer.

  OR ☐ **Buyer waives the purchase of a home warranty plan. Nothing in this paragraph precludes Buyer's purchasing a home warranty plan during the term of this Agreement.**

8. ITEMS INCLUDED IN AND EXCLUDED FROM SALE:

 A. NOTE TO BUYER AND SELLER: Items listed as included or excluded in the MLS, flyers or marketing materials are **not** included in the purchase price or excluded from the sale unless specified in paragraph 8 B or C.

 B. ITEMS INCLUDED IN SALE: Except as otherwise specified or disclosed,

  (1) All EXISTING fixtures and fittings that are attached to the Property;

  (2) EXISTING electrical, mechanical, lighting, plumbing and heating fixtures, ceiling fans, fireplace inserts, gas logs and grates, solar power systems, built-in appliances, window and door screens, awnings, shutters, window coverings, attached floor coverings, television antennas, satellite dishes, air coolers/conditioners, pool/spa equipment, garage door openers/remote controls, mailbox, in-ground landscaping, trees/shrubs, water features and fountains, water softeners, water purifiers, security systems/alarms and the following if checked: ☐ all stove(s), except _____; ☐ all refrigerator(s) except _____; ☐ all washer(s) and dryer(s), except _____;

  (3) Existing integrated phone and home automation systems, including necessary components such as intranet and Internet-connected hardware or devices, control units (other than non-dedicated mobile devices, electronics and computers) and applicable software, permissions, passwords, codes and access information, are (☐ are NOT) included in the sale.

  (4) LEASED OR LIENED ITEMS AND SYSTEMS: Seller shall, within the time specified in paragraph 14A, (i) disclose to Buyer if any item or system specified in paragraph 8B or otherwise included in the sale is leased, or not owned by Seller, or specifically subject to a lien or other encumbrance, and (ii) Deliver to Buyer all written materials (such as lease, warranty, etc.) concerning any such item. Buyer's ability to assume any such lease, or willingness to accept the Property subject to any such lien or encumbrance, is a contingency of this Agreement as specified in paragraph 14B.

  (5) The following additional items: _____.

  (6) Seller represents that all items included in the purchase price, unless otherwise specified, (i) are owned by Seller and shall be transferred free and clear of liens and encumbrances, except the items and systems identified pursuant to 8B(4) and _____, and (ii) are transferred without Seller warranty regardless of value.

 C. ITEMS EXCLUDED FROM SALE: Unless otherwise specified, the following items are excluded from sale: (i) audio and video components (such as flat screen TVs, speakers and other items) if any such item is not itself attached to the Property, even if a bracket or other mechanism attached to the component or item is attached to the Property; (ii) furniture and other items secured to the Property for earthquake purposes; and (iii) _____
_____. **Brackets attached to walls, floors or ceilings for any such component, furniture or item shall remain with the Property (or ☐ will be removed and holes or other damage shall be repaired, but not painted).**

Buyer's Initials (_____)(_____)   Seller's Initials (_____)(_____)

FIGURE 5.7 (Continued)

Property Address: _____   Date: _____

9. **CLOSING AND POSSESSION:**

   A. Buyer intends (or ☐ does not intend) to occupy the Property as Buyer's primary residence.

   B. **Seller-occupied or vacant property:** Possession shall be delivered to Buyer: (i) at 6 PM or (_____ ☐ AM/☐ PM) on the date of Close Of Escrow; (ii) ☐ no later than ___ calendar days after Close Of Escrow; or (iii) ☐ at _____ ☐ AM/☐ PM on _____.

   C. **Seller remaining in possession After Close Of Escrow:** If Seller has the right to remain in possession after Close Of Escrow, (i) the Parties are advised to sign a separate occupancy agreement such as ☐ C.A.R. Form SIP, for Seller continued occupancy of less than 30 days, ☐ C.A.R. Form RLAS for Seller continued occupancy of 30 days or more; and (ii) the Parties are advised to consult with their insurance and legal advisors for information about liability and damage or injury to persons and personal and real property; and (iii) Buyer is advised to consult with Buyer's lender about the impact of Seller's occupancy on Buyer's loan.

   D. **Tenant-occupied property: Property shall be vacant** at least **5 (or ___) Days** Prior to Close Of Escrow, unless otherwise agreed in writing. **Note to Seller: If you are unable to deliver Property vacant in accordance with rent control and other applicable Law, you may be in breach of this Agreement.**

   OR ☐ **Tenant to remain in possession** (C.A.R. Form TIP).

   E. At Close Of Escrow: Seller assigns to Buyer any assignable warranty rights for items included in the sale; and Seller shall Deliver to Buyer available Copies of any such warranties. Brokers cannot and will not determine the assignability of any warranties.

   F. At Close Of Escrow, unless otherwise agreed in writing, Seller shall provide keys, passwords, codes and/or means to operate all locks, mailboxes, security systems, alarms, home automation systems and intranet and Internet-connected devices included in the purchase price, and garage door openers. If the Property is a condominium or located in a common interest subdivision, Buyer may be required to pay a deposit to the Homeowners' Association ("HOA") to obtain keys to accessible HOA facilities.

10. **STATUTORY AND OTHER DISCLOSURES (INCLUDING LEAD-BASED PAINT HAZARD DISCLOSURES) AND CANCELLATION RIGHTS:**

    A. **(1)** Seller shall, within the time specified in paragraph 14A, Deliver to Buyer: (i) if required by Law, a fully completed: Federal Lead-Based Paint Disclosures (C.A.R. Form FLD) and pamphlet ("Lead Disclosures"); and **(ii)** unless exempt, fully completed disclosures or notices required by sections 1102 et. seq. and 1103 et. seq. of the Civil Code ("Statutory Disclosures"). Statutory Disclosures include, but are not limited to, a Real Estate Transfer Disclosure Statement ("TDS"), Natural Hazard Disclosure Statement ("NHD"), notice or actual knowledge of release of illegal controlled substance, notice of special tax and/or assessments (or, if allowed, substantially equivalent notice regarding the Mello-Roos Community Facilities Act of 1982 and Improvement Bond Act of 1915) and, if Seller has actual knowledge, of industrial use and military ordnance location (C.A.R. Form SPQ or SSD).

    (2) Any Statutory Disclosure required by this paragraph is considered fully completed if Seller has answered all questions and completed and signed the Seller section(s) and the Listing Agent, if any, has completed and signed the Listing Broker section(s), or, if applicable, an Agent Visual Inspection Disclosure (C.A.R. Form AVID). Nothing stated herein relieves a Buyer's Broker, if any, from the obligation to (i) conduct a reasonably competent and diligent visual inspection of the accessible areas of the Property and disclose, on Section IV of the TDS, or an AVID, material facts affecting the value or desirability of the Property that were or should have been revealed by such an inspection or (ii) complete any sections on all disclosures required to be completed by Buyer's Broker.

    (3) Note to Buyer and Seller: Waiver of Statutory and Lead Disclosures is prohibited by Law.

    (4) Seller, unless exempt from the obligation to provide a TDS, shall, within the time specified in paragraph 14A, complete and provide Buyer with a Seller Property Questionnaire (C.A.R. Form SPQ) **OR** ☐ Supplemental Contractual and Statutory Disclosure (C.A.R. Form SSD).

    (5) Buyer shall, within the time specified in paragraph 14B(1), return Signed Copies of the Statutory, Lead and other disclosures to Seller.

    (6) In the event Seller or Listing Broker, prior to Close Of Escrow, becomes aware of adverse conditions materially affecting the Property, or any material inaccuracy in disclosures, information or representations previously provided to Buyer, Seller shall promptly provide a subsequent or amended disclosure or notice, in writing, covering those items. **However, a subsequent or amended disclosure shall not be required for conditions and material inaccuracies** of which Buyer is otherwise aware, or which are **disclosed in reports provided to or obtained by Buyer or ordered and paid for by Buyer.**

    (7) If any disclosure or notice specified in paragraph 10A(1), or subsequent or amended disclosure or notice is Delivered to Buyer after the offer is Signed, Buyer shall have the right to cancel this Agreement within **3 Days** After Delivery in person, or **5 Days** After Delivery by deposit in the mail, by giving written notice of cancellation to Seller or Seller's agent.

    B. **NATURAL AND ENVIRONMENTAL HAZARD DISCLOSURES AND OTHER BOOKLETS:** Within the time specified in paragraph 14A, Seller shall, if required by Law: (i) Deliver to Buyer earthquake guide(s) (and questionnaire), environmental hazards booklet, and home energy rating pamphlet; (ii) disclose if the Property is located in a Special Flood Hazard Area; Potential Flooding (Inundation) Area; Very High Fire Hazard Zone; State Fire Responsibility Area; Earthquake Fault Zone; and Seismic Hazard Zone; and (iii) disclose any other zone as required by Law and provide any other information required for those zones.

    C. **WITHHOLDING TAXES:** Within the time specified in paragraph 14A, to avoid required withholding, Seller shall Deliver to Buyer or qualified substitute, an affidavit sufficient to comply with federal (FIRPTA) and California withholding Law (C.A.R. Form AS or QS).

    D. **MEGAN'S LAW DATABASE DISCLOSURE:** Notice: Pursuant to Section 290.46 of the Penal Code, information about specified registered sex offenders is made available to the public via an Internet Web site maintained by the Department of Justice at **www.meganslaw.ca.gov.** Depending on an offender's criminal history, this information will include either the address at which the offender resides or the community of residence and ZIP Code in which he or she resides. (Neither Seller nor Brokers are required to check this website. If Buyer wants further information, Broker recommends that Buyer obtain information from this website during Buyer's inspection contingency period. Brokers do not have expertise in this area.)

    E. **NOTICE REGARDING GAS AND HAZARDOUS LIQUID TRANSMISSION PIPELINES:** This notice is being provided simply to inform you that information about the general location of gas and hazardous liquid transmission pipelines is available to the public via the National Pipeline Mapping System (NPMS) Internet Web site maintained by the United States Department of Transportation at **http://www.npms.phmsa.dot.gov/.** To seek further information about possible transmission pipelines near the Property, you may contact your local gas utility or other pipeline operators in the area. Contact information for pipeline operators is searchable by ZIP Code and county on the NPMS Internet Web site.

Buyer's Initials (_____)(_____)   Seller's Initials (_____)(_____)

FIGURE 5.7 (Continued)

Property Address: _____ Date: _____

F. **CONDOMINIUM/PLANNED DEVELOPMENT DISCLOSURES:**
(1) **SELLER HAS: 7 (or ___) Days** After Acceptance to disclose to Buyer if the Property is a condominium, or is located in a planned development or other common interest subdivision (C.A.R. Form SPQ or SSD).
(2) If the Property is a condominium or is located in a planned development or other common interest subdivision, Seller has **3 (or ___) Days** After Acceptance to request from the HOA (C.A.R. Form HOA1): **(i)** Copies of any documents required by Law; **(ii)** disclosure of any pending or anticipated claim or litigation by or against the HOA; **(iii)** a statement containing the location and number of designated parking and storage spaces; **(iv)** Copies of the most recent 12 months of HOA minutes for regular and special meetings; and **(v)** the names and contact information of all HOAs governing the Property (collectively, "CI Disclosures"). Seller shall itemize and Deliver to Buyer all CI Disclosures received from the HOA and any CI Disclosures in Seller's possession. Buyer's approval of CI Disclosures is a contingency of this Agreement as specified in paragraph 14B(3). The Party specified in paragraph 7, as directed by escrow, shall deposit funds into escrow or direct to HOA or management company to pay for any of the above.

11. **CONDITION OF PROPERTY:** Unless otherwise agreed in writing: **(i)** the Property is sold (a) "AS-IS" in its PRESENT physical condition as of the date of Acceptance and (b) subject to Buyer's Investigation rights; **(ii)** the Property, including pool, spa, landscaping and grounds, is to be maintained in substantially the same condition as on the date of Acceptance; and **(iii)** all debris and personal property not included in the sale shall be removed by Close Of Escrow.
A. Seller shall, within the time specified in paragraph 14A, DISCLOSE KNOWN MATERIAL FACTS AND DEFECTS affecting the Property, including known insurance claims within the past five years, and make any and all other disclosures required by law.
B. Buyer has the right to conduct Buyer Investigations of the Property and, as specified in paragraph 14B, based upon information discovered in those investigations: (i) cancel this Agreement; or (ii) request that Seller make Repairs or take other action.
C. **Buyer is strongly advised to conduct investigations of the entire Property in order to determine its present condition. Seller may not be aware of all defects affecting the Property or other factors that Buyer considers important. Property improvements may not be built according to code, in compliance with current Law, or have had permits issued.**

12. **BUYER'S INVESTIGATION OF PROPERTY AND MATTERS AFFECTING PROPERTY:**
A. Buyer's acceptance of the condition of, and any other matter affecting the Property, is a contingency of this Agreement as specified in this paragraph and paragraph 14B. Within the time specified in paragraph 14B(1), Buyer shall have the right, at Buyer's expense unless otherwise agreed, to conduct inspections, investigations, tests, surveys and other studies ("Buyer Investigations"), including, but not limited to, the right to: **(i)** inspect for lead-based paint and other lead-based paint hazards; **(ii)** inspect for wood destroying pests and organisms. Any inspection for wood destroying pests and organisms shall be prepared by a registered Structural Pest Control company; shall cover the main building and attached structures; may cover detached structures; shall NOT include water tests of shower pans on upper level units unless the owners of property below the shower consent; shall NOT include roof coverings; and, if the Property is a unit in a condominium or other common interest subdivision, the inspection shall include only the separate interest and any exclusive-use areas being transferred, and shall NOT include common areas; and shall include a report ("Pest Control Report") showing the findings of the company which shall be separated into sections for evident infestation or infections (Section 1) and for conditions likely to lead to infestation or infection (Section 2); **(iii)** review the registered sex offender database; **(iv)** confirm the insurability of Buyer and the Property including the availability and cost of flood and fire insurance; **(v)** review and seek approval of leases that may need to be assumed by Buyer; and **(vi)** satisfy Buyer as to any matter specified in the attached Buyer's Inspection Advisory (C.A.R. Form BIA). Without Seller's prior written consent, Buyer shall neither make nor cause to be made: **(i)** invasive or destructive Buyer Investigations except to the extent required to prepare a Pest Control Report; or **(ii)** inspections by any governmental building or zoning inspector or government employee, unless required by Law.
B. Seller shall make the Property available for all Buyer Investigations. Buyer shall **(i)** as specified in paragraph 14B, complete Buyer Investigations and either remove the contingency or cancel this Agreement, and **(ii)** give Seller, at no cost, complete Copies of all such Investigation reports obtained by Buyer, which obligation shall survive the termination of this Agreement.
C. Seller shall have water, gas, electricity and all operable pilot lights on for Buyer's Investigations and through the date possession is made available to Buyer.
D. **Buyer indemnity and seller protection for entry upon property:** Buyer shall: **(i)** keep the Property free and clear of liens; **(ii)** repair all damage arising from Buyer Investigations; and **(iii)** indemnify and hold Seller harmless from all resulting liability, claims, demands, damages and costs. Buyer shall carry, or Buyer shall require anyone acting on Buyer's behalf to carry, policies of liability, workers' compensation and other applicable insurance, defending and protecting Seller from liability for any injuries to persons or property occurring during any Buyer Investigations or work done on the Property at Buyer's direction prior to Close Of Escrow. Seller is advised that certain protections may be afforded Seller by recording a "Notice of Non-Responsibility" (C.A.R. Form NNR) for Buyer Investigations and work done on the Property at Buyer's direction. Buyer's obligations under this paragraph shall survive the termination of this Agreement.

13. **TITLE AND VESTING:**
A. Within the time specified in paragraph 14, Buyer shall be provided a current preliminary title report ("Preliminary Report"). The Preliminary Report is only an offer by the title insurer to issue a policy of title insurance and may not contain every item affecting title. Buyer's review of the Preliminary Report and any other matters which may affect title are a contingency of this Agreement as specified in paragraph 14B. The company providing the Preliminary Report shall, prior to issuing a Preliminary Report, conduct a search of the General Index for all Sellers except banks or other institutional lenders selling properties they acquired through foreclosure (REOs), corporations, and government entities. Seller shall within 7 Days After Acceptance, give Escrow Holder a completed Statement of Information.
B. Title is taken in its present condition subject to all encumbrances, easements, covenants, conditions, restrictions, rights and other matters, whether of record or not, as of the date of Acceptance except for: **(i)** monetary liens of record (which Seller is obligated to pay off) unless Buyer is assuming those obligations or taking the Property subject to those obligations; and **(ii)** those matters which Seller has agreed to remove in writing.
C. Within the time specified in paragraph 14A, Seller has a duty to disclose to Buyer all matters known to Seller affecting title, whether of record or not.
D. At Close Of Escrow, Buyer shall receive a grant deed conveying title (or, for stock cooperative or long-term lease, an assignment of stock certificate or of Seller's leasehold interest), including oil, mineral and water rights if currently owned by Seller. Title shall vest as designated in Buyer's supplemental escrow instructions. THE MANNER OF TAKING TITLE MAY HAVE SIGNIFICANT LEGAL AND TAX CONSEQUENCES. CONSULT AN APPROPRIATE PROFESSIONAL.

Buyer's Initials (_____)(_____)   Seller's Initials (_____)(_____)

EQUAL HOUSING OPPORTUNITY

FIGURE 5.7 (Continued)

Property Address: _____ Date: _____

   E.   Buyer shall receive a CLTA/ALTA "Homeowner's Policy of Title Insurance", if applicable to the type of property and buyer. If not, Escrow Holder shall notify Buyer. A title company can provide information about the availability, coverage, and cost of other title policies and endorsements. If the Homeowner's Policy is not available, Buyer shall choose another policy, instruct Escrow Holder in writing and shall pay any increase in cost.

14. **TIME PERIODS; REMOVAL OF CONTINGENCIES; CANCELLATION RIGHTS: The following time periods may only be extended, altered, modified or changed by mutual written agreement. Any removal of contingencies or cancellation under this paragraph by either Buyer or Seller must be exercised in good faith and in writing (C.A.R. Form CR or CC).**

   A.   **SELLER HAS: 7 (or ___) Days** After Acceptance to Deliver to Buyer all Reports, disclosures and information for which Seller is responsible under paragraphs 5, 6, 7, 8B(4), 10A, B, C, and F, 11A and 13A. If, by the time specified, Seller has not delivered any such item, Buyer after first Delivering to Seller a Notice to Seller to Perform (C.A.R. Form NSP) may cancel this Agreement.

   B.   **(1) BUYER HAS: 17 (or ___) Days** After Acceptance, unless otherwise agreed in writing, to:

      (i) complete all Buyer Investigations; review all disclosures, reports, lease documents to be assumed by Buyer pursuant to paragraph 8B(4), and other applicable information, which Buyer receives from Seller; and approve all matters affecting the Property; and **(ii)** Deliver to Seller Signed Copies of Statutory and Lead Disclosures and other disclosures Delivered by Seller in accordance with paragraph 10A.

      (2) Within the time specified in paragraph 14B(1), Buyer may request that Seller make repairs or take any other action regarding the Property (C.A.R. Form RR). Seller has no obligation to agree to or respond to (C.A.R. Form RRRR) Buyer's requests.

      (3) By the end of the time specified in paragraph 14B(1) (or as otherwise specified in this Agreement), Buyer shall Deliver to Seller a removal of the applicable contingency or cancellation (C.A.R. Form CR or CC) of this Agreement. However, if any report, disclosure or information for which Seller is responsible is not Delivered within the time specified in paragraph 14A, then Buyer has **5 (or ___) Days** After Delivery of any such items, or the time specified in paragraph 14B(1), whichever is later, to Deliver to Seller a removal of the applicable contingency or cancellation of this Agreement.

      (4) **Continuation of Contingency:** Even after the end of the time specified in paragraph 14B(1) and before Seller cancels, if at all, pursuant to paragraph 14C, Buyer retains the right, in writing, to either (i) remove remaining contingencies, or (ii) cancel this Agreement based on a remaining contingency. Once Buyer's written removal of all contingencies is Delivered to Seller, Seller may not cancel this Agreement pursuant to paragraph 14C(1).

   C.   **SELLER RIGHT TO CANCEL:**

      (1) **Seller right to Cancel; Buyer Contingencies:** If, by the time specified in this Agreement, Buyer does not Deliver to Seller a removal of the applicable contingency or cancellation of this Agreement, then Seller, after first Delivering to Buyer a Notice to Buyer to Perform (C.A.R. Form NBP), may cancel this Agreement. In such event, Seller shall authorize the return of Buyer's deposit, except for fees incurred by Buyer.

      (2) **Seller right to Cancel; Buyer Contract Obligations:** Seller, after first delivering to Buyer a NBP, may cancel this Agreement if, by the time specified in this Agreement, Buyer does not take the following action(s): **(i)** Deposit funds as required by paragraph 3A, or 3B or if the funds deposited pursuant to paragraph 3A or 3B are not good when deposited; **(ii)** Deliver a notice of FHA or VA costs or terms as required by paragraph 3D(3) (C.A.R. Form FVA); **(iii)** Deliver a letter as required by paragraph 3J(1); **(iv)** Deliver verification, or a satisfactory verification if Seller reasonably disapproves of the verification already provided, as required by paragraph 3C or 3H; **(v)** Return Statutory and Lead Disclosures as required by paragraph 10A(5); or **(vi)** Sign or initial a separate liquidated damages form for an increased deposit as required by paragraphs 3B and 21B; or **(vii)** Provide evidence of authority to sign in a representative capacity as specified in paragraph 19. In such event, Seller shall authorize the return of Buyer's deposit, except for fees incurred by Buyer.

   D.   **NOTICE TO BUYER OR SELLER TO PERFORM:** The NBP or NSP shall: **(i)** be in writing; **(ii)** be signed by the applicable Buyer or Seller; and **(iii)** give the other Party at least **2 (or ___) Days** After Delivery (or until the time specified in the applicable paragraph, whichever occurs last) to take the applicable action. A NBP or NSP may not be Delivered any earlier than **2 Days** Prior to the expiration of the applicable time for the other Party to remove a contingency or cancel this Agreement or meet an obligation specified in paragraph 14.

   E.   **EFFECT OF BUYER'S REMOVAL OF CONTINGENCIES:** If Buyer removes, in writing, any contingency or cancellation rights, unless otherwise specified in writing, Buyer shall conclusively be deemed to have: **(i)** completed all Buyer Investigations, and review of reports and other applicable information and disclosures pertaining to that contingency or cancellation right; **(ii)** elected to proceed with the transaction; and **(iii)** assumed all liability, responsibility and expense for Repairs or corrections pertaining to that contingency or cancellation right, or for the inability to obtain financing.

   F.   **CLOSE OF ESCROW:** Before Buyer or Seller may cancel this Agreement for failure of the other Party to close escrow pursuant to this Agreement, Buyer or Seller must first Deliver to the other Party a demand to close escrow (C.A.R. Form DCE). The DCE shall: **(i)** be signed by the applicable Buyer or Seller; and **(ii)** give the other Party at least **3 (or ____) Days** After Delivery to close escrow. A DCE may not be Delivered any earlier than **3 Days** Prior to the scheduled close of escrow.

   G.   **EFFECT OF CANCELLATION ON DEPOSITS:** If Buyer or Seller gives written notice of cancellation pursuant to rights duly exercised under the terms of this Agreement, the Parties agree to Sign mutual instructions to cancel the sale and escrow and release deposits, if any, to the party entitled to the funds, less fees and costs incurred by that party. Fees and costs may be payable to service providers and vendors for services and products provided during escrow. Except as specified below, **release of funds will require mutual Signed release instructions from the Parties, judicial decision or arbitration award.** If either Party fails to execute mutual instructions to cancel, one Party may make a written demand to Escrow Holder for the deposit (C.A.R. Form BDRD or SDRD). Escrow Holder, upon receipt, shall promptly deliver notice of the demand to the other Party. If, within 10 Days After Escrow Holder's notice, the other Party does not object to the demand, Escrow Holder shall disburse the deposit to the Party making the demand. If Escrow Holder complies with the preceding process, each Party shall be deemed to have released Escrow Holder from any and all claims or liability related to the disbursal of the deposit. Escrow Holder, at its discretion, may nonetheless require mutual cancellation instructions. **A Party may be subject to a civil penalty of up to $1,000 for refusal to sign cancellation instructions if no good faith dispute exists as to who is entitled to the deposited funds (Civil Code §1057.3).**

15. **FINAL VERIFICATION OF CONDITION:** Buyer shall have the right to make a final verification of the Property within **5 (or ☐ ___) Days** Prior to Close Of Escrow, NOT AS A CONTINGENCY OF THE SALE, but solely to confirm: **(i)** the Property is maintained pursuant to paragraph 11; **(ii)** Repairs have been completed as agreed; and **(iii)** Seller has complied with Seller's other obligations under this Agreement (C.A.R. Form VP).

Buyer's Initials (_____)(_____)   Seller's Initials (_____)(_____)

FIGURE 5.7 (Continued)

Property Address: _____ Date: _____

16. **REPAIRS:** Repairs shall be completed prior to final verification of condition unless otherwise agreed in writing. Repairs to be performed at Seller's expense may be performed by Seller or through others, provided that the work complies with applicable Law, including governmental permit, inspection and approval requirements. Repairs shall be performed in a good, skillful manner with materials of quality and appearance comparable to existing materials. It is understood that exact restoration of appearance or cosmetic items following all Repairs may not be possible. Seller shall: **(i)** obtain invoices and paid receipts for Repairs performed by others; **(ii)** prepare a written statement indicating the Repairs performed by Seller and the date of such Repairs; and **(iii)** provide Copies of invoices and paid receipts and statements to Buyer prior to final verification of condition.

17. **PRORATIONS OF PROPERTY TAXES AND OTHER ITEMS:** Unless otherwise agreed in writing, the following items shall be PAID CURRENT and prorated between Buyer and Seller as of Close Of Escrow: real property taxes and assessments, interest, rents, HOA regular, special, and emergency dues and assessments imposed prior to Close Of Escrow, premiums on insurance assumed by Buyer, payments on bonds and assessments assumed by Buyer, and payments on Mello-Roos and other Special Assessment District bonds and assessments that are now a lien. The following items shall be assumed by Buyer WITHOUT CREDIT toward the purchase price: prorated payments on Mello-Roos and other Special Assessment District bonds and assessments and HOA special assessments that are now a lien but not yet due. Property will be reassessed upon change of ownership. Any supplemental tax bills shall be paid as follows: **(i)** for periods after Close Of Escrow, by Buyer; and **(ii)** for periods prior to Close Of Escrow, by Seller (see C.A.R. Form SPT or SBSA for further information). TAX BILLS ISSUED AFTER CLOSE OF ESCROW SHALL BE HANDLED DIRECTLY BETWEEN BUYER AND SELLER. Prorations shall be made based on a 30-day month.

18. **BROKERS:**
   A. **COMPENSATION:** Seller or Buyer, or both, as applicable, agree to pay compensation to Broker as specified in a separate written agreement between Broker and that Seller or Buyer. Compensation is payable upon Close Of Escrow, or if escrow does not close, as otherwise specified in the agreement between Broker and that Seller or Buyer.
   B. **SCOPE OF DUTY:** Buyer and Seller acknowledge and agree that Broker: **(i)** Does not decide what price Buyer should pay or Seller should accept; **(ii)** Does not guarantee the condition of the Property; **(iii)** Does not guarantee the performance, adequacy or completeness of inspections, services, products or repairs provided or made by Seller or others; **(iv)** Does not have an obligation to conduct an inspection of common areas or areas off the site of the Property; **(v)** Shall not be responsible for identifying defects on the Property, in common areas, or offsite unless such defects are visually observable by an inspection of reasonably accessible areas of the Property or are known to Broker; **(vi)** Shall not be responsible for inspecting public records or permits concerning the title or use of Property; **(vii)** Shall not be responsible for identifying the location of boundary lines or other items affecting title; **(viii)** Shall not be responsible for verifying square footage, representations of others or information contained in Investigation reports, Multiple Listing Service, advertisements, flyers or other promotional material; **(ix)** Shall not be responsible for determining the fair market value of the Property or any personal property included in the sale; **(x)** Shall not be responsible for providing legal or tax advice regarding any aspect of a transaction entered into by Buyer or Seller; and **(xi)** Shall not be responsible for providing other advice or information that exceeds the knowledge, education and experience required to perform real estate licensed activity. Buyer and Seller agree to seek legal, tax, insurance, title and other desired assistance from appropriate professionals.

19. **REPRESENTATIVE CAPACITY:** If one or more Parties is signing this Agreement in a representative capacity and not for him/herself as an individual then that Party shall so indicate in paragraph 31 or 32 and attach a Representative Capacity Signature Disclosure (C.A.R. Form RCSD). Wherever the signature or initials of the representative identified in the RCSD appear on this Agreement or any related documents, it shall be deemed to be in a representative capacity for the entity described and not in an individual capacity, unless otherwise indicated. The Party acting in a representative capacity (i) represents that the entity for which that party is acting already exists and (ii) shall Deliver to the other Party and Escrow Holder, within 3 Days After Acceptance, evidence of authority to act in that capacity (such as but not limited to: applicable trust document, or portion thereof, letters testamentary, court order, power of attorney, resolution, or formation documents of the business entity).

20. **JOINT ESCROW INSTRUCTIONS TO ESCROW HOLDER:**
   A. **The following paragraphs, or applicable portions thereof, of this Agreement constitute the joint escrow instructions of Buyer and Seller to Escrow Holder,** which Escrow Holder is to use along with any related counter offers and addenda, and any additional mutual instructions to close the escrow: paragraphs 1, 3, 4B, 5A, 6, 7, 10C, 13, 14G, 17, 18A, 19, 20, 26, 29, 30, 31, 32 and paragraph D of the section titled Real Estate Brokers on page 10. If a Copy of the separate compensation agreement(s) provided for in paragraph 18A, or paragraph D of the section titled Real Estate Brokers on page 10 is deposited with Escrow Holder by Broker, Escrow Holder shall accept such agreement(s) and pay out from Buyer's or Seller's funds, or both, as applicable, the Broker's compensation provided for in such agreement(s). The terms and conditions of this Agreement not set forth in the specified paragraphs are additional matters for the information of Escrow Holder, but about which Escrow Holder need not be concerned. Buyer and Seller will receive Escrow Holder's general provisions, if any, directly from Escrow Holder and will execute such provisions within the time specified in paragraph 7C(1)(c). To the extent the general provisions are inconsistent or conflict with this Agreement, the general provisions will control as to the duties and obligations of Escrow Holder only. Buyer and Seller will execute additional instructions, documents and forms provided by Escrow Holder that are reasonably necessary to close the escrow and, as directed by Escrow Holder, within 3 (or ___) Days, shall pay to Escrow Holder or HOA or HOA management company or others any fee required by paragraphs 7, 10 or elsewhere in this Agreement.
   B. A Copy of this Agreement including any counter offer(s) and addenda shall be delivered to Escrow Holder within **3** Days After Acceptance (or _____). Buyer and Seller authorize Escrow Holder to accept and rely on Copies and Signatures as defined in this Agreement as originals, to open escrow and for other purposes of escrow. The validity of this Agreement as between Buyer and Seller is not affected by whether or when Escrow Holder Signs this Agreement. Escrow Holder shall provide Seller's Statement of Information to Title company when received from Seller. If Seller delivers an affidavit to Escrow Holder to satisfy Seller's FIRPTA obligation under paragraph 10C, Escrow Holder shall deliver to Buyer a Qualified Substitute statement that complies with federal Law.
   C. Brokers are a party to the escrow for the sole purpose of compensation pursuant to paragraph 18A and paragraph D of the section titled Real Estate Brokers on page 10. Buyer and Seller irrevocably assign to Brokers compensation specified in paragraph 18A, and irrevocably instruct Escrow Holder to disburse those funds to Brokers at Close Of Escrow or pursuant to any other mutually executed cancellation agreement. Compensation instructions can be amended or revoked only with the written consent of Brokers. Buyer and Seller shall release and hold harmless Escrow Holder from any liability resulting from Escrow Holder's payment to Broker(s) of compensation pursuant to this Agreement.

Buyer's Initials (_____)(_____)   Seller's Initials (_____)(_____)

RPA-CA REVISED 11/14 (PAGE 7 OF 10) Print Date
CALIFORNIA RESIDENTIAL PURCHASE AGREEMENT (RPA-CA PAGE 7 OF 10)

EQUAL HOUSING OPPORTUNITY

FIGURE 5.7 (Continued)

Property Address: _____   Date: _____

D. Upon receipt, Escrow Holder shall provide Seller and Seller's Broker verification of Buyer's deposit of funds pursuant to paragraph 3A and 3B. Once Escrow Holder becomes aware of any of the following, Escrow Holder shall immediately notify all Brokers: **(i)** if Buyer's initial or any additional deposit or down payment is not made pursuant to this Agreement, or is not good at time of deposit with Escrow Holder; or **(ii)** if Buyer and Seller instruct Escrow Holder to cancel escrow.

E. A Copy of any amendment that affects any paragraph of this Agreement for which Escrow Holder is responsible shall be delivered to Escrow Holder within **3** Days after mutual execution of the amendment.

21. REMEDIES FOR BUYER'S BREACH OF CONTRACT:

A. **Any clause added by the Parties specifying a remedy (such as release or forfeiture of deposit or making a deposit non-refundable) for failure of Buyer to complete the purchase in violation of this Agreement shall be deemed invalid unless the clause independently satisfies the statutory liquidated damages requirements set forth in the Civil Code.**

B. **LIQUIDATED DAMAGES: If Buyer fails to complete this purchase because of Buyer's default, Seller shall retain, as liquidated damages, the deposit actually paid. If the Property is a dwelling with no more than four units, one of which Buyer intends to occupy, then the amount retained shall be no more than 3% of the purchase price. Any excess shall be returned to Buyer. Except as provided in paragraph 14G, release of funds will require mutual, Signed release instructions from both Buyer and Seller, judicial decision or arbitration award. AT THE TIME OF ANY INCREASED DEPOSIT BUYER AND SELLER SHALL SIGN A SEPARATE LIQUIDATED DAMAGES PROVISION INCORPORATING THE INCREASED DEPOSIT AS LIQUIDATED DAMAGES (C.A.R. FORM RID).**

Buyer's Initials_____/_____   Seller's Initials_____/_____

22. DISPUTE RESOLUTION:

A. **MEDIATION:** The Parties agree to mediate any dispute or claim arising between them out of this Agreement, or any resulting transaction, before resorting to arbitration or court action through the C.A.R. Real Estate Mediation Center for Consumers (**www.consumermediation.org**) or through any other mediation provider or service mutually agreed to by the Parties. The Parties **also agree to mediate any disputes or claims with Broker(s), who, in writing, agree to such mediation prior to, or within a reasonable time after, the dispute or claim is presented to the Broker.** Mediation fees, if any, shall be divided equally among the Parties involved. If, for any dispute or claim to which this paragraph applies, any Party (i) commences an action without first attempting to resolve the matter through mediation, or (ii) before commencement of an action, refuses to mediate after a request has been made, then that Party shall not be entitled to recover attorney fees, even if they would otherwise be available to that Party in any such action. THIS MEDIATION PROVISION APPLIES WHETHER OR NOT THE ARBITRATION PROVISION IS INITIALED. **Exclusions from this mediation agreement are specified in paragraph 22C.**

B. **ARBITRATION OF DISPUTES:**

The Parties agree that any dispute or claim in Law or equity arising between them out of this Agreement or any resulting transaction, which is not settled through mediation, shall be decided by neutral, binding arbitration. The Parties also agree to arbitrate any disputes or claims with Broker(s), who, in writing, agree to such arbitration prior to, or within a reasonable time after, the dispute or claim is presented to the Broker. The arbitrator shall be a retired judge or justice, or an attorney with at least 5 years of residential real estate Law experience, unless the parties mutually agree to a different arbitrator. The Parties shall have the right to discovery in accordance with Code of Civil Procedure §1283.05. In all other respects, the arbitration shall be conducted in accordance with Title 9 of Part 3 of the Code of Civil Procedure. Judgment upon the award of the arbitrator(s) may be entered into any court having jurisdiction. Enforcement of this agreement to arbitrate shall be governed by the Federal Arbitration Act. Exclusions from this arbitration agreement are specified in paragraph 22C.

"NOTICE: BY INITIALING IN THE SPACE BELOW YOU ARE AGREEING TO HAVE ANY DISPUTE ARISING OUT OF THE MATTERS INCLUDED IN THE 'ARBITRATION OF DISPUTES' PROVISION DECIDED BY NEUTRAL ARBITRATION AS PROVIDED BY CALIFORNIA LAW AND YOU ARE GIVING UP ANY RIGHTS YOU MIGHT POSSESS TO HAVE THE DISPUTE LITIGATED IN A COURT OR JURY TRIAL. BY INITIALING IN THE SPACE BELOW YOU ARE GIVING UP YOUR JUDICIAL RIGHTS TO DISCOVERY AND APPEAL, UNLESS THOSE RIGHTS ARE SPECIFICALLY INCLUDED IN THE 'ARBITRATION OF DISPUTES' PROVISION. IF YOU REFUSE TO SUBMIT TO ARBITRATION AFTER AGREEING TO THIS PROVISION, YOU MAY BE COMPELLED TO ARBITRATE UNDER THE AUTHORITY OF THE CALIFORNIA CODE OF CIVIL PROCEDURE. YOUR AGREEMENT TO THIS ARBITRATION PROVISION IS VOLUNTARY."

"WE HAVE READ AND UNDERSTAND THE FOREGOING AND AGREE TO SUBMIT DISPUTES ARISING OUT OF THE MATTERS INCLUDED IN THE 'ARBITRATION OF DISPUTES' PROVISION TO NEUTRAL ARBITRATION."

Buyer's Initials _____/_____   Seller's Initials _____/_____

C. **ADDITIONAL MEDIATION AND ARBITRATION TERMS:**

(1) **EXCLUSIONS: The following matters are excluded from mediation and arbitration: (i) a judicial or non-judicial foreclosure or other action or proceeding to enforce a deed of trust, mortgage or installment land sale contract as defined in Civil Code §2985; (ii) an unlawful detainer action; and (iii) any matter that is within the jurisdiction of a probate, small claims or bankruptcy court.**

(2) **PRESERVATION OF ACTIONS: The following shall not constitute a waiver nor violation of the mediation and arbitration provisions: (i)The filing of a court action to enable the recording of a notice of pending action, for order of attachment, receivership, injunction, or other provisional remedies; or (ii) the filing of a mechanic's lien.**

(3) **BROKERS: Brokers shall not be obligated nor compelled to mediate or arbitrate unless they agree to do so in writing. Any Broker(s) participating in mediation or arbitration shall not be deemed a party to this Agreement.**

Buyer's Initials (_____)(_____)   Seller's Initials (_____)(_____)

FIGURE 5.7 (Continued)

Property Address: _____ Date: _____

23. **SELECTION OF SERVICE PROVIDERS:** Brokers do not guarantee the performance of any vendors, service or product providers ("Providers"), whether referred by Broker or selected by Buyer, Seller or other person. Buyer and Seller may select ANY Providers of their own choosing.

24. **MULTIPLE LISTING SERVICE ("MLS"):** Brokers are authorized to report to the MLS a pending sale and, upon Close Of Escrow, the sales price and other terms of this transaction shall be provided to the MLS to be published and disseminated to persons and entities authorized to use the information on terms approved by the MLS.

25. **ATTORNEY FEES:** In any action, proceeding, or arbitration between Buyer and Seller arising out of this Agreement, the prevailing Buyer or Seller shall be entitled to reasonable attorney fees and costs from the non-prevailing Buyer or Seller, except as provided in paragraph 22A.

26. **ASSIGNMENT:** Buyer shall not assign all or any part of Buyer's interest in this Agreement without first having obtained the separate written consent of Seller to a specified assignee. Such consent shall not be unreasonably withheld. Any total or partial assignment shall not relieve Buyer of Buyer's obligations pursuant to this Agreement unless otherwise agreed in writing by Seller (C.A.R. Form AOAA).

27. **EQUAL HOUSING OPPORTUNITY:** The Property is sold in compliance with federal, state and local anti-discrimination Laws.

28. **TERMS AND CONDITIONS OF OFFER:**
This is an offer to purchase the Property on the above terms and conditions. The liquidated damages paragraph or the arbitration of disputes paragraph is incorporated in this Agreement if initialed by all Parties or if incorporated by mutual agreement in a counter offer or addendum. If at least one but not all Parties initial, a counter offer is required until agreement is reached. Seller has the right to continue to offer the Property for sale and to accept any other offer at any time prior to notification of Acceptance. The Parties have read and acknowledge receipt of a Copy of the offer and agree to the confirmation of agency relationships. If this offer is accepted and Buyer subsequently defaults, Buyer may be responsible for payment of Brokers' compensation. This Agreement and any supplement, addendum or modification, including any Copy, may be Signed in two or more counterparts, all of which shall constitute one and the same writing.

29. **TIME OF ESSENCE; ENTIRE CONTRACT; CHANGES:** Time is of the essence. All understandings between the Parties are incorporated in this Agreement. Its terms are intended by the Parties as a final, complete and exclusive expression of their Agreement with respect to its subject matter, and may not be contradicted by evidence of any prior agreement or contemporaneous oral agreement. If any provision of this Agreement is held to be ineffective or invalid, the remaining provisions will nevertheless be given full force and effect. Except as otherwise specified, this Agreement shall be interpreted and disputes shall be resolved in accordance with the Laws of the State of California. **Neither this Agreement nor any provision in it may be extended, amended, modified, altered or changed, except in writing Signed by Buyer and Seller.**

30. **DEFINITIONS:** As used in this Agreement:
A. **"Acceptance"** means the time the offer or final counter offer is accepted in writing by a Party and is delivered to and personally received by the other Party or that Party's authorized agent in accordance with the terms of this offer or a final counter offer.
B. **"Agreement"** means this document and any incorporated addenda, counter offers and written terms Signed by all Parties collectively forming the binding agreement between the Parties. All terms and conditions of any addenda checked and Signed are incorporated into this Agreement.
C. **"C.A.R. Form"** means the most current version of the specific form referenced or another comparable form agreed to by the parties.
D. **"Close Of Escrow"**, including "COE", means the date the grant deed, or other evidence of transfer of title, is recorded.
E. **"Copy"** means copy by any means including photocopy, NCR, facsimile and electronic.
F. **"Days"** means calendar days. However, after Acceptance, the last **Day** for performance of any act required by this Agreement (including Close Of Escrow) shall not include any Saturday, Sunday, or legal holiday and shall instead be the next Day.
G. **"Days After"** means the specified number of calendar days after the occurrence of the event specified, not counting the calendar date on which the specified event occurs, and ending at 11:59 PM on the final day.
H. **"Days Prior"** means the specified number of calendar days before the occurrence of the event specified, not counting the calendar date on which the specified event is scheduled to occur.
I. **"Deliver"**, **"Delivered"** or **"Delivery"**, unless otherwise specified in writing, means and shall be effective upon: personal receipt by Buyer or Seller or the individual Real Estate Licensee for that principal as specified in the section titled Real Estate Brokers on page 10, regardless of the method used (i.e., messenger, mail, email, fax, other).
J. **"Electronic Copy"** or **"Electronic Signature"** means, as applicable, an electronic copy or signature complying with California Law. Buyer and Seller agree that electronic means will not be used by either Party to modify or alter the content or integrity of this Agreement without the knowledge and consent of the other Party.
K. **"Law"** means any law, code, statute, ordinance, regulation, rule or order, which is adopted by a controlling city, county, state or federal legislative, judicial or executive body or agency.
L. **"Repairs"** means any repairs (including pest control), alterations, replacements, modifications or retrofitting of the Property provided for under this Agreement.
M. **"Signed"** means either a handwritten or electronic signature on an original document, Copy or any counterpart.

31. **EXPIRATION OF OFFER:** This offer shall be deemed revoked and the deposit, if any, shall be returned to Buyer unless the offer is Signed by Seller and a Copy of the Signed offer is personally received by Buyer, or by _____, who is authorized to receive it, by 5:00 PM on the third Day after this offer is signed by Buyer (or by ☐ _____ ☐AM/☐PM, on _____(date)).

☐ One or more Buyers is signing this Agreement in a representative capacity and not for him/herself as an individual. See attached Representative Capacity Signature Disclosure (C.A.R. Form RCSD) for additional terms.

Date _____ BUYER _____

(Print name) _____

Date _____ BUYER _____

(Print name) _____

☐ Additional Signature Addendum attached (C.A.R. Form ASA).

RPA-CA REVISED 11/14 (PAGE 9 of 10) Print Date   Seller's Initials (_____)(_____)

CALIFORNIA RESIDENTIAL PURCHASE AGREEMENT (RPA-CA PAGE 9 OF 10)

FIGURE 5.7 (Continued)

Property Address: _____   Date: _____

32. **ACCEPTANCE OF OFFER:** Seller warrants that Seller is the owner of the Property, or has the authority to execute this Agreement. Seller accepts the above offer and agrees to sell the Property on the above terms and conditions. Seller has read and acknowledges receipt of a Copy of this Agreement, and authorizes Broker to Deliver a Signed Copy to Buyer.

☐ (If checked) SELLER'S ACCEPTANCE IS **SUBJECT TO ATTACHED COUNTER OFFER (C.A.R. Form SCO or SMCO) DATED:**
_____.

☐   One or more Sellers is signing this Agreement in a representative capacity and not for him/herself as an individual. See attached Representative Capacity Signature Disclosure (C.A.R. Form RCSD) for additional terms.

Date _____   SELLER _____

(Print name) _____

Date _____   SELLER _____

(Print name) _____

☐   Additional Signature Addendum attached (C.A.R. Form ASA).

(____/____) **(Do not initial if making a counter offer.)** CONFIRMATION OF ACCEPTANCE: A Copy of Signed Acceptance was
(Initials)   personally received by Buyer or Buyer's authorized agent on (date) _____ at _____
☐AM/☐PM. **A binding Agreement is created when a Copy of Signed Acceptance is personally received by Buyer or Buyer's authorized agent whether or not confirmed in this document. Completion of this confirmation is not legally required in order to create a binding Agreement; it is solely intended to evidence the date that Confirmation of Acceptance has occurred.**

REAL ESTATE BROKERS:
A.   **Real Estate Brokers are not parties to the Agreement between Buyer and Seller.**
B.   **Agency relationships are confirmed as stated in paragraph 2.**
C.   If specified in paragraph 3A(2), Agent who submitted the offer for Buyer acknowledges receipt of deposit.
D.   **COOPERATING BROKER COMPENSATION:** Listing Broker agrees to pay Cooperating Broker **(Selling Firm)** and Cooperating Broker agrees to accept, out of Listing Broker's proceeds in escrow, the amount specified in the MLS, provided Cooperating Broker is a Participant of the MLS in which the Property is offered for sale or a reciprocal MLS. If Listing Broker and Cooperating Broker are not both Participants of the MLS, or a reciprocal MLS, in which the Property is offered for sale, then compensation must be specified in a separate written agreement (C.A.R. Form CBC). Declaration of License and Tax (C.A.R. Form DLT) may be used to document that tax reporting will be required or that an exemption exists.

Real Estate Broker (Selling Firm) _____ CalBRE Lic. # _____
By _____ CalBRE Lic. # _____ Date _____
By _____ CalBRE Lic. # _____ Date _____
Address _____ City_____ State _____ Zip _____
Telephone _____ Fax _____ E-mail _____
Real Estate Broker (Listing Firm) _____ CalBRE Lic. # _____
By _____ CalBRE Lic. # _____ Date _____
By _____ CalBRE Lic. # _____ Date _____
Address _____ City_____ State _____ Zip _____
Telephone _____ Fax _____ E-mail _____

ESCROW HOLDER ACKNOWLEDGMENT:
Escrow Holder acknowledges receipt of a Copy of this Agreement, (if checked, ☐ a deposit in the amount of $ _____),
counter offer numbers _____ ☐ Seller's Statement of Information and _____
_____ , and agrees to act as Escrow Holder subject to paragraph 20 of this Agreement, any supplemental escrow instructions and the terms of Escrow Holder's general provisions.

Escrow Holder is advised that the date of Confirmation of Acceptance of the Agreement as between Buyer and Seller is _____

Escrow Holder _____ Escrow # _____
By _____ Date _____
Address _____
Phone/Fax/E-mail _____
Escrow Holder has the following license number # _____
☐ Department of Business Oversight, ☐ Department of Insurance, ☐ Bureau of Real Estate.

PRESENTATION OF OFFER: (_____) Listing Broker presented this offer to Seller on_____(date).
Broker or Designee Initials

REJECTION OF OFFER: (_____)(_____) No counter offer is being made. This offer was rejected by Seller on_____(date).
Seller's Initials

Reviewed by _____
Broker or Designee _____

Buyer's Initials (_____)(_____)

RPA-CA REVISED 11/14 (PAGE 10 of 10)   Print Date

CALIFORNIA RESIDENTIAL PURCHASE AGREEMENT   (RPA-CA PAGE 10 OF 10)

FIGURE 5.8

REAL ESTATE TRANSFER DISCLOSURE STATEMENT
(CALIFORNIA CIVIL CODE §1102, ET SEQ.)
(C.A.R. Form TDS, Revised 4/14)

THIS DISCLOSURE STATEMENT CONCERNS THE REAL PROPERTY SITUATED IN THE CITY OF _____ _____, COUNTY OF _____, STATE OF CALIFORNIA, DESCRIBED AS _____.

THIS STATEMENT IS A DISCLOSURE OF THE CONDITION OF THE ABOVE DESCRIBED PROPERTY IN COMPLIANCE WITH SECTION 1102 OF THE CIVIL CODE AS OF (date) _____. IT IS NOT A WARRANTY OF ANY KIND BY THE SELLER(S) OR ANY AGENT(S) REPRESENTING ANY PRINCIPAL(S) IN THIS TRANSACTION, AND IS NOT A SUBSTITUTE FOR ANY INSPECTIONS OR WARRANTIES THE PRINCIPAL(S) MAY WISH TO OBTAIN.

I. COORDINATION WITH OTHER DISCLOSURE FORMS

This Real Estate Transfer Disclosure Statement is made pursuant to Section 1102 of the Civil Code. Other statutes require disclosures, depending upon the details of the particular real estate transaction (for example: special study zone and purchase-money liens on residential property).

Substituted Disclosures: The following disclosures and other disclosures required by law, including the Natural Hazard Disclosure Report/Statement that may include airport annoyances, earthquake, fire, flood, or special assessment information, have or will be made in connection with this real estate transfer, and are intended to satisfy the disclosure obligations on this form, where the subject matter is the same:

☐ Inspection reports completed pursuant to the contract of sale or receipt for deposit.
☐ Additional inspection reports or disclosures: _____
_____

II. SELLER'S INFORMATION

The Seller discloses the following information with the knowledge that even though this is not a warranty, prospective Buyers may rely on this information in deciding whether and on what terms to purchase the subject property. Seller hereby authorizes any agent(s) representing any principal(s) in this transaction to provide a copy of this statement to any person or entity in connection with any actual or anticipated sale of the property.

THE FOLLOWING ARE REPRESENTATIONS MADE BY THE SELLER(S) AND ARE NOT THE REPRESENTATIONS OF THE AGENT(S), IF ANY. THIS INFORMATION IS A DISCLOSURE AND IS NOT INTENDED TO BE PART OF ANY CONTRACT BETWEEN THE BUYER AND SELLER.

Seller ☐ is ☐ is not occupying the property.

A. The subject property has the items checked below:*

☐ Range	☐ Wall/Window Air Conditioning	☐ Pool:
☐ Oven	☐ Sprinklers	☐ Child Resistant Barrier
☐ Microwave	☐ Public Sewer System	☐ Pool/Spa Heater:
☐ Dishwasher	☐ Septic Tank	☐ Gas ☐ Solar ☐ Electric
☐ Trash Compactor	☐ Sump Pump	☐ Water Heater:
☐ Garbage Disposal	☐ Water Softener	☐ Gas ☐ Solar ☐ Electric
☐ Washer/Dryer Hookups	☐ Patio/Decking	☐ Water Supply:
☐ Rain Gutters	☐ Built-in Barbecue	☐ City ☐ Well
☐ Burglar Alarms	☐ Gazebo	☐ Private Utility or
☐ Carbon Monoxide Device(s)	☐ Security Gate(s)	Other_____
☐ Smoke Detector(s)	☐ Garage:	☐ Gas Supply:
☐ Fire Alarm	☐ Attached ☐ Not Attached	☐ Utility ☐ Bottled (Tank)
☐ TV Antenna	☐ Carport	☐ Window Screens
☐ Satellite Dish	☐ Automatic Garage Door Opener(s)	☐ Window Security Bars
☐ Intercom	☐ Number Remote Controls ____	☐ Quick Release Mechanism on
☐ Central Heating	☐ Sauna	Bedroom Windows
☐ Central Air Conditioning	☐ Hot Tub/Spa:	☐ Water-Conserving Plumbing Fixtures
☐ Evaporator Cooler(s)	☐ Locking Safety Cover	

Exhaust Fan(s) in _____ 220 Volt Wiring in _____ Fireplace(s) in _____
☐ Gas Starter _____ ☐ Roof(s): Type: _____ Age: _____ (approx.)
☐ Other: _____
Are there, to the best of your (Seller's) knowledge, any of the above that are not in operating condition? ☐ Yes ☐ No. If yes, then describe. (Attach additional sheets if necessary): _____
_____

(*see note on page 2)

Buyer's Initials (_____)(_____)   Seller's Initials (_____)(_____)

TDS REVISED 4/14 (PAGE 1 OF 3) Print Date

Reviewed by _____ Date _____

EQUAL HOUSING OPPORTUNITY

REAL ESTATE TRANSFER DISCLOSURE STATEMENT (TDS PAGE 1 OF 3)

FIGURE 5.8 (Continued)

Property Address: _____ Date: _____

B. Are you (Seller) aware of any significant defects/malfunctions in any of the following? ☐ Yes ☐ No. If yes, check appropriate space(s) below.

☐ Interior Walls ☐ Ceilings ☐ Floors ☐ Exterior Walls ☐ Insulation ☐ Roof(s) ☐ Windows ☐ Doors ☐ Foundation ☐ Slab(s) ☐ Driveways ☐ Sidewalks ☐ Walls/Fences ☐ Electrical Systems ☐ Plumbing/Sewers/Septics ☐ Other Structural Components
(Describe: _____
_____)

If any of the above is checked, explain. (Attach additional sheets if necessary.): _____
_____
_____

*Installation of a listed appliance, device, or amenity is not a precondition of sale or transfer of the dwelling. The carbon monoxide device, garage door opener, or child-resistant pool barrier may not be in compliance with the safety standards relating to, respectively, carbon monoxide device standards of Chapter 8 (commencing with Section 13260) of Part 2 of Division 12 of, automatic reversing device standards of Chapter 12.5 (commencing with Section 19890) of Part 3 of Division 13 of, or the pool safety standards of Article 2.5 (commencing with Section 115920) of Chapter 5 of Part 10 of Division 104 of, the Health and Safety Code. Window security bars may not have quick-release mechanisms in compliance with the 1995 edition of the California Building Standards Code. Section 1101.4 of the Civil Code requires all single-family residences built on or before January 1, 1994, to be equipped with water-conserving plumbing fixtures after January 1, 2017. Additionally, on and after January 1, 2014, a single-family residence built on or before January 1, 1994, that is altered or improved is required to be equipped with water-conserving plumbing fixtures as a condition of final approval. Fixtures in this dwelling may not comply with section 1101.4 of the Civil Code.

C. Are you (Seller) aware of any of the following:

1. Substances, materials, or products which may be an environmental hazard such as, but not limited to, asbestos, formaldehyde, radon gas, lead-based paint, mold, fuel or chemical storage tanks, and contaminated soil or water on the subject property .... ☐ Yes ☐ No

2. Features of the property shared in common with adjoining landowners, such as walls, fences, and driveways, whose use or responsibility for maintenance may have an effect on the subject property .... ☐ Yes ☐ No

3. Any encroachments, easements or similar matters that may affect your interest in the subject property.................. ☐ Yes ☐ No

4. Room additions, structural modifications, or other alterations or repairs made without necessary permits................ ☐ Yes ☐ No

5. Room additions, structural modifications, or other alterations or repairs not in compliance with building codes......... ☐ Yes ☐ No

6. Fill (compacted or otherwise) on the property or any portion thereof... ☐ Yes ☐ No

7. Any settling from any cause, or slippage, sliding, or other soil problems.. ☐ Yes ☐ No

8. Flooding, drainage or grading problems .... ☐ Yes ☐ No

9. Major damage to the property or any of the structures from fire, earthquake, floods, or landslides .... ☐ Yes ☐ No

10. Any zoning violations, nonconforming uses, violations of "setback" requirements .... ☐ Yes ☐ No

11. Neighborhood noise problems or other nuisances .... ☐ Yes ☐ No

12. CC&R's or other deed restrictions or obligations... ☐ Yes ☐ No

13. Homeowners' Association which has any authority over the subject property... ☐ Yes ☐ No

14. Any "common area" (facilities such as pools, tennis courts, walkways, or other areas co-owned in undivided interest with others)... ☐ Yes ☐ No

15. Any notices of abatement or citations against the property .... ☐ Yes ☐ No

16. Any lawsuits by or against the Seller threatening to or affecting this real property, claims for damages by the Seller pursuant to Section 910 or 914 threatening to or affecting this real property, claims for breach of warranty pursuant to Section 900 threatening to or affecting this real property, or claims for breach of an enhanced protection agreement pursuant to Section 903 threatening to or affecting this real property, including any lawsuits or claims for damages pursuant to Section 910 or 914 alleging a defect or deficiency in this real property or "common areas" (facilities such as pools, tennis courts, walkways, or other areas co-owned in undivided interest with others) .... ☐ Yes ☐ No

If the answer to any of these is yes, explain. (Attach additional sheets if necessary.): _____
_____
_____
_____

D. 1. The Seller certifies that the property, as of the close of escrow, will be in compliance with Section 13113.8 of the Health and Safety Code by having operable smoke detector(s) which are approved, listed, and installed in accordance with the State Fire Marshal's regulations and applicable local standards.

    2. The Seller certifies that the property, as of the close of escrow, will be in compliance with Section 19211 of the Health and Safety Code by having the water heater tank(s) braced, anchored, or strapped in place in accordance with applicable law.

Buyer's Initials (_____)(_____)   Seller's Initials (_____)(_____)

TDS REVISED 4/14 (PAGE 2 OF 3) | Reviewed by _____ Date _____ | EQUAL HOUSING OPPORTUNITY

REAL ESTATE TRANSFER DISCLOSURE STATEMENT (TDS PAGE 2 OF 3)

FIGURE 5.8 (Continued)

Property Address: _____ Date:_____

Seller certifies that the information herein is true and correct to the best of the Seller's knowledge as of the date signed by the Seller.

Seller_____ Date _____

Seller_____ Date _____

III. AGENT'S INSPECTION DISCLOSURE

(To be completed only if the Seller is represented by an agent in this transaction.)

THE UNDERSIGNED, BASED ON THE ABOVE INQUIRY OF THE SELLER(S) AS TO THE CONDITION OF THE PROPERTY AND BASED ON A REASONABLY COMPETENT AND DILIGENT VISUAL INSPECTION OF THE ACCESSIBLE AREAS OF THE PROPERTY IN CONJUNCTION WITH THAT INQUIRY, STATES THE FOLLOWING:

☐ See attached Agent Visual Inspection Disclosure (AVID Form)

☐ Agent notes no items for disclosure.

☐ Agent notes the following items: _____

_____

_____

_____

Agent (Broker Representing Seller) _____ By _____ Date_____
                                        (Please Print)   (Associate Licensee or Broker Signature)

IV. AGENT'S INSPECTION DISCLOSURE

(To be completed only if the agent who has obtained the offer is other than the agent above.)

THE UNDERSIGNED, BASED ON A REASONABLY COMPETENT AND DILIGENT VISUAL INSPECTION OF THE ACCESSIBLE AREAS OF THE PROPERTY, STATES THE FOLLOWING:

☐ See attached Agent Visual Inspection Disclosure (AVID Form)

☐ Agent notes no items for disclosure.

☐ Agent notes the following items: _____

_____

_____

_____

Agent (Broker Obtaining the Offer) _____ By _____ Date_____
                                        (Please Print)   (Associate Licensee or Broker Signature)

V. BUYER(S) AND SELLER(S) MAY WISH TO OBTAIN PROFESSIONAL ADVICE AND/OR INSPECTIONS OF THE PROPERTY AND TO PROVIDE FOR APPROPRIATE PROVISIONS IN A CONTRACT BETWEEN BUYER AND SELLER(S) WITH RESPECT TO ANY ADVICE/INSPECTIONS/DEFECTS.

I/WE ACKNOWLEDGE RECEIPT OF A COPY OF THIS STATEMENT.

Seller _____ Date _____   Buyer _____ Date_____

Seller _____ Date _____   Buyer _____ Date_____

Agent (Broker Representing Seller) _____   By _____ Date_____
                    (Please Print)   (Associate Licensee or Broker Signature)

Agent (Broker Obtaining the Offer) _____   By _____ Date_____
                    (Please Print)   (Associate Licensee or Broker Signature)

SECTION 1102.3 OF THE CIVIL CODE PROVIDES A BUYER WITH THE RIGHT TO RESCIND A PURCHASE CONTRACT FOR AT LEAST THREE DAYS AFTER THE DELIVERY OF THIS DISCLOSURE IF DELIVERY OCCURS AFTER THE SIGNING OF AN OFFER TO PURCHASE. IF YOU WISH TO RESCIND THE CONTRACT, YOU MUST ACT WITHIN THE PRESCRIBED PERIOD.

A REAL ESTATE BROKER IS QUALIFIED TO ADVISE ON REAL ESTATE. IF YOU DESIRE LEGAL ADVICE, CONSULT YOUR ATTORNEY.

Published and Distributed by:
REAL ESTATE BUSINESS SERVICES, INC.
a subsidiary of the California Association of REALTORS®
525 South Virgil Avenue, Los Angeles, California 90020

Reviewed by _____ Date _____

TDS REVISED 4/14 (PAGE 3 OF 3)

REAL ESTATE TRANSFER DISCLOSURE STATEMENT (TDS PAGE 3 OF 3)

FIGURE 5.9

CALIFORNIA ASSOCIATION OF REALTORS®

BUYER'S INSPECTION ADVISORY
(C.A.R. Form BIA, Revised 11/14)

Property Address _____ ("Property")

1. IMPORTANCE OF PROPERTY INVESTIGATION: The physical condition of the land and improvements being purchased is not guaran- teed by either Seller or Brokers. You have an affirmative duty to exercise reasonable care to protect yourself, including discovery of the legal, practical and technical implications of disclosed facts, and the investigation and verification of information and facts that you know or that are within your diligent attention and observation. A general physical inspection typically does not cover all aspects of the Property nor items affecting the Property that are not physically located on the Property. If the professionals recommend further investigations, including a rec- ommendation by a pest control operator to inspect inaccessible areas of the Property, you should contact qualified experts to conduct such additional investigations.

2. BROKER OBLIGATIONS: Brokers do not have expertise in all areas and therefore cannot advise you on many items, such as those listed below. If Broker gives you referrals to professionals, Broker does not guarantee their performance.

3. YOU ARE STRONGLY ADVISED TO INVESTIGATE THE CONDITION AND SUITABILITY OF ALL ASPECTS OF THE PROPERTY, INCLUDING BUT NOT LIMIITED TO THE FOLLOWING. IF YOU DO NOT DO SO, YOU ARE ACTING AGAINST THE ADVICE OF BROKERS.

    A. GENERAL CONDITION OF THE PROPERTY, ITS SYSTEMS AND COMPONENTS: Foundation, roof (condition, age, leaks, useful life), plumbing, heating, air conditioning, electrical, mechanical, security, pool/spa (cracks, leaks, operation), other structural and non- structural systems and components, fixtures, built-in appliances, any personal property included in the sale, and energy efficiency of the Property.

    B. SQUARE FOOTAGE, AGE, BOUNDARIES: Square footage, room dimensions, lot size, age of improvements and boundaries. Any numerical statements regarding these items are APPROXIMATIONS ONLY and have not been verified by Seller and cannot be verified by Brokers. Fences, hedges, walls, retaining walls and other barriers or markers do not necessarily identify true Property boundaries.

    C. WOOD DESTROYING PESTS: Presence of, or conditions likely to lead to the presence of wood destroying pests and organisms.

    D. SOIL STABILITY: Existence of fill or compacted soil, expansive or contracting soil, susceptibility to slippage, settling or movement, and the adequacy of drainage.

    E. WATER AND UTILITIES; WELL SYSTEMS AND COMPONENTS;WASTE DISPOSAL: Water and utility availability, use restrictions and costs. Water quality, adequacy, condition, and performance of well systems and components. The type, size, adequacy, capacity and condition of sewer and septic systems and components, connection to sewer, and applicable fees.

    F. ENVIRONMENTAL HAZARDS: Potential environmental hazards, including, but not limited to, asbestos, lead-based paint and other lead contamination, radon, methane, other gases, fuel oil or chemical storage tanks, contaminated soil or water, hazardous waste, waste disposal sites, electromagnetic fields, nuclear sources, and other substances, materials, products, or conditions (including mold (airborne, toxic or otherwise), fungus or similar contaminants).

    G. EARTHQUAKES AND FLOODING: Susceptibility of the Property to earthquake/seismic hazards and propensity of the Property to flood.

    H. FIRE, HAZARD AND OTHER INSURANCE: The availability and cost of necessary or desired insurance may vary. The location of the Property in a seismic, flood or fire hazard zone, and other conditions, such as the age of the Property and the claims history of the Property and Buyer, may affect the availability and need for certain types of insurance. Buyer should explore insurance options early as this information may affect other decisions, including the removal of loan and inspection contingencies.

    I. BUILDING PERMITS, ZONING AND GOVERNMENTAL REQUIREMENTS: Permits, inspections, certificates, zoning, other governmental limitations, restrictions, and requirements affecting the current or future use of the Property, its development or size.

    J. RENTAL PROPERTY RESTRICTIONS: Some cities and counties impose restrictions that limit the amount of rent that can be charged, the maximum number of occupants, and the right of a landlord to terminate a tenancy. Deadbolt or other locks and security systems for doors and windows, including window bars, should be examined to determine whether they satisfy legal requirements.

    K. SECURITY AND SAFETY: State and local Law may require the installation of barriers, access alarms, self-latching mechanisms and/ or other measures to decrease the risk to children and other persons of existing swimming pools and hot tubs, as well as various fire safety and other measures concerning other features of the Property.

    L. NEIGHBORHOOD, AREA, SUBDIVISION CONDITIONS; PERSONAL FACTORS: Neighborhood or area conditions, including schools, law enforcement, crime statistics, registered felons or offenders, fire protection, other government services, availability, adequacy and cost of internet connections or other technology services and installations, commercial, industrial or agricultural activities, existing and proposed transportation, construction and development that may affect noise, view, or traffic, airport noise, noise or odor from any source, wild and domestic animals, other nuisances, hazards, or circumstances, protected species, wetland properties, botanical diseases, historic or other governmentally protected sites or improvements, cemeteries, facilities and condition of common areas of common interest subdivisions, and possible lack of compliance with any governing documents or Homeowners' Association requirements, conditions and influences of significance to certain cultures and/or religions, and personal needs, requirements and preferences of Buyer.

By signing below, Buyers acknowledge that they have read, understand, accept and have received a Copy of this Advisory. Buyers are encouraged to read it carefully.

Buyer _____   Buyer _____

Published and Distributed by:
REAL ESTATE BUSINESS SERVICES, INC.
a subsidiary of the California Association of REALTORS®
525 South Virgil Avenue, Los Angeles, California 90020

Reviewed by _____ Date _____

EQUAL HOUSING OPPORTUNITY

BIA REVISED 11/14 (PAGE 1 OF 1)   Print Date
BUYER'S INSPECTION ADVISORY (BIA PAGE 1 OF 1)

STUDENT LEARNING OUTCOMES, PART I

In Part I of this chapter, you will study land descriptions, stressing the lot, block, and tract; metes and bounds; and U.S. government survey methods for describing and locating land.

You will also explore five ways of acquiring title to real estate, including an explanation of deeds used in California. At the conclusion of Part I, you will be able to do the following:

- List the three methods used to legally describe and locate land.
- Find a parcel of land using each of the three location methods and be able to calculate acreage.
- Outline five ways of acquiring title to real estate.
- Discuss the difference between a grant deed, quitclaim deed, and warranty deed.
- Briefly describe the purpose of the California recording system.

PART I: LEGAL DESCRIPTIONS, METHODS OF ACQUIRING TITLE, AND DEEDS

6.1 LAND DESCRIPTIONS

Three reasons the description of real property is essential are as follows:

1. To specifically identify and locate areas of real property ownership.
2. To satisfy buyers who are interested in the precise dimensions and area of their property.
3. To minimize land description disputes between neighbors by establishing set boundary lines.

In addition to these three reasons, the law requires that every parcel of land sold, mortgaged, or leased must be properly described or identified. Legal descriptions are usually based upon the field notes of a civil engineer or a surveyor. When dealing with real property, recorded descriptions usually can be obtained from title insurance policies, deeds, deeds of trust, or mortgages.

Engineers and surveyors establish exact directions and distances by means of transits and measuring devices. Aerial photography and Global Positioning Systems (GPS) are also used in modern mapping.

Early Methods Used

Today's survey methods are a far cry from the methods used in early California. One early method of land measurement employed two people on horseback. Each rider dragged an end of a cord or rawhide strip, called a *thong*, which was about 100 *varas* in length. (A *vara* is about 33 inches.) One rider remained stationary while the other rode past. When the length of the thong was reached, the process was repeated by the other rider until one of them arrived at the end of the property. The number of thong lengths passed was counted, and the dimensions of the property were determined.

In another early method, the circumference of a wagon wheel was measured. A leather strip was tied to a spoke, and then, by rolling the wheel on the ground, the revolutions of the wheel were counted and the distance recorded.

Present-Day Land Descriptions

Three major methods are used today to legally describe and locate land. They are as follows:

1. Lot, block, and tract system.
2. Metes and bounds system.
3. U.S. government survey, commonly called the *U.S. section and township system.*

Lot, Block, and Tract System

Dividing a large parcel of land into smaller parcels is called *subdividing.* The California Subdivision Map Act requires that all new subdivisions be either mapped or platted. A map of each subdivision is recorded in the recorder's office of the county in which the land is located.

At the time a subdivision map is filed in the county recorder's office, it is assigned a tract name and/or number. Once subdivision maps are recorded, legal descriptions are created by making reference to a particular lot in the block in that tract in which the property is located.

> Example: "All of lot 4 in Block A of Tract number 2025 in the city of Bellflower, Los Angeles County, California. As per map recorded in Book 76 page 83 of maps in the office of the recorder of said county." This type of identification is commonly found in urban areas of California, where extensive subdividing has taken place. (See Figure 6.1.)

Metes and Bounds System

The **metes and bounds** system of land location is used most often when the property in question is not covered by a recorded subdivision map or when the property is so irregular in shape that it is impractical to describe under the section and township system.

Metes refer to the measurement of length, using items such as inches, feet, yards, rods, meters, and miles. *Bounds* refer to the

FIGURE 6.1

Tract 2025

1	6	1	6
2	7	2	7
3 A 8		3 B 8	
4	9	4	9
5	10	5	10

Source: © 2015 OnCourse Learning

use of boundaries, both natural and artificial, such as rivers, roads, fences, boulders, creeks, and iron pipes. So the term *metes and bounds* means to measure the boundaries. This system is one of the oldest methods used to describe land, and it is used in both rural and urban areas. A common term used in the metes and bounds system is *benchmark*. A benchmark is a mark on a fixed or enduring object, such as a metal stake or rock, and it is often used as an elevation point by a surveyor.

Another term is *angular lines*. Many surveys using metes and bounds descriptions are based on angles and directions from a given north–south line, which is obtained with a compass. Angles are a deflection from this north–south line. Deflections are to the east or west of the north–south line.

There are 360° in a circle and 180° in a half-circle. Each degree is divided into 60 minutes, and each minute is divided into 60 seconds. The bearing of a course is described by measuring easterly or westerly from the north and south lines. (See Figure 6.2.) Although the metes and bounds land description is one of the oldest forms, it is also one of the most complicated. The system ranges from simple distances between given landmarks to surveyor readings based on angles found in the arc of a circle.

FIGURE 6.2

Source: © 2015 OnCourse Learning

In using the metes and bounds method, three important points must be stressed:

1. You must start at a given point of beginning.
2. You must follow, in detail, the boundaries of the land in courses, distances, and directions from one point to another.
3. You must return to the point of beginning, thus enclosing the boundary lines.

Example: Here is a legal description using the metes and bounds method. "Beginning at a point on the southerly line of Harbor Ave., 200 ft. westerly of the southwest corner of the intersection of Harbor Ave. and 8th St.; running thence due south 300 ft. to the northerly line of Cribbage St.; thence westerly along the northerly line of Cribbage St., 200 ft.; thence northerly and parallel to the first course, 300 ft. to the southerly line of Harbor Ave.; thence easterly along the southerly line of Harbor Ave., 200 ft. to the point of beginning." (See Figure 6.3.)

One major weakness in using a metes and bounds system is that markers or points of beginning often disappear or are moved or replaced. In later years, this makes it difficult to find the exact corners of a parcel.

FIGURE 6.3

Source: © 2015 OnCourse Learning

U.S. Government Section and Township System

The U.S. government section and township method of survey is used primarily to describe agricultural or rural land. The system originated in the late 1780s with a survey of public lands made by the U.S. surveyor general. The **U.S. government survey system** establishes monuments as points of beginning. The monuments are intersected by two imaginary lines: one running east and west, called a *base line*, and another running north and south, called a *meridian line*.

Because of its peculiar shape, the state of California requires three of these principal base lines and meridians, as shown in Figure 6.4. They are as follows:

1. *Humboldt Base Line and Meridian*, which is the point of beginning for describing land in the northwestern part of California. The actual point of beginning is on Mt. Pierce, just south of Eureka, California. (See Figure 6.4.)

2. *Mt. Diablo Base Line and Meridian*, which is the point of beginning for describing land in the central and northeastern part of California. The actual point of beginning is on Mt. Diablo, near Walnut Creek, California.

FIGURE 6.4

CALIFORNIA BASE LINES AND MERIDIANS

Source: © 2015 OnCourse Learning

3. *San Bernardino Base Line and Meridian*, which is used to describe land in southern California. The actual point of beginning is the intersection of Base Line Street and Meridian Avenue in the city of San Bernardino, California.

Range lines run parallel to the principal meridians at six-mile intervals. *Township lines* (sometimes referred to as *tier lines*) run parallel to the principle base lines at six-mile intervals. The result is a grid of squares, or townships, each township containing approximately 36 square miles.

To identify each of these townships, a numbering system utilizing an assignment of two location numbers was devised. The identity of each township is determined by its position north or south of the base line and east or west of the meridian line. An example of a legal description might be "Township 2 North, Range 3 East, San Bernardino Base Line and Meridian. (T2N, R3E, SBBL & M)." The *X* indicates the township. (See Figure 6.5.)

Sections in a Township

Townships are, in turn, divided into sections. Each township contains 36 squares, or sections. Each section is one mile square. These sections

FIGURE 6.5

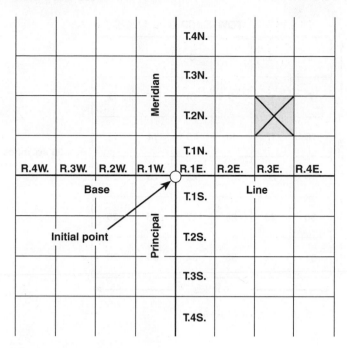

Source: © 2015 OnCourse Learning

are uniformly numbered from 1 to 36, with Section 1 located in the northeast corner of the township.

Not only is each section one mile square, but also each contains 640 acres. Each section can be divided into smaller parcels of land, as follows:

A quarter of a section = 160 acres

A quarter of a ¼ section = 40 acres

A quarter of a ¼ of a ¼ section = 10 acres

The division can be smaller and smaller until the size of the parcel is identified. The division need not be in quarters; it can also be in halves. (See Figures 6.6 and 6.7.)

Pitfall

Because of the earth's curvature, some sections in townships are distorted and may not contain a full 640 acres; thus, computing acreage under the U.S. government system provides approximate figures. An accurate measure of actual acreage is best left to licensed civil engineers and surveyors.

These additional measurements will help in computing land measurements:

One mile = 5,280 feet

FIGURE 6.6

TOWNSHIP

6	5	4	3	2	1
7	8	9	10	11	12
18	17	16	15	14	13
19	20	21	22	23	24
30	29	28	27	26	25
31	32	33	34	35	36

6 miles (vertical)   = 36 sq. miles

6 miles (horizontal)

Source: © 2015 OnCourse Learning

FIGURE 6.7

MAP OF A SECTION

N 1/2 OF NW 1/4

SW 1/4 OF NW 1/4

80A.

20A.

5A. 5A.

10A.

40A.

1320'

1 mile / 5280'

SW 1/4

160 A.

2640'

1 mile

Source: © 2015 OnCourse Learning

One acre = 43,560 square feet

One square acre = 208.71 feet

Commercial acre = standard acre less land needed for streets, sidewalks, and curbs

6.2 METHODS OF ACQUIRING TITLE

Chapter 2 discussed the difference between real and personal property. Section 6.1 of this chapter illustrated the three main ways of legally describing real property. The next logical step is to describe how a person goes about acquiring legal title to real property. According to the California Civil Code, the five legal ways of acquiring property are by will, succession, accession, occupancy, and transfer.

Acquiring Property by Will

A will is a legal instrument by which a person over the age of 18 and of sound mind disposes of property upon his or her death. California law recognizes three types of wills: (1) a witnessed will, (2) a holographic will, and (3) a statutory will. (See Figure 6.8.)

A **witnessed will** is a formal typewritten document signed by the individual who is making it, wherein he or she declares in the presence of at least two witnesses that it is his or her will. The two witnesses, in turn, sign the will. This document should be prepared by an attorney. Because of the attorney's expertise, this is usually considered the best type of will.

A **holographic will** is a document written, dated, and signed in its entirety in the handwriting of the maker. It requires no witnesses. A **statutory will** is a preprinted form approved by the state in which a person merely fills in the blanks, usually without formal legal assistance. This statutory will requires at least two witnesses. At one time, another will—an oral will in contemplation of death, called a *nuncupative will*—was occasionally recognized. But today oral dying declarations are, for the most part, ignored by the probate courts.

FIGURE 6.8

TYPES OF WILLS

WITNESSED	**HOLOGRAPHIC**	**STATUTORY**
... in writing ... two witnesses	... handwritten ... no witness	... preprinted form ... approved by state

Source: © 2015 OnCourse Learning

Special Terms

A will is also called a *testament*. Special terms relating to wills are as follows:

Testator: Male person who makes a will.

Testatrix: Female person who makes a will.

Executor: Male person named in the will by the maker to handle the estate of the deceased.

Executrix: Female person named in the will by the maker to handle the estate of the deceased.

Administrator: Male person appointed by the court to handle the estate when no will is left.

Administratrix: Female person appointed by the court to handle the estate when no will is left.

Devise: A gift of real property by will.

Devisee: Person receiving real property by will.

Bequest, legacy: A gift of personal property by will.

Legatee: Person receiving personal property by will.

Codicil: A change in a will.

Intestate: A situation in which a person dies without leaving a will; he or she is said to have died intestate.

Testate: A situation in which a person dies leaving a will.

Probate

Legal title to property being acquired by will is subject to the control of the probate court. The purpose of a **probate** hearing is to identify the creditors of the deceased and to pay off these creditors. Then if any property remains, the probate court determines the identity of the rightful heirs and distributes the remaining property.

The law requires that upon the death of the owner, all property is subject to the temporary possession of an **executor** (or **executrix**, if female) or an **administrator** (or **administratrix if female**).

Probate action takes place in superior court, and the estate property may be sold during the probate period for the benefit of the heirs or to cover court costs. If a probate sale takes place, certain guidelines are set by the court. The general guidelines are as follows:

1. The initial offer in a probate real estate sale must be for at least 90 percent of the appraised value of the property.

2. Once the initial offer is made, the court is petitioned to confirm the sale, and at the hearing, the court may accept additional bids.

3. The first additional bid must be an increase of at least 10 percent of the first $10,000 of the original bid and 5 percent of any excess. For example, if the original bid is in the amount of $500,000, the first overbid would be 10 percent of the first $10,000, which is $1,000, and the remaining excess of $490,000 is then multiplied by 5 percent which would be $24,500. The first overbid would then be $525,500 or more. Subsequent bids may be for any amount set by the court as the judge would start an auction in the courtroom.

4. The court confirms the final sale and sets the broker's commissions if a broker is involved. Frequently, the listing agent, the selling agent, AND the agent who brings in the initial offer all receive a commission. The rationale is that the agent who brought in the initial offer should be compensated since that agent created a situation which led to the sale of the property!

Probate fees paid to executors, administrators, and attorneys are set by the courts and vary depending on the size and complexity of the estate. Certain types of property holdings need not be probated, which is discussed in Part II of this chapter.

Independent Administration of Estate Act

Under this act, if all heirs agree in advance, the complicated open-court probate sale rules mentioned above are avoided. Under the Independent Administration of Estate Act, the executor/executrix or administrator/administratrix can sell the property directly to a specific buyer, similar to a regular real estate sale. The sale is still subject to court approval, but no open-court hearing for other potential bidders is required. But if all heirs do not agree, which is occasionally the case, the previously described open-court sale rules apply. The advantage here is by being able to avoid the overbid confirmation process, buyers are more likely to make offers on the property and the property will sell in a shorter period of time.

Acquiring Property by Succession

When a deceased person leaves no will, the law provides for the disposition of his or her property. The state of California dictates who will get the property under the law of **intestate** succession. **Succession** means the handing down of property to another person. (See Figure 6.9.)

When a person dies intestate, the property of the deceased is divided into two categories: separate property and community property. The laws of intestate succession are different for each of these categories.

FIGURE 6.9

Source: © 2015 OnCourse Learning

When a person dies without a will and leaves separate property, this means that the surviving spouse or registered domestic partner, a person, other than a spouse, with whom one cohabits, did not have an interest in said property. If a person leaves community property, this means a surviving spouse or registered domestic partner has a one-half interest in the property.

When *separate property* is involved, the following disposition of property is made:

1. When a deceased person leaves a spouse or registered domestic partner and no children, the separate property is divided one-half to the spouse or registered domestic partner and one-half to the parents of the deceased person.

2. When a deceased person leaves a spouse or registered domestic partner and one child, the separate property is divided one-half to the spouse or registered domestic partner and one-half to the child.

3. When a deceased person leaves a spouse and two or more children, the spouse/registered domestic partner receives one-third and the children equally divide the other two-thirds.

4. Other divisions are made by the courts in the event that a person dies leaving no spouse or registered domestic partner and no children. The usual rule is that the property goes to the next of kin, such as parents, brothers, sisters, and so on.

When a person dies intestate and leaves community property, the deceased person's community interest passes to the surviving spouse or registered domestic partner. The children, if any, get nothing.

Key Point

On matters regarding wills and estates, always consult an experienced attorney! Do-it-yourself estate planning is not recommended!

Acquiring Property by Accession

You may acquire title to property that is added to your existing real estate. This process is called accession.

Examples include (1) accretion, (2) avulsion, (3) addition of fixtures, and (4) improvements made in error. (See Figure 6.10.)

Accretion

The gradual accumulation of soil on property bordering a stream, a river, or an ocean shoreline is called accretion. The soil thus deposited is referred to as alluvion or *alluvion deposits*. The gradual wearing away of land by the action of water and wind is known as *erosion*. Reliction occurs when the waterway, sea, or river recedes permanently below the usual water line. When this takes place, the owner of the property that borders on the waterway, sea, or river may acquire title to the newly exposed land.

Avulsion

Avulsion occurs when a river or stream, during a storm or earthquake, carries away a part of the bank and bears it to the opposite bank or

FIGURE 6.10

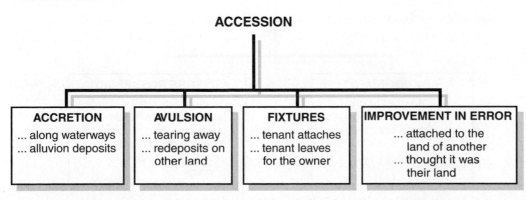

Source: © 2015 OnCourse Learning

to another part of the same bank. The owner of the part carried away may reclaim it within one year after the avulsion. However, the owner must reclaim the title by applying some act of ownership, such as cultivation of the soil, within one year; if not, the land belongs to the owner of the property to which the land is now attached.

For urban readers, this discussion regarding rivers and water rights may seem out of place. But in rural California, especially northern California, these topics are an important aspect of real estate principles.

Addition of Fixtures

Addition of fixtures occurs when a person affixes something to the land of another without an agreement permitting removal. The thing so affixed may then become the property of the landowner.

Improvements Made in Error

An improvement made in error occurs when a person, in good faith, erroneously affixes improvements to the land of another. In some cases, these erroneous improvements may pass to the landowner. But in most cases, the person who made the improvements in error is permitted to remove the improvements and pay the cost to restore the property to its original condition.

Acquiring Property by Occupancy

Real property or the use of real property may be gained through (1) abandonment and (2) adverse possession. (See Figure 6.11.)

FIGURE 6.11

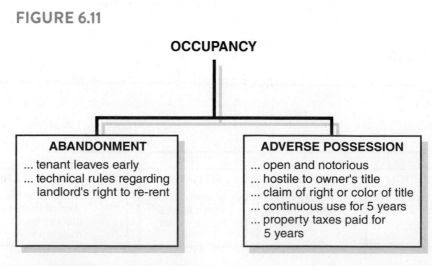

Source: © 2015 OnCourse Learning

Abandonment

A party who holds a leasehold interest (the tenant) in a piece of property may abandon his or her interest or any improvements made thereon. If this should occur, the landlord may reacquire possession and full control of the premises. In other words, when a tenant leaves before the lease expires, the landlord may reacquire the use of the property at that time and in some cases not be obligated to refund rental payments or return any improvements made on the property. There are technical rules regarding the landlord's right to re-rent the property. If a tenant abandons the premises and leaves personal property, the landlord may, after due notification, dispose of such personal property.

Adverse Possession

Adverse possession is the process by which title to another's property is acquired without compensation. Ownership may develop into legal title if five conditions are met.

Five elements of adverse possession

1. There must be actual occupation, open and notorious. This means the claim of possession must not be kept a secret. In other words, if the present owner inspects the property, the possession or use by another person should be apparent. You do not actually have to reside on the property, but you must show your intentions of holding and possessing the land through some type of improvement to the land. For example, if the property were farmland, the cultivation of crops, the grazing of cattle, or the fencing of the property might constitute possession.
2. There must be occupancy hostile to the true owner's title (wishes). Hostile does not mean physical confrontation. Hostile means a person is using the property without permission and not making rental payment of any kind to the owner. Permission to use the property defeats the hostile use and prevents acquiring title by adverse possession.
3. There must be a *claim of right or color of title*. Under claim of right, the claimant enters as an intruder and remains with the intent to claim the property; under color of title, claimants base their right on some court decree or upon a defective written instrument.
4. There must be *continuous and uninterrupted possession* for a period of five years.
5. There must be the *payment by the possessor of all real property taxes* levied and assessed for a period of five consecutive years.

The fact that the true owner is also paying the taxes does not necessarily defeat the rights of the adverse possessor, as long as the possessor pays the taxes first.

Adverse possession is not common in California because of the five requirements listed previously. It is not possible to obtain title by adverse possession to public lands or against an incompetent private landowner. Title insurance and marketable title cannot be obtained until a court, under a quiet title action, rules that the adverse possession vested valid title. In short, if you acquire title by adverse possession, it will be difficult to finance or sell the property without first going to court.

Acquiring Property by Transfer

Without question, the most common method of acquiring property is by transfer. When property is conveyed from one person to another by act of the parties or by act of law, title is acquired by transfer. There are five basic types of property transfers: (1) private grant, (2) public grant, (3) gift, (4) public dedication, and (5) court action (or involuntary transfer). (See Figure 6.12.)

Private Grant

Private grant occurs when an owner voluntarily conveys his or her ownership rights to another. The basic instrument used in this transaction is a deed. (Deeds are discussed in detail in Section 6.3.)

FIGURE 6.12

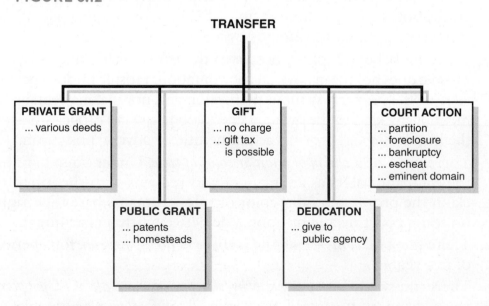

Source: © 2015 OnCourse Learning

Public Grant

When a governmental agency deeds property to an individual or institution, it is called a **public grant**. In the early years of U.S. history, public grants were made through laws enacted by Congress.

The Preemption Act of 1862 allowed persons living on federal land, who were known as *squatters*, to acquire 160 acres of land at a small fee. The Homestead Act of 1862 allowed vast stretches of public land to be homesteaded. Heads of families or persons over 21 years of age could obtain 160 acres. They had to file a declaration of homestead with the county recorder or at a land office and had to agree to occupy and improve the land. After residing on it for five years and paying a small fee, they received a document from the government called a *patent*, which conveyed the title from the government to the homesteader. Other public grants were made by the government for railroads, educational institutions, national parks, cities, and towns.

Gift

A property owner may voluntarily transfer property to a private person or an organization without giving or receiving any consideration or compensation. In the case of real property, the transfer normally is evidenced by a gift deed. Depending on the value of the gift, there may or may not be a gift tax liability. The person who gives the gift is called the *donor;* the person who receives the gift is called the *donee*.

Public Dedication

A property owner may also give land to the government for a particular use such as a street, a park, bridges, schools, playgrounds, and so on. This act is called *public dedication*. The dedication is valid only if the public body accepts the property.

Court Action (Involuntary Transfer)

A court of law may be called upon to transfer legal title in a variety of situations. The most common of these involuntary transfers are partition action, foreclosure action, bankruptcy, escheat, and eminent domain. (See Figure 6.13.)

Partition action is a court action wherein the co-owners of property may sue other co-owners for severance of their respective interests. If the property cannot be physically divided, the court can order a sale and divide the proceeds among the former owners.

Foreclosure action takes place when a person holding a delinquent lien on a property institutes proceedings requesting the forced sale

FIGURE 6.13

COURT ACTION

Partition action
Foreclosure action
Bankruptcy
Escheat
Eminent domain

Source: © 2015 OnCourse Learning

of property. In California, delinquent real estate loans are foreclosed using a process called a *trustee's sale*, which is discussed in Chapter 8.

Bankruptcy can be either voluntary or involuntary. When an individual cannot meet credit obligations, he or she may voluntarily file bankruptcy or may be adjudged bankrupt by the courts. Title to real property is then vested in a court-appointed trustee, who sells the property to pay the claims of creditors. Under certain circumstances, a family home can be protected against forced sale by the bankruptcy court.

Escheat is the legal process whereby ownership of property reverts to the state due to lack of heirs or want of legal ownership. The probate courts do all in their power to locate possible heirs. After escheat proceedings are instituted, the title is held in trust by the state for a set time. If at the end of that time no heirs have been located, title to the property transfers to the state. Every year, millions of dollars' worth of property escheats to the state of California because of the lack of heirs.

Eminent domain is the power of the state to take land from private ownership by due process of law. Use of eminent domain is often referred to as *condemnation proceedings*. These proceedings may be instituted by all levels of government and by public utilities or railroads.

Two conditions are legally required to use the power of eminent domain:

1. The property must be taken for a public use, *as found to be the case in *Kelo v. New London* (Connecticut), a U.S. Supreme Court ruling.

2. The owner must be paid just compensation. Most courts have ruled that the "fair market value" based on an appraisal is the proper method for determining just compensation.

---

*See *Kelo v. City of New London*, 545 U.S. 469 (2005).

6.3 INSTRUMENTS USED IN THE TRANSFER OF REAL PROPERTY

Under English common law, a written document was not needed to transfer title to real property. Rather, a twig, a stone, or a handful of dirt passing from one owner to the next owner in the presence of witnesses was symbolic of the transfer of property. Other methods of transfer were simply a statement made before witnesses in sight of the land, followed by entry upon the land by the new owner. Today under California law, the transfer of ownership of real property may be done by a single written instrument known as a *deed*.

A deed is a written document by which (when properly executed, delivered, and accepted) title to real property is transferred from one person, called a grantor, to another person, called a grantee. The grantor is the person who gives title, and the grantee is the person who receives title. In a real estate sale, the grantor is the seller and the grantee is the buyer. Throughout this book, you will find words to designate the parties in an agreement that end in the letters *or* and *ee*, such as the following:

Trustor and trustee

Lessor and lessee

Vendor and vendee

Optionor and optionee

To understand these terms, remember this rule:

The or *ending denotes the giver, and the* ee *ending indicates the receiver.*

Example: A lessor (owner or landlord) gives a lease to the lessee (tenant).

Essentials of a Valid Deed

To be valid, a deed must contain certain essential elements:

1. *The deed must be in writing.* Legal instruments required to be in writing come under the Statute of Frauds. According to this statute, when the title to real property is to be voluntarily conveyed, it must be accomplished by an instrument in writing, usually a deed.
2. *Parties must be correctly described and identified.* For a deed to be valid, the parties must be properly described. This means that the grantor (seller) and the grantee (buyer) must be certain and absolute.

FOR DEED TO BE VALID

It must be...
1 in writing,
2 with the parties correctly described,
3 with a competent grantor and capable grantee,
4 with a clear description,
5 granting clause, and
6 bearing the signature of the grantor.

Example: A deed from A to B or C is not absolute. The word *or* creates the problem. A deed from A to B and C is absolute. The word *and* makes it certain.

Because so many individuals have like or similar names, the parties to a deed must be identified as clearly as possible to avoid any later confusion as to true identity.

If possible, the full legal name should be used and the legal status of the individual should be shown. Remember, the full name includes middle name or initial, if any, and the legal status refers to the relationship between parties, such as husband and wife.

3. *Grantor must be competent to convey and grantee capable of receiving title.* Everyone is competent to convey except:

   a. *Minors:* persons under the age of 18 years, unless the minor is classified as emancipated, in which case a minor can legally contract for real estate. An emancipated minor is normally a person under 18 years who is married or in the armed services.

   b. *Incompetents:* persons of unsound mind, judicially declared incompetent.

   c. *Convicts:* persons imprisoned for life or under a death penalty.

Question: Can an infant take title to real property?
Answer: Yes, an infant can receive title by gift or inheritance but cannot convey title without a guardian or other court approval.
Question: Can a person take title under an assumed name?
Answer: Yes, but upon resale, he or she may have difficulty proving identity for a notary public.

4. *Description of the property must be clear.* The property in the deed must be correctly described; this means any description that clearly identifies the property so it can be located with certainty meets the test of the law. In most cases, the legal description is a lot, block, and tract; a metes and bounds; or a U.S. government survey description.

5. *There must be a granting clause.* A granting clause means the deed must contain words indicating the intention of the owner to convey the property. The exact words are not specified; however, the words *I hereby grant, I hereby convey,* or *I hereby transfer* satisfy the requirements of a granting clause.

6. *Deed must contain the signature of the grantor.* To be valid, a deed must be signed by all grantors named in the deed. If there is more than one owner, all owners must sign. For instance, both husband

and wife must sign a deed to convey community property. Only the grantor(s) sign a deed, not the grantee(s).

Under certain guidelines, state law allows a grantor's name to be signed by an *attorney in fact*, a person acting under a valid power of attorney.

California permits a person who is unable to sign his or her name to sign by mark as long as two witnesses are present. One of the witnesses then signs the deed according to the manner prescribed by law.

Delivery of the Deed Is Required

A deed is not effective unless it is delivered to and accepted by the grantee. This does not mean a mere turning over of the physical possession of the document. The grantor must have a clear and honest intention to pass title immediately, before there is a legal delivery.

1. *Evidence of delivery.* The best evidence is actually handing the deed to the grantee. However, manual delivery is not necessary, as a deed may be delivered to a third party for the benefit of the grantee—for example, depositing the deed in escrow. Again, manual delivery does not in itself constitute delivery; the proof lies in the intent of the grantor to pass title. Recording of the deed, if and when it happens, presumes valid delivery.

2. *Time of delivery.* To be effective, a deed must be delivered to the grantee during the grantor's lifetime. It cannot be used to take the place of a will. A deed that is delivered to a grantee with the condition that it is not to take effect until the death of the grantor is not valid because the intent to pass title would not occur during the lifetime of the grantor.

3. *Date of delivery.* A deed is presumed to be delivered as of its date of writing or execution. If no date exists on the deed, the legal date is presumed to be the date of delivery. The lack of a date on the deed does not invalidate the deed.

4. *Unconditional delivery.* Delivery of a deed must be absolute. It cannot be delivered to a grantee subject to conditions. For example, in an attempt to avoid the cost of probate, A gives a deed to B, telling B she is not to record the deed until A dies. This is a conditional delivery and is not a valid deed or transfer.

Acceptance

The deed must be accepted by the grantee, and this acceptance must be voluntary and unconditional. Acceptance is usually accomplished by words, acts, or conduct on the grantee's part that lead to the presumption of voluntary acceptance. An example of acceptance is the recording of the deed by the grantee.

Acknowledgment

A deed is a real estate document that need not be recorded to be valid. However, if the grantee wishes to record the deed, it must first be acknowledged.

An **acknowledgment** is a formal declaration before a duly authorized officer (usually a notary public) by the person who signed a document, stating that the signature is voluntarily given and that he or she is the person whose signature appears on the document.

Nonessentials in a Deed

Many of the items listed previously are essential for a deed to be valid. Some items, however, are not legally required but are commonly found in a deed.

Legally, a deed *does not* need to contain but commonly has (1) an acknowledgment, (2) a date, and (3) a recording number issued by the county.

However, it must be remembered that a deed is void or invalid if the:

1. grantor is incompetent.
2. deed is signed in blank.
3. deed is not delivered.
4. deed is a forgery.
5. grantee does not exist (fictitious or deceased).
6. deed is altered in escrow.

TYPES OF DEEDS

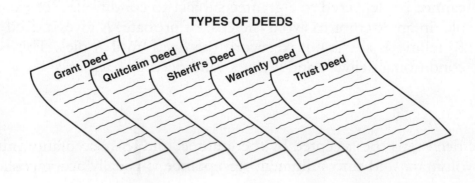

Grant Deed

In California, the **grant deed** is the most commonly used instrument for transferring title to real estate. A grant deed carries two *implied warranties*—meaning that although the warranties are not written in the deed, the law says they apply. An example of a grant deed is shown in Figure 6.14.

The implied warranties in a grant deed are that:

1. the grantor has not already conveyed title to any other person.
2. the estate being conveyed is free from encumbrances made by the grantor or any other person claiming under the grantor, other than those disclosed to the grantee.

Notice that these implied warranties do not state that the grantor is the owner or that the property is not encumbered. Rather, they state that the grantor has not deeded to others and that the property is free of encumbrances made by the grantor. This is why a potential buyer should insist that a policy of title insurance be issued as a condition of the purchase.

In addition to transferring legal ownership, a grant deed can be used to create easements and land use restrictions. A grant deed also conveys any after acquired title. *After acquired title* means that after the grantor deeds the property to the grantee, if the grantor should later acquire an additional interest in the property, that interest automatically passes to the grantee.

Quitclaim Deed

A **quitclaim deed** provides the grantee with the least protection of any deed. A quitclaim deed carries no implied warranties and no after acquired title provisions. Under a quitclaim deed, the grantor merely relinquishes any right or claim he or she has in the property. If the grantor has absolute ownership, that is what is conveyed. If the grantor has no claim or ownership right, this type of deed transfers what the grantor has—nothing! In other words, a quitclaim deed merely says, "Whatever interest I have in the property is yours; it may be something, or it may be nothing."

The quitclaim deed is usually used to remove certain items from the public record, such as the removal of an easement or a recorded restriction. It is not normally used in a buy-and-sell transaction.

Sheriff's Deed

The court may order an owner's property sold after a lawsuit and the rendering of a money judgment against the owner. The successful

FIGURE 6.14

RECORDING REQUESTED BY

AND WHEN RECORDED MAIL DOCUMENT AND
TAX STATEMENT TO:

NAME

STREET
ADDRESS

CITY, STATE &
ZIP CODE

TITLE ORDER NO.   ESCROW NO.   SPACE ABOVE THIS LINE FOR RECORDER'S USE ONLY

GRANT DEED

APN:

The undersigned grantor(s) declare(s)_____
DOCUMENTARY TRANSFER TAX $
☐ computed on full value of property conveyed, or
☐ computed on full value less linens and encumbrances remaining at time of sale.
☐ Unincorporated Area   City of _____

FOR VALUABLE CONSIDERATION, receipt of which is hereby acknowledged, I (we)

hereby remise, release and grant to

the following described real property in the City of _____, County of _____
State of California, with the following legal description:

_____   _____
          Date   _____

STATE OF _____

COUNTY OF _____

On _____ before me, _____ ,
          (Date)   (Name and title of the officer)
personally appeared _____ , who proved to me on the basis of
                                (Name of person signing)
satisfactory evidence to be the person(s) whose name(s) is/are subscribed to the within instrument and acknowledged to me that he/she/
they executed the same in his/her/their authorized capacity(ies), and that by his/her/their signature(s) on the instrument the person(s), or the
entity upon behalf of which the person(s) acted executed the instrument.

I certify under PENALTY OF PERJURY under the laws of the State of California that the foregoing paragraph is true and correct.

WITNESS my hand and official seal.

_____
          Signature of officer

MAIL TAX STATEMENT AS DIRECTED ABOVE

* There are various types of deed forms depending on each person's legal status. Before you use this form you many want to consult an attorney
if you have questions concerning which document form is appropriate for your transaction.

Source: © 2015 OnCourse Learning

bidder at this type of sale receives a sheriff's deed, which contains no warranties. In some courts, this sale is conducted by a commissioner instead of the sheriff, and the deed issued is called a *commissioner's deed*.

Gift Deed

A person who wishes to give real estate to another may convey title by using a gift deed. The legal consideration given in a gift deed is usually "love and affection." A gift deed is valid unless it is being used to defraud creditors, in which case the creditors may institute legal action to void the deed.

Tax Deed

A tax deed is issued by the tax collector after the sale of land that previously reverted to the state because of nonpayment of property taxes. The tax sale procedure is presented in Chapter 14.

Warranty Deed

A **warranty deed** is seldom used in California. Under a warranty deed, the grantor is legally responsible to the grantee for the condition of the title. Sellers in California are reluctant to assume this liability and rarely sign warranty deeds. Instead, sellers sign grant deeds and leave the legal responsibility for the condition of the title to title insurance companies.

Deed of Trust (Trust Deed)

A **deed of trust** conveys "bare legal title" (but no right of use or possession) to a third party called a *trustee*. This deed differs from others in that title is held by the trustee merely as security for a loan (lien) until such time as the loan is paid off or until the borrower defaults on his or her payments. Deeds of trust are financing instruments, and they are explained in Chapter 8.

Deed of Reconveyance

This deed is executed by the trustee to the borrower (trustor). When a beneficiary (the lender) notifies the trustee that the trustor has repaid a loan that used a deed of trust, the trustee reconveys the title back to the trustor using a deed of reconveyance. This instrument is also involved with the financing of real estate and is discussed in Chapter 8.

Trustee's Deed

This deed conveys title to a successful bidder at a trustee's sale (foreclosure). A trustee's deed contains no warranties. A trustee's deed and the foreclosure process are discussed in Chapter 8.

6.4 THE RECORDING SYSTEM

The recording of a deed and many other title instruments, although not required by law, protects the new owner's rights. Under the Spanish and Mexican governments, there were no recording laws in California. Shortly after California became a state, the legislature adopted a recording system by which evidence of title or interest in real property could be collected and held for public view at a convenient and safe place. This safe public place is the county recorder's office.

To be accepted for recording by a county recorder, the deed must have the following:

1. An acknowledgment (be notarized)
2. Name and address to which future tax statements can be mailed
3. Basis for computing the transfer tax
4. Names of all parties involved in the transaction
5. An adequate legal description
6. Payment of a recording fee

Once a document is recorded, it is said that the world has constructive notice of the contents of the document.

The recording system also shows sequential transfers of property from the original owner to the present owner. This successive list of owners is called a *chain of title*.

Recorded documents are filed in books called *grantor–grantee indexes*. Most counties have reduced their title records to microfilm or microfiche for easy handling and storage. These title records are frequently transferred by title companies to computers, making it easier for the title company to research a property.

A general rule says, "The first to record is the first in right."

Example: A deeds to B, who does not record. If A then deeds to C, who does record, under the general rule, C would probably get the property because C recorded first.

However, there are two exceptions to this rule:

1. If a party or grantee is the first to record, but is aware of another party (an earlier grantee for example) who has an interest in the

property, the first party to record would be second to the interest of the other earlier party.

2. If the first party failed to record but took possession of the property, the possession by an unrecorded owner can defeat a later recorded deed by another person.

Example: A deeds to B, who does not record, but B takes physical possession of the property. A then deeds to C, who does not make a physical inspection of the property. C then records the deed. Who will probably win?

Answer: B, because physical possession gives actual notice to all parties, including C, that B has a prior interest in the property.

Moral: Always physically inspect a property before you purchase. Do not rely on the public records only!

Chapter Summary, Part I

There are three major types of land descriptions: lot, block, and tract; metes and bounds; and the U.S. government survey system. Five ways of acquiring title to property are by will, succession, accession, occupancy, and transfer.

To be valid, a deed must contain certain essential elements, and the deed must have proper delivery and acceptance. Major types of deeds are grant deed, quitclaim deed, warranty deed, sheriff's deed, and gift deed. The most common is the grant deed, and it contains two implied warranties.

California has adopted a recording system designed to protect the rights of property owners and lien holders.

Important Terms and Concepts

accession	eminent domain
accretion	escheat
acknowledgment	executor (or executrix)
addition of fixtures	foreclosure action
administrator (or administratrix)	grant deed
adverse possession	grantee
alluvion	grantor
avulsion	holographic will

intestate	registered domestic partner
metes and bounds	statutory will
partition action	succession
private grant	trust deed
probate	U.S. government survey system
public grant	warranty deed
quitclaim deed	witnessed will

Practical Application

1. S ½ of SW ¼ of the SW ¼ of the NW ¼, **and** the SW ¼ of Section 5. How many acres? Using the grid below, shade in the parcel.

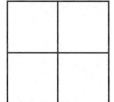

Section 5

2. At a probate sale for a vacant lot, the initial accepted offer to purchase is $200,000. If you wish to place the next additional bid, what is the minimum you must bid?

3. Garcia deeds real property to Williams using a grant deed. Shortly thereafter, the county abandons an alley easement at the rear of the property. Garcia maintains that the alley area is his, whereas Williams says it belongs to her. Based on your knowledge of grant deeds, who is probably right?

Reviewing Your Understanding

1. Ms. Jones was killed in an automobile accident. When the courts were called upon to distribute her property, they found she had died intestate. This means that she died:

   a. leaving no property.

   b. leaving no heirs.

   c. in debt.

   d. without a will.

2. If a married man with two children died without leaving a will, separate property that was purchased by him before he married and was maintained as separate property during the marriage would be distributed as follows:

   a. One-half to the children

   b. One-half to the widow

   c. All to the widow

   d. One-third to the widow and two-thirds to the children

3. How many acres are there in a parcel of property that includes the following: the NW ¼ of the SW ¼, the E ½ of the NW ¼, and the NE ¼ of the SW ¼ of Section 5?
   a. 320 acres
   b. 160 acres
   c. 40 acres
   d. 80 acres

4. The state urgently needs a piece of property to complete a project for public use. The owner did not wish to sell. Which method could be used to acquire the property?
   a. Dedication
   b. Escheat
   c. Police power
   d. Eminent domain

5. The term *escheat* is a legal term meaning:
   a. a fraud has been committed.
   b. an agent's license has been revoked.
   c. property with a mortgage can be conveyed.
   d. title has reverted to the state.

6. The water flowing down a river gradually builds up the land along the bank by leaving deposits of soil; this action is called:
   a. accretion.
   b. reliction.
   c. avulsion.
   d. erosion.

7. All of the following statements concerning wills are correct, EXCEPT:
   a. a statutory will uses a form in compliance with state law.
   b. a holographic will can be signed by an X.
   c. an administratrix is appointed by a probate court.
   d. a person who receives real property by will is known as a devisee.

8. Deeds are used to transfer property. Which deed contains no implied or expressed warranties?
   a. Warranty deed
   b. Grant deed
   c. Quitclaim deed
   d. Interspousal grant deed

9. The executrix of an estate is:
   a. selected by the heirs.
   b. appointed by the superior court.
   c. named in the testator's will.
   d. named by the decedent's attorney.

10. To be valid, a deed must:
    a. contain a proper description of the property.
    b. be signed by a competent grantee.
    c. be recorded.
    d. be dated.

11. "Beginning on a point on the North line of Bard Avenue distant 218.00 feet East from the Northeast corner of Bard Avenue and Elm Street." This legal description is:
    a. metes and bounds.
    b. lot, block, and tract.
    c. U.S. government survey.
    d. townships and sections.

12. Which of the following is not a base and meridian found in California?
    a. Humboldt
    b. Mt. Diablo
    c. Mt. Shasta
    d. San Bernardino

13. Which measurement is incorrect?
    a. Acre = 43,800 square feet
    b. Mile = 5,280 feet
    c. One square acre = 208.71 feet
    d. Township = 6 miles square

14. Hostile, open, and notorious use of another person's land for five years is required for title by:
    a. will.
    b. succession.
    c. accession.
    d. adverse possession.

15. An instrument by which the government grants title to a person is a(n):
    a. homestead.
    b. partition action.
    c. patent.
    d. escheat.

16. Recording of a deed gives:
    a. actual notice.
    b. constructive notice.
    c. physical notice.
    d. vested notice.

17. A deeds to B, who does not record the deed or take physical possession of the property. A then deeds to C, who had no notice of the prior deed to B. C records the deed. In a dispute over title between B and C, which rule would be important?
    a. All deeds must be recorded to be valid.
    b. He or she who records first is the first in right.
    c. All deeds must be acknowledged to be valid.
    d. The date of the deed determines who is first.

18. All of the following are true statements regarding deeds EXCEPT:
    a. a minor who is not emancipated can receive title but cannot convey title without court action.
    b. incompetent persons cannot convey title without court action.
    c. a person cannot take legal title under an assumed name.
    d. a valid deed need not be recorded.

19. An after acquired title provision occurs in a:
    a. grant deed.
    b. quitclaim deed.
    c. sheriff's deed.
    d. tax deed.

20. Who signs a grant deed?
    a. Lessor
    b. Mortgagor
    c. Grantee
    d. Grantor

© Shutterstock / Martin M303

STUDENT LEARNING OUTCOMES PART II

Part II discusses freehold and less-than-freehold estates. In addition, various methods of holding title (including joint tenancy, tenancy in common, community property, living trust, and tenancy in partnership) are presented, stressing the characteristics, advantages, and disadvantages of each. At the conclusion of Part II, you will be able to do the following:

- Explain the difference between freehold and less-than-freehold estates.
- Describe the key differences in taking title to property as joint tenants as opposed to tenants in common.
- Explain the difference between community property and separate property.
- Discuss the concepts of cohabitation, equity sharing, and living trusts.

PART II: ESTATES AND METHODS OF HOLDING TITLE

6.5 ESTATES

An **estate** is defined as the degree, quantity, nature, and extent of interest a person has in property. If the estate is in real property, you have a real estate interest. Real property estates fall into two major classifications: freehold estates and less-than-freehold estates.

Freehold Estates (Estates of Ownership)

A **freehold estate** refers to one's interest as an owner of real property. The term "freehold" refers to feudal times when only free men could own real property. Back then, women and servants could lease real property, but they could not own it. Freehold estates can be subdivided into fee estates and life estates. (See Figure 6.15.)

1. Fee estates or fee simple estates can be divided into the following:
   a. **Fee simple absolute**, which the owner holds without any qualifications or limitations, such as private deed restrictions. All government ordinances and limitations still apply. This is the highest form of interest an individual can have in land.
   b. **Fee simple qualified** (*defeasible*), which the owner holds subject to special conditions, limitations, or private deed restrictions that limit the use of the property.

   Example: A parcel of land may carry a restriction that prohibits the sale of alcoholic beverages on the premises. If the owner fails to adhere to the restriction, the owner may be liable in a lawsuit for damages, or in extreme cases the title may revert back to the grantor or creator of the restriction.

2. **Life estates** are created by deed or will for the life of one or more designated human beings. The life tenant has all the rights of

FIGURE 6.15

Source: © 2015 OnCourse Learning

possession, or income, during the life of the designated person(s). However, the holder of a life estate cannot deed or lease a property beyond the life of the designated person. If the person granting the life estate designates that the title is to go to some other person upon the death of the life estate holder, the person so designated is said to have an **estate in remainder**.

Example: In **Figure 6.16**, A deeds a life estate to B for the life of B.

When B dies, the property passes to C. B holds the life estate; C holds the estate in remainder.

If the property is to be returned to the person who gave the life estate or to his or her heirs, that person is said to have an **estate in reversion**.

FIGURE 6.16

Source: © 2015 OnCourse Learning

FIGURE 6.17

Estate in Reversion

Source: © 2015 OnCourse Learning

Example: In **Figure 6.17**, A deeds a life estate to B for B's life, with the provision that when B dies, the title reverts back to A. B holds a life estate; A holds the *estate in reversion.*

Another possibility is a *grant reserving a life estate.* Among life estates, this is probably the most common situation.

Example: In **Figure 6.18**, A deeds title to B, but A reserves or keeps a life estate for the rest of A's life. Upon the death of A, possession and use pass to B.

As previously mentioned, a holder of a life estate cannot deed or lease property beyond the length of the life of the designated person. For example, assume that A holds title for life and, upon A's death, title is to pass to B, the remainder person. If, during A's life, A leases the property to C, upon A's death the lease is canceled and B, the remainder person, receives title free of the lease. If C wishes to continue to lease the property, C needs to negotiate a new lease with B.

Finally, freehold estates, both fee simple and certain parts of life estates, are considered durable and capable of being transferred by inheritance upon death. Therefore, freehold estates are sometimes called *estates of inheritance.*

FIGURE 6.18

Reserving a Life Estate

Source: © 2015 OnCourse Learning

Less-than-Freehold Estates (Leasehold- Estates of Possession)

Less-than-freehold estates are interests held by tenants who rent or lease property. Tenants are also called *lessees* or *leaseholders* and are discussed in detail in Chapter 12.

6.6 METHODS OF HOLDING TITLE

When people acquire ownership of real property, they must decide how to hold title. Title may be held separately in one person's name alone or concurrently with other people.

Ownership in Severalty

When a person acquires real property and holds title solely in his or her own name, it is technically known as **ownership in severalty**. In other words, he or she alone enjoys the ownership benefits, including the complete bundle of rights, and "severs" his or her relationship with others.

A person can hold title in severalty in one of the following ways, depending on the owner's legal status:

As single (never been married)

As unmarried (a person who is no longer married)

As married (currently married)

As a registered domestic partner

As a widow or widower (a person whose spouse has died)

A person who wishes to indicate **separate property** ownership can add the words *sole* and *separate property* to any of the choices listed. A corporation can hold title in severalty, such as "Acme Company, a California Corporation."

Concurrent Ownership

Concurrent ownership is when two or more people hold title together. There are numerous types of concurrent ownership, but the most important are joint tenancy, tenancy in common, community property, and tenancy in partnership.

Joint Tenancy

Joint tenancy exists when two or more persons are joint and equal owners of the same undivided interest in real property. To create and maintain a valid joint tenancy, four unities must exist:

1. *Unity of time.* This means that the owners must have acquired their interest at the same time.

2. *Unity of title.* This means that all owners must come into title on the same document. Consider this example: A and B are joint tenants. B sells her interest to C. A and C are tenants in common because they each took title on a different document at a different time.

3. *Unity of interest.* This means that all owners must have equal shares or interest in the property. For example, if there are two owners, each must have a one-half interest; with four owners, each must have a one-quarter interest; with eight owners, each must have a one-eighth interest; and so on.

4. *Unity of possession.* This means that all owners must have equal rights of possession. No one owner can be prevented from using the property by the other owner(s).

If any of these unities are missing, the joint tenancy is invalid and the rules of tenancy in common apply.

Important Characteristics

The most important characteristic of joint tenancy is the **right of survivorship**. This means that if one tenant dies, the surviving joint tenant(s) acquire the deceased's interest without a court action such as a probate.

Example:
1. A and B take title to property as joint tenants. B dies; A becomes the sole owner because of the right of survivorship.
2. A, B, and C take title to a property as joint tenants. C dies and her interest automatically passes to the survivors, A and B. A and B are still joint tenants between each other, each owning a one-half interest in the property.

Other Characteristics of Joint Tenancy

In addition to the four unities (time, title, interest, and possession) and the right of survivorship, joint tenancy has these important characteristics:

1. You cannot will your interest in joint tenancy property.

2. Interest in the property is undivided. In other words, just as we will see in all forms of co-ownership, each owner can use every square foot, and he or she cannot say, "This is my half and this is yours."

3. No probate procedure is required to distribute the interest upon the death of one of the owners. The interest goes to the surviving co-owners. However, some paperwork is required to shift the remaining interest to the surviving joint tenant. But this paperwork is minor in comparison to a complete probate.

4. A joint tenant may sell or convey his or her interest without approval of the other tenant(s). This action may break the joint tenancy and create a tenancy in common. For example, A, B, and C are joint tenants. C sells his interest to X. A and B are still joint tenants with each other, but now they are also tenants in common with X.

    Example: A and B are joint tenants. B sells her interest to C. A and C are now tenants in common. Why? Because B's act of selling to C violated the unities of time and title.

5. A corporation is not allowed to hold title as a joint tenant because, in theory, a corporation never "dies."

6. A surviving tenant acquires the interest of the deceased joint tenant and is free from the debts created individually by the deceased joint tenant.

Tenancy in Common

When two or more persons are owners of an undivided interest in property, they can hold title as tenants in common. **Tenancy in common** has these characteristics:

1. There is no right of survivorship, meaning that upon the death of a tenant in common, his or her interest passes to the heirs, not the surviving co-tenants. This requires a probate proceeding.

2. Each owner may own unequal shares.

    Example: A, B, C, and D hold title as tenants in common. These owners might share their ownership as follows:

    A might own one-quarter share or interest.
    B might own one-eighth share or interest.
    C might own one-eighth share or interest.
    D might own one-half share or interest.

    Contrast this with joint tenancy, which requires all owners to have equal shares or interest. Just as in joint tenancy, all owners share equal rights of possession for the full property.

3. Each owner has equal rights of possession and must pay his or her share of the expenses, such as property taxes.

4. Each owner may will his or her interest to his or her heirs, and upon death, the heirs take their place along with the other owners as tenants in common.

5. Each co-tenant may sell, convey, or encumber his or her interest without the consent of the co-tenants.

Example: A and B are tenants in common. A dies and his interest passes to his heir, X. X and B become tenants in common.
or
A, B, and C are tenants in common. If C sells her interest to D, then A, B, and D become tenants in common.

What If?

To test your understanding of the difference between joint tenancy and tenants in common, answer the following questions.

1. A and B are joint tenants. If B dies, who gets what?
2. A and B are joint tenants. If B sells to C, what is the relationship between A and C?
3. A and B are tenants in common. If B dies, who gets what?
4. A, B, and C are joint tenants. C sells his interest to D. What is the relationship between A, B, and D?

Answers

1. B's interest passes to A, who now holds title in severalty.
2. A and C are tenants in common.
3. A and the heirs of B are tenants in common.
4. A and B are joint tenants to each other and tenants in common with D.

Tenancy in Business Partnership

Tenancy in partnership exists when two or more persons, as partners, pool their interests, assets, and efforts in a business venture, with each to share in the profits or the losses. This type of business organization includes general partnerships and limited partnerships, and many rules and regulations are involved. The following discussion outlines only the real estate aspects of partnerships, not the legal or accounting aspects. Tenancy in partnership has the following real estate characteristics:

1. Each partner has an equal right with other partners to possession of specific partnership property for partnership purposes. This means a partner only has the right to use the property for business, not for personal purposes, unless the other partners agree to the personal use.

2. A partner's right in the partnership property is not assignable except in connection with the assignment of rights of all the partners in the same property.

3. A partner's right in the partnership property is not subject to attachment or execution, except on a claim against the partnership.

4. There is a form of survivorship when one partner dies.

> **Example:** A and B own property as partners. A dies; B receives title in trust until the disposition of the property. In other words, the title rests in the survivor only long enough to carry on the business for the sole purpose of winding up the partnership affairs.

Limited Partnership

Sometimes title to real estate is held by a limited partnership. Under a limited partnership, one or more general partners have unlimited liability and usually a series of limited partners have limited liability. *Limited liability* means that if all legal requirements have been met, the limited partners can lose only their investment and cannot be held liable for partnership debts. Most real estate syndicates hold title as a limited partnership.

Community Property

Community property ownership is another form of ownership held by more than one person, but in this case, the property can be held only by married spouses or by registered domestic partners. Community property is defined as all property acquired during a valid marriage or registered domestic partnership. California is a community property state; therefore, all California property acquired by married spouses or by registered domestic partners during marriage is presumed to be community property. However, there are a few exceptions.

1. All property owned by a spouse before marriage or registered domestic partnership can remain separate property after marriage or registered domestic partnership as long as the property is not commingled with community property, causing it to lose its separate property identity.

2. All property acquired by gift or inheritance by either spouse during marriage or registered domestic partnership remains separate property as long as it is not commingled with community property.

3. All income and profits from separate property as well as any property acquired from the proceeds of separate property remain separate property as long as said income and profits are not commingled with community property.

In effect, married spouses are general partners, as are registered domestic partners, each owning one-half of the community property.

Each spouse or partner has equal management and control of the community property. Neither spouse or partner may convey or encumber real estate held as community property unless the other spouse or partner also signs the contracts or documents involved.

Each spouse or partner has the right to dispose of his or her half of the community property by will to whomever he or she wishes. But if either spouse or partner dies intestate, the surviving spouse or partner receives all the property; the children, if any, get nothing.

Another Choice

Effective for deeds or documents recorded after July 2, 2001, a married couples or registered domestic partners may hold title as "community property with right of survivorship." This means upon the death of one spouse or partner, the surviving spouse or partner receives title without a special spousal or partner probate. In short, married couples and registered domestic partners now have a choice. They may (1) hold title as regular community property and keep the right to will their separate interest or (2) hold title with the right of survivorship and automatically guarantee that upon death of one spouse or partner, the property will go to the surviving spouse or partner without any probate. In addition, there are some tax differences between the two choices. If a married couple acquired title as community property prior to July 2, 2001, and wish to switch, they need to discuss with their tax and legal experts the pros and cons of redeeding to take advantage of this more recent choice (see California Civil Code Sec.682.1).

Community property does not need to be probated if the deceased spouse or partner leaves his or her interest to the surviving spouse or partner. But if the deceased spouse's or partner's interest is left to someone other than the surviving spouse or partner, the estate must be probated.

For Married Couples or Registered Domestic Partners, Which Is Best: Joint Tenancy or Community Property?

The answer is complicated and should be discussed with a tax attorney. Some of the main issues to compare are income tax basis upon death, estate taxes, and probate procedures (if any). Also, the trend toward deeding title into a **living trust** may need to be discussed with a tax attorney. Real estate licensees and escrow officers are neither qualified nor allowed to give buyers and existing owners advice on how to hold title. Typically licensees may define the options but not recommend which would be the best choice. (See Table 6.1.)

TABLE 6.1   The Basics of Co-Ownership.

	Tenancy in Common	Joint Tenancy	Community Property
Who Can Hold Title?	Any 2 or more persons	Any 2 or more persons	Married spouses and registered domestic partners
Ownership Interest	Can be any percentage, equal or not	All shares must be equal	Equal shares
Upon Death	Probate usually required	No probate, right of survivorship, no will allowed	Special probate; right to will; in-testate goes to surviving spouse or partner; after July 2001, optional right of survivorship
Disposition of Title	Convey interest without others' permission	Convey interest without others' permission	Need both signatures to convey title

Source: © 2015 OnCourse Learning

Special Interest Topic

Cohabitation and Property Rights

In 1976, in the famous *Marvin v. Marvin* case involving the late actor Lee Marvin, California courts held that unmarried persons who cohabitate may create property rights and obligations by oral agreement. The bottom line is that unmarried people who cohabitate might need to discuss this situation with an attorney. They may find it advisable to reduce to contract form an agreement on how to handle previously owned property and property accumulated during cohabitation, in the event they separate at a later date.

The Future of Registered Domestic Partners

State law requires registered domestic partners to register with the California Secretary of State's Office; marriages are registered with the County Recorders' Office. This statute-created relationship began prior to the legalization of same-sex marriages. Now that California allows same-sex marriages, will we see the continuation of registered domestic partners? For the time being, probably yes since same-sex marriage is being litigated in other states and it is still a politically charged issue. Those who fought hard for a legal bond for same-sex couples are not likely to give up those rights. However, once same-sex marriages are upheld, there is really no need for registered domestic partners. In fact, having both could create a legal paradox as some courts may rule one way on a property settlement with a registered domestic partnership dissolution and a different court could rule a different way in a similar property dispute in a same-sex marriage. This could create a legal nightmare as the laws between one set of couples could be different that another set of couples, depending on if they had a registered domestic partnership or a marriage. This will probably be settled in a few years, but for now, we have two parallel courses for same-sex couples.

Equity Sharing

Equity sharing is when an owner-occupant and a nonresident owner-investor pool their money to buy a home. The down payment is split according to an agreed percentage, and both parties are on the deed and mortgage. The owner-occupant pays rent to the nonresident owner-investor for a portion of the home owned by the investor. The nonresident owner-investor then uses the rent money to join with the owner-occupant to pay the monthly mortgage payments. The equity share contract spells out who is responsible for taxes, insurance, and upkeep. Some day in the future, the home is either refinanced or sold, and the parties split the net proceeds according to a prearranged percentage. Equity share arrangements are complicated and should not be undertaken without advice from legal and tax experts.

Living Trust

As the value of estates increases, the tendency is for people to look for ways to minimize the cost of probate. One trend has been to place all real estate and other valuable property into a living trust. The owner transfers the property to the trust and frequently names himself or herself as trustee with the right to change the terms and scope of the trust as he or she sees fit. While in the trust, he or she enjoys all the privileges of ownership. Upon death, title passes to the named beneficiaries without the time and delay of a probate. A living trust does not eliminate estate taxes but rather eliminates the cost of probate. A person should contact an attorney before entering into a living trust to discuss its pros and cons.

Chapter Summary, Part II

Freehold estates consist of fee estates and life estates, representing the rights of an owner of real property. Fee estates are either fee simple absolute with no private restrictions or fee simple qualified with some private limitations and restrictions. Life estates are granted for the life of one or more persons and may be a remainder, reversion, or reservation type.

Ownership in severalty is when title is held in sole ownership. Concurrent ownership is when title is held by two or more persons. Common examples of concurrent ownership are joint tenancy, tenancy in common, tenancy in partnership, and community property. In California, property acquired by a husband and wife during marriage and by partners while domestically registered is considered to be community property. Property acquired by a spouse or partner before marriage or registration, or property acquired by inheritance or gift during marriage or registration, is considered separate property unless it is commingled with the community property. An increasing number of people are choosing to hold title in a living trust. Methods of holding title have important estate and income tax consequences that should be discussed with a qualified attorney before a selection is made.

Important Terms and Concepts

community property	less-than-freehold estate
estate	life estate
estate in remainder	living trust
estate in reversion	ownership in severalty
fee simple absolute	right of survivorship
fee simple qualified	separate property
freehold estate	tenancy in common
joint tenancy	tenancy in partnership

Practical Application

1. Chan owns real property and deeds a life estate to Washington. Upon Washington's death, title is to pass to Adams. While holding a life estate, Washington leases the property for five years to Santos. Two years later, Adams dies; one year later, Chan and Washington both die. Upon Washington's death, who is entitled to possession of the property?

2. Nguyen and Harris purchased 20 acres as joint tenants. Harris then sold one-half of her undivided interest to Battino. Shortly thereafter, Harris died. What is the legal relationship between Nguyen and Battino, and what percentage interest is owned by each?

3. Bill and Sara Belinski, husband and wife, purchased a home in California as community property. Later, Sara's parents died and left her a five-unit apartment building in Los Angeles. The apartments are professionally managed, and all rental proceeds are placed in a separate account under Sara's name alone. Sara uses the rental proceeds to pay tuition for the children, who are still in college. The Belinskis are now in the process of a divorce. What are the community property issues?

Reviewing Your Understanding

1. Which of the following statements is false?
   a. The right of survivorship is present in a tenancy in common.
   b. A life estate tenant is responsible for payment of the property tax.
   c. A leasehold estate is a less-than-freehold estate.
   d. Unity of possession is present in joint tenancy and tenancy in common ownerships.

2. Which of the following terms do not belong together?
   a. Joint tenancy, probate hearing
   b. Tenancy in common, equal interest
   c. Tenancy in common, severalty estate
   d. All of the above

3. Which of the following is considered to be a less-than-freehold estate?
   a. Fee simple absolute
   b. Life estate
   c. Leasehold estate
   d. Fee simple defeasible

4. The single most important characteristic of joint tenancy is:
   a. equal rights of use.
   b. equal interest.
   c. right of survivorship.
   d. right to encumber.

5. It is impossible for a corporation to legally hold title as a:
   a. trustee.
   b. joint tenant.
   c. tenant in common.
   d. California corporation.

6. Which of the following is not one of the four unities of joint tenancy?
   a. Time
   b. Interest
   c. Security
   d. Title

7. A deeds a life estate to B; upon B's death, title is to pass to C. This is an example of a:
   a. perpetual estate.
   b. less-than-freehold estate.
   c. remainder estate.
   d. fee simple estate.

8. The term *fee simple defeasible* is best described in which statement?
   a. Owner holds a title without limitations.
   b. Owner holds a less-than-freehold estate.
   c. Owner holds title subject to deed restrictions.
   d. Owner holds an estate in remainder.

9. Smith and Dang are joint tenants; Dang sells his half of the property to Brown. Brown will take title with Smith as:
   a. joint tenants.
   b. tenants in common.
   c. ownership in severalty.
   d. separate property.

10. Community property is defined as property acquired by married spouses or registered domestic partners:
    a. before marriage or domestic registration.
    b. after marriage or domestic registration.
    c. by either party by gift or inheritance.
    d. before or after marriage or registration.

11. Real estate syndicates usually hold title to property as:
    a. a general partnership.
    b. a limited partnership.
    c. tenants in common.
    d. a tenancy in partnership.

12. Freehold estates are sometimes called estates of:
    a. inheritance.
    b. will.
    c. accession.
    d. years.

13. Ownership in severalty refers to holding title as:
    a. joint tenants.
    b. an individual.
    c. co-ownership.
    d. partners.

14. Garcia owned a life estate in a property. Garcia leased the property to Williams for five years. Two years later, Garcia died. The lease is:
    a. valid and in force for the rest of the term.
    b. valid for a two-year period after the death of Garcia.
    c. invalid from the beginning; a life estate owner cannot sign a lease.
    d. canceled and invalid upon Garcia's death.

15. A, B, and C are joint tenants, and they hold title to the NW ¼ of Section 24 in some township. C deeds her interest to D.
    a. D is a joint tenant with A and B.
    b. A and B now each own half of the property.
    c. D owns a one-third interest in 160 acres.
    d. A, B, and D are all tenants in common with each other.

16. In California, without any evidence to the contrary, married spouses or registered domestic partners are presumed to hold title as:
    a. tenants in common.
    b. joint tenants.
    c. community property.
    d. tenancy in partnership.

17. To be valid, all owners must have equal shares, except for:
    a. community property.
    b. joint tenancy.
    c. tenants in common.
    d. All of the above must have equal shares.

18. For a married person or registered domestic partner, which of the following is most likely to be separate property? Real estate recently acquired by:
    a. gift.
    b. severalty.
    c. purchase.
    d. foreclosure.

19. Which real estate owner is usually considered to be liable only for the amount of invested capital, not the owner's personal assets?
    a. Tenant in common
    b. General partner
    c. Joint tenant
    d. Limited partner

20. Regarding the best method for buyers to hold title:
    a. real estate agents should tell buyers the best way.
    b. buyers should seek advice from their attorneys.
    c. joint tenancy is always the best method.
    d. for married couples and registered domestic partners in California, community property is the only method allowed.

© Shutterstock / SNEHIT

STUDENT LEARNING OUTCOMES

In this chapter, you will study money and nonmoney encumbrances. The discussion of nonmoney encumbrances centers on easements, encroachments, and private and public restrictions.

Money encumbrances are defined as liens. The liens discussed include mechanics' liens, tax liens, special assessment liens, attachments, and judgment liens.

In addition, the California homestead law is presented, illustrating how homeowners can protect their homes against a forced sale by certain types of creditors. At the conclusion of this chapter, you will be able to do the following:

- Define the types of encumbrances: lien, easement, and encroachment.
- Explain the difference between private deed restrictions and public restrictions.
- Describe the key characteristics of mechanics' liens and the enforcement of judgment liens.
- Discuss the details of the California homestead law.

ENCUMBRANCES, LIENS, AND HOMESTEADS

7.1 ENCUMBRANCES

In real estate, an **encumbrance** is anything that burdens the owner's title with a legal obligation. It is any right or interest in the property possessed by someone other than the owner.

Encumbrances fall into two basic categories: *nonmoney encumbrances* and *money encumbrances*.

Nonmoney (Physical) Encumbrances

Nonmoney encumbrances affect the physical condition or use of the property. Examples include easements, public and private restrictions, and encroachments—as opposed to money encumbrances, such as real estate loans or property taxes, where the property is held as security for repayment of a debt.

Easements

An easement is a right to enter or use another person's property, or a portion thereof, within certain limitations without paying rent or being considered a trespasser. In California, the most common type of easement is for access, also called an easement for ingress (entering) and egress (exiting) the property.

Two important terms used in connection with a right-of-way are **dominant tenement** and **servient tenement**. The property that benefits from the use of the easement (Property B in Figure 7.1) is described as the dominant tenement. The property subject to the easement or upon which the easement is imposed (Property A in Figure 7.1) is described as the servient tenement.

FIGURE 7.1

Source: © 2015 OnCourse Learning

An easement is usually designated as nonexclusive, meaning that when it is created, it doesn't prevent the owner from using the land, including that part covered by the easement. The owner's use (servient tenement), however, cannot interfere with the right of use by the dominant tenement.

In addition to an easement for access,, other examples of easements include the right to take water, wood, minerals, and other named items; the right to receive air and light; or the right to use a wall as a **party wall**. A party wall is a dividing partition between two adjoining buildings (or units) that is shared by the tenants of each residence or business.

When an easement is created, it is usually considered to be appurtenant or belonging to the land. This means the easement is considered real property and stays attached to the property in the event of a sale or another title transfer. When an easement '"runs with the land," it is called an **easement appurtenant**.

Some easements do not have a dominant tenement. This is known as an **easement in gross**. For example, when a utility company erects poles or strings wire over private lands, the utility company obtains an easement in gross. Easements in gross allow someone to pass over the land for personal use, not to reach an adjoining parcel of land. This means no dominant landowner is being served; hence, no dominant tenement exists.

Creation of Easements

Easements can be created in a number of ways. The most common ways are by (1) deed, (2) necessity, (3) dedication, (4) condemnation, and (5) prescription. (See Figure 7.2.)

FIGURE 7.2

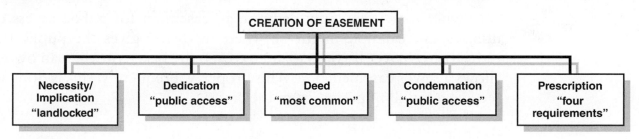

Source: © 2015 OnCourse Learning

By Deed

Easements are not created orally; instead, they are set forth in the form of a written grant (known as an easement deed). An easement must comply with all the legal requirements of a deed and be signed by the owner of the property (servient tenement) over which the easement lies.

> *Example:* (1) **A** deeds an easement to **B** to cross A's property, or (2) **A** deeds title to **B** but reserves an easement over **B's** property for **A's** use. Easements created by a written deed or contract are also called *expressed easements.*

By Necessity or by Implication

When a buyer discovers that he or she has no access to the street without passing over the property of another, the buyer's property is considered "landlocked." In this situation, the landlocked buyer can appeal to the courts and ask for an easement by necessity over the portion of land, if any, which the seller of the landlocked parcel may still own. If the seller of the landlocked parcel does not own an adjoining parcel to cross over, the buyer of the landlocked parcel may be permanently landlocked. However, a recent court case, *Kellogg v. Garcia* 102 Cal. App. 4th 796 (2002), may allow under some circumstances an easement over nearby property.

An easement can also be implied. For example, A deeds a portion of his or her land to B, but fails to grant an easement for access. However, an existing road runs over the remaining portion of the land owned by A. In this circumstance, B usually has an implied right to use the road over A's property to get to B's property. To obtain an easement by necessity, previous common ownership is required. Some people mistakenly think that if you have a landlocked parcel you may simply sue the adjoining landowner for access; this is not the case any more than a buyer can sue a property owner and force that owner to sell him his property!

By Dedication

An owner may voluntarily dedicate an easement for public access or utilities. An example might be when an owner gives the public the right to cross over his or her land to reach the beach or when an owner allows a sewer easement across his property. Frequently, this is done to receive a building permit from the city.

By Condemnation

Often, an easement is created through condemnation. This means that government, as well as utility companies and railroads, may acquire an easement against the wishes of an owner through a legal process known as *eminent domain*. The law states that the condemned easement must be acquired for public use and the owner reimbursed for the value lost to the property.

By Prescription

An easement by prescription is created when a person acquires an easement in another person's property by reason of use. To obtain an easement by prescription in another person's property, a person must comply with four basic requirements:

1. A person must openly and notoriously use the land of another.
2. The easement use must be continuous and uninterrupted for five years.
3. The easement use must be hostile to the true owner's wishes, meaning without the owner's permission.
4. There must be a claim of right or color of title. This means the easement user must believe he or she has some right to cross the land of another or have a document that falsely purports to give the easement user an easement right.

Termination of an Easement

Easements can be terminated in several ways. (See Figure 7.3.)

1. The most common way to terminate an easement is by express release. The dominant tenement usually issues a quitclaim deed to the servient tenement owner, which extinguishes the easement.
2. Another way easements can be terminated is by a court proceeding called a *quiet title action*. The purpose of a quiet title action is to establish title against adverse claims to real property or any interest in the property. (Code Civ. Proc. §760.020)

FIGURE 7.3

Source: © 2015 OnCourse Learning

3. When the owner of the dominant tenement property becomes the owner of the servient tenement property, the easement is terminated by merger of title. In other words, you cannot have an easement over your own property!

4. The filing of a formal abandonment can terminate an easement.

5. A prescription easement can be terminated automatically by nonuse for a period of five years. However, termination by nonuse applies only to prescriptive easements, not deeded easements.

Other Types of Nonmoney Encumbrances

In addition to easements, other examples of nonmoney encumbrances include private deed restrictions, public restrictions, and encroachments.

Private Deed Restrictions

A seller of property can place in a deed certain legal restrictions or limits on the use of the property being sold. The restrictions can apply not only to the new owner, but also to all subsequent owners. These restrictions are often referred to as *CC&Rs*, which stands for covenants, conditions, and restrictions.

A **covenant** is a promise or an agreement on the part of the individual accepting it to do or not do certain things. If a grantee (buyer) violates a covenant, he or she has broken a promise or an agreement, and the grantor (seller) may institute court proceedings. The grantor may sue for dollar damages or get an injunction against the grantee prohibiting continuation of the violation of the promise.

A **condition** is a restriction that places a limitation on the grantee's (buyer's) ownership. The main difference between a covenant and a condition is the degree of punishment if a violation occurs. If a condition is violated, the grantor may have the right to demand the forfeiture of the grantee's title to the property. However, a violation of a covenant normally only allows money damages, or a cease-and-desist order may be issued by a judge or other governmental authority.

Some restrictions are legal and some are not. A classic example of restrictions that are unethical, illegal, and unenforceable is those relating to discrimination. Any discrimination based on race; color; creed; religion; national origin; sex; sexual orientation; marital, registered domestic partnership; family status; physical handicap; or gender identification is prohibited by state and/or federal law. A detailed discussion of fair housing laws is presented in Chapter 13.

Public Restrictions

When the government imposes restrictions on property, they are called **public restrictions.** Using a provision called *police power,* government has the right to impose restrictions on the use of private property to protect the health, safety, morals, and welfare of its citizens.

Police power includes such public restrictions as the following:

1. Zoning regulations that dictate what type of land use may exist in a given geographical area
2. Building codes that mandate rules and regulations governing the quality and size of construction
3. Health codes to protect and regulate the quality of domestic water and the effectiveness of sanitation systems. If there is a difference between a public restriction and a private restriction, the strictest rule applies.

Encroachments

Another type of physical nonmoney encumbrance is an encroachment. An **encroachment** is the wrongful construction of a building or

FIGURE 7.4

Source: © 2015 OnCourse Learning

an improvement on or over the land of another. Examples of possible encroachments are shown in Figure 7.4.

According to the statute of limitations, the party whose land is encroached upon has only three years in which to bring action for the removal of any such encroachment. If the owner allows the time limitation to run out, the owner runs the risk that the encroachment on the property becomes permanent. However, some encroachments are above the ground, such as a neighbor's tree limb extending into your airspace. This type of encroachment has no statute of limitation, and an action for removal can be brought at any time for a vegetation encroachment.

7.2 LIENS

A lien is a money encumbrance. In this type of encumbrance, a specific property is held as security for the payment of a money debt. Liens can be classified as voluntary or involuntary and general or specific. (See Figure 7.5.)

Voluntary Lien

A voluntary lien is freely accepted by the property owner. An example of a voluntary lien is a mortgage or a deed of trust, which an owner signs when obtaining a real estate loan. (Deeds of trust and mortgages are discussed in detail in Chapter 8.)

Involuntary Lien

An involuntary lien is one imposed by law that the owner does not freely accept. Examples of involuntary liens include mechanics' liens, tax liens, attachments, and judgment liens.

FIGURE 7.5

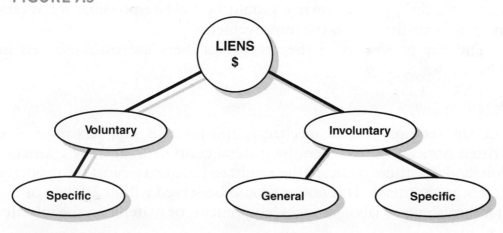

Source: © 2015 OnCourse Learning

General Lien

An involuntary lien that applies to all the property of an owner, unless exempt by law, is a general lien. Examples of general liens include income tax and judgment liens against the owner of the property.

Specific Lien

A voluntary or involuntary lien against a particular single piece of property is a specific lien. Examples of voluntary specific liens include mortgages and trust deeds. Involuntary specific liens include property taxes and mechanics' liens.

Types of Liens

Mechanics' Liens

Before discussing the details of a mechanics' lien, you need to know what is meant by a *mechanic*. A mechanic is anyone hired to do work that improves real property. In short, a mechanic is anyone who performs labor, bestows services, or furnishes material or equipment on a construction project. This includes contractors, subcontractors, carpenters, plumbers, painters, plasterers, laborers, material and equipment suppliers, architects, and landscape gardeners, as well as those workers involved in the demolition and removal of old buildings and the grading and filling of land.

The California State Constitution allows any qualified mechanic who does not receive payment to file a lien against the specific property upon which work was done. The mechanics' lien must be based on a valid contract, written or verbal, between the claimant and the owner or the owner's general contractor. The mechanics' lien law is based on the theory that improvements contribute additional value to the land; therefore, the property owner should be held responsible for wages and materials that led to the improvements.

The key provisions of the mechanics' lien law are illustrated in Figure 7.6.

Preliminary Notice

The law requires that all mechanics and material suppliers must give written notice to the owner, the general contractor, and the construction lender, if there is one, of their right to file a lien against the property if they are not paid. This notice should be served within 20 days of the first furnishing of labor, services, equipment, or material to the job site.

FIGURE 7.6

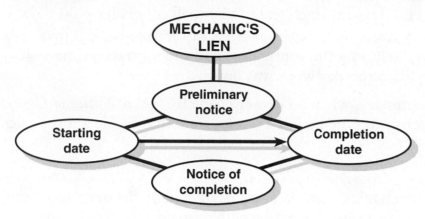

Source: © 2015 OnCourse Learning

Failure to give the *Preliminary Notice* within 20 days does not preclude the right to give a *Preliminary Notice* at a later time, but the mechanic's claim rights may be subordinated to other claims.

Starting Date

For a valid mechanics' lien to be created, the law requires that the lien must be recorded within a specified period of time after completion of the project. The law has determined the following situations to be equivalent to completion:

1. Owner occupies the property, and work stops.
2. Owner accepts the work as being completed and files a document called a *Notice of Completion*.
3. Work on the project ceases for a continuous 60-day period.
4. Work ceases for a continuous period of 30 days or more, and the owner files a notice of cessation.

Notice of Completion

A *Notice of Completion*, if filed by the owner or the general contractor, must show the date of the completion, the name and address of the owner, the nature of the interest or estate of the owner, a description of the property, and the name of the contractor (if any). To be valid, a *Notice of Completion* must be recorded within 10 days after the completion of the project.

Statutory Time Period

Two situations establish time periods for filing a mechanics' lien.

1. If the owner files a *Notice of Completion*, the original contractor has 60 days in which to file a lien; all others have 30 days.
2. If no *Notice of Completion* is filed or if the notice is invalid, all parties, including the contractors and subcontractors, have 90 days to file from the day work was finished.

In summary, when an owner correctly files a *Notice of Completion*, it shortens the time period a work person has to file a mechanics' lien.

Termination of a Mechanics' Lien

1. A mechanics' lien is terminated when the debt has been paid, either by voluntary action or by forced foreclosure sale.
2. A mechanics' lien is automatically terminated if the mechanic fails to institute a court foreclosure within 90 days after filing the mechanics' lien. In other words, once a mechanics' lien is recorded, a mechanic has only 90 days to bring foreclosure action. If mechanics wait more than 90 days, they lose their right to foreclose upon the property. They still can personally sue the owner for the amount owed, but they cannot foreclose on the mechanics' lien and force the sale of the property.

Notice of Non-responsibility

If a tenant orders work on a property without the landlord's approval, can the landlord be held responsible for any unpaid work? The answer is yes. However, a landlord can protect against mechanics' liens resulting from work ordered by a tenant if the landlord files a **Notice of Non-responsibility**.

This *Notice of Non-responsibility* must be filed within 10 days of the date of discovery that the work is being done. It is filed by recording a copy of a *Notice of Non-responsibility* in the county recorder's office and posting a notice on the property. This gives the workers notice that the owner will not be financially responsible for the work being done, and the workers must look to the tenant for payment.

Priority of Claim

When a mechanics' lien is placed against a given piece of property, its priority over a construction loan is determined by the beginning date of the project. The law states that even though a mechanics' lien is recorded after a construction loan is recorded, the mechanics' lien is given priority if any work has been done or materials furnished prior to recording the construction loan. Ordinarily, a title insurance company first inspects the property to make sure no work has been done or materials delivered prior to the recording of the construction loan.

If there are multiple mechanics' liens against a property, they all share on a parity with each other. This means that the first mechanic to record a lien does not have a superior right over the second mechanics' lien, and so on. If there are multiple mechanics' liens and the property is sold for lien payments, each mechanic receives a share of the proceeds based on his or her *pro rata* (proportionate) share of the work.

Summary of Mechanics' Lien Dates

1. *Preliminary Notice* should be given within 20 days of the beginning of work.
2. If the owner files a *Notice of Completion* within 10 days of completion of the project:
   a. Original contractors have 60 days to file.
   b. All others have 30 days to file.
3. If the owner does not file a *Notice of Completion* or if the notice is invalid, all mechanics have 90 days to file from the day that work was finished.
4. Once a valid mechanics' lien is filed, the mechanic must bring a court foreclosure action within 90 days to enforce the lien.
5. A *Notice of Non-responsibility* must be filed by the landlord within 10 days of the discovery of work ordered by a tenant.

Finally, a property owner who hires a contractor might consider having the contractor provide a performance bond in which, for a fee, an insurance company guarantees payment in the event the general contractor fails to complete the project and/or fails to pay the subcontractors.

Tax Liens

The purpose of taxation is to provide money to cover government expenses. An involuntary tax lien arises when a person does not pay taxes when they are due and his or her property and personal assets may be encumbered to ensure payment.

Tax liens may include these:

1. Unpaid real property taxes - specific lien has priority over all other liens on the property
2. Unpaid income taxes - general lien does not have priority
3. Unpaid estate taxes - general lien does not have priority
4. Unpaid gift taxes - general lien does not have priority

Taxes and their consequences are covered in detail in Chapter 14. The point stressed here is that government has the power to levy taxes. If the taxpayer refuses to pay the levy, government has the right to place a lien against the taxpayer's real and personal property. If the lien is for property taxes, the lien will take priority over any other lien on the property, such as a first deed of trust or mortgage.

Special Assessments

Special assessments are levied against property owners in a certain assessment district or neighborhood. The assessment is typically based on the front footage or street front of the lot since the improvements defray the cost of specific local improvements, such as streets, sidewalks, lighting, sewers, and so on. They differ in that property taxes are a general tax levied to pay general government expenses, whereas assessments are for a single purpose. Special assessment liens take priority behind property tax liens. Special assessments are discussed in Chapter 14.

Attachments and Judgments

An **attachment** is a legal process whereby property, personal or real, is seized pending the outcome of a court action. A **judgment** is a decision of the court as a result of a lawsuit. A judgment is the final determination of the rights of the parties involved in a court proceeding.

The purpose of the attachment is to have the property of the defendant available to satisfy a judgment if it is rendered in favor of the plaintiff. In some cases, it may take several months before the case is tried and a judgment issued. During this time, an unscrupulous defendant might secretly sell or give away his or her property, making it impossible for the plaintiff to satisfy the judgment.

Under an attachment, the seizure and holding of the property is merely symbolic. The defendant may still keep the property, but a notice is posted on the property and the attachment is recorded. The attachment remains a lien upon all real property attached, three days from the date of levy. However, so much property is exempt from attachment (such as a personal residence, most of the debtor's wages, and so on) that the use of an attachment has declined in recent years. Instead of seeking an attachment, many creditors go directly for a judgment.

A judgment (court decision) does not automatically create a lien on real property. For a judgment to become a lien, an *abstract of the judgment* (summary of the judgment) must be recorded with the county recorder. It then becomes a general lien on all real property located in the county in which the abstract is recorded.

The judgment lien normally runs for 10 years. Any real property acquired during the 10-year period in the county where the abstract is filed automatically becomes encumbered by the judgment lien. The abstract of judgment may be recorded in any number of California counties. If a creditor wishes to tie up anything a debtor might own in California, the creditor can record the abstract of judgment in all 58 counties. Abstracts of judgments from California courts cannot normally be recorded in other states. A separate court proceeding is needed in each state.

Writ of Execution

To collect on a judgment, the creditor requests a writ of execution. Under a writ of execution, the court orders the sheriff to seize and sell the property to satisfy the judgment. A public auction is then held, and the property is sold to the highest bidder.

In the event that the judgment is paid before the sale, the judgment creditor issues to the judgment debtor a satisfaction of judgment. When this notice is recorded, the judgment is released and the lien is lifted from the property.

7.3 HOMESTEAD LAW

The California homestead law is designed to protect a homeowner's equity in a personal residence from forced sale by certain types of creditors. The term homestead means a personal dwelling and should not be confused with the federal homestead laws of early American history, where the government gave away land to encourage settlement.

Declared Versus Automatic Homestead

There are two types of homesteads in California: a formal declared homestead and an automatic homestead called a *dwelling house exemption*. The formal declared homestead requires an owner to correctly complete and file a homestead document at the county recorder's office, whereas a dwelling house exemption is available to all valid homeowners who have not previously filed a document at the county recorder's office. The dollar protections are the same, but there are other differences that will be pointed out in the following discussion.

Requirements for a Formal Declared Homestead

Certain essentials must be observed in the filing of a formal homestead exemption. If these rules are not followed, the formal homestead is void and the automatic dwelling exemption usually applies.

1. A formal homestead must be recorded to be valid. A homestead declaration must be recorded in the recorder's office, showing that the claimant is a head of family, if such is the case, or when the declaration is made by the wife, that the husband has not made such a declaration and that she, therefore, makes it for their joint benefit. In addition to a husband or wife, the state liberally interprets a *head of family* to be any person who lives in his or her home and provides for any relative living in the same home. Registered domestic partners are entitled to head-of-household homestead rights.

2. The formal homestead statement must declare that the claimant is residing on the premises and claims this as a homestead.

3. The formal homestead statement must include a description of the premises. The dwelling house may be a single- or multiple-family dwelling, a condominium, a stock cooperative, a community apartment project, a mobile home, or a yacht. Any owner-occupied residential property can be used, but the owner may have only one homestead exemption at a time.

No previous formal filing is required for the automatic dwelling house exemption, but the home must be a principal residence and the debtor-homeowner must appear in court and claim the dwelling house exemption.

Dollar Protection for Formal and Automatic Homestead

Effective January 1, 2010, the head of the household is entitled to exemption protection of $100,000. Heads of households 65 years and older and certain low-income homeowners 55 to 64 years old are allowed a $175,000 exemption. Single persons who are not considered low income and are under the age of 65 years are usually allowed a $75,000 exemption. These exemption figures do not reflect the actual value of the property. The homestead exemption is intended to protect the equity the owner has in the property.

When the courts rule that a home has too much equity and, therefore, is to be sold to satisfy the debts of the homeowner, the owner retains the exemption portion and the creditor is awarded the difference.

Example:

Homestead Property A $500,000 home
                       –$460,000 loan
                        $40,000 equity

This home cannot be sold by judgment creditors as the equity is within the homestead exemption.

Homestead Property B $500,000 home
                      –$0 loan
                      $500,000 equity

This home can be sold by judgment creditors as the equity exceeds the homestead exemption. However, the homeowner (debtor) is allowed to keep the amount of the exemption, and the creditor only gets the excess.

$500,000 equity
–$100,000 exemption for head of household
$400,000 excess to creditor if needed

The proceeds from any forced sale are allocated in the following order:

1. To the discharge of all prior liens and encumbrances exempt from the homestead.
2. To the homestead claimant (homeowner), the amount of the exemption.
3. To the satisfaction of the execution.
4. To the homestead claimant if a balance is left over.

The Six-Month Rule

In the event the homeowner wishes to sell to move to another home or if the owner is forced to sell the home to satisfy an execution and the homeowner's equity is converted to cash, a homeowner with a valid formal declaration of homestead applies what is known as the six-month rule.

The owner has six months in which to invest his or her equity money in a new home. The homeowner may then file a homestead on the new home and thereby continue to protect the equity against creditors up to the exemption amount. *The homeowner who relies on the automatic dwelling house exemption does not get to use this six-month rule to protect the equity exemption upon resale.*

Remember that the law states that a party cannot have more than one homestead at the same time and that a homestead can be placed only on owner-occupied residential property.

Homestead Protection

Homesteads, both formally declared and automatic, protect against forced sale of a family home because of execution of judgments from unsecured creditors as long as the equity in the home does not exceed the homestead exemption.

Homesteads do not protect against forced sale of a family home resulting from mortgage or trust deed foreclosures and mechanics' liens. Even if the homestead is recorded before the trust deed and mechanics' lien, *a homestead never defeats a trust deed or mechanics' lien.*

Termination of Homestead

A homestead may be terminated in one of two ways:

1. The owner may sell the home, which automatically terminates a homestead. On the other hand, a formally declared homestead is not terminated if the owner merely moves out and rents the home. The rule is that a property must be owner occupied at the time of filing the formal homestead. An owner can later move and rent the property and still have a valid homestead. *But when a homeowner relies on the automatic dwelling exemption and then moves out, there is a loss of the homestead protection.*

2. A homeowner who has filed a formal declaration of homestead can terminate a homestead by filing a notice of abandonment. If one spouse or registered domestic partner dies, the homestead stays in force for the surviving spouse or partner. A dissolution of marriage or registered domestic partnership does not terminate a homestead if one spouse or partner remains in possession of the property. However, when death or dissolution results in only one occupant, the exemption will be reduced from $100,000 to $75,000, due to the homeowner becoming single again, unless the person is 65 years or older or 55 to 64 years and of low income; then the exemption remains $175,000.

Chapter Summary

Encumbrances are burdens on title that can be either physical or money encumbrances. Physical (nonmoney) encumbrances include easements, private and public restrictions, and encroachments. Money encumbrances are called *liens*, and they include mechanics' liens, tax liens, judgment liens, mortgages, and deeds of trust. An easement is a right to use the land of another. The most common easement is a right-of-way for ingress and egress. Easements are created by deed, implication, necessity, dedication, condemnation, and prescription. They may be removed by deed, court action, merger of title, filing of an abandonment, or nonuse for five years in the case of prescriptive easements.

Private restrictions placed in a deed are known as *CC&Rs*, a term that stands for covenants, conditions, and restrictions. Public restrictions such as zoning, building codes, health regulations, and so on, are imposed by governments.

An encroachment is the wrongful extension of a building or improvement on or over the land of another. There are statutory time periods in which an owner must sue to force removal.

Liens (money encumbrances) may be voluntary or involuntary and may be general or specific. Mechanics' liens are involuntary liens placed upon a property by anyone who performs labor, provides a service, or furnishes equipment or supplies on a construction project to guarantee that they are paid for their services. Starting dates and completion dates are extremely important, and the law specifies the exact time limits involved in carrying out a mechanics' lien right.

Judgments are considered general liens and may attach all property owned by the debtor in the county in which the abstract of judgment is filed. An abstract of judgment creates a lien for 10 years on real estate located within the county where the judgment is recorded.

The homestead law provides a limited amount of protection in the event a judgment is obtained against a homeowner. If a homestead is properly completed and recorded, the head of a household is entitled to a $100,000 exemption; persons 65 or over and low-income people 55 to 64 get $175,000, whereas a single person under 65 years receives $75,000. A homestead can be applied only on owner-occupied residential property, and only one homestead can be held at a time. Homesteads can be terminated by selling the property or filing a declaration of abandonment or, in the case of the automatic dwelling house exemption, by moving out of the home.

Important Terms and Concepts

attachment	dominant tenement
condition	easement appurtenant
covenant	easement in gross

encroachment

encumbrance

general lien

homestead

involuntary lien

judgment

lien

mechanics' lien

notice of completion

notice of nonresponsibility

party wall

public restrictions

servient tenement

six-month rule

specific lien

voluntary lien

writ of execution

Practical Application

1. How does an easement by prescription differ from adverse possession?

2. You wish to have a contractor build a home on your lot. You insist that the contractor be licensed, be bonded, and carry adequate workers' compensation insurance and other liability insurance.

   You are also concerned about the mechanics' lien rules. Fill in the correct days for each situation.

   a. Preliminary notice should be served within _____ days from the first furnishing of labor or materials on your home site.

   b. A notice of completion should be filed by you within _____ days after the completion of the home.

   c. After filing your notice of completion, the general contractor has _____ days to file a lien, while the subcontractors have _____ days.

   d. If your notice of completion is filed incorrectly and hence is invalid, all workers have _____ days to file a lien.

   e. If a mechanics' lien is filed, it automatically terminates if court action is not instituted within _____ days.

3. A 45-year-old head of household has correctly filed a formal declaration of homestead. The condo is worth $300,000 and has a first loan of $125,000, plus a $35,000 homeowner equity second loan. A judgment creditor petitions the court to force the sale of the condo for the payment of a $25,000 debt. Assuming the court orders the sale of the condo, how will the proceeds be distributed?

Reviewing Your Understanding

1. An easement on a parcel of land may be removed from the records by:
   a. a reconveyance deed.
   b. an unlawful detainer action.
   c. recording a quitclaim deed executed by the user of the easement to the servient tenement.
   d. a lis pendens action.

2. Materials were delivered to a building site for the construction of a commercial building. To be sure the supplier can collect for the cost of the material, he or she should file a:
   a. homestead declaration.
   b. preliminary notice.
   c. surety bond.
   d. subordination lien.

3. The terms *ingress* and *egress* refer to:
   a. utilities.
   b. streams.
   c. encroachments.
   d. easements.

4. An easement is an example of a(n):
   a. general lien on real property.
   b. encumbrance on real property.
   c. equitable restriction on real property.
   d. specific lien on real property.

5. A formally declared homestead can be terminated in all of the following ways, except by:
   a. renting the property.
   b. making untrue statements in the homestead declaration.
   c. selling the property.
   d. filing an abandonment of homestead.

6. When a property owner discovers that a neighbor has built a structure on a portion of his or her property, how long does the property owner normally have to bring an action against the neighbor?
   a. Six months
   b. Two years
   c. Three years
   d. Fifteen years

7. A mechanics' lien can be filed and recorded for the benefit of:
   a. painters.
   b. subcontractors.
   c. material suppliers.
   d. all of the above.

8. Which document does not need to be recorded to be valid?
   a. Mechanics' lien
   b. Deed
   c. Formal homestead declaration
   d. None of the above need to be recorded to be valid.

9. One way of acquiring an easement is by prescription. All of the following are required for the creation of this type of easement, except:
   a. paying the property taxes for five years.
   b. using the property hostile to the true owner's wishes.
   c. using the property openly and notoriously.
   d. having some right of claim or color of title.

10. A plaintiff takes a case to court and obtains a judgment. To create a lien on the defendant's property, the plaintiff must record a(n):
    a. writ of attachment.
    b. abstract of judgment.
    c. writ of execution.
    d. lis pendens action.

11. A telephone company's right to enter your property to maintain power lines is an example of a(n):
    a. servient tenement.
    b. mechanics' lien.
    c. easement in gross.
    d. easement appurtenant.

12. A 35-year-old head of household files a legally declared homestead against a $480,000 home that has a $370,000 loan against the property. A judgment creditor attempts to force the sale of the home. If the home is sold, the judgment creditor is allowed how much from the sale proceeds?
    a. $10,000
    b. $35,000
    c. $100,000
    d. Nothing

13. If zoning laws allow a property to be used in such a manner that is prohibited by a lawful deed restriction, the:
    a. owner must file a quiet title action.
    b. zoning allowance should prevail over a deed restriction.
    c. deed restriction should prevail.
    d. owner must file a quitclaim deed.

14. Which of the following is an involuntary lien?
    a. Homestead
    b. Encroachment
    c. Mortgage
    d. Judgment

15. Private deed restrictions are known as *CC&Rs*. The first *C* stands for:
    a. condition.
    b. covenant.
    c. convenient.
    d. cooperative.

16. Once properly recorded, an abstract of judgment is good for:
    a. ten years.
    b. seven years.
    c. five years.
    d. three years.

17. If an owner files a notice of completion, a general contractor has how many days to file a mechanics' lien?
    a. 90
    b. 60
    c. 30
    d. 10

18. If an owner files a notice of completion, a subcontractor has how many days to file a mechanics' lien?
    a. 90
    b. 60
    c. 30
    d. 10

19. If a landlord wishes to be protected from a mechanics' lien on work ordered by a tenant, upon discovery of the work, the landlord must file a notice of nonresponsibility within how many days?

a. 90

b. 60

c. 30

d. 10

20. Which of the following is a general lien?

a. Real estate property taxes

b. Special assessment

c. Mortgage

d. Judgment

©Shutterstock / jessicakirsh

STUDENT LEARNING OUTCOMES

This chapter stresses the legal aspects of real estate finance. At the conclusion of this chapter, you will be able to do the following:

- Name the three types of promissory notes in general use.
- Describe at least five of the characteristics of an adjustable rate loan.
- Define the following special clauses: acceleration, alienation, subordination, and prepayment penalty.
- Outline the principles of the Real Property Loan Law.

INTRODUCTION TO REAL ESTATE FINANCE

8.1 REAL ESTATE FINANCING INSTRUMENTS

Access to money and credit is the key factor in most real estate transactions. Real estate is expensive, and few people ever accumulate enough savings to pay all cash for property. Therefore, the completion of a real estate sale hinges on the buyer's ability to obtain financing. Even people who have sufficient funds rarely pay cash for real estate. Income tax deductions and an investment concept called *leverage* in some cases favor purchasing real estate with borrowed funds. Thus, whether by necessity or by choice, financing is essential for most real estate transactions.

Real Estate Financing Process

Real estate financing usually involves five phases: (1) application, (2) analysis, (3) processing, (4) closing, and (5) servicing. (See Figure 8.1.)

The lending process begins by having the prospective borrower complete a lender's loan application. A loan application form requests information about the borrower's financial status, such as level and consistency of income, personal assets, existing debts, and current expenses. The loan application form also asks for data concerning the property, including its location, its age, the size of the lot, and any existing improvements.

Once the application is completed, the lender reviews the form and uses it as a screening device to determine whether the prospective borrower and the subject property appear to meet the lender's requirements. If it becomes obvious that the borrower or the property is unacceptable for a loan, the lender informs the applicant. If it appears that the borrower and the property might be acceptable, the analysis phase begins.

Analysis involves a professionally compiled credit report on the prospective borrower and an in-depth appraisal of the property. After

FIGURE 8.1

REAL ESTATE FINANCING PROCESS

| Loan application | → | Loan analysis | → | Approval and processing | → | Closing | → | Servicing |

Source: © 2015 OnCourse Learning

the credit report and appraisal are completed (and assuming both are favorable), the lender presents the terms and cost of financing to the borrower. The borrower may accept, reject, or attempt to negotiate the financing terms with the lender. Assuming an agreement is reached, the processing phase begins.

Processing involves drawing up loan papers, preparing disclosure forms regarding loan costs, and issuing instructions for the escrow and title insurance company. Each lender establishes its own processing pattern in view of its special in-house needs.

Once the loan package has been processed, the closing phase begins. Closing the loan involves signing all loan papers and then, in conjunction with the other terms of the sale, transferring the property. In southern California, an independent escrow company, the escrow department of a title company, or (in some cases) the broker handles the entire escrow. In much of northern California, once the loan papers are signed, they are forwarded to the escrow department of a title insurance company, which closes the sale.

After the title has been transferred and the escrow is closed, the loan-servicing phase begins. *Loan servicing* refers to the record-keeping process once the loan has been placed. Many lenders do their own servicing, while others pay independent mortgage companies to handle the paperwork. The goal of loan servicing is to see that the lender makes the expected yield on the loan by promptly collecting and processing the loan payments with minimum cost.

Promissory Notes

When money is borrowed to purchase real estate, the borrower agrees to repay the loan by signing a *promissory note,* which outlines the terms of repayment and sets the due date. The promissory note is legal evidence that a debt is owed. The types of promissory notes in general use are the *straight note, installment note,* and *negative amortized note.*

Straight Note

The straight note is frequently referred to as an interest-only note. Under a **straight note**, the borrower agrees to pay the interest, usually monthly, and to pay the entire principal in a lump sum on the due date. For example, if you borrow $100,000 for 30 years at 10 percent interest using a straight note, the monthly payments would be $833.33 per month. The $833.33 payments cover just the monthly interest. Thus, 30 years hence, on the due date, you must pay back the entire $100,000 principal. In other words, the payments were only large enough to cover the monthly interest and did not reduce the $100,000 principal. (Proof: $100,000 × 10% = $10,000 ÷ 12 months = $833.33 per month.) (Ten percent is used for illustration purposes only. Actual interest rates will vary.)

Installment Note

The second and by far the most common type of real estate promissory note is the installment note. An **installment note** requires payments that include both principal and interest. If you borrow $100,000 for 30 years at 10 percent interest payable at $877.57 per month, including both principal and interest, you will find that at the end of 30 years, the entire debt is liquidated. Each monthly payment of $877.57 includes the monthly interest due and reduces a portion of the $100,000 principal. By the time the due date arrives 30 years hence, the entire principal has been paid back. *An installment loan that includes principal and interest of equal installment payments that liquidate the debt is called a fully amortized loan.* Under a fully amortized loan, no large balloon payment must be paid on the due date of the loan, as the loan is completely paid off.

One variation of the installment note is to have monthly payments that are large enough to pay the monthly interest and reduce some of the principal, but the monthly principal portion is not sufficient to entirely liquidate the debt by the due date. Thus, on the due date, the remaining unpaid principal must be paid in a lump sum, often referred to as a **balloon payment**. (Any payment more than twice the lowest payment amount is called a *balloon payment*.) A $100,000 loan for 30 years at 10 percent interest payable at $850 per month would require a balloon payment of $62,325.20 on the due date. Why? Because the $850 per month was enough to cover the monthly interest ($833.33), but it was not enough to cover the monthly interest and the monthly principal, which would have taken $877.57 per month. Thus, the difference over the 30-year life of the loan comes to $62,325.20, which must be paid on the due date in the form of a balloon payment. Loan payments and balloon payments can be calculated using financial tables or financial calculators.

Finally, some borrowers sign negative amortized promissory notes. **Negative amortization** means that the loan payment does not cover even the monthly interest. Each month, this shortage is added to the principal owed, resulting in an increased loan balance, which, in turn, incurs additional interest. As mentioned above, a $100,000 loan at 10 percent payable interest would be a monthly payment of only $833.33 ($100,000 × 10% ÷ 12 mo.). If a borrower paid only $750 per month, the difference between the interest-only payment of $833.33 and the $750 payment would be $83.33. Each month this additional $83.33 amount would be added to the $100,000 loan and begin to accrue interest.

If this continued for 30 years, the borrower would still owe a balloon payment of $288,373.99 on top of paying $750 per month for 30 years! The total paid would be $750 × 360 payments (30 years × 12) = $270,000 + $288,373.99 balloon payment, for a grand total of $558,373.99 to pay off a $100,000 negative amortized loan payable for $750 per month at 10 percent over 30 years! Of course, in the real world, most people do not stay in a home and pay for 30 years. They usually sell or refinance long before 30 years, and the balance owed on a negative amortized loan is far less than that illustrated above. But the lesson learned is that a negative amortized loan is one where a loan balance grows each and every year prior to payoff.

Adjustable Rate Loans

Most real estate lenders qualify a borrower for either a fixed interest rate or an adjustable rate loan. The fixed interest rate is the traditional real estate loan where the interest rate does not change over the life of the loan. Under an **adjustable rate loan,** the rate may move up or down. Therefore, the monthly payment may decrease or increase over the life of the loan.

How Does It Work?

Adjustable rate loans, usually called *adjustable rate mortgages* (ARMs), have the following characteristics:

1. They are usually offered at a lower initial interest rate than traditional fixed interest rate loans.
2. Once the initial interest rate is established, the rate is tied to some neutral index, which is beyond the control of the lender or the borrower.
3. The index is usually a government index. Examples are the One-Year Treasury Spot Index, the Treasury 12-Month Average Index, or the 11th District Cost-of-Funds Index. Other indexes used

are tied to certificate of deposit (CD) rates, prime rates, or even a European rate known as the London Interbank Offered Rate (LIBOR). The distance between the actual rate paid by the borrower and the index is called the *margin*. A typical margin is two percent to three percent.

4. Although not required, most lenders place a cap on how high the rate can climb. A typical cap is five percent or six percent; therefore, if the initial interest rate is six percent, the maximum it can rise to is 11 percent or 12 percent.

5. The adjustment period can vary, with some lenders adjusting the rate at six-month, one-year, or three-year intervals.

6. The maximum increase or decrease per period is established in the lender's contract, with a maximum change of one percent per six-month adjustment period being typical.

7. If the interest rate increases because of a change in the index, in some cases, the borrower may have the option of (a) increasing the monthly payment so the term of the loan remains the same or (b) maintaining the same monthly payment and increasing the term of the loan. Usually, the maximum term to which a 30-year loan may be extended is 40 years. Once a 40-year term is reached, any increase in interest rate must increase the monthly payment. If the interest rate drops below the initial rate, the borrower can continue the existing payments (which will shorten the term) or decrease the monthly payments. However, in recent years, fewer lenders are offering this feature.

8. The borrower must be given advance notice prior to a change in rate.

9. Some ARMs may be negative amortized loans. This means the payments may not cover the annual interest. The unpaid interest is added to the principal, making the loan larger. This can cause some problems in later years.

10. Some lenders offer a convertible feature that allows the borrower to convert an ARM loan to a fixed interest rate loan or a fixed rate loan to an ARM. The conversion is only offered during a certain "window period," usually from the beginning of the second year through the end of the fifth year. The borrower may be required to meet credit standards at the time of the conversion and is usually required to pay extra fees.

Other Alternative Types of Real Estate Loans

Other experimental types of loans include names such as FLIP (flexible payment mortgage), GPM (graduated payment mortgage), and

SAM (shared appreciation mortgage), in addition to many other loans called *alphabet soup financing*. The details of these alternative loan types can be studied in a Real Estate Financing course.

Purpose of Adjustable Rate and Other Alternative Loans

Alternative real estate loans have been recommended by financial experts and real estate economists for many years. Here are some of the lender's reasons for using adjustable rate loans.

Institutional lenders and secondary market investors have a constant problem with cycles of tight and loose money. This unsteady flow of funds is disruptive to their operations and the housing industry. When money is tight, it flows out of savings institutions because depositors can obtain higher yields elsewhere.

Advocates of alternative loans say this problem can be reduced through the use of ARMs. If money gets tight and interest rates rise, the savings institutions should be allowed to increase the rate they pay their depositors in order to prevent an outflow of savings. However, to pay higher interest on savings accounts, lenders must receive a higher interest rate on their existing loans. With an ARM, lenders can increase interest rates on their existing loans when they increase the interest they pay on a depositor's savings account.

Another problem facing lending institutions and secondary market investors deals with old, low fixed interest rate loans currently on the lender's books. If the current cost of money exceeds the interest rates on these older loans, the institutions are losing money on these loans. That means that the interest rate on new loans must be increased to compensate for the loss on these old loans. In effect, new borrowers are subsidizing the old borrowers. If all borrowers were on an adjustable rate, this subsidizing process would not be as severe. Those who are opposed to alternative loans argue that lenders are merely shifting the risk of rising interest rates to the borrower.

Adjustable rate mortgages are not new. They have been used for many years in Canada and in some European countries. In California, the Cal-Vet loan program has been using adjustable rates since the program was started over 80 years ago.

Deeds of Trust

To give added insurance that a borrower will repay a loan, lenders require collateral or security for the loan. To give something as security for a loan without giving possession is called **hypothecation**. A real estate lender's most logical security is real property owned or about to be acquired by the borrower. To secure an interest in the borrower's

FIGURE 8.2

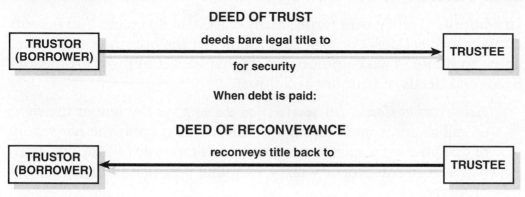

DEED OF TRUST

TRUSTOR (BORROWER) — deeds bare legal title to / for security → TRUSTEE

When debt is paid:

DEED OF RECONVEYANCE

TRUSTOR (BORROWER) ← reconveys title back to — TRUSTEE

Source: © 2015 OnCourse Learning

real property, lenders in California use a deed of trust (also called a *trust deed*).

A **deed of trust** is a three-party instrument consisting of a borrower (**trustor**), a lender (**beneficiary**), and a neutral third party (**trustee**). Under a deed of trust (trust deed), the trustor deeds legal title (sometimes called *bare legal title* or *naked title*) to the trustee, who keeps the title as security until the promissory note is repaid. Once the debt is repaid, the beneficiary orders the trustee to reconvey the title back to the trustor. If the trustor should default on the loan, the beneficiary can order the trustee to hold a trustee's sale and sell the property to obtain the cash needed to pay the loan. Figure 8.2 illustrates how title is passed between a trustor and a trustee in a deed of trust and a deed of reconveyance.

In other states, frequently a mortgage is used to secure a real estate loan instead of a deed of trust. But in California, mortgages are rare—most lenders insist on deeds of trust instead. Why? Because in nearly all cases, deeds of trust favor the lender over the borrower. If the borrower should default under a deed of trust, the lender can order the trustee to sell the property without a court proceeding, and it can be accomplished in approximately four months. Once the sale takes place, the borrower loses all rights to redeem the property.

Foreclosure under a mortgage usually requires a court proceeding and can take up to one year. Why does it take so long? Under a mortgage, the title does not pass to a third party, such as a trustee under a deed of trust. So an expensive court action is needed to divest the borrower from the title. Then, after a court foreclosure, the borrower may have up to a one-year right of redemption. In short, California real estate lenders prefer to use deeds of trust rather than mortgages as a security instrument because foreclosure is quicker and cheaper with a deed of trust.

Special Clauses

In addition to repayment terms, many real estate financing instruments contain special clauses or loan conditions that the borrower and lender agree to honor. Two common clauses that appear in most promissory notes and deeds of trust are as follows:

1. *Acceleration clause.* An acceleration clause gives the lender the right to call all sums immediately due and payable upon the happening of certain events, such as nonpayment of monthly obligations, nonpayment of real property taxes, or willful destruction of the subject property.

2. *Alienation (due-on-sale) clause.* An alienation (due-on-sale) clause is a specific type of acceleration clause that gives the lender the right to call the loan due and payable if the borrower conveys legal title to a new owner. After a period of controversy, the due-on-sale issue has been settled. Per federal law, effective October 15, 1985, all due-on-sale clauses are enforceable, except for transfers between spouses and family trusts.

Other major clauses, although not as common, that occasionally appear in promissory notes and deeds of trust include the following:

1. *Subordination clause.* A subordination clause is where the holder of a senior (first) deed of trust agrees to become a junior lien (second) to pave the way for a new senior (first) deed of trust. This is most common when the holder of the first loan on vacant land agrees to allow a new construction loan to be put on record as a first deed of trust.

2. *Prepayment penalty clause.* A prepayment penalty clause allows a lender to charge the borrower a penalty if the loan is paid before the scheduled due date. A typical prepayment penalty is 80 percent of six months' interest on the remaining balance of the loan.

However, penalties do vary with each lender. In today's real estate market, most loans do not have a prepayment penalty.

As of 2006, California law prohibits lenders from charging a prepayment penalty on owner-occupied home loans if the loan has been on the lender's books for three years or longer. But if the lender is supervised by a federal agency, this California regulation does not apply. There is no prepayment penalty on FHA-insured, VA-guaranteed, or Cal-Vet home loans.

A financing instrument may contain several other special clauses depending on the operating policies of the lender. Borrowers should carefully read all documents to make certain they completely understand what all clauses mean. This will help to assure harmony between the lender and the borrower during the life of the loan.

Junior Deed of Trust

Any trust deed other than a first is called a **junior deed of trust**, a junior loan, or a junior lien. When a buyer does not have enough cash down payment to cover the gap between the sales price and the first deed of trust loan, a junior (or second) deed of trust loan is frequently carried back by the seller.

> **Example:** Sales price $500,000; buyer has a $50,000 cash down payment and is willing to secure a first deed of trust bank loan of $400,000. Therefore, $400,000 + 50,000 = $450,000. The buyer is short $50,000. To cover the gap, the seller agrees to carry back a $50,000 promissory note secured by a second deed of trust. This can be illustrated as follows:

$500,000	Sales price
−$400,000	First deed of trust
$100,000	Required to close the sale (excluding closing costs)
−$50,000	Cash down payment
$50,000	Size of second deed of trust

Homeowner equity loans are another common example of the use of junior (second) deeds of trust. Many banks and finance companies advertise their home equity loan programs, where the lender grants a loan based on the homeowner's increase in equity caused by appreciation of property values or earlier loan pay down. Home equity loans are usually secured by junior deeds of trust. Because junior trust deeds are less secure than first trust deeds, lenders usually demand a higher interest rate on home equity loans.

Taking Over a Seller's Existing Loan

The placement of a new real estate loan from an institutional lender requires the payment of loan fees, appraisal fees, credit report charges, and other loan closing costs.

In addition, the interest rate paid by a buyer is at the current prevailing market rate. If a buyer has enough cash down payment and if legally possible, it is usually cheaper to take over the seller's existing loan, rather than obtain a new loan. Many of the loan costs are avoided, and in some cases, the interest rate on the seller's loan is less than the prevailing interest rates on new real estate loans.

There are two ways a buyer can take over a seller's existing loan. A buyer can *assume* a seller's existing loan, or a buyer can purchase subject to a seller's existing loan. When a buyer assumes a seller's existing loan, the buyer agrees to take over the payments and to become personally liable for the debt. But when a buyer purchases subject to the existing loan, the buyer agrees to take over the payments, but not the primary liability for the debt; the seller remains personally liable. This distinction becomes important if a lender should foreclose and sue for a deficiency judgment.

A **deficiency judgment** is where a lender sues a borrower after a foreclosure when the proceeds from a foreclosure are not enough to cover the outstanding loan amount. For example, suppose a real estate lender is owed $300,000, there is a default on the loan, and the lender sells the property in a foreclosure sale for $250,000. The amount owed was $300,000, and the proceeds from the foreclosure were $250,000; therefore, the deficiency is $50,000.

If the lender is allowed to sue for the $50,000 deficiency, the question arises, "Who will be sued?" The answer is "Whoever is personally liable for the debt." If a buyer assumed a seller's existing loan, the action would be brought against the buyer, as he or she is personally liable. On the other hand, if a buyer purchased subject to a seller's existing loan, the seller is still primarily liable and the deficiency action would be brought against the seller. Deficiency judgments on residential dwellings are difficult to obtain in California because of special laws protecting purchase money, owner-occupied homeowners. But deficiency judgments are obtainable on VA-guaranteed home loans because these are federally backed loans, and federal law supersedes state antideficiency laws.

Loan Terms

These are common terms used on a daily basis by lenders and real estate professionals working with seller and buyers.

Equity

Equity is a function of value minus all debt against a property. The equation is: value today minus debt today. If the current value is $200,000 and the owner owes $150,000 today the equity in the property is $50,000. Tomorrow the equity would change due to variety of issues, the property could appreciate or a payment could lower the debt.

Loan to Value LTV

Loan to value or LTV is how the amount the lender will loan a borrower is determined. The lender takes the sales price or appraised value, whichever is lower and then offers the borrower loan terms off that amount. Typically, LTV is between 80% to 95%, the lower the number the lower the risk since the borrower has more equity.

Loan Origination Fee

Loan origination fees are what the lender charges to do the loan, typically 1% of loan is amount. An easy way to remember this fee is to think of it as the lenders commission.

Discount Points

Discount points are charges from the lender for giving the buyer a lower than par interest rate. The points help to increase the lenders yield when charging less interest. Each point is 1% of the loan amount.

Example: Current interest is 3% with no points
A rate of 2.75 would have an extra charge of 1.5 points
A rate of 2.5 would have an extra charge of 2 points
A rate of 2.25 would have an extra charge 2.5 points

Below this the lender would not offer a discount. A borrower with a loan amount of $100,000 wanting a rate of 2.25% would need to pay $2,500 in discount points and $1,000 in loan origination fees.

Leverage

Leverage can be described as using a small amount of your money (equity capital) and a large amount of someone else's money (borrowed capital) to buy real estate. Leverage can be advantageous if the property increases in value.

For example, assume you can purchase land for $100,000 and resell it later for $150,000. If you pay $100,000 all cash and sell the property for $150,000, you realize a $50,000 gain, or a 50 percent return on your investment.

All-Cash Transaction

$150,000   Resale price
$-100,000$ Purchase price
$50,000   Gain

$$\frac{\$50,000 \text{ Gain}}{\$100,000 \text{ Investment}} = 50\%$$

On the other hand, if you could obtain a $90,000 real estate loan, you would need to invest only $10,000 as a down payment. If you resell the land for $150,000 and pay off the $90,000 loan, you would have a $50,000 gain, or a 500 percent return on your investment.

Leverage Transaction

$100,000	Purchase price
– 90,000	Loan
$10,000	Down payment (investment)
$150,000	Resale price
– 90,000	Loan
$60,000	
$10,000	Down payment
$50,000	Gain

$$\frac{\$50,000 \text{ Gain}}{\$10,000 \text{ Investment}} = 500\%$$

Of course, the percentage return is reduced by income taxes, closing costs, and interest on the loan, but they have been omitted to stress the impact of leverage. However, leverage is rosy only if property values increase. If property values decrease, look out! See the following section on pitfalls.

PITFALLS

Leverage can work in reverse if the value of the property declines. Here is what happens if the land in the example has declined in value by 10% upon resale.

All-Cash Transaction

$100,000	Purchase price
– 90,000	Resale price
$(10,000)	Loss on resale

$$\frac{\$10,000 \text{ Loss}}{\$100,000 \text{ Invested}} = -10\% \text{ Loss on investment}$$

Leverage Transaction

$90,000	Resale price
− 90,000	Loan
$0	Gain

$$\frac{\$0\ Gain}{\$100,000\ Invested} = -10\%\ \text{Loss on investment}$$

If you paid $100,000 all cash, your loss was 10 percent. But if you paid $100,000 by borrowing $90,000 and making a $10,000 down payment and the property resold for only $90,000, you were just able to repay the lender, and you lost all of your $10,000 down payment! If the property were to decline in value more than 10 percent, you would owe more than what the property is worth. If this becomes the case and the buyer "walks away" from the property and the lender forecloses, the buyer's credit rating is destroyed. In addition, any difference between the loan amount and the lower amount the lender receives from the resale of the property can, in some cases, result in an income tax liability for the former owner.

Example:

$90,000 Loan balance owed at the time of foreclosure
−70,000 Resale price lender receives for the property after foreclosure
$20,000 Difference is known as *debt forgiveness* and could be taxable to the former owner as income (see a tax expert for details)

Installment Sales Contracts (Land Contracts)

Another real estate financing instrument is an installment sales contract, also called a contract of sale or agreement of sale or land contract. An installment sales contract is an agreement between the seller, called the *vendor,* and the buyer, called the *vendee,* where the buyer is given possession and use of the property. In exchange for possession and use, the buyer agrees to make regular payments to the seller. Legal title to the property remains with the seller until an agreed amount has been paid, at which time the seller formally deeds title to the buyer. In essence, under an installment sales contract, the seller becomes the lender. Outside lending institutions, such as banks and mortgage companies, are not needed in such a transaction.

The lack of immediate title poses some risks for the buyer. If the seller should die, become bankrupt, or become incompetent or encumber the title during the contract, the buyer could become involved in legal entanglements.

Recent court cases have greatly restricted the ease by which a seller can remove a buyer if he or she defaults on the payments. A long, expensive court action may be needed to remove a defaulted buyer from possession. In light of the disadvantage for the buyer and the seller, installment sales contracts are no longer popular in California. They are still used on a regular basis in other states.

8.2 FORECLOSURE PROCESS: TRUSTEE'S SALE

Borrowers default on repayment of loans for a variety of reasons, usually because of events beyond their control. Financial reversals such as loss of a business or job probably head the list, but other circumstances are closely related: death, disability, bankruptcy, dissolution of marriage, drop in property values, and poor budgeting. When a borrower defaults on a real estate loan, unless arrangements can be made with the lender to work out a satisfactory schedule for repayment, foreclosure takes place. However, most lenders try to avoid foreclosure whenever possible and use it only as a last resort. Lenders are in the business of lending money and do not want to become involved in owning and managing real estate.

A borrower can be in default for reasons other than nonpayment. There may be a violation of other terms listed on the trust deed, such as failure to maintain the property or failure to pay property taxes and fire insurance. Regardless of the violation, lenders in California must follow a prescribed procedure to take title from a delinquent debtor. Here is a summary of the process, which is also illustrated in Figure 8.3.

Trustee's Sale

Virtually all trust deeds contain a power-of-sale clause, which empowers the trustee, in the event of default by the trustor, to sell the property at public auction. Although the provisions of the power-of-sale clause

FIGURE 8.3

TRUSTEE'S SALE (FORECLOSURE)

Borrower defaults → Trustee records notice of default → Starts reinstatement period; runs until 5 business days prior to sale → Trustee records and publishes notice of sale → Trustee's sale is held → Successful bidder receives trustee's deed

Source: © 2015 OnCourse Learning

are a matter of contract and may vary from instrument to instrument, there are laws that specifically regulate foreclosure through a trustee's sale. The statutory requirements are as follows:

1. *Notice of default (NOD).* Once the beneficiary is reasonably certain that a trustor is unable to make good on the loan and any statutory grace period required by law (90 days as of 2011), the beneficiary orders the trustee to record a notice of default in the county where the property is located. This begins a reinstatement period. The notice must contain a correct legal description of the property, the name of the trustor, the nature of the breach, and a statement to the effect that the party executing the notice of default has elected to sell the property to satisfy the obligation. Within 10 days after filing the notice of default, a copy must be sent by registered or certified mail to the borrower, junior lienholders, and anyone whose "request for notice" appears on record. During this reinstatement period, which runs until five days before the date of sale, the trustor (borrower) can reinstate the loan by paying all delinquent installments. The trustor must also pay foreclosure costs and trustee's fees. This is referred to as the *right of reinstatement.*

2. *Notice of sale.* In addition to recording a notice of default, a trustee must also record a notice of sale. This notice of sale is filed if the borrower fails to reinstate the loan. The notice must contain a correct identification of the property, such as the street address or legal description. It must be published in a newspaper of general circulation in the county or jurisdiction in which the property is located. The publication must appear at least once a week for three consecutive calendar weeks. Moreover, the notice must also be posted in a public place, such as a courthouse, and in some conspicuous place on the property, such as the front door. The sale must be held in a public place during business hours on a weekday (Monday through Friday).

3. *Final sale.* Any person, including the trustor and beneficiary, may bid on the property via public auction. All bids must be in cash or its equivalent. However, the lender foreclosing can submit the amount owed the lender as a bid in lieu of cash. A trustee's deed is issued to the highest bidder. Any surplus funds (that is, funds remaining after paying off the lender; foreclosure costs; and junior liens, if any) are given to the trustor.

No right of redemption exists after a trustee's sale. The purchaser acquires all rights held by the former owner, becoming the successor in interest, and is entitled to immediate possession, subject to those having superior rights over the trust deed that was foreclosed.

Rights of Holders of Junior Trust Deeds

When a trustee's sale is held on behalf of a first trust deed lender, junior trust deeds can be eliminated. Therefore, it is important to examine what rights a junior trust deed holder has in the foreclosure process.

Assume a homeowner has a first and a second trust deed loan against the property and is in default on the loans. If the first trust deed lender begins to foreclose, the second trust deed lender can step in and make the payments due on the first loan. This will stop the first lender from foreclosing. *The second trust deed lender then adds the payments made on the first trust deed loan to the balance the borrower owes on the second trust deed loan.* The holder of the second trust deed loan then demands repayment from the borrower. If the borrower fails to repay, the holder of the second trust deed forecloses under the trustee sale provisions of the second trust deed. The successful bidder at the trustee's sale becomes the owner of the property, subject to the first trust deed—that is, takes over the property and is required to make all future payments on the first trust deed loan. In short, a holder of a junior trust deed can stop the first lender from foreclosing on the first trust deed. This, in turn, keeps the second trust deed from being eliminated. The holder of the second trust deed gets title to the property as the lone bidder at the trustee's sale or cash from a third party who is the successful bidder at the trustee's sale on the second trust deed.

How does a holder of a second trust deed know when a borrower has defaulted on the first trust deed? The law requires senior trust deed holders to send a certified copy of any notice of default and sale to all holders of junior trust deeds. To be doubly sure, a holder of a junior trust deed may also wish to record an instrument called a *request for copy of notice of default*. This places on public record a notice to the senior trust deed holder that the junior trust deed holder wishes to be informed when a default is declared on the first loan.

Loan Modifications

Rather than facing foreclosure, borrowers may try to renegotiate their loan terms with their lender; this is known as a *loan modification*. Borrowers need to understand that the lender is not required to participate in a loan modification but may do so if the property is worth less than the loan amount and the lender believes it may see a larger loss if it forecloses on the property. To be successful, a borrower will need to present the following to the lender:

- A formal application, including a description of the hardship created by the mortgage

- Proof of income, such as two recent pay stubs or the most recent profit-and-loss statement for self-employed borrowers
- A form authorizing the Internal Revenue Service to release tax data to the servicer

It is also helpful if the borrower provides an estimate of what the property is worth, either an appraisal from a licensed appraiser or a broker price opinion from a reputable real estate agent.

8.3 TRUTH-IN-LENDING, EQUAL CREDIT OPPORTUNITY, AND THE REAL ESTATE SETTLEMENT PROCEDURES ACT

Many years ago, Congress passed the Truth-in-Lending Law, which resulted in a provision called *Regulation Z*. The purpose of the law is to help borrowers understand how much it costs to borrow money. The law requires all lenders to show loan costs in the same way. This allows borrowers to compare one lender's cost against another lender's cost. The law requires lenders to quote the cost of borrowing, using what is called an annual percentage rate (APR). The APR is not an interest rate, but rather a percentage rate that reflects the effective interest rate on the loan, including other prepaid financing charges such as loan fees, prepaid interest, and tax service fees.

Regulation Z requires a lender to give the borrower a disclosure statement showing a complete breakdown of all loan costs, in addition to other loan information. The law also says that certain loans are rescindable within three business days. This means borrowers have three days after they agree to a loan to cancel if they so wish. Generally, the rescindable right applies only to loans to refinance a borrower's home and to certain types of junior deeds of trust, including home improvement loans. First deeds of trust to purchase a home do not carry a three-day right to rescind, nor do loans carried back by a seller of real estate.

Real Estate Advertisements

Real estate advertisements must comply with Regulation Z. If one financial term (such as *interest rate* or *no money down*) is mentioned, all financing terms (*interest rate, monthly payments, length of loan,* and so on) must be stated in the ad. There are severe penalties for people who incorrectly advertise real estate loan terms.

Equal Credit Opportunity Act

The Equal Credit Opportunity Act, a federal law, prohibits lenders from discriminating on the basis of race, color, religion, national origin, age, sex, family size, handicap, or marital status or on the grounds of receipt of income from a public assistance program.

Some of the basic provisions of the act are as follows:

1. A lender cannot ask if the borrower is divorced or widowed. The lender can ask if the borrower is married, unmarried, or separated. For purposes of the law, *unmarried* means single, divorced, or widowed.

2. A lender cannot ask the borrower about receiving alimony or child support unless the borrower is first notified that the information need not be revealed; unless the borrower wishes to use such income to qualify for a loan, he or she need not disclose the source of income. However, the lender can ask about obligations to pay alimony or child support.

3. A lender cannot ask about birth control practices or childbearing intentions or capabilities.

4. A lender must notify the borrower within 30 days about what action has been taken on his or her loan application. In case of disapproval, if requested, the reason must be given.

5. If the borrower requests, the lender must consider information provided by the borrower indicating that a bad history of a joint account does not reflect on his or her credit.

In short, the Equal Credit Opportunity Act assures that all qualified persons shall have equal access to credit. This law has been especially helpful in assuring that women are not discriminated against because of their gender.

Real Estate Settlement Procedures Act

The **Real Estate Settlement Procedures Act (RESPA)** is a federal law requiring that certain forms be provided with regard to closing costs. The law applies whenever a person purchases an owner-occupied residence using funds obtained from institutional lenders that are regulated by a federal agency. Virtually all banks and thrift institutions, and most other lenders, fall directly or indirectly under RESPA's rules. The one major exception is real estate loans made by private parties.

RESPA rules require the lender to furnish the borrower with a special information booklet and a good faith estimate of closing costs three days from the time the prospective borrower files an application for a real estate loan. RESPA rules prohibit any kickbacks or unearned fees from being charged or listed as closing costs. The law states that only valid, earned closing costs shall be charged to the buyer or seller. Violators can be punished by up to one year in jail and/or a $10,000 fine. Most of the burden for implementing RESPA falls upon the real estate lender. However, escrow agents are also involved. RESPA requires the use of a Uniform Settlement Statement, which itemizes all final closing charges. Upon request, the escrow agent must let the borrower-buyer inspect the Uniform Settlement Statement one day before the close of escrow. In addition, the escrow officer must see that all parties receive a copy of the Uniform Settlement Statement after the close of escrow.

Effective August 1, 2015 the Consumer Financial Protection Bureau consolidated four separate disclosures into two combined disclosures. This merger of the Truth in Lending Act (TILA) and the Real Estate Settlement Procedures Act (RESPA) is commonly known as the TILA/RESPA Rule. This rule combines the Good Faith Estimate and the preliminary Truth in Lending Disclosure into a preliminary disclosure known as the Loan Estimate. The Loan Estimate is to be given to the borrower no later than three business days from submitting a loan application to a lender. The rule consolidates the HUD-1 Form and the final Truth in Lending Disclosure into a disclosure known as Closing Disclosure. The Closing Disclosure is to be given to the borrower three business days prior to the consummation of the loan. The purpose of this new rule is to make it easier for consumers to locate and compare key information such as interest rates, monthly payments and closing costs of a loan and to better compare loan programs offered by competing lenders.

8.4 REAL PROPERTY LOAN LAW

Another consumer-oriented law is the Real Property Loan Law found in Sections 1024048 of the California Business and Professions Code (Article 7). This segment of the law is commonly called the *Mortgage Loan Broker Law*. The purpose of this law is to protect borrowers who use the services of mortgage loan brokers. The law requires mortgage brokers to give a loan disclosure statement to all borrowers before they become obligated for the loan. The disclosure statement itemizes all closing costs, loan expenses, and commissions to be paid, thereby showing the borrower how much he or she will net from the loan.

Exceptions to the Mortgage Loan Broker Law

It is easier to state which lenders and what transactions are not covered by the law than to list those that are. As of January 2011, the following are exempt from the Real Property Loan Law:

1. Regulated institutional lenders, such as banks, thrift institutions, credit unions, and finance companies.

2. Purchase money transactions where a seller carries back the loan as part of the sale price; however, if a seller carries back the loan for more than seven transactions in one year, the Mortgage Loan Broker Law does apply.

3. Loans secured by first trust deeds when the principal amount is $30,000 or more.

4. Loans secured by junior trust deeds when the principal amount is $20,000 or more.

Maximum Commissions

Mortgage loan brokers are limited in the amount of commissions they can charge as a percentage, as shown in Table 8.1. As is evident in Table 8.1, the shorter the term of the loan, the less commission the

TABLE 8.1　Maximum Commission as a Percentage.

	Less Than Two Years	Two Years but Less Than Three	Three Years and Over	Exempt Transactions
Type and Length of Loan	5%	5%	10%	Loans of $30,000 and over
First Trust Deeds				
Junior Trust Deeds	5%	10%	15%	Loans of $20,000 and over

Source: © 2015 OnCourse Learning

Special Interest Topic

Usury Law

Many states have passed laws establishing the maximum rate of interest that can be charged on various types of loans. Interest rates that exceed the maximum rate are considered usurious and, therefore, illegal. In some instances, if a lender is found guilty of usury, the borrower does not have to repay the interest due on the loan.

In California, the maximum rate is 10 percent or 5 percent above the Federal Reserve discount rate, which ever is greater, unless the lender is exempt from the law. California regulations exempt banks, thrift institutions, and several other recognized lenders from the usury law. Any real estate transaction handled by a licensed broker

(Continued)

is also exempt from the usury law. However, private parties lending directly to private borrowers are not exempt. For example, real estate loans from institution all enders can be at any rate agreed upon, while reale state loans from private lenders cannot. There is at least one exception: Sellers carrying back a purchase money deed of trust as part of their equity on a real estate sale can charge interest at any agreed-upon rate. However, this transaction should be cleared with an attorney to makesure the law has not changed.

The pros and cons of usury laws are currently being debated. Proponents believe that usury laws protect consumers against lenders, while opponents believe usury laws restrict the supply of loan funds and drive some borrowers to illegal loan sharks. From time to time, the federal government passes temporary laws that override state usury laws during periods of tight mortgage money.

Source: From R. J. Bond, D. J. McKenzie, J. Fesler, and Rick Boone, *California Real Estate Finance*, 9th ed. (Cincinnati, OH: Cengage, 2011).

broker can charge as a percentage of the face amount of the loan. On loans of $30,000 and over for first liens and $20,000 for junior liens, the broker can charge as much as the borrower agrees to pay. For loans covered by the law, however, competition frequently keeps rates below the maximum allowed.

Other Costs and Expenses

Under transactions covered by the Real Property Loan Law, brokers are also limited in the amount of costs and expenses, other than commissions, they can charge a borrower for arranging a loan. Such costs and expenses cannot exceed 5 percent of the amount of the loan. However, if 5 percent of the loan is less than $390, the broker can charge up to that amount, provided the charges do not exceed actual costs and expenses paid, incurred, or reasonably earned by the broker.

Regardless of the size of the loan, the borrower cannot be charged more than $700 for miscellaneous costs and expenses, excluding commission and title and recording fees as of January 2011.

Balloon Payments

A balloon payment is prohibited if (1) the term of the loan is for six years or less and (2) the loan is secured by the dwelling place of the borrower. Again, this provision does not apply to loans carried by sellers.

Insurance

A borrower is not required to purchase credit life or disability insurance as a condition for obtaining a loan. However, a lender may insist, for self-protection, that fire and hazard insurance be obtained on the property until the loan has been repaid. If licensed to sell such insurance, the mortgage broker can act as the agent for the borrower, but the borrower is not obligated to purchase the insurance coverage through the mortgage loan broker.

Miscellaneous Provisions

Mortgage brokers are prohibited from charging a borrower for loan-servicing or collection fees. Late charges, if any, may not exceed $5 or 10 percent of the principal and interest part of an installment payment, whichever is greater. If an installment payment is made within 10 days of its due date, however, no late charge can be assessed.

In case of early repayment of a loan, there can be no prepayment penalty against the borrower when the loan is over seven years old. During the first seven years, a borrower is allowed to pay up to 20 percent of the remaining principal balance of the loan during any 12-month period without a penalty. The remaining balance may then be subjected to a maximum prepayment penalty of six months' unearned interest. Mortgage brokers must keep copies of all loan papers for at least four years.

Chapter Summary

The financing of real estate usually involves a five-phase process consisting of the loan application, analysis, processing, closing, and servicing phases. In California, the major instruments of finance are promissory notes and deeds of trust (trust deeds). Promissory notes can be straight notes, which contain interest-only payments, or installment notes, which include payments of principal and interest. The most common promissory note is the fully amortized installment note. In addition to fixed interest rate loans, adjustable rate loans are also popular.

Real estate loans in California are secured by deeds of trust, also called trust deeds. A deed of trust is a three-party instrument consisting of a trustor (borrower), a trustee (neutral third party), and a beneficiary (lender). Upon repayment of a loan, the trustee reconveys title back to the trustor. If the trustor should default on the loan, the trustee forecloses on the property under what is called a trustee's sale.

Many promissory notes and deeds of trust contain special clauses that outline the duties and responsibilities of the borrower. Acceleration and alienation (due-on-sale) clauses are the most common. Subordination and prepayment penalty clauses are also used. Junior deeds of trust are used in any real estate transactions when the buyer does not have enough money to cover the gap between the sales price and the first loan. Installment sales contracts are no longer popular for the purchase and financing of real estate.

The Truth-in-Lending Act, the Equal Credit Opportunity Act, and the Real Estate Settlement Procedures Act (RESPA) are examples of federal laws designed to assure proper disclosure to and equal treatment of prospective real estate borrowers. The Real Property Loan Law is a California law that requires full disclosure when a borrower procures a loan through a mortgage loan broker. This law also regulates maximum commissions and closing costs that can be charged to a borrower. The Real Property Loan Law, in California, does not apply to first deed of trust loans of $30,000 or more or second deed of trust loans of $20,000 or more.

Important Terms and Concepts

acceleration clause	installment sales contract
adjustable rate	junior deed of trust
alienation (due-on-sale) clause	leverage
annual percentage rate (APR)	loan origination
balloon payment	negative amortized
beneficiary	prepayment penalty clause
deed of trust	Real Estate Settlement Procedures Act (RESPA)
deficiency judgment	
discount points	straight note
Equal Credit Opportunity Act	subordination clause
equity	trustee
hypothecation	trustor
installment note	Truth-in-Lending Law

Practical Application

1. A homeowner has a $200,000 interest-only ARM loan with a current interest rate of six percent with a two percent margin over the 11th District Cost-of-Funds Index with a cap rate of 11 percent. What are the current monthly loan payments? With an annual maximum increase of two percent per year, under

worst-case circumstances, what are the maximum monthly loan payments for the second, third, and fourth years?

2. An owner is in financial trouble and is behind $2,000 in payments on a $175,000 studio condo loan. The lender files a notice of default and begins to foreclose. To date, foreclosure costs total $1,000, plus the $2,000 back payments. Explain what the owner must do to save the home.

3. Using the services of a mortgage loan broker, a homeowner borrows a $15,000 junior loan for a 10-year period to pay off consumer debts. Assuming the loan broker charges the maximum commission and fees allowed by law, how much will the homeowner net after paying these fees?

Reviewing Your Understanding

1. A real estate promissory note reads "$557.50 per month for 239 payments, then a final monthly payment of $2,011.19." This is an example of a(n):

   a. alienation payment.
   b. prepayment.
   c. balloon payment.
   d. amortized payment.

2. Under a deed of trust the:

   a. trustor deeds to the beneficiary.
   b. trustee deeds to the trustor.
   c. trustor deeds to the trustee.
   d. trustee deeds to the beneficiary.

3. An enforceable due-on-sale clause is correctly called a(n):

   a. acceleration clause.
   b. alienation clause.
   c. wraparound clause.
   d. prepay clause.

4. A negative amortized ARM means:

   a. it can cause some problems in later years.
   b. the payments may not cover the annual interest.
   c. the unpaid interest is added to the principal.
   d. all of the above.

5. Late charges on a loan:

   a. are charged at a standard $50.00 per month.
   b. cannot legally be charged.
   c. are added to the balance of the loan.
   d. may not exceed five dollars or 10 percent of the principal and interest part of an installment payment, whichever is greater.

6. A type of financing instrument in which the owner (vendor) retains the legal title until the buyer (vendee) fulfills the terms of the purchase contract is called a(n):

   a. lease contract.
   b. installment sales contract.
   c. wraparound contract.
   d. junior lien contract.

7. The Equal Credit Opportunity Act requires a lender to:

   a. quote interest rates as annual percentage rates (APR).
   b. disclose all closing costs.
   c. an approved loan estimate form
   d. not discriminate on the basis of race, creed, color, sex, origin, plus other protected categories.

8. The successful bidder at a trustee's sale (foreclosure) receives what type of deed?

   a. Trustee's
   b. Grant
   c. Quitclaim
   d. Sheriff's

9. If a real estate loan is paid off in advance of the due date, some lenders are legally allowed to charge a penalty. This is what type of penalty?

   a. Acceleration
   b. Alienation
   c. Prepayment
   d. Balloon

10. The Real Property Loan Law does not apply to first loans of $30,000 or more and second deed of trust loans of:

    a. $5,000.
    b. $17,500.
    c. $19,500.
    d. $20,000.

11. RESPA stands for:

    a. Real Estate Settlement Procedures Act.
    b. Real Estate Salesperson Association.
    c. Real Estate Syndication Planning Act.
    d. Real Estate Settlement Program Act.

12. An owner sells and the buyer takes over the existing loan. To relieve the seller of primary liability, the buyer must:

    a. sign a nonrecourse agreement.
    b. take title contingent upon the note and trust deed.
    c. take title subject to the note and trust deed.
    d. assume the note and deed of trust.

13. An annual percentage rate (APR):

    a. is not an interest rate but rather a percentage rate that reflects the effective interest rate on the loan.
    b. is an interest rate that includes tax service fees.
    c. is not an interest rate; it is a fee for lending.
    d. is an interest rate that only applies to refinancing.

14. A $300,000 loan at eight percent, payable as interest only at $2,000 per month, is what type of note?

 a. Installment
 b. Straight
 c. ARM
 d. Amortized

15. An ARM loan would not be a good option for which of the following borrowers?

 a. One who does not plan on being in the home very long.
 b. A borrower on a fixed income.
 c. One who is likely to receive raises during the term of the loan.
 d. A borrower who has little money down but good income.

16. In an ARM loan, the distance between the borrower's rate and the index is called the:

 a. cap.
 b. adjustment.
 c. margin.
 d. teaser.

17. A copy of a mortgage loan disclosure statement prepared by the broker and signed by the borrower must be retained by the broker for at least:

 a. five years.
 b. four years.
 c. three years.
 d. two years.

18. A clause in a deed of trust which states that the lender's rights shall become secondary to a new trust deed is called a(n):

 a. alienation clause.
 b. subordination clause.
 c. submortgage.
 d. escalation clause.

19. The loan-to-value ratio on a mortgage is defined as the:

 a. loan amount as a percentage of sales price or appraised value, whichever is lower.
 b. loan amount as a percentage of assessed value.
 c. loan amount as a percentage of appraised value or sales price, whichever is higher.
 d. monthly payments as a percentage of the face amount of the loan.

20. A buyer asking a seller to carry back a loan on the purchase of a residential lot which the buyer plans to build a house would be most interested in a(n):

 a. alienation clause
 b. subordination clause
 c. acceleration clause
 d. prepayment penalty

STUDENT LEARNING OUTCOMES, PART I

This chapter is divided into two parts. Part I covers the main types of real estate lenders found in California. Part II discusses government's role in real estate financing, stressing the main points of the Federal Housing Administration (FHA), Department of Veterans Affairs (VA), and California Department of Veterans Affairs (Cal-Vet) programs.

At the conclusion of Part I, you will be able to do the following:

- List three institutional and three noninstitutional real estate lenders.
- Describe the difference between a mortgage loan broker and a mortgage loan banker.
- Identify three characteristics of private lenders.
- Explain private mortgage insurance and why it is important to the housing market.

PART I: REAL ESTATE LENDERS

9.1 QUALIFYING FOR A REAL ESTATE LOAN

When qualifying a borrower, a lender tries to determine whether a borrower will make his or her loan payments in the future. To make this determination, a loan officer analyzes two major characteristics:

1. *Capacity to pay.* To determine capacity to pay, these questions must be asked: Does the borrower make enough money to make the payments? If so, is it a stable source of income? Does the borrower have enough cash to buy this property? What other assets does the borrower have? The answers to all of these questions affect the borrower's capacity to pay.

2. *Desire to pay.* Desire to pay is the other major factor a lender must analyze. A person may have the capacity to pay but lack the desire to do so. The desire to pay is just as important as the capacity to pay, but it is more difficult to measure. The desire to pay is generally reflected by the past credit history of a borrower.

Credit (FICO) Score

Credit scoring is how most lenders evaluate a person's credit history. Credit scores are also called *FICO scores,* a term that comes from Fair, Isaac & Company, who designed a matrix of more than 30 items used to predict the likelihood that a loan will be repaid as agreed. Scores range from a low of 30 to a high of approximately 900. A score below 650 usually triggers a closer examination by a lender. Most lenders used to require a score of 720; however, lenders are frequently requiring scores of 740 and above for a borrower to get the best loan terms. Examples of major items that influence a credit score include the following:

1. The number of credit accounts and cards. Are the cards "maxed out" or at a zero balance? Too many credit accounts, even with

zero balances, lower a score. Why? Because they may be "maxed out" after a loan is granted, overloading the borrower.

2. The number of credit inquiries. How recent were the inquiries? A lot of recent inquiries indicate a hunt for credit.

3. Any late payments, collections, judgments, credit charge-offs, bankruptcy, or other similar items.

Three credit-reporting agencies—Equifax, Experian, and Trans-Union—issue a credit score. A lender tends to use the mid-score of all three scores. After a credit report has been issued, a borrower has the right to see a copy and his or her credit score.

In short, for a potential borrower, a good credit score is good news. A low score is not good news. The Federal Fair Credit Report Act allows a person to obtain a free copy of a credit report once per year. Contact the credit agencies for details. For information about your credit score, access www.myfico.com, www.equifax.com, or another website you locate using a search engine. A fee may be charged.

Old Rule of Thumb Is Inadequate

The old lender's rule, "A home should not cost more than two and a half times a buyer's (borrower's) gross income," is inadequate. The rule ignores the real issue—the buyer's ability to pay the monthly housing payment. This rule also ignores the issue of a buyer's personal debts. Isn't a buyer who is free of debt able to pay more for housing than a buyer heavily in debt? Most lenders today recognize that "two and a half times the gross income" rule is riddled with errors and pitfalls.

Use of Multipliers and Ratios

Most lenders qualify borrowers by using income multipliers or ratios. The ratios can vary from lender to lender; however, the traditional 4:1 multiplier has been used by conservative real estate lenders for many years.

A 4:1 multiplier simply means that the monthly income of the borrower should be approximately four times the monthly housing payment. Thus, if the monthly housing payment (principal + interest + monthly taxes, private mortgage insurance [if any], and hazard insurance) will be $1,000, four times this amount ($1,000 × 4), or $4,000, should be the borrower's gross monthly income. When converted to a ratio, the 4:1 multiplier means that a borrower's monthly housing payment should not be much more than 25 percent of the borrower's gross monthly income. Gross income must include all stable income of the borrower and co-borrowers, such as a spouse's income, alimony payments, and public assistance payments as well as regular wages, commissions, and salaries.

Trend Toward More Liberal Ratios

Recently there has been a move toward the use of 3.5:1 multipliers. This means that the borrower's monthly housing payments should not exceed approximately 30 percent of the borrower's gross income. Lenders recognize that because of higher costs for homes in California, more of a borrower's income must be used to cover housing payments. Therefore, if a borrower's monthly housing payment (principal + interest + monthly taxes, private mortgage insurance [if any], and hazard insurance) will be $1,000, three and one-half times this amount, or $3,500, should be the borrower's gross monthly income. Contrast this $3,500 with the $4,000 required when a lender uses the 4:1 multiplier, and you can see that the lower the ratio, the less gross income is needed to qualify for a real estate loan.

What Counts as Income?

Generally, lenders would like the borrower to have at least a two-year work history, preferably with the same employer or in the same vocation. Acceptable income includes wages, commissions, alimony, child support, pensions, Social Security benefits, positive cash flow from rentals, and self-employment income. In most cases, the lender would want to see current pay stubs, and in the case of alimony and child support a history of consistent payments. Rental and self-employment income are usually verified by submitting the last two years of income tax filings. Under some circumstances, a lender may also count overtime, bonuses, and part-time work if the borrower can show a consistent pattern of receiving steady payment from these sources.

Debts

A lender must also consider a borrower's debts in order to determine the capacity to pay. A borrower's debts may be short term or long term.

Short-term debts may be ignored, and long-term debts are counted. The definition of long- versus short-term debts can vary depending on the lender. However, many lenders consider long-term debts to be obligations that exist for six to ten months or more.

When considering debts, conventional lenders traditionally have used the following guidelines: the monthly housing payment + long-term debts = total monthly expenses. Traditionally, the total monthly expenses should not exceed 33 to 38 percent of the borrower's gross monthly income. However, in times of liberal financing, some lenders will boost this to 40 percent.

> **Example:** $1,000 monthly housing expense + $250 long-term monthly debts = $1,250 × 3 = $3,750, the gross monthly income required from the borrower.

Summary of Qualifying Guidelines

1. (Principal + interest + monthly taxes, PMI, and hazard insurance)

$$\frac{\text{Monthly housing payments}}{\text{Gross monthly income}} = \text{Percentage \%}$$

Ideally this rate should not exceed 25 to 30 percent, with 28 percent commonly used by many lenders.

2. (Monthly housing payments + long-term monthly debts)

$$\frac{\text{Total monthly expenses}}{\text{Gross monthly income}} = \text{Percentage \%}$$

This ratio should not exceed 33 to 38 percent, with 36 percent commonly used by many lenders.

Most real estate lenders require that borrowers qualify under both tests. Some borrowers can qualify on the first test but not on the second because they are too heavily in debt. These guidelines can vary from lender to lender; thus, consumers and real estate professionals should contact local lenders to obtain specific guidelines. Market conditions, the secondary mortgage market, and government regulations may also affect lender policies; the previous examples should be used as a guide. (See the case study on qualifying for a home loan in the appendix of this chapter.)

9.2 INSTITUTIONAL LENDERS

An institutional lender is a financial depository that gathers deposits from the general public and then invests these funds. As indicated in Figure 9.1, California has three major types of institutional lenders: commercial banks, savings banks (formerly called savings and loan associations), and life insurance companies. All three of these institutions pour billions of dollars into California real estate loans. Before studying institutional lenders, it is helpful to review the characteristics

FIGURE 9.1

Source: © 2015 OnCourse Learning

of the California mortgage market and the concept of savings forming the pool for borrowing.

The California Mortgage Market

The characteristics of the California mortgage market can be summarized as follows:

1. *Usually high demand.* Because of its large economy, California traditionally has needed large amounts of mortgage funds. However, in periods of recession and economic slowdown, the demand for real estate loans declines.

2. *Population growth.* California is the most populous state. High population means high demand for housing to own or rent.

3. *Financial institutions.* California has many of the nation's largest commercial and savings banks.

4. *Mortgage loan correspondents.* California has many experienced mortgage companies that represent out-of-state life insurance companies and other lenders that, in boom times, are eager to invest in California real estate loans.

5. *Title and escrow companies.* Title insurance and escrow companies originated in California. Many of the nation's largest are in California, and they provide fast and efficient service for real estate lenders.

6. *Use of deeds of trust.* The deed of trust (trust deed) is used rather than mortgage instruments for securing real estate loans. Deeds of trust give lenders more flexibility than mortgages.

7. *Active secondary market.* Existing real estate loans are sold to out-of-state lenders. These include mutual savings banks, which are not located in California but which make the capital available through secondary purchases.

Savings Form the Pool for Borrowing

Profits and income can be taxed, spent, or saved. For most people, taxes are taken out first, and the remainder is used for consumer or business expenditures. If any funds remain after expenditures, they are saved or invested, which is a form of saving.

Sometimes people spend more than they earn and need to borrow to cover the excess spending. Where do the funds come from when people borrow? (Answer: from someone else's savings.) If all income were taxed or spent, there wouldn't be any savings left over to borrow, and it would be impossible to obtain a loan. Thus, all private funds for loans, including real estate loans, can be traced back to some form of savings. These savings can come from both domestic and foreign sources. With this background, turn your attention to the characteristics of institutional real estate lenders.

Commercial Banks

Commercial banks operate under a license or charter from the state or federal government. As far as real estate loans are concerned, there is little difference between a state and a national bank.

In recent years, commercial banks have been a powerful source for home loans, whether for purchase or refinance. Commercial banks also specialize in short-term construction financing, where the builder or developer has a "take-out" commitment from some other lender—most often, an insurance company or a savings bank—for the permanent mortgage loan. Large commercial banks play a major role in financing business and commercial properties, whereas some smaller banks deal exclusively with home loans.

Bankers may make conventional real estate loans for up to 95 percent or more of appraised value and for as long as 30–50 years on single-family dwellings. Many banks require private mortgage insurance on loans whose loan-to-value ratio is in excess of 80 percent. Bankers are sometimes authorized to grant FHA-insured and VA-guaranteed loans. Bankers are active seekers of home improvement and home equity loans.

Savings Banks (Formerly Called Savings and Loans)

A **savings bank** is a financial institution that accepts savings from the public and invests these savings mainly in real estate trust deeds and mortgages. The majority of savings bank loans are in residential properties, mostly single-family dwellings. A savings bank is also classified as either a state-chartered or a federally chartered institution. As far as real estate lending is concerned, there is little difference.

Under certain conditions, up to 95 percent or more loan-to-value ratio loans are obtainable at some savings banks if the loans are covered by private mortgage insurance. Most savings banks limit their loans to 30 years. Their prime real estate loan is on owner-occupied dwellings. But in a favorable market, savings banks also grant mobile home loans and apartment loans. Also common are combination loans that unite home construction and long-term take-out financing in one package.

The Savings and Loan Crisis

What happened? Why was there a massive savings and loan crisis in the 1980s? Some blame the economic stimulus provisions in the Economic Recovery Act of 1981. In the act, savings and loans were allowed to compete with commercial banks in more risky ventures; previously, they were restricted to single-family residential loans. Then in 1986, significant changes were made to the tax code that took away many of the tax advantages or shelters associated with investment real estate and the deductibility of interest. As a result, investment properties lost value and borrowers, unable to cover their mortgage payments, walked away from their properties.

Life Insurance Companies

Life insurance companies are another important source for real estate financing, particularly for large commercial and industrial properties such as shopping centers, office buildings, and warehouses. Life insurance companies also provide a significant amount of money for new housing subdivisions. In general, life insurance companies have broad lending powers.

Loan-to-value ratios are usually on the conservative side, generally in the 60 to 75 percent range for conventional financing, commonly with 30-year terms. Historically, insurance companies have preferred to grant large commercial and industrial real estate loans, but only if they are occupied by owners and tenants who have excellent credit and good company balance sheets.

Loan correspondents, such as mortgage companies, are widely used as agents of insurance companies. In this way, the insurance company is relieved of the burden of originating and processing loans as well as the responsibility of some administrative and service functions.

9.3 NONINSTITUTIONAL LENDERS

Institutional lenders such as commercial banks, savings banks, and life insurance companies accept deposits from the general public and are highly regulated by state and federal agencies.

Noninstitutional lenders do not accept deposits from the general public and are not as strictly regulated as institutional lenders. Major noninstitutional lenders include mortgage companies, private parties, real estate investment trusts, credit unions, and pension funds.

Mortgage Companies

Mortgage companies are a major type of noninstitutional real estate lender. When a mortgage company represents a life insurance company, a commercial bank, a savings bank, or another lender, it is called a *mortgage or loan correspondent*. It "corresponds" on behalf of its principal(s) in dealing with prospective borrowers. The mortgage correspondent is paid a fee in exchange for originating, processing, closing, and servicing loans. A loan correspondent serves a valuable function in the field of real estate financing for lenders whose headquarters or principal offices are located great distances from the properties on which they make loans.

Rules Regarding Mortgage Companies

Mortgage companies that do not use their own funds are subject in their lending activities to the same restrictions that govern their principal(s). Thus, if a California mortgage correspondent or banker represents an eastern life insurance company, the correspondent would have the same loan-to-value limitations placed on its loans as the insurance company.

Mortgage companies have special restrictions placed upon them. In California, they must be licensed and state approved. Even though they may not be lending money belonging to third parties, they are subject to the Real Property Loan Law when they make loans that are not specifically exempt under that law. They are also subject to some lending and other business regulations.

Mortgage Banker Versus Mortgage Broker

A mortgage company could be a mortgage banker, a mortgage broker, or both. Mortgage bankers lend their own money and then either resell the loan to another lender or keep the loan for an investment. Mortgage brokers do not lend their own money; rather, they find a lender and a borrower and get a fee for bringing them together.

Major Player

Mortgage companies have become a dominant force in the California real estate market. In some areas, mortgage companies place more home loans than do institutional lenders. Many traditional real estate brokerage offices have added a mortgage brokerage division to give buyers a "one-stop shopping" option of buying and financing a purchase at the same office.

The Financial Crisis of 2008

One might have thought lenders would have learned their lesson in the early 1990s. But as real estate prices began soaring in 2002, fueled by low interest rates and increasing demand, lenders again began making risky loans. These loans were based on the "stated income" (without any documentation) of the borrower and provided straight or "interest-only" junior loans to achieve 100 percent financing without any type of mortgage insurance. As the market continued to heat up, lenders in increasing competition with each other began extending financing to borrowers with lower credit scores.

When the market began to slow down due to rising interest rates, borrowers unable to meet the interest rate adjustments on their adjustable rate loans began defaulting. This time, not only were commercial banks and savings banks caught off-guard, but also insurance companies, investment banks, and pension funds saw their investments in mortgage-backed securities lose value.

Far more extensive than the recession of the early 1990s, in 2008 Wall Street investment firms saw their portfolios filled with mortgage investments drop in value as much as 50 percent. As the economy entered 2010, a stabilization of the real estate market began, but with a continuance of borrower defaults and a flat real estate market, most economists predicted a slow economic recovery.

New Regulations for Mortgage Companies

As a result of the financial crisis of 2008, Congress enacted the Secure and Fair Enforcement for Mortgage Licensing (SAFE) Act on July 30, 2008, which requires the federal registration of all mortgage lenders, brokers, branches, and mortgage loan originators (MLOs) making loans secured by real estate. Implemented in California by SB 36, mortgage brokers are now required to obtain an MLO endorsement from the California Bureau of Real Estate to do loans in California.

The SAFE Act is designed to enhance consumer protection and reduce fraud through the setting of minimum standards for the licensing and registration of state-licensed mortgage loan originators. Additional educational requirements, licensing, and background checks will be required as these laws are implemented in 2010 for all real estate lenders, including mortgage brokers. Specifically, the licensing requirements include a 20-hour pre-licensing education course, which is to be completed through a Nationwide Mortgage Licensing System (NMLS) approved provider and contains the following:

- Three hours of federal law and regulations
- Three hours of ethics, including fraud, consumer protection, and fair lending issues
- Two hours of training related to lending standards for the nontraditional mortgage product marketplace

Upon completion of the pre-license course, all applicants must pass a national and state-specific exam. Real estate licensees acting as mortgage brokers who fail to obtain this endorsement will face fines of $50 a day up to a maximum fine of $10,000.

Private Lenders

Private lenders are individuals who invest their savings in real estate loans. Private individuals can invest directly by granting loans to borrowers, or they can invest indirectly by turning to mortgage brokers who find borrowers for the private lender. Sellers frequently become private lenders when they carry back deeds of trust in order to facilitate the sale of their property.

The prime motivation of private lenders is to earn a high yield, with some degree of safety. Some private lenders become investors by entering into partnership with young home buyers in equity-share programs for the purchasing and financing of homes.

On seller carry loans on one to four residential units, a *seller financial disclosure statement* (see CAR Form: Seller Financing Addendum and Disclosure) is required. This disclosure statement gives the buyer-borrower and the seller-lender an extensive breakdown of the major financial terms in the seller carry loan. Most real estate brokers have preprinted forms that satisfy this disclosure requirement.

Characteristics of Private Lenders

Private lenders generally share common characteristics, regardless of whether the loan is made directly by the individual or indirectly through a loan broker:

1. Most private lenders operate in the second deeds of trust market. Frequently, these loans are seller carry-back seconds that, thereafter, are sold to investors, usually at a discount, when the seller needs cash.

2. Most loans are on single-family homes and condos because this type of property is most familiar to the typical private investor and because the size of the loan is usually small.

3. The term of a private loan is usually short and often calls for a balloon payment. Three to six years are the most common maturities.

Real Estate Investment Trusts

The **real estate investment trust (REIT)** is a creature of the federal tax law. It was created in 1960 with the goal of encouraging small investors to pool their resources with others in order to raise venture capital for real estate transactions. It has been called the "mutual funds" of the real estate business. Just as mutual funds invest in a diversified portfolio of corporate stocks and bonds, REITs invest in a diversified portfolio of real estate and mortgage investments. Some examples of REIT's are shopping malls, office buildings, hotels, and medical facilities.

To qualify as a trust, there are many tests that must be met, such as the requirement that at least 95 percent of the REIT's net income be distributed annually to the investors to qualify for favorable tax treatment. The legal ramifications of REITs are beyond the scope of this course; anyone interested in forming or participating in REITs should seek legal counsel.

Credit Unions

A **credit union** is a mutual, voluntary-membership, cooperative organization of people who agree to save their money together to provide money for loans to each other. There are many credit unions throughout the United States, and their numbers are growing rapidly. For the most part, credit union lending in the field of real estate has been short term, but law changes now allow long-term real estate loans.

Syndicates, pension funds, trust funds, and various types of endowment funds are also noninstitutional real estate lenders. However, their lending practices are beyond the scope of this course.

Special Interest Topic

Investing in Trust Deeds

TRUST DEEDS

Some private investors prefer to purchase existing notes and deeds of trust instead of granting a loan directly to a borrower. These investors search for a sale where the seller carries back the paper. They then attempt to purchase existing seller carry loans at a discount. Many times the seller is willing to sell the note for cash rather than wait several years for the buyer to pay off the loan.

The investor usually buys the note at a discount, which increases the investor's yield to a rate higher than the amount of interest on the face of the note. The size of the discount varies with the quality of the borrowers, the equity in the property, and current money market conditions. Some mortgage brokers earn commissions by bringing buyers and sellers of notes together.

Here are two legal terms regarding the selling of existing notes and trust deeds:

1. *Negotiable instrument.* This is a promissory note that is a written promise or order to pay an amount of money at a definite time or on demand. Negotiable instruments are allowed to be freely sold.

2. *Holder in due course.* This is a person who in good faith has purchased a note for value without any knowledge about defects or past due payments. A person who purchased a note as a holder in due course has some superior rights if the borrower on the note refuses to pay based on certain disputes with the former owner of the note.

9.4 PRIVATE MORTGAGE INSURANCE

What is **private mortgage insurance (PMI)**? It is insurance that is used to guarantee lenders the payment of the upper portion of a conventional loan if a borrower defaults and a deficiency occurs at the foreclosure sale. Private mortgage insurance, formerly called *mortgage guaranty* *insurance,* is sold by private insurance companies, and in the lending business it is referred to as *PMI.*

The private mortgage system stimulates the housing market by allowing buyers with smaller down payments to qualify for a loan. Lenders who normally want buyer-borrowers to have a LTV of 80% will allow qualified buyer-borrowers to put less down and have a higher LTV if they purchase private mortgage insurance.

Coverage and Cost of Private Mortgage Insurance

Private mortgage insurance is available on one- to four-unit dwellings. It generally covers the top 20 to 25 percent of the loan amount based on the value of the property. For example, if a condo sold for $380,000 and the loan was 90 percent, the loan would be $380,000 × 90% = $342,000. The private mortgage insurance coverage to the lender would be 20% × $342,000 loan = $68,400.

The initial insurance premium fee varies with PMI companies, but it is usually paid by the borrower. In addition, an annual premium that is divided by 12 is added to the borrower's monthly payment. There are also plans whereby you can pay one fee at the time of closing and no annual premium. Recent laws allow the borrower to cancel the PMI once the homeowner achieves 20 percent or more equity.

Chapter Summary, Part I

Real estate lenders are concerned about a borrower's ability to repay a loan. To screen loan applicants, lenders use qualifying ratios coupled with an examination of the borrower's credit history and net worth.

Real estate lenders can be divided into three categories: (1) institutional lenders, (2) noninstitutional lenders, and (3) government-backed programs. Institutional real estate lenders are commercial banks, savings banks (savings and loan associations), and life insurance companies.

Noninstitutional real estate lenders include mortgage companies, private lenders, REITs, credit unions, and pension funds. The main government-backed programs include FHA, VA, and Cal-Vet.

Private mortgage insurance (PMI) is used to guarantee a lender the payment of the upper portion of a loan if a borrower should default and a foreclosure sale does not generate enough money to cover the loan. PMI allows lenders to grant higher loans, thereby requiring less for a down payment.

Important Terms and Concepts

commercial banks

credit union

institutional lenders

life insurance companies

mortgage bankers

mortgage brokers

mortgage companies

noninstitutional lenders

private lenders

private mortgage insurance (PMI)

real estate investment trust (REIT)

savings bank

Practical Application

1. A borrower earns $5,000 gross income per month and has $600 in long-term monthly debts. The lender's maximum qualifying ratios are 28 and 36 percent. Assuming good credit, what is the maximum monthly housing payment this borrower is qualified to pay?

2. Buyers make $85,000 per year gross. Their recurring debts total $1,050 monthly. They are applying for a conventional loan for 30 years at 6.5%. What maximum payment (PITI) do they qualify for?

3. Stories have surfaced about borrowers being overcharged for their PMI coverage. A recent law requires PMI insurers to cancel the PMI coverage once a loan amount is reduced to 80 percent or less of the value of the home. Assume that a loan balance is $180,000 and represents 80 percent or less of the value of the condo. If the annual PMI charge is .0025 of the loan amount (.25 of one percent), how much will a borrower's loan payment be reduced by canceling the PMI?

Reviewing Your Understanding

1. Which of the following is an institutional lender?

   a. Credit union

   b. Mortgage company

   c. Life insurance company

   d. Pension fund

2. The three major credit reporting agencies are:

   a. Experian, TRW, and Equifax.

   b. Experian, Equifax, and TransUnion.

   c. TRW, Equifax, and FICO.

   d. Equifax, Experian, and Franklin.

3. A seller financial disclosure statement must be signed by:
   a. the buyer.
   b. the seller.
   c. the broker.
   d. all of the above.

4. The ultimate source of all loan funds is:
   a. taxes.
   b. government spending.
   c. transfer payments.
   d. savings.

5. Real estate investment trusts (also known as REITs):
   a. were created to encourage small investors to invest in real estate transactions with other small investors.
   b. operate in the second deed of trust market.
   c. are usually a two-year loan.
   d. invest in savings banks.

6. Traditionally, the total monthly expenses should not exceed _____ of the borrower's gross monthly income.
   a. 33 percent to 38 percent
   b. 33 percent to 36 percent
   c. 28 percent to 30 percent
   d. 25 percent to 30 percent

7. Which of the following are major types of California lenders?
   a. Commercial banks
   b. Savings banks
   c. Life insurance companies
   d. All of the above

8. Who does not lend their money, but instead earns a fee for bringing a borrower and lender together?
   a. Mortgage banker
   b. Mortgage broker
   c. Mortgage consultant
   d. Mortgage investor

9. A borrower has monthly income of $1,400 and expenses of $448 what is the expense ratio for the borrower?
   a. 36%
   b. 32%
   c. 28%
   d. 3%

10. For an REIT to avoid double taxation, it must distribute what percentage of its income each year to the shareholders/investors?
   a. 85 percent
   b. 90 percent
   c. 95 percent
   d. 100 percent

STUDENT LEARNING OUTCOMES PART II

Part II of this chapter focuses on specific government programs designed to help people acquire their own home. Three programs presented in detail are the Federal Housing Administration (FHA), Department of Veterans Affairs (VA), and California Department of Veterans Affairs (Cal-Vet) programs. In addition, the purpose and function of the secondary mortgage market are discussed. At the conclusion of Part II, you will be able to do the following:

- List the advantages of FHA-insured loans.
- Describe the disadvantages of VA-guaranteed loans.
- Explain who is eligible for Cal-Vet loans.
- Define the secondary mortgage market and discuss the role played by government agencies in this market.

PART II: FHA, VA, AND CAL-VET LOANS AND THE SECONDARY MORTGAGE MARKET

9.5 GOVERNMENT ROLE IN REAL ESTATE FINANCING

The government has become heavily involved in helping consumers acquire decent housing. There are many government housing programs, but in this text, only FHA-insured, VA-guaranteed, Cal-Vet loan, and CalHFA programs are discussed.

Federal Housing Administration (FHA)

The Federal Housing Administration (FHA), a part of the Department of Housing and Urban Development (HUD), was established in 1934 to improve the construction and financing of housing. Since its creation, the FHA has had a major influence on real estate financing. Some of today's loan features that are taken for granted were initiated by the FHA.

The FHA is not a lender; *it does not make loans*. Approved lenders such as mortgage companies, insurance companies, and banks make the loans. However, the loans must be granted under FHA guidelines. Once the loan is granted, if the borrower defaults on the loan, the FHA insures the lender against foreclosure loss.

The FHA collects a fee for this insurance, which is called the *Mortgage Insurance Premium (MIP)*. The MIP fees are paid up front in cash or financed as part of the loan. MIP premiums are used to protect the lender against loss in the event of foreclosure.

This insurance should not be confused with credit life insurance. An FHA mortgage insurance policy does not insure the borrower's life. A mortgage insurance policy is used by the FHA to reimburse a lender if the borrower defaults on mortgage payments and the foreclosure results in a loss for the insured lender.

Advantages of FHA Loans

1. *Low down payment.* The main advantage of an FHA-insured loan is the low down payment. It used to be that FHA interest rates were

set below the conventional rates. But deregulation now allows the FHA interest rate to float with the market. Therefore, sellers are no longer required to pay discount points to increase the lender's yield. Any loan fees or points charged by the lender are an item of negotiation and can be paid by the buyer or the seller.

2. *No prepayment penalty.* An FHA-insured loan does not allow a prepayment penalty.

3. *Under some circumstances, FHA-insured loans are assumable.* FHA-insured loans do not allow alienation clauses (due-on-sale clauses). This makes it possible to buy property and, with FHA approval, take over the seller's existing FHA-insured loan. At one time, all FHA-insured loans were assumable without requiring a credit and/or income check. But beginning with FHA-insured loans originating as of December 15, 1989, all assumptions must be approved by the FHA. In addition, non-owner-occupied assumptions are prohibited on FHA-insured loans as of the same date.

4. *All cash to the seller.* New FHA-insured loans cash out the seller. In a down real estate market, many sellers may need to carry a second, also known as a piggyback loan which is a combination of two loans that close at the same time to purchase a home to help finance a conventional loan for a buyer. Under FHA terms, the high loan-to-value ratio gives the seller all cash.

5. *Minimum property standards.* FHA will not allow a lender to grant a loan unless the property meets FHA housing standards, which, in some cases, are more stringent than what some conventional lenders allow.

Disadvantages of FHA Loans

1. *Low loan amounts.* As a result of high home prices in many areas of California, the FHA program is often not practical because of the cap the FHA sets on its maximum loan amount allowed. (See "How to Calculate FHA-Insured Loan Amounts.")

2. *Red tape and processing time.* The FHA is a large federal agency; therefore, the problem of dealing with a bureaucracy becomes an issue. However, some FHA-insured lenders have preapproval rights that can speed up the FHA process.

3. *Repairs on existing property.* The FHA-appointed appraiser also checks for repairs that he or she believes are necessary. The FHA then requires that these repairs be made before the property is approved. Sellers may not wish to make these repairs and may refuse to sell to an FHA-insured buyer.

Federal Housing Administration Programs

Here are some general rules that apply to all FHA homeowner programs:

1. FHA will approve loans on owner-occupied 1- to 4-unit residential dwellings, planned unit developments (PUDs), condominiums, and mobile homes.

2. The maximum loan fee is 1 percent of the loan amount, and the buyer normally pays this fee.

3. The Mortgage Insurance Premium upfront fees vary by program and are based on the outstanding principal balance.

4. The maximum loan term is 30 years or three-quarters of the remaining economic life of the property, whichever is less.

5. The FHA requires that monthly payments include principal, interest, and one-twelfth of the annual property taxes, hazard insurance premium, and Mortgage Insurance Premium.

6. There is no maximum purchase price. The buyer can pay more than the FHA appraisal. The loan is based on whichever is lower: the appraisal or the sales price.

7. The interest rates on FHA-backed loans now float with the market instead of being fixed by the FHA.

8. FHA appraisals are good for six months on existing property and one year on new construction.

How to Calculate FHA-Insured Loan Amounts (As of 2014)

FHA calculates the loan amount based on the home's sales price or the FHA-approved appraisal, whichever is less.

As of 2014, the maximum loan amount was set at 96.5 percent (or a three and a half percent down payment). FHA then sets a ceiling on the maximum loan allowed based on the median home prices in various geographic areas. The dollar amounts can change each year depending on the trend in home prices. Of California's 58 counties, the following 15 counties are considered especially high-cost areas and are allowed the largest FHA loan amounts in the continental United States: Alameda, Contra Costa, Los Angeles, Marin, Monterey, Orange, San Diego, San Francisco, San Joaquin, San Mateo, Santa Barbara, Santa Clara, Santa Cruz, Sonoma, and Ventura counties. In the remaining 43 California counties, the maximum FHA loan amounts are less. Dollar amounts are not quoted here because they vary among California counties. For the maximum FHA-approved loan amount for your area, contact any local FHA-approved lender.

You can also access HUD's website at www.hud.gov and get the latest quote for your county.

Required Cash Investment

The FHA requires a minimum three and a half percent cash investment based on the sales price or appraisal, whichever is less. This three and a half percent cash investment can come from an approved gift and need not be the FHA buyer's own personal money (larger down payments may be required for borrowers with low credit scores).

Therefore, with a three and a half percent required cash investment, the buyer will be paying for some of the closing costs. If the buyer pays no more than the required three and a half percent cash investment, the remaining closing costs, after applying the three and a half percent rule, must be paid by the seller or some other party. The buyer can finance the required MIP by increasing the loan amount.

Under previous FHA rules, only the seller, not the buyer, must pay for the following closing costs: tax service fee, loan document fee, processing fee, flood certification fee, and termite costs, if any.

Currently, the payment of nonrecurring closing costs is negotiable between the seller and the buyer. See Chapter 11, "The Role of Escrow and Title Insurance Companies," for a complete discussion of the difference between recurring and nonrecurring closing costs.

FHA Programs

The National Housing Act of 1934 created the Federal Housing Administration. The act has 11 subdivisions, or "Titles," with further subdivisions called "Sections." This chapter deals only with Section 203b because this is the most important section for the average homebuyer or real estate agent.

Section 203b

Under the **FHA 203b program**:

1. Anyone who is financially qualified is eligible.
2. Loans are available on properties from one to four units.
3. The maximum FHA loan amounts vary from county to county, with high-cost areas of California allowed larger loan amounts than lower-cost areas within the state.
4. Although a buyer's credit history is important, it does not need to be perfect.

5. The buyer must make a minimum cash investment of Three and a half percent, but this can come from an approved gift from family members and certain nonprofit groups.

6. The Mortgage Insurance Premium (MIP) must be obtained and can be purchased up front or financed as part of the loan. The MIP added to the loan is allowed to exceed maximum FHA loan limits.

7. FHA permits a borrower to carry more debt than most conventional lenders will allow.

Example: A buyer wishes to purchase a small condo under the FHA 203b program. The buyer agrees to pay $230,000, and the FHA-approved appraisal comes in at $232,000. What is the maximum FHA loan amount? What is the minimum cash the buyer must invest?

Step 1: The lesser of the price or appraisal is $230,000 × 96.5% = $221,950, or the maximum loan for the area, whichever is less, plus any amount for the MIP.

Step 2: The lesser of the price or appraisal is $230,000 × 3.5% = $8,050, minimum cash investment required from the buyer. If more cash is needed to pay for closing costs, the buyer can add more money or the seller or some other party can agree to pay the remaining costs. This will be determined on a case-by-case basis.

Department of Veterans Affairs (VA or G.I.) Loans

In 1944, Congress passed the G.I. Bill of Rights to provide benefits to veterans, including provisions for making real estate loans.

Like the FHA, the VA is not a lender. However, if no approved private lender is located in the area, the VA will make direct loans under certain conditions. One difference between the FHA and the VA is that the **Department of Veterans Affairs (VA)** *guarantees* a portion of the loan, while the Federal Housing Administration *insures* the loan.

The VA guaranteed amount is calculated as 25 percent of the current Federal Home Loan Mortgage Corporation (Freddie Mac) conforming loan amount. Each year, if the Freddie Mac conforming loan amount increases, the VA guarantee to an approved lender also increases. For example, as of February, 2014 the maximum Freddie Mac conforming loan was $417,000; thus, 25% × $417,000 = $104,250 was the maximum VA lender guarantee.

Then, most VA-approved lenders simply reverse the process and will grant a no-money-down loan to qualified veterans that is four times the VA guarantee. For 2014, this would be the $104,250 guarantee divided by .25 = $417,000 maximum no-down-payment VA-guaranteed loan. The bottom line is that the maximum VA no-money-down loan amount is usually the same as the maximum Freddie Mac conforming loan amount.

As of 2014, VA limits were increased based on property values in the county where the property is located. Since these limits change, you are encouraged to go to the Department of Veterans Affairs website at www.homeloans.va.gov to get the latest quote for your county.

Whether a loan is insured or guaranteed is important only if a foreclosure occurs. If a foreclosure does occur, the VA has two options:

1. It can pay the lender the loan balance and take over the property.

2. It can give the lender the property and pay it the amount of the deficiency, if any, up to the maximum amount of the VA guarantee.

However, if a foreclosure occurs under the FHA program, the lender is paid off and the property is taken over by the FHA.

Advantages and Disadvantages of VA (G.I.) Loans

Advantages of VA Loans

1. *No down payment 100% LTV.* The VA does not require a borrower to make any down payment on loans up to the current maximum loan amount if the borrower pays the VA-appraised value for the property. *Caution:* VA no-down loan amounts can change. Access the VA's website at www.homeloans.va.gov for the latest loan amounts.

2. *No private mortgage insurance*

3. *No prepayment penalty.*

4. *Creditworthiness qualification for assumptions.* VA loans are assumable, with qualifications, by the buyer. This allows the buyer to take over the loan and not pay the costs of obtaining a new loan.

Disadvantages of VA Loans

1. *Seller may need to pay discount points.* The VA point system is explained later.

2. *Red tape and processing time.* Processing time, inflexibility, and paperwork occasionally are problems in dealing with a large government agency.

3. *Loans can only be obtained by qualified veterans.*

Who Is Eligible for VA Loans?

To be eligible, a veteran must have a discharge or release that is not dishonorable. The veteran must have served a minimum number of days depending on the qualifying wartime and peacetime periods and qualifying active duty dates in the military. The National Guard and other military reserves who served at least six years are eligible. Also eligible is the spouse of a service member who died while serving or from a service-connected disability.

Those who served less than the required time but were released or discharged because of a service-connected disability are also eligible for VA loans. In addition, many other classifications of veterans are eligible for a VA-guaranteed loan depending on the circumstances. Also, a veteran can use his or her VA loan more than once, provided that the prior VA loan has been paid in full.

General Information on VA Loans

1. *Type of property.* The VA will guarantee loans on properties of one to four units, planned unit developments (PUDs), condominiums, and mobile homes.

2. *Interest rate.* Within VA guidelines, the interest rate is negotiable between the veteran and the lender.

3. *Loan fee.* The amount of the loan origination fee paid by the borrower is negotiable. Prior to a 1993 law change, the loan fee could be only 1 percent of the loan amount.

4. *Funding fee.* A separate fee on top of the loan fee is paid by the borrower for granting the loan. This fund fee usually varies from two to 3.three percent of the loan amount. The funding fee can be financed by adding it to the loan amount.

5. *Term of loan.* The maximum term is 30 years.

6. *Down payment.* The VA does not require a down payment on loans up to current designed amounts. The veteran is frequently allowed to borrow the full amount of the purchase price. What happens if the VA appraisal is less than the purchase price? The loan amount cannot exceed the appraisal. The difference between the purchase price and the appraisal must be paid by the borrower in cash.

7. *Maximum loan.* There is no maximum loan amount on a VA loan. This does not mean you can obtain a no-down-payment VA loan in any amount. Since the VA guarantees only a portion of the loan, lenders limit the amount they will lend on VA loans. Many lenders will not lend more than four times the guarantee.

8. *Occupying the property*. The veteran must occupy the property; if purchasing a multi-unit the veteran must live in one of the units.

9. *Monthly payments*. Included are principal, interest, and one-twelfth the annual property taxes and hazard insurance premiums.

10. *Appraisal*. The VA appraisal is called the *certificate of reasonable value (CRV)*. To the VA, *reasonable value* means current market value.

11. *Structural pest control report*. The VA requires that a report be obtained from a licensed structural pest control company. Any required work must be done, and the veteran must certify that the work has been done satisfactorily.

Calculating Discount Points for VA Loans

Under VA terms, a lender and the veteran negotiate the interest rate. If this negotiated rate is not sufficient to cope with today's cost of overhead and profit, a lender simply refuses to grant a loan under VA terms. This may cause the sale to fall through. Under these circumstances, a motivated seller might be willing to pay a discount fee to increase the lender's yield, thereby encouraging the lender to grant a VA loan and allow the sale to close.

> **Example:** Assume the home sales price and appraisal both are $333,700 and the maximum VA-guaranteed loan available is $333,700. Also assume the negotiated VA interest rate the veteran qualifies for is four percent, but lenders can get five percent interest on government-backed real estate loans. To entice the lender to make the VA-backed loan at four percent, the seller agrees to pay discount points to make up the difference.

As a rule of thumb, points are calculated as follows: each one percent of discount (one point) is equal to one-sixth of one percent interest. For a lender to increase the yield on a loan by one percent, the lender must charge four percent, or four points, of the loan amount, which is deducted from the seller's net proceeds from the sale. The seller agreed in the purchase contract to pay this cost for the buyer's loan.

Thus, in the following example:

$$5\% - 4\% = 1\% = 4/4 = 4 \text{ points or } .04 \text{ of the loan amount}$$

Therefore:

$$\text{\$333,700 loan amount} \times .04 = \text{\$13,348, which is the}$$
discount fee the seller must pay the lender up front
from the seller's sale proceeds

The one percent difference in the previous example is used for simplicity's sake to explain VA discount points. In the real world, the interest rate spread between the VA and conventional rate may be only one-eighth percent to one-quarter percent, resulting in only one to two discount points to be paid by the seller.

In an active market, where there are numerous buyers, sellers are reluctant to sell to VA buyers who require the payment of discount points. But in a slow market, a seller may be more than willing to pay discount points just to get rid of the property.

Cal-Vet Loans

The **Cal-Vet loans** program is administered by the State of California, Department of Veterans Affairs, Division of Farms and Home Purchases. The veteran (buyer) normally deals directly with this agency, although recent rules allow a mortgage loan broker to start the loan process on behalf of the buyer. No other lender is involved; the state makes the loan to the veteran directly. The money is obtained from the sale of State Veteran Bonds.

Who Is Eligible for Cal-Vet Loans?

To qualify, a veteran must meet these requirements:

1. Have had 90 days' active duty.
2. Have been given an honorable discharge or, if still on active duty, a *Statement of Service* verifying his or her status. Generally, a medical discharge is acceptable if it was a service-connected disability. In addition, "Under Honorable Terms" is usually acceptable but the VA should be called for clarification.
3. Be willing to buy a California home or farm as his or her primary residence, owner occupied.

Both peacetime and wartime veterans are eligible for a Cal-Vet loan. But if loan funds are limited, a preference is given to wartime veterans. The highest priority is given to war veterans with a service-connected disability. Surviving spouses or registered domestic partners of an eligible veteran, who have not remarried, may also be qualified for a Cal-Vet loan. A Cal-Vet loan may be used more than once, as long as the previous Cal-Vet loan has been paid in full or awarded in a divorce to a nonveteran spouse.

General Information About Cal-Vet Loans

1. *Property.* Cal-Vet has generally the same property standards as FHA and VA. The property must be a single-family dwelling or a unit in a PUD, condominium, or mobile home. Certain farm loans are also approved. Cal-Vet requires both a structural pest control report and a roof inspection.

2. *Maximum loan.* The maximum Cal-Vet loan amounts can vary each year. There are separate maximums for single-family dwellings, farms, and mobile homes. To find the current maximum for each, go to the Cal-Vet website (www.cdva.ca.gov).

3. *Down payment and loan fees.* Cal-Vet loans guaranteed by the VA are called *Cal-Vet/VA loans* and are available for no money down up to the current maximum VA-guaranteed loan, which is usually four times the maximum VA guarantee (discussed earlier in the chapter). On straight Cal-Vet loans, without the VA guarantee, the down payment is usually two to three percent of the purchase price or appraised value, whichever is the lesser.

4. *Term of loan.* Most loans are approved for a term of 30 years.

5. *Interest rate.* The interest rate is variable. The rate is checked periodically to determine whether a change is necessary. The costs of the bonds and of running the program determine the interest rate.

6. *Secondary financing.* This is permitted under special circumstances. However, the provisions are too complex to be covered in this text.

7. *No prepayment penalty.* There is no penalty to pay off a Cal-Vet Loan early.

8. *Occupancy.* The veteran must occupy the property.

9. *Monthly payments.* Principal, interest, and one-twelfth the annual property taxes, hazard insurance, disability, and life insurance premiums are included in monthly loan payments.

10. *Title to property.* When a property is being financed with a regular Cal-Vet loan, title is first conveyed to the Department of Veterans Affairs by the seller. The department then sells the property to the veteran under an installment land contract. The department continues to hold title until the veteran has paid the loan in full.

Advantages and Disadvantages of Cal-Vet Loans

The main advantages of Cal-Vet loans are low interest rate, inexpensive life and hazard insurance, and low closing costs. In the past, the main disadvantage was the long time it took to process a Cal-Vet loan. But recent changes by the California Department of Veterans Affairs have attempted to address this issue. Cal-Vet now has several district offices throughout the state with trained personnel to provide the latest information and the help needed to prepare the required forms for faster loan processing. In addition, many mortgage brokers have completed Cal-Vet loan-processing seminars and are equipped to help a veteran process a loan. If a private mortgage loan broker is used, the seller and buyer must pay the broker's fee; it cannot be financed as part of a Cal-Vet loan. For more information, the website is www.cdva.ca.gov.

See Table 9.1 for a comparison of the government programs designed for obtaining loans.

9.6 THE CALIFORNIA HOUSING FINANCE AGENCY (CalHFA) PROGRAM

The **CalHFA** program is designed to help first-time homebuyers acquire a home in California's expensive housing market. This state agency sells mortgage revenue bonds to investors, and then uses the funds to buy loans from approved lenders who make loans under CalHFA guidelines. Thus, like FHA and VA, CalHFA does not make loans directly to borrowers. Instead, this state agency purchases the loans

TABLE 9.1　Comparison of Government-Backed Loans (excluding CalHFA) as of July 2006.

	Federal Housing Administration (FHA)	Department of Veterans Affairs (VA)	Cal-Vet
Purpose of loan	1–4 units	1–4 units	Home or farm
Eligibility	Any U.S. resident	U.S. veteran	U.S. veteran
Maximum purchase price	None	None	None
Maximum loan	Varies by geographic area	None by the VA, but the VA restricts the guarantee	Varies each year
Down payment	3.5% minimum cash investment	None, but loan limited to the CRV	2% or 3% of sale price or appraisal, whichever is less
Maximum term	Usually 30 years	Usually 30 years	Usually 30 years
Interest rate	Market rate	Negotiated rate	Variable rate
Prepayment penalty	None	None	None

Source: © 2015 OnCourse Learning

made by approved lenders. CalHFA prides itself on not using state funds and taxpayer dollars to operate its program. Full details regarding CalHFA can be found at (www.calhfa.ca.gov).

Two Main Programs

CalHFA offers a 30-year fixed-rate conventional loan program and what it calls an interest-only PLUS plan.

30-Year, Fixed-Rate Conventional Loan Program

This program features a below-market fixed interest rate amortized for 30 years and a maximum loan-to-value ratio of 100 percent. In special circumstances, the loan can be as high as a 110 percent loan-to-value ratio. The loan origination fee cannot exceed one and a half percent of the loan amount. Mortgage insurance is required, and CalHFA provides this coverage at a very low fee.

Property Eligibility: The property must meet all of the following requirements:

1. Sales price of the home cannot exceed CalHFA price limits. Said price limits vary by county. See the CalHFA website for your area.
2. It must be an owner-occupied, single-family, one-unit home, condo, or PUD.
3. Manufactured homes are allowed if they meet CalHFA construction standards.

Borrower Eligibility: The borrower must meet the following requirements:

1. Be a U.S. citizen, permanent resident, or qualified alien.
2. Be a first-time homebuyer, unless the home is located in a federally designated *targeted area* that is deemed to need an infusion of investment.
3. Occupy the home as a principal or primary residence; non-owner-occupied loans are not allowed.
4. Meet credit, income limits, and loan requirements of CalHFA lender and mortgage insurer.
5. CalHFA borrowers must complete "homebuyer education counseling" and obtain a certificate of completion through an eligible counseling organization.

There are certain special circumstances in which homes or borrowers may still qualify even if they cannot quite meet all the requirements listed above. See the CalHFA website for additional details.

Interest-Only PLUS Program

This CalHFA plan features a conventional loan with a below-market fixed interest rate, a 35-year term, and interest-only payments for the first five years. Then the payments switch to an amortized loan for the remaining 30 years. The interest rate remains fixed for the entire 35-year term. The loan- to-value ratio is 100 percent, rising to 110 percent under special circumstances. Mortgage insurance is required and is provided by CalHFA at very low rates. The property and borrower eligibility requirements are identical to the ones listed above under the 30-year fixed-rate program.

For more information about this first-time homebuyer program, contact CalHFA at (www.calhfa.ca.gov).

9.7 SECONDARY MORTGAGE MARKET

The **secondary mortgage market** is a market where existing real estate loans are bought and sold—in other words, lenders sell their loans to other lenders and investors. The secondary mortgage market should not be confused with secondary financing. Secondary financing is a loan secured by a second or junior deed of trust, whereas a secondary market is the sale of an existing loan by one lender to another lender or investor. (See Figure 9.2.)

Purpose of the Secondary Mortgage Market

Flow of Money

Why do lenders need a secondary mortgage market? Why don't they just make a loan and keep it? That would be fine if every lender always had a perfect balance between the demand for loans and its supply of money. However, in the real world, this balance rarely exists. For example, a lender in California may have a greater demand for loans than it can meet. Another lender in Texas might have the opposite

FIGURE 9.2

SECONDARY MARKET

Source: © 2015 OnCourse Learning

problem—surplus funds because of lack of demand in Texas. The solution to this problem is to have the Texas lender buy loans from the California lender. Both would be satisfying their needs. The Texas lender would be putting idle money to work, and the California lender would obtain additional funds to use to make new loans. Thus, one of the main purposes of the secondary market is to shift mortgage funds to areas where they are needed.

Generate New Loan Fees

A second reason why lenders resell their loans in the secondary market is to generate loan and collection fees. When a lender grants a loan, the lender generates a loan fee.

Some lenders prefer to sell a recently granted loan quickly to reinvest the proceeds into another new loan and generate a new loan fee (and so on). In addition, when a lender sells a loan, the purchaser of the loan may ask the original lender to continue to collect the loan payments and forward said payments to the purchaser. The original lender is paid a collection fee for this service.

Stabilize the Mortgage Market

The mortgage market is never static. Instead, it moves through cycles of tight and loose money. The market can be stabilized by providing funds to buy loans during tight money periods and providing loans to be purchased during loose money periods. Three main organizations are designed to help stabilize the mortgage market:

1. Federal National Mortgage Association
2. Federal Home Loan Mortgage Corporation
3. Government National Mortgage Association

Federal National Mortgage Association

The **Federal National Mortgage Association (Fannie Mae)** is usually called by its nickname. Established in 1938 by the U.S. Congress, its main job is to provide a secondary market for mortgages. Fannie Mae remained a part of the federal government until 1968, when it became a private corporation. Its main function today is still to maintain a secondary market.

To maintain a secondary market, Fannie Mae buys and sells mortgages. Where does it get the money to do this? It borrows money in the capital market by selling notes and bonds. Fannie Mae can usually obtain a more favorable rate than another corporate borrower because its obligations carry the indirect backing of the U.S. government.

What type of loans can Fannie Mae buy and sell? Fannie Mae can purchase government-backed and conventional loans on one- to four-unit dwellings, units in PUDs, and condominiums. Fannie Mae buys conventional loans only if the loans have been issued using Fannie Mae guidelines. Once purchased, the loans are either held as an investment or resold to other lenders and investors.

For more consumer information about Fannie Mae, access its website at www.fanniemaefoundation.org.

Federal Home Loan Mortgage Corporation

The **Federal Home Loan Mortgage Corporation (Freddie Mac)** was created in 1970 under the Emergency Home Finance Act. The main function of Freddie Mac was to provide a secondary mortgage market for the savings and loan associations. However, today it also deals with other institutional lenders.

Freddie Mac buys FHA, VA, and conventional loans. It purchases conventional loans on one- to four-unit buildings, units in PUDs, and condominiums. Freddie Mac and Fannie Mae usually have identical loan applications, maximum loan amounts, appraisal standards, and borrower loan qualification guidelines. Freddie Mac is a government-chartered stockholder-owned corporation, and information on it and its programs can be found at www.freddiemac.com.

The Secondary Mortgage Market Financial Crisis

Due to the large number of foreclosures following the depreciating real estate market in 2008, the federal government took conservatorship over both Fannie Mae and Freddie Mac. In 2008, the U.S. Treasury advanced funds to Fannie Mae and Freddie Mac for the purpose of stabilizing the secondary mortgage market. In May 2013, Fannie Mae announced it would pay a dividend of $59.4 billion to the U.S. Treasury.

Government National Mortgage Association

The **Government National Mortgage Association (Ginnie Mae)** is a wholly owned corporation of the U.S. government. It was created in 1968, when Fannie Mae became a private corporation. At the time, Fannie Mae was relieved of two of its duties, which were given to Ginnie Mae. These were as follows:

1. The management and liquidation of certain mortgages previously acquired by the U.S. government

2. Special assistance functions, including the development of a mortgage-backed security program

By directly and indirectly providing low-interest-rate loans, Ginnie Mae encourages people to buy new homes. The increased demand for new homes results in more work and more jobs for the construction industry.

The real impact of Ginnie Mae is in its mortgage-backed security program. This program was established to attract additional money into the housing market. The mortgage-backed security was created to make investing in mortgages as simple as buying stocks and bonds. Under this mortgage program, an investor purchases a pool of mortgages and receives a certificate. There is no need to examine each mortgage. All the time-consuming paperwork is eliminated. Since Ginnie Mae is a federal corporation, its guarantee is backed by the "full faith and credit" of the U.S. government.

In short, the Ginnie Mae programs in the secondary mortgage market have added to the funds made available for real estate borrowers.

Special First-Time Homebuyer Programs

The Federal National Mortgage Association (Fannie Mae) has a first-time homebuyer program called the Community Home Buyer's Program. This program has lower down payment requirements and more generous qualifying ratios. See the Fannie Mae website noted above for more details.

Some local lenders, in an effort to place loans throughout the communities they serve, have their own first-time homebuyer programs.

Many of these lower-cost programs are for people who purchase in designated zip codes and U.S. census tracts.

Real Estate Loan Jargon

Real estate lenders speak a language of their own. Here are some key terms regarding real estate loans:

Conventional loans. Any non-government-backed loan

Conforming loans. Loans that meet the guidelines of Fannie Mae or Freddie Mac

Nonconforming loans. Loans that do not meet the guidelines of Fannie Mae or Freddie Mac

Jumbo loans. Loans that exceed the loan limits of Fannie Mae or Freddie Mac

Portfolio loans. Loans that will not be sold in the secondary mortgage market, but will be held by the lender as an investment

Chapter Summary, Part II

Government has taken an active role in the field of real estate finance. On the federal level, the Federal Housing Administration (FHA) has several programs. The 203b program is the most popular. The Department of Veterans Affairs (VA) has a no-down-payment program for qualified veterans. The state of California's Cal-Vet loan program has been a huge success, with demand usually exceeding the supply of loans available. The low interest rate paid by the California veteran is the main attraction.

The secondary mortgage market consists of real estate lenders who sell existing mortgages to other real estate lenders. The main purpose of the secondary mortgage market is to help strike a balance between the demand for real estate loans and the supply of money available for them. The Federal National Mortgage Association (Fannie Mae), the Federal Home Loan Mortgage Corporation (Freddie Mac), and the Government National Mortgage Association (Ginnie Mae) participate in this secondary mortgage market.

Important Terms and Concepts

CalHFA

Cal-Vet loans

Department of Veterans Affairs (VA)

Federal Home Loan Mortgage Corporation (Freddie Mac)

Federal Housing Administration (FHA)

Federal National Mortgage Association (Fannie Mae)

FHA 203b program

Government National Mortgage Association (Ginnie Mae)

secondary mortgage market

Practical Application

1. A buyer agrees to purchase an older studio condo using the FHA 203b program. The price and FHA-approved appraisal are both $150,000, and the seller agrees to pay all closing costs above the buyer's minimum cash investment. Based only on this information, how much cash is the buyer required to invest to close escrow?

2. Referring to question one, assume the buyer used the VA program and paid a 1 percent loan fee, plus a one and a half percent funding fee and $500 in other closing costs. Based only on this

information, how much cash does the buyer-veteran need to close escrow?

3. Referring to question one, assume the buyer used the Cal-Vet program and paid the two percent down payment and $700 in closing costs, with the seller agreeing to pay all other remaining costs. Based only on this information, how much cash does the buyer-veteran need to close escrow?

Reviewing Your Understanding

1. The CalHFA program:
   a. is a secondary mortgage market.
   b. is designed to help first-time homebuyers.
   c. is used as a last resort by lenders to make loans to borrowers with less than perfect credit.
   d. charges the least amount of money in closing costs compared to any other program.

2. A secondary mortgage market is where:
   a. existing lenders sell to other lenders and investors.
   b. a seller carries a junior trust deed.
   c. the supply of funds available for real estate loans is decreased.
   d. the Federal Reserve tightens mortgage interest rates.

3. Fannie Mae is the:
   a. Federal Home Loan Mortgage Corporation.
   b. Federal National Mortgage Association.
   c. Government National Mortgage Association.
   d. Federal Deposit Insurance Corporation.

4. Of the following government-backed loans, which usually has the lowest interest rate?
   a. FHA
   b. Cal-Vet
   c. Fannie Mae
   d. VA

5. Which organization requires a CRV appraisal before approving a loan?
   a. California Department of Veteran's Affairs
   b. Federal Housing Administration
   c. U.S. Department of Veterans Affairs
   d. Federal National Mortgage Association

6. Which of the following types of loans are made only to individuals who intend to occupy the property as a personal residence?
   a. VA
   b. Conventional
   c. Purchase money
   d. Jumbo

7. When a borrower pays mortgage insurance on an FHA loan, this type of insurance:

   a. protects the lender against a shortage in the event of a default.

   b. is an expense that is borne entirely by the lender.

   c. pays the borrower the loan balance in the event of a fire loss.

   d. prevents foreclosure in the event of the trustor's death.

8. Which program has the seller deed title to the government?

   a. VA

   b. Cal-Vet

   c. FHA

   d. FNMA

9. When the Department of Veterans Affairs "guarantees" a loan, it does so in order to protect the:

   a. lender.

   b. veteran.

   c. seller.

   d. assets of the Federal National Mortgage Association.

10. The VA will guarantee loans on:

    a. mobile homes.

    b. townhomes.

    c. both a and b.

    d. none of the above.

CASE STUDY—QUALIFYING FOR A HOME LOAN

As a general rule of thumb, there are ideally two percentages to be aware of: 28 percent and 36 percent.

1. No more than 28 percent of your gross monthly income should be used for your total monthly house payment, consisting of principal, interest, taxes, insurance, and (if need be) association dues and private mortgage insurance.

$$\frac{\text{Total monthly house payment}}{\text{Gross monthly income}} = \text{No more than 28\%}$$

2. No more than 36 percent of your gross monthly income should be used for your total monthly credit obligations (monthly house payments plus all other monthly credit obligations such as car loans, credit cards, and so on, which have six months or more to run).

$$\frac{\text{Total monthly credit obligation}}{\text{Gross monthly income}} = \text{No more than 36\%}$$

Mr. and Mrs. First-Time Buyer wish to purchase a small older $180,000 condo. Mr. Buyer has a yearly salary of $33,000, and Mrs. Buyer earns $34,000 per year. They have both been with their employers for more than four years. Their monthly bills are as follows: car payments, three years remaining at $375 per month; furniture payment, $125 per month for 13 months; and a student loan, $75 per month with four months remaining. If they buy the home, their annual property taxes will be $2,100, and homeowner's insurance and dues will cost $504 per year.

A local lender is willing to make a $162,000 (90 percent) loan at eight and a half percent for 30 years, payable at $1,245 per month, plus $38 per month for private mortgage insurance. Assuming the buyers have the required cash down payment and have a good credit history, do they have the income to qualify for this loan? Do they meet the 28 and 36 percent ratios?

After you have done your computations, check your answer by turning to the section titled "Answers to Reviewing Your Understanding Questions" toward the end of the book.

© Shutterstock / Sai Yeung Chan

STUDENT LEARNING OUTCOMES

An appraisal is an essential part of a real estate transaction. Many times the decision to buy, sell, or grant a loan on real estate hinges on a real estate appraiser's estimate of a property's value. At the conclusion of this chapter, you will be able to do the following:

- Define appraisal and list the essential elements of value.
- Distinguish between utility value and market value.
- Discuss the three approaches or methods used to determine value.
- Define reconciliation and explain how it applies to the final estimate of value.

REAL ESTATE APPRAISAL

10.1 APPRAISAL CONCEPTS

An **appraisal** is defined as an estimate or an opinion of value. Real estate appraisals are used to do the following:

1. Estimate property value for loans
2. Set listing prices on property
3. Help set premiums on fire insurance policies.

Other reasons include determining estate taxes and values for government acquisition. Real estate appraisal is not an exact science; therefore, the accuracy of an appraisal is related to the skill, education, experience, and judgment of the appraiser. A competitive market analysis (CMA) is similar to an appraisal, but it is done by a real estate professional when helping a seller set the price for listing or buyer determine the amount to offer. It is important that the real estate professional make clear in the CMA that is not an appraisal, which can only be done by licensed appraisers.

Real Estate Appraisal License Requirements

Any appraisal for a real estate transaction involving federal insurance or assistance must be done by a licensed or certified appraiser. This includes an appraisal for any lender whose deposits are insured or regulated by a federal agency. For these appraisals, the appraiser must have a special license or certificate issued by the Bureau of Real Estate Appraisers (BREA). There are four levels of real estate appraisal licensing as of January 2015:

1. *AT-Trainee License*: No experience requirements must work under a supervising appraiser. The scope of practice allows any property that the supervising appraiser is permitted to appraise.

2. *AL-Residential License:* Allowed to appraise noncomplex one- to four-unit residential properties up to $1 million. On nonresidential transactions, the dollar limit is up to $250,000.

3. *AR-Certified Residential:* Allowed to appraise all one- to four-unit residential properties regardless of the value or complexity. On nonresidential transactions with a value up to $250,000.

4. *AG-Certified General:* Allowed to appraise any real estate regardless of type or value.

All appraisers must take a minimum number of hours of real estate appraisal and related educational courses as follows:

Trainee License: 150 hours
Residential License: 150 hours
Certified Residential: 200 hours
Certified General: 300 hours

All of the educational hours listed above must include the 15-hour course on the Uniform Standards of Professional Appraisal Practice (USPAP). USPAP is considered the quality control standards for real property appraisal reports. *Minimum on-the-job experience requirements are as follows:*

Residential License: 2,000 hours and no less than 12 months of appraisal experience
Certified Residential: 2,500 hours plus two and a half years of experience
Certified General: 3,000 hours (at least 1,500 hours must be with nonresidential properties) plus two and a half years of experience

Effective January 1, 2015, any new residential license applicant will need 30 semester credit hours of college level education from an accredited community college or university OR an associate's degree or higher in any field. Any new certified residential license applicant will need a bachelor's degree or higher from an accredited college or university in any field. Any new certified general license applicant will need a bachelor's degree or higher from an accredited college or university, in any field. For more information, go to the Bureau of Real Estate Appraisers website at www.brea.ca.gov.

After meeting these requirements, a person must pass an examination and then apply for an appraisal license or certification is issued for a two-year period. To renew the license, a designated number of hours of approved continuing education courses must be taken. For more information about a real estate appraiser's license, access the BREA's website at www.brea.ca.gov.

Professional Designations

In addition to a state-issued license or certificate, several professional real estate appraisal organizations in the United States issue highly prized professional designations. Two of the appraisal trade associations are the American Institute of Real Estate Appraisers, which issues the widely recognized Member of the Appraisal Institute (MAI) designation. This designation is held by appraisers who are experienced in the valuation of commercial, industrial, residential, and other types of properties. The Society of Real Estate Appraisers issues the designation SRPA to those appraisers who are experienced in the valuation of commercial, industrial, and residential properties.

Home Valuation Code of Conduct (HVCC)

Fannie Mae and Freddie Mac will not purchase loans from lenders who do not subscribe to the Home Valuation Code of Conduct (HVCC). The HVCC is designed to prevent lenders, borrowers, and sellers from influencing an appraisal report in single-family residential transactions. Specifically, the HVCC does the following:

- Prohibits lenders and third parties from influencing appraisers in the preparation of their appraisal reports.
- Mandates standards for appraisal reports, and for hiring and compensating appraisers in the preparation of reports.
- Lenders must provide a copy of the appraisal report to the borrower within three business days prior to closing.
- Requires independence of appraisers from the influence of lenders and third parties and limits communication.

Because of Fannie Mae and Freddie Mac's dominance in the secondary mortgage market, the Home Valuation Code of Conduct has standardized the appraisal process in residential lending.

Market Value

The purpose of an appraisal is to determine the market value for a property. Although there are various types of value—sales/listing value, loan value, tax value, and insurance value—two major categories of value are market value and value in use (utility value).

Market value is value in exchange as determined by supply and demand in the open real estate market. Market value is also referred to as *objective value*. Market value can be briefly defined as "the highest price in terms of money for which a property would sell in the open market, with the ready, willing, and able seller not being obligated to sell, and a ready, willing, and able buyer not being obligated to buy, in an "arm's length" transaction with a reasonable length of time to effect the sale." This assumes that the buyer and the seller are fully knowledgeable persons. An appraiser's job is to estimate market value.

Another value that impacts property is value in use (utility value) which is the value of a particular property to a particular owner or user of real estate. The value of property to a particular owner may be emotional as well as economic; thus, value in use is also known as *subjective value*. For example, the value that you place in a property that has been in your family for over 100 years might be different than what an outside buyer views as value.

Both subjective and objective values play apart in the sale of real estate. A buyer makes an offer on a property, based on the listing price which is typically the seller's and their agent's estimate of market value. The buyer working with her agent then determines what to offer, which begins the negotiation process. Throughout the negotiations subjective value often plays a part as the parties determine what they are willing to take or pay for the property

Market Value Versus Market Price

Market price is the price that is actually paid at close of escrow. It is used by appraisers and real estate professionals to determine market value of other properties in the area.

The key point is the sales price establishes market price for that property, but for any given single sale, the price actually paid may be equal to, higher than, or lower than listing price or estimated market value.

Essential Elements of Value

For property to have value, four essential elements or characteristics must be present: (1) demand, (2) utility, (3) scarcity, and (4) transferability. *Demand* refers to the desire to own real estate, coupled with the financial ability to buy. Assuming a scarce number of properties for sale, the greater the number of ready, willing, and able buyers (demand), the greater the likelihood that the property offered for sale will increase in value. *Utility* refers to usefulness—the more useful a property in the market, the greater its potential value. Therefore a three bedroom home has more utility and value than a one bedroom home. *Scarcity* means lack of abundance; without scarcity values drop. The more scarcity the higher the values. This element explains why prices tend to be higher on islands and in the center of cites, where scarcity is built in.

Transferability refers to the ability to transfer identifiable ownership. A beautiful home on the California coast may be a scarce commodity, with great utility and high demand. But if the property's title is clouded and uncertain, not many people will be willing to buy the home. With clear title, the property is more valuable. When a title is clouded, the property is less valuable.

Demand, utility, scarcity, and transferability are the essential elements that create value. If all are present in a favorable combination, a property's value may increase. If one or more elements are flawed or missing, a property's value may be declining, or in a worst-case scenario it becomes worthless. (See Figure 10.1.) To remember the essential elements of value think DUST: Demand, Utility, Scarcity, Transferability.

FIGURE 10.1

Source: © 2015 OnCourse Learning

Four Forces that Influence Value

Once a property's value has been established, there are four forces that can change its value. These forces (shown in Figure 10.1) are as follows:

1. *Social forces,* such as changes in population, marriage trends, and family size, and changes in attitudes toward education, recreation, and lifestyles.

2. *Economic forces,* which include changes in income levels, employment opportunities, the cost of money, and natural resources.

3. *Political forces,* such as changes in zoning, building codes, construction moratoriums, government housing programs, and pro-growth or no-growth government philosophies.

4. *Physical forces* that affect the physical aspects of the property, such as size and shape of the parcel, location, climate, and soil conditions.

These four forces continually bombard every parcel of real estate and cause values to shift positively or negatively. Which of these forces is the single most important? There is no simple answer! This is where the skill, experience, and judgment of an appraiser weigh in. However, an old saying states, "The three most important factors of value are location, location, location."

Basic Principles of Valuation

A number of principles used to support appraisal theory. These include:

1. *Principle of highest and best use.* The best use of land is that which produces the greatest net return to the land. It may or may not be the current use. Example: A residential home zoned for commercial use, not typically part of a CMA but always in an appraisal.

2. *Principle of change.* Real estate values are constantly changing as a result of social, economic, political, and physical forces within a region, city, and neighborhood.

3. *Principle of supply and demand.* The interaction of supply and demand causes real estate values to change in both sales and rentals. For example, assuming a fixed supply of homes for sale, an increase in demand should cause prices to increase. With an increase in supply typically demand will go down along with values. Conversely, if demand stays high despite more supply then prices will stay high.

4. *Principle of substitution.* This principle underlies all approaches to value. Substitution states the value of a property tends to be influenced by the price of acquiring an equally desirable substitute

property. For example, the value of property A is determined by the value of comparable properties B, C, and D. Buyers will choose the highest value for the lowest price. Appraisers must always determine if the market value of the property fits within the current values of area and comparable properties no matter which approach to value is used.

5. *Principle of conformity*. In a residential neighborhood, the maximum value is found where there is a high degree of conformity, such as homes of similar design, size, architecture, and upkeep. Example: a large home in an area of small home will have less value than if the home was in an area of similar sized properties.

6. *Principle of contribution*. Involves what value improving a property will add to the market value. Depending upon the improvement made it may have an increasing or decreasing return on the market value. The value of the improvement is not what it costs to add but what the value the market place gives the improvement. For example swimming pools in California tend to add more value than they cost to install. Where in Minnesota, which has is limited time to use a pool, the market often will not see an increase in the value of a property that has a pool.

10.2 DEPRECIATION

Depreciation as used in the cost approach to value, is defined as a loss in value from any cause. Depreciation is usually measured as the difference between the new replacement cost of a building or improvement and its value as of the date of the appraisal. If an existing building (excluding land) is appraised at $450,000, but its replacement cost (if it were destroyed and needed to be rebuilt) is calculated to be $500,000, the $50,000 difference ($500,000 less $450,000) is the amount of the depreciation. Deprecation is classified as curable or incurable based on the principle of contribution. Curable depreciation means if repairs and/or remodeling are undertaken, the expense incurred will be less than the value added to the property. If you spend $30,000 to repair your home and in the process this adds $35,000 or more in value, this is considered curable. Incurable depreciation means the cost to repair or remodel exceeds the value added to the property. If you pay $30,000 to repair your home and in the process this adds $25,000 in value, this is considered incurable (in other words, it violates the principle of contribution). Physical deterioration and functional obsolescence can be classified as curable or incurable per the guidelines noted earlier. However, economic obsolescence is most often incurable.

Causes of Depreciation

The causes or reasons for a loss in real estate value can be grouped into three categories.

1. **Physical deterioration** is a loss in value caused by (a) wear and tear from use; (b) deferred maintenance and lack of upkeep; (c) damage by termites, dry rot, and so on; and (d) weather conditions. A run-down home in need of paint and repairs is an example of depreciation caused by physical deterioration. Typically, this is considered to be curable as making the repairs will increase the value more than the cost of the materials.

2. **Functional obsolescence** is a loss in value caused by (a) an unpopular floor plan and layout; (b) a lack of updated, modern appliances and equipment; and (c) a poor or unpopular architectural design and style. A three-bedroom, one-bath home with a wall heater and single-car garage is an example of depreciation caused by functional obsolescence. Why? Because most buyers of three-bedroom homes prefer one and one-half or two bathrooms, a two-car garage, and a forced-air heating system. Therefore, all other things being equal, the three-bedroom, one-bath home usually sells at a lower price. Functional obsolescence may be curable or incurable. Once again the appraiser would have to determine if the cost to cure was greater or less than the value it would add. If it is less it is curable; if it is greater it is incurable.

3. **Economic obsolescence** is a loss in value resulting from (a) zoning and other government actions; (b) misplaced improvements, such as a home built next to an all-night service station; and (c) a drop in demand for real estate, or overbuilding, creating an excessive supply of homes. An example of economic obsolescence would be a neighborhood street, recently declared a truck route, whose increased traffic brings noise and fumes into the area. This could cause home values to decline. In short, economic obsolescence is caused by factors outside the boundaries of the property—items beyond the control of the owners. This is almost always considered incurable because the loss in value is caused by negative factors outside the property's boundaries. Therefore, it is assumed that these negative factors are beyond the control of any single property owner to correct.

Accrued Depreciation Versus Recapture for Depreciation

Accrued depreciation is the loss in value that has already occurred in a building. Recapture for depreciation (sometimes called *accrual for depreciation*) is an estimate for depreciation that will occur in the future. Accrued (past) depreciation is used in the *cost approach.*

An Additional Word about Depreciation

Depreciation for appraisal purposes is different from depreciation for income tax purposes. The appraiser looks at depreciation as being an actual decline in value. For income tax purposes, an accountant uses book depreciation (also called *cost recovery*) as a basis for an income tax deduction. The two concepts are not the same. The accountant uses a theoretical figure allowed by the Internal Revenue Service, whereas an appraiser uses economic analysis to arrive at an actual decline in value.

Appreciation is an increase in value that can result from inflation or from the interaction of supply and demand forces. All real estate improvements suffer some form of depreciation, but simultaneously many properties are appreciating. The question then becomes this: Is the rate of appreciation exceeding the rate of depreciation? If so, overall value of the property increases. But if the rate of depreciation is exceeding appreciation, the overall value of the property decreases.

10.3 APPRAISAL REPORTS

When an appraiser is hired, the appraiser's estimate of value is submitted as a report.

Currently, only two types of reports meet the minimum requirements and reporting standards of Uniform Standards of Professional Appraisal Practice (USPAP): the restricted report and the appraisal report. Due to the lack of information contained in the restricted report it does not meet most lender requirements and is typically not used.

The appraisal report is most commonly used by real estate appraisers when appraising property for loan purposes, which is the majority of the work done by appraisers. It contains a moderate or extensive level of detail. The appraisal report is only required to meet minimum applicable legal standards so it contains a moderate amount of detail.

There are two report styles:

1. Form report
2. Narrative report

The form report style consists of check sheets and spaces to be filled in by the appraiser. (See Figure 10.2.) The narrative report style is formatted as an essay. Appraisers generally have more freedom in developing the look of this report.

FIGURE 10.2

Uniform Residential Appraisal Report
File #

The purpose of this summary appraisal report is to provide the lender/client with an accurate, and adequately supported, opinion of the market value of the subject property.

SUBJECT

Property Address		City		State	Zip Code

Borrower | Owner of Public Record | County

Legal Description

Assessor's Parcel #   Tax Year   R.E. Taxes $

Neighborhood Name   Map Reference   Census Tract

Occupant ☐ Owner ☐ Tenant ☐ Vacant   Special Assessments $ ☐ PUD   HOA $ ☐ per year ☐ per month

Property Rights Appraised ☐ Fee Simple ☐ Leasehold ☐ Other (describe)

Assignment Type ☐ Purchase Transaction ☐ Refinance Transaction ☐ Other (describe)

Lender/Client   Address

Is the subject property currently offered for sale or has it been offered for sale in the twelve months prior to the effective date of this appraisal? ☐ Yes ☐ No

Report data source(s) used, offering price(s), and date(s).

CONTRACT

I ☐ did ☐ did not analyze the contract for sale for the subject purchase transaction. Explain the results of the analysis of the contract for sale or why the analysis was not performed.

Contract Price $ Date of Contract   Is the property seller the owner of public record? ☐Yes ☐No Data Source(s)

Is there any financial assistance (loan charges, sale concessions, gift or downpayment assistance, etc.) to be paid by any party on behalf of the borrower? ☐ Yes ☐ No
If Yes, report the total dollar amount and describe the items to be paid.

NEIGHBORHOOD

Note: Race and the racial composition of the neighborhood are not appraisal factors.

Neighborhood Characteristics	One-Unit Housing Trends	One-Unit Housing	Present Land Use %
Location ☐ Urban ☐ Suburban ☐ Rural	Property Values ☐ Increasing ☐ Stable ☐ Declining	PRICE AGE	One-Unit %
Built-Up ☐ Over 75% ☐ 25–75% ☐ Under 25%	Demand/Supply ☐ Shortage ☐ In Balance ☐ Over Supply	$ (000) (yrs)	2-4 Unit %
Growth ☐ Rapid ☐ Stable ☐ Slow	Marketing Time ☐ Under 3 mths ☐ 3–6 mths ☐ Over 6 mths	Low	Multi-Family %
		High	Commercial %
		Pred.	Other %

Neighborhood Boundaries

Neighborhood Description

Market Conditions (including support for the above conclusions)

SITE

Dimensions   Area   Shape   View

Specific Zoning Classification   Zoning Description

Zoning Compliance ☐ Legal ☐ Legal Nonconforming (Grandfathered Use) ☐ No Zoning ☐ Illegal (describe)

Is the highest and best use of the subject property as improved (or as proposed per plans and specifications) the present use? ☐ Yes ☐ No If No, describe

Utilities	Public	Other (describe)		Public	Other (describe)	Off-site Improvements—Type	Public	Private
Electricity	☐	☐	Water	☐	☐	Street	☐	☐
Gas	☐	☐	Sanitary Sewer	☐	☐	Alley	☐	☐

FEMA Special Flood Hazard Area ☐ Yes ☐ No FEMA Flood Zone   FEMA Map #   FEMA Map Date

Are the utilities and off-site improvements typical for the market area? ☐ Yes ☐ No If No, describe

Are there any adverse site conditions or external factors (easements, encroachments, environmental conditions, land uses, etc.)? ☐ Yes ☐ No If Yes, describe

IMPROVEMENTS

General Description	Foundation	Exterior Description materials/condition	Interior materials/condition
Units ☐ One ☐ One with Accessory Unit	☐ Concrete Slab ☐ Crawl Space	Foundation Walls	Floors
# of Stories	☐ Full Basement ☐ Partial Basement	Exterior Walls	Walls
Type ☐ Det. ☐ Att. ☐ S-Det./End Unit	Basement Area sq. ft.	Roof Surface	Trim/Finish
☐ Existing ☐ Proposed ☐ Under Const.	Basement Finish %	Gutters & Downspouts	Bath Floor
Design (Style)	☐ Outside Entry/Exit ☐ Sump Pump	Window Type	Bath Wainscot
Year Built	Evidence of ☐ Infestation	Storm Sash/Insulated	Car Storage ☐ None
Effective Age (Yrs)	☐ Dampness ☐ Settlement	Screens	☐ Driveway # of Cars
Attic ☐ None	Heating ☐ FWA ☐ HWBB ☐ Radiant	Amenities ☐ Woodstove(s) #	Driveway Surface
☐ Drop Stair ☐ Stairs	☐ Other Fuel	☐ Fireplace(s) # ☐ Fence	☐ Garage # of Cars
☐ Floor ☐ Scuttle	Cooling ☐ Central Air Conditioning	☐ Patio/Deck ☐ Porch	☐ Carport # of Cars
☐ Finished ☐ Heated	☐ Individual ☐ Other	☐ Pool ☐ Other	☐ Att. ☐ Det. ☐ Built-in

Appliances ☐Refrigerator ☐Range/Oven ☐Dishwasher ☐Disposal ☐Microwave ☐Washer/Dryer ☐Other (describe)

Finished area above grade contains: Rooms Bedrooms Bath(s) Square Feet of Gross Living Area Above Grade

Additional features (special energy efficient items, etc.)

Describe the condition of the property (including needed repairs, deterioration, renovations, remodeling, etc.).

Are there any physical deficiencies or adverse conditions that affect the livability, soundness, or structural integrity of the property? ☐ Yes ☐ No If Yes, describe

Does the property generally conform to the neighborhood (functional utility, style, condition, use, construction, etc.)? ☐ Yes ☐ No If No, describe

FIGURE 10.2 (Continued)

Uniform Residential Appraisal Report

File #

There are	comparable properties currently offered for sale in the subject neighborhood ranging in price from $					to $	.
There are	comparable sales in the subject neighborhood within the past twelve months ranging in sale price from $					to $	.

FEATURE	SUBJECT	COMPARABLE SALE # 1		COMPARABLE SALE # 2		COMPARABLE SALE # 3	
Address							
Proximity to Subject							
Sale Price	$		$		$		$
Sale Price/Gross Liv. Area	$ sq. ft.	$ sq. ft.		$ sq. ft.		$ sq. ft.	
Data Source(s)							
Verification Source(s)							
VALUE ADJUSTMENTS	DESCRIPTION	DESCRIPTION	+(-) $ Adjustment	DESCRIPTION	+(-) $ Adjustment	DESCRIPTION	+(-) $ Adjustment
Sale or Financing Concessions							
Date of Sale/Time							
Location							
Leasehold/Fee Simple							
Site							
View							
Design (Style)							
Quality of Construction							
Actual Age							
Condition							
Above Grade	Total Bdrms. Baths	Total Bdrms. Baths		Total Bdrms. Baths		Total Bdrms. Baths	
Room Count							
Gross Living Area	sq. ft.	sq. ft.		sq. ft.		sq. ft.	
Basement & Finished Rooms Below Grade							
Functional Utility							
Heating/Cooling							
Energy Efficient Items							
Garage/Carport							
Porch/Patio/Deck							
Net Adjustment (Total)		☐ + ☐ -	$	☐ + ☐ -	$	☐ + ☐ -	$
Adjusted Sale Price of Comparables		Net Adj. % Gross Adj. %	$	Net Adj. % Gross Adj. %	$	Net Adj. % Gross Adj. %	$

I ☐ did ☐ did not research the sale or transfer history of the subject property and comparable sales. If not, explain

My research ☐ did ☐ did not reveal any prior sales or transfers of the subject property for the three years prior to the effective date of this appraisal.

Data source(s)

My research ☐ did ☐ did not reveal any prior sales or transfers of the comparable sales for the year prior to the date of sale of the comparable sale.

Data source(s)

Report the results of the research and analysis of the prior sale or transfer history of the subject property and comparable sales (report additional prior sales on page 3).

ITEM	SUBJECT	COMPARABLE SALE # 1	COMPARABLE SALE # 2	COMPARABLE SALE # 3
Date of Prior Sale/Transfer				
Price of Prior Sale/Transfer				
Data Source(s)				
Effective Date of Data Source(s)				

Analysis of prior sale or transfer history of the subject property and comparable sales

Summary of Sales Comparison Approach

Indicated Value by Sales Comparison Approach $

Indicated Value by: Sales Comparison Approach $ Cost Approach (if developed) $ Income Approach (if developed) $

This appraisal is made ☐ "as is", ☐ subject to completion per plans and specifications on the basis of a hypothetical condition that the improvements have been completed, ☐ subject to the following repairs or alterations on the basis of a hypothetical condition that the repairs or alterations have been completed, or ☐ subject to the following required inspection based on the extraordinary assumption that the condition or deficiency does not require alteration or repair:

Based on a complete visual inspection of the interior and exterior areas of the subject property, defined scope of work, statement of assumptions and limiting conditions, and appraiser's certification, my (our) opinion of the market value, as defined, of the real property that is the subject of this report is $, as of   , which is the date of inspection and the effective date of this appraisal.

FIGURE 10.2 (Continued)

Uniform Residential Appraisal Report

File #

ADDITIONAL COMMENTS

COST APPROACH TO VALUE (not required by Fannie Mae)

Provide adequate information for the lender/client to replicate the below cost figures and calculations.

Support for the opinion of site value (summary of comparable land sales or other methods for estimating site value)

ESTIMATED ☐ REPRODUCTION OR ☐ REPLACEMENT COST NEW	OPINION OF SITE VALUE	= $
Source of cost data	Dwelling Sq. Ft. @ $	= $
Quality rating from cost service Effective date of cost data	Sq. Ft. @ $	= $
Comments on Cost Approach (gross living area calculations, depreciation, etc.)		
	Garage/Carport Sq. Ft. @ $	= $
	Total Estimate of Cost-New	= $
	Less Physical Functional External	
	Depreciation	= $( )
	Depreciated Cost of Improvements	= $
	"As-is" Value of Site Improvements	= $
Estimated Remaining Economic Life (HUD and VA only) Years	Indicated Value By Cost Approach	= $

INCOME APPROACH TO VALUE (not required by Fannie Mae)

Estimated Monthly Market Rent $ _____ X Gross Rent Multiplier _____ = $ _____ Indicated Value by Income Approach

Summary of Income Approach (including support for market rent and GRM)

PROJECT INFORMATION FOR PUDs (if applicable)

Is the developer/builder in control of the Homeowners' Association (HOA)? ☐ Yes ☐ No Unit type(s) ☐ Detached ☐ Attached

Provide the following information for PUDs ONLY if the developer/builder is in control of the HOA and the subject property is an attached dwelling unit.

Legal name of project

Total number of phases _____ Total number of units _____ Total number of units sold _____

Total number of units rented _____ Total number of units for sale _____ Data source(s) _____

Was the project created by the conversion of an existing building(s) into a PUD? ☐ Yes ☐ No If Yes, date of conversion

Does the project contain any multi-dwelling units? ☐ Yes ☐ No Data source(s)

Are the units, common elements, and recreation facilities complete? ☐ Yes ☐ No If No, describe the status of completion.

Are the common elements leased to or by the Homeowners' Association? ☐ Yes ☐ No If Yes, describe the rental terms and options.

Describe common elements and recreational facilities

FIGURE 10.2 (Continued)

Uniform Residential Appraisal Report   File

This report form is designed to report an appraisal of a one-unit property or a one-unit property with an accessory unit; including a unit in a planned unit development (PUD). This report form is not designed to report an appraisal of a manufactured home or a unit in a condominium or cooperative project.

This appraisal report is subject to the following scope of work, intended use, intended user, definition of market value, statement of assumptions and limiting conditions, and certifications. Modifications, additions, or deletions to the intended use, intended user, definition of market value, or assumptions and limiting conditions are not permitted. The appraiser may expand the scope of work to include any additional research or analysis necessary based on the complexity of this appraisal assignment. Modifications or deletions to the certifications are also not permitted. However, additional certifications that do not constitute material alterations to this appraisal report, such as those required by law or those related to the appraiser's continuing education or membership in an appraisal organization, are permitted.

SCOPE OF WORK: The scope of work for this appraisal is defined by the complexity of this appraisal assignment and the reporting requirements of this appraisal report form, including the following definition of market value, statement of assumptions and limiting conditions, and certifications. The appraiser must, at a minimum: (1) perform a complete visual inspection of the interior and exterior areas of the subject property, (2) inspect the neighborhood, (3) inspect each of the comparable sales from at least the street, (4) research, verify, and analyze data from reliable public and/or private sources, and (5) report his or her analysis, opinions, and conclusions in this appraisal report.

INTENDED USE: The intended use of this appraisal report is for the lender/client to evaluate the property that is the subject of this appraisal for a mortgage finance transaction.

INTENDED USER: The intended user of this appraisal report is the lender/client.

DEFINITION OF MARKET VALUE: The most probable price which a property should bring in a competitive and open market under all conditions requisite to a fair sale, the buyer and seller, each acting prudently, knowledgeably and assuming the price is not affected by undue stimulus. Implicit in this definition is the consummation of a sale as of a specified date and the passing of title from seller to buyer under conditions whereby: (1) buyer and seller are typically motivated; (2) both parties are well informed or well advised, and each acting in what he or she considers his or her own best interest; (3) a reasonable time is allowed for exposure in the open market; (4) payment is made in terms of cash in U. S. dollars or in terms of financial arrangements comparable thereto; and (5) the price represents the normal consideration for the property sold unaffected by special or creative financing or sales concessions* granted by anyone associated with the sale.

*Adjustments to the comparables must be made for special or creative financing or sales concessions. No adjustments are necessary for those costs which are normally paid by sellers as a result of tradition or law in a market area; these costs are readily identifiable since the seller pays these costs in virtually all sales transactions. Special or creative financing adjustments can be made to the comparable property by comparisons to financing terms offered by a third party institutional lender that is not already involved in the property or transaction. Any adjustment should not be calculated on a mechanical dollar for dollar cost of the financing or concession but the dollar amount of any adjustment should approximate the market's reaction to the financing or concessions based on the appraiser's judgment.

STATEMENT OF ASSUMPTIONS AND LIMITING CONDITIONS: The appraiser's certification in this report is subject to the following assumptions and limiting conditions:

1. The appraiser will not be responsible for matters of a legal nature that affect either the property being appraised or the title to it, except for information that he or she became aware of during the research involved in performing this appraisal. The appraiser assumes that the title is good and marketable and will not render any opinions about the title.

2. The appraiser has provided a sketch in this appraisal report to show the approximate dimensions of the improvements. The sketch is included only to assist the reader in visualizing the property and understanding the appraiser's determination of its size.

3. The appraiser has examined the available flood maps that are provided by the Federal Emergency Management Agency (or other data sources) and has noted in this appraisal report whether any portion of the subject site is located in an identified Special Flood Hazard Area. Because the appraiser is not a surveyor, he or she makes no guarantees, express or implied, regarding this determination.

4. The appraiser will not give testimony or appear in court because he or she made an appraisal of the property in question, unless specific arrangements to do so have been made beforehand, or as otherwise required by law.

5. The appraiser has noted in this appraisal report any adverse conditions (such as needed repairs, deterioration, the presence of hazardous wastes, toxic substances, etc.) observed during the inspection of the subject property or that he or she became aware of during the research involved in performing this appraisal. Unless otherwise stated in this appraisal report, the appraiser has no knowledge of any hidden or unapparent physical deficiencies or adverse conditions of the property (such as, but not limited to, needed repairs, deterioration, the presence of hazardous wastes, toxic substances, adverse environmental conditions, etc.) that would make the property less valuable, and has assumed that there are no such conditions and makes no guarantees or warranties, express or implied. The appraiser will not be responsible for any such conditions that do exist or for any engineering or testing that might be required to discover whether such conditions exist. Because the appraiser is not an expert in the field of environmental hazards, this appraisal report must not be considered as an environmental assessment of the property.

6. The appraiser has based his or her appraisal report and valuation conclusion for an appraisal that is subject to satisfactory completion, repairs, or alterations on the assumption that the completion, repairs, or alterations of the subject property will be performed in a professional manner.

FIGURE 10.2 (Continued)

Uniform Residential Appraisal Report   File

APPRAISER'S CERTIFICATION: The Appraiser certifies and agrees that:

1. I have, at a minimum, developed and reported this appraisal in accordance with the scope of work requirements stated in this appraisal report.

2. I performed a complete visual inspection of the interior and exterior areas of the subject property. I reported the condition of the improvements in factual, specific terms. I identified and reported the physical deficiencies that could affect the livability, soundness, or structural integrity of the property.

3. I performed this appraisal in accordance with the requirements of the Uniform Standards of Professional Appraisal Practice that were adopted and promulgated by the Appraisal Standards Board of The Appraisal Foundation and that were in place at the time this appraisal report was prepared.

4. I developed my opinion of the market value of the real property that is the subject of this report based on the sales comparison approach to value. I have adequate comparable market data to develop a reliable sales comparison approach for this appraisal assignment. I further certify that I considered the cost and income approaches to value but did not develop them, unless otherwise indicated in this report.

5. I researched, verified, analyzed, and reported on any current agreement for sale for the subject property, any offering for sale of the subject property in the twelve months prior to the effective date of this appraisal, and the prior sales of the subject property for a minimum of three years prior to the effective date of this appraisal, unless otherwise indicated in this report.

6. I researched, verified, analyzed, and reported on the prior sales of the comparable sales for a minimum of one year prior to the date of sale of the comparable sale, unless otherwise indicated in this report.

7. I selected and used comparable sales that are locationally, physically, and functionally the most similar to the subject property.

8. I have not used comparable sales that were the result of combining a land sale with the contract purchase price of a home that has been built or will be built on the land.

9. I have reported adjustments to the comparable sales that reflect the market's reaction to the differences between the subject property and the comparable sales.

10. I verified, from a disinterested source, all information in this report that was provided by parties who have a financial interest in the sale or financing of the subject property.

11. I have knowledge and experience in appraising this type of property in this market area.

12. I am aware of, and have access to, the necessary and appropriate public and private data sources, such as multiple listing services, tax assessment records, public land records and other such data sources for the area in which the property is located.

13. I obtained the information, estimates, and opinions furnished by other parties and expressed in this appraisal report from reliable sources that I believe to be true and correct.

14. I have taken into consideration the factors that have an impact on value with respect to the subject neighborhood, subject property, and the proximity of the subject property to adverse influences in the development of my opinion of market value. I have noted in this appraisal report any adverse conditions (such as, but not limited to, needed repairs, deterioration, the presence of hazardous wastes, toxic substances, adverse environmental conditions, etc.) observed during the inspection of the subject property or that I became aware of during the research involved in performing this appraisal. I have considered these adverse conditions in my analysis of the property value, and have reported on the effect of the conditions on the value and marketability of the subject property.

15. I have not knowingly withheld any significant information from this appraisal report and, to the best of my knowledge, all statements and information in this appraisal report are true and correct.

16. I stated in this appraisal report my own personal, unbiased, and professional analysis, opinions, and conclusions, which are subject only to the assumptions and limiting conditions in this appraisal report.

17. I have no present or prospective interest in the property that is the subject of this report, and I have no present or prospective personal interest or bias with respect to the participants in the transaction. I did not base, either partially or completely, my analysis and/or opinion of market value in this appraisal report on the race, color, religion, sex, age, marital status, handicap, familial status, or national origin of either the prospective owners or occupants of the subject property or of the present owners or occupants of the properties in the vicinity of the subject property or on any other basis prohibited by law.

18. My employment and/or compensation for performing this appraisal or any future or anticipated appraisals was not conditioned on any agreement or understanding, written or otherwise, that I would report (or present analysis supporting) a predetermined specific value, a predetermined minimum value, a range or direction in value, a value that favors the cause of any party, or the attainment of a specific result or occurrence of a specific subsequent event (such as approval of a pending mortgage loan application).

19. I personally prepared all conclusions and opinions about the real estate that were set forth in this appraisal report. If I relied on significant real property appraisal assistance from any individual or individuals in the performance of this appraisal or the preparation of this appraisal report, I have named such individual(s) and disclosed the specific tasks performed in this appraisal report. I certify that any individual so named is qualified to perform the tasks. I have not authorized anyone to make a change to any item in this appraisal report; therefore, any change made to this appraisal is unauthorized and I will take no responsibility for it.

20. I identified the lender/client in this appraisal report who is the individual, organization, or agent for the organization that ordered and will receive this appraisal report.

FIGURE 10.2 (Continued)

Uniform Residential Appraisal Report   File

21. The lender/client may disclose or distribute this appraisal report to: the borrower; another lender at the request of the borrower; the mortgagee or its successors and assigns; mortgage insurers; government sponsored enterprises; other secondary market participants; data collection or reporting services; professional appraisal organizations; any department, agency, or instrumentality of the United States; and any state, the District of Columbia, or other jurisdictions; without having to obtain the appraiser's or supervisory appraiser's (if applicable) consent. Such consent must be obtained before this appraisal report may be disclosed or distributed to any other party (including, but not limited to, the public through advertising, public relations, news, sales, or other media).

22. I am aware that any disclosure or distribution of this appraisal report by me or the lender/client may be subject to certain laws and regulations. Further, I am also subject to the provisions of the Uniform Standards of Professional Appraisal Practice that pertain to disclosure or distribution by me.

23. The borrower, another lender at the request of the borrower, the mortgagee or its successors and assigns, mortgage insurers, government sponsored enterprises, and other secondary market participants may rely on this appraisal report as part of any mortgage finance transaction that involves any one or more of these parties.

24. If this appraisal report was transmitted as an "electronic record" containing my "electronic signature," as those terms are defined in applicable federal and/or state laws (excluding audio and video recordings), or a facsimile transmission of this appraisal report containing a copy or representation of my signature, the appraisal report shall be as effective, enforceable and valid as if a paper version of this appraisal report were delivered containing my original hand written signature.

25. Any intentional or negligent misrepresentation(s) contained in this appraisal report may result in civil liability and/or criminal penalties including, but not limited to, fine or imprisonment or both under the provisions of Title 18, United States Code, Section 1001, et seq., or similar state laws.

SUPERVISORY APPRAISER'S CERTIFICATION: The Supervisory Appraiser certifies and agrees that:

1. I directly supervised the appraiser for this appraisal assignment, have read the appraisal report, and agree with the appraiser's analysis, opinions, statements, conclusions, and the appraiser's certification.

2. I accept full responsibility for the contents of this appraisal report including, but not limited to, the appraiser's analysis, opinions, statements, conclusions, and the appraiser's certification.

3. The appraiser identified in this appraisal report is either a sub-contractor or an employee of the supervisory appraiser (or the appraisal firm), is qualified to perform this appraisal, and is acceptable to perform this appraisal under the applicable state law.

4. This appraisal report complies with the Uniform Standards of Professional Appraisal Practice that were adopted and promulgated by the Appraisal Standards Board of The Appraisal Foundation and that were in place at the time this appraisal report was prepared.

5. If this appraisal report was transmitted as an "electronic record" containing my "electronic signature," as those terms are defined in applicable federal and/or state laws (excluding audio and video recordings), or a facsimile transmission of this appraisal report containing a copy or representation of my signature, the appraisal report shall be as effective, enforceable and valid as if a paper version of this appraisal report were delivered containing my original hand written signature.

APPRAISER

Signature_____
Name _____
Company Name _____
Company Address_____
_____
Telephone Number _____
Email Address_____
Date of Signature and Report _____
Effective Date of Appraisal _____
State Certification # _____
or State License # _____
or Other (describe) _____ State # _____
State _____
Expiration Date of Certification or License _____

ADDRESS OF PROPERTY APPRAISED
_____
_____
APPRAISED VALUE OF SUBJECT PROPERTY $ _____
LENDER/CLIENT
Name _____
Company Name _____
Company Address_____
_____
Email Address_____

SUPERVISORY APPRAISER (ONLY IF REQUIRED)

Signature_____
Name_____
Company Name _____
Company Address _____
_____
Telephone Number _____
Email Address _____
Date of Signature _____
State Certification # _____
or State License # _____
State _____
Expiration Date of Certification or License _____

SUBJECT PROPERTY
☐ Did not inspect subject property
☐ Did inspect exterior of subject property from street
　Date of Inspection _____
☐ Did inspect interior and exterior of subject property
　Date of Inspection _____

COMPARABLE SALES
☐ Did not inspect exterior of comparable sales from street
☐ Did inspect exterior of comparable sales from street
　Date of Inspection _____

FIGURE 10.2 (Continued)

Instructions

Uniform Residential Appraisal Report

This report form is designed to report an appraisal of a one-unit property or a one-unit property with an accessory unit; including a unit in a planned unit development (PUD), based on an interior and exterior inspection of the subject property. This report form is not designed to report an appraisal of a manufactured home or a unit in a condominium or cooperative project.

Use

This report form is designed to report an appraisal of a one-unit property or a one-unit property with an accessory unit; including a unit in a planned unit development (PUD), based on an interior and exterior inspection of the subject property. This report form is not designed to report an appraisal of a manufactured home or a unit in a condominium or cooperative project.

Modifications, Additions, or Deletions

This appraisal report is subject to the scope of work, intended use, intended user, definition of market value, statement of assumptions and limiting conditions, and certifications contained in the report form. Modifications, additions, or deletions to the intended use, intended user, definition of market value, or assumptions and limiting conditions are not permitted. The appraiser may expand the scope of work to include any additional research or analysis necessary based on the complexity of this appraisal assignment. Modifications or deletions to the certifications are also not permitted. However, additional certifications that do not constitute material alterations to this appraisal report, such as those required by law or those related to the appraiser's continuing education or membership in an appraisal organization are permitted.

Scope of Work

The scope of work for this appraisal is defined by the complexity of this appraisal assignment and the reporting requirements of this appraisal report form, including the following definition of market value, statement of assumptions and limiting conditions, and certifications. The appraiser must, at a minimum: (1) perform a complete visual inspection of the interior and exterior areas of the subject property, (2) inspect the neighborhood, (3) inspect each of the comparable sales from at least the street, (4) research, verify, and analyze data from reliable public and/or private sources, and (5) report his or her analysis, opinions, and conclusions in this appraisal report.

Required Exhibits

- A street map that shows the location of the subject property and of all comparables that the appraiser used;

- An exterior building sketch of the improvements that indicates the dimensions. The appraiser must also include calculations to show how he or she arrived at the estimate for gross living area. A floor plan sketch that indicates the dimensions is required instead of the exterior building or unit sketch if the floor plan is atypical or functionally obsolete, thus limiting the market appeal for the property in comparison to competitive properties in the neighborhood;

- Clear, descriptive photographs (either in black and white or color) that show the front, back, and a street scene of the subject property, and that are appropriately identified. (Photographs must be originals that are produced either by photography or electronic imaging.);

- Clear, descriptive photographs (either in black and white or color) that show the front of each comparable sale and that are appropriately identified. Generally, photographs should be originals that are produced by photography or electronic imaging; however, copies of photographs from a multiple listing service or from the appraiser's files are acceptable if they are clear and descriptive;

- Any other data--as an attachment or addendum to the appraisal report form--that are necessary to provide an adequately supported opinion of market value.

Instructions Page

Appraisal Process

As in many other professional occupations, real estate appraisers have developed a system for conducting their work. The appraisal of real estate can be viewed as a series of steps, with each step logically following the preceding, until a final estimate of value is reached. Figure 10.3 is a flowchart of the real estate appraisal process.

As shown in Figure 10.3, the appraiser starts with a definition of the problem. What is the reason for the appraisal? Why does the client need the appraisal? What type of property is in need of analysis? The appraiser is determining the approaches to value that will most likely solve the problem and what data will need to gathered. The data is then gathered and classified and used for the appropriate approach. Sometimes the appraiser uses all three approaches to value sometimes only two. A separate value is arrived at under each approach, and these values are correlated, or reconciled. From this reconciliation process, one final estimate of value is given to the client. Reconciliation is not the averaging of the results from the three approaches, but rather a weighted blend based on what approach is most appropriate for the property.

Although this appraisal process has its roots in scientific analysis, the appraisal of real estate is still somewhat judgmental. Therefore, the accuracy of the appraisal depends not only on the data gathered but also on the judgment, skill, education, and experience of the person doing the appraisal.

Three Approaches to Value

Cost Approach to Value

The cost approach is appropriate for appraising newly constructed buildings and unique special-purpose properties and public buildings such as schools and libraries. The process used is to determine what the building would cost to build new, based either on reproduction or replacement costs, then subtracting the accrued depreciation and adding in the value of the land, which does not depreciate. The cost approach usually sets the highest limits on value—the thought being that the most a person will pay for real property is what it would cost to replace the property.

The four basic steps are:

1. Estimate the value of the land. Compare recent lot sales prices using the market date approach.
2. Estimate the current replacement or reproduction costs of the improvements. Building square footage × cost per square foot; also estimate price of fencing, cement work, and landscaping.

FIGURE 10.3

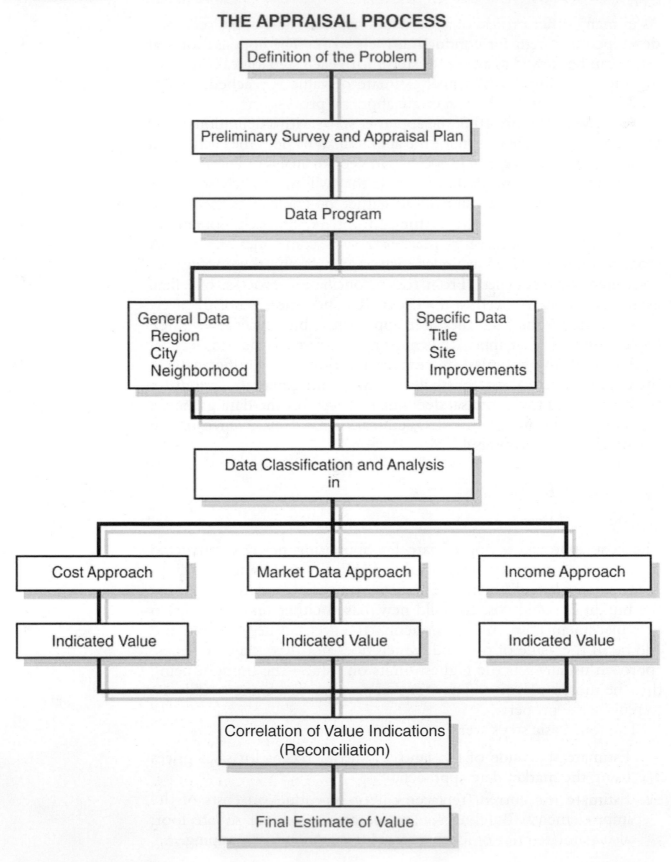

THE APPRAISAL PROCESS

Definition of the Problem

Preliminary Survey and Appraisal Plan

Data Program

General Data
Region
City
Neighborhood

Specific Data
Title
Site
Improvements

Data Classification and Analysis
in

Cost Approach

Market Data Approach

Income Approach

Indicated Value

Indicated Value

Indicated Value

Correlation of Value Indications
(Reconciliation)

Final Estimate of Value

Source: © 2015 OnCourse Learning

3. Estimate and then subtract accrued depreciation to arrive at the present value of the improvement. Current cost to build new less depreciation = present value of the improvements.

4. Add value of land to the present value of the improvements.

Improvement value + land value = estimated market value for the cost approach.

Estimating Replacement or Reproduction Cost

Depending on what the client is seeking the appraiser will either estimate replacement or reproduction costs. Reproduction is the price to create an exact duplicate where replacement cost is for a building of similar utility. Old wood trim in a home would have to be exactly the same type of wood and carving for reproduction, whereas for replacement the trim could even be resin if given a different look. Replacement cost is what is most often used in this approach. To estimate the current cost of buildings, appraisers first measure the square footage (exterior length × width). The square footage of the house is measured separately from the garage, patios, and porches. Based on the construction quality of the building they are appraising, appraisers obtain estimates from local contractors regarding construction costs per square foot. In addition to local contractors, square foot costs and other construction information can be obtained by subscribing to cost-estimating publications. Once accurate costs per square foot are obtained, the appraiser multiplies this figure by the square footage of the building. Figures for fencing, cement work, and landscaping are then added to arrive at the current replacement cost of all the improvements.

Estimating Depreciation

To estimate accrued depreciation, appraisers can use several techniques. The two most common methods of determining depreciation are the straight-line/age-life method and the cost-to-cure/observed condition method. The straight-line/age-life method assumes that depreciation occurs annually at an even rate over the estimated life of the improvement. For example, if a new building has an estimated life of 50 years, the straight-line/age-life method would assume a rate of depreciation of 2 percent per year (100% ÷ 50-year life = 2%). Thus, if an appraiser were appraising a building with an effective age of 10 years, the subtraction for depreciation would be 20 percent of the current replacement cost (10 years × 2% per year = 20%).

To estimate accrued depreciation using the cost-to-cure/observed condition method requires the appraiser to carefully observe physical, functional, and economic depreciation; then the appraiser estimates what it would cost to cure this depreciation. If some of the depreciation is incurable, the appraiser estimates the permanent loss in value. The sum of the cost to cure plus the permanent loss in value equals the estimated depreciation. Once the accrued depreciation has been estimated, this figure is subtracted from the current replacement cost to arrive at the present value of the improvements.

The final step in the cost approach is the easiest. The estimated value of the land is added to the estimated present value of the improvements to arrive at the estimated market value of the total real property.

Advantages and Disadvantages of the Cost Approach

The **cost approach** is appropriate for appraising newly constructed buildings and unique special-purpose properties and public buildings such as schools and libraries. The cost approach usually sets the highest limits on value—the thought being that the most a person will pay for real property is what it would cost to replace the property.

On the negative side, the cost approach does not always measure the individual amenities of the property, such as location, or the outside influences, such as neighborhood surroundings. Also, it is difficult to accurately convert depreciation into dollar figures. Thus, on older properties, the likelihood of errors in estimating depreciation increases with the age of the building. Also, in a declining real estate market, the cost to build a property may be much higher than what buyers are currently willing to pay. Figure 10.4 is an example of an appraisal using the cost approach.

Income Approach

The income approach to value is based on the premise that property that generates income is worth the present value of the future income to be produced by the property. In other words, what an investor should be willing to pay today for a property is directly related to what the investor expects to receive from the property in the future. Financial analysts have developed a technique called *capitalization*, which mathematically computes the present value of the future income produced by real estate. Capitalization or Cap Rate is what an investor in the market wants in return for her money or the rate of return for current income properties in an area. A cap rate can be defined as the rate necessary to attract an average investor to invest in the property being appraised. The cap rate reflects a return on the funds invested, as well as a return (recapture) of the investment. This

FIGURE 10.4

Example Using Cost Approach

Cost New per Square Foot
Home = $150 per sq. ft.
Garage = $50 per sq. ft.

Depreciation Information	**Land Value**
Estimated life new = 50 years	$150,000 based on recent comparable sales
Present effective age = 10 years	

Solution

$$\begin{array}{ll} 30 & \text{ft.} \\ \times\,40 & \text{ft.} \qquad \text{(Home)} \\ \hline 1{,}200 & \text{sq. ft.} \end{array}$$

$$\begin{array}{ll} 1{,}200 & \text{sq. ft.} \\ \times\,\$150 & \text{per sq. ft.} \\ \hline \$180{,}000 & \text{replacement value of home} \end{array}$$

$$\begin{array}{ll} 20 & \text{ft.} \\ \times\,20 & \text{ft.} \qquad \text{(Garage)} \\ \hline 400 & \text{sq. ft.} \end{array}$$

$$\begin{array}{ll} 400 & \text{sq. ft.} \\ \times\,\$50 & \text{per sq. ft.} \\ \hline \$20{,}000 & \text{replacement value of garage} \end{array}$$

$$\begin{array}{ll} \$180{,}000 & \text{replacement value of home} \\ +20{,}000 & \text{replacement value of garage} \\ \hline \$200{,}000 & \text{before depreciation} \end{array}$$

Depreciation

$$\frac{100\%}{50 \text{ yrs.}} = 2\% \text{ depreciation per year} \times 10 \text{ years} = 20\%$$

($200,000 × 20% depreciation = $40,000 depreciation)

$$\begin{array}{ll} \$200{,}000 & \text{before depreciation} \\ -40{,}000 & \text{depreciation} \\ \hline \$160{,}000 & \text{present value of improvement} \\ +150{,}000 & \text{land} \\ \hline \$310{,}000 & \text{estimate of value} \end{array}$$

is not unlike opening a savings account with $100. If at the end of the year you received $10 in interest, you would have a 10 percent return or 10 percent cap rate. The cap rate for an area is determined by using sold income properties and determing what rate other like properties are returning to their owners. If the appraiser found three similar income properties in the area that had cap rates of 3% to 4% the appraiser might decide to use 3.5% to determine the market value of the subject.

The computation for cap rate to determine value is:

Income (net operating) divided by the cap rate or I/R=V.

To determine the net operating income needed for a given rate the formula is cap rate times current value or R × V=I.

To determine the current cap rate the formula is Income divided by value (typically what the property sold for) or I/V=R.

The determination of value by the income approach can be viewed as a series of steps:

Step 1. Estimate gross annual income. Gross annual income is the maximum amount of income a property can expect to make if fully occupied 100 percent of the time and assuming rents are at the going market rate.

Step 2. Estimate vacancies and uncollectible rents and fees; these tend to be factors. Local vacancy rates are published monthly, and all property will have a percentage of loss of income in uncollected rents and fees. Once the amount is determined it is subtracted from gross annual income to arrive at the effective gross income, also called the gross operating income.

Step 3. After computing the effective gross income, the appraiser totals the annual operating expenses. Operating expenses are all the costs of running and maintaining the property. Examples include the following:

Property taxes	Supplies
Insurance premiums	Utilities
Repairs	Accounting and legal advice
Maintenance	Advertising
Management fees	Reserves for replacement

Real estate loan payments and income tax depreciation deductions are not considered operating expenses because they are not costs incurred to run the building. Therefore, they are not deducted to arrive at net income.

Once annual operating expenses are calculated, they are subtracted from the effective gross income to arrive at the net operating income. Net operating income is the income the property produces after the deduction of operating expenses, but before the payment of real estate loans.

Once the net operating income has been found the appraiser can then use the capitalization formula to determine the property value.

These steps can be summarized as follows:

Gross annual income

Less   –Vacancy factor and uncollectible rents

Equals   Effective gross income

Less   –Annual operating expenses

Equals   Net operating income

$$\frac{\text{Net operating income}}{\text{Capitalization rate}} = \text{Estimate of property's value}$$

The income approach to value is appropriate for income-producing properties such as apartment buildings, commercial office buildings, and retail stores. Figure 10.5 is an example of an appraisal using the income approach.

Market date or sales comparison approach

The market data approach or sales comparison approach is used primarily for residential properties where there are enough current sales of similar properties to make its use feasible. As with all approaches to value, the principle of substitution plays a large part in this approach because it is the buyer's decision on which property has the best price and suits her needs, compared to others in the area, that creates the sale.

To apply the market data approach, an appraiser gathers data on the subject property and then seeks current sales of comparable properties to the subject. Ideally, the comparable properties should be in the same neighborhood; be similar in size, style, and quality; and contain similar internal characteristics as the subject property. The more current the sale the better representation of market value the appraiser can make. Appraisers must use comparable sales within the last 12 months but typically want sales no older than 6 months. If the area market is rapidly appreciating or depreciating the appraiser may have to make a date of sale adjustment to reflect this difference.

FIGURE 10.5

Example Using Income Approach

The property is a clean, but modest, 15-unit apartment with fair market rents of $700 per unit. The estimated factor for vacancies and uncollectibles is 5%.
Annual operating expenses include:

Property taxes	$9,450
Insurance	$1,000
Management and accounting	$10,000
Repairs and others	$12,000

The capitalization rate selected by the appraiser is 7%.

Solution

Gross annual income	$126,000	($700 × 15 units × 12 months)
Less vacancies and uncollectibles	−6,300	($126,000 × 5%)
Effective gross income	$119,700	
Less annual expenses	−32,450	($9,450 + $1,000 + $10,000 + $12,000)
Net operating income	$87,250	

$$\frac{\text{Net operating income}}{\text{Capitalization rate}} \quad \frac{\$87,250}{7\%} = \$1,246,000 \text{ Estimate of value}$$
(rounded to nearest $1,000)

If the capitalization rate selected had been 6%, the value would be:

$$\frac{\$87,250}{6\%} = \$1,454,000 \text{ rounded to nearest } \$1,000$$

If the capitalization rate were 8%, the value would be:

$$\frac{\$87,250}{8\%} = \$1,091,000 \text{ rounded to nearest } \$1,000$$

Observe this rule: *The higher the capitalization rate, the lower the value.* Therefore, you can see that the selection of the appropriate capitalization rate is very critical! *The selection of an inappropriate capitalization rate can greatly distort value.*

Once three to five comparable properties are selected and the appraiser makes adjustments for the differences between the comparable properties and the subject property, the appraiser takes the sales prices of the comparable properties and adjusts the prices to reflect what the comparable properties would have sold for if they had the same features or characteristics of the subject property. Only the comparables can be adjusted since the subject does not have sold price to make adjustments to, and this is what the appraisal is to determine. The results of this process produce an indicated market value range for the property being appraised. Figure 10.6 is an example of an appraisal using the market approach

Value Range for Market Approach Example

The comparables in the market approach example (Figure 10.6) were near the location of the subject home and had the same lot size and overall condition of the subject home. With some minor adjustments to the comparables A, B, and C would have sold for somewhere between $319,900 and $320,500 if they were exactly like the subject, which means the figures reflect the indicated market value range.

Value Conclusions for Market Approach Example

The subject home in Figure 10.6 should sell for somewhere between $319,900 and $320,500. The final estimate is $320,000, as Comparable B is most comparable in the opinion of the appraiser.

This is a highly simplified example of the market approach, but it does show the basic concept of how the market approach attempts to adjust known comparable sales to reflect what the comparables should have sold for if the comparables had the characteristics of the subject property. As consumers, people use an informal market approach when they shop for automobiles, furniture, clothes, and most other types of consumer purchases. When it comes to real estate, appraisers simply formalize the process by reducing the comparative facts to writing.

The market data approach is also what real estate professionals use when completing CMA's for listing residential property or for helping a buyer make an offer.

Use of Gross Multipliers

Appraisers have designed a method for quickly obtaining a rough estimate of value using what are called *gross monthly rent multipliers*

FIGURE 10.6

Assume that the subject property is an older two-bedroom home with a one-car garage. The square footage for the home is 1,100 square feet. The appraiser locates three similar homes that have recently sold in the neighborhood at fair market prices. All have identical square footage and number of rooms.

Comparables (Comps)

Data	Subject Market Value?	Comp A	Sold $323,900	Comp B	Sold $321,500	Comp C	Sold $316,000
Location	Average for area	better	− 1,000	equal	0	equal	0
Lot size	¼ acre	equal	0	larger	− 1,500	smaller	+1,500
Condition	Average	better	− 3,500	equal	0	worse	+3,000
Adjustment			+4,500		− 1,500		+4,500
		Value	$319,000		$320,000		$320,500

Dollar Adjustment Factors per the Opinion of the Appraiser

Location difference	$1,000
Lot size difference	$1,500
Overall condition difference	$3,000

_____   _____   _____

(GMRM), also known as *gross rent multipliers* (GRM), if annual rents, instead of monthly rents, are used. A gross multiplier is a ratio between sales price and rental rates. The GMRM is found by dividing the sales price of a home by its monthly rent.

Example:

$$\frac{\text{Sales price}}{\text{Monthly rental rate}} \quad \frac{\$300,000}{\$2,000} = \begin{array}{l}\text{150 Gross monthly}\\ \text{rent multiplier}\end{array}$$

The gross rent multiplier is found by dividing the sales price of a home by its annual rent.

$$\begin{array}{l}\text{Sales price}\\ \text{Annual rate}\\ (\$2,000/\text{mo} \times 12)\end{array} \quad \frac{\$300,000}{\$24,000} = \begin{array}{l}\text{12.5 Annual gross}\\ \text{rent multiplier}\end{array}$$

An appraiser does this for many sales until a trend develops. When asked to conduct an appraisal on a home, the appraiser does a complete market approach (comparable sales) to arrive at an estimate of value. To recheck the results of the market approach, the appraiser may also do a cost approach and an income approach. For a home, a full-blown income approach is not needed, so the gross rent multiplier approach is often used instead.

The appraiser locates comparable homes, determines their gross multipliers, and selects the most appropriate multiplier. Next, the appraiser determines the fair market rent of the subject home. Then the gross multiplier is multiplied by the fair market rent to arrive at an estimate of value.

Example:

After carefully selecting comparable sales, the appraiser determines that the gross monthly rent multiplier should be 200. The fair market rent of the home is $1,500. Therefore, gross monthly rent multiplier × monthly rent = estimate of value

$$200 \times \$1,500 = \$300,000 \text{ Estimate of value}$$

Because smaller residential properties have a higher expense ratio, gross multipliers are more frequently used on one to four residential units, while larger properties are values with a capitalization rate.

Reconciliation and Final Estimate of Value

The process of bringing together the three indications of value derived through the market, cost, and income approaches is the final step in the appraisal process. This process is called **correlation (reconciliation)**. When reconciling, the appraiser gives full consideration to each approach; then, based on judgment and experience, the appraiser arrives at one final value or price.

Correlation or reconciliation is not the averaging of the three approaches! Averaging gives equal weight to each approach, which is wrong. For any given property, one of the approaches is better and should be given more weight such as market data for residential.

The final value estimate is not given in odd dollars and cents. The final estimate of value usually is rounded to the nearest $100, $500, or $1,000, depending on the value of the property.

Chapter Summary

Appraisers are required to be licensed or certified for all transactions involving federal insurance or regulation. An appraisal license or certificate is distinct and separate from a real estate license.

An appraisal is defined as an estimate or opinion of value. Although there are many types of value, the value sought most often is the market value.

For a property to have value, four elements are necessary: demand, scarcity, utility, and transferability. Once value has been established, social, economic, political, and physical forces cause value to change. Appraisal theory rests on certain principles, such as highest and best use, change, supply and demand, substitution, contribution and conformity, in addition to several others.

Depreciation is defined as a loss in value from any cause. Depreciation of real estate is caused by physical deterioration, functional obsolescence, and economic obsolescence. Depreciation can be classified as curable or incurable or as accrued or accrual for depreciation.

The appraisal process can be viewed as a series of steps leading to a final estimate of value. The appraisal techniques include the cost approach, income approach, and market approach. In certain instances, the gross multiplier technique is also used to estimate value.

The selection of a single final estimate of value is called correlation or reconciliation. Final value conclusions are submitted in a written report, which may be a restricted appraisal report or an appraisal report.

Important Terms and Concepts

appraisal	correlation (reconciliation)
appreciation	cost approach
capitalization rate	curable depreciation

depreciation

economic obsolescence

functional obsolescence

gross multiplier

income approach

incurable depreciation

market data/sales comparison approach

market value

physical deterioration

principle of substitution

value in use (utility value)

Practical Application

1. A steel building property consists of the following: the land value is $300,000, the main structure is 200 feet × 40 feet, and a storage building is 35 feet × 15 feet. A cement slab and other improvements have a present value of $27,000. The main structure has an effective age of 20 years with an estimated life of 50 years. The replacement cost of the main structure is $65 per square foot. The storage building has an effective age of 15 years with an estimated life new of 30 years. The replacement cost of the storage building is $20 per square foot. Using the cost approach, what is the estimated value of the property? (Round answer to nearest $1,000.)

2. An 11,000-square-foot commercial property rents for $1 per square foot per month on a triple net lease to a highly rated tenant with 10 years to go on the lease. The only cost to the landlord is five percent of gross rents for miscellaneous expenses not covered by the net lease. A comparable property sold for $1,500,000 and had a net operating income of $135,000. Based only on this information, what is the estimated value of the commercial property? (Round answer to nearest $1,000.)

3. You are doing a listing presentation for Ms. Seller's home, which does not have a spa. You found three comparable homes that sold recently in the subdivision: Comparable A sold for $357,000, is in better condition, and has a larger lot in addition to a spa. Comparable B sold for $340,000 and is in similar condition to Ms. Seller's home, but it has a smaller lot and no spa. Comparable C sold for $325,000, is in worse condition than Ms. Seller's home, and has a smaller lot and no spa. The adjustments are as follows: for spa, $1,000; condition, $3,000; and lot size, $10,000. Based only on this information, what do you think should be the listing price of Ms. Seller's home? (Round answer to nearest $1,000.)

Reviewing Your Understanding

1. The most important consideration in an appraisal is the:
   a. method used.
   b. experience, license, and integrity of the appraiser.
   c. data gathered.
   d. inspection of the title records.

2. The market data (sales comparison) approach to value is most important for determining the value of:
   a. special purpose properties.
   b. commercial property.
   c. existing residential homes.
   d. income-producing property.

3. Which of the following is a political force that influences value?
   a. Rate of changes in population
   b. Income levels
   c. Size and shape of the parcel
   d. Zoning changes

4. The essentials of value include all of the following, except:
   a. age.
   b. utility.
   c. scarcity.
   d. demand.

5. The appraisal principle which states that the value of a property tends to be influenced by the price of acquiring an equally desirable property is the:
   a. principle of supply and demand.
   b. principle of highest and best use.
   c. principle of substitution.
   d. principle of change.

6. The difference between the current replacement cost new and the estimated value of the building as of the date of the appraisal is called:
   a. market depreciation.
   b. remainder depreciation.
   c. past or accrued depreciation.
   d. future or accrual for depreciation.

7. A loss in value because of a poor floor plan is an example of:
   a. economic obsolescence.
   b. accrual for depreciation.
   c. functional obsolescence.
   d. physical deterioration.

8. The cost approach would be given the least weight if appraising a(n):
   a. new home.
   b. new apartment.
   c. old home.
   d. Special-purpose property.

9. Land is valued at $80,000. New construction cost for a minimum quality home 35 ft. × 45 ft. is $100 per square foot. For a garage 25 ft. × 25 ft., the cost is $40 per square foot. Depreciation is 10 percent of new replacement cost. What is the value estimate?
   a. $262,500
   b. $182,500
   c. $164,250
   d. $244,250

10. Find the value by use of the income approach for an older three-unit apartment that rents for $1,000 per month per unit and has a vacancy factor of five percent, annual operating expenses of $10,000, and a capitalization rate of 8 percent. (Round to the nearest $100.)
    a. $302,500
    b. $288,000
    c. $276,500
    d. $275,000

11. You are appraising Home X in an affordable area. You find comparables A, B, and C, which have sold recently.

Sales Prices	A = $300,000	B = $304,000	C = $296,000
Condition	poorer than X	poorer than X	equal to X
Lot Size	equal to X	better than X	poorer than X
Location	equal to X	equal to X	poorer than X

Adjustment Figures
Difference in condition use $8,000
Difference in lot size use $4,000
Difference in location use $8,000
Home X should have a value of:
    a. $300,000.
    b. $304,000.
    c. $308,000.
    d. $312,000.

12. With a gross monthly multiplier of 150, a duplex that rents one unit for $575 per month and the other for $625 should have an estimated value of:
    a. $173,000.
    b. $176,000.
    c. $180,000.
    d. $197,000.

13. "Value in use" refers to:
    a. how a particular property can be used.
    b. the value of a particular property to a particular owner or user of real estate.
    c. what the property is worth.
    d. market value.

14. Capitalization is the
    a. process of establishing the cost of capital improvements.
    b. present value of future income.
    c. computing of gross income and reproduction costs.
    d. determining reserves for depreciation.

15. Objective value is also known as:
    a. value in use.
    b. market value.
    c. utility value.
    d. emotional value.

16. The principle which states that the best use of land is the use that generates the greatest net return is known as:

    a. highest and best use.

    b. conformity.

    c. supply and demand.

    d. substitution.

17. In the cost approach, the most difficult item to measure accurately is:

    a. square footage.

    b. accrued depreciation.

    c. lot size.

    d. replacement cost.

18. In evaluating a house that has an actual age of 15 years, the appraiser assigned it an age of only 10 years because of the home's excellent condition. This is an example of:

    a. effective age.

    b. chronological age.

    c. economic age.

    d. physical age.

19. All things being equal, the higher the cap rate, the:

    a. higher the value.

    b. lower the return.

    c. higher the rent.

    d. lower the value.

20. Accrued depreciation is used in what appraisal technique?

    a. Market data approach

    b. Cost approach

    c. Income approach

    d. Sales comparison approach

© Shutterstock / V. S

STUDENT LEARNING OUTCOMES

Closing a real estate transaction is a highly technical process. Escrow and title insurance companies provide valuable services that help consumers and real estate agents smoothly and efficiently close a real estate transaction. At the conclusion of this chapter, you will be able to do the following:

- Define escrow and list the legal requirements for a valid escrow.
- Describe the basic services provided by title insurance companies.
- Explain the difference between a CLTA standard and an ALTA extended-coverage policy of title insurance.
- Explain various closing costs and indicate who normally pays for each closing cost.

THE ROLE OF ESCROW AND TITLE INSURANCE COMPANIES

11.1 ESCROW

Definition of Escrow

In a real estate sale, an **escrow** is a process whereby a neutral third party acts as the closing agent for the buyer and the seller. (See Figure 11.1.) The escrow officer assumes the responsibility of handling all the paperwork and disbursement of funds to close out a real estate transaction. California Civil Code Section 1057 defines an escrow as follows:

A grant may be deposited by the grantor with a third person, to be delivered on the performance of a condition, and, on delivery by the depository, it will take effect. While in the possession of the third person, and subject to condition, it is called an escrow.

Escrows can be used for a variety of business transactions, such as sale or exchange of real estate, sale or encumbrance of personal property, sale or pledging of securities, sale of the assets of a business (bulk sale), sale of a promissory note secured by a deed of trust, and transfer of liquor licenses. By far, the most common reason for the use of an escrow is to handle the sale and transfer of real estate. The clerical aspects of transferring title to real estate are detailed and complicated; therefore, buyers, sellers, lenders, and real estate agents prefer to use trained escrow officers.

Legal Requirements for a Valid Escrow

There are two essential requirements for a valid real estate escrow:

1. There must be a binding contract between the seller (grantor) and the buyer (grantee).
2. There must be the conditional delivery of transfer instruments and monies to a neutral third party.

The binding contract can be in any legal form, such as a deposit receipt, an agreement of sale, an exchange agreement, or mutual

FIGURE 11.1

Source: © 2015 OnCourse Learning

instructions from the buyer and the seller. The escrow instructions signed by the buyer and seller supplement the terms of the original purchase agreement, and the two contracts are interpreted together. If there is a conflict between the purchase contract and the escrow instructions, the usual rule is that the most recent contract prevails. In most cases, this is the signed escrow instructions. Prior to signing the escrow instructions, every signee should check to see that the instructions reflect the most current purchase agreement.

Confidentiality of Escrows

Escrow instructions are confidential. Only the principals and their agents in the transaction are entitled to see the escrow instructions, and then only insofar as the instructions pertain to mutual items in the transaction. For example, the buyer and the seller are entitled to see each other's escrow instructions regarding the sales price, down payment, and other terms of the sale. But how much the seller is netting from the sale is no business of the buyer. Likewise, the buyer's financing arrangement with an institutional lender is no business of the seller, who is cashing out of the transaction.

If the escrow holder receives conflicting instructions from the principals, the escrow officer simply refuses to proceed until the parties settle their differences. An escrow officer cannot give legal advice and may bring an action in court forcing the principals in the escrow to litigate their differences. This legal action is called an *interpleader action*.

Status of the Escrow Holder

An escrow is a limited agency. The only obligations to be fulfilled by the escrow holder are those set forth in the instructions connected with the transaction. Before a real estate sale is recorded, the escrow officer is the dual agent for the buyer and the seller. After the deed is recorded, the escrow officer becomes the individual agent for each party.

This distinction is important, especially if an unethical escrow officer should steal money from the escrow company. If the escrow officer embezzles the money before the seller is entitled to it, the buyer suffers the loss. But if the money is embezzled after the seller becomes entitled to it, the loss falls on the seller because the money is now considered to be the seller's.

Regulation of Escrow Holders

Title insurance companies, banks, trust companies, savings and loan institutions, and insurance companies can handle escrows without obtaining an escrow license. Real estate brokers performing escrow services for a client and attorneys with a client relationship to the transaction also do not need an escrow license. However, independent escrow companies must be incorporated and can handle escrows only after obtaining an escrow license from the Department of Business Oversight, formerly the Department of Corporations. Independent escrow companies are common in southern California, whereas title insurance companies handle most of the escrows in northern California.

Who Decides Which Escrow Company to Use?

The selection of an escrow company is negotiated between the buyer and seller. The real estate agent cannot dictate which escrow company to use. If a real estate agent has a financial interest in an escrow company, the law requires the agent to disclose this interest to the buyer and the seller before a final selection is made. Real estate brokers can legally handle escrows without obtaining a special escrow license if the broker is an agent for the buyer or the seller in the transaction.

Once an escrow company is selected, who pays the fee? The payment of the escrow fee is an item that is negotiable between buyer and seller. The decision as to who pays this fee varies throughout the state. In some geographic areas, the seller usually pays; in other areas, the buyer usually pays; in some areas, the fee is split between the buyer and the seller.

Services Provided by Escrow Holders

For a fee, the escrow holder carefully collects, prepares, and safeguards the instructions, documents, and monies required to close the transaction. Upon receipt of written instructions from all parties (i.e., buyer, seller, lender, and real estate agent), the escrow instructions are compared to determine whether the parties are in mutual agreement. An escrow officer can do no more or no less than the instructions dictate.

When the parties are in agreement and all instruments and monies have been deposited, the escrow officer sees that title is transferred. The following are some of the services performed by an escrow company:

1. Prepares buyer's and seller's escrow instructions; prepares deed and other needed documents, such as promissory notes and deeds of trust as instructed from all parties

2. Orders title search which produces a preliminary title report from the title company and reviews the report for items such as unrecorded liens, judgments, etc.

3. Requests the demand for payoff for the seller's loan from the lending institution or, in the case of an assumption, requests a beneficiary statement from the lending institution

4. Collects the structural pest control report and the notice of work completed, if any

5. Collects the required fire insurance policy

6. Balances the accounting details, including adjustments and prorations of the taxes, interest, insurance, and assessments and rents (if any)

7. Collects the balance of monies required to close the transaction

8. Verifies that the appropriate documents are recorded; after transfer has occurred, the escrow file is audited; the escrow officer then disburses the monies, issues itemized closing statements to all parties, and orders the title insurance policy

Special Interest Topic

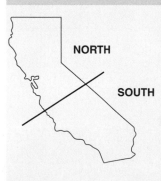

North Versus South

Escrow practices differ between southern and northern California. In southern California, independent escrow companies are common, and they handle a considerable number of the real estate transactions. Title insurance companies provide the title services, but escrow companies do the actual closing of the sale. Some lending institutions also provide escrow services in southern California. In northern California, most escrows are handled by title insurance companies that have extensive escrow departments with many branch offices.

One other point of difference has to do with the timing of the signing of escrow instructions. In southern California, it is common to have the buyer and seller sign escrow instructions shortly after they sign their purchase agreement. This may be 30 or 60 days before the actual close of escrow. In many northern California counties, escrow instructions are usually not signed until a day or two before the actual close of escrow.

Termination of Escrows

Escrows are usually terminated by completion of the sale and, in the case of a refinance, upon completion of the loan process. If the transaction is not completed, the escrow may be canceled by mutual agreement of all parties. The escrow company is entitled to receive partial payment of escrow fees for services rendered to date.

All the conditions required by escrow instructions must be performed within the time limit set forth in the escrow agreement. The escrow officer has no authority to enforce or accept the performance after the time limit provided in the instructions. When the time limit provided in the escrow has expired and neither party to the escrow has performed in accordance with the terms, upon receiving mutual written releases, the parties are entitled to the return of their respective papers, documents, and money from the escrow officer.

Escrow and TRID

Over the years, both the Truth in Lending Act (TILA) and the Real Estate Settlement Procedure Act (RESPA) provided protection, safeguards, and disclosures to consumers who were shopping for loans. However, they required lenders and settlement agents to provide borrowers with two sets of different but overlapping disclosure forms explaining the loan's terms and costs. Under new laws from the Consumer Financial Protection Bureau (CFPB), which now administers both TILA and RESPA, the disclosure requirement has been combined so the consumer now receives two forms instead of four. The disclosures are used to inform the borrower of the true cost of credit which is when all costs are added into the principle amount being borrowed.

The Loan Estimate form gives the borrower information on estimated costs of the loan and closing and must be received by the borrower no later than three days after completing an application. The form also alerts the borrower to items that may be shopped for, such as title work versus those fees that will be a direct charge such as the appraisal costs. The borrower should also receive the "Your Home Loan Toolkit: A Step-by-Step Guide," booklet at the same time as the loan estimate form.

The Closing Disclosure form is the final accounting for the closing and must be received by the borrower no later than three business days prior to closing of the loan. This is to give the borrower time to review all the costs and terms and to verify they match what was received in the loan estimate.

Most of the burden for implementing RESPA falls upon the real estate lender. However, escrow agents are also involved. RESPA requires the use of a Uniform Settlement Statement, which must itemize all closing charges. Upon request, the escrow agent must let the borrower-buyer inspect the Uniform Settlement Statement one day before the close of escrow. In addition, the escrow officer must see that all parties receive a copy of the Uniform Settlement Statement after the close of escrow.

11.2 PRORATIONS

Ownership of real property entails certain expenses. Some of these expenses are paid in advance; others, in arrears. They may be paid for by the seller prior to the sale of the property, or the buyer may assume costs owed by the seller at the close of escrow.

It is only fair that expenses paid in advance should be credited (allocated) to the seller and debited (charged) to the buyer; by the same token, expenses owed by the seller and not paid by the seller

Escrows—Summarized

An escrow holder is a neutral third party who, for a fee, will handle the paperwork involved in transferring title and/or in placing a new loan on real property. Escrow companies are licensed by the state of California. However, banks and title insurance companies can act as escrow holders without obtaining an escrow license. A real estate broker can act as an escrow holder only if the broker is an agent for the buyer or the seller. An attorney can also handle an escrow for a client involved in the transaction, without an escrow license.

TECHNICAL REASONS FOR AN ESCROW

1. To provide a custodian for funds and documents who can make concurrent delivery
2. To provide a clearinghouse for payments
3. To provide an agency for computing prorations

ESSENTIALS OF A VALID ESCROW

1. Must have a binding contract between buyer and seller
2. Must have conditional delivery of transfer instruments to a third party

TERMINATION OF AN ESCROW

1. By full performance and closing
2. By mutual cancellation by the parties
3. By revocation by a party

prior to the close of escrow, but to be paid later by the buyer, should be debited to the seller and credited to the buyer.

Proration is the act of making an equitable distribution of these expenses in escrow at the close of the sale.

There are four basic steps in proration:

1. Determine whether the amount should be a credit or a debit to the seller or the buyer.
2. Determine the number of days to be prorated.
3. Tabulate the cost per day.
4. Multiply the number of days by the cost per day.

Remember

For simplicity in determining prorations, assume there are 30 days in a month and 360 days in a year.

Expenses that are normally subject to proration are real property taxes and assessments, interest on loans assumed, hazard insurance, and prepaid rents if the property is income producing.

Example: Ms. A sells her rural cabin on September 1, 2014. She has an existing loan of $100,000 on the cabin. The interest on the loan is 9 percent. Buyer B assumes Ms. A's loan with interest paid to August 15, 2014. The seller has paid for an existing three-year hazard insurance policy for $360 per year, paid by Ms. A until October 15, 2015. Ms. A also neglected to pay her property taxes of $1,800 for the year. The tax year runs July 1, 2014, through June 30, 2015. What is the interest proration, and who is credited or debited? What is the insurance proration, and who is credited or debited? What is the tax proration, and who is credited or debited?

To figure the proration on the interest:
Step 1: August 15 to September 1, 2014 = 15 days
Step 2: $100,000 × 9% ÷ 360 = $25 per day
Step 3: 15 days × $25 per day = $375 interest
Step 4: Credit the buyer and debit the seller.

To figure the proration on the insurance policy:
Step 1: September 1, 2014, through October 15, 2015 = 405 days
Step 2: $360 ÷ 360 = $1 per day
Step 3: 405 days × $1 per day = $405
Step 4: Credit the seller and debit the buyer.

To figure the tax proration:
Step 1: July 1 to September 1, 2014 = 60 days
Step 2: $1,800 ÷ 360 = $5 per day
Step 3: 60 days × $5 per day = $300
Step 4: Debit the seller and credit the buyer.

Note

A general rule to use in proration is: When the expenses are paid beyond escrow, credit the seller and debit the buyer. When the expenses are paid short of escrow, debit the seller and credit the buyer.

11.3 DOCUMENTARY TRANSFER TAX

When real property is transferred, state law allows the county recorder to apply a **documentary transfer tax**. The amount of the tax is placed on the deed and is computed based on the following schedule:

1. $0.55 for every $500 of value transferred or fraction thereof. (Another option for determining the amount is $1.10 per $1,000 transferred.)
2. When the terms of the sale are all cash or a new loan, the documentary transfer tax is paid on the entire sales price.
3. When the buyer assumes the seller's existing loan, the amount of the loan on property is exempt and is subtracted from the total selling price. The tax is computed only on the equity amount. The transfer tax can be paid by the buyer or the seller, but custom usually has the seller pay the tax.

In some areas, cities are allowed to levy a real estate transfer tax on top of this statewide documentary tax. These transfer taxes are not standardized and vary from city to city. They are not presented in this book.

Example: A home is sold for $510,000. The buyer puts some cash down and obtains new financing for the balance of the sales price. What is the documentary transfer tax?

$$\frac{\$510,000}{\$500} = 510 \times \$.55 = \$561 \text{ documentary transfer tax}$$

11.4 TITLE INSURANCE COMPANIES

Title insurance companies are incorporated businesses that provide these basic services:

1. Search and gather public records relating to the legal title of real property.

2. Examine and interpret the title records that have been gathered.

3. Insure an owner or lender against financial loss resulting from certain unreported defects in the title.

Title Search

A *title search* can be conducted in one of two ways. The first is the *courthouse search*. Under this method, a title person goes to the county courthouse and searches through the public records, seeking information pertaining to a particular property under examination. The title searcher reproduces the information and presents the items to a title examiner for interpretation.

The second method is for a title company to maintain its own *title plant*. A title plant is really a condensed courthouse where records affecting real property are copied, usually microfilmed or computerized, and filed for future reference. When a title search is ordered, the title person has only to select the needed information from the title plant. This reduces the need for frequent trips to the county courthouse, thereby saving valuable time for the title company and the customer.

Title Examination

The actual examination and interpretation of a title is done by a highly skilled title examiner (not an attorney) whose task is to review each document and create what is known as a **chain of title**. A chain of title is an unbroken history of all the title transfers, beginning with the document originally transferring title from the government to private ownership and ending with the document vesting title in the current owner.

In addition to identifying the correct owner, the title examiner determines what and how various encumbrances (such as taxes, deeds of trust, easements, and so on) affect the ownership. When the examination is complete, the information is compiled into a *preliminary title report* that lists the name of the owner(s), the legal description of the property, the status of property taxes and special assessments, and the various encumbrances against the property. This preliminary title report is not the actual title policy, but it is the basis upon which a title company is willing to insure the owner's title.

Title Insurance

In the early days of California, title insurance did not exist. Land holdings were large, and population was sparse. Property frequently was transferred simply by the delivery of a symbol in the presence of a witness.

As population and migration increased, land holdings were divided and sold to incoming strangers. Boundaries became confused, and it was difficult to identify ownership. To combat this confusion, when California became a state in 1850, the legislature enacted recording statutes. These recording statutes created depositories (namely, the county recorder's office) to collect and file title documents for public use. Soon the recorder's offices became too complex for many laypeople to use. Specialists called **abstractors** began searching and compiling courthouse records. For a fee, these abstractors would publish their findings on a specific parcel of land.

To protect the public, the need arose for a system to guard against the errors, omissions, and incorrect judgments that abstractors might make. This need for additional assurance led to the concept of title insurance.

Today a title insurance policy insures the ownership of land and the priority of a lien (deed of trust, contract of sale, and so on) subject to the encumbrances revealed in the title examination. The owner and/or lender is assured that a thorough search has been made of all public records affecting a particular property. (See Figure 11.2.)

Types of Title Insurance Policies

Title insurance policies are divided into two basic groups, the standard policy and the extended-coverage policy. The **standard policy** is the most widely used and can be divided into three subtypes:

1. *Standard owner's policy,* which insures the owner for the amount of the purchase price
2. *Standard lender's policy,* which insures the lender for the amount of the loan
3. *Standard joint protection policy,* which co-insures the owner and lender under one policy

The standard policy is frequently referred to as a **CLTA policy**. CLTA stands for California Land Title Association, a state trade association for title insurance companies.

FIGURE 11.2

TITLE INSURANCE PROCESS

Search ⟶ Examination ⟶ Chain of title ⟶ Preliminary report ⟶ Escrow ⟶ Title policy

Source: © 2015 OnCourse Learning

Included in the standard coverage policy is the assurance that title is free and clear of all encumbrances of public record, other than the items revealed in the title examination and listed as exceptions in the title policy. Under the standard policy, the title company does not make a physical inspection of the property and therefore excludes from coverage unrecorded items that could affect the title. For example, unrecorded easements are excluded, as well as the rights of parties in possession other than the owner, such as tenants or squatters. Also excluded from standard policy coverage are encroachments, violations of environmental laws, zoning and other government ordinances affecting the use of the property, non-declared assessments, and some items regarding mining and water claims.

Extended-Coverage Policy

The **extended-coverage policy** was originally established for real estate lenders. This policy requires the title company to make a physical inspection of the property and insures against certain unrecorded title risks excluded under the standard policy. In some cases, the extended-coverage policy is requested and issued to homeowners, but not to other types of property owners. The extended-coverage policy is commonly referred to as an **ALTA policy**. ALTA stands for American Land Title Association, a national trade association for title insurance companies.

How Much Does Title Insurance Cost?

Title insurance premiums, like most other types of insurance premiums, are calculated based upon the dollar amount of insurance coverage. Owners' title policies are issued for the purchase price of the property, whereas lenders' title policies are issued for the loan amount. Therefore, owners of more expensive property pay higher title fees than owners of less expensive property. Title fees are established by title companies themselves, not by any government agency. Competition keeps rates between title companies comparable.

Unlike other forms of insurance (such as automobile, fire, and life insurance), which require annual premiums, a title insurance fee is paid only once. The title policy stays in force as long as the owner retains title to the property. A new title insurance policy is required by the lender; otherwise, the lender will not make the loan on the property.

Who Pays for the Title Insurance?

The payment of the owner's policy fee is a negotiable item between the buyer and the seller. However, in different geographic areas, the method of payment varies. In some areas, it is customary to split the title fee between the buyer and the seller. In some areas, the seller normally pays the title fee; in others, the buyer pays. The lender's policy title fee is almost always paid by the borrower-buyer.

Special Interest Topic

Evolution of Title Protection

FIRST CAME — *Abstract of Title*
A summary of title prepared by an early-day specialist, with no guarantee of accuracy

THEN — *Certificate of Title*
A certificate stating the name of the owner and a list of encumbrances, with no guarantee of accuracy

THEN — *Guarantee of Title*
A title search in which an abstract company guaranteed the accuracy of the search

AND TODAY — *Title insurance*
Creation of an insurance company that issue satitle policy and insures the accuracy of results. If insured suffers an insured loss, a claim is filed similar in nature to any other type of insurance. Title insurance led to the use of the grant deed and elimination of the warranty deed in California. (See Chapter 2 for details regarding deeds.)

Who Decides Which Title Insurance Company to Use?

This is another negotiable item between the buyer and the seller. The usual custom is for the party paying the title fee to select the title company. As discussed above, real estate regulations prohibit a real estate agent from dictating which title insurance company to use. If the real estate agent should happen to have a financial interest in the title company selected, the agent must disclose this fact to the buyer and the seller.

Title Insurance Summarized

A title insurance policy ensures that a thorough examination has been made of all public records affecting the property in question and that the owner has acquired ownership free from title defects of public record, subject only to the encumbrances revealed in the title examination and the exceptions recited in the title insurance policy. It means that the owner has a marketable title that can be transferred to others.

STANDARD COVERAGE POLICY (CLTA)

1. Risks normally insured against the following:
   (a) Most matters disclosed by public records
   (b) Certain off-record risks, such as forgery or incompetence of parties
2. Risks not normally insured against the following:
   (a) Matters not disclosed by public records
   (b) Environmental laws, zoning, and other government ordinances regarding the use of the property
   (c) Certain mining and water claims
   (d) Defects known to the insured before the property was purchased and not revealed to the title company before the sale

EXTENDED-COVERAGE POLICY (ALTA)

1. Risks covered:
   (a) All those listed under the standard coverage policy
   (b) Unperfected mechanics' liens
   (c) Unrecorded physical easements
   (d) Facts a correct survey would show
   (e) Certain water claims
   (f) Rights of parties in possession, including tenants and owners under unrecorded instruments
2. Risks not normally covered:
   (a) Environmental laws, zoning, and other government ordinances affecting the use of the property
   (b) Defects known to the insured before the property was insured but not revealed to title company by the insured

For an additional charge, an insured can purchase special endorsements to cover items normally excluded under the CLTA or ALTA policies.

11.5 CLOSING COSTS

Closing costs refer to the expenses paid by the buyer and the seller upon the sale of property. Some people attempt to estimate closing costs by using simple rules of thumb, such as "3 percent of the sales price" or some other rough figure. However, rules of thumb are not accurate. The only sure way to determine actual closing costs is to list and price each individual item.

The payment of the closing costs is a negotiable topic between the buyer and seller. No law requires that certain closing costs are the responsibility of the buyer or the seller. The only exception deals with some government-backed loans where regulations prohibit the buyer from paying certain closing costs. However, by custom, certain closing costs are typically paid by the buyer, and other costs are usually paid by the seller.

Buyer's Closing Costs

A buyer's (borrower) closing costs can be divided into two categories: (1) nonrecurring closing costs and (2) recurring closing costs.

Nonrecurring closing costs are one-time charges paid upon the close of escrow. Recurring closing costs are prepaid items that the buyer pays in advance to help offset expenses that will continue as long as the buyer owns the property.

Nonrecurring Closing Costs Usually Paid by the Buyer

1. *Loan origination fee.* A fee charged by a lender to cover the expenses of processing a loan. The fee is usually quoted as a percentage of the loan amount. For example, a 1% loan fee for a $300,000 loan would be 1% × $300,000 = $3,000 loan fee.

2. *Appraisal fee.* A fee charged by an appraiser for giving an estimate of property value. The fee for a simple appraisal varies throughout the state, with $350 to $450 or more being a typical charge for a single-family residence. Appraisal fees for income properties such as apartments and office buildings are considerably higher.

3. *Credit report fee.* Before a lender grants a loan, the borrower's credit is checked at a credit agency. The credit report usually costs from $40 to $60.

4. *Structural pest control inspection fee.* A fee charged by a licensed inspector who checks for termites, fungus, dry rot, pests, and other items that might cause structural damage. For a home in an urban area, the fee is usually $75 to $125.

5. *Tax service fee.* A fee paid to a tax service company that, for the life of the loan, each year reviews the tax collector's records. If a borrower fails to pay property taxes, the tax service company reports this fact to the lender, who then takes steps to protect the loan against a tax foreclosure sale. This fee usually runs from $50 to $80.

6. *Recording fees.* This covers the cost of recording the deed, the deed of trust, and other buyer-related documents. Most counties charge $10 to $15 to record a single-page document.

7. *Notary fees.* Signatures on documents to be recorded must be notarized. The buyer will pay the notary for the buyers signatures on the promissory note and mortgage or deed of trust Notary public fees are set by law.

8. *Assumption fee.* A fee paid to a lender if the buyer "assumes" the loan, that is, agrees to take over and continue to pay the seller's existing loan.

9. *Title and escrow fees.* Buyer's responsibility in buyer-pays areas, areas where it is customary for the buyer to pay the title and escrow fees.

Recurring Closing Costs Usually Paid by the Buyer

1. *Hazard insurance.* A one-year premium for insurance against fire, storm, and other risks. The minimum coverage is the amount of the real estate loan, but buyers are advised to purchase greater amounts if they make a large down payment toward the purchase price. Many owners purchase comprehensive homeowner's packages.

2. *Tax proration.* In California, the property tax year runs from July 1 through June 30 of the following year. If the seller has prepaid the taxes, the buyer reimburses the seller for the prepaid portion.

3. *Tax and insurance reserves.* This is also known as an *impound account* or *reserve account.* If a buyer's (borrower's) monthly loan payment is to include taxes and insurance, as well as principal and interest, the lender sets up a reserve account. Depending on the time of the year (the date taxes and insurance are due relative to the date escrow closes), a lender will want the buyer to prepay one to six months of taxes and insurance premiums into this reserve account. Once an adequate reserve account is established, tax and insurance bills are forwarded to the lender for payment. At the end of the year, adjustments are made to assure that adequate amounts are in the trust fund for the next year.

4. *Interest due before the first loan payment.* Interest on real estate loans is typically paid in arrears. For example: Escrow closes September 15 with the first loan payment due November 1.

The payment due November 1 covers the interest due for the month of October. How is the interest from September 15 to September 30 collected? It is collected in advance at the close of escrow and is called *prepaid interest*. If escrow closed on the first of the month, there would be no prepaid interest if the first payment was due on the first of the following month.

Seller's Closing Costs

The closing costs paid by a seller are one-time, nonrecurring expenses. After the close of escrow, the seller is divested of ownership and, therefore, has no recurring expenses attached to ownership such as property taxes and hazard insurance. Remember that the payment of a particular closing expense is negotiable between the buyer and seller. The following list is merely a guideline to closing costs usually paid by the seller as the result of custom and/or agreement.

Closing Costs Usually Paid by the Seller

1. *Transfer tax.* A tax charged when title is transferred. The county has a documentary transfer tax that is computed at $1.10 per $1,000 (or 55 cents per $500 or fraction thereof) of the sales price. For example, if a $500,000 home is sold for cash or all-new financing, the state documentary transfer tax would be as follows:

   $500,000 sales price ÷ $1,000 = 500 × $1.10 = $550 tax

   In addition to the documentary transfer tax, some cities in California have enacted a municipal transfer tax that must be collected and disbursed at the close of escrow.

2. *Prepayment penalty.* A charge by a lender when a borrower pays off a loan before the required due date. Many times when a property is sold, the buyer obtains financing to cover the sales price. In the process, the seller's existing mortgage is paid off to make way for the buyer's new mortgage. If the seller's mortgage has a prepayment clause, the seller pays this penalty as a closing cost. Most loans do not have prepayment penalties. But if they do, the actual prepayment penalties vary by lender. A typical prepayment penalty might be six months' interest on the outstanding loan balance at the time of payoff, after subtracting 20 percent of the original loan amount.

3. *Structural pest control work.* In certain areas, the buyer pays for the structural pest control inspection fee, and the seller pays for

corrective work. However, in some areas, the seller pays for both the inspection and the corrective work.

4. *Real estate brokerage commission.* The commission is normally quoted as a percentage of the sales price. A 6 percent commission with a sales price of $500,000 would be $30,000, shown as part of the closing costs to the seller on the closing statement.

5. *Discount points.* On some government-backed loans, the seller may pay discount points to increase a lender's yield on a loan. One point is equal to 1 percent of the buyer's loan amount.

6. *Recording and notary fees.* Fees for recording seller-oriented documents, such as a deed of reconveyance to clear off an old loan.

7. *Title and escrow fees.* Seller's responsibility in seller-pays areas, where it is customary for the seller to pay the title and escrow fees.

8. *Natural hazard disclosure fees.* To provide seller-required disclosures for earthquake, flood, fire, and other hazards.

Summary of Closing Costs

BUYER USUALLY PAYS

1. Loan origination fee
2. Appraisal fee
3. Credit report
4. Structural pest control inspection fee
5. Tax service fee
6. Recording fees
7. Notary fees
8. Assumption fee, if any
9. Title and escrow fees in buyer-pays areas
10. Hazard insurance
11. Interest on loan before first payment

SELLER USUALLY PAYS

1. Transfer tax
2. Prepayment penalty
3. Structural pest control work and report fee

(Continued)

4. Real estate brokerage commission
5. Discount points on government-backed loans
6. Recording and notary fees
7. Title and escrow fees in seller-pays areas
8. Natural hazard disclosure fees

USUALLY PRORATED BETWEEN THE BUYER AND SELLER

1. Property taxes
2. Interest if loan is assumed by buyer
3. Rents if the property is tenant-occupied income property

Chapter Summary

Escrow is the use of a neutral third party to act as the closing agent in a real estate transaction. To be valid, an escrow requires a binding contract and a conditional delivery of transfer instruments. Escrow companies must comply with the requirements of TRID for the closing disclosures forms.

Title insurance companies, institutional lenders, attorneys, and independently licensed companies can handle escrows. A real estate broker can handle an escrow if he or she is an agent for the buyer or the seller in the transaction.

Title insurance companies search and gather public title records, examine and interpret the records, and then issue policies of title insurance. The two major types of title insurance policies are the CLTA standard and the ALTA extended-coverage policies. Certain items are not included in title insurance coverage; therefore, consumers should be aware that these excluded items are their responsibility.

Closing costs can be classified as recurring and nonrecurring. Recurring closing costs are prepaid items that the buyer pays in advance to help offset expenses that will continue as long as the buyer owns the property. Nonrecurring closing costs are one-time charges paid upon the close of escrow.

The payment of escrow fees, title insurance, and closing costs is an item of negotiation between the buyer and the seller. However, by custom, certain closing costs are typically paid by the buyer, whereas other costs are usually paid by the seller. This custom varies throughout the state of California. Escrow and closing practices differ between northern and southern California.

Important Terms and Concepts

abstractors

ALTA policy

chain of title

closing costs

CLTA policy

documentary transfer tax

escrow

extended-coverage policy

proration

Real Estate Settlement Procedures
   Act (RESPA)

standard policy

Practical Application

1. Seller and buyer are in escrow for the sale of a home. In the area, it is customary for the seller to pay for the CLTA title policy. The deposit receipt states that the seller will pay for the title policy, but the escrow instructions signed by all parties state that all title and escrow fees will be split 50/50. Just prior to close of escrow, the buyer submits amended instructions for the escrow officer to charge the entire CLTA policy to the seller. The seller refuses to proceed with the escrow. As the buyer's real estate agent, what might you do to solve this problem?

2. Acme Title Company has a policy of giving real estate licensees who refer business to the company a dinner for two and tickets to a professional sporting event. Without your suggestion, the buyer and the seller asked that Acme Title Company be the title insurer. As the real estate agent in the transaction, what are the legal and ethical issues?

3. A $413,575 existing ARM loan at seven percent will be assumed by the buyer. The seller has made the October 1 payment, and escrow will close on October 19 (use 18 days since buyer is responsible for the day escrow closes). Using a 360-day year, what are the escrow debit and credit charges to the buyer and seller for the interest proration?

Reviewing Your Understanding

1. For an escrow to be valid, there must be a:
   a. conditional delivery of transfer documents to a third party.
   b. real estate agent in the transaction.
   c. title insurance policy.
   d. 60-day limit on the closing date.

2. In a real estate transaction, who decides which escrow company to use?
   a. The seller
   b. The buyer
   c. It is negotiated between the buyer and the seller
   d. The real estate agent

3. A history of title transfers for a particular parcel of land is a(n):
   a. preliminary report.
   b. title insurance policy.
   c. abstracter index.
   d. chain of title.

4. Most homeowners in California have which type of title insurance policy?
   a. ALTA lender's
   b. ALTA owner's
   c. CLTA lender's
   d. CLTA owner's

5. Which insurance policy requires the title company to make a physical inspection of the property?
   a. CLTA
   b. Standard
   c. RESPA
   d. ALTA

6. Sales price $295,000, buyer puts on new 80 percent loan and pays one percent loan fee, $45 tax service fee, $400 tax prorations, $175 structural pest control inspection fee, $20 credit report, $20 recording fees, $910 hazard insurance fee, and a $600 escrow fee. How much will the buyer need to close escrow?
   a. $4,530
   b. $37,740
   c. $63,530
   d. $68,360

7. In northern California, most escrows are handled by:
   a. escrow companies.
   b. real estate agents.
   c. title companies.
   d. all of the above.

8. Escrow is a process whereby a neutral third party acts on behalf of the:
   a. buyer, seller, buyer's agent, and seller's agent.
   b. title company.
   c. selling agent and listing agent.
   d. buyer and seller only.

9. A standard title insurance policy insures against:
   a. encroachments.
   b. incompetent parties on record.
   c. unrecorded easements.
   d. mining claims.

10. Who decides what title company to use?
    a. The seller
    b. The buyer
    c. The listing agent
    d. This is negotiable between the buyer and the seller

11. Termination of an escrow can occur:
    a. when the escrow officer completes the paperwork.
    b. when the listing agent says it is okay.
    c. upon completion of the sale.
    d. none of the above.

12. Which of the following is a recurring closing cost?
    a. Fire insurance
    b. Recording fees
    c. Notary fees
    d. Appraisal fee

13. On behalf of the buyer and seller, the escrow officer acts as a(n):
    a. employee.
    b. independent contractor.
    c. agent.
    d. licensee.

14. With the approval of all parties, real estate brokers can act as escrow holders in transactions in which they have:
    a. the listing.
    b. the buyer.
    c. the ownership.
    d. all of the above.

15. TRID requires the buyer receive what document three days before closing the loan?
    a. Loan estimate
    b. Closing disclosure
    c. Lending booklet
    d. Escrow instructions

16. Which of the following must be licensed to be an escrow holder?
    a. Bank
    b. Attorney
    c. Trust company
    d. Independent corporation

17. The buyer's closing costs are divided into categories. They are:
    a. recurring and seller's costs.
    b. buyer's costs and seller's costs.
    c. recurring and nonrecurring costs.
    d. nonrecurring costs only because the buyer does not pay recurring costs.

18. A joint protection title policy insures:
    a. the buyer and seller.
    b. the buyer and lender.
    c. the buyer and broker.
    d. two unrelated owners.

19. The tax service fee is usually paid by the:
    a. buyer.
    b. seller.
    c. lender.
    d. broker.

20. The sales price is $800,000. The buyer is to put $200,000 down and to obtain a new first loan for $500,000, and the seller is to carry back a second loan for $100,000. The documentary transfer tax is:
    a. $880.
    b. $770.
    c. $550.
    d. $220.

STUDENT LEARNING OUTCOMES

The relationship between landlords and tenants can be calm and enjoyable, or it can be turbulent, with frustration and confusion on both sides. The California legislature is constantly passing laws related to landlords and tenants. Many problems between landlords and tenants are caused by a lack of understanding of the legal rights and duties of each party. At the conclusion of this chapter, you will be able to do the following:

- Define a lease and list four types of leasehold estates.
- Outline the requirements needed for a valid lease.
- Explain the difference between a sublease and an assignment of a lease.
- Discuss the duties and responsibilities that landlords and tenants owe to each other.
- Describe how tenants can be lawfully evicted.
- Explain the services provided by professional property managers.

LANDLORD AND TENANT RELATIONS

12.1 LEASES

A lease is a contract between an owner, called a **lessor** (or landlord), and a **lessee** (or tenant). A tenant is given the right to possess and use the landlord's property in exchange for rent. *California law requires that all leases for more than one year must be in writing to be valid.*

A lease for one year or less need not be in writing to be valid. However, a prudent person should reduce all rental and lease agreements to writing. The terms *lease* and *rental agreement* are often used interchangeably, although commonly people will refer to agreements of a month-to-month duration as a rental agreement and agreements of longer duration as a lease. In this chapter we will use lease.

Types of Leasehold Estates

In Chapter 6, a distinction was made between a *freehold estate* and a *less-than-freehold estate*. A freehold estate is an interest in real property as an owner; a less-than-freehold estate is an interest in real property as a tenant. Less-than-freehold estates are also known as *leasehold estates*. There are four types of leasehold estates, as illustrated in Figure 12.1 and described in the following list.

1. **Estate for years** *(tenancy for a fixed term)*. A leasehold that continues for a fixed time span. The term *estate for years* is misleading because the fixed time span can be for a day, a week, a month, a year, or years. Therefore, a signed lease for five years and a signed lease for one month are both estates for years. To eliminate this confusion, the term *estate for years* is beginning to be called a *tenancy for a fixed term*.

FIGURE 12.1

Source: © 2015 OnCourse Learning

2. **Estate from period to period** (*periodic tenancy*). A leasehold that continues from period to period (day, week, month, or year) with no specified termination date. Each party agrees to renew or terminate at the end of each period. A month-to-month lease is an example of an estate from period to period.

3. **Estate at will.** A leasehold at the landlords will. An estate at will has no definite termination date listed in the lease and often has no written lease. This estate is often verbal, such as a friend agreeing to allow another friend to stay in his extra room for a remuneration at some point. If the landlord set an amount and due date a periodic estate would be created. Estate at will can be terminated without notice at any time by the landlord or the tenant. The California legislature has passed laws stating that the lessor and the lessee must give advance notice prior to the termination of an estate at will.

4. **Estate at sufferance.** A leasehold where a tenant retains possession of the property after the expiration of a lease. This is how the law differentiates between someone who has had a right of possession and will need due process to be removed and a trespasser who has no right to due process. For example, a tenant has an estate for years that expired today. The assumption of the lease if there is no other language is the lease and possession terminate on the date listed in the lease. Under these circumstances, the lessee's estate for years is converted to an estate at sufferance until a decision is made about the future rights of the lessee. The landlord can ask the tenant to leave, enter into another lease agreement or start eviction. If the landlord accepts rent typically a month to month tenancy is created.

Requirements for a Valid Lease

For a lease to be valid, it must have the following characteristics:

1. Meet all the requirements of valid contracts; competent parties, mutual consent, lawful objective and consideration.

2. Be in writing if the term is for more than one year. Any alterations must also be in writing.

3. Contain the names of the lessor and lessee.

4. Contain a sufficient description of the property. In some cases, a street address is sufficient for a simple residential lease. In other cases, it may be wise to include a complete legal description in addition to the common street address.

5. Show the amount of rent and the manner of payment. An example might be a rent of $60,000, payable $1,000 per month for five years.

6. State the duration or time period the lease is to run or, in the case of a periodic tenancy, the periods involved. *According to law, urban property cannot be leased for more than 99 years and rural agricultural land for more than 51 years.*

7. Be signed by the lessor. Technically, a lessee does not need to sign the lease to make it valid. The lessee's possession of the property is considered to be acceptance of the agreement. However, to eliminate misunderstanding, a landlord should insist that the tenant sign the lease.

8. Have any renewal or extension provisions in boldface type. A renewal or extension provision is a clause that automatically renews or extends the lease if the lessee remains in possession after expiration of the lease.

See Figure 12.2 for a sample residential lease form.

Other Provisions

Although not legally required, a lease should also state who is responsible for utilities and maintenance. If there are special rules regarding noise, guests, parking, pets, and so on, they should be noted in the lease. The intended use of the property should be specified, as well as the maximum number of tenant occupants per rental unit as allowed by law. A lease should also note the right, if any, the tenant may have to remove fixtures attached by him or her.

FIGURE 12.2

CALIFORNIA
ASSOCIATION
OF REALTORS ®

**RESIDENTIAL LEASE OR
MONTH-TO-MONTH RENTAL AGREEMENT**
(C.A.R. Form LR, Revised 12/13)

Date _____, _____ ("Landlord") and
_____ ("Tenant") agree as follows:

1. PROPERTY:
    A. Landlord rents to Tenant and Tenant rents from Landlord, the real property and improvements described as:_____
                                                                                ("Premises").
    B. The Premises are for the sole use as a personal residence by the following named person(s) **only:** _____
        _____.
    C. The following personal property, maintained pursuant to paragraph 11, is included: _____
        _____ or ☐ (if checked) the personal property on the attached addendum.
    D. The Premises may be subject to a local rent control ordinance _____.
2. TERM: The term begins on (date) _____ ("Commencement Date"), **(Check A or B):**
    ☐ **A. Month-to-Month:** and continues as a month-to-month tenancy. Tenant may terminate the tenancy by giving written notice at
        least 30 days prior to the intended termination date. Landlord may terminate the tenancy by giving written notice as provided by
        law. Such notices may be given on any date.
    ☐ **B. Lease:** and shall terminate on (date) _____ at _____ ☐ AM/ ☐ PM. Tenant
        shall vacate the Premises upon termination of the Agreement, unless: **(i)** Landlord and Tenant have extended this Agreement
        in writing or signed a new agreement; **(ii)** mandated by local rent control law; or **(iii)** Landlord accepts Rent from Tenant (other
        than past due Rent), in which case a month-to-month tenancy shall be created which either party may terminate as specified in
        paragraph 2A. Rent shall be at a rate agreed to by Landlord and Tenant, or as allowed by law. All other terms and conditions of
        this Agreement shall remain in full force and effect.
3. RENT: "Rent" shall mean all monetary obligations of Tenant to Landlord under the terms of the Agreement, except security deposit.
    A. Tenant agrees to pay $ _____ per month for the term of the Agreement.
    B. Rent is payable in advance on the **1st (or ☐ _____) day** of each calendar month, and is delinquent on the next day.
    C. If Commencement Date falls on any day other than the day Rent is payable under paragraph 3B, and Tenant has paid one full
        month's Rent in advance of Commencement Date, Rent for the second calendar month shall be prorated and Tenant shall pay
        1/30th of the monthly rent per day for each day remaining in prorated second month.
    D. **PAYMENT:** Rent shall be paid by ☐ personal check, ☐ money order, ☐ cashier's check, or ☐ other _____, to
        (name) _____ (phone) _____ at (address) _____
        _____, (or at any other location subsequently
        specified by Landlord in writing to Tenant) (and ☐ if checked, rent may be paid personally, between the hours of _____ and _____
        on the following days _____). If any payment is returned for non-sufficient
        funds ("NSF") or because tenant stops payment, then, after that: (i) Landlord may, in writing, require Tenant to pay Rent in cash for
        three months and (ii) all future Rent shall be paid by ☐ money order, or ☐ cashier's check.
4. SECURITY DEPOSIT:
    A. Tenant agrees to pay $ _____ as a security deposit. Security deposit will be
        ☐ transferred to and held by the Owner of the Premises, or ☐ held in Owner's Broker's trust account.
    B. All or any portion of the security deposit may be used, as reasonably necessary, to: **(i)** cure Tenant's default in payment of Rent (which
        includes Late Charges, NSF fees or other sums due); **(ii)** repair damage, excluding ordinary wear and tear, caused by Tenant or by a guest
        or licensee of Tenant; **(iii)** clean Premises, if necessary, upon termination of the tenancy; and **(iv)** replace or return personal property or
        appurtenances. **SECURITY DEPOSIT SHALL NOT BE USED BY TENANT IN LIEU OF PAYMENT OF LAST MONTH'S RENT.**
        If all or any portion of the security deposit is used during the tenancy, Tenant agrees to reinstate the total security deposit within five
        days after written notice is delivered to Tenant. Within 21 days after Tenant vacates the Premises, Landlord shall: **(1)** furnish Tenant
        an itemized statement indicating the amount of any security deposit received and the basis for its disposition and supporting
        documentation as required by California Civil Code § 1950.5(g); and **(2)** return any remaining portion of the security deposit to Tenant.
    C. **Security deposit will not be returned until all Tenants have vacated the Premises and all keys returned. Any security
        deposit returned by check shall be made out to all Tenants named on this Agreement, or as subsequently modified.**
    D. No interest will be paid on security deposit unless required by local law.
    E. If the security deposit is held by Owner, Tenant agrees not to hold Broker responsible for its return. If the security deposit is held
        in Owner's Broker's trust account, **and** Broker's authority is terminated before expiration of this Agreement, **and** security deposit is
        released to someone other than Tenant, **then** Broker shall notify Tenant, in writing, where and to whom security deposit has been
        released. Once Tenant has been provided such notice, Tenant agrees not to hold Broker responsible for the security deposit.
5. MOVE-IN COSTS RECEIVED/DUE: Move-in funds made payable to _____ shall be
    paid by ☐ personal check, ☐ money order, or ☐ cashier's check.

Category	Total Due	Payment Received	Balance Due	Date Due
Rent from _____ to _____ (date)				
*Security Deposit				
Other _____				
Other _____				
Total				

*The maximum amount Landlord may receive as security deposit, however designated, cannot exceed two months' Rent for unfurnished
 premises, or three months' Rent for furnished premises.

Tenant's Initials (_____)(_____)   Landlord's Initials (_____)(_____)

LR REVISED 12/13 (PAGE 1 OF 6) Print Date

Reviewed by _____ Date _____

EQUAL HOUSING
OPPORTUNITY

FIGURE 12.2 (Continued)

Premises: _____ Date: _____

6. **LATE CHARGE; RETURNED CHECKS:**

   A. Tenant acknowledges either late payment of Rent or issuance of a returned check may cause Landlord to incur costs and expenses, the exact amounts of which are extremely difficult and impractical to determine. These costs may include, but are not limited to, processing, enforcement and accounting expenses, and late charges imposed on Landlord. If any installment of Rent due from Tenant is not received by Landlord within **5 (or ☐ _____) calendar days** after the date due, or if a check is returned, Tenant shall pay to Landlord, respectively, an additional sum of $ _____ or _____% of the Rent due as a Late Charge and $25.00 as a NSF fee for the first returned check and $35.00 as a NSF fee for each additional returned check, either or both of which shall be deemed additional Rent.

   B. Landlord and Tenant agree that these charges represent a fair and reasonable estimate of the costs Landlord may incur by reason of Tenant's late or NSF payment. Any Late Charge or NSF fee due shall be paid with the current installment of Rent. Landlord's acceptance of any Late Charge or NSF fee shall not constitute a waiver as to any default of Tenant. Landlord's right to collect a Late Charge or NSF fee shall not be deemed an extension of the date Rent is due under paragraph 3 or prevent Landlord from exercising any other rights and remedies under this Agreement and as provided by law.

7. **PARKING: (Check A or B)**

   ☐ A. Parking is permitted as follows: _____
   _____.
   The right to parking ☐ is ☐ is not included in the Rent charged pursuant to paragraph 3. If not included in the Rent, the parking rental fee shall be an additional $ _____ per month. Parking space(s) are to be used for parking properly licensed and operable motor vehicles, except for trailers, boats, campers, buses or trucks (other than pick-up trucks). Tenant shall park in assigned space(s) only. Parking space(s) are to be kept clean. Vehicles leaking oil, gas or other motor vehicle fluids shall not be parked on the Premises. Mechanical work or storage of inoperable vehicles is not permitted in parking space(s) or elsewhere on the Premises.

   OR ☐ B. Parking is not permitted on the Premises.

8. **STORAGE: (Check A or B)**

   ☐ A. Storage is permitted as follows: _____
   The right to separate storage space ☐ is, ☐ is not, included in the Rent charged pursuant to paragraph 3. If not included in the Rent, storage space fee shall be an additional $ _____ per month. Tenant shall store only personal property Tenant owns, and shall not store property claimed by another or in which another has any right, title or interest. Tenant shall not store any improperly packaged food or perishable goods, flammable materials, explosives, hazardous waste or other inherently dangerous material, or illegal substances.

   OR ☐ B. Except for Tenant's personal property, contained entirely within the Premises, storage is not permitted on the Premises.

9. **UTILITIES:** Tenant agrees to pay for all utilities and services, and the following charges: _____ except _____, which shall be paid for by Landlord. If any utilities are not separately metered, Tenant shall pay Tenant's proportional share, as reasonably determined and directed by Landlord. If utilities are separately metered, Tenant shall place utilities in Tenant's name as of the Commencement Date. Landlord is only responsible for installing and maintaining one usable telephone jack and one telephone line to the Premises. Tenant shall pay any cost for conversion from existing utilities service provider.

10. **CONDITION OF PREMISES:** Tenant has examined Premises and, if any, all furniture, furnishings, appliances, landscaping and fixtures, including smoke detector(s).

    (Check all that apply:)

    ☐ A. Tenant acknowledges these items are clean and in operable condition, with the following exceptions: _____
    _____.

    ☐ B. Tenant's acknowledgment of the condition of these items is contained in an attached statement of condition (C.A.R. Form MIMO).

    ☐ C. **(i)** Landlord will Deliver to Tenant a statement of condition (C.A.R. Form MIMO) ☐ within **3 days** after execution of this Agreement; ☐ prior to the Commencement Date; ☐ within **3 days** after the Commencement Date.
    (ii) Tenant shall complete and return the MIMO to Landlord within **3 (or ☐_____) days** after Delivery. Tenant's failure to return the MIMO within that time shall conclusively be deemed Tenant's Acknowledgement of the condition as stated in the MIMO.

    ☐ D. Tenant will provide Landlord a list of items that are damaged or not in operable condition within **3 (or ☐ _____) days** after Commencement Date, not as a contingency of this Agreement but rather as an acknowledgment of the condition of the Premises.

    ☐ E. Other: _____.

11. **MAINTENANCE:**

    A. Tenant shall properly use, operate and safeguard Premises, including if applicable, any landscaping, furniture, furnishings and appliances, and all mechanical, electrical, gas and plumbing fixtures, and smoke alarms, and keep them and the Premises clean, sanitary and well ventilated. Tenant shall be responsible for checking and maintaining all carbon monoxide detectors and any additional phone lines beyond the one line and jack that Landlord shall provide and maintain. Tenant shall immediately notify Landlord, in writing, of any problem, malfunction or damage with any item on the property. Tenant shall be charged for all repairs or replacements caused by Tenant, pets, guests or licensees of Tenant, excluding ordinary wear and tear. Tenant shall be charged for all damage to Premises as a result of failure to report a problem in a timely manner. Tenant shall be charged for repair of drain blockages or stoppages, unless caused by defective plumbing parts or tree roots invading sewer lines.

    B. ☐ Landlord ☐ Tenant shall water the garden, landscaping, trees and shrubs, except: _____
    _____.

    C. ☐ Landlord ☐ Tenant shall maintain the garden, landscaping, trees and shrubs, except: _____
    _____.

    D. ☐ Landlord ☐ Tenant shall maintain _____.

    E. Tenant's failure to maintain any item for which Tenant is responsible shall give Landlord the right to hire someone to perform such maintenance and charge Tenant to cover the cost of such maintenance.

    F. The following items of personal property are included in the Premises without warranty and Landlord will not maintain, repair or replace them: _____.

Tenant's Initials (_____)(_____)   Landlord's Initials (_____)(_____)

LR REVISED 12/13 (PAGE 2 OF 6)

| Reviewed by _____ Date _____ |

EQUAL HOUSING OPPORTUNITY

RESIDENTIAL LEASE OR MONTH-TO-MONTH RENTAL AGREEMENT (LR PAGE 2 OF 6)

FIGURE 12.2 (Continued)

Premises: _____ Date: _____

12. NEIGHBORHOOD CONDITIONS: Tenant is advised to satisfy him or herself as to neighborhood or area conditions, including schools, proximity and adequacy of law enforcement, crime statistics, proximity of registered felons or offenders, fire protection, other governmental services, availability, adequacy and cost of any wired, wireless internet connections or other telecommunications or other technology services and installations, proximity to commercial, industrial or agricultural activities, existing and proposed transportation, construction and development that may affect noise, view, or traffic, airport noise, noise or odor from any source, wild and domestic animals, other nuisances, hazards, or circumstances, cemeteries, facilities and condition of common areas, conditions and influences of significance to certain cultures and/or religions, and personal needs, requirements and preferences of Tenant.

13. PETS: Unless otherwise provided in California Civil Code § 54.2, no animal or pet shall be kept on or about the Premises without Landlord's prior written consent, except: _____.

14. ☐ (If checked) **NO SMOKING:** No smoking of any substance is allowed on the Premises or common areas. If smoking does occur on the Premises or common areas, (i) Tenant is responsible for all damage caused by the smoking including, but not limited to stains, burns, odors and removal of debris; (ii) Tenant is in breach of this Agreement; (iii) Tenant, guests, and all others may be required to leave the Premises; and (iv) Tenant acknowledges that in order to remove odor caused by smoking, Landlord may need to replace carpet and drapes and paint the entire premises regardless of when these items were last cleaned, replaced. or repainted. Such actions and other necessary steps will impact the return of any security deposit. The Premises or common areas may be subject to a local non-smoking ordinance.

15. RULES/REGULATIONS:
    A. Tenant agrees to comply with all Landlord rules and regulations that are at any time posted on the Premises or delivered to Tenant. Tenant shall not, and shall ensure that guests and licensees of Tenant shall not, disturb, annoy, endanger or interfere with other tenants of the building or neighbors, or use the Premises for any unlawful purposes, including, but not limited to, using, manufacturing, selling, storing or transporting illicit drugs or other contraband, or violate any law or ordinance, or commit a waste or nuisance on or about the Premises.
    B. (If applicable, check one)
        ☐ **1.** Landlord shall provide Tenant with a copy of the rules and regulations within _____days
        or _____.
    OR ☐ **2.** Tenant has been provided with, and acknowledges receipt of, a copy of the rules and regulations.

16. ☐ (If checked) **CONDOMINIUM;PLANNED UNIT DEVELOPMENT:**
    A. The Premises are a unit in a condominium, planned unit development, common interest subdivision or other development governed by a homeowners' association ("HOA"). The name of the HOA is _____ Tenant agrees to comply with all HOA covenants, conditions and restrictions, bylaws, rules and regulations and decisions ("HOA Rules"). Landlord shall provide Tenant copies of HOA Rules, if any. Tenant shall reimburse Landlord for any fines or charges imposed by HOA or other authorities, due to any violation by Tenant, or the guests or licensees of Tenant.
    B. (Check one)
        ☐ **1.** Landlord shall provide Tenant with a copy of the HOA Rules within _____ days
        or _____.
    OR ☐ **2.** Tenant has been provided with, and acknowledges receipt of, a copy of the HOA Rules.

17. ALTERATIONS; REPAIRS: Unless otherwise specified by law or paragraph 29C, without Landlord's prior written consent, **(i)** Tenant shall not make any repairs, alterations or improvements in or about the Premises including: painting, wallpapering, adding or changing locks, installing antenna or satellite dish(es), placing signs, displays or exhibits, or using screws, fastening devices, large nails or adhesive materials; **(ii)** Landlord shall not be responsible for the costs of alterations or repairs made by Tenant; **(iii)** Tenant shall not deduct from Rent the costs of any repairs, alterations or improvements; and **(iv)** any deduction made by Tenant shall be considered unpaid Rent.

18. KEYS; LOCKS:
    A. Tenant acknowledges receipt of (or Tenant will receive ☐ prior to the Commencement Date, or ☐ _____):
        ☐ _____ key(s) to Premises,   ☐ _____ remote control device(s) for garage door/gate opener(s),
        ☐ _____ key(s) to mailbox,   ☐ _____,
        ☐ _____ key(s) to common area(s),   ☐ _____.
    B. Tenant acknowledges that locks to the Premises ☐ have, ☐ have not, been re-keyed.
    C. If Tenant re-keys existing locks or opening devices, Tenant shall immediately deliver copies of all keys to Landlord. Tenant shall pay all costs and charges related to loss of any keys or opening devices. Tenant may not remove locks, even if installed by Tenant.

19. ENTRY:
    A. Tenant shall make Premises available to Landlord or Landlord's representative for the purpose of entering to make necessary or agreed repairs (including, but not limited to, installing, repairing, testing, and maintaining smoke detectors and carbon monoxide devices, and bracing, anchoring or strapping water heaters), decorations, alterations, or improvements, or to supply necessary or agreed services, or to show Premises to prospective or actual purchasers, tenants, mortgagees, lenders, appraisers, or contractors.
    B. Landlord and Tenant agree that 24-hour written notice shall be reasonable and sufficient notice, except as follows: (1) 48-hour written notice is required to conduct an inspection of the Premises prior to the Tenant moving out, unless the Tenant waives the right to such notice. (2) If Landlord has in writing informed Tenant that the Premises are for sale and that Tenant will be notified orally to show the premises (C.A.R. Form NSE), then, for the next 120 days following the delivery of the NSE, notice may be given orally to show the Premises to actual or prospective purchasers. (3) No written notice is required if Landlord and Tenant orally agree to an entry for agreed services or repairs if the date and time of entry are within one week of the oral agreement. (4) No notice is required: **(i)** to enter in case of an emergency; **(ii)** if the Tenant is present and consents at the time of entry; or **(iii)** if the Tenant has abandoned or surrendered the Premises.
    C. ☐ (If checked) Tenant authorizes the use of a keysafe/lockbox to allow entry into the Premises and agrees to sign a keysafe/lockbox addendum (C.A.R. Form KLA).

20. SIGNS: Tenant authorizes Landlord to place FOR SALE/LEASE signs on the Premises.

21. ASSIGNMENT; SUBLETTING: Tenant shall not sublet all or any part of Premises, or assign or transfer this Agreement or any interest in it, without Landlord's prior written consent. Unless such consent is obtained, any assignment, transfer or subletting of Premises or this Agreement or tenancy, by voluntary act of Tenant, operation of law or otherwise, shall, at the option of Landlord, terminate this Agreement. Any proposed assignee, transferee or sublessee shall submit to Landlord an application and credit information for Landlord's approval and, if approved, sign a separate written agreement with Landlord and Tenant. Landlord's consent to any one assignment, transfer or sublease, shall not be construed as consent to any subsequent assignment, transfer or sublease and does not release Tenant of Tenant's obligations under this Agreement.

Tenant's Initials (_____)(_____)   Landlord's Initials (_____)(_____)

Reviewed by _____ Date _____

FIGURE 12.2 (Continued)

Premises: _____ Date: _____

22. **JOINT AND INDIVIDUAL OBLIGATIONS:** If there is more than one Tenant, each one shall be individually and completely responsible for the performance of all obligations of Tenant under this Agreement, jointly with every other Tenant, and individually, whether or not in possession.

23. ☐ **LEAD-BASED PAINT (If checked):** Premises were constructed prior to 1978. In accordance with federal law, Landlord gives and Tenant acknowledges receipt of the disclosures on the attached form (C.A.R. Form FLD) and a federally approved lead pamphlet.

24. ☐ **MILITARY ORDNANCE DISCLOSURE:** (If applicable and known to Landlord) Premises are located within one mile of an area once used for military training, and may contain potentially explosive munitions.

25. ☐ **PERIODIC PEST CONTROL:** Landlord has entered into a contract for periodic pest control treatment of the Premises and shall give Tenant a copy of the notice originally given to Landlord by the pest control company.

26. ☐ **METHAMPHETAMINE CONTAMINATION:** Prior to signing this Agreement, Landlord has given Tenant a notice that a health official has issued an order prohibiting occupancy of the property because of methamphetamine contamination. A copy of the notice and order are attached.

27. **MEGAN'S LAW DATABASE DISCLOSURE:** Notice: Pursuant to Section 290.46 of the Penal Code, information about specified registered sex offenders is made available to the public via an Internet Web site maintained by the Department of Justice at www. meganslaw.ca.gov. Depending on an offender's criminal history, this information will include either the address at which the offender resides or the community of residence and ZIP Code in which he or she resides. (Neither Landlord nor Brokers, if any, are required to check this website. If Tenant wants further information, Tenant should obtain information directly from this website.)

28. **POSSESSION:**
    A. Tenant is not in possession of the Premises. If Landlord is unable to deliver possession of Premises on Commencement Date, such Date shall be extended to the date on which possession is made available to Tenant. If Landlord is unable to deliver possession within **5 (or ☐ _____) calendar days** after agreed Commencement Date, Tenant may terminate this Agreement by giving written notice to Landlord, and shall be refunded all Rent and security deposit paid. Possession is deemed terminated when Tenant has returned all keys to the Premises to Landlord.
    B. ☐ Tenant is already in possession of the Premises.

29. **TENANT'S OBLIGATIONS UPON VACATING PREMISES:**
    A. Upon termination of this Agreement, Tenant shall: **(i)** give Landlord all copies of all keys or opening devices to Premises, including any common areas; **(ii)** vacate and surrender Premises to Landlord, empty of all persons; **(iii)** vacate any/all parking and/or storage space; **(iv)** clean and deliver Premises, as specified in paragraph C below, to Landlord in the same condition as referenced in paragraph 10; **(v)** remove all debris; **(vi)** give written notice to Landlord of Tenant's forwarding address; and **(vii)**
    _____.
    B. All alterations/improvements made by or caused to be made by Tenant, with or without Landlord's consent, become the property of Landlord upon termination. Landlord may charge Tenant for restoration of the Premises to the condition it was in prior to any alterations/improvements.
    C. **Right to Pre-Move-Out Inspection and Repairs: (i)** After giving or receiving notice of termination of a tenancy (C.A.R. Form NTT), or before the end of a lease, Tenant has the right to request that an inspection of the Premises take place prior to termination of the lease or rental (C.A.R. Form NRI). If Tenant requests such an inspection, Tenant shall be given an opportunity to remedy identified deficiencies prior to termination, consistent with the terms of this Agreement. **(ii)** Any repairs or alterations made to the Premises as a result of this inspection (collectively, "Repairs") shall be made at Tenant's expense. Repairs may be performed by Tenant or through others, who have adequate insurance and licenses and are approved by Landlord. The work shall comply with applicable law, including governmental permit, inspection and approval requirements. Repairs shall be performed in a good, skillful manner with materials of quality and appearance comparable to existing materials. It is understood that exact restoration of appearance or cosmetic items following all Repairs may not be possible. **(iii)** Tenant shall: **(a)** obtain receipts for Repairs performed by others; **(b)** prepare a written statement indicating the Repairs performed by Tenant and the date of such Repairs; and **(c)** provide copies of receipts and statements to Landlord prior to termination. Paragraph 29C does not apply when the tenancy is terminated pursuant to California Code of Civil Procedure § 1161(2), (3) or (4).

30. **BREACH OF CONTRACT; EARLY TERMINATION:** In addition to any obligations established by paragraph 29, in the event of termination by Tenant prior to completion of the original term of the Agreement, Tenant shall also be responsible for lost Rent, rental commissions, advertising expenses and painting costs necessary to ready Premises for re-rental. Landlord may withhold any such amounts from Tenant's security deposit.

31. **TEMPORARY RELOCATION:** Subject to local law, Tenant agrees, upon demand of Landlord, to temporarily vacate Premises for a reasonable period, to allow for fumigation (or other methods) to control wood destroying pests or organisms, or other repairs to Premises. Tenant agrees to comply with all instructions and requirements necessary to prepare Premises to accommodate pest control, fumigation or other work, including bagging or storage of food and medicine, and removal of perishables and valuables. Tenant shall only be entitled to a credit of Rent equal to the per diem Rent for the period of time Tenant is required to vacate Premises.

32. **DAMAGE TO PREMISES:** If, by no fault of Tenant, Premises are totally or partially damaged or destroyed by fire, earthquake, accident or other casualty that render Premises totally or partially uninhabitable, either Landlord or Tenant may terminate this Agreement by giving the other written notice. Rent shall be abated as of the date Premises become totally or partially uninhabitable. The abated amount shall be the current monthly Rent prorated on a 30-day period. If the Agreement is not terminated, Landlord shall promptly repair the damage, and Rent shall be reduced based on the extent to which the damage interferes with Tenant's reasonable use of Premises. If damage occurs as a result of an act of Tenant or Tenant's guests, only Landlord shall have the right of termination, and no reduction in Rent shall be made.

33. **INSURANCE:** Tenant's or guest's personal property and vehicles are not insured by Landlord, manager or, if applicable, HOA, against loss or damage due to fire, theft, vandalism, rain, water, criminal or negligent acts of others, or any other cause. **Tenant is advised to carry Tenant's own insurance (renter's insurance) to protect Tenant from any such loss or damage.** Tenant shall comply with any requirement imposed on Tenant by Landlord's insurer to avoid: **(i)** an increase in Landlord's insurance premium (or Tenant shall pay for the increase in premium); or **(ii)** loss of insurance.

34. **WATERBEDS:** Tenant shall not use or have waterbeds on the Premises unless: **(i)** Tenant obtains a valid waterbed insurance policy; **(ii)** Tenant increases the security deposit in an amount equal to one-half of one month's Rent; and **(iii)** the bed conforms to the floor load capacity of Premises.

35. **WAIVER:** The waiver of any breach shall not be construed as a continuing waiver of the same or any subsequent breach.

Tenant's Initials (_____)(_____)   Landlord's Initials (_____)(_____)

| Reviewed by _____ Date _____ |

LR REVISED 12/13 (PAGE 4 OF 6)

RESIDENTIAL LEASE OR MONTH-TO-MONTH RENTAL AGREEMENT (LR PAGE 4 OF 6)

FIGURE 12.2 (Continued)

Premises: _____ Date: _____

36. NOTICE: Notices may be served at the following address, or at any other location subsequently designated:

Landlord: _____   Tenant: _____

_____   _____

_____   _____

37. TENANT ESTOPPEL CERTIFICATE: Tenant shall execute and return a tenant estoppel certificate delivered to Tenant by Landlord or Landlord's agent within **3 days** after its receipt. Failure to comply with this requirement shall be deemed Tenant's acknowledgment that the tenant estoppel certificate is true and correct, and may be relied upon by a lender or purchaser.

38. REPRESENTATION

A. TENANT REPRESENTATION; OBLIGATIONS REGARDING OCCUPANTS; CREDIT: Tenant warrants that all statements in Tenant's rental application are accurate. Landlord requires all occupants 18 years of age or older and all emancipated minors to complete a lease rental application. Tenant acknowledges this requirement and agrees to notify Landlord when any occupant of the Premises reaches the age of 18 or becomes an emancipated minor. Tenant authorizes Landlord and Broker(s) to obtain Tenant's credit report periodically during the tenancy in connection with the modification or enforcement of this Agreement. Landlord may cancel this Agreement: **(i)** before occupancy begins; **(ii)** upon disapproval of the credit report(s); or **(iii)** at any time, upon discovering that information in Tenant's application is false. A negative credit report reflecting on Tenant's record may be submitted to a credit reporting agency if Tenant fails to fulfill the terms of payment and other obligations under this Agreement.

B. LANDLORD REPRESENTATIONS: Landlord warrants that, unless otherwise specified in writing, Landlord is unaware of **(i)** any recorded Notices of Default affecting the Premise; **(ii)** any delinquent amounts due under any loan secured by the Premises; and **(iii)** any bankruptcy proceeding affecting the Premises.

39. MEDIATION:

A. Consistent with paragraphs B and C below, Landlord and Tenant agree to mediate any dispute or claim arising between them out of this Agreement, or any resulting transaction, before resorting to court action. Mediation fees, if any, shall be divided equally among the parties involved. If, for any dispute or claim to which this paragraph applies, any party commences an action without first attempting to resolve the matter through mediation, or refuses to mediate after a request has been made, then that party shall not be entitled to recover attorney fees, even if they would otherwise be available to that party in any such action.

B. The following matters are excluded from mediation: **(i)** an unlawful detainer action; **(ii)** the filing or enforcement of a mechanic's lien; and **(iii)** any matter within the jurisdiction of a probate, small claims or bankruptcy court. The filing of a court action to enable the recording of a notice of pending action, for order of attachment, receivership, injunction, or other provisional remedies, shall not constitute a waiver of the mediation provision.

C. Landlord and Tenant agree to mediate disputes or claims involving Listing Agent, Leasing Agent or property manager ("Broker"), provided Broker shall have agreed to such mediation prior to, or within a reasonable time after, the dispute or claim is presented to such Broker. Any election by Broker to participate in mediation shall not result in Broker being deemed a party to this Agreement.

40. ATTORNEY FEES: In any action or proceeding arising out of this Agreement, the prevailing party between Landlord and Tenant shall be entitled to reasonable attorney fees and costs, except as provided in paragraph 39A.

41. C.A.R. FORM: C.A.R. Form means the specific form referenced or another comparable form agreed to by the parties.

42. OTHER TERMS AND CONDITIONS;SUPPLEMENTS: ☐ Interpreter/Translator Agreement (C.A.R. Form ITA); ☐ Keysafe/Lockbox Addendum (C.A.R. Form KLA); ☐ Lead-Based Paint and Lead-Based Paint Hazards Disclosure (C.A.R. Form FLD); ☐ Landlord in Default Addendum (C.A.R. For LID) _____

The following ATTACHED supplements are incorporated in this Agreement: _____

_____

43. TIME OF ESSENCE; ENTIRE CONTRACT; CHANGES: Time is of the essence. All understandings between the parties are incorporated in this Agreement. Its terms are intended by the parties as a final, complete and exclusive expression of their Agreement with respect to its subject matter, and may not be contradicted by evidence of any prior agreement or contemporaneous oral agreement. If any provision of this Agreement is held to be ineffective or invalid, the remaining provisions will nevertheless be given full force and effect. Neither this Agreement nor any provision in it may be extended, amended, modified, altered or changed except in writing. This Agreement is subject to California landlord-tenant law and shall incorporate all changes required by amendment or successors to such law. This Agreement and any supplement, addendum or modification, including any copy, may be signed in two or more counterparts, all of which shall constitute one and the same writing.

44. AGENCY:

A. CONFIRMATION: The following agency relationship(s) are hereby confirmed for this transaction:

Listing Agent: (Print firm name) _____ is the agent of (check one): ☐ the Landlord exclusively; or ☐ both the Landlord and Tenant.

Leasing Agent: (Print firm name) _____ (if not same as Listing Agent) is the agent of (check one): ☐ the Tenant exclusively; or ☐ the Landlord exclusively; or ☐ both the Tenant and Landlord.

B. DISCLOSURE: ☐ (If checked): The term of this lease exceeds one year. A disclosure regarding real estate agency relationships (C.A.R. Form AD) has been provided to Landlord and Tenant, who each acknowledge its receipt.

45. ☐ **TENANT COMPENSATION TO BROKER:** Upon execution of this Agreement, Tenant agrees to pay compensation to Broker as specified in a separate written agreement between Tenant and Broker.

Tenant's Initials (_____)(_____)   Landlord's Initials (_____)(_____)

LR REVISED 12/13 (PAGE 5 OF 6)

Reviewed by _____ Date _____

RESIDENTIAL LEASE OR MONTH-TO-MONTH RENTAL AGREEMENT (LR PAGE 5 OF 6)

FIGURE 12.2 (Continued)

Premises: _____ Date: _____

46. ☐ **INTERPRETER/TRANSLATOR:** The terms of this Agreement have been interpreted for Tenant into the following language: _____. Landlord and Tenant acknowledge receipt of the attached interpreter/translator agreement (C.A.R. Form ITA).

47. FOREIGN LANGUAGE NEGOTIATION: If this Agreement has been negotiated by Landlord and Tenant primarily in Spanish, Chinese, Tagalog, Korean or Vietnamese, pursuant to the California Civil Code, Tenant shall be provided a translation of this Agreement in the language used for the negotiation.

48. OWNER COMPENSATION TO BROKER: Upon execution of this Agreement, Owner agrees to pay compensation to Broker as specified in a separate written agreement between Owner and Broker (C.A.R. Form LCA).

49. RECEIPT: If specified in paragraph 5, Landlord or Broker, acknowledges receipt of move-in funds.

> Landlord and Tenant acknowledge and agree Brokers: **(a)** do not guarantee the condition of the Premises; **(b)** cannot verify representations made by others; **(c)** cannot provide legal or tax advice; **(d)** will not provide other advice or information that exceeds the knowledge, education or experience required to obtain a real estate license. Furthermore, if Brokers are not also acting as Landlord in this Agreement, Brokers: **(e)** do not decide what rental rate a Tenant should pay or Landlord should accept; and **(f)** do not decide upon the length or other terms of tenancy. Landlord and Tenant agree that they will seek legal, tax, insurance and other desired assistance from appropriate professionals.

Tenant agrees to rent the Premises on the above terms and conditions.

Tenant _____ Date _____
Address _____ City _____ State _____ Zip_____
Telephone _____ Fax_____ E-mail _____
Tenant _____ Date _____
Address _____ City _____ State _____ Zip_____
Telephone _____ Fax_____ E-mail _____

☐ **GUARANTEE:** In consideration of the execution of this Agreement by and between Landlord and Tenant and for valuable consideration, receipt of which is hereby acknowledged, the undersigned ("Guarantor") does hereby: **(i)** guarantee unconditionally to Landlord and Landlord's agents, successors and assigns, the prompt payment of Rent or other sums that become due pursuant to this Agreement, including any and all court costs and attorney fees included in enforcing the Agreement; **(ii)** consent to any changes, modifications or alterations of any term in this Agreement agreed to by Landlord and Tenant; and **(iii)** waive any right to require Landlord and/or Landlord's agents to proceed against Tenant for any default occurring under this Agreement before seeking to enforce this Guarantee.

Guarantor (Print Name) _____
Guarantor _____ Date _____
Address _____ City _____ State _____ Zip_____
Telephone _____ Fax_____ E-mail _____

Landlord agrees to rent the Premises on the above terms and conditions.

Landlord _____ Landlord _____
Address _____
Telephone _____ Fax_____ E-mail _____

> **REAL ESTATE BROKERS:**
> **A.** Real estate brokers who are not also Landlord under this Agreement are not parties to the Agreement between Landlord and Tenant.
> **B.** Agency relationships are confirmed in paragraph 44.
> **C.** **COOPERATING BROKER COMPENSATION:** Listing Broker agrees to pay Cooperating Broker (Leasing Firm) and Cooperating Broker agrees to accept: **(i)** the amount specified in the MLS, provided Cooperating Broker is a Participant of the MLS in which the Property is offered for sale or a reciprocal MLS; or **(ii)** ☐ (if checked) the amount specified in a separate written agreement between Listing Broker and Cooperating Broker.

Real Estate Broker (Listing Firm)_____ DRE Lic. # _____
By (Agent) _____ DRE Lic. # _____ Date _____
Address _____ City _____ State _____ Zip _____
Telephone _____ Fax_____ E-mail _____

Real Estate Broker (Leasing Firm)_____ DRE Lic. # _____
By (Agent) _____ DRE Lic. # _____ Date _____
Address _____ City _____ State _____ Zip _____
Telephone _____ Fax_____ E-mail _____

Published and Distributed by:
REAL ESTATE BUSINESS SERVICES, INC.
a subsidiary of the California Association of REALTORS®
525 South Virgil Avenue, Los Angeles, California 90020

LR REVISED 12/13 (PAGE 6 OF 6)

Reviewed by _____ Date _____   EQUAL HOUSING OPPORTUNITY

RESIDENTIAL LEASE OR MONTH-TO-MONTH RENTAL AGREEMENT (LR PAGE 6 OF 6)

Source: Reprinted with permission of California Association of REALTORS®

Security Deposits

On a residential rental, a security deposit cannot exceed more than two months' rent on unfurnished dwellings or three months' rent on furnished units. The security deposit must be refunded within 21 days after the tenant vacates the property.

However, if properly worded, the security deposit can be used to offset back rent and damages caused by the tenant or to clean the premises left dirty by the tenant. If an offset is used, the landlord must provide the tenant with an itemized statement showing all charges within 21 days after the tenant vacates. *No security deposit can be labeled as nonrefundable.* The landlord is still allowed to collect the first month's rent in addition to the security deposit already noted.

Assignment Versus Sublease of the Lease

An assignment of a lease transfers the entire leasehold interest to another party, including the prime liability and responsibility to make payments to the lessor (landlord). Figure 12.3 illustrates an assignment of a lease.

Under an assignment, the original Lessee A is removed from the transaction and all rights and duties pass to Assignee B. Assignee B is now primarily liable for the lease.

A **sublease** transfers only a part of the term of the lessee to a sublessee. The original lessee is still liable to the lessor (landlord) for the terms and conditions of the lease. Figure 12.4 illustrates a sublease.

Sublessee B pays Lessee A, who pays the lessor. In essence, there are two contracts—the original lease between lessor and Lessee A and another contract between Lessee A and Sublessee B. Each contract stands alone. If Sublessee B does not pay Lessee A, Lessee A must still pay the lessor. In Figure 12.4, Lessee A is said to hold a **sandwich lease**. In other words, Lessee A is wedged between the lessor and the sublessee. A lessor can insert a clause in the lease, prohibiting any assignment or sublease without the prior written approval of the lessor.

FIGURE 12.3

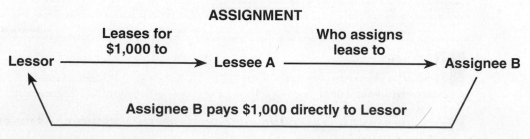

Source: © 2015 OnCourse Learning

FIGURE 12.4

SUBLEASE

Source: © 2015 OnCourse Learning

Lease with Option to Buy

Under a **lease with option to buy** (purchase), property is rented for a period of time, at the end of which the lessee is given the option to purchase per a set of agreed terms. The lessee (tenant/optionee) is not required to buy, but may if he or she wishes. If the lessee does exercise the option, the lessor/optionor must sell.

A lease with option to buy should not be confused with a concept known as *first right of refusal*. Under a first right of refusal, the lessor (landlord) is not required to sell. However, if the lessor does wish to sell, the lessee (tenant) is given the first chance to buy.

Major Types of Leases

1. **Gross/fixed lease**. The tenant pays a fixed rental amount, and the landlord is responsible for taxes, maintenance, and insurance.
2. **Net lease**. The tenant pays a fixed rent plus, per the lease, pays a portion of the landlord's property taxes, hazard insurance, and maintenance (a helpful acronym is *TIM*). If the tenant pays only one item it is net lease if three items it called a triple net lease. This type of lease is used when commercial property is leased on a long-term basis.
3. **Percentage lease**. Rent is based on a percentage of the tenant's gross sales—this type of lease often uses a combination fixed rent plus a certain percentage of the tenant's gross sales. Usually, the higher the tenant's gross sales, the smaller the percentage; and the lower the tenant's sales volume, the higher the percentage.

Important Concepts

1. *Extension of a lease*. The continuation of an old lease is an *extension*. For example, an existing lease is about to expire, so the lessor and lessee agree to extend the lease for one year using the same terms and conditions.

2. *Renewal of a lease.* This occurs when the existing lessor and lessee renegotiate a new lease upon the expiration of the existing lease. The terms and conditions are frequently different from those of the old lease.

3. *Escalator clause.* This clause allows the landlord to increase the rent during the term of the lease if costs increase. It is frequently tied to the Consumer Price Index or Producer Price Index.

12.2 DUTIES AND RESPONSIBILITIES OF LANDLORDS AND TENANTS

Landlord's Duties and Rights

In exchange for rent, a landlord surrenders use and possession of the property to a tenant. Under this arrangement, a landlord owes the tenant certain duties and responsibilities, which include these:

1. If the property is residential, there is an *implied right of habitability.* The landlord, in essence, guarantees that the dwelling meets minimum housing and health codes, such as having hot and cold running water.

2. Landlords have the right to inspect the property periodically, but they must give *advance notice.* Most lease agreements state that the landlord must give 24 or 48 hours' notice. In cases of emergency, to protect the property, a landlord is allowed to enter the premises without giving advance notice.

3. With residential property, a landlord is usually held liable for injuries resulting from unsafe conditions in common areas such as stairwells, hallways, and the surrounding grounds. If the defects or dangers are caused by tenant negligence, the liability for injuries may shift from the landlord to the tenant. On nonresidential structures, the liability for keeping the premises safe is frequently shifted from landlord to tenant via the use of triple net lease terms.

4. A landlord is not allowed to interfere with the tenant's use and quiet enjoyment of the property. If the tenant is abiding by the terms of the lease, frequent and uncalled-for intrusions by a pesky landlord can be grounds for the tenant to cancel the lease and possibly seek damages in court.

5. According to state and federal laws, a landlord cannot refuse to rent to a tenant based on (1) race, color, or national origin; (2) religion or creed; (3) sex, sexual orientation, or marital status and registered domestic partnership; and (4) physical handicap unless it can be proven that the building poses a danger to the

handicapped person. Also, landlords cannot refuse to rent to families with children; however, certain senior citizen housing projects are allowed to exclude children.

6. Under current law a landlord can terminate a month-to-month lease by serving the tenant with a 60-day notice if the tenant has been in the property for over a year. If the tenant has occupied the property for less than a year, then the landlord can give the tenant a 30-day notice. The landlord does not need to give the tenant a reason, nor does the tenant need to be in violation of the terms of the lease. However, if the tenant can prove that the landlord's actions are unfair based upon the antidiscriminatory laws noted above, the tenant can sue the landlord. Also, if a tenant has a signed lease for a specified duration (estate for years), a landlord cannot force the tenant (lessee) to leave unless the tenant violates the terms of the lease agreement. *Note:* If a landlord has entered into a Section 8 agreement with a local housing authority to provide housing for low- and moderate-income tenants, special rules apply that may be different from those noted above.

Tenant's Duties and Rights

A tenant owes a landlord certain duties and responsibilities. In turn, a tenant has certain rights. Tenant duties and rights are summarized as follows:

1. Tenants are expected to pay the rent when due and not to damage the property beyond normal wear and tear.

2. Tenants who have month-to-month leases are required to give at least a 30-day notice (regardless of how long the tenant has occupied the property) before vacating the property. A landlord can sue for 30 days' rent if a tenant fails to give the landlord a 30-day notice before vacating.

3. Tenants can be held liable for injuries to guests or customers resulting from unsafe conditions caused by the tenant's negligence. Tenants should purchase their own renter's insurance policy to protect their valuables in case of fire, storm damage, and theft. Most renter's insurance policies also provide personal liability protection for the tenant.

4. Tenants have a duty not to interfere with the rights of other tenants.

5. A tenant has the right to use and enjoy the property. If the property becomes uninhabitable the tenant may choose to give notice and move. This process is called constructive eviction.

Special Interest Topic

Rent Controls

Rent control is a controversial topic, with emotions and misconceptions running rampant on both sides of the issue. From a purely economic point of view, rent controls make little sense. The issue has been studied repeatedly by liberal and conservative economists, and most agree that rent controls do not solve housing problems. Rents are high because demand for apartment housing is high and supply is inadequate. The solution is to decrease demand for rental units or increase supply.

Rent controls do neither. Rent controls artificially depress rent levels, which, in turn, stimulates demand instead of reducing demand. Rent controls reduce returns and yields on apartment investments, thereby discouraging the construction of new units or the conversion of large homes into apartments. In the long term, rent controls can actually cause landlords to defer needed maintenance, resulting in a property's deterioration. In short, rent controls tend to perpetuate the ill they are supposed to cure!

A danger accompanying long-term rent control is the departure of investors in rental property altogether. If investors are unable to make a reasonable return on any specific type of investment, they will abandon it as an investment vehicle. The result over time is likely to be an ever-decreasing number of available rental opportunities for tenants.

Never fully explored is the hostage-like situation that is established for tenants unwilling to move from their rent-controlled apartments. Artificially maintained low rents can create difficult decisions for tenants who may have to move to areas where market rents prevail even when such a move may be to their overall economic benefit.

Source: From *California Real Estate Finance*, 9th ed., by R. J. Bond, D. J. McKenzie, John Fesler, and Rick Boone (Cincinnati, OH: Cengage Learning, 2011).

6. In California, all residential rentals must meet minimum housing and health codes. The responsibility for meeting the codes rests with the landlord. If the property falls below standards because of damage or negligence caused by the tenant, the landlord can bring legal action against the tenant. On the other hand, if, through no fault of the tenant, the dwelling falls below housing codes, the tenant can demand that the landlord make the needed repairs. If the landlord refuses, the tenant can abandon the property and not be liable for future rent. The tenant may elect to use a rental offset procedure outlined in the California Civil Code.

Rental Offset

If a residential landlord refuses to make needed repairs, Section 1942 of the Civil Code allows a tenant to spend up to one month's rent to make the repairs. The paid repair bill can then be used to offset the next month's rent. The basic rules are as follows:

1. The tenant must give the landlord written notice and adequate time to make the repairs.

2. If the landlord refuses, the tenant can spend up to one month's rent on the repairs and then deduct the cost of repairs from the following month's rent.

3. A tenant can use a rental offset only twice in any 12-month period and can use it only for needed repairs, not decorative changes. In most cases, a tenant cannot charge for his or her own labor, only for repair parts. However, if a tradesperson makes the repairs, both parts and labor can be used for the offset. If a tenant spends more than one month's rent, the excess cannot be applied against subsequent rental payments. *Note:* It is probably best for tenants to use the rental offset for repairs affecting habitability only.

Current law prohibits a landlord from taking retaliatory action, such as serving an eviction notice or raising the rent, for a period of 180 days after the tenant's use of the rental offset.

Rental Payments to Neutral Escrow

In some instances, needed repairs may exceed one month's rent and a tenant may be reluctant to use the limited offset provisions noted earlier. Under these circumstances, a tenant may be able to make rental payments to a neutral escrow, with instructions to deliver the rents to the landlord after the property has been brought up to minimum housing standards. *Caution: This is a controversial legal concept and should not be exercised without the advice of an attorney.*

12.3 EVICTIONS AND OTHER WAYS TO TERMINATE A LEASE

Eviction occurs when a tenant is dispossessed by operation of law. The eviction process is a legal procedure in court. Landlords cannot resort to "self-help" actions such as changing the locks, shutting off utility services, seizing the tenant's property in lieu of rent, or threatening the tenants with bodily harm. If a landlord commits an illegal act, such as the ones noted previously, the tenant can sue the landlord under the aforementioned theory known as *constructive eviction*.

Unlawful Detainer Action

The process of legally removing a tenant from possession involves a series of steps.

1. Landlord serves the tenant with a three-day or 30-day notice, depending on the circumstances.
2. If the tenant fails to abide by the notice, the landlord files an unlawful detainer action in court.
3. If the landlord wins, the court awards the landlord a judgment. The landlord then asks for a writ of possession authorizing the sheriff to evict the tenant.
4. The sheriff sends the tenant an eviction notice; if the tenant fails to leave, the sheriff physically removes the tenant.

Three-Day Notice Versus 30- or 60-Day Notice

A tenant is served a three-day notice when the tenant has defaulted on rent or has violated other terms of the lease.

A 30-day notice is served when the landlord is giving the tenant notice to return possession. Typically, the tenant has not violated the lease, but the landlord is giving them notice she is not going to renew a periodic tenancy or estate for years. This notice may also be used if the tenant is in violation of other terms though a the 3 day notice is more typical.

Serving Notice

The procedure for serving notice can be summarized as follows:

1. The notice must be personally delivered to the tenant(s).
   OR

2. If the tenant(s) is absent, a copy should be left with someone of suitable age (typically 18 years old or older) and then a copy must be mailed to the tenant(s) at place of residence.

OR

3. If no one is home, a copy may be affixed in a conspicuous place on the property and then a copy must be mailed to the tenant(s).

Slipping the notice under the door or putting it in the mailbox is not sufficient delivery. Also, it is a good idea to have the notice served by someone other than the landlord. If a sheriff, marshal, or constable serves the notice, it will have the maximum impression on the tenant(s).

Superior Court

Landlords bring unlawful detainer actions in superior court. In superior court, these actions have a priority on the court's calendar, and an early hearing is usually granted. An attorney generally is needed for a superior court action, and this helps assure the landlord that legal procedures will be correctly followed. This is important if a landlord or tenant appeals to a higher court. Unlawful detainer actions can no longer be heard in small claims court.

Sheriff Evicts the Tenant

After a writ of possession has been granted to the landlord, the sheriff sends the tenant an eviction notice. After approximately five days, if the tenant has not left, the sheriff physically removes the tenant, but not the tenant's possessions. The tenant's possessions are impounded according to the lien laws.

Delays and Appeals

With an increasing awareness of tenants' rights, many tenant action groups have effectively designed delay and appeal processes that can extend an unlawful detainer action for many months. This dramatically increases the landlord's costs, in both attorney time and lost rents. From the landlord's point of view, the best protection is to make sure that a lawful, careful screening takes place before a tenant moves in. Once an unethical tenant moves in, it can become very expensive to have the tenant removed.

Termination of Lease

Few leases are ever terminated because of eviction. Most leases are terminated for the following reasons:

1. *Expiration of time.* The time period for the lease is up, and new terms are not negotiated.
2. *Mutual consent.* The lessor and lessee agree to terminate the lease with no additional liability on either side.

In addition, leases can be terminated because of destruction of the premises; government action, such as condemnation; or a breach of terms and conditions by the lessor or lessee.

Mobile (Manufactured) Home Park Tenants*

A mobile home park is usually a development where lots are rented to mobile home owners. The tenants own their mobile homes, but they are tenants of the land. In California, special laws for mobile home park tenants differ from the typical landlord–tenant laws. A mobile home tenant in a park *cannot be evicted unless one of the following applies:*

1. The tenant fails to comply with local and state laws.
2. The tenant annoys other tenants.
3. The tenant fails to abide by reasonable park rules.
4. The tenant fails to pay the rent and other agreed-upon charges.
5. The tenant has his or her rights condemned by government.
6. The use of the park changes.

The mobile home tenant who is in violation must be given at least a 60-day notice, rather than the three-day or 30-day notice rules for regular tenants.

If the mobile home cannot be moved without a permit, the law requires that a tenant must be given a reasonable notice to vacate. The tenant cannot be required to move merely to make space for a person purchasing a mobile home from the park owner. In addition, many other special rules apply to tenants in mobile home parks.

12.4 PROPERTY MANAGEMENT

As an investment, real estate offers a hedge against inflation; offers income tax advantages; and, in some cases, provides annual cash income. However, real estate needs managerial attention, which

---

*Mobile and manufactured homes are one and the same for this discussion.

frequently discourages investors who do not wish to be bothered by tenants. An alternative might be to employ a professional property manager.

Field of Property Management

Property management is a specialty within the real estate business. Property managers represent owners by screening tenants, negotiating leases, hiring personnel to maintain the building and grounds, and hiring on-site residential managers. California rules state that an apartment building or complex with 16 or more rental units must have an on-site residential manager (a real estate license is not required for on-site residential managers but is for off-site property managers). In addition, property managers are responsible for rent collection and the keeping of accounting records for income tax purposes.

Property managers range from real estate brokers who handle a few properties for their clients to large corporate firms that manage hundreds or thousands of units, including commercial properties such as office buildings and shopping centers.

As mentioned above, an off-site property manager must be a licensed real estate broker, but on-site residential managers do not need a real estate license. Key employees of the property management company must be bonded. The Institute of Real Estate Management, affiliated with the National Association of REALTORS®, issues the nationally recognized designation **Certified Property Manager (CPM)**. The CPM designation is achieved after meeting rigorous educational and experience requirements.

Compensation

Property management firms are usually paid a percentage of the rents collected. The percentage is negotiable and varies from firm to firm. For a large structure with many rental units, the fee may be as low as 1 percent or 2 percent of gross rents collected. On small units such as rental homes and duplexes, the fee may be 10 percent or more. The fee for renting resort properties may be 25 percent or more of rents collected. Some property managers may charge a flat rate rather than a percentage of rents collected. It is important to remember that property management compensation, like commissions, is negotiable.

Property management fees do not include the cost of maintenance, only the management of the property. If maintenance or repairs are needed, the manager sees that the work is done, but the bill is paid by the property owner or is deducted from the rent proceeds.

When a property manager is hired, the manager and the owner sign a management contract. This contract designates the property manager as the owner's agent and lists all the duties and responsibilities of the parties. To be enforceable, the management contract must meet the legal requirements of California contract law.

Chapter Summary

A lease is a contract between an owner, called the lessor, and a tenant, called the lessee. A lessee is given possession in exchange for rent. Leases for more than one year must be in writing to be valid.

Types of leasehold estates are estate for years, estate from period to period, estate at will, and estate at sufferance. Leases on urban property cannot exceed 99 years, whereas leases for agricultural land cannot exceed 51 years. Security deposits on residential properties cannot exceed two months' rent on unfurnished dwellings and three months' rent on furnished dwellings.

An assignment of a lease transfers the entire leasehold interest to another person, whereas a sublease transfers only a part of the leasehold interest to a sublessee.

Rental payments can be paid on a gross, net, or percentage basis. An escalator clause allows the landlord to raise the rent during the term of the lease.

A landlord's duties and rights include an implied condition of habitability, advance notice prior to inspection, 30- or 60-day advance notice when ordering the tenant to vacate, and an obligation not to discriminate when renting property.

A tenant's duties and rights include paying the rent when due, not damaging the property, and giving the landlord 30 days' notice when vacating. Under certain conditions, a tenant can use a rent offset for repairs if the property falls below minimum housing standards. Eviction occurs when a tenant is dispossessed by process of law. The tenant must be served with a 3-, 30-, or 60-day notice, depending on the circumstances.

The action of suing for eviction is called unlawful detainer action. If a writ of possession is granted, the sheriff evicts the tenant. Delays and appeals by a tenant can extend the eviction process by several months.

In addition to eviction, leases can be terminated by expiration of time, mutual consent, destruction of the premises, government action, and breach of terms and conditions.

Property management is a specialty within the real estate business. Property managers represent owners by finding tenants, caring for the property, and maintaining proper accounting records. Property managers are usually paid a fee based on the rents collected.

Important Terms and Concepts

Certified Property Manager (CPM)	lessee
estate at sufferance	lessor
estate at will	net lease
estate for years	percentage lease
estate from period to period	sandwich lease
gross lease	sublease
lease with option to buy	triple net lease

Practical Application

1. An apartment is rented for $800 per month with a $1,000 security deposit. While moving out, the tenant informs the landlord that the water heater leaks. After inspecting the water heater, the landlord believes the leak was the result of the tenant banging the water heater while moving out. The cost of the repair is $100. How would you handle the security deposit issue if you were the landlord?

2. A tenant has a one-year lease that terminates December 1, 20XX. The terms of the lease state that no pets are allowed. On October 1, 20XX, a neighbor calls the landlord to complain that the tenant's dog barks too much. The landlord tells the tenant that the dog must go, but the tenant refuses to remove the dog. List the next legal steps the landlord must take to get rid of the dog.

3. An owner of a five-unit apartment complex, is hiring a professional property manager. The property manager quotes a fee of 8 percent of annual collected rents. Each apartment rents for $750 per month with a vacancy factor of 5 percent. What is the total fee to the property manager for the year?

Reviewing Your Understanding

1. Ms. Alvarez leases her summer cabin to Mr. Greene for the months of June, July, and August of a designated year. Mr. Greene has an estate:
   a. for years.
   b. from period to period.
   c. at sufferance.
   d. at will.

2. Urban property cannot be leased for more than:
   a. 99 years.
   b. 51 years.
   c. 15 years.
   d. There is no time limit on urban property.

3. An assignment of a lease differs from a sublease in that an assignment:
   a. transfers liability to the new occupant.
   b. involves two lease contracts: (1) lessor to lessee and (2) lessee to sublessee.
   c. requires that the original lessee still be primarily liable to the lessor.
   d. none of the above.

4. Under which lease does the tenant pay rent, property taxes, maintenance, and hazard insurance?
   a. Gross lease
   b. Triple net lease
   c. Fixed lease
   d. Escalator lease

5. A residential tenant can expect the landlord to make necessary repairs to keep the dwelling habitable. If the landlord does not, the tenant can make repairs and offset the rent up to:
   a. $700 maximum.
   b. one month's rent.
   c. a reasonable cost.
   d. $1,000 maximum.

6. It is illegal to screen and eliminate potential tenants based on:
   a. marital status, sex, sexual orientation, and family status.
   b. race, color, and creed.
   c. religion and physical handicap.
   d. all of the above.

7. If a tenant has violated the terms of the lease, before the tenant can be evicted, the tenant must be served a:
   a. one-day notice.
   b. three-day notice.
   c. 30-day notice.
   d. 60-day notice.

8. If a small unfurnished apartment rents for $800 per month, the maximum security deposit the landlord can ask for is:
   a. $100.
   b. $500.
   c. $800.
   d. $1,600.

9. The legal process by which a tenant is evicted is called a(n):
   a. eviction action.
   b. ejectment action.
   c. possessory action.
   d. unlawful detainer action.

10. The professional designation CPM stands for:
    a. Certificate of Public Management.
    b. Certified Practical Manager.
    c. Certificate of Practical Management.
    d. Certified Property Manager.

11. At the end of the lease, the lessee can purchase the property under agreed terms and the lessor must sell. This is an example of:
    a. a lease with option to buy.
    b. first right of refusal.
    c. a sublease.
    d. assignment of lease.

12. The law which states that certain leases must be in writing to be enforceable is the:
    a. statute of escribe.
    b. statute of limitations.
    c. statute of conveyance.
    d. statute of frauds.

13. A landlord wants to ask the month-to-month tenant who has occupied the property for six months to leave because the landlord plans to occupy the rental home. Under state law, the landlord must serve the tenant with a(n):
    a. 30-day notice.
    b. three-day notice.
    c. eviction order.
    d. writ of possession.

14. A landlord who is uniform in application can refuse to rent based upon all of the following, except:
    a. poor credit.
    b. inadequate income.
    c. the existence of children.
    d. too many pets.

15. Assuming the tenant takes possession, in order to be valid, a lease for thirteen months must contain:
    a. signatures of the lessor and lessee.
    b. written terms.
    c. a legal description of the property.
    d. none of the above.

16. The interest a tenant has in real estate is known as a:
    a. freehold estate.
    b. less-than-freehold estate.
    c. tenant right estate.
    d. fee simple absolute estate.

17. Regarding security deposits:
    a. the maximum for an unfurnished apartment is three months' rent.
    b. no security deposit can be labeled nonrefundable.
    c. the deposit must be less than the first month's rent.
    d. all unused deposits must be refunded in seven days.

18. Month-to-month tenants in a mobile home park can be requested to leave only for specified reasons and must be served with at least a:
    a. 90-day notice.
    b. 60-day notice.
    c. 30-day notice.
    d. three-day notice.

19. Most unlawful detainer actions are heard in:

a. a superior court.

b. a small claims court.

c. an appellate court.

d. the Supreme Court.

20. In an apartment complex, an on-site resident manager is required if there are:

a. four or more units.

b. eight or more units.

c. 12 or more units.

d. 16 or more units.

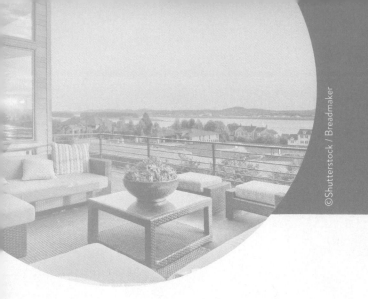

STUDENT LEARNING OUTCOMES

This chapter highlights the principles of government land-use planning and stresses zoning and subdivision regulations. Condominiums, planned unit developments, and the selling of undivided interests are also discussed. The chapter concludes with an explanation of fair housing laws. At the conclusion of this chapter, you will be able to do the following:

- Describe the main goals of a community general plan.
- Explain the difference between government use of police power and eminent domain, and give two examples of each.
- List the major characteristics of the Subdivision Map Act and the Subdivided Lands Law.
- Describe a common interest development and discuss the differences between a condominium and a planned unit development.
- List the major fair housing laws that prohibit discrimination in the selling or renting of real estate.

CHAPTER

13

LAND-USE PLANNING, SUBDIVISIONS, FAIR HOUSING, AND OTHER PUBLIC CONTROLS

13.1 GOVERNMENT LAND-USE PLANNING

Government land-use controls are controversial. Some people believe land is a commodity to be bought and sold like any other product. They consider any type of land-use control an infringement on free enterprise. At the other extreme are those who believe land is a resource that belongs to all the people, the use of which should be completely controlled by government. Somewhere in the middle is the view that land is a commodity and a resource that should be privately owned, but used constructively to benefit society.

Private Deed Restrictions

Most attention regarding land-use control has focused on government regulations. However, for many years, covenants, conditions, and restrictions (CC&Rs) in deeds have been used by private individuals to regulate real estate usage.

California owners are allowed to limit the use of land by contract as long as the restrictions are not a violation of the law. Thus, land-use controls are not new, but in the last 70 years, the bulk of the controls have shifted from private imposition to government imposition. Private deed restrictions were discussed in more detail in Chapter 7.

Public Land-Use Controls

Industrialization and urban crowding have created a need for public controls to maintain order and promote social harmony. One way to maintain order is to control the use of land. The two main powers that allow government to control land use are police power and the power of eminent domain.

Police power refers to the constitutional right of government to regulate private activity to promote the general health, welfare, and safety of society. Police power has often been used in the United States to direct land use. Major real estate examples of police power include zoning ordinances, building and health codes, setback requirements, environmental regulations, and rent controls. Of the many police power enactments, zoning, subdivision, and environmental regulations emerge as the most influential methods for controlling land use.

Police power allows government to regulate private land use without the payment of compensation. The power of eminent domain is different in that it allows the government to acquire title to private land for public use in exchange for the payment of just compensation. Eminent domain is used for a variety of government land-use projects, such as highways, public housing, and urban renewal.

Redevelopment agencies also have the power of eminent domain under California's Redevelopment Law. A redevelopment agency may condemn land within a redevelopment district that has been determined as being blighted and resell it to a private developer in an effort to revitalize urban areas or improve an area's economic climate; see *Kelo v. City of New London*, 545 U.S. 469 (2005).

All levels of government can exercise the power of eminent domain regardless of how unwilling the property owner may be. The main issue in most eminent domain cases is the amount of compensation. The courts have ruled that the property's fair market value is the proper basis for determining compensation. In addition, most federal and some state agencies must pay for moving and other miscellaneous expenses incurred by those being displaced.

Planning

The dictionary defines *planning* as "thinking out acts and purposes beforehand." When applied to cities and counties, planning can be defined as anticipating and achieving community goals in light of social, economic, and physical needs. Planning requires that a community analyze its assets and liabilities, establish its goals, and attempt to achieve these goals using land-use control as a primary tool. California law requires that every incorporated city and county must have a planning commission. A planning commission is composed of citizens appointed by the members of the city council or board of supervisors (in some smaller cities, the city council acts as the planning commission). Planning commissioners advise the elected officials on land-use matters. The planning commission typically only makes recommendations; the final decision on planning rests with the city council or board of supervisors, depending on who has jurisdiction.

In addition to planning commissions, many cities and counties have planning departments. Planning departments are agencies within city and county government, staffed with professionally trained planners. Planning department employees provide technical services for planning commissions, elected officials, and citizens.

State law requires every city and county to develop a general plan, which outlines the goals and objectives for the community. The general plan also lists the steps needed to achieve these goals.

General Plan

The establishment of a community general plan requires three major steps: (1) resource analysis, (2) formulation of community goals, and (3) implementation of the plan.

Resource Analysis

The first step is to recognize the individual character of the community. What are its strong points? What are its weaknesses? To accomplish this, several substudies are required, including an economic base study, a population trend study, a survey of existing land use, a housing needs study, a city facilities study, and an analysis of the community's financial resources. Once a resource inventory has been taken, the next step is to formulate community goals in light of the resources.

Formulation of Community Goals

The formulation of community goals is the most difficult phase of urban planning because of the conflict between various special interest groups, each trying to secure and establish its own definition of the community goal. In spite of this problem, citizen input should be encouraged. A community plan must be based on the desires of community residents as a whole, not on the desires of staff planners alone.

Once the goals are established, a comprehensive plan to achieve the objectives must be formulated. The plan is frequently referred to as the general plan or the master plan, and it should encompass all social, economic, and physical aspects of the projected growth. The plan should be long-range but provide for short-range flexibility as the need for modification arises. Under no circumstances must the general plan be viewed as an inflexible, permanent fixture that never requires modification. A community's attitude and resources can change, and the general plan must be modified to comply with these changes.

Implementation of the Plan

The final step in urban planning is to implement the general plan. The implementation phase requires local government to use police power, eminent domain, taxation, and control over government spending to enact the plan. As previously indicated, the three most powerful tools for implementing a community plan are zoning, subdivision, and environmental regulations.

Zoning

Zoning refers to the division of land into designated land-use districts. In its simplest form, zoning districts are divided into residential use, commercial use, industrial use, and rural use. Each use, in turn, can have several subclasses. For example, residential can be broken down into single-family, multifamily, and mobile home zones. Commercial zones are usually divided into retail, office, and wholesale space. Industrial zones are divided into light industry and heavy industry and rural zones into agricultural, resource, and recreational use.

Zoning as a land-control tool was not common in the United States until the 1920s; prior to this time, there was some doubt about the constitutionality of zoning, although early zoning laws can be traced to colonial times. However, in 1926, the U.S. Supreme Court held that zoning was a reasonable exercise of government police power. Since this decision, every state has passed legislation allowing individual cities and counties to enact zoning ordinances.

Early zoning ordinances were aimed at safety and nuisance control. The idea was to use zoning to protect individual property values by prohibiting offensive use of surrounding land. The use of zoning has gradually been expanded, and now it is used to "promote the general welfare" of the entire community.

Inclusionary Zoning

Inclusionary zoning is an ordinance that requires a builder of new residential housing to set aside a designated number of units for low- and moderate-income people. If the developer refuses to provide the designated units, the building permit is denied.

In some cases, instead of providing inclusionary units, the builder is required to pay into a fund that the government uses to provide low- and moderate-income housing. To encourage participation in the program, the builder is allowed to construct more units per acre than normal.

The economic reality is that the prices of the regular units are frequently increased to offset the builder's losses on the inclusionary units. This shifts the burden of providing affordable housing from the government to the private market.

Controversy: Local Versus State and Federal Planning

Historically, planning has been a local matter. Each community developed its own plans within the confines of its own territorial limits. In the process, each community attempted to optimize its own social and economic well-being, frequently at the expense of surrounding areas. For example, the planning of a smelly industrial plant on the border of one city has a spillover effect on the neighboring community located downwind.

The growth of multicity metropolitan areas has led the state to mandate planning on a regional basis. Water and sewage systems, rapid transit, highway traffic patterns, airports, and pollution controls are examples of regional planning. However, from a political point of view, there is wide-scale resistance to the creation of another layer of government. Moreover, local government officials are reluctant to surrender some of their power to regional or state commissioners.

Opposition to federal and state controls also comes from individuals who believe that the power of land regulation should be limited to local government. They fear that planning on a state and federal level is insensitive to local needs. Who is correct? Like most land-use controls, the correct answer depends on one's value judgment. However, the current trend is toward more regional, state, and federal control over land use.

Examples of federal laws include the National Environmental Policy Act, which requires an environmental impact report on all projects using federal funding, and the Clean Air Act, which requires businesses (including real estate developers) to meet air quality standards. The federal government has declared that development cannot take place in "wetlands" for fear of damaging wildlife habitat. The definition of what constitutes *wetlands* has created numerous lawsuits.

Examples of state laws include the Coastline Conservation Act, creating controls on the 1,000-mile California coast; the California Environmental Quality Act, which requires an environmental impact report on major real estate projects; and the Subdivision Map Act and Subdivided Lands Law, which control the creation of subdivisions in the state.

13.2 SUBDIVISIONS

Another important use of police power is *subdivision regulation*. Poorly conceived subdivisions, with inadequate streets and facilities, can become a burden to taxpayers in later years, when expensive redevelopment is needed to correct earlier oversights. Proponents of subdivision controls believe that the origin of slums and urban blight can be traced to inadequate regulations. Opponents disagree, stating that today's slums are the result of government ordinances that prevent land from rising to its economic highest and best use.

Today subdivision regulations are used in all areas of California. Real estate developers are frequently required to provide water, sewer, paved streets, sidewalks, street lights, and school and park sites as a condition of being allowed to subdivide. The idea is to plan for the

Summary of Planning Terms

Planning commission. An appointed body of citizens charged with the responsibility of advising the elected board of supervisors or city council members in matters of land use.

Planning department. City or county staff employees who lend professional and technical assistance to elected officials and citizens.

Zone. An area defined on a map by a boundary line within which the land-use regulations are the same.

Rezoning. The process of changing land-use regulations on property from one zone to another.

Variance. A deviation from the zoning regulations for a structure on a particular parcel.

Conditional use permit. A requirement imposed by government in connection with the approval of a permit or a division of property relating to its use.

Development plans. Plans showing the details of the proposed development. Normally includes plot plan, architectural renderings, and statistical information relative to acreage, building area, units, and parking. In most cases, an environmental impact study will be required.

Standard subdivision. A division of property into lots that does not include common areas.

Minor subdivision or lot split. A division of residential property into two, three, or four parcels.

Major subdivision. A division of residential property into five or more parcels.

Architectural review. Certain zoning areas where a special citizens' group approves or rejects the proposal based on its architectural compatibility with the surrounding area.

Appeal. The right to request review of a negative planning commission decision. The appellate process goes from the planning commission to the board of supervisors or city council to the courts.

Source: From *Essentials of Real Estate Economics*, 6th ed., by D. J. McKenzie and R. M. Betts (OnCourse Learning, 2011).

future at the inception and to require the purchaser of the subdivided lot, not the community as a whole, to pay the expense of added community facilities. Like all public controls, subdivision regulations are controversial because they require the surrender of some individual rights in an attempt to promote the general welfare.

Subdivision Laws

There are two basic laws under which subdivisions are controlled in California—the Subdivision Map Act and the Subdivided Lands Law. The Subdivision Map Act covers the division of land into two or more lots for the purpose of sale, lease, or financing, whether now or in the future. The Subdivision Map Act is administered by local officials and is concerned with the physical aspects of the subdivision, such as design, streets, water, sewers, and so on. The Subdivision Map Act outlines the procedure for filing subdivision maps to legally create a subdivision. (See Figure 13.1.)

The Subdivided Lands Law defines a subdivision as the division of land into five or more lots for the purpose of sale, lease, or financing, whether now or in the future. The Subdivided Lands Law is administered by the California real estate commissioner and is primarily concerned with the marketing aspects of the subdivision. The basic objective of the Subdivided Lands Law is to protect the purchasers of property in new subdivisions from fraud and misrepresentation when buying new subdivided land.

No new subdivision of five or more parcels located in California can be offered for sale until the real estate commissioner issues a public report. The final public report is not issued until the commissioner is satisfied that the developer has met all statutory requirements, with particular emphasis on the establishment of financial arrangements to assure completion of any promised facilities. *The issuance of a public report does not mean that in the eyes of the commissioner, the subdivision is a good investment.* It merely means that the subdivider has conformed to all laws and regulations.

Before each lot in a new subdivision can be sold, the subdivider must deliver a copy of the commissioner's final public report to the prospective buyer. The prospective buyer must then sign a statement acknowledging that he or she received and read the public report, and this signed copy must be kept on file by the subdivider for three years. Only after these steps have taken place can the subdivider sell each lot.

The public report is good for five years; however, the law requires the commissioner to issue an amended public report when a material change occurs regarding the subdivision. Examples of material changes include changes in contract forms, physical changes such as lot lines or street lines, and a sale of five or more lots to a single buyer.

FIGURE 13.1

BASIC OUTLINE OF SUBDIVISION MAP PREPARATION AND APPROVAL

PRELIMINARY PLANNING

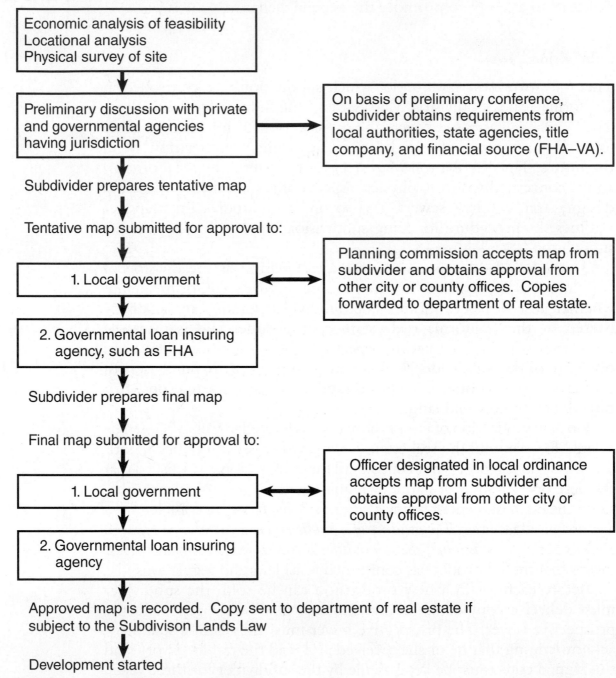

Source: From *Reference Book*, California Department of Real Estate.

Under certain circumstances, the commissioner can issue a preliminary **public report**, which allows the subdivider to take reservations for purchase pending the issuance of the final public report. A reservation is not binding upon the prospective buyer. The prospective buyer is allowed to back out and receive a full refund up until the final report is issued and a binding purchase agreement is signed.

The public report process applies only to the first sale of each lot in a new subdivision. A subsequent resale of a lot by the original purchaser does not require that the second buyer receive a public report.

Out-of-State and Foreign Land

Subdivided land projects located in other states and offered for sale in California do not need to obtain a formal public report from the California Bureau of Real Estate (CalBRE). Instead, out-of-state subdividers must include specific disclaimers in all advertising and sales agreements. Foreign properties offered for sale in California have very few restrictions; a sale is basically a buyer-beware situation. All California buyers should seek legal advice before purchasing an out-of-state or out-of-country property. Out-of-state and out-of-country purchases also need to conform to the Interstate Land Sales Act, which is discussed below.

Red Tape

The actual processing of a subdivision is frequently a costly and time-consuming process. The data needed to complete the required forms are highly technical and beyond the skills of average property owners. The services of title officers, surveyors or engineers, contractors, and attorneys often are required. The average subdivision takes many months to process and major development can take years. Delays are costly; in the end, these costs are borne by the consumer.

Land Project Right to Rescind Sale

A *land project* is defined as a speculative subdivision of 50 or more lots located in a sparsely populated area of the state. These types of subdivisions are frequently sold only after intensive promotion in urban areas, long distances away from the development.

A purchaser of a lot in the land project is allowed a limited time after the sale to "cool off" and rescind, or cancel, the purchase contract and receive a full refund with no further obligations. As of July 2007, the right to rescind extends for 14 days after the signing of the purchase agreement. But in the future, regulations might extend this period. (Also see the section "Time-Sharing Ownership" regarding the right to rescind sale.)

Interstate Land Sales Full-Disclosure Act

A federal law known as the Interstate Land Sales Full-Disclosure Act regulates land sales between two or more states. If a developer

Subdivision Laws Summarized

Subdivided Lands Act	Subdivision Map Act
Five or more lots or parcels	Two or more lots or parcels
No contiguity requirement	Land must be contiguous units
160-acre and larger parcels designated as such by government survey are exempt	No exemption for 160 acres and larger
Administered by California real estate commissioner	Administered by local officials
Requires a final public report	No public report required

Currently a debate is raging. On one hand, increased regulations are designed to protect the consumer and the environment; on the other hand, consumers must pay for these regulations via higher prices. Are the protections worth the price? This is a value judgment question that each person must answer.

of 50 or more lots located in one state wishes to market the lots in another state(s), the developer must conform to this law.

Basically, the law requires the developer to obtain a public report issued by the Department of Housing and Urban Development (HUD) and to deliver a copy of the public report to each prospective buyer. This law is an attempt to reduce the number of fraudulent land sales that take place by mail or through out-of-state advertising.

13.3 COMMON INTEREST DEVELOPMENTS (CIDS)

An increase in population has caused an increase in urban land prices. As land becomes scarcer and prices begin to rise, there is a tendency to intensify development to obtain more living units per acre. Common interest developments (CIDs) in the form of condominiums, planned unit developments, stock cooperatives, and community apartments are examples of intensified owner-occupied developments that differ from the traditional single-family-home type of subdivision. All of these developments are considered subdivisions and are regulated by state law.

Condominiums

A condominium is a type of real estate ownership, not a type of structure. Condominiums can be any type of use e.g. office, warehouse, not just residential. In a legal sense, a condominium owner acquires a fee title interest in the airspace of the particular unit and an undivided interest (with other condominium owners) in the land in addition to all other common areas, such as hallways, elevators, carports, and recreational facilities. A condominium is sometimes called a *vertical subdivision or a subdivision of airspace.*

Each condominium owner has his or her own individual deed, real estate loan, and property tax assessment. A condominium interest is bought and sold like any other parcel of real estate.

All condominiums have owners' associations that elect a governing board. The governing board is responsible for the management of the complex and sees that the building and common areas are maintained. The owners' association also sets the dues for each owner's share of the maintenance.

Condominium developments are expected to continue to gain an increasing share of the housing market. In some areas, there has been a tendency to convert existing renter-occupied apartments into owner-occupied condominiums. This has caused controversy because condo conversion reduces the supply of rental units, thereby making it more difficult for renters to find affordable housing. On the other hand, a condo conversion increases the supply of owner-occupied housing, thereby making it easier for owners to find affordable housing.

Planned Unit Development (PUD)

A planned unit development (PUD) or planned development (PD) is often confused with a condominium. They are not the same. In a PUD, a person owns his or her own living unit and lot, in addition to an undivided interest in the common areas. A condominium owner owns his or her own living unit, but not his or her own lot. A PUD is often referred to as a *townhouse development,* but this is incorrect. A townhouse is a type of architecture and not a type of ownership. In a PUD, no one lives in the airspace above or below the owner, as is found in a condominium. PUDs are frequently located in the suburbs, whereas condominiums are usually located in urban areas. They are both found in resort areas such as Lake Tahoe and Palm Desert.

PUDs are similar in operation to condominiums. A owners' association levies dues for upkeep and maintenance of the common areas.

In addition, each property owner has CC&Rs in his or her deed that dictate the do's and don'ts of ownership.

Stock Cooperatives and Community Apartments

A **stock cooperative** is a corporation formed for the purpose of holding title to a building. Each shareholder of the entire corporation is given the right to occupy a living unit, but the entire building is owned by the corporation. A sale of a share in the corporation also passes the right of occupancy to a living unit within the stock cooperative.

A community apartment is created when a group of people jointly purchase an undivided interest in an entire apartment complex. Then each person is given the right to occupy a particular apartment unit. The undivided share can be sold, and the new purchaser acquires the right to live in the particular apartment.

Under a stock cooperative and a community apartment, each person does not receive an individual deed, real estate loan, or property tax assessment. All the shareholders and undivided interest owners must agree to pool their funds each month to make the mortgage payment, pay the property taxes, and pay for upkeep and maintenance.

Stock cooperatives and community apartments are not as popular as condominiums and PUDs. Most people prefer their own individual deed, real estate loan, and property tax assessment, which are present in condominiums and PUDs but not in stock cooperatives or community apartments.

Disclosure Requirements

When a unit in an existing common interest development is offered for sale, the seller must provide, as a *minimum,* to a prospective buyer prior to the close of escrow:

1. A copy of the existing conditions, covenants, and restrictions; the articles of incorporation; the owners' association by-laws; the governing documents; and a current financial statement on the owners' association

2. A written statement of any known pending special assessments, claims, or litigation against the seller or the owners' association

3. A current statement showing whether the seller has any unpaid assessments or dues owed to the owners' association

Recreational Developments Selling Undivided Interests

Recreational land developments can be found throughout California. The developer usually begins with a large parcel of land, subdivides the land, and then sells parcels to individual owners. In some cases, the parcels are fully developed; in other cases, vacant lots are sold.

An alternative to subdividing recreational land into individual parcels is keeping the original large parcel intact and selling undivided interests or shares in the whole. An example is a developer who has 1,000 acres of land and is considering subdividing the land into 1,000 one-acre lots to be sold to 1,000 recreational users. An alternative might be to sell a 1/1,000 undivided interest to 1,000 recreational users. With selling 1,000 undivided interests, each owner has the right to use all 1,000 acres instead of just one acre, as would be the case if a traditional subdivision were created.

The buyer of an undivided interest in a recreational land development has seven days (from receipt of the public report or signing the contract) to rescind the purchase contract under the California Business and Professions Code for any reason and receive a full refund. The marketing of an undivided interest is controlled by the state subdivision laws and private deed restrictions, similar to condominiums and PUDs.

Time-Sharing Ownership

Another interesting concept is that of time-sharing ownership. Under time-sharing, a person buys an interest in a building—for example, a condominium in a resort area—where the right of occupancy is limited to a specified calendar time period. An example is 12 people who pool their funds and each person purchases a 1/12 interest in a Lake Tahoe condominium. Each person's 1/12 interest gives that person the right to occupy the condominium for a month. The month or the time period is designated in the deed or by a separate instrument. This is a way to own a vacation home for the exact time period you desire, for an expense that covers just the pro rata time of occupancy.

There are other derivations of time-sharing ownership, such as purchasing the right of occupancy for a designated time period each year. But the purchaser does not acquire an interest in the land. Many timeshare resorts have exchange privileges with other resorts, allowing a time-share owner to move from location to location.

The time-sharing owners need CC&Rs in deeds, as well as an owners' association to govern the use and maintenance of the unit. The buyer of a time-share has seven days (from receipt of the public report or signing the contract) to rescind the purchase contract under the California Business and Professions Code for any reason and receive a full refund.

13.4 HOUSING AND CONSTRUCTION LAWS

State Laws and Regulations

State housing laws. State housing laws, or codes, establish minimum housing standards for the entire state. State housing and health and safety codes are enforced by local, not state, building inspectors. The state housing law is a uniform code that must be adopted by all cities and counties in California.

Local building codes. Until 1970, local codes were allowed to deviate from state housing laws. However, with the passage of the state uniform housing codes, local variances are permitted only if a study finds sufficient reason to deviate from the state uniform code.

Contractor's license law. State law requires every person who engages in the business of a contractor to be licensed. A property owner doing his or her own work for his or her own use must build according to codes, but is exempt from the contractor license law. On the other hand, if an owner wishes to build with the intention to offer the finished real estate project for sale, a licensed contractor must do the work.

Environmental impact regulations. A housing or real estate development usually requires an environmental review before a building permit is issued. The builder must prepare a negative impact report (NIR) if a project is minor, with no or limited environmental concern, or a costly, fully documented environmental impact report (EIR) if a project is major. The purpose of both reports is to address what impact the real estate construction will have on the social, economic, physical, and biological environment. Then the report must state what steps the builder will take to reduce the impact on the environment, including not building the project in the first place.

13.5 FAIR HOUSING

State Laws and Regulations

EQUAL HOUSING OPPORTUNITY

Over the years, several federal and state laws have been passed making it against public policy to discriminate in real estate based on race, color, religion, sex, sexual orientation, gender identification, marital status or registered domestic partnership, national origin, ancestry, family status, genetic background, citizenship, foreign language, legal status, or mental or physical disability. The courts do not tolerate discrimination, and violators can expect to be fined and/or jailed.

Unruh Civil Rights Act. This state law makes it unlawful for people engaged in business in California, including real estate agents, to discriminate when providing business products and services. Examples of unlawful real estate agent conduct include steering and block busting.

Steering is the unlawful directing of a prospective buyer or tenant to certain neighborhoods or the refusal to tell about the availability of housing in another neighborhood. *Block busting* is attempting to create panic selling by telling existing property owners that minority groups have targeted their neighborhoods for purchase. Steering and block busting are illegal; the penalties include loss of a real estate license and severe criminal and civil charges, in addition to fines.

California Fair Housing Act (Rumford Act). This state law forbids discrimination in the sale, rental, lease, or financing of practically all types of housing. The staff of the Department of Fair Employment and Housing investigates complaints from people who believe they have been discriminated against in housing. If the staff thinks a violation has occurred, a hearing is held with the Commission of Fair Employment and Housing. If the commission rules that discrimination has occurred, it has the power to order the sale or rental of the property. In addition, the commission has the power to levy fines. A person who has suffered discrimination has a right to bypass the commission process and bring a direct lawsuit in court. The state of California believes that fair housing is so important that it requires all real estate agents to take a three-hour fair-housing course as a condition for keeping a real estate license.

Housing Financial Discrimination Act (Holden Act). This state law prohibits financial institutions from engaging in discriminatory loan practices. This law attempts to prohibit redlining. *Redlining* is a loan practice under which a lender refuses to grant a housing loan in certain geographic areas based on neighborhood trends, regardless of the merits of the borrower or of the individual home.

Commissioner's Rules and Regulations. The California real estate commissioner has issued numerous regulations regarding housing discrimination. These regulations detail the types of discriminatory conduct that, if practiced by a real estate licensee, are the basis for disciplinary action that can result in a suspension or fine or even in prosecution by the local district attorney. The policy of the commission is to create an equal opportunity industry.

Federal Laws

Civil Rights Act of 1866, 1964, 1968, and 1988 Amendments. Also know as the federal fair housing act. This comprehensive law states that within constitutional limits, fair housing should prevail throughout the United States. This act left it up to the courts to determine the constitutionality of this law.

Jones v. Mayer Case. In this landmark case, the U.S. Supreme Court interpreted and applied an act of Congress passed in 1866 immediately after the Civil War. The constitutionality rested on the

Thirteenth Amendment, which prohibits slavery. Using the Act of 1866 and the Thirteenth Amendment, the U.S. Supreme Court held that the Civil Rights Act of 1866 bars all racial discrimination, private as well as public, in the sale or rental of property, and that the statute was a valid exercise of the power of Congress to enforce the Thirteenth Amendment.

1988 Amendments to the Civil Rights Act of 1968. The 1988 Amendments broaden the definition of *handicap* to include anyone with a disability that impairs "major life activities." Thus, property owners cannot discriminate because of AIDS, cancer, and alcoholism. People with mental disorders, including past drug users, are also protected (current abusers of alcohol or illegal substances are not protected). Per the 1988 Amendments, current drug abusers or anyone who can be proved to be a current threat to the health, safety, or property of others is not considered a protected class. To be safe, any refusal to sell or rent for any reason other than inadequate income or credit should first be reviewed by the property owner's attorney. The 1988 Amendments also make it a federal violation to discriminate against families with children unless the development is an approved senior citizen project.

Senior Citizen Housing

Due to public policy concerns for the availability of affordable housing for seniors, federal law provides an exception to antidiscrimination laws based on age, allowing certain apartment complexes, CIDs, and detached dwelling communities to designate themselves as senior communities.

There are two classifications for senior communities. The first is where every dwelling is occupied solely by persons age 62 or older. The second classification is where 80 percent or more of the dwellings must have at least one person age 55 or older and the community adheres to a policy that demonstrates intent to house persons who are 55 or older. The remaining 20 percent of the dwellings may be occupied solely by those under age 55. The purpose of the 20 percent classification is for surviving spouses. Let's say Ed, age 56 and Lavonne, age 52, move into a senior community. A year later, Ed dies, leaving his widow in the dwelling. If not for the 20 percent category, Lavonne would have to vacate since she is not 55 or older. Instead, she now moves over to the 20 percent category, and upon reaching age 55 would return to the 80 percent category.

While occupancy is restricted by age, ownership is not. For example, a 53-year-old couple could purchase a home in a 55-year-or-older community but would not be able to move in until one of them turns age 55. They could rent the residence to a qualifying tenant during the meantime. Agents representing buyers and sellers in senior communities must be very careful to fully disclose the community's requirements. Senior community management companies and homeowners' associations are diligent about disclosing to agents the requirements of occupancy. An agent is wise to attach any correspondence received from the community's management to their disclosure (see Chapter 5) for the buyer.

Many Other Laws

In addition to the laws listed previously, numerous other laws and regulations directly or indirectly attempt to prohibit discrimination in housing. All real estate owners, agents, managers, and lenders must give the public an equal opportunity to acquire real estate.

Chapter Summary

Two powers that allow government to control land use are police power and the power of eminent domain. Major police power tools include zoning, building and health codes, and subdivision regulations.

Cities and counties in California must have a planning commission. In addition, most cities and counties also have planning departments. The planning commission and elected officials must adopt a general plan that outlines the goals and objectives for the community. The three most powerful tools for implementing the general plan are zoning, subdivision regulations, and environmental regulations. The two major subdivision laws are the Subdivision Map Act and the Subdivided Lands Law. The Subdivision Map Act is administered by local officials and is mostly concerned with the physical aspects of a subdivision. The Subdivided Lands Law is administered by the California real estate commissioner and is primarily concerned with the marketing aspects of a subdivision. The key element of the Subdivided Lands Law is the required public report, which must be delivered to each prospective buyer of a lot in a new California subdivision.

Common interest developments in the form of condominiums, PUDs, stock cooperatives, and community apartments are examples of intensified owner-occupied developments, which differ from the traditional single-family-dwelling type of subdivision.

Over the years, laws have been passed making it against public policy to discriminate in the selling, leasing, or renting of housing. The Unruh Civil Rights Act and the California Fair Housing Act (Rumford Act) are two California antidiscrimination laws. The Civil Rights Acts of 1866, 1964, 1968, and 1988 Amendments is a federal law that prohibits discrimination in housing.

Important Terms And Concepts

California Fair Housing Act
  (Rumford Act)
Civil Rights Act of 1968 and 1988
  Amendments
Clean Air Act
Commissioner's Rules and
  Regulations
common interest developments
  (CIDs)
condominium
eminent domain
Housing Financial Discrimination
  Act (Holden Act)
inclusionary zoning

National Environmental Policy Act
planned unit development (PUD)
planning commission
planning departments
police power
public report
selling undivided interests
steering
stock cooperative
Subdivided Lands Law
Subdivision Map Act
Unruh Civil Rights Act
zoning

Practical Application

1. You are the real estate agent for an owner of vacant land currently zoned residential. You and the owner believe that growth trends have changed and that the highest and best use of the land would be for commercial development. You apply to the planning commission for a rezone to commercial use. The planning commission turns down your proposal. The owner wishes to appeal the planning commission decision. What is the appeal process?

2. Explain how a condominium differs from a PUD and a stock cooperative. Why are they all called *common interest developments*?

3. You just listed a $750,000 home for sale. Twenty days later, the seller calls to tell you that the neighbors are concerned that the home might be sold to a minority person and that the seller does not want the home shown to potential minority buyers. How should you respond?

Reviewing Your Understanding

1. Which of the following is an example of government use of police power?
   a. Rent controls
   b. Building codes
   c. Zoning ordinances
   d. All of the above

2. The Subdivision Map Act is administered by:
   a. the California real estate commissioner.
   b. local officials.
   c. the California Department of Urban Planning.
   d. the Department of Housing and Urban Development (HUD).

3. Before a developer can sell a lot in a new California subdivision containing five or more lots, the prospective buyer must receive a copy of the:
   a. preliminary title report.
   b. builder's warranties.
   c. public report.
   d. zoning ordinances.

4. A developer from Nevada wishes to sell 300 Las Vegas lots to California residents and open sales offices in Los Angeles and San Francisco. The developer need not conform to the:
   a. Subdivision Map Act.
   b. California Bureau of Real Estate sales agreement disclosures requirements.
   c. California Bureau of Real Estate advertising disclosures requirements.
   d. Interstate Land Sales Full-Disclosure Act.

5. The right of the consumer, within a specified time, to rescind a land purchase contract and receive a full refund applies to new:
   a. urban subdivisions of 50 lots or more.
   b. suburban subdivisions of 50 lots or more.
   c. farmland of 50 acres or more.
   d. land projects of 50 lots or more.

6. A development where a person individually owns his or her living unit but has an undivided interest with the other owners in the land and common areas is a:
   a. planned unit development.
   b. common interest development.
   c. condominium.
   d. all of the above.

7. The selling of a 1/2,500 share in a northern California recreational ranch is an example of a(n):
   a. undivided interest.
   b. condominium.
   c. PUD.
   d. time-sharing ownership.

8. A person cannot refuse to sell a home based on a buyer's:
   a. physical handicap.
   b. marital status.
   c. sex.
   d. all of the above.

9. The law that prevents California business including real estate professionals from discriminating when providing real estate services is the:
   a. Fair Housing Act.
   b. Rumford Act.
   c. Unruh Civil Rights Act.
   d. Housing Financial Discrimination Act.

10. The law that makes it illegal for real estate lenders to redline a neighborhood is the:
    a. California Fair Housing Act.
    b. Rumford Act.
    c. Unruh Civil Rights Act.
    d. Housing Financial Discrimination Act.

11. Which of the following is the best example of a common interest development?
    a. Condominium
    b. Single-family home
    c. Tenant-occupied apartment building
    d. Mobile home park

12. Recorded CC&Rs and a homeowners' association are mandatory for a:
    a. condominium.
    b. single-family home.
    c. tenant-occupied apartment building.
    d. mobile home park.

13. A deviation from the established zone requirements is called:
    a. a lot split.
    b. a negative impact report.
    c. rezoning.
    d. a variance.

14. If private deed restrictions allow some use that is prohibited by zoning, the rule is that:
    a. zoning prevails.
    b. private deed restrictions prevail.
    c. rezoning is allowed.
    d. spot zoning is required.

15. A simple lot split is governed by the:
    a. Subdivided Lands Law.
    b. Subdivision Lot Division Act.
    c. Subdivision Map Act.
    d. Subdivision Land Project Act.

16. The Civil Rights Act of 1968 and 1988 Amendments does not protect against discrimination in housing if a person is:
    a. a current controlled-substance abuser.
    b. an alcoholic.
    c. an AIDS victim.
    d. confined to a wheelchair.

17. The illegal act of directing potential buyers and tenants to certain neighborhoods is called:
    a. block busting.
    b. directing.
    c. locating.
    d. steering.

18. If the real estate commissioner issues a Preliminary Public Report for a subdivision, a developer is allowed to:
    a. sell the lots.
    b. reserve the lots.
    c. finance the lots.
    d. escrow the lots.

19. The power of eminent domain requires government agencies to:

a. regulate but not buy the private property.

b. pay just compensation for the private property.

c. include the private property in the general plan.

d. take public property.

20. Prior to issuing a building permit involving a minor project with little if any environmental damage, the local government may require a(n):

a. environmental impact report.

b. public subdivision report.

c. property tax report.

d. negative impact report.

STUDENT LEARNING OUTCOMES

Government levies taxes to generate revenue to help pay for government expenditures. This chapter presents the principles of real property and income taxation, two forms of taxation that have a direct impact on real estate ownership. At the conclusion of this chapter, you will be able to do the following:

- Describe the real property assessment procedure as required by Proposition 13.
- List the rules regarding the date and manner of payment of real property taxes, and describe the tax sale procedure in the event of nonpayment of property taxes.
- Explain homeowners', veterans', and senior citizens' property tax exemptions.
- List the income tax advantages of real estate ownership, including the changes resulting from recent revisions in tax laws.

INTRODUCTION TO TAXATION

14.1 REAL PROPERTY TAXES

In California, property taxes used to be levied by cities and counties on an ad valorem basis. **Ad valorem** is a Latin phrase that means "according to value." Under the concept of ad valorem, owners of higher valued property pay more in property taxes than owners of lower valued property. With the passage of Proposition 13, property taxes in California are now levied using a system based upon date of acquisition, which is not a pure ad valorem system.

Assessment Procedure

On June 6, 1978, the voters of California passed Proposition 13, the Jarvis-Gann initiative. **Proposition 13** limits real property taxes to one percent of the full cash value of the real property, plus an amount for local assessments and bonds.

No Change in Ownership Since March 1, 1975

Under the terms of Proposition 13, if there has been no change in ownership since March 1, 1975, the 1975 value shall be the initial full cash value. To this figure the assessor is allowed to add an inflation factor of two percent per year, *compounded* to arrive at full cash value for the present tax year. For example, assume that a person has owned his or her home since March 1, 1975. The 1975 value was $60,000. The 1976 full cash value would be $60,000 plus two percent (or $61,200), 1977 would be $61,200 plus two percent (or $62,424), and so on, until the present tax year is reached. In this example, for the year 2011, the value for tax purposes will be $113,073. Therefore, the maximum real property tax for the 2011–2012 tax year will be one percent of $113,073, or only $1,130.73, plus any amount needed to pay for voter-approved bonds, less any exemptions such as the California homeowner's exemption. Again, this applies only if there is no change in ownership since March 1, 1975.

In this example, the value for tax purposes bears no relationship to the actual current market value of the property. A home worth $60,000 in 1975 may be worth $500,000 or more currently. But the property would be taxed at a value of $113,073—a bargain for the property owner.

Change in Ownership Since March 1, 1975

When there is a change in ownership (such as a sale, a gift, or an inheritance), *the new owner's full cash value for tax purposes shall be the sales price or value of the property as of the date of transfer.* A supplemental tax bill is then mailed to the new owner.

Using the previous example, if a property worth $60,000 in 1975 is sold in January 2011 for $500,000, the new owner's full cash value for that tax year will be $500,000. Therefore, the maximum real property tax for the 2011–2012 tax year will be one percent of $500,000, or $5,000, plus any amount needed to pay for voter-approved bonds, less any exemptions such as the California homeowner's exemption.

As you can see, whenever there is a change in ownership, the full cash value for tax purposes is adjusted to the current market value of the property. In many cases, this can result in a dramatic increase in real property taxes from what the former owner was paying.

Supplemental Property Tax Bill

When a real estate transfer occurs that triggers a new property tax assessment, a supplemental tax bill is sent to the new owner. For example, assume that a transfer occurs in the middle of a tax year. The new owner will be required to pay the remaining portion of the former owner's property tax bill, plus an increase (or decrease, in some cases) in the form of a supplemental bill that reflects the increase in assessment due to the title transfer. This prevents a new owner from getting a windfall tax break based on the former owner's lower Proposition 13 assessment.

Is This Discrimination?

Opponents of Proposition 13 have long contended that this law discriminates against recent buyers. Opponents point out that similar properties side by side could have dramatically different property tax bills depending on when each owner purchased the property. Is this a form of discrimination based on unequal taxation? In a U.S. Supreme Court case, it was held that Proposition 13 is constitutional and not a form of illegal discrimination.

Other Adjustments

On new construction since March 1, 1975, full cash value for tax purposes is the real estate value at the time of completion plus the inflation factor of two percent per year to the present tax year. If you add improvements to your existing home, such as a swimming pool or a new bathroom, does this affect your tax bill? Yes. Does it mean that the entire home is brought up to current market value for tax purposes? No. What happens is that your home keeps its present full cash value as shown on the tax records before your new improvements. Then the new improvements are valued separately as of the date of completion. Each of these figures is adjusted by the two percent yearly figure, and the sum of these two figures equals full cash value for tax purposes.

Transfer Exclusions

Transfers between spouses and registered domestic partners—such as changing title from joint tenancy to community property or a deed from one spouse or partner to another—or deeding property to a living trust are not considered transfers for property tax purposes. A transfer of a principal residence worth $1 million or less from a parent(s) to children also is not considered a transfer for property tax purposes. Other transfer exclusions include replacing a property due to government eminent domain or replacing a property due to a disaster. This means that the county assessor *will not* reappraise the property and increase the property tax.

During the real estate crash of the early to mid-1990s, and again from 2007–2011, when property values dropped, the tax assessor did not automatically increase tax values by the 2 percent factor allowed under Proposition 13. In some cases, property tax values were lowered and property taxes owed declined.

Special Treatment for Senior Citizens

Another law, Proposition 60, allows homeowners 55 years of age and over to transfer their base-year property tax value to another home of equal or less value in the *same county* and keep the low assessment they had on their former home. Example: A couple purchased a home in 1985 for $100,000. For property tax purposes, the assessed value is now $121,900 but the home is worth $500,000. If the couple sells for $500,000 and buys a home in the same county for $490,000, they can take their $121,900 assessment to the new home, rather than be assessed for the $490,000 purchase price. This results in the following property tax savings: $121,900 × 1% = $1,219 property tax, versus $490,000 × 1% = $4,900 property tax.

Proposition 90 allows the same concept to be applied if a home is purchased in *another county,* but only if that county's Board of Supervisors chooses to apply Proposition 90.

Real Property Tax Dates

Real property taxes cover a fiscal year that begins July 1 and runs through June 30 of the following year. For example, the fiscal tax year for 2013–2014 would begin July 1, 2013, and end June 30, 2014. The real property tax becomes a lien on the January 1 preceding the fiscal tax year. Using the previous example, on January 1, 2013, a lien is placed on all taxable real estate for the 2013–2014 tax year, which begins July 1, 2013. (See Figure 14.1.)

The real property tax can be paid in two equal installments. The first installment is due November 1 and is delinquent if not paid by 5 P.M. on December 10. If December 10 falls on a weekend or holiday, the tax is due by 5 P.M. the next business day. The second installment is due on February 1 and is delinquent if not paid by 5 P.M. on April 10. Again, if April 10 falls on a weekend or holiday, the tax is due by 5 P.M. the next business day.

If a taxpayer wishes, both installments can be paid when the first installment is due. A 10 percent penalty is added to each installment that is not paid on time. If both installments become delinquent, a small additional charge is added to the 10 percent penalty. As a memory tool, some people use the acronym NDFA, which stands for "November, December, February, and April"—or "No Darn Fooling Around" with property taxes!

> **MEMORY TOOL "NDFA"**
>
> November 1
> December 10
> February 1
> April 10

FIGURE 14.1

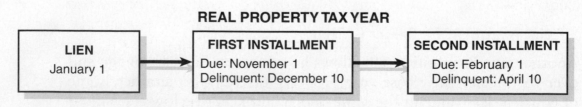

REAL PROPERTY TAX YEAR

LIEN	FIRST INSTALLMENT	SECOND INSTALLMENT
January 1	Due: November 1	Due: February 1
	Delinquent: December 10	Delinquent: April 10

Source: © 2015 OnCourse Learning

Tax Sale

If an owner fails to pay real property taxes when due, on June 30 the tax collector publishes a notice of "intent to sell" the property to the state of California because of unpaid taxes. This sale is not a real sale, but rather what is known as a *book sale*. The property owner still owns the real estate, but the owner's name is entered into a delinquent account book, which begins a five-year redemption period. During this five-year period, an owner can redeem the property by paying back taxes, interests, and other penalties and costs. Delinquent taxes can be paid in five annual installments as long as the current taxes are paid on time. For example, assume that a taxpayer owes three years' worth of back property taxes. If the owner pays the current year's taxes, the tax collector will allow the owner to make partial payments on the back taxes, rather than demand full payment of all back taxes.

If after five years the property taxes are still unpaid, the delinquent property is deeded to the state, and the former owner loses title. But as long as the state holds title, the former owner still has the right of redemption.

However, the state also has the right to sell tax-deeded property to other public agencies or to private parties. Once the state sells the property, the former owner loses the right of redemption.

Public Auction

The sale of tax-deeded property is conducted by the county tax collector, who must first obtain the permission of the local board of supervisors and the state controller.

The actual sale is a public auction that begins with a minimum bid that varies with each parcel being sold. All tax sales are for cash, as the state or county will not finance the sale. The successful bidder receives a *tax deed*. Under current title insurance practices, the holder of tax-deeded property can acquire title insurance after a period of one year.

Real Property Tax Exemptions

Because of special laws, certain owners of real estate are partially or totally exempt from the payment of property taxes. For example, government-owned real estate such as public buildings, parks, and school sites are exempt from property taxation. Some churches and other religious properties are not charged property taxes. In addition, there are special exemptions for homeowners, veterans, and senior citizens.

California Homeowner's Exemption

Under current law (January 2007), an owner-occupied residential dwelling is entitled to a $7,000 deduction from full assessed value. For example, if an owner-occupied home is assigned a $350,000 full cash value by the assessor, a $7,000 homeowner's exemption is subtracted from this figure to obtain a $343,000 taxable value.

$350,000	Full cash value
−7,000	Less homeowner's exemption
$343,000	Taxable value

Then, according to Proposition 13, the actual tax will be $3,430 ($343,000 × 1%), plus any amount needed to pay for voter-approved bonds. In short, the California homeowner's exemption is worth $70 ($7,000 × 1%).

To claim the homeowner's exemption, a person must have been the owner and in residence on or before January 1 and must file for the exemption with the assessor's office by February 15. Once filed, the exemption remains in effect until title is transferred or the exemption is terminated by actions of the owner. If a home-owner should miss the February 15 deadline, he or she can still file by December 1, but will receive only 80 percent ($5,600) of the $7,000 exemption.

Veteran's Exemption

A California resident who has served in the military during time of war is entitled to a $4,000 exemption on the full value of the property. However, a person may not have a homeowner's exemption and a veteran's exemption on the same property. Therefore, a veteran who owns one home is wise to take the homeowner's exemption of $7,000 instead of the veteran's exemption of $4,000. If a veteran owns other real estate in addition to a personal residence, the veteran's exemption can be applied against the other property. But current rules prohibit a veteran whose net worth exceeds a designated sum from using the veteran's exemption. The designated net worth is subject to change, so a veteran should contact a veteran's official or tax consultant before applying for the veteran's exemption.

Upon the death of an eligible veteran, the exemption rights are extended to the unmarried surviving spouse, registered domestic partner, or a pensioned father or mother. *Special rules exist for veterans who are disabled* because of injuries incurred in military service. In some cases, the disabled veteran may not be required to pay any property tax. The California Department of Veterans

Affairs should be contacted regarding the special rules for disabled California veterans.

Exemptions for Senior Citizens

In recent years, several laws have been enacted to help senior citizens, many of whom live on fixed incomes. Under some laws, a senior citizen is defined as a person 55 years of age or older; under other laws, the age limit is moved up to 62 years or older.

In California, the property tax postponement for senior citizens, blind, or disabled persons was suspended effective February 20, 2009. As a result of the program suspension, the state controller no longer accepts applications for property tax postponement. Chapter 369, Statutes of 2011, allows each county to implement a voluntary tax postponement program for properties located within that county.

The rules that determine the eligibility of senior citizens for special tax treatment are constantly changing; therefore, senior citizens should contact the California state controller's office website at sco.ca.gov or call 1-800-952-5661 for current information on the property tax postponement program.

Other Exemptions

Property tax exemptions of one sort or another also exist for a variety of other owners of real estate. Owners who use the land for timber, growing crops, young orchard trees, grapevines less than three years old, as well as churches and nonprofit organizations all qualify in some way for property tax exemptions. In addition, property tax incentives are used to keep agricultural land from being converted to urban use.

Special Assessments

Special assessments are different from real property taxes. Real property taxes help pay for the general operation of local government, whereas special assessments are levied to pay for a specific improvement, such as streets and sewers. Special assessment liens usually are on a parity with property tax liens and often are collected at the same time.

A frequently used special assessment law is the Street Improvement Act of 1911. This law is used by cities and counties for street improvements. According to this law, local government or a specially formed district hires a contractor to install or improve streets. Each owner along the street is liable for a pro rata share of the cost. The owner can pay in full within 30 days after completion, or the local government can sell bonds to raise the revenue to pay the contractor. If the project goes to bond, the property owners can pay their pro-rated share in installments over a period of time. Failure to pay a special assessment can result in a loss in the property owner's title, similar in nature to a tax sale.

Another program is the Mello-Roos Community Facilities Act of 1982. This law is used to finance public services in newly developed areas. Examples of services include waste treatment plants, parks, schools, fire stations, and so on. Under this program, the owners in the assessment district pay for the facilities in their neighborhood, rather than owners in other neighborhoods paying for the facilities. The Mello-Roos Act can result in very high taxes, well above the normal property tax, and must be made known to any new buyer before a purchase takes place.

Taxing Personal Property

As a general rule, only tangible personal property used in business is subject to taxes. Intangible property (such as shares of stock, or loans due) as well as household furnishings and personal effects are not taxed.

Personal property taxes are divided into secured and unsecured categories, depending on whether the owner of the personal property also owns the real estate where the personal property is located. Many rules apply to personal property, but they are beyond the scope of this book. Local tax assessors have numerous pamphlets available that explain the personal property tax procedures. All businesspeople are encouraged to obtain and read these pamphlets.

14.2 INCOME TAXES

Income taxes are levied by the federal government and by the state of California. The income tax is a progressive tax. *Progressive* means that the federal and state rates increase as the income levels being taxed increase.

The buying and selling of real estate have significant income tax consequences. In some cases, the income tax aspects may be as important as the price of the property. Income tax aspects of a real estate transaction should be considered before the sale, not after. Once a sale takes place, it is too late to go back and restructure the sale to take advantage of any tax laws that were overlooked.

Special Interest Topic

Persons and Agencies Involved in Property Taxes

COURTHOUSE

County board of supervisors. Establishes county budgets and sets county property tax rates up to the maximum allowed by law.

City council members. Establish city budgets and set city property tax rates up to the maximum allowed by law.

City or county auditor. Maintains the tax rolls.

City or county assessor. Appraises property for tax purposes.

City or county tax collector. Is responsible for actually collecting the taxes.

Local board of equalization. Is composed of the members of the board of supervisors; hears appeals from citizens who believe they have been taxed unfairly. In some areas, this function is handled by an assessment appeals board, which consists of citizens appointed by the board of supervisors.

State board of equalization. Audits and offers guidance to local taxing agencies.

Special note: Registered domestic partners cannot file joint income tax forms for federal taxes. Therefore, the income tax privileges extended to married couples do not apply to registered domestic partners when filing federal income tax.

Income tax laws are complicated and constantly changing. Before entering into a complicated real estate transaction, a person should seek the advice of an income tax specialist, such as an attorney or accountant.

Major Income Tax Advantages for Homeowners

Income tax laws favor homeowners over renters by granting various income tax incentives for becoming a homeowner.

1. Interest paid on real estate loans is deductible against personal income to reduce tax liability, subject to the interest limitation noted on the next pages.

2. Property taxes paid are also deductible against personal income.

3. Capital gains are not charged against primary residences up to the limit of $250,000 for singles and $500,000 for married couples who file joint returns. Unmarried co-owners get up to a $250,000 exclusion for each person if each meets the ownership and occupancy rules. Registered domestic partners come under this unmarried co-owner rule. To qualify, the home must have been the principal residence for at least two of the five years prior to the sale. Homeowners may use this law repeatedly as long as they have lived full time in the primary residence for the required 2 out of 5 years.

    Example: A couple sell their primary home that they lived in for fifteen years for $700,000 and will owe capital gains taxes on $200,000 ($700,000 - $500,000 excluded = $200,000).

4. The full exclusion can be used only once every two years. When the home is sold for a gain before the two-year holding period is achieved, the gain is fully taxable unless the sale is due to a job change, a major illness, or unforeseen circumstances. Then a pro rata formula is used to separate tax exempt from taxable gain.

    Example: Owned and lived in a home only 18 months; then due to a job change, sold it for a gain. The formula is as follows:

$$\frac{18 \text{ months}}{24 \text{ months}} = 75\%$$

For single $250,000 × 75% = $187,500 maximum exclusion
For married $500,000 × 75% = $375,000 maximum exclusion

1997 Tax Law: Homeowner Problems

1. Homeowners with gains of more than $250,000 for singles and $500,000 for married couples filing jointly will be taxed at capital gain rates for the excess over these dollar amounts. No deferral techniques are available.
2. Loss on the sale of a personal home will not be tax deductible.

Major Income Advantages for Investment Property Owners

1. Interest on real estate loans and property taxes paid is deductible against the rental income earned by the property.

2. Repairs, maintenance, management, insurance, and other operating expenses are also deductible. *Note: Repairs, maintenance, and other operating expenses are not deductible for homeowners on their own residences, only on investment real estate.*

3. Depreciation deduction allowances, technically called *cost recovery*, can be used to shelter income. The depreciation deduction consists of a yearly allowance (the length depending on if it is residential or nonresidential) for wear, tear, and obsolescence, which permits the property owner to recover the original cost over the useful life of the property. Land is not depreciable, only the improvements such as buildings, fences, and so on. Depreciation cannot be taken on owner-occupied residential homes; it can be taken only on income real estate. Depreciation deductions reduce the taxable income, thereby giving the property owner more after-tax cash flow. However, tax law changes place restrictions on how real estate losses can be used to shelter income other than rents.

4. Under certain circumstances, an investment property owner can enter into a tax-deferred exchange. If properly structured, an investor can exchange one like property for another (typically defined as real for real, in business or investment use, for equal or greater value) without paying immediate income taxes on the former property. The tax liability is not eliminated, but rather postponed until the investor disposes of the new property in a taxable transaction—usually a sale. Some people incorrectly call this a "tax-free" exchange; technically it is only a tax-deferred exchange. To structure an Internal Revenue Code, Section 1031, tax-deferred exchange, an investor must not receive what is referred to as *boot*. Boot is defined as unlike property received in an exchange. The receipt of boot creates a tax liability on the boot. Examples of boot include cash, notes, personal property, mortgage relief, and so on. There are many technical rules regarding a tax-deferred exchange, and no one should proceed without the advice of tax counsel.

5. An installment sale is another way to reduce tax liability upon the sale of real estate. This method of selling allows the seller to carry back paper and spread the gain from the sale over a period of years. Rather than paying the entire tax in the year of sale, the seller pays income taxes only on that portion of the gain received in the form of payments in any one year. Once again, advice of tax counsel should be sought to make sure the sale qualifies for installment reporting.

REAL ESTATE ASPECTS OF THE TAX REFORM ACT OF 1986, TAX REVENUE ACT OF 1987, TAXPAYER RELIEF ACT OF 1997, AND OTHER RECENT REVISIONS

Summary of Rules for Homeowners

1. Mortgage interest deductions are allowed for acquisition debt (purchase money loan) up to a maximum loan of $1 million on all combined mortgages on a first and second residence. If you borrow more than $1 million, the interest paid on the excess over $1 million is not deductible. No interest deduction is allowed for three or more personal-use homes.

2. For the refinance of an existing home, the remaining loan balance on acquisitions loan(s) plus $100,000 will be the maximum refinance loan allowed if the homeowner wishes to deduct all the interest as a qualified home loan. However, if a refinance loan exceeds the home's value, a portion of the interest paid is not deductible.

3. The $250,000 for singles and $500,000 for joint-filing married couples exemptions noted on previous pages are still valid.

4. Installment sale treatment is still allowed for homeowners.

Summary of Rules for Income Property Owners

1. Depreciation (cost recovery) on buildings and improvements is 27½ years for residential rental properties and 39 years for nonresidential properties. The straight-line method must be used.

2. Rental property mortgage interest is fully deductible against rental income, with no dollar loan limits such as the $1 million cap placed on homeowners. However, any tax loss created by interest and depreciation deductions falls under the passive tax loss rules listed herein.

3. Real estate rentals are considered "passive" investments and produce either passive income or passive loss, depending on the property's cash flow. The general rule is that a passive real estate loss can only be used to offset other passive income, not active or portfolio income such as salaries, commissions, profits, interest, and dividends. Prior to tax law changes, real estate losses could be used to offset active or portfolio income.

(Continued)

4. There is a special $25,000 exception to the passive loss rules if a person meets the following test:

   a. Is an individual owner of 10 percent or more interest in rental real estate

   b. Is actively involved in the management (owner can use property managers, but he or she must make the key decisions)

   c. Has a modified adjusted gross income of $100,000 or less

   If the owner of rental real estate meets this test, he or she can use up to $25,000 in passive losses from real estate to offset active or portfolio income, such as salaries and interest, after first offsetting passive income.

5. If the rental property owner's modified adjusted gross income exceeds $100,000, the $25,000 amount is reduced $1 for every $2 above the $100,000. Any unused passive losses from rental real estate can be carried forward to reduce future passive income and gain upon sale of the property. The passive loss rules do not eliminate the investor's right to use real estate losses. However, the law's changes will, in some cases, delay the right to use the loss until a later date, such as the date of resale.

6. The right for a real estate investor to do a 1031 tax-deferred exchange remains the same; recent tax law changes have not eliminated this technique.

7. Installment sales treatment for real estate investors is still allowed. Installment sale treatment for real estate dealers has been abolished.

There are many other tax law changes, but these are the items that have a major impact on real estate. The preceding is listed for information purposes and should not be considered tax advice. For tax advice, a person should seek competent tax advisors.

State Income Tax

In some ways, California income tax law is patterned after the federal laws. However, some notable differences should be discussed with a tax expert. For example, the tax brackets for individuals and corporations are different for state income tax as opposed to federal income taxes. There are special rules regarding new residents and their need to file a

California income tax statement. All of these state tax laws, in addition to many others, are administered by the California Franchise Tax Board.

For most real estate transactions, the impact of federal income taxes is more important than the impact of state income taxes. But careful tax planning should attempt to minimize both federal and state income taxes.

Special Withholding Rules for Foreign and Out-of-State Sellers

Under the Foreign Investment in Real Property Tax Act (FIRPTA), the federal government requires that 10 percent of the sales price of property owned by a foreigner must be withheld for a possible income tax liability. California Revenue and Taxation Code Sections 18805 and 26131 require a three and a third percent withholding for state income taxes if the seller is a foreigner or a resident of another state. A recent law change also allows the state to withhold three and a third percent from California residents who sell certain types of investment property. Both of these laws put the burden for compliance on the buyer, not the seller. Both of these laws have exceptions and exemptions that can be complicated and tricky. If a person is purchasing California property from a foreigner or a U.S. citizen who lives in another state, the buyer might wish to check with a tax expert before the sale takes place to make sure the income tax laws are being correctly applied.

14.3 OTHER TAXES

Documentary Transfer Tax

Upon the transfer of real estate, a documentary transfer tax of $0.55 per $500 of consideration, or fraction thereof (at a rate of $1.10 per $1,000), is levied. If the property being transferred is in an unincorporated area, all of the tax goes to the county where the property is located. If the property is located in an incorporated city, the city and county divide the tax proceeds.

The tax is levied on the full price of the property if there is an all-cash sale or if the buyer obtains a new loan that cashes the seller out. If the buyer assumes the seller's existing loan, the transfer tax is levied only on the equity being transferred. (See Chapter 6 for detailed examples of the documentary transfer tax.)

Estate and Inheritance Tax

In some cases, the federal government taxes the estates of deceased persons. The state of California has eliminated inheritance taxes.

There are several ways to reduce or, in some cases, avoid the payment of estate taxes. The methods are technical and complicated, and the services of an attorney should be used. For further information, see Internal Revenue Publication 559.

Gift Taxes

The federal government, but not the state of California, has tax laws that apply to gifts of real and personal property. A gift is a voluntary transfer of property from the owner, called the *donor,* to the receiver, called the *donee.*

The federal law allows a tax-free gift (as of January 2014) of $14,000 of value per donee per year. This $14,000 is scheduled to increase slowly over time. The use of gift tax exclusions during the life of the donor can often be used to save estate taxes upon death. Gift tax laws are complicated, and professional tax advice should be sought when planning an estate to minimize taxes by use of gifts.

Miscellaneous Taxes

Sales and use taxes occasionally arise in certain broker transactions—for example, in the sale of a business opportunity or a mobile home. In circumstances where sales tax is involved, the real estate agent is responsible for seeing that escrow instructions are correctly drafted to account for the tax liability.

Unemployment insurance fees, worker's compensation fees, and Social Security taxes may need to be collected when a real estate sales-person is hired by a broker and acts as an employee instead of as an independent contractor.

Chapter Summary

Property taxes in California are levied on a modified ad valorem basis and usually change when a property is transferred to a new owner. Two classifications of property taxes are real property taxes and personal property taxes. With passage of the Jarvis-Gann initiative (Proposition 13), the maximum real property tax allowed is one percent of full cash value, plus two percent annual inflationary factor, plus an additional sum to pay for voter-approved bonds that affect the property.

If there has been no change in ownership since March 1, 1975, the tax year 1975–1976 is the base year for computing full cash value. A change in ownership after March 1, 1975, causes the full cash value for tax purposes to be increased to the sales price or value as of the date of transfer. There are special rules for the handling of remodeling and additions that cause the taxable value to rise.

Real property taxes are paid over a fiscal year beginning July 1 and ending June 30. The first installment is due November 1 and is delinquent if not paid by December 10. The second installment is due February 1 and is delinquent if not paid by April 10. Real property taxes become a lien on the January 1 preceding the fiscal tax year. If the required taxes are not paid, the owner's title will eventually revert to the state of California for delinquent taxes.

Real property tax exemptions include $7,000 on appraised value for homeowners, $4,000 for qualified veterans, and special exemptions for senior citizens. There are several other property tax exemptions for certain classes of property, such as timber and growing crops.

Income taxes are levied by both federal and state government. Income taxes are progressive—that is, the tax rate increases as the income level increases. The buying and selling of real estate have significant income tax consequences. Sometimes the income tax aspects are more important than the price. Income tax laws are complicated and constantly changing. Before entering into a real estate transaction, a person should seek the advice of a qualified tax expert.

Other taxes that can have an impact on real estate are estate taxes, gift taxes, transfer taxes, and use and sales taxes.

Important Terms and Concepts

ad valorem   Proposition 13

boot   special assessments

depreciation deduction

Practical Application

1. Counting local bonds, the typical property tax in your community runs .0125 of the sales price, and homeowner's insurance runs .005 of the sales price. As a real estate agent, you are showing potential buyers a $225,000 condo that requires an 80 percent loan at 8 percent amortized for 30 years. Based on this information, what will be the initial monthly housing payment of PITI (principal, interest, one twelfth taxes, and one twelfth insurance)? *Hint:* You need to use a financial calculator and the amortization table in Appendix B.

2. Married homeowners who have owned and lived in their main home for eight years sell their $750,000 home and have a $300,000 gain. They file joint returns and their federal capital gain tax bracket is 20 percent. Based on this information, how much do they owe in federal taxes due to the sale of their home?

3. A homeowner refinances and takes out a 125 percent equity loan. How much of the interest on this loan is deductible for federal income taxes?

Reviewing Your Understanding

1. The homeowner's exemption, excluding local assessments, saves approximately how much in property taxes?
   a. $100
   b. $80
   c. $70
   d. $40

2. The proposition that allows certain homeowners to transfer their property tax base to another home in the same county is:
   a. Proposition 13.
   b. Proposition 57.
   c. Proposition 60.
   d. Proposition 90.

3. For a homeowner, which of the following is tax deductible?
   a. Fire insurance premiums
   b. Roof repairs
   c. Mortgage interest
   d. Two of the above are deductible for homeowners

4. City council members:
   a. set city property tax rates as allowed by law.
   b. establish city budgets.
   c. do both a and b.
   d. do neither a nor b.

5. The second installment of real property taxes is delinquent if not paid by:
   a. November 1.
   b. December 10.
   c. February 1.
   d. April 10.

6. Which of the following is true?
   a. A person cannot use a homeowner's exemption and a veteran's exemption on the same home.
   b. Real property taxes become a lien on the first Monday in March.
   c. A 12 percent penalty is added for delinquent property taxes.
   d. California has special property tax exemptions for senior citizens 45 years or older.

7. A frequently used special assessment law is:
   a. the Street Improvement Act of 1911.
   b. the Mello-Roos Community Facilities Act of 1982.
   c. Proposition 13.
   d. Proposition 60.

8. Under certain conditions, married couples may exempt up to how much in gains from the sale of a home?
   a. $500,000
   b. $250,000
   c. $125,000
   d. $50,000

9. When foreigners sell U.S. property, the Foreign Investment in Real Property Tax Act (FIRPTA) may require what percentage to be withheld from the sale proceeds?
   a. 3½ percent
   b. 5 percent
   c. 10 percent
   d. 13 percent

10. Property taxes become a lien on:
    a. July 1.
    b. November 1.
    c. February 1.
    d. January 1.

11. Private property is deeded to the state for delinquent property taxes after:
    a. one year.
    b. two years.
    c. three years.
    d. five years.

12. When a special assessment is made on a piece of property under the Street Improvement Act of 1911:
    a. the property owner can deduct principal and interest.
    b. it is based on the front footage of the property.
    c. it is appraised as per the amount of square footage.
    d. assessment must be paid within six months.

13. In a 1031 real estate exchange, a tax liability arises if the person exchanging receives:
    a. like-kind property.
    b. boot.
    c. income property.
    d. investment property.

14. Which of the following is TRUE of the exclusion on paying capital gains on primary residence?
    a. The owner must have lived in the property at least five consecutive years.
    b. Single people may exclude up to $500,000.
    c. The exclusion can be used repeatedly if ownership requirements are met.
    d. Only those over 55 and married may use the exclusion.

15. Under certain conditions, a single homeowner may exempt up to how much in gains from the sale of a home?
    a. $500,000
    b. $300,000
    c. $250,000
    d. $125,000

16. Which of the following events could trigger a new property tax assessment?
    a. A refinance by the current owner
    b. A real estate transfer
    c. A construction loan
    d. The rental of a single-family residence

17. Ad valorem is a Latin phrase that means:
    a. according to value.
    b. buyer beware.
    c. and others.
    d. none of the above.

18. The county tax assessor's duty is to determine:
    a. the tax rate to be applied to assessed values.
    b. assignment of parcel numbers to current secured tax rolls.
    c. tax to be paid by the property owner.
    d. value of the property for tax purposes.

19. A law used to finance public services in newly developed areas that can lead to high assessments for the affected owners is called:
    a. Mello-Roos.
    b. Holden-Aspen.
    c. Alvarez-Greene.
    d. Brown-Miller.

20. For investors, losses on the operation of rental real estate are what type of losses?
    a. Passive
    b. Active
    c. Actual
    d. Portfolio

© Shutterstock / Martin M303

STUDENT LEARNING OUTCOMES

This chapter explores the characteristics of a house, including construction details, roof styles, and architectural designs. Mobile homes, condominiums, and vacation or second homes are also discussed. At the conclusion of this chapter, you will be able to do the following:

- Identify major construction terms associated with home building.
- Differentiate among various architectural styles.
- List the advantages and disadvantages of buying versus renting a home.
- Discuss the advantages and disadvantages of owning a mobile (manufactured) home, condominium, and vacation home.

SINGLE-FAMILY HOMES AND MOBILE HOMES

15.1 HOME CONSTRUCTION STYLES AND TERMS

There are many varieties of home construction styles, but the three most common types are one-story, split-level, and two-story homes.

The one-story home is the simplest to build and the easiest to maintain, but it occupies more land per square foot of living space than the other styles.

The split-level home is popular in California because of the better utilization of land of varying topography as well as the pleasing cosmetic effect. However, it is usually more expensive to build.

The two-story home has a lower cost per square foot because a single foundation and roof support two floors of living area. But the principal disadvantage is the stairs that must be climbed to reach the second floor. Also, the difficulty of reaching exterior portions for repair and maintenance presents some problems.

Foundations are the base of all construction. Three types of typical home foundations are concrete slab, crawl space, and basements. Foundations can be made of wood, stacked stone, or block, but most modern foundations are poured concrete. The first building component is the footing, which is the concrete support for the foundation; it sets the footprint of the structure. Then the foundation walls are poured. From this the sills, which support the floor joists, are positioned to start the support system for the upper structure. Typically a subfloor is laid with the finished flooring attached to it. The sole plate attaches to the subfloor and creates the base from which the exterior and interior walls will be built. Studs, typically 2×4's, are vertical members that create the support and structure for the walls. The top plate is attached to the top of the studs to create the ceiling and roof support. Headers are beams used above doors and windows to spread weight and support the opening. Roof joist are then set on the walls. Often a center bearing wall, especially in older homes, also supports the roof joist and cannot be removed without support being added. The roof decking is added on top of the roof joist, and the roofing materials – shingles or tiles – are attached to the decking. Gutters are typically added to move the water away from the structure. In California there are a number of building requirements added for earthquake resistance. See Roof styles and Construction Details on the following pages.

Roof Styles

The major roof styles are illustrated below.

Gable Roof

Victorian Roof

Hip Roof
All sides slope to eaves.

Shed Roof

Gambrel Roof
Found on barns and Dutch colonial homes.

Gable Roof
with shed dormer

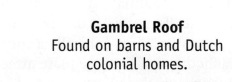

Pyramid Roof
All sides slope from one point (no ridge line).

Mansard Roof
(French style)

Source: © OnCourse Learning 2015.

New England Colonial
A box-shaped two-story house with a center entrance, wood siding, and shutters.

Georgian Colonial
A brick two-story house with a center entrance and a hip roof.

Southern Colonial
A two-story house with pillars and shutters.

Dutch Colonial
A two-story house with a gambrel roof.

California Bungalow
A small one-story house with a low-pitched roof.

California Ranch
A one-story house with a low-pitched roof and a sprawling floor plan.

Spanish
A house with a tile roof and arches.

Cape Cod
A house with a second story above the eaves, a high-pitched roof, wood siding, and a large chimney.

French Provincial
A formal house with a high-pitched slate hip roof, a stone or brick exterior, and shutters.

Victorian
A house with
ornate gables.

English Elizabethan
A house with a high-
pitched slate roof,
rough half-timbers,
and a plaster exterior.

Monterey
A two-story
house with a
front balcony.

French Norman
A house with a tower
as the main entrance
and a steep roof.

English Tudor
A house with a high-pitched
slate roof, a cathedral-
like entrance, and a
masonry exterior.

Mediterranean or Italian
A house with a tile roof,
a stucco exterior, and
rounded decorative work
above the windows.

Contemporary
A house of
modern design.

Source: © OnCourse Learning 2015.

CONSTRUCTION DETAILS

A CEILING JOIST. Horizontal beams supporting ceiling
B COLLAR BEAM. A beam that connects opposite rafters above the floor
C CRIPPLES. Short vertical piece 2 × 4 above or below an opening
D DIAGONAL BRACE. A brace across corner of structure to prevent swaying
E FIRE STOP. Short board or wall between studs to prevent fire spreading
F FLASHING. Metal sheet usually around chimney to prevent water seepage
G FLOOR JOIST. Horizontal beams supporting floor
H FOOTING. Base or bottom of a foundation wall
I FOUNDATION. The supporting portion of structure resting on footing
J LINTEL. A horizontal board over a door or window, also called header
K MUDSILL. Perimeter board anchored directly to foundation
L RAFTERS. Boards designed to support roof loads
M RIDGE BOARD. Highest board in the house supporting upper ends
N SOLE PLATE. Usually 2 × 4 on which wall and studs rest
O STUDS. Vertical boards 2 × 4 supporting the walls every 16″ (on center)
P TOP PLATE. A horizontal board fastened to upper end of studs

Other Construction Terms
    Board Foot = used to measure lumber, contains 144 cubic inches
    R–VALUE = ranking of insulation materials
    EER = Energy Efficiency Rating

15.2 MOBILE (MANUFACTURED) HOMES

Because building codes, zoning laws, and other practices, as well as inflation, make it difficult to build low-cost conventional houses, many families have turned to mobile homes as a solution.

The name *mobile* was changed to *manufactured* over 20 years ago, but most people still call them mobile homes. A mobile or manufactured home is defined by the California Health and Safety Code as "a vehicle designed and equipped to contain no more than two dwelling units, to be used without permanent foundation." Mobile homes in the past were confused with trailers. The major difference is that trailers usually provide temporary housing only, whereas a mobile home is a permanent living unit. The word *mobile* may be confusing; actually, studies show that once in place, mobile homes are seldom moved. They are usually located in mobile home parks, although in many rural areas, they can be found on individual lots. The Mobile Home Parks Act defines a mobile home park as "any area or tract of land where one or more mobile home lots are rented or leased." The rental operation of a mobile home park is within the jurisdiction of the State Department of Housing and Community Development. If a mobile home park has five or more lots for sale or lease, it is considered a subdivision and consequently subject to subdivision laws. Under certain circumstances, mobile homes purchased after July 1, 1980, can be taxed as real property if they are attached to a permanent foundation.

Types of Mobile Homes

The four basic types of mobile homes are illustrated here.

Single, 8-foot, and 10-foot-wide units

Single, 12-foot-wide units

Multiple-wide, double-wide, or triple-wide units

Quads—four units together

Legal Requirements Related to Mobile Homes

In order to list or sell a mobile home, a real estate licensee must comply with special aspects of the real estate law.

1. *New mobile homes cannot be sold by real estate licensees,* but only through mobile home dealers licensed by the Department of Housing and Community Development.

2. *A real estate licensee can sell used mobile homes* provided the mobile homes have already been registered with the state and are on a lot or in a mobile home park.

3. The mobile home must be capable of being transported over a road. The hitch must be attached to the unit or stored underneath, and the axles must still be attached to the frame.

4. The licensee is responsible to see that there is proper completion and delivery of the title to the buyer.

5. Notification of transfer of ownership must be made within 10 days of the sale date.

6. All fees must be paid to the state within 10 days of the sale date.

7. No concealment of a material fact or any other fraudulent act may be committed.

8. Mobile homeowners must pay an in lieu tax similar to regular property taxes paid by homeowners.

9. If the mobile home was manufactured after June 15, 1976, it must have a Department of Housing and Urban Development (HUD) tag, guaranteeing its proper construction.

Violations of Business and Professions Code

Under this code, real estate licensees may have their licenses suspended or revoked if they are found guilty of any of the following:

1. Failed to provide for the delivery of proper certificate of ownership of a mobile home
2. Knowingly participated in the purchase or sale of a stolen mobile home
3. Submitted a check, draft, or money order to the state for payment of mobile home fees and the draft is dishonored upon presentation to the bank

Financing Mobile Homes

Because mobile homes are considered to be personal property, the method of encumbering the ownership is through a security agreement instead of a deed of trust.

Mobile homes can be financed through FHA, VA, and Cal-Vet loans (see Chapter 9). In addition, conventional loans are available from banks and other real estate lenders. Most mobile home loans are amortized over a 15-year period. Interest rates on mobile home loans are usually higher than on conventional home loans.

Termination of Tenancy in a Mobile Home Park

The Civil Code provides for the termination of tenancy by the landlord of a mobile home park tenant when any of these occur:

1. Failure of the tenant to comply with local ordinances and state laws and regulations related to mobile homes
2. Conduct of the tenant upon park premises that constitutes a substantial annoyance to other tenants
3. Failure of the tenant to comply with reasonable rules and regulations of the mobile home park
4. Nonpayment of rent, utility charges, or incidental service charges
5. Failure to maintain the mobile home in a reasonable state of repair acceptable to park management

In recent years, there has been considerable legislation, as well as many disputes and lawsuits, regarding rents and other occupancy issues at mobile home parks. The complete rights and duties of landlords and tenants in a mobile home park are too extensive to cover in this textbook. Interested parties should research The Mobile Home

Residency Law, Civil Code 798, and The Mobile-Home Parks Act, Sections 18200, et. seq., of the California Health and Safety Code.

Advantages of Mobile Home Ownership

1. The price of traditional homes has risen so rapidly that many families, young adults, and senior citizens are purchasing mobile homes because of their lower prices as compared to conventional homes.
2. Mobile home parks are relatively quiet places to live.
3. Residents feel secure because there is usually only one entrance or exit to the mobile home and most residents know the other owners who live in the mobile home park.
4. Mobile homes are transportable.
5. The quality and amenities of mobile homes have improved over the years.
6. Better financing terms are now available for mobile home purchasers.
7. There is minimal yard maintenance or none at all.

Disadvantages of Mobile Home Ownership

1. Mobile homes can depreciate rapidly.
2. Mobile homes usually have a lower resale value than conventional houses.
3. The terms of loans offered by lenders are usually not as favorable as those for conventional homes.
4. When a mobile home is located in a mobile home park, the owner may be required to buy extras, such as steps with handrails or skirting to conceal wheels.
5. Cities and counties may have restrictions regarding the placement of mobile homes; therefore, sites may be difficult to obtain.

Converting a Mobile Home to Real Property

For a mobile home to become real property, the following four conditions must be met:

1. The mobile homeowner must obtain a building permit.
2. The mobile home must be placed on a permanent foundation.
3. The mobile homeowner must obtain a certificate of occupancy.
4. A document stating that the mobile home is attached to a permanent foundation must be recorded.

Once these conditions are met, a mobile home is considered real property, and all the laws of real estate apply.

Modular Homes

Although there are slight technical differences between a modular and a pre-paneled home, for our purposes a modular home will be considered a factory-built home, without wheels, that is intended from the beginning to be placed on a permanent foundation. Modular homes are not considered vehicles, as are mobile homes, and they immediately become real estate upon placement. Once placed, all the rules of real property apply to modular homes. They are allowed in areas zoned for single-family dwellings and compete in the marketplace with on-site constructed homes (sometimes called *stick-built homes*). Advocates of modular homes stress the consistent quality guaranteed in a factory setting, plus the lower cost per square foot, and the homes arrive at the building site 90 percent finished, which saves on-site construction time.

There are communities where lots are sold primarily for the placement of modular homes. Most of these are subdivisions with private deed restrictions and an owners' association for the common areas. Modular homes are entitled to all the financing packages that are granted to on-site constructed homes.

As with mobile homes, a real estate licensee is not allowed to sell a new modular unit from the factory or off a sales lot. But once a modular home is set in place, a real estate licensee is allowed to handle the sale of the property. If a real estate agent wishes to sell new mobile or modular homes, said agent must conform to retailer rules that come under the California State Board of Equalization and obtain additional special licenses that apply to mobile and modular homes.

15.3 CONDOMINIUMS

A condominium is a system of individual fee ownership of a unit in a complex that can be for any use, combined with ownership in common with the other owner's of common areas of the structure and the land.

Advantages of Condominium Ownership

1. Owners can sell their units as they would a regular home.
2. Insurance companies offer special packages for condominium owners.
3. It combines the benefits of owning a house with the advantages of apartment living.

4. Owners receive the same income tax benefits as homeowners.
5. Owners build equity with each payment, as they do in a regular home.
6. There is little or no yard work to perform.
7. Common areas that are part of ownership can include game rooms, swimming pools, tennis courts, and putting greens.
8. The law offers some protection to owners, in that they cannot be made to leave because of certain infractions of by-laws and regulations of the governing owners' association.

Disadvantages of Condominium Ownership

1. Each owner is responsible for all maintenance problems in his or her unit.
2. Owners may be required to pay their share of the association fees to cover maintenance costs in common areas even if they disagree with the expenditure.
3. Sometimes the developer controls parking and recreation areas, for which he or she may charge extra fees.
4. Owners may find themselves living rather compactly in close proximity to neighbors. Noises emanating from swimming pool and game areas may be distracting.

Basic Items to Check When Buying a Condominium

1. If the building is new, check on the reputation of the builder. If it is an existing building, check with agents, neighbors, homeowners' associations, and government agencies to see if there have been complaints regarding the quality of construction.
2. Read all legal documents carefully, most importantly all current financial documents and any other items including any conditions, covenants, and restrictions, as well as governing documents of the owners' association.
3. Make sure you know the amount and coverage of any owners' association fees. What are they now? When were they raised last? Are there any pending lawsuits against the owners' association?
4. Ask yourself these specific questions:
   a. Is exterior and/or interior maintenance included in the established fees?
   b. Are there any restrictions on the sale or lease of individual units? How many units are tenant occupied, as opposed to owner occupied?

    c. Are there any warranties on equipment? If so, for how long?

    d. Does the developer and/or the association have reserve funds in case of an emergency?

    e. Are owners required to pay maintenance costs for unsold units?

    f. Is there enough insurance to protect against fire, liability, theft, and other risks?

5. What experience has the real estate agent had regarding the sale and financing of condominiums?

15.4 VACATION HOMES

Many people own a vacation or second home. Second homes typically include a cabin in the mountains, a cottage by the lake, a house near the beach, a chalet near a ski slope, or a home in a desert resort area.

Where You Buy Is Important

You should ask yourself these questions before you make your final decision regarding ownership of a second home:

1. Can I tolerate close neighbors, or do I want complete privacy?

2. Do I want a place close to everyday conveniences or one that is "out of sight and sound"?

3. Depending on the area chosen, can I afford it? If not, can I interest someone in a joint venture?

4. What is the resale potential? Will the home be difficult to resell if I need to get my money out?

A Second Home as an Investment

Five major factors determine investment potential. They are risk, liquidity, management, tax aspects, and appreciation potential. **Risk** is the possibility that you will lose all or part of your initial investment. The risk involved in a second home as an investment depends on the market conditions at the time of purchase and resale. Second-home investments are usually considered a greater risk than a principal residence, and this is reflected in the higher interest rates a lender may charge for a second-home loan compared to the interest rate on a loan to buy a principal residence.

    Liquidity refers to the ability to convert your investment to cash quickly. Real estate is not as liquid as other investments, such as stocks and bonds. However, if the second home is priced right, it can usually be sold in a reasonable amount of time. Before you buy a second home, check out the resale history of the area.

Management refers to the cost and time involved in overseeing the investment. Real estate requires a considerable amount of management. On nearby real estate investments, you may choose to manage the property yourself. But when the second home is a considerable distance away, you need to pay for local management to oversee, maintain, and check up on the property.

Tax aspects refer to the income tax laws and their impact on the investment. Owners of second homes are allowed to deduct the interest on loans and payment of property taxes. If the second home is rented out for a portion of time, a complex set of income tax rules applies. If a second home is sold for a gain, homeowners are not allowed to use the $250,000 for singles and $500,000 for married couples income tax exclusions. A vacation or second home is no longer the tax haven it once was—see your tax advisor before you buy. Today most vacation homes are purchased to enjoy; they are not purchased as tax shelters.

Appreciation refers to an increase in value when demand exceeds supply. California real estate, as a whole over a length of time, has tended to increase significantly in value. But at any given time, prices can decline because of a current decline in demand. The vacation or second-home market is usually more volatile than the regular home market.

15.5 SHOULD YOU RENT OR BUY?

Keep in mind that the advantages of renting closely parallel the disadvantages of buying, and the disadvantages of renting closely relate to the advantages of buying.

Advantages of Renting and Disadvantages of Buying

1. Only a comparatively small outlay of money is required to rent, usually the first and last months' rents and a security deposit. When you purchase a home, the lender may require a down payment of 5 to 20 percent of the price. If you put less money down on a home, you are usually charged a higher interest rate and loan fees, because of the risk involved to the lender.

2. There is less risk in renting because your initial outlay is limited. You do not stand to lose much even if you decide to move earlier

than you had planned. In purchasing, whenever you invest money, there is a greater risk you might lose some or all of it if property values decline.

3. In the short run, when renting, your costs are fixed. You know how much your rent will be each month, so you can usually budget accordingly. In buying, the mortgage payment may or may not remain stable depending on whether the loan has a fixed or adjustable rate. When you own your property, taxes and maintenance costs increase over time.

4. In renting, if the neighborhood should decline, you can move without suffering a personal loss because of a decline in real estate values. Renting provides greater mobility than owning.

5. When you rent, you can take the money that otherwise would be used to buy a home and deposit it in a savings account or buy stocks and bonds, giving you greater liquidity. When you purchase real estate, your money is usually tied up and may be difficult to pull out to meet a financial emergency.

6. When you rent, you do not have the same responsibility for maintenance as you do when you own property. You can take a vacation trip without worrying about the maintenance and upkeep of the property. When you own, the responsibility for maintenance is yours.

Advantages of Buying and Disadvantages of Renting

1. Buying a home can be an investment for the future. Well-located properties usually increase in value over the long run. During recessions, there may be a short-term drop in prices, but over the long term, the average California home has experienced appreciation. When you rent, you have only rent receipts to show for your expenditure at the end of each month.

2. As a homeowner, you can deduct your property taxes and interest payments from personal income before paying federal or state income taxes.

3. Pride of ownership and security make people feel comfortable and permanent in their homes. Many homeowners cement that security by becoming involved in community affairs, working around the yard, and making minor repairs. On the other hand, it is difficult to establish permanence in a rented home. At the whim of the landlord, you may be asked to leave or to pay higher rent in order to stay.

4. A home is usually larger than an apartment unit, allowing plenty of room for activities. Few apartment units provide the same freedom of movement as a home. In addition, you can build on to your home if you need more space.

5. There are fewer restrictions placed on homeowners. They can have pets if they wish.

6. Homeowners are frequently viewed as more secure credit risks than renters.

These items are just a few of the advantages and disadvantages of owning versus renting.

Chapter Summary

This chapter discussed the characteristics of one-story, two-story, and split-level homes. Various architectural designs, roof styles, and construction details were illustrated. The principles of mobile home, condominium, and vacation home ownership were discussed. The chapter ended with an explanation of the pros and cons of buying versus renting real estate.

Important Terms and Concepts

appreciation

condominium

liquidity

management

mobile home park

modular homes

risk

tax aspects

Practical Application

1. Using the construction illustration in the book, starting from the ground and moving to the sole plate of a standard home, give the construction name for each item in the correct sequence.

2. List the four conditions required in California to convert a mobile home to real property.

3. As a real estate agent, you are attempting to convince a renter that buying a home makes more economic sense than renting. List five advantages of owning a home.

Reviewing Your Understanding

1. This type of roof has all sides slope downward toward the eaves.
   a. hip.
   b. gambrel.
   c. gable.
   d. mansard.

2. A real estate licensee can sell used mobile homes provided the mobile homes have been registered with the:
   a. Department of Housing and Community Development.
   b. Federal Housing Administration.
   c. Department of Veterans Affairs.
   d. Bureau of Real Estate

3. Title to a mobile home is transferred by use of a:
   a. document of title.
   b. deed.
   c. certificate of ownership.
   d. contract of sale.

4. Which of the following regarding mobile homes is true?
   a. Interest rates on loans are usually lower than on conventional homes.
   b. They usually depreciate more rapidly than a conventional home.
   c. They cannot be financed using FHA, VA, or Cal-Vet programs.
   d. In most cities, they are allowed to be placed in any residential area.

5. One advantage a two-story home has over a one-story home is:
   a. that it usually costs less per square foot to build.
   b. that it has ease of access to the roof.
   c. that it has a convenient floor plan for disabled people.
   d. that it is easier to maintain.

6. Vertical pieces of 2 × 4 used to create the inner wall structure are called:
   a. diagonal braces.
   b. headers.
   c. studs.
   d. rafters.

7. A footing is what the:
   a. floor sits upon.
   b. foundation sits upon.
   c. mudsill sits upon.
   d. heater sits upon.

8. A new mobile home from the factory can be sold by:
   a. the developer.
   b. a real estate licensee.
   c. the Department of Veterans Affairs.
   d. none of the above.

9. When a buyer purchases a property, there is a risk of:
   a. losing some or all of their investment if property values decline.
   b. not being viewed as a secure credit risk as compared to renters.
   c. having too many restrictions placed on the homeowner versus a renter.
   d. not having any additional tax advantages.

10. A ranch home offers ease of use and:
    a. has the advantage of being less expensive to construct.
    b. is not a typical type of home in California.
    c. has a disadvantage of using the most land.
    d. is expensive to maintain.

11. What portion of the building do the upright beams, known as studs, rest upon?
    a. Collar beam
    b. Floor joist
    c. Fire stops
    d. Sole plate

12. A mobile home park, consisting of five or more lots, is considered a:
    a. PUD.
    b. subdivision.
    c. community development.
    d. stock cooperative.

13. Before major remodeling of the interior of a home, structural care must be given in regard to:
    a. mechanics' liens.
    b. pitch of the roof.
    c. the bearing wall.
    d. easements on the property.

14. Which of the following is false regarding condominium ownership?
    a. There are commercial as well as residential condos.
    b. Each owner has an undivided interest in common areas.
    c. Airspace within each unit is held as fee simple ownership.
    d. All condos are single-level buildings.

15. For a mobile home to be legally considered real property, it must:
    a. be insured as a home by an insurance company.
    b. rest on a permanent foundation.
    c. be certified by a proper government agency (building permit).
    d. both b and c are correct.

16. The rental operation of a mobile home park is within the jurisdiction of the:
    a. Bureau of Real Estate.
    b. Department of Housing and Urban Development.
    c. Department of Veterans Affairs.
    d. State Department of Housing and Community Development.

17. A real estate licensee should have a basic understanding of construction terms. One thing he or she should know is that the beam above the door and windows is know as the:
    a. floor joist.
    b. sole plate.
    c. header.
    d. roof joist.

18. Instead of buying a vacation home, many people buy:
    a. RVs.
    b. time shares.
    c. an undivided interest in recreational developments.
    d. all of the above.

19. Which of the following roof styles is best described as a "pitched roof sloping from two sides with the sides meeting at the top"?

    a. Gable roof

    b. Gambrel roof

    c. Hip roof

    d. Mansard roof

20. What is not a factor to consider when determining investment potential?

    a. Risk

    b. Liquidity

    c. Carpet quality

    d. Management requirements

THE CALIFORNIA STATE EXAMINATION

THE REAL ESTATE LICENSE EXAMINATION IN DETAIL

The requirements to become a real estate salesperson or broker were discussed in Chapter 1. The discussion below outlines in more detail the state examination and the steps required to obtain a license once the examination has been passed.

The state real estate examination was created using guidelines originally outlined by a research project conducted by the University of California. The examination has been updated several times using generally accepted scientific studies. All questions are based on the knowledge necessary to competently perform the tasks of a real estate broker and salesperson. The real estate salesperson examination and the real estate broker examination are weighted by topics chosen to reflect the differences in the level and amount of knowledge required by each job. As the real estate business changes and the separate roles of a salesperson and a broker change, the Bureau of Real Estate attempts to alter the examination to reflect these changes. **The examination weightings as of September 2015 follow. The weightings may be subject to change in the future.**

Special Interest Topic

AREA 1—PROPERTY OWNERSHIP AND LAND USE CONTROLS AND REGULATIONS

Approximately 15 percent of the Sales Exam and 15 percent of the Broker Exam

Classes of Property
Property Characteristics
Encumbrances
Types of Ownership
Description of Property
Government Rights in Land
Public Controls
Environmental Hazards and Regulations
Private Controls
Water Rights
Special Categories of Land

AREA 2—LAWS OF AGENCY AND FIDUCIARY DUTIES

Approximately 17 percent of the Sales Exam and 17 percent of the Broker Exam

Law, Definition, and Nature of Agency Relationships, Types of Agencies, and Agents
Creation of Agency and Agency Agreements
Responsibilities of Agent to Seller and Buyer as a Principal
Disclosure of Agency
Disclosure Acting as a Principal or Other Interest
Termination of Agency
Commissions and Fees
Responsibilities of Agent to Non-Client Third Parties

AREA 3—PROPERTY VALUATION AND FINANCIAL ANALYSIS

Approximately 14 percent of the Sales Exam and 9 percent of the Broker Exam

Value
Methods of Estimating Value
Financial Analysis

AREA 4—FINANCING

Approximately 9 percent of the Sales Exam and 9 percent of the Broker Exam

General Concepts
Types of Loans
Sources of Financing
Government Programs
Mortgages/Deeds of Trust/Notes
Financing/Credit Laws
Loan Brokerage
Types of Loan Originators

AREA 5—TRANSFER OF PROPERTY

Approximately 8 percent of the Sales Exam and 8percent of the Broker Exam

Title Insurance
Deeds
Escrow
Tax Aspects
Special Process
Transfer through Court Supervision
Types of Vesting

AREA 6—PRACTICE OF REAL ESTATE AND MANDATED DISCLOSURES (INCLUDES SPECIALTY AREAS)

Approximately 25 percent of the Sales Exam and 25 percent of the Broker Exam

Trust Account Management
Fair Housing Laws
Truth in Advertising
Recordkeeping Requirements
Agent Supervision
Permitted Activities of Unlicensed Sales Assistants
CalBRE Jurisdiction and Disciplinary Actions
Licensing and Continuing Education Requirements and Procedures
California Real Estate Recovery Fund

General Ethics

Technology

Property Management

Commercial/Industrial/Income Properties

Specialty Areas

Transfer Disclosure Statements

Natural Hazard Disclosure Statements

Disclosure of Material Facts Affecting Property Value

Need for Inspection and Obtaining/Verifying Information

Reports

Servicing Diverse Populations

AREA 7—CONTRACTS

Approximately 12 percent of the Sales Exam and 12 percent of the Broker Exam

General

Listing Agreements

Buyer Broker Agreements

Offers/Purchase Contracts

Agreements

Promissory Notes/Securities

Purchase/Lease Options

Advanced Fee

BASIC RULES AND PROCEDURES

Conduct that constitutes subversion and is grounds for denial, suspension, revocation, or restriction of a license includes, but is not limited to, the following:

1. Removing or reproducing examination material without authorization
2. Paying a test taker to reconstruct the examination
3. Using improperly obtained test questions to prepare for the examination
4. Selling, distributing, or buying state examination material
5. Cheating during the examination

6. Possessing unauthorized equipment or information during the examination

7. Impersonating an examinee or having an impersonator take the examination

EXAMINATION BOOKLET		ANSWER SHEET				
22. When examinees and licensees refer to the Reference Book, as published by the Department of Real Estate, they should use: (a) the first edition (b) any edition available (c) the 1960 edition (d) the latest edition published		22	A ○	B ○	C ○	D ○
		23	A ○	B ○	C ○	D ○
		24	A ○	B ○	C ○	D ○
		25	A ○	B ○	C ○	D ○

All examinations are multiple-choice tests. Each question gives four possible answers, only one of which is correct. You may think more than one answer has some element of correctness, but only one answer is the most complete and best answer. No question is intended to be tricky; therefore, you should interpret words according to their common meaning.

The only materials allowed are CalBRE-provided materials. The Los Angeles, Sacramento, San Diego, Fresno, and Oakland locations offer the examination in an electronic format.

HOW TO APPLY FOR THE SALESPERSON EXAMINATION

1. Complete an original Salesperson Examination Application (RE 400A) or a combination Examination and License Application (RE 435). No changes of any kind can be made to an application once it has been received by the CalBRE. Do not submit more than one application.

2. Attach the current examination fee. This fee varies from time to time. The CalBRE accepts checks, money orders, and (in most cases) credit cards. For the current fee and payment procedure, visit the CalBRE website at www.bre.ca.gov or call the CalBRE at (916) 227-0900.

3. Send official transcripts or photocopies of approved certificates of completion.

4. Applicants with limitations requiring special accommodations must submit a physician's letter with the application to verify the nature of the limitation. The CalBRE's ability to honor special requests is limited by scheduling constraints and cannot be guaranteed.

5. Send the application, official transcripts, and appropriate fee to the most current CalBRE address in Sacramento. The wait time for a response depends on the CalBRE's workload. If you do not receive an official notice within four weeks, contact the CalBRE for a follow-up. Your official Examination Schedule Notice (RE 401A) will list the date, time, and official location based on your selection on the application form.

RESCHEDULING PROCEDURES

If you change your mind and do not wish to take the examination as scheduled, you can apply for another examination date or location. You do this by completing and returning the Examination Schedule Notice (RE 401A). A fee is charged for any rescheduled examination.

NOTIFICATION OF EXAMINATION RESULTS

Examination results are provided at the completion of the exam. The passing score is 70 percent or better. You are not given your test score when you pass. You are given your test score when you fail.

REEXAMINATION IF YOU FAIL

You may apply for reexamination after you receive notification that you failed the prior test. There is no limit on the number of reexaminations you can take during a two-year period following the filing of your original examination application. If you wish to be reexamined after this two-year period, you must file a new application. All reexaminations require the payment of a fee.

ONCE YOU PASS THE EXAMINATION

When you pass, you are sent a Salesperson License Application (RE 202), if you have not already completed RE 435. Within one year of the examination date, you must complete this form and send it to the CalBRE along with the appropriate license fee. A complete fingerprint set on the Live Scan is required. Out-of-state applicants must complete different forms.

(See the CalBRE website for details.) The application must also include proof of legal residence (e.g., a birth certificate or resident alien card). This must be submitted with a State Public Benefits Statement (RE 205) before a license will be issued. In addition, a license may be denied if an applicant has violated California law regarding the payment of child support. If you fail to apply for your license within one year of passing the examination, your test score is no longer valid and you need to retake and pass the examination again before being eligible to apply for a real estate salesperson license.

HOW TO APPLY FOR THE BROKER EXAMINATION

1. Complete an original Broker Examination Application (RE 400B) or a combination Examination and License Application (RE 436). No changes of any kind can be made to an application once it has been received by the CalBRE. Do not submit more than one application.

2. Attach the current examination fee. This fee varies from time to time. The CalBRE accepts checks, money orders, and (in most cases) credit cards. For the current fee and payment procedure, visit the CalBRE website at www.bre.ca.gov or call the CalBRE at (916) 227-0900.

3. Submit an official transcript or approved certificate of completion showing successful completion of all of the eight required statutory college-level real estate courses. Photocopies of transcripts are not acceptable.

4. Submit a completed Employment Verification form(s) (RE 226) to verify the required two years of licensed real estate salesperson experience or a copy of a diploma or transcript to verify a four-year college degree, showing real estate as a major or minor for that degree, earned through a regionally accredited college, or an Equivalent Experience Verification form(s) (RE 227) to verify nonlicensed real estate–related experience.

5. Applicants with limitations requiring special accommodations must submit a physician's letter with the application to verify the nature of the limitation. The CalBRE's ability to honor special requests is limited by scheduling constraints and cannot be guaranteed.

6. Send the application, official transcripts, and appropriate fee to the most current CalBRE address in Sacramento. The wait time for a response depends on the CalBRE's workload. If you do not receive an official notice within four weeks, contact the CalBRE for a follow-up. Your official Examination Schedule Notice (RE 401B) will list the date, time, and official location based on your selection on the application form.

RESCHEDULING PROCEDURES

If you change your mind and do not wish to take the examination as scheduled, you can apply for another examination date or location. You do this by completing and returning the Examination Schedule Notice (RE 401B). A fee is charged for any rescheduled examination.

NOTIFICATION OF EXAMINATION RESULTS

Examination results are provided at the completion of the examination. The passing score is 75 percent or better. You are not given your test score when you pass. You are given your test score when you fail.

REEXAMINATION IF YOU FAIL

You may apply for reexamination after you receive notification that you failed the prior test. There is no limit on the number of reexaminations you can take during a two-year period following the filing of your original examination application. If you wish to be reexamined after this two-year period, you must file a new application. All reexaminations require the payment of a fee.

ONCE YOU PASS THE EXAMINATION

When you pass, you are sent a Broker License Application (RE 200) if you have not completed RE 436. Within one year of the examination date, you must complete this form and send it to the DRE along with the appropriate license fee and a complete fingerprint set on Live Scan.

Out-of-state applicants must complete different forms. (See the CalBRE website for details.) The application must also include proof of legal residence (e.g., birth certificate or resident alien card). This must be submitted with a State Public Benefits Statement (RE 205) before a license will be issued. In addition, a license may be denied if an applicant has violated California law regarding the payment of child support. If you fail to apply for your license within one year of passing the examination, your test score is no longer valid and you need to retake and pass the examination again before being eligible to apply for a real estate broker's license.

COMPREHENSIVE REAL ESTATE PRINCIPLES PRACTICE EXAMINATION WITH ANSWERS

An old education adage says the best way to learn is to "read, recite, and review." To help with your review, a 150-question practice examination is presented. Real estate principles cover such a vast amount of material that every single topic cannot be tested.

But the questions that follow are a representative sample of the types of questions that may appear in examinations. The questions have been created to be similar to the weighting breakdown found in the state examination. Answers appear at the end of the examination.

Test-Taking Tips

1. Take three passes through the examination. The first time through, answer only the questions you know for sure, skipping everything else. This will give you a sense of success and allow you to get a feel for the examination. The second time through, answer those questions you think you know, skipping those that are completely unfamiliar to you. The third time through, guess. **Remember to go back and answer all the questions**.

2. Reading pitfalls: Make sure you read all the answer choices. Sometimes an answer may appear correct, but another reading reveals the actual correct answer. Watch out for questions that say "except for," "which is not," and so on. The wording is confusing and you may select the wrong answer if you are not careful.

3. Here are some guessing suggestions:
   a. Choose the longest answer.
   b. Do not choose "all of the above" unless you can identify two answers as being right.
   c. Two answers will be close, and two answers will be obviously wrong. Eliminate the obviously wrong two answers, and select the most logical of the remaining two.

4. Take the entire exam in one sitting in quiet surroundings. Upon completion, check your answers and look up the textbook discussion regarding the questions you missed.

DO NOT WRITE IN THE TEXTBOOK. INSTEAD, RUN SEVERAL COPIES OF THE QUESTIONS. THIS PROCEDURE WILL ALLOW YOU TO RETAKE THE EXAMINATION SEVERAL TIMES FOR PRACTICE.

Practice Examination

1. A "loss in value from any cause" is a definition of:
   a. economic obsolescence.
   b. depreciation.
   c. leverage.
   d. goodwill.

2. A couple recently married and each person had children from a previous marriage. They wish to take title to property so they can pass their share to their own children by will. The best form of title would be:
   a. joint tenancy.
   b. severalty.
   c. community property.
   d. tenancy in whole.

3. A valid deed passes title when it is:
   a. signed.
   b. recorded.
   c. delivered and accepted.
   d. acknowledged.

4. In July, a buyer bought a home through the listing broker at ABC Realty and received a property disclosure. After a hard rain in November, the roof developed a severe leak. The buyer sued the seller and listing broker for the cost of a new roof. Testimony in court revealed that the seller mentioned needing to add the roof leak to the disclosure, which the listing broker failed to do. The listing broker also failed to inform the buyer of the issue. What was most likely the outcome of the court case?
   a. The broker not the seller is liable for payment and for not disclosing the material fact.
   b. The buyer cannot collect since the house has closed escrow.
   c. The buyer could only recover from the seller since the broker is not liable for disclosures.
   d. The buyer cannot recover from either the seller or buyer based on the principle of caveat emptor.

5. The main purpose of the Truth-in-Lending Law is to:
   a. prevent usury.
   b. require disclosure of credit terms.
   c. reduce the cost of credit.
   d. regulate annual percentage rates.

6. The difference between judgment liens and mechanics' liens is that:
   a. mechanics' liens are general liens.
   b. mechanics' liens can take priority before they are recorded.
   c. mechanics' liens are voluntary liens.
   d. judgment liens are involuntary liens.

7. Broker Santos is in the process of listing a home. The agency disclosure must be given:
   a. within five days.
   b. prior to close of escrow.
   c. prior to the seller signing the listing agreement.
   d. immediately after the seller signs the listing agreement.

8. On October 1, 2014, Garcia agreed to purchase Chan's home. Both parties agreed that escrow would close on December 1, 2014, and that property taxes would be prorated as of date of possession. On November 1, 2014, Chan paid the property taxes for the year 2014–2015. According to the escrow closing statement, which of the following is true?
   a. Garcia paid Chan for seven months' taxes.
   b. Garcia paid Chan for one month's taxes.
   c. Chan paid Garcia for eight months' taxes.
   d. Chan paid Garcia for one month's taxes.

9. A quitclaim deed conveys only the present rights of the:
   a. grantor.
   b. servient tenant.
   c. grantee.
   d. trustee.

10. To have a valid recorded homestead, certain elements are essential. Which of the following is not essential?
    a. A description of the property
    b. A statement of residence
    c. To be a married person
    d. To be recorded

11. A licensed loan broker arranged for a loan on a home purchase and has the borrower sign the required statement. The title work shows clouds on the title that the seller cannot clear in a timely manner. If the loan cannot be closed, the borrower is liable for:
    a. cost and expenses incurred to date.
    b. no cost and expenses.
    c. all cost and expenses and half the commission.
    d. none of the above.

12. A person purchased a property for $200,000, which was equal to $4.75 per square foot. The rectangular lot was 300 feet deep. The cost per front foot was:
    a. $1,425.
    b. $950.
    c. $827.
    d. $793.

13. Which of the following is not essential to form an agency?
    a. A fiduciary relationship
    b. Agreement of the parties
    c. Consideration
    d. Competent parties

14. An owner sells a lot for cash and receives $67,100 from escrow. The only expenses were a 6 percent commission and $517 in other expenses. The property sold for:
    a. $71,643.
    b. $71,933.
    c. $72,591.
    d. $73,137.

15. A real estate agent must disclose all material facts to a seller principal. Which of the following is considered a material fact?
    a. The buyer's racial background
    b. The agent's knowledge of a pending better offer
    c. The lender's requirement that a buyer pay a loan fee
    d. That the buyer has a medical problem

16. In appraising improved property, the least important factor is:
    a. sales price.
    b. highest and best use.
    c. prices of comparables.
    d. assessed value.

17. Common interest developments in the form of community apartments and condominium projects fall within the California Subdivision Act and:
    a. are illegal.
    b. are regulated by state law.
    c. are rarely approved.
    d. have fewer units per acre.

18. Studs are attached to rest upon the:
    a. mud sill.
    b. subfloor.
    c. header.
    d. sole plate.

19. A person borrowed 80 percent of the value of a studio condo. The loan interest rate was 7 percent. The first-year interest was $10,500. The value of the condo was:
    a. $173,500.
    b. $182,900.
    c. $187,500.
    d. none of the above.

20. Adams, Brown, and Chow are owners of commercial land as joint tenants. Adams dies and is survived by Brown and Chow. Which is correct?
    a. Brown and Chow receive title by succession.
    b. The joint tenancy is terminated.
    c. Adams's interest terminates.
    d. Brown and Chow are now tenants in common.

21. How many acres are in the NW ½ of the SW ¼ of the NE ¼ of Section 10?
    a. 40
    b. 20
    c. 80
    d. 640

22. When the landlord and the tenant mutually agree to cancel a lease, their action is called a(n):
    a. mutually agreed upon termination.
    b. rescission.
    c. release.
    d. abandonment.

23. An amortized loan has equal monthly installments consisting of:
    a. interest alone.
    b. principal alone.
    c. principal and interest.
    d. principal, interest, taxes, and insurance.

24. Which of the following is an operating expense to be subtracted from gross income when appraising a property using the income approach?
    a. Interest payments
    b. Principal payments
    c. Property taxes
    d. All of the above

25. The word *emblements* refers to:
    a. attachments to a contract.
    b. annual crops.
    c. machinery.
    d. fixtures on a building.

26. A salesperson working for a broker had been wrongfully selling information to a loan company. When the broker, who had been using reasonable supervision, discovered this, the salesperson was fired. Based upon the information given:
    a. the broker is probably not liable if he or she had no knowledge of the wrongdoing.
    b. both the salesperson and the broker are liable.
    c. there is no liability.
    d. a salesperson is licensed to sell loan information in his or her name only.

27. The primary function of the secondary mortgage market is to:
    a. originate loans for the primary mortgage market.
    b. supply private mortgage insurance to borrowers.
    c. buy loans to fund the primary mortgage market.
    d. protect consumers from fraudulent lenders.

28. Williams entered into a nine-month oral lease on July 1 to start on September 1 at a rate of $1,000 per month. On August 15, Williams backed out of the lease. The lease is:
    a. unenforceable.
    b. enforceable.
    c. void.
    d. restricted by the statute of frauds.

29. Title insurance does not protect a buyer against:
    a. forgery in the chain of title.
    b. lack of capacity of the grantor.
    c. recorded easements.
    d. zoning restrictions.

30. If state housing codes conflict with local codes, usually:
    a. state codes prevail.
    b. local codes prevail.
    c. the stricter of the two prevails.
    d. the more lenient of the two prevails.

31. A broker received deposits from principals and incorrectly placed the funds in the firms operations account for several days before moving the funds to the broker's trust fund account at the bank. The broker is guilty of:
    a. conversion.
    b. commingling.
    c. misrepresentation.
    d. fraud.

32. A husband dies intestate in California. How is his separate property distributed to his wife and two children?
    a. All to the wife
    b. Half to the wife and half to the children
    c. All to the children
    d. One-third to the wife, the rest to the children

33. Under the Subdivided Lands Law, the real estate commissioner is primarily concerned with:
    a. physical design and layout.
    b. health facilities.
    c. financing and marketing arrangements.
    d. none of the above.

34. Jones leases a home from Santos under a three-month written lease. Upon expiration of the lease, Jones retains possession. Santos has not decided on the next step. Jones has an estate at:
    a. will.
    b. sufferance.
    c. years.
    d. tenancy.

35. An investor has an apartment building with no vacancies in which each unit rents for $600. The investor raises the rent 15 percent and suffers a 15 percent vacancy factor. Rental income:
    a. increases.
    b. decreases.
    c. remains the same.
    d. The question cannot be answered with the information given.

36. A real estate agent is asked to hold the buyer's deposit uncashed until acceptance of the offer by the seller. Upon the seller's acceptance, the agent must put the deposit in escrow or in a trust fund or give the deposit to the seller within how many business days?
    a. 5
    b. 3
    c. 2
    d. 1

37. The maximum amount of personal funds a broker may have in a trust fund account to cover charges and not be guilty of commingling is:
    a. $50.
    b. $200.
    c. $500.
    d. $1,000.

38. Property is being sold where the buyer is going to take over the seller's existing loan. To avoid legal conflict before closing, the real estate agent should check to be sure the loan does not include a(n):
    a. release clause.
    b. prepayment penalty.
    c. alienation clause.
    d. subordination clause.

39. The stated policy of the real estate commissioner is to create an equal opportunity industry. This means agents should:
    a. maintain an attitude free from bias.
    b. realize that race, creed, and color are not material facts.
    c. do unto others as you would have them do unto you.
    d. do all of the above.

40. A California subdivider sold five lots to one buyer and optioned five other lots to another buyer. The subdivider must:

    a. notify the Bureau of Real Estate of a material change.

    b. close the option sales within three business days.

    c. record the sales within five business days.

    d. not sell five lots to a single purchaser.

41. Under the federal Truth-in-Lending Law (Regulation Z), certain borrowers have _____ days to rescind the loan.

    a. 30

    b. 10

    c. 5

    d. 3

42. A seller employed a broker under an open listing. The seller indicated to the broker that the roof leaked. While showing the home to a buyer, the broker stated that the roof was in good condition. After the sale, the buyer discovered that the roof leaked. The broker is guilty of:

    a. false promise.

    b. the statute of frauds.

    c. misrepresentation.

    d. all of the above.

43. Under Division 6 of the Uniform Commercial Code (Bulk Sale), a public notice must be given 12 days before transfer by:

    a. the seller.

    b. the buyer.

    c. the creditors.

    d. all of the above.

44. The value of the subject property as set by the price of comparable properties is based on the principle of:

    a. change.

    b. regression.

    c. substitution.

    d. highest and best use.

45. A California real estate broker sold a ranch in Montana to a California resident. A Montana broker assisted in the sale. To show appreciation, the California broker gave part of the commission to the Montana broker. This action was:

    a. unlawful because the California broker was not licensed in Montana.

    b. unlawful because the Montana broker was not licensed in California.

    c. lawful.

    d. none of the above.

46. Income tax benefits for homeowners include deductions for:

    a. interest on home loans.

    b. depreciation on buildings.

    c. expenses and repairs.

    d. all of the above.

47. All REALTORS® in California are bound by which code of ethics?

    a. National Mortgage Brokers Association

    b. National Association of Real Estate Brokers

    c. National Association of REALTORS®

    d. All of the above

48. In issuing a policy of title insurance, the title company is least likely to make an on-site inspection if the policy is a(n):
   a. CLTA standard owner's policy.
   b. ALTA extended policy.
   c. construction loan policy.
   d. lender's policy.

49. A real estate broker must retain copies of all listings and deposit receipts for how many years?
   a. 1
   b. 3
   c. 4
   d. 5

50. The first half of real property taxes is due and payable on November 1. The taxes become delinquent after December 10, at which time, if not paid, a penalty is added to the amount. The penalty is:
   a. 10 percent.
   b. 8 percent.
   c. 6 percent.
   d. 3 percent.

51. A Notice of Nonresponsibility is usually posted and recorded by an owner when a:
   a. bulk sale takes place.
   b. tenant approves repairs without consent from the landlord.
   c. transfer of title takes place.
   d. mechanic's lien is filed.

52. The maximum ownership rights in property are known as:
   a. fee simple absolute.
   b. estate for years.
   c. fee simple defeasible.
   d. life estate.

53. Which of the following is not a fiduciary relationship?
   a. Broker to seller
   b. Trustor to beneficiary
   c. Attorney to client
   d. Attorney-in-fact to principal

54. An appraiser determines that the market rent for a parcel of land is $700 per month and that interest (capitalization) rates should be 11 percent. The approximate value is:
   a. $54,545.
   b. $69,280.
   c. $76,364.
   d. $105,000.

55. An owner plans to divide a parcel of land into nine parcels, with the intention of selling three parcels per year for each of the next three years. The owner:
   a. must satisfy the Subdivision Map Act.
   b. must report to the real estate commissioner, but need not conform to the Subdivision Map Act.
   c. must comply with the Subdivision Map Act and the Subdivided Lands Law.
   d. need not comply with any special law, as fewer than five lots are being sold in any one year.

56. Which of the following is a less-than-freehold estate?
   a. Fee simple defeasible
   b. Fee simple absolute
   c. Leasehold estate
   d. Life estate

57. A lease that lies between the primary lease and the sublessee is a:
   a. sandwich lease.
   b. percentage lease.
   c. ground lease.
   d. wedge lease.

58. A California easement by prescription requires a minimum period of hostile use of:
   a. five years.
   b. three years.
   c. two years.
   d. one year.

59. A corporation built a large tract of homes and hired a handyperson to take care of the maintenance. The handyperson was given extra compensation for showing the homes on weekends to prospective buyers.
   a. The corporation is not in violation of real estate regulations.
   b. The handyperson could be fined for showing homes without a license.
   c. As an employee, the handyperson does not need a license to show homes.
   d. All corporate employees and officers selling the homes must be licensed.

60. After a trustee's sale, any money remaining after paying lienholders and costs is remitted to the:
   a. trustor.
   b. trustee.
   c. beneficiary.
   d. mortgagor.

61. The person who acquires title to real property under the terms of a will is known as the:
   a. devisee.
   b. administrator.
   c. testator.
   d. executrix.

62. A "commercial acre: is:
   a. 43,560 sq. ft.
   b. a normal acre, less deductions for streets and setbacks.
   c. an acre zoned for commercial use.
   d. 42,513 sq. ft.

63. As required by law and regulations, a real estate broker must have a:
   a. trust fund account.
   b. trust fund logbook.
   c. credit card for business use only.
   d. Both a and b are correct.

64. An owner gives a quitclaim deed to Wilson for a parcel of real estate. Wilson does not record the deed. Which of the following is true the deed?

    a. It is not valid since an essential element is recording.

    b. It will not become valid until recorded.

    c. It is valid, but Wilson may lose title if another party records a deed.

    d. Recording is not required if the party is in possession.

65. When public records are used to establish a chain of title, a written summary of the results is known as a(n):

    a. guarantee of title.

    b. abstract of title.

    c. opinion of title.

    d. affidavit of title.

66. After a mortgage is executed and recorded, title:

    a. remains with the mortgagor.

    b. transfers to the mortgagee.

    c. is given to the trustee.

    d. remains with the trustor.

67. A real estate contract by an emancipated minor is:

    a. void.

    b. voidable.

    c. unenforceable.

    d. valid.

68. An exclusive agency listing differs from an exclusive right-to-sell listing in that:

    a. only the exclusive right-to-sell listing must have a definite termination date.

    b. the broker is entitled to a commission if the owner sells the property under the exclusive agency listing.

    c. only the exclusive right-to-sell listing must be in writing to be enforceable.

    d. under the exclusive right-to-sell listing, the broker is entitled to a commission no matter who sells the property during the term of the listing.

69. A buyer in a land project can rescind the purchase for any reason and obtain a refund within:

    a. three days.

    b. five days.

    c. ten days.

    d. fourteen days.

70. Which of the following represents the four essentials of value?

    a. Scarcity, cost, demand, utility

    b. Utility, transferability, cost, demand

    c. Transferability, utility, demand, scarcity

    d. Demand, cost, utility, price

71. All of the following are contracts, except:

    a. escrow instructions.

    b. a listing agreement.

    c. a deed.

    d. a deposit receipt.

72. The cost approach to value has limited use when appraising:
    a. a new building.
    b. tract homes.
    c. museum buildings.
    d. special-purpose properties.

73. When an agent violates antidiscrimination regulations, the real estate commissioner can:
    a. sue for damages.
    b. file a criminal action.
    c. revoke a license.
    d. do all of the above.

74. Zowski holds a life estate measured by his own life. He leased the property to Anderson for five years, but died two months later. The lease is:
    a. still valid.
    b. no longer valid.
    c. invalid from the inception.
    d. binding on the heirs of Zowski.

75. An owner sold a lot for $70,400, realizing a 20 percent profit over what was originally paid for the lot. The profit is:
    a. $11,733.
    b. $14,080.
    c. $13,714.
    d. $12,509.

76. Which of the following is not essential to a general contract?
    a. That it be in writing
    b. Mutual consent
    c. Capable parties
    d. Lawful object

77. An example of a lender that frequently uses loan correspondents and funds large commercial loans is a:
    a. savings bank.
    b. commercial bank.
    c. credit union.
    d. life insurance company.

78. The TRID closing disclosure is required to be delivered to the borrower no later than:
    a. three days after application.
    b. five days before the appraisal.
    c. ten days after loan approval.
    d. three days before closing.

79. A deeds a title to B with the condition that B never sell alcoholic beverages on the property. B has a:
    a. less-than-freehold estate.
    b. fee simple absolute.
    c. fee simple defeasible.
    d. periodic tenancy.

80. An abstract of judgment can be recorded:
    a. in any county.
    b. only in the county where the judgment is to be placed.
    c. only in the county where the debtor has real property.
    d. only in the county where the creditor resides.

81. The amount of real estate sales commission is:
    a. regulated by the real estate commissioner.
    b. subject to negotiation.
    c. fixed by trade groups.
    d. governed by state law.

82. A roof that is pitched with two sloping sides is called a:
    a. hip.
    b. gable.
    c. mansard.
    d. gambrel.

83. A contract that is executory:
    a. has not been performed.
    b. has been signed.
    c. is completed.
    d. has been notarized.

84. How much money would have to be invested at a 7 percent return to give an investor $200 per month?
    a. $34,286
    b. $48,000
    c. $43,705
    d. $39,325

85. A person who believes he or she has been discriminated against in seeking housing can file a complaint with the:
    a. Federal Trade Commission.
    b. Rumford Commission.
    c. Unruh Commission.
    d. Fair Employment and Housing Commission.

86. A borrower decides to apply for a loan with a 90% LTV which requires PMI. The borrower did this to:
    a. create more equity.
    b. have a smaller down payment.
    c. get a better interest rate.
    d. to pay off the principle sooner.

87. After a loan has been granted, rapid unanticipated inflation would most benefit a:
    a. borrower with an ARM loan.
    b. fixed-interest rate beneficiary.
    c. trustor with a fixed interest rate.
    d. trustee.

88. The most difficult depreciation to correct is:
    a. physical.
    b. economic.
    c. functional.
    d. accrued.

89. Properties A and B each have a value of $200,000. Property A was appraised using a capitalization rate of 6 percent, whereas Property B was appraised using a capitalization rate of 7 percent.
    a. Property B has more income than Property A.
    b. Property B has less income than Property A.
    c. Property A and Property B have the same income.
    d. None of the above

90. Which of the following is not appurtenant or incidental to the land?
    a. Stock in a mutual water company
    b. An easement
    c. Reasonable airspace
    d. A picked crop

91. Recording of an instrument gives:
    a. actual notice.
    b. constructive notice.
    c. preliminary notice.
    d. recorded notice.

92. A rate of interest that exceeds the legal rate is:
    a. the nominal rate.
    b. the going rate.
    c. the stated rate.
    d. none of the above.

93. The Federal National Mortgage Association (Fannie Mae) was primarily created to:
    a. insure low-income housing loans.
    b. increase the amount of money available to finance housing.
    c. insure bank depositors for up to $250,000 per account.
    d. lengthen the term for real estate loans.

94. Broker Sanchez and Broker Roberts both have an open listing on a home. Broker Sanchez showed the home to a buyer who decided not to make an offer. A month later, Broker Roberts showed the same home to the same buyer, who then decided to buy. The seller owes a commission to:
    a. Broker Sanchez only.
    b. Broker Sanchez and Broker Roberts.
    c. Broker Roberts only.
    d. Broker Sanchez, who needs to split it with Broker Roberts.

95. Both the buyer and the seller initial the liquidated damages clause in a deposit receipt. Later the buyer backs out. The seller is entitled to:
    a. actual damages.
    b. no damages.
    c. punitive damages.
    d. liquidated damages.

96. A person borrowed $2,500 on a straight note. In eight months, $150 in interest was paid. The interest rate is:
    a. 8.4 percent.
    b. 9 percent.
    c. 10.1 percent.
    d. 10.6 percent.

97. If a dispute arises during escrow and the buyer and seller cannot agree, the escrow holder may legally:
    a. file an interpleader action.
    b. return all funds to the respective parties.
    c. cancel the escrow.
    d. do all of the above.

98. The SW ¼ of the NW ¼ of the SE ¼ of the SE ¼ of the NW ¼ of a section contains:
   a. 1¼ acres.
   b. 2½ acres.
   c. 5 acres.
   d. none of the above.

99. Which of the following requires a real estate agent to do a physical inspection of a home and then report the results of said inspection?
   a. Disclosure Regarding Real Estate Agency Relationship
   b. Real Estate Transfer Disclosure Statement
   c. Natural Hazard Disclosure Statement
   d. Independent Real Estate Inspection Report

100. An owner hired a broker to act as property manager and collect rent from tenants. Rents are due on the first of the month. On June 1, the broker collected rents from all but one of the tenants. The next day, the owner died. On June 2, the broker asked the remaining tenant for the rent. The tenant refused to give the rent money to the broker. The tenant:
   a. must give the rent to the broker.
   b. should not give the rent to anyone but the heirs or the court.
   c. is in default by not giving the rent to the broker.
   d. need not pay the rent.

101. Which of the following employment situations would require withholding taxes?
   a. Independent contractor
   b. Jobber
   c. Employer–employee
   d. Agent

102. If there is no notice of completion, a subcontractor must file a mechanic's lien in:
   a. 10 days.
   b. 30 days.
   c. 60 days.
   d. 90 days.

103. Which of the following is not issued by the Bureau of Real Estate?
   a. Real estate broker license
   b. Prepaid rental listing license
   c. Real estate sales license
   d. Escrow license

104. The fine for an unlicensed individual who receives a real estate commission is:
   a. $20,000.
   b. $2,000.
   c. $200.
   d. none of the above.

105. When a buyer purchases a condominium, the buyer must be given which of the following regarding CC&Rs, the amount of homeowner dues, and financial and pending lawsuits (if any) about the homeowners' association?
   a. Common Interest Development General Information
   b. Real Estate Transfer Disclosure Statement
   c. Natural Hazard Disclosure Statement
   d. Seller Financing Disclosure Statement

106. An out-of-state developer wishes to sell lots to Californians. All of the following apply, EXCEPT:
    a. The sales agreements must carry a disclaimer approved by the California real estate commissioner.
    b. All advertising must carry a disclaimer approved by the California real estate commissioner.
    c. The Subdivision Map Act will be enforced.
    d. All of the above apply.

107. The $500,000 exemption on the profits from the sale of a qualified principal residence applies for homeowners who are:
    a. 50 years or older.
    b. married and file joint tax returns.
    c. native Californians only.
    d. earning an income of $125,000 or less.

108. Equity in real property is the:
    a. cash flow value.
    b. total of all mortgages.
    c. difference between the mortgage balance and current value.
    d. appraised value.

109. The maximum time that urban real estate can be leased is:
    a. 99 years.
    b. 51 years.
    c. 30 years.
    d. 15 years.

110. Which of the following is not required to obtain title to unimproved land by adverse possession?
    a. Minimum of five years
    b. Open and notorious use
    c. Color of title or claim of right
    d. That the acquiring party live on the property

111. Certain unities are required to maintain a joint tenancy relationship. They are:
    a. grantee, unity, possession, and claim.
    b. time, title, interest, and unity.
    c. interest, time, title, and possession.
    d. ownership, time, title, and interest.

112. The Health and Safety Code specifies minimum standards for water and sewer facilities in a new subdivision. Approval and control for local water and sewer rest with the:
    a. local officials.
    b. real estate commissioner.
    c. state officials.
    d. planning commissioner.

113. Most real estate syndicates in California use which form of ownership?
    a. Corporation
    b. Limited partnership
    c. Real estate investment trust
    d. Joint venture

114. The words *procuring cause* would have the most important meaning under which circumstance?
    a. A lawsuit by the buyer
    b. A dispute between brokers over a commission
    c. A disagreement between buyer and seller
    d. A dispute over loan proceeds

115. Which of the following would violate the advertising provisions of the Truth-in-Lending Law? Ads that state:
    a. no money down.
    b. $100,000 all-cash sale.
    c. $200,000 price, easy terms.
    d. qualification for FHA financing.

116. In the event that a seller backs out of a valid purchase contract, all of the following are true, except:
    a. the buyer could sue for damages.
    b. the buyer could sue for specific performance.
    c. the broker could sue for damages.
    d. the broker could sue for specific performance.

117. A federal law regarding the sale of subdivided lots is the:
    a. Subdivision Map Act.
    b. Interstate Land Sales Full Disclosure Act.
    c. Land Project Act.
    d. Subdivided Lands Law.

118. The instrument used to transfer title to personal property is the:
    a. deed.
    b. bill of lading.
    c. lease.
    d. bill of sale.

119. An example of functional obsolescence is a:
    a. one bath, four bedroom home.
    b. cracked foundation.
    c. truck route in front of a home.
    d. detrimental change in zoning.

120. When the real estate commissioner receives a valid complaint against a licensee, the commissioner institutes action against the licensee under the:
    a. Business and Professions Code.
    b. Administrative Procedures Code.
    c. Real Estate Code.
    d. Rules and Regulations Code.

121. When a business opportunity is sold, a price is often paid for continued patronage. This continued patronage is called:
    a. goodwill.
    b. blue sky.
    c. turnover.
    d. future sales.

122. A cloud on the title could be created by:
    a. a recorded homestead.
    b. a deed of trust paid, but never reconveyed.
    c. an easement for utility poles.
    d. recorded covenants and conditions.

123. A written agency between a real estate broker and a principal would not be:
    a. executed.
    b. implied.
    c. expressed.
    d. a contract.

124. Which act of California law prohibits real estate agents from discriminating while conducting business?
    a. Unruh Civil Rights Act
    b. Housing Financial Discrimination Act
    c. Holden Act
    d. Civil Rights Act of 1968 and 1988 Amendments

125. When a real estate broker acts exclusively for the buyer or seller, but not for both, it is called a(n):
    a. dual agency.
    b. exclusive agency.
    c. divided agency.
    d. single agency.

126. The most important factor in estimating the value of residential homes is:
    a. square footage.
    b. demand by ready, willing, and able buyers.
    c. floor plan.
    d. rent.

127. In an exclusive-agency listing:
    a. only the broker who is the procuring cause gets paid.
    b. to be paid the listing broker must be the one who sells the property.
    c. a buyer's agent from MLS and the listing broker would be paid if the property closes.
    d. if the seller sells the property the listing broker will be reimbursed for marketing fees.

128. Once an abstract of judgment is recorded, it remains in force for:
    a. 1 year.
    b. 3 years.
    c. 5 years.
    d. 10 years.

129. The *secondary mortgage market* refers to:
    a. the resale of existing loans.
    b. the granting of second loans.
    c. mortgage brokers who arrange loans.
    d. none of the above.

130. Real estate loans that are pegged to some index and in which the interest rate may change during the term of the loan are called:
    a. conventional loans.
    b. FHA loans.
    c. ARM loans.
    d. seller carry loans.

131. The unauthorized use of the term REALTOR® is:
    a. a criminal offense.
    b. a violation of California Real Estate Law.
    c. not a problem if the person is a licensed broker.
    d. not punishable in California.

132. If a tenant is late on the rent, an owner should serve a(n):
    a. 30-day notice.
    b. 3-day notice.
    c. unlawful detainer warrant.
    d. eviction notice.

133. Once a real estate broker's license has been revoked or suspended, his or her sales associates can:
    a. be paid commissions earned prior to the suspension.
    b. collect rents as property managers.
    c. continue to work on existing listings.
    d. take new listings with a post date on the contract.

134. A woman died and left an estate. Thirty-seven percent went to her husband; 18 percent went to each of the two sons and one daughter. The rest went to a college foundation. The college foundation received $37,000. The daughter's share was:
    a. $74,000.
    b. $84,000.
    c. $96,000.
    d. $124,000.

135. Adams sells his property to Baker. Baker places the deed to the property in his safety deposit box without recording. Adams also sells the property to Collins who records her deed and takes possession with no knowledge of the Baker transfer. Who is most likely to be deemed the owner of the property?
    a. Baker and Collins will have title as joint tenants
    b. Baker
    c. Baker and Collins in severalty
    d. Collins

136. Personal property attached to a building in such a way that it becomes part of the building is known as a(n):
    a. appurtenance.
    b. fixture.
    c. attachment.
    d. dedication.

137. The situation by which property reverts to the state for lack of heirs is called:
    a. escheat.
    b. eminent domain.
    c. condemnation.
    d. intestate succession.

138. When work is done per the Street Improvement Act of 1911, property owners are allowed to pay their pro rata share within how many days before it goes to bond?
    a. 30
    b. 60
    c. 90
    d. 180

139. The real property tax year runs from:
    a. January 1 to December 31.
    b. March 1 to February 28.
    c. July 1 to June 30.
    d. December 10 to December 9.

140. Which of the following is correct regarding an "as is" home sale?
    a. Caveat emptor is the only rule.
    b. The real estate agent is not required to physically inspect the home.
    c. All material facts about the home must still be disclosed.
    d. "As is" home sales are not allowed in California.

141. In qualifying married buyers for a loan, the least important is:
    a. regular income.
    b. spouse's income.
    c. monthly debts.
    d. overtime pay.

142. Rates for title insurance are established by:
    a. title insurance companies.
    b. the Bureau of Real Estate.
    c. the Department of Insurance.
    d. the corporation commissioner.

143. A duly licensed real estate salesperson may lawfully receive a commission from:
    a. the seller.
    b. the escrow holder.
    c. the broker.
    d. all of the above.

144. A real estate broker would not be disciplined by the real estate commissioner for:
    a. making a secret profit.
    b. making a false promise.
    c. making a misrepresentation.
    d. acting as a dual agent with the full knowledge and approval of all parties.

145. A California Real Estate Purchase Contract is frequently referred to as a(n):
    a. purchase agreement.
    b. listing agreement.
    c. option.
    d. lease.

146. The important case of the U.S. Supreme Court that prohibits discrimination in housing is:
    a. *Wellenkamp v. Wilson.*
    b. *Jones v. Mayer.*
    c. *Unruh v. Smith.*
    d. *Rumford v. Brown.*

147. The maximum mortgage broker commission allowed on a $5,000 second trust deed loan due in seven years is:
    a. $250.
    b. $500.
    c. $750.
    d. $1,000.

148. The maximum amount allowed from the Real Estate Recovery Fund for all parties in a single-judgment case against a broker is:
    a. $100,000.
    b. $125,000.
    c. $150,000.
    d. $250,000.

149. A corporation is prohibited from holding title as:
    a. joint tenants.
    b. tenancy in partnership.
    c. tenants in common.
    d. severalty.

150. In a 1031 real estate exchange, taxable unlike property is called:
    a. like for like.
    b. basis.
    c. foreign property.
    d. boot.

ANSWERS TO PRACTICE EXAMINATION

As you grade your practice examination, keep track of each question missed. A passing score is 105 questions correct (70 percent).

After you compute your score, go back and reread each question missed; then look up the explanation in the textbook. Wait a day or two, review the glossary in the textbook, and take the examination again.

1. (b) Chapter 10

2. (c) Chapter 6

3. (c) Chapter 6

4. (a) Chapter 4

5. (b) Chapter 8

6. (b) Chapter 8

7. (c) Chapter 4

8. (a) Appendix B

9. (a) Chapter 6

10. (c) Chapter 8

11. (b) Chapter 8

12. (a) $200,000/$4.75
= 42,105.26 sq. ft./300
= 140.35 front ft., then
$200,000/140.35
= $1,425

13. (a) Chapter 5 (fiduciary is a result of agency, but not needed to form an agency)

14. (b) $67,100 + $517
= (94 percent of total)
$67,617/0.94
= $71,933

15. (b) Chapter 5

16. (d) Chapter 10

17. (b) Chapter 13 (Subdivision Map Act 2 or more units)

18. (d) Chapter 15

19. (c) $10,500/0.07
= $150,000/0.80
= $187,500 value

20. (c) Chapter 6

21. (b) Chapter 6

22. (a) Chapter 12

23. (c) Chapter 8

24. (c) Chapter 10

25. (b) Chapter 2

26. (b) Chapter 4

27. (c) Chapter 9

28. (b) Chapter 12

29. (d) Chapter 11

30. (c) Chapter 13

31. (b) Chapter 4

32. (d) Chapter 6

33. (c) Chapter 13

34. (b) Chapter 12

35. (b) Chapter 10 (15 percent rent increase will not cover 15 percent vacancy)

36. (b) Chapter 4

37. (b) Chapter 4

38. (c) Chapter 8

39. (d) Chapter 13

40. (a) Chapter 13

41. (d) Chapter 8

42. (c) Chapter 4

43. (b) Chapter 1

44. (c) Chapter 10

45. (a) Chapter 4

46. (a) Chapter 14

47. (c) Chapter 1

48. (a) Chapter 11

49. (b) Chapter 5

50. (a) Chapter 14

51. (b) Chapter 7

52. (a) Chapter 6

53. (b) Chapter 8

54. (c) $700 × 12 mo. = $8,400/0.11 = $76,364

55. (c) Chapter 13

56. (c) Chapter 12

57. (a) Chapter 12

58. (a) Chapter 7

59. (b) Chapter 1

60. (a) Chapter 8

61. (a) Chapter 6

62. (b) Chapter 6

63. (b) Chapter 4

64. (c) Chapter 6

65. (b) Chapter 12

66. (a) Chapter 8

67. (d) Chapter 5

68. (d) Chapter 5

69. (d) Chapter 13

70. (c) Chapter 10

71. (c) Chapter 5

72. (b) Chapter 10

73. (c) Chapter 1

74. (b) Chapter 7

75. (a) $70,400/1.20 = $58,667, then $70,400 less $58,667 = $11,733

76. (a) Chapter 5 (only contracts under the statute of frauds need be in writing, not a general contract)

77. (d) Chapter 9

78. (d) Chapter 11

79. (c) Chapter 6

80. (a) Chapter 7

81. (b) Chapter 5

82. (b) Chapter 15

83. (a) Chapter 5

84. (a) $200 × 12 mo. = $2,400/0.07 = $34,286

85. (d) Chapter 13

86. (b) Chapter 8

87. (c) Chapter 8

88. (b) Chapter 10

89. (a) Appendix B

90. (d) Chapter 2

91. (b) Chapter 6

92. (d) Chapter 8 (usury)

93. (b) Chapter 9

94. (c) Chapter 5

95. (d) Chapter 5

96. (b) $150/8 = $18.75 mo.
× 12 mo. = $225 int. yr./
$2,500 loan = 9%

97. (a) Chapter 11

98. (d) Chapter 6

99. (b) Chapter 5

100. (b) Chapter 4

101. (c) Chapter 4

102. (d) Chapter 7

103. (d) Chapter 1

104. (a) Chapter 1

105. (a) Chapter 5

106. (c) Chapter 13

107. (b) Chapter 14

108. (c) Chapter 8

109. (a) Chapter 12

110. (d) Chapter 6

111. (c) Chapter 6

112. (a) Chapter 13

113. (b) Chapter 6

114. (b) Glossary

115. (a) Chapter 8

116. (d) Chapter 5

117. (b) Chapter 13

118. (d) Chapter 1

119. (a) Chapter 10

120. (b) Chapter 1

121. (a) Chapter 1

122. (b) Chapter 8

123. (b) Chapter 5

124. (a) Chapter 13

125. (d) Chapter 4

126. (b) Chapter 10

127. (c) Chapter 5

128. (d) Chapter 7

129. (a) Chapter 9

130. (c) Chapter 8

131. (b) Chapter 1

132. (b) Chapter 12

133. (a) Chapter 1

134. (a) 18% × 3 = 54% children's share, then 54% + 37% = 91% husband and children combined, then 100% − 91% = 9% college share, then daughter has twice as much as college, $37,000 × 2 = $74,000

135. (d) Chapter 6

136. (b) Chapter 2

137. (a) Chapter 6

138. (a) Chapter 14

139. (c) Chapter 14

140. (c) Chapter 4

141. (d) Chapter 9

142. (a) Chapter 11

143. (c) Chapter 1

144. (d) Chapter 4

145. (a) Chapter 5

146. (b) Chapter 13

147. (c) Chapter 8

148. (d) Chapter 4

149. (a) Chapter 6

150. (d) Chapter 14

PRACTICAL REAL ESTATE MATHEMATICS

Over the last several years, we have seen the California Bureau of Real Estate place less emphasis on mathematics. It is not unusual to hear license examinees say there were no math questions on the exam or that only one or two math questions were included. The authors of your text felt allocating an entire chapter to a subject that only concerns one or two questions out of 150 questions on the sales examination (200 for the broker's examination) created an unrealistic preparation for the exam.

Not that mathematics is not important. Students looking to enter property management or investment real estate need a firm grasp of mathematics. However, most real estate licensees are in the field of residential real estate where mathematics is not a significant part of their practice. Regardless of the reasons behind CalBRE's decision to lessen the importance of mathematics on the state exam, examinees will find fewer math questions than what was in earlier exams.

REVIEW OF FUNDAMENTALS

The practical application of real estate mathematics creates apprehension in some people. The use of calculators and the development of tables can help alleviate the fear of math. An understanding of the simple formulas presented in this lesson can help you gain confidence in your ability to solve everyday real estate mathematical problems.

The difficulty some people have with mathematics comes from a lack of knowledge or a forgetfulness of some of the basic rules of mathematics, particularly with regard to percentages, decimals, and fractions.

Decimals

Before solving various real estate mathematical problems, it is helpful to review the concept of decimals. A decimal is the period that sets apart the whole number from the fractional part of a number.

The position of the decimal in a number determines the value of the number.

All numbers to the right of the decimal are less than one. The first position to the right of the decimal is the "tenth" position, the second is the "hundredth," the third is the "thousandth," the fourth is the "ten thousandth," the fifth is the "hundred thousandth," and so on.

To the left of the decimal are the whole numbers. The first position is known as the "units" position, the second is the "tens," the third is the "hundreds," the fourth is the "thousands," the fifth is the "ten thousands," the sixth is the "hundred thousands," and so on. Table 1 may help you clarify the relationships among percentages, decimals, and fractions.

Converting Percentages to Decimals

To remove the percent sign, simply move the decimal two places to the left to form a usable decimal number. (See Table 2.)

Many times an answer will appear as a decimal. If you wish to convert the answer to an answer with a percent sign (%), simply reverse the procedure. (See Table 3.)

TABLE 1

Percentage(%)	Decimal	Fraction
4.5	0.045	45/1000
6.67	0.0667	1/15
10	0.10	1/10
12.5	0.125	1/8
16.67	0.1667	1/6
25	0.25	1/4
33.33	0.333	1/3
50	0.50	1/2
66.67	0.6667	2/3
75	0.75	3/4
100	1.00	1/1

TABLE 2

8%	converts	.08
25%	converts	.25
9.5%	converts	.095
105%	converts	1.05

TABLE 3

.08	converts to	8%
.25	converts to	25%
0.95	converts to	9.5%
1.05	converts to	105%

Addition of Decimal Numbers

When adding numbers with decimals, place figures in a vertical column, making sure each decimal is in a direct vertical line.

Example:

$$
\begin{array}{r}
126.06 \\
5.715 \\
400.8 \\
\hline
532.575
\end{array}
$$

Subtraction of Decimal Numbers

The same procedure is used to subtract one decimal number from another.

Example:

$$
\begin{array}{r}
\$18,450.60 \\
-\ 425.20 \\
\hline
\$18,025.40
\end{array}
$$

Multiplication of Decimal Numbers

Multiply the two numbers in the normal fashion and then mark off as many decimal places in the answer as there are in the two numbers being multiplied.

Example:

$$
\begin{array}{r}
7.064 \quad \text{(multiplicand)} \\
\times\ 37.6 \quad \text{(multiplier)} \\
\hline
265.6064 \quad \text{(product)}
\end{array}
$$

Division of Decimal Numbers

In a division problem that contains a decimal in the divisor, you must remove that decimal before proceeding with the problem. Mentally move the decimal in the dividend the same number of places shown in the divisor. Add zeros to the dividend if the dividend has fewer digits than are needed to carry out the division process. The decimal point in the quotient (answer) will appear directly above the imaginary decimal in the dividend.

Example:

$$\begin{array}{r} 6000 \text{ (quotient)} \\ \text{(divisor)}.045\overline{\smash{\big)}\,270.000 \text{ (dividend)}} \end{array}$$

When no decimal appears in the divisor, the decimal in the quotient will appear directly above the decimal in the dividend.

Example:

$$\begin{array}{r} 3.02 \\ 24\overline{\smash{\big)}\,72.48} \end{array}$$

VARIABLES

Most real estate problems involve three variables—two known and one unknown. You must find the unknown variable. The three variables are termed *paid*, *made*, and *rate* (%). These basic formulas evolve from the illustration:

$$\text{Made} = \text{Paid} \times \text{Rate}$$
$$\text{Paid} = \text{Made} \div \text{Rate}$$
$$\text{Rate} = \text{Made} \div \text{Paid}$$

In any problem involving these formulas, one quantity is unknown. You must determine from the given information whether to multiply or divide the other variables to compute the third variable.

TABLE 4

Amount Made	Amount Paid	Rate (%)
1. Income (earned per year)	Amount of investment	Percentage return
2. Sales commission	Selling price	Rate of commission
3. Documentary transfer tax	Taxable equity	Transfer tax rate
4. Monthly rent	Investment amount	Rate of return
5. Annual net income	Property value	Capitalization rate
6. Interest	Principal	Rate × Time
7. Discount amount	Loan balance	Rate of discount
8. Area of property	Length	Width

To assist in this process, Table 4 equates various real estate terms with the terms *made*, *paid*, and *rate*.

Investment Problems

To find the amount of money to be invested when the **income and** rate of return are known:

$$\text{Amount invested (paid)} = \frac{\text{Income (made)}}{\text{Rate (\% of return)}}$$

To find the rate (%) of return when the income and **the amount** invested are known:

$$\text{Rate (\%)} = \frac{\text{Income (made)}}{\text{Amount invested (paid)}}$$

To find the income when the amount invested and the **rate (%) are** known:

$$\text{Income (made)} = \text{Amount invested (paid)} \times \text{Rate (\%)}$$

Sample investment problems using the preceding formulas **follow**.

Caution

When you are given monthly figures, convert them to annual figures (for example, $80 per month × 12 months = $960 per year).

Problem 1

If an investor wants to earn $50 per month from a savings **account** and the account pays 5 percent simple interest, how much **must be put** in the account?

The given variables are:

Income = $600 per year ($50 × 12 months)
Rate of Return = 5%

The unknown variable is the amount of investment. By **substituting in** the formula, you obtain:

$$\text{Amount} = \frac{\$600}{5\% \text{ or } .05} \qquad .05\overline{)600.00}^{\,12,000}$$

Amount of investment = $12,000

Problem 2

An investor bought a small lot for $85,000 cash. Assume the lot was later listed for sale and sold for $125,000. What is the rate (%) of profit the investor made on this sale?

The given variables are:

> Paid = $85,000
> Made = $40,000 ($125,000 − $85,000)

The unknown variable is the rate of profit. By substituting in the formula, you obtain

$$85{,}000\overline{)40{,}000}^{\,.4706} \quad \text{or} \quad 47.06\%$$

Discounting Notes

Problem 3

A $5,000 note for a loan from a private lender is to be paid off in 12 months. The borrower is to pay the $5,000 plus 8 percent interest on the due date. An investor purchases the note today at a discount rate of 10 percent. What is the investor's rate of return on the amount invested?

The first step is to determine the amount made.

> Paid × Rate = Made

By substituting in the formula, you obtain:

> $5,000 × .08 = $400 (interest to the lender on due date)
> $5,000 × .10 = $500 (discount allowed investor)
> Made = $900 ($400 + $500)
> Paid = $5,000 less 10%, or $4,500

The given variables are:

> Made = $900
> Paid = $4,500

The unknown variable is the rate (%).

> Made ÷ Paid = Rate

Substitution results in:

$$\begin{array}{r} .20 \text{ or } 20\% \\ 4500\overline{)\ 900.00} \end{array}$$

Rate or percent of profit = .20, or 20%

Appraisal Problems

In appraisal problems, use the formula:

Paid × Rate (%) = Made

Reconstructed, the choices become:

1. Value of property × Capitalization rate = Net income or net loss
2. Value = Made ÷ Rate (capitalization rate)
3. Capitalization rate = Made ÷ Paid (value of property)
4. Income or loss = Paid × Capitalization rate

Problem 4

After all operating expenses have been deducted, an older triplex nets an income of $500 per month per apartment unit. A prospective investor is interested in purchasing the property, and he or she demands an investment rate (capitalization rate) of 6 percent. What is the maximum the investor should pay for the triplex?

$500 per unit × 3 units = $1,500 net income per month
$1,500 × 12 months = $18,000 annual net income

The given variables are:

Made = $18,000
Rate = 6%

The unknown variable is the paid. Substitution in the formula results in:

$$\begin{array}{r} 300,000 \\ .06\overline{)18,000.00} \end{array}$$

The investor should pay no more than $300,000.

Problem 5

An investor pays $600,000 for an older six-unit apartment house that has a gross income of $700 rent per month per unit with total expenses of $14,400 per year. What capitalization rate (%) will the investor make on the purchase price?

$$\text{Gross income} = 12 \text{ months} \times 700 = \$8,400 \times 6 \text{ units}$$

$$
\begin{aligned}
&= \$50,400 \\
\text{Less expenses} \quad &\quad -14,400 \\
\text{Net income (made)} \quad &\quad \$36,000
\end{aligned}
$$

By substituting in the formula:

$$
600,000 \overline{)36,000.00} \quad .06
$$

The capitalization rate = 6%.

Commission Problems

In commission problems:

Paid figure refers to the selling price.
Rate is the commission rate.
Made is the amount of commission.

Problem 6

A real estate salesperson found a buyer for a $300,000 condo. The seller agreed to pay the broker a 6 percent commission on the sale. The broker pays the salesperson 40 percent of the commission. What is the salesperson's commission?

The unknown variable is the made. Substitution in the formula results in:

Paid = $300,000 (selling price)
Rate = 40% of 6%
Made (commission) = Paid (selling price) × Rate

$$
\begin{array}{ll}
\$300,000 & \$18,000 \\
\underline{\times .06} & \underline{\times .40} \\
\$18,000 \quad \text{Total commission} & \$7,200 \quad \text{Salesperson's commission}
\end{array}
$$

The amount of the salesperson's share of the $18,000 total commission is $7,200.

Problem 7

A real estate office lists a parcel of land for $800,000 with an agreed commission of 10 percent. The broker presents an offer for 10 percent less than the listed price, which the seller agrees to accept if the broker reduces the amount of commission by 25 percent. If the broker agrees to the reduction, what is the amount of the commission?

The missing variable is the made.

> Paid = $800,000 less 10% ($80,000) = $720,000
> Rate = 10% less 25% = 7.5% or (.075)

Thus, the formula becomes Selling Price × Commission Rate = Commission Amount.

> Therefore: $800,000 listing price – 10% = $720,000 selling price
> 10% – 25% = 7.5% commission rate (.10 – .025 = .075)
> Then: $720,000 × 7.5% = $54,000 commission

There are a variety of commission splits in actual practice.

A broker may take a listing, make the sale, and receive the entire commission. One or more salespersons in a broker's office may be involved; if so, they divide the commission with the broker.

A listing may be taken by Broker A and placed in multiple listing. If the sale is made by Broker B, he or she splits the commission with Broker A's office. One of Broker B's salespersons may make the sale. If so, the salesperson splits the office's share of the commission with Broker B.

Commission splits between multiple listing brokers vary, with 50/50 being the most common. In some cases, this split is 40 percent to the listing broker's office and 60 percent to the selling broker's office.

When the listing and the sale are in-house, the splits may be as follows:

- 20 percent to the listing salesperson
- 40 percent to the salesperson making the sale
- 40 percent to the broker

  OR

- 35 percent to the listing salesperson
- 35 percent to the salesperson making the sale
- 30 percent to the broker

The amount of the commission split depends on the individual broker's commission schedule. An example of a possible commission

FIGURE 1

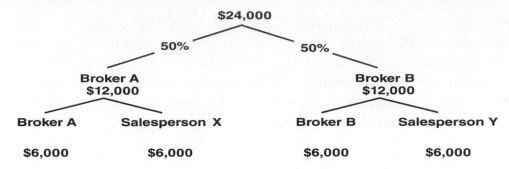

split between real estate brokers and salespersons may be as follows: Assume that $400,000 is the sales price for a home and the seller agrees to pay a 6 percent commission. Then 6% × $400,000 = $24,000 commission. The $24,000 commission may be divided up between brokers and salespeople as shown in Figure 1.

Interest and Loan Problems

Interest is the charge for the use of money. The dollar amount of interest is determined by the rate of interest charged and the amount of money borrowed. When borrowing money, the borrower is obligated to pay back the amount borrowed as well as interest per agreed terms between the borrower and the lender.

Note
When working with interest problems, be sure to convert monthly figures to annual figures.

To solve interest problems, you will use these terms and formulas. Interest is the charge for the use of money expressed as dollars. Principal is the amount of money borrowed.

Rate is the percentage of interest charged on the principal.

Time represents the interval between payments on principal and/or interest. In the formula, time is expressed as years or a fraction of a year. Interest = Principal × Rate × Time (I = P × R × T).

By applying this formula to the standard "made, paid, rate" formula, the paid figure refers to the amount of the loan or the principal, rate (%) is the rate of interest multiplied by the years or fraction of a year, and made is the amount of interest expressed in money. As a result, the following formulas are derived:

$$\text{Amount of loan} = \frac{\text{Amount of interest}}{\text{Rate of interest} \times \text{time}} \text{ or } P = \frac{I}{R \times T}$$

$$\text{Rate of interest} = \frac{\text{Amount of interest}}{\text{Amount of loan} \times \text{time}} \text{ or } R = \frac{I}{P \times T}$$

$$\text{Amount of interest} = \text{Amount of loan} \times \text{Rate of interest} \times \text{Time or}$$

$$I = P \times R \times T$$

Problem 8

If you borrowed $8,000 for one year and paid $640 interest, what rate of interest did you pay?

The known variables are:

Paid = $8,000
Made = $640 × 1 year = $640 per year

Substitution results in:

$$\text{Rate} = \text{Made} \div \text{Paid or } \frac{I}{P \times T}$$

$$\$8000\overline{)640.00}^{\ .08} \quad \text{or} \quad \frac{640}{8000 \times I}$$

Problem 9

If one month's interest is $1,000 on a seven-year straight note (interest-only note) and the note calls for interest at 6 percent per year, what is the amount of the loan?

The know variables are:

Rate = 6%
Made = $1,000 × 12 months = $12,000 interest per year

Substitution in the formula results in:

$$\text{Paid} = \text{Made} \div \text{Rate}$$

$$.06\overline{)12,000.00}^{\ 200,000} \quad \text{Proof:} \quad \begin{array}{r} \$200,00 \\ \times\ .06 \\ \hline \$12,000 \end{array} \quad \begin{array}{l} \text{Principal} \\ \text{Rate} \\ \text{Interest paid for year} \end{array}$$

Cost and Selling Price Problems

When dealing with cost problems, you are given a selling price and are asked to calculate the profit or the cost before a fixed profit. The first step is to consider the cost figure as 100 percent. Next, add the profit percent to the 100 percent and divide the total percentage into the selling price.

Problem 10

A person sold a rural property for $60,000, which allowed her to make a 20 percent profit. What did she pay for the property?
  Substitution in the formula results in:

$$\text{Cost} = \text{Selling price} \div (\text{Profit \%} + 100\%)$$

$$\text{Cost} = 1.20 \overline{)60,\!000.00}^{\,50,\!000}$$

She paid $50,000 for the property.

Problem 11

Another problem arises when the seller receives a given net amount and you are asked to establish the selling price or amount of the loan.

  For instance, you offer your lot for sale, asking for a certain net amount. A broker who found a buyer delivered a check to you for $85,500. The broker had already deducted 10 percent for commission and seller closing cost. What did the lot sell for?
  The formula used to solve this problem is:

$$\text{Selling price} = \frac{\text{Net amount received}}{100\% - \text{Commission rate}}$$

Substitution in this formula results in:

$$\text{Selling price} = \$85,\!000 \div (100\% - 10\%) \text{ or } 90\%$$

$$\text{Selling price} = .90 \overline{)85,\!500.00}^{\,95,\!000}$$

SQUARE FOOTAGE AND AREA CALCULATION

Problems related to square footage are simple. This technique is used when you want to know the number of square feet in a property. Once you determine the square footage, you can refer to an index on residential property to determine the cost per square foot or to obtain estimates per square foot from local contractors. The cost per square foot multiplied by the square footage gives an estimated new construction cost of a building.

The basic formula for determining the area of a piece of property is:

$$Area = Length \times Width$$

The following formulas can be used:

$$Area = Length \times Width$$
$$Length = Area \div Width$$
$$Width = Area \div Length$$

Problem 12

What is the depth, or length, of a piece of vacant land containing six acres with a width, or front footage, of 400 feet on a county road? (Remember, there are 43,560 square feet in an acre.)

Convert the piece of property into square feet by multiplying 43,560 by 6 = 261,360 square feet.

Substitution in the formula results in

$$Length = Area \div Width$$
$$Length = 261,360 \div 400 = 653.4 \text{ feet}$$
$$Proof: 400 \text{ feet} \times 653.4 \text{ feet} = 261,360 \text{ square feet}$$

If the piece of property you are measuring is irregular in shape, try to make rectangles and triangles of the area given (Area of a triangle = Altitude × Base ÷ 2). An example of this type of computation is given in Problem 13.

Problem 13

Use Figures 2 and 3 to compute the square footage of the lot and then find the total construction cost of the garage and house. Assume contractors are quoting $50 per square foot for garages and $100 per square foot for homes.

Insert dotted lines in the diagram to form a rectangle A and a triangle B.

FIGURE 2

FIGURE 3

Improvements

1. Compute the area in rectangle A as follows: 110 × 100 = 11,000 square feet.

2. Compute the area of triangle B as follows: 40 × 100 ÷ 2 = 2,000 square feet.

Thus, the size of the lot is 11,000 + 2,000 = 13,000 square feet. To figure the area in the house:

1. Place dotted lines as indicated in the diagram, thus forming three rectangles (C, D, E) in the house.

2. Compute the area of each rectangle as follows:
    Rectangle C = 25 × 20 = 500 square feet

Rectangle D = 60 × 20 = 1,200 square feet
Rectangle E = 20 × 35 = 700 square feet

3. Compute the area of the garage as follows: 20 × 25 = 500 square feet

4. Compute the costs as follows:

2,400 square feet × $100 per square foot	=	$240,000
500 square feet × $50 per square foot	=	$ 25,000
Total	=	$265,000

Answers

13,000 square feet in the lot; $265,000 cost of construction for the total improvements

PRORATIONS

Ownership of real property entails certain expenses. Some of these expenses are paid in advance; others, in arrears. They may be paid for by the seller prior to the sale of the property, or the buyer may assume costs owed by the seller at the close of escrow.

It is only fair that expenses paid in advance should be credited (allocated) to the seller and debited (charged) to the buyer; by the same token, expenses owed by the seller and not paid by the seller prior to the close of escrow, but to be paid later by the buyer, should be debited to the seller and credited to the buyer.

Proration is the act of making an equitable distribution of these expenses in escrow at the close of the sale.

There are four basic steps in proration:

1. Determine whether the amount should be a credit or a debit to the seller or the buyer.
2. Determine the number of days to be prorated.
3. Tabulate the cost per day.
4. Multiply the number of days by the cost per day.

Remember

For simplicity in determining proration's, assume there are 30 days in a month and 360 days in a year.

Expenses that are normally subject to proration are real property taxes and assessments, interest on loans assumed, hazard insurance, and prepaid rents if the property is income producing.

Problem 14

Ms. A sells her rural cabin on September 1, 2013. She has an existing loan of $100,000 on the cabin. The interest on the loan is 9 percent. Buyer B assumes Ms. A's loan with interest paid to August 15, 2013. The seller has paid for an existing three-year hazard insurance policy for $360 per year, paid by Ms. A until October 15, 2014. Ms. A also neglected to pay her property taxes of $1,800 for the year. The tax year runs July 1, 2013, through June 30, 2014. What is the interest proration, and who is credited or debited? What is the insurance proration, and who is credited or debited? What is the tax proration, and who is credited or debited?

To figure the proration on the interest:

Step 1: August 15 to September 1, 2013 = 15 days
Step 2: $100,000 × 9% ÷ 360 = $25 per day
Step 3: 15 days × $25 per day = $375 interest
Step 4: Credit the buyer and debit the seller.

To figure the proration on the insurance policy:

Step 1: September 1, 2013, through October 15, 2014 = 405 days
Step 2: $360 ÷ 360 = $1 per day
Step 3: 405 days × $1 = $405
Step 4: Credit the seller and debit the buyer.

To figure the tax proration:

Step 1: July 1 to September 1, 2013 = 60 days
Step 2: $1,800 ÷ 360 = $5 per day
Step 3: 60 days × $5 = $300
Step 4: Debit the seller and credit the buyer.

Note

A general rule to use in proration is: When the expenses are paid beyond escrow, credit the seller and debit the buyer. When the expenses are paid short of escrow, debit the seller and credit the buyer.

DOCUMENTARY TRANSFER TAX

When real property is transferred, state law allows the county recorder to apply a documentary transfer tax. The amount of the tax is placed on the deed and is computed based on the following schedule:

1. $1.10 for $1,000 of value transferred, or $0.55 for every $500 or fraction thereof.
2. When the terms of the sale are all cash, the documentary transfer tax is paid on the entire sales price. A new loan by the buyer is treated the same as an all-cash sale.
3. When the buyer assumes the seller's existing loan, the amount of the loan on property is exempt and is subtracted from the total selling price. The tax is computed only on the equity amount. The transfer tax can be paid by the buyer or the seller, but custom usually has the seller pay the tax.

In some areas, cities are allowed to levy a real estate transfer tax on top of this statewide documentary tax. These transfer taxes are not standardized and vary from city to city. They are not presented in this book.

Problem 15

A home is sold for $510,000. The buyer puts some cash down and obtains new financing for the balance of the sales price. What is the documentary transfer tax?

$$\frac{\$510,000}{\$1,000} = 510 \times \$1.10 = \$561 \text{ Documentary transfer tax}$$

Problem 16

A one-bedroom condo is sold for $237,500. But in this case, the buyer assumes the seller's existing $200,000 loan. What is the documentary transfer tax?

$237,500 Sales price
− 200,000 Existing loan assumed
$37,500 Equity transferred

$$\frac{\$37,500}{\$1,000} = 37.5 \times \$1.10 = \$41.25 \text{ Documentary transfer tax}$$

USE OF FINANCIAL TABLES

To facilitate mathematical computations, financial calculators, computers, and/or tables are used.

Interest Computation

This appendix previously discussed how to compute the amount of interest to be paid using the formula $I = P \times R \times T$. Remember that computations are usually based on a 30-day month and 360-day year.

Take a look at an example using the conventional method and an interest table. (See Table 5.)

Problem 17

What is the interest on a $6,500 loan for one year, three months, and 20 days at 9 percent interest?

TABLE 5   Interest Table Figured on $1,000 360 Days to the Year.

Days	5%	6%	7%	8%	9%	10%
1	0.1389	0.1667	0.1944	0.2222	0.2500	0.2778
2	0.2778	0.3333	0.3889	0.4444	0.5000	0.5556
3	0.4167	0.5000	0.5833	0.6666	0.7500	0.8334
4	0.5556	0.6667	0.7778	0.8888	1.0000	1.1112
5	0.6944	0.8333	0.9722	1.1111	1.2500	1.3890
6	0.8333	1.0000	0.1667	1.3333	1.5000	1.6668
7	0.9722	1.1667	1.3611	1.5555	1.7500	1.9446
8	1.1111	1.3333	1.5556	1.7777	2.0000	2.2224
9	1.2500	1.5000	1.7500	2.0000	2.2500	2.5002
10	1.3889	1.6667	1.9444	2.2222	2.5000	2.7780
11	1.5278	1.8333	2.1389	2.4444	2.7500	3.0558
12	1.6667	2.0000	2.3333	2.6666	3.0000	3.3336
13	1.8056	2.1667	2.5278	2.8888	3.2500	3.6114
14	1.9444	2.3333	2.7222	3.1111	3.5000	3.8892
15	2.0833	2.5000	2.9167	3.3333	3.7500	4.1670
16	2.2222	2.6667	3.1111	3.5555	4.0000	4.4448
17	2.3611	2.8333	3.3055	3.7777	4.2500	4.7226
18	2.5000	3.0000	3.5000	4.0000	4.5000	5.0004
19	2.6389	3.1667	3.6944	4.2222	4.7500	5.2782
20	2.7778	3.3333	3.8889	4.4444	5.0000	5.5560
21	2.9167	3.5000	4.0833	4.6666	5.2500	5.8338
22	3.0556	3.6667	4.2778	4.8888	5.5000	6.1116
23	3.1944	3.8333	4.4722	5.1111	5.7500	6.3894
24	3.2222	4.0000	4.6667	5.3333	6.0000	6.6672
25	3.4722	4.1667	4.8611	5.5555	6.2500	6.9450
26	3.6111	4.3333	5.0555	5.7777	6.5000	7.2228
27	3.7500	4.5000	5.2500	6.0000	6.7500	7.5006
28	3.8889	4.6667	5.4444	6.2222	7.0000	7.7784
29	4.0278	4.8333	5.6389	6.4444	7.2500	8.0562
30	4.1667	5.0000	5.8333	6.6666	7.5000	8.3340

31st day

Conventional Method

$P \times R \times T = I$

Principal is $6,500

Rate is 9%

Time is 470 days (1 year + 3 months + 20 days)
Thus

$$\$6,500 \times .09 \times 1.3056^* = \$763.78 \text{ (actual)}$$

$$\frac{^*470 \text{ days}}{360 \text{ days}} = 1.3056$$

Use of Interest Table

1 year and 3 months = 15 months
Under the 9% column in Table 5, the 30-day factor = 7.5000.
15 months × 7.5000 = 112.50 + the 20-day factor of 5.00 = 117.50
117.50 × 6.5 (number of thousands in $6,500) = $763.75

Amortization Tables

Amortization tables can be used to compute monthly payments for various loan amounts at various interest rates and terms. A typical table showing various rates of interest and length of loans (called *terms*) is shown in Table 6.

A typical table shows along one axis a list of various loan terms expressed in years and along the other axis various amounts of interest. At the intersection of any two axes in the table is found the monthly payment to pay off $1,000 at various interest rates.

TABLE 6   Table of Monthly Payments to Amortize $1,000 Loan.

Term of Years	6%	7%	8%	9%	10%	11%	12%
10	11.11	11.62	12.14	12.67	13.22	13.78	14.35
15	8.44	8.99	9.56	10.15	10.75	11.37	12.00
20	7.17	7.76	8.37	9.00	9.66	10.32	11.01
25	6.45	7.07	7.72	8.40	9.09	9.80	10.53
30	6.00	6.66	7.34	8.05	8.78	9.52	10.29
40	5.51	6.22	6.96	7.71	8.49	9.28	10.09

Problem 18

A $100,000 loan for 30 years at 7 percent interest will have what monthly payment? To solve this problem using an amortization table, use the following procedure:

Go to the 7 percent interest column in Table 6, and follow it down to the 30-year line. There you will find the factor 6.66. This means $6.66 per month will pay off $1,000 in 30 years. The loan amount is $100,000; therefore,

$$\frac{\$100,000}{\$1,000} = 100$$

Thus, $100 \times \$6.66 = \$660$ per month (rounded), which will pay off a $100,000 loan at 7 percent in 30 years.

Problem 19

If an individual made payments of $1,234.60 per month, including 9 percent on a fully amortized 30-year loan, what was the original amount of the loan?

In Table 6, the point where the 30-year line intersects with the 9 percent interest line is $8.05 for a $1,000 loan.

$1,234.60 ÷ 8.05 = $153.37 × 1,000 = $153,366 loan (approximate)

Problem 20

If you borrowed $48,000 from a personal finance company using a fully amortized home equity loan and were to make payments of $495.45, including 11 percent interest, how many years would it take to pay off the loan?

Solution:

Reduce $48,000 to the amount of each payment per $1,000 as follows:

$495.45 ÷ 48 = $10.32

Using the 11 percent interest column in Table 6, locate the amount $10.32. This amount falls on the 20-year loan term line. It will take approximately 20 years to pay off the $48,000 loan.

Problem 21

If an individual borrowed $250,000 for a home loan, payable $1,834.41 per month, including interest, for a period of 30 years, what would be the rate of interest?

Solution:

Divide $1,834.41 by 250 to determine the amount of each payment per $1,000:

$$\$1,834.41 \div 250 = \$7.34$$

Using Table 6, the intersection of the 30-year line and $7.34 = 8 percent interest rate.

Real World of Real Estate

Today's real estate professionals use financial calculators and computers to do real estate math problems. Due to the large variety of models and software, it is impossible to illustrate the keystrokes and software used to arrive at the answers presented in this appendix. The California Bureau of Real Estate (CalBRE) will provide calculators to be used during the state real estate examination.

ANSWER KEY

Answers to Chapter Practical Application Questions

Chapter 1

1. As a new California real estate salesperson licensee, the educational requirements during the first four years of your license are as follows: you must complete four 3-hour Cal-BRE-approved courses in ethics, agency, fair housing, and trust fund handling. After July 1, 2007, you must also take a 3-hour course in risk management.

2. As a California real estate broker licensee, the continuing educational requirements during the first four years of your license are as follows: You must complete 45 hours of CalBRE-approved continuing education, including one 8-hour survey course updating ethics, agency, fair housing, trust fund handling, risk management, and management and supervision, or six 3-hour courses in those topics, along with a minimum of 18 clock hours in consumer protection courses.

3. A bulk sale occurs when a business that has inventory is sold. When the bulk sale rules are not followed, a buyer of a business may find that he or she paid twice for the same inventory: once to the seller who did not own the inventory outright and again to the creditor who has a claim on the inventory. All purchasers of businesses should seek the advice and guidance of an attorney to be sure that all bulk sale rules are followed.

Chapter 2

1. To determine fixtures the listing broker would use the memory aid of MARIA to determine what items are fixtures. Then the listing broker would ask the sellers if they were going to include the attached mirror and built-in bookshelves and sound system since they are considered to be fixtures. If the seller stated that the bookshelves and sound system would be part of the sale but the mirror they were taking, the listing broker might suggest that the seller remove the mirror and make any repairs to the wall before the listing went live so there would be no confusion in the buyer's mind. Freestanding items are considered to be personal property but if transferring are typically listed in the listing contract and MLS.

2. In the absence of an agreement to the contrary, all items of personal property can usually be removed by the seller. If the facts of the case show that the

prefab storage shed merely rested on the ground, it is probably personal property. If it was bolted down on a cement slab or attached to a foundation, it probably is real property and should stay with the land. If the issue is too close to call, the courts tend to favor the buyer. This entire issue could have been avoided if the parties had mentioned the outcome of the shed in the purchase contract.

3. Trade fixtures are added by tenants as items needed to run a business, while regular fixtures are added by tenants for personal use. The presumption is that business tenants are automatically allowed to remove trade fixtures when they leave. Personal fixtures carry no automatic removal presumption. Whether regular fixtures can or cannot be removed depends on individual circumstances. In both cases, any legal removal carries with it the responsibility to repair all damages the removal may cause. Once again, any conflict can be avoided by discussing the issue in the rental contract.

Chapter 3

1. Vista Realty is a dual agent for Alvarez and Patel because both salespeople work for the same real estate office.

2. Both Acme Properties and Lake Realty are probably guilty of misrepresentation. The incorrect square footage and wrong lot size were probably honest mistakes and not outright fraud, but a misrepresentation is a misrepresentation. Acme Properties will have a difficult time declaring they are innocent because they relied on the information supplied by Lake Realty. The salesperson from Acme Properties should have said, "Here are the measurements provided by Lake Realty, the listing agent. I have not verified the numbers, and you should not make any decisions until you have an appraiser or another qualified person check their accuracy."

3. The heirs are right. The seller's death prior to accepting the offer automatically canceled the listing contract with Excellent Realty. Excellent Realty's contention that a commission was earned prior to the seller's death due to the $360,000 offer is incorrect. $360,000 is less than the listed price of $375,000, and it would take the seller's formal acceptance of the $360,000 offer to waive the required $375,000 listing price.

Chapter 4

1. A freshly painted ceiling of an older home could well be a red flag of an attempt to cover up evidence of a roof leak. The agent should ask the sellers if they have had any roof leaks and perhaps ask why they did not repaint the walls when the ceiling was repainted.

2. It is irrelevant whether the buyer believes in ghosts. The issue is whether or not the community belief that the house is haunted affects the value of the home. The fact that the listing has been on the market for a long time indicates that

this belief may affect the value of the property. The buyer, eight years from now, may find it difficult to sell the property due to the concern over the house being haunted. If it affects the value of the property, it is a material fact.

3. Because a death by illness is not normally considered a material fact, a disclosure probably does not have to be made. In light of the fact that the decedent was gay (a protected class in California) and the cause of death was AIDS (considered to be a disability and also a protected area), an agent would be careful not to disclose the sexual orientation or the cause of death as it could constitute a fair housing violation.

Chapter 5

1. Sara has a bilateral (promise for a promise; e.g., rent for occupancy), expressed (written), executed (signed and moved in), valid real estate contract (lease). Although she is only 17, by virtue of her military service, she is an emancipated minor and legally able to contract.

2. The legal issues to consider: Sunrise Realty was given the exclusive authorization and right to sell the listing for 180 days. Vargas canceled the listing in 90 days without a legal release from Sunrise Realty. The sale took place through Ambrosini Properties during the 180-day time period that Vargas had given to Sunrise Realty. In a similar situation, a California court ruled that a seller could not unilaterally cancel the listing, that the permission of the listing agent was required, and that the seller must pay a second full commission to the original listing company.

3. Since the buyer has not released their continences, the deposit is fully refundable. The buyer does not have to give a reason for cancellation, as long as their cancellation is done in good faith.

Chapter 6: Part 1

1. 165 acres, which looks like the shaded area below.

160 acres + 5 acres = 165 acres

2. The basic rule is that the first additional bid over the initial accepted bid must be 10% of the first $10,000 and 5% of any excess.

Therefore: $200,000 initial bid
    − 10,000 × 10%   = $1,000
    $190,000 × 5%   = $9,500
    $10,500

$200,000 initial bid + $10,500 = $210,500 required for the first additional bid over the initial bid. Any bids after this may be in any amounts at the pleasure of the probate judge.

3. Williams is probably right because a grant deed carries after- acquired title, which means that after the grantor deeds the property, if he or she should later acquire an additional interest in the property, that interest automatically passes to the grantee.

Chapter 6: Part 2

1. Upon Washington's death, the lease with Santos is canceled since a life tenant cannot lease beyond the life of the designated person in a life estate. Possession will go to the heirs of Adams.

2. Nguyen and Battino are tenants in common as they do not have the unities of time, title, or interest. The percentage of interest in the properties is as follows: Nguyen now has his original 50% + Harris's 25%, for a total of 75% interest in the 20 acres Battino has a 25% interest in the 20 acres. When Harris sold one half to Battino, Harris was still a joint tenant with Nguyen on the remaining one half, and the right of survivorship applies. This illustrates how confusing things can get when joint tenants sell off portions of their interest in real estate.

3. The community property issues for the court to look at are as follows: The family home is obviously community property, but the five-unit apartment is going to be a legal issue. When Sara's parents left her the apartments, the inheritance was her separate property. The placing of the rental money in a separate account in her name alone showed intent to keep it separate property. But Sara's using the rental income to pay for the children's college tuition may be perceived as using the funds for a community property responsibility and a form of commingling. Sara's attorney will try to prove the money was a mere gift and not a pledging of the rental proceeds for a community purpose. Bill's attorney may take the opposite argument, which could create a nasty situation. The moral to the story is that if you are married and wish to maintain separate property, it is best to operate under the guidance of a competent attorney.

Chapter 7

1. An easement by prescription is an attempt to obtain the right to travel over the land of another, while adverse possession is an attempt to take title to the land of another. Both require hostile, open, and notorious use for at least five years under a claim of right or color of title. But adverse possession also requires the payment of the property taxes for at least five years, while easement by prescription does not.

2. a. Preliminary Notice should be served within 20 days from the first furnishing of labor or materials on your home site.

   b. A Notice of Completion should be filed by you within 10 days after the completion of the home.

   c. After filing your Notice of Completion, the general contractor has 60 days to file a lien, while the subcontractors have 30 days.

   d. If your Notice of Completion is filed incorrectly and, therefore, is invalid, all workers have 90 days to file a lien.

   e. If a mechanics' lien is filed, it will automatically terminate if court action is not instituted within 90 days.

3.

$300,000	condo value
− 125,000	to holder of first loan
− 35,000	to holder of home equity second loan
− 100,000	to owner of home per head of household exemption
$ 40,000	remainder to be applied toward the judgement creditor's $25,000 debt

Chapter 8

1. $200,000 interest-only loan × 6% = $12,000 ÷ 12 months = $1,000 current monthly payment. Second year equals $200,000 × 8% = $16,000 ÷ 12 months = $1,333.33 monthly payment. Third year equals $200,000 × 10% = $20,000 ÷ 12 months = 1,666.67 monthly payment. Fourth year 11% cap rate is reached; therefore, $200,000 × 11% = $22,000 ÷ 12 months = $1,833.33 monthly payment.

2. The homeowner has until five days prior to the date of the fore- closure sale to make up back payments and all foreclosure costs to save the home. Using the figures given, that would be $2,000 back payments + $1,000 foreclosure costs, for a total of $3,000. If the homeowner waits until the five days prior or the date of sale, the lender can then demand the entire loan balance of $175,000 + $2,000 back payments + $1,000 in foreclosure costs. Some owners who find themselves in this predicament use the services of an attorney to file bankruptcy in an attempt to buy some time against the foreclosure.

3. $15,000 junior lien for ten years has a maximum commission rate of 15%, plus a maximum of 5% of the loan amount for additional costs and expenses,

not to exceed $700. Therefore, $15,000 × 15% = $2,250 commission; $15,000 × 5% = $750 other costs, with a maximum allowed of only $700. Thus, $15,000 less $2,250 commission less $700 additional costs and expenses = $12,050 net to the homeowner. But the homeowner will be required to repay $15,000 plus interest on the $15,000, driving the effective rate of interest considerably higher than the interest rate stated on the note.

Chapter 9: Part 1

1. $5,000 gross monthly income × 28% = $1,400 qualified maximum housing payments not counting debts. $5,000 × 36% = $1,800 less $600 long-term monthly debts = $1,200 qualified, counting monthly debts. Therefore, $1,200—the lesser of the two—applies. This illustrates how too much long-term debt reduces a person's ability to qualify for a larger loan, which, in turn, reduces his or her ability to qualify for a more expensive home.

2. $84,000 ÷ 12 = $7,000 per month

   $7,000 × 28% = $1,960.00

   $7,000 × 36% = 2,520.00

   $2,520.00 - $1,050 = $1,470.00 maximum payment

3. $180,000 loan balance × .0025 = $450 annual PMI cost divided by 12 months = $37.50 reduction in the monthly loan payment if the PMI coverage is canceled.

Chapter 9: Part 2

1. Minimum cash required is 3.5%; therefore, $150,000 price × 3.5% = $5,250 cash required to close escrow if the seller pays all other closing costs.

2. Due to no down payment on this VA-guaranteed loan, the sales price and the loan amount are the same. Therefore, $150,000 loan 2.5% × (1% loan fee + 1.5% funding fee) = $3,750 + $500 other closing costs = $4,250 cash to close escrow.

3. $150,000 Cal-Vet price × 2% down payment = $3,000 + $700 other costs = $3,700 cash required to close escrow.

Chapter 10

1. 200-foot × 40-foot main structure = 8,000 square feet × $65 per square foot = $520,000 replacement cost new; 20-year effective life × 2% (100% ÷ 50 years) = 40% depreciation. Therefore:

$520,000	replacement cost new
−208,000	depreciation
$312,000	present value of main structure

   35-foot × 15-foot storage building = 525 square feet × $20 per square foot = $10,500 replacement cost new; 15-year effective life × 3.33% (100% ÷ 30 years) = 50% depreciation factor; $10,500 × 50% = $5,250 depreciation. Therefore:

$ 10,500	replacement cost new
− 5,250	depreciation
$ 5,250	present value of storage building
$312,000	present value of main structure
+ 5,250	present value of storage building
+ 27,000	present value of cement slab and other improvements
+300,000	land value
$644,250	or $644,000 estimated value of special use property

2. 11,000 square feet × $1 × 12 months = $132,000 gross rents

$132,000	gross rents
− 6,000	expenses ($132,000 × 5%)
$125,400	net operating income

$$\frac{\$135,000 \text{ net income of comparable property}}{\$1,500,000 \text{ comparable property}} = 9\% \text{ comparable cap rate}$$

$$\frac{\$125,400 \text{ net operating income}}{09 \text{ capitalization rate}} = \$1,393,333 \text{ or } \$1,393,000 \text{ estimated value}$$

3.

	Comparable A	Comparable B	Comparable C
Price paid	$357,000	$340,000	$325,000
Spa	− 1,000	0	0
Condition	− 3,000	0	+ 3,000
Lot size	− 10,000	+ 10,000	+ 10,000
	$343,000	$350,000	$338,000

$350,000 is the best listing price estimate based on Comparable B having the least number of adjustments.

Chapter 11

1. The issue here is to save the transaction. The buyer's agent might mention that the buyer signed escrow instructions to split the title fee 50/50, even though the original deposit receipt said the seller would pay. The latest contract usually applies unless the buyer made an honest mistake and misread the instructions. The agent might mention that if the transaction falls through, the buyer could lose his or her deposit. Also, the issue of a court action interpleader might be pursued by the escrow holder. The bottom line is that if the transaction falls apart, the buyer will not get the home, the seller will not get the full sale proceeds, and the agent will not get a full commission. If the issue is a total stumbling block, ultimately the agent might agree to pay the buyer's 50 percent portion just to close the transaction. This may not be "fair," but it might be what is needed to solve the problem.

2. There are many issues here: California has an anti-rebate law that prohibits title companies from paying real estate licensees for the placement of title insurance. The fine can be up to $10,000 and/or one year in jail for both the title representative and the real estate agent. Federal RESPA rules prohibit kickbacks and unearned fees paid to real estate agents. Real estate commissioner regulations prohibit "secret profit" by real estate agents. The issue is whether unsolicited dinner and sporting event tickets come under the anti-rebate, RESPA, and secret profit rules. It would take an attorney to check out each law! It is probably best to pass on the whole thing and tell the title company, "NO THANKS!"

3. $413,575 × 7% = $28,950.25 ÷ 360 days = $80.42 per day × 18 days = $1,447.51 pro ration, which will be a debit for the seller and a credit for the buyer because interest is paid in arrears on real estate loans.

Chapter 12

1. The landlord could proceed as follows: Within 21 days, refund the security deposit, less damages beyond normal wear and tear. If the $100 damage to the water heater is beyond normal, the landlord should withhold the $100 from the security deposit. The problem is proving that the leak was caused by damage, not normal wear and tear. From a practical point of view, many landlords will not hold the $100 from the security deposit for fear the tenant will make an issue, causing legal hassles, which could end up costing a landlord much more than $100.

2. The landlord should serve a three-day (not a 30-day) notice to remove the dog or quit possession. If the tenant complies, the issue is settled. If the tenant does not remove the dog or move out, the next step for the landlord is to proceed with a formal unlawful detainer action. From a pure cost point of view, some- times it is cheaper to pay the tenant to move, rather than bear the cost of an unlawful detainer action.

3. 5 units × $750 per month × 12 months = $45,000 gross scheduled income per year; then:

$ 45,000	
− 2,250	vacancy factor ($45,000 × 5%)
$ 42,750	collected rents
× .08	property management rate
$ 3,420	property management fee paid

Chapter 13

1. The appeal process is as follows: The planning commission decision can be appealed to the city council or to the board of super- visors depending on who has jurisdiction. If a person does not like the decision of the city council

or board of supervisors, he or she can appeal to the courts. The decision of the highest court is final.

2. An owner of a condominium owns exclusively his or her airspace within the condo unit and has an undivided interest with the other owners in the building and land. A PUD owner owns his or her individual unit, inside and out, and owns the land immediately under the PUD. He or she has an equal undivided interest with the other PUD owners in the common areas. Under a stock cooperative, a corporation owns the property and each shareholder in the corporation is given the right to occupy a living unit. They are all called common interest developments because they feature some joint form of ownership in common with other co-owners.

3. The agent should respond by stating that any form of discrimination is illegal and carries a stiff fine and/or jail term for agents and owners. Also, good business ethics and a sense of fair play mean that all financially qualified people should have an equal right to own a home. Finally, if the owner insists upon discriminating, the agent should immediately cancel the listing.

Chapter 14

1. $225,000 × 80% = $180,000 loan at 8% for 30 years = $1,320.78 monthly payment using a financial calculator or 7.34 × 180 = $1,321.20 approximate monthly payment using the amortization table in Appendix B. $225,000 price × .017 (.012 property taxes plus .005 insurance) = $3,825 ÷ 12 months = $318.75 per month for property taxes and insurance. Therefore, $1,320.78 + $318.75 = $1,639.53 by financial calculator or $1,321.20 + $318.75 = $1,639.95 using the amortization table in Appendix B.

2. No federal capital gains tax is owed as the first $500,000 of gain is excluded for married homeowners who file joint returns and live in their main home for more than two years.

3. The federal tax code allows homeowners to deduct interest on the home equity loan up to the market value of the home. The interest paid on 25% of a 125% loan that exceeds the market value of the home will not be deductible if said funds are used to pay personal debts or expenditures. Homeowners should check with a tax specialist before entering into an equity loan to determine the current IRS rulings.

Chapter 15

1. Using the illustration in the book, starting with the ground and building up, a standard home has the footings, then the foundation, then the mudsill, then the floor joist, and finally the sole plate.

2. The four conditions are as follows: (1) must obtain a building permit, (2) must be placed on a permanent foundation, (3) must obtain a certificate of occupancy, and (4) must record a document stating that the mobile home is attached to a permanent foundation.

3. Advantages of owning your home include appreciation potential, tax advantages, privacy and control, pride of ownership, and better access to credit.

Answers to Chapter Reviewing Your Understanding Quesions

Chapter 1

1.	(b)	8.	(c)	15.	(c)
2.	(d)	9.	(d)	16.	(d)
3.	(c)	10.	(d)	17.	(d)
4.	(b)	11.	(d)	18.	(d)
5.	(d)	12.	(c)	19.	(c)
6.	(b)	13.	(d)	20.	(d)
7.	(d)	14.	(c)		

Chapter 2

1.	(c)	8.	(d)	15.	(b)
2.	(b)	9.	(d)	16.	(c)
3.	(d)	10.	(d)	17.	(b)
4.	(c)	11.	(c)	18.	(a)
5.	(a)	12.	(a)	19.	(d)
6.	(d)	13.	(b)	20.	(a)
7.	(b)	14.	(d)		

Chapter 3

1.	(b)	5.	(d)	9.	(b)
2.	(d)	6.	(a)	10.	(d)
3.	(b)	7.	(d)	11.	(b)
4.	(b)	8.	(c)	12.	(a)

13. (c)	18. (c)	23. (c)
14. (c)	19. (b)	24. (c)
15. (c)	20. (d)	25. (b)
16. (b)	21. (a)	
17. (a)	22. (c)	

Chapter 4

1. (b)	8. (c)	15. (b)
2. (c)	9. (a)	16. (b)
3. (a)	10. (c)	17. (a)
4. (b)	11. (b)	18. (b)
5. (b)	12. (b)	19. (b)
6. (d)	13. (d)	20. (a)
7. (b)	14. (d)	

Chapter 5

1. (d)	10. (c)	19. (c)
2. (d)	11. (a)	20. (a)
3. (c)	12. (b)	21. (b)
4. (b)	13. (c)	22. (d)
5. (d)	14. (a)	23. (a)
6. (a)	15. (b)	24. (a)
7. (b)	16. (c)	25. (c)
8. (d)	17. (a)	
9. (c)	18. (b)	

Chapter 6: Part 1

1. (d)	6. (a)	11. (a)
2. (d)	7. (b)	12. (c)
3. (b)	8. (c)	13. (a)
4. (d)	9. (c)	14. (d)
5. (d)	10. (a)	15. (c)

16. (b)	18. (c)	20. (d)
17. (b)	19. (a)	

(Hint: Question 3: Read legal description backward and divide to solve for acres. Thus, Section 5 has 640 acres, so the SW 1/4 of that totals 160 acres, and the NE 1/4 of that totals 40 acres. The word "and" or a comma means "the sum of." Next, go back to Section 5's 640 acres, then jump to the NW 1/4 of that, which is 160 acres, and then you can see that the E 1/2 of that is 80 acres. Now go back again to Section 5's 640 acres, then the SW 1/4 of that has 160 acres, and the NW 1/4 of that has 40 acres. Thus, 40 + 80 + 40 = 160 acres.)

Chapter 6: Part 2

1. (a)	8. (c)	15. (c)
2. (d)	9. (b)	16. (c)
3. (c)	10. (b)	17. (c)
4. (c)	11. (b)	18. (a)
5. (b)	12. (a)	19. (d)
6. (c)	13. (b)	20. (b)
7. (c)	14. (d)	

Chapter 7

1. (c)	8. (b)	15. (b)
2. (b)	9. (a)	16. (a)
3. (d)	10. (b)	17. (b)
4. (b)	11. (c)	18. (c)
5. (a)	12. (a)	19. (d)
6. (c)	13. (c)	20. (d)
7. (d)	14. (d)	

Chapter 8

1. (c)	5. (d)	9. (c)
2. (c)	6. (b)	10. (d)
3. (b)	7. (d)	11. (a)
4. (d)	8. (a)	12. (d)

13. (a)   16. (c)   19. (a)
14. (b)   17. (b)   20. (b)
15. (b)   18. (b)

Chapter 9: Part 1

1. (c)   5. (a)   9. (b)
2. (b)   6. (a)   10. (c)
3. (d)   7. (d)
4. (d)   8. (b)

Chapter 9: Part 2

1. (b)   5. (c)   9. (a)
2. (a)   6. (a)   10. (c)
3. (b)   7. (a)
4. (d)   8. (b)

Appendix Case Study

$1,245	Principal and interest
+ 175	Property taxes (2,100 ÷ 12)
+ 42	Property insurance and dues (504 ÷ 12)
+ 38	Private mortgage insurance (PMI)
$1,500	Total monthly housing payments

$33,000 + 34,000 = $67,000 per year ÷ 12 months = $5,583 per month

$1,500 ÷ $5,583 = 26.9%

$1,500	Total monthly housing payment
+ 375	Car payment
+ 125	Furniture payment
$2,000	Total monthly credit obligations

$2,000 ÷ $5,583 = 35.8%

Yes, they qualify for the loan.

Chapter 10

1. (b)   4. (a)   7. (c)
2. (c)   5. (c)   8. (c)
3. (d)   6. (c)   9. (d)

10. (a)   14. (b)   18. (a)
11. (c)   15. (b)   19. (d)
12. (c)   16. (a)   20. (b)
13. (b)   17. (b)

Chapter 11

1. (a)   8. (d)   15. (b)
2. (c)   9. (b)   16. (d)
3. (d)   10. (d)   17. (c)
4. (d)   11. (c)   18. (b)
5. (d)   12. (a)   19. (a)
6. (c)   13. (c)   20. (a)
7. (c)   14. (d)

Chapter 12

1. (a)   8. (d)   15. (b)
2. (a)   9. (d)   16. (b)
3. (a)   10. (d)   17. (b)
4. (b)   11. (a)   18. (b)
5. (b)   12. (d)   19. (a)
6. (d)   13. (a)   20. (d)
7. (b)   14. (c)

Chapter 13

1. (d)   9. (c)   17. (d)
2. (b)   10. (d)   18. (b)
3. (c)   11. (a)   19. (b)
4. (a)   12. (a)   20. (d)
5. (d)   13. (d)
6. (c)   14. (a)
7. (a)   15. (c)
8. (d)   16. (a)

Chapter 14

1.	(c)	8.	(a)	15.	(c)
2.	(c)	9.	(c)	16.	(b)
3.	(c)	10.	(d)	17.	(a)
4.	(b)	11.	(d)	18.	(d)
5.	(d)	12.	(b)	19.	(a)
6.	(a)	13.	(b)	20.	(a)
7.	(a)	14.	(c)		

Chapter 15

1.	(a)	8.	(d)	15.	(d)
2.	(a)	9.	(a)	16.	(d)
3.	(c)	10.	(c)	17.	(c)
4.	(b)	11.	(d)	18.	(d)
5.	(a)	12.	(b)	19.	(a)
6.	(c)	13.	(c)	20.	(c)
7.	(b)	14.	(d)		

GLOSSARY

A

ALTA Owner's Policy A residential owner's extended coverage policy that provides buyers or owners the same protection the ALTA policy gives to lenders. Also called an ALTA-R policy.

ALTA Title Policy An American Land Title Association–approved title policy. A type of title insurance policy that expands the risks normally insured against under the standard type of policy to include unrecorded mechanics' liens; unrecorded physical easements; facts a physical survey would show; water and mineral rights; and rights of parties in possession, such as tenants and buyers under unrecorded instruments.

Absolute Fee-Simple Title Title that is absolute and unqualified. It is the best title one can have.

Abstract of Judgment A condensation of the essential provisions of a court judgment.

Abstract of Title A summary or digest of the conveyances, transfers, and any other facts relied on as evidence of title, together with any other elements of record that may impair the title.

Abstraction A method of valuing land. The indicated value of the improvement is deducted from the sales price.

Acceleration Clause A clause in a trust deed or mortgage giving the lender the right to call all sums owed to the lender to be immediately due and payable upon the happening of a certain event.

Acceptance When the seller or agent's principal agrees to the terms of the agreement of sale and approves the negotiation on the part of the agent and acknowledges receipt of the deposit in subscribing to the agreement of sale.

Access Right The right of an owner to have ingress and egress to and from his or her property. Also called right of way.

Accretion An addition to land from natural causes as, for example, from gradual action of the ocean or river waters.

Accrued Depreciation The difference between the cost of replacement new as of the date of the appraisal and the present appraised value.

Accrued Items of Expense Those incurred expenses that are not yet payable. The seller's accrued expenses are credited to the purchaser in a closing statement.

Acknowledgment A formal declaration before a duly authorized officer by a person who has executed an instrument that such execution is his or her act and deed.

Acquisition The act or process by which a person procures property.

Acre A measure of land equaling 160 square rods, or 4,840 square yards, or 43,560 square feet, or a tract about 208.71 feet square.

Ad Valorem A Latin phrase meaning "according to value." Usually used in connection with real estate taxation.

Administrator/Administratrix A person appointed by the probate court to administer the estate of a person deceased.

Adjustable Rate Loan A mortgage where the interest rate may go up or down, thereby the monthly payment may decrease or increase over the life of the loan.

Advance Commitment The institutional investor's prior agreement to provide long-term financing upon completion of construction.

Advance Fee A fee paid in advance of any services rendered. The practice of obtaining a fee in advance for the advertising of property or businesses for sale. Said fees can be incorrectly obtained, thereby becoming a violation of real estate laws and regulations.

Adverse Possession The open and notorious possession and occupancy under an evident claim or right, in denial or opposition to the title of another claimant.

Affiant A person who makes an affidavit.

Affidavit A statement or declaration reduced to writing, sworn to or affirmed before some officer who has authority to administer an oath or affirmation.

Agency The relationship between principal and agent that arises out of a contract, either expressed or implied, written or oral, wherein the agent is employed by the principal to do certain acts dealing with a third party.

Agent One who represents another from whom he or she has derived authority.

Agreement of Sale A written agreement or contract between seller and purchaser in which they reach a meeting of minds on the terms and conditions of the sale. Often called a deposit receipt.

Air Rights The rights in real property to use the airspace above the surface of the land.

Alienation The transferring of property to another; the transfer of property and possession of lands or other things from one person to another.

Alienation Clause A clause that gives the lender the right to call a loan upon sale of real estate. Also called a due-on-sale clause.

Alluvion (Alluvium) Soil deposited by accretion; increase of earth on a shore or bank of a river.

Amenities Satisfaction of enjoyable living to be derived from a home; conditions of agreeable living or a beneficial influence arising from location or improvements.

AMO Accredited Management Organization.

Amortization The liquidation of a financial obligation on an installment basis; also, recovery, over a period, of cost or value.

Amortized Loan A loan that is completely paid off, interest and principal, by a series of regular payments that are equal or nearly equal. Also called a level payments loan.

Annual Percentage Rate (APR) Not an interest rate, but rather percentage rate that reflects the effective interest rate on the loan, including other prepaid financing charges such as loan fees, prepaid interest, and tax service fees.

Annuity A series of assured equal or nearly equal payments to be made over a period of time or a lump sum payment to be made in the future. The series of installment payments due to the landlord under a lease. The series of installment payments due to a lender. Real estate finance is most concerned with the first definition.

Anticipation, Principle of Affirms that value is created by anticipated benefits to be derived in the future.

Appraisal An estimate and opinion of value; a conclusion resulting from the analysis of facts.

Appraiser One qualified by education, training, and experience and tested by the state who is hired to estimate the value of real and personal property based on experience, judgment, facts, and use of formal appraisal processes.

Appreciation An increase in value that can result from inflation or from the interaction of supply and demand forces.

Appropriation of A legal term including the act or acts involved in the taking and reducing to personal possession of water occurring in a stream or another body of water and of applying such water to beneficial uses or purposes.

Appurtenance Something annexed to another thing that may be transferred incident to it. That which belongs to another thing, such as a barn, a dwelling, a garage, or an orchard, is incident to the land to which it is attached.

Architectural Style Generally, the appearance and character of a building's design and construction.

Assessed Valuation A valuation placed upon property by a public officer or board as a basis for taxation.

Assessed Value Value placed upon property as a basis for taxation.

Assessment The valuation of property for the purpose of levying a tax or the amount of the tax levied.

Assessor The official who has the responsibility of determining assessed values for property taxes.

Assignment A transfer or making over to another of the whole of any property, real or personal, in possession or in action, or of any estate or right therein.

Assignment of Lease The original lessee is removed from the transaction and the rights and duties pass to a new assignee, who is now primarily liable for the lease.

Assignor One who assigns or transfers property.

Assigns; Assignees Those to whom property is transferred.

Assumption Agreement An undertaking or adoption of a debt or an obligation resting primarily upon another person.

Assumption Fee A lender's charge for changing over and processing new records for a new owner who is assuming an existing loan.

Assumption of Mortgage The taking of title to property by a grantee, wherein he or she assumes liability for payment of an existing note secured by a mortgage or deed of trust against the property; becoming a coguarantor for the payment of a mortgage or deed of trust note.

Attachment Seizure of property by court order, usually done to have the property available in the event a judgment is obtained in a pending suit.

Attest To affirm to be true or genuine; an official act establishing authenticity.

Attorney in Fact One who is authorized to perform certain acts for another under a power of attorney; power of attorney may be limited to a specific act or acts or be general.

Avulsion The sudden tearing away or removal of land by action of water flowing over or through it.

Axial Growth City growth that occurs along main transportation routes. Usually takes the form of star shaped extensions outward from the center.

B

Backfill The replacement of excavated earth into a hole or against a structure.

Balloon Payment Where the final installment payment on a note is more than twice as great as the preceding installment payments, paying the note in full.

Baseboard A board placed against the wall around a room next to the floor.

Baseline and Meridian Imaginary lines used by surveyors to find and describe the location of private or public lands.

Batten Narrow strips of wood or metal used to cover joints interiorly or exteriorly; also used for decorative effect.

Beam A structural member transversely supporting a load.

Bearing Wall or Partition A wall or partition supporting any vertical load in addition to its own weight.

Bench Marks A location indicated on a durable marker by surveyors.

Beneficiary (1) One entitled to the benefit of a trust; (2) one who receives profit from an estate, the title of which is vested in a trustee; or (3) the lender on the security of a note and deed of trust.

Bequeath To give or hand down by will; to leave by will.

Bequest That which is given by the terms of a will.

Betterment An improvement upon property that increases the property value and is considered a capital asset, as distinguished from repairs or replacements where the original character or cost is unchanged.

Bilateral Contract Contract in which a promise from one person is made in exchange for a promise from another person.

Bill of Sale A written instrument given to pass title of personal property from the vendor to the vendee.

Binder An agreement to consider a down payment for the purchase of real estate as evidence of good faith on the part of the purchaser. Also, a notation of coverage on an insurance policy that is issued by an agent and given to the insured prior to the issuing of the policy.

Blacktop Asphalt paving used in streets and driveways.

Blanket Mortgage A single mortgage that covers more than one piece of real estate.

Board Foot A unit of measurement of lumber that is one foot wide, one foot long, and one inch thick; 144 cubic inches.

Bona Fide In good faith; without fraud.

Boot Unlike property received in an exchange that creates an income tax liability; for example, cash, notes, and personal property.

Bracing Framing lumber nailed at an angle to provide rigidity.

Breach The breaking of a law or failure of duty by either omission or commission.

Breezeway A covered porch or passage that is open on two sides and that connects the house and the garage or two parts of the house.

Bridging Small wood or metal pieces used to brace floor joists.

Broker A person employed by another for a fee to carry on any of the activities listed in the license law definition of a broker.

B.T.U. (British thermal unit) The quantity of heat required to raise the temperature of one pound of water by one degree Fahrenheit.

Building Code A systematic regulation of construction of buildings within a municipality established by ordinance or law.

Building Line A line set by law a certain distance from a street line in front of which an owner cannot build on his or her lot (a setback line).

Building, Market Value of The sum of money that the presence of a structure adds to or subtracts from the value of the land it occupies. Land valued on the basis of highest and best use.

Built-in Cabinets or similar features built as part of a house.

Bundle of Rights Rights the law designates that accompany ownership.

Buyer's Agent Real estate broker appointed by a buyer to be the buyer's agent to find property for the buyer.

C

California Association of Realtors (CAR) State affiliated group that provides services for California members.

California Housing Finance Agency Program (CalHFA) Program designed to help first-time homebuyers acquire a home in California's expensive housing market.

California Land Title Association (CLTA) Trade association for title insurance companies that issues standard policies of title insurance.

Cal-Vet Loan Loan made directly to a veteran by the state of California. The money is obtained from the sale of State Veteran Bonds.

California Fair Housing Act (Rumford Act) State law that forbids discrimination in the sale, rental, lease, or financing of practically all types of housing.

Capital Assets Assets of a permanent nature used in the production of an income, such as land, buildings, machinery, and equipment. Under income tax law, they are usually distinguishable from "inventory," which comprises assets held for sale to customers in ordinary course of the taxpayers' trade or business.

Capital Gain Income from the sale of an asset rather than from the general business activity. Capital gains are generally taxed at a lower rate than ordinary income.

Capitalization In appraising, determining value of property by considering net income and percentage of reasonable return on the investment. Thus, the value of an income property is determined by dividing annual net income by the capitalization rate.

Capitalization Rate The rate of interest that is considered a reasonable return on the investment and used in the process of determining value based on net income. It may also be described as the yield rate that is necessary to attract the money of the average investor to a particular kind of investment. This amortization factor can be determined in various ways; for example, by the straight-line depreciation method. (To explore this subject in greater depth, refer to current real estate appraisal texts.)

Casement Window Frames of wood or metal that swing outward.

Cash Flow The net income generated by a property before depreciation and other noncash expenses.

Caveat Emptor Let the buyer beware. The buyer must examine the goods or property and buy at his or her own risk.

CBD Central business district.

CC&Rs Covenants, conditions, and restrictions.

Center of Influence One who, by nature of his or her relationships, is in a position to sway others.

Central Business District (CBC) An area in a city's downtown core noted for its commercial, office, and other business-related activities.

Certificate of Reasonable Value (CRV) The Department of Veterans Affairs appraisal commitment of property value.

Certificate of Taxes Due A written statement or guarantee of the condition of the taxes on a certain property made by the county treasurer of the county in which the property is located.

Any loss resulting to any person from an error in a tax certificate is paid by the county the treasurer represents.

Chain A unit of measurement used by surveyors. A chain consists of 100 links equal to 66 feet.

Chain of Title A history of conveyances and encumbrances affecting the title from the time the original patent was granted or as far back as records are available.

Change, Principle of Holds that it is the future, not the past, that is of prime importance in estimating value.

Characteristics Distinguishing features of a (residential) property.

Chattel Mortgage A claim on personal property (instead of real property) used to secure or guarantee a promissory note. (See Security Agreement and Security Interest.)

Chattel Real An estate related to real estate, such as a lease on real property.

Chattels Goods or every species of property, movable or immovable, that are not real property.

Circuit Breaker An electrical device that automatically interrupts an electric circuit when an overload occurs. Used instead of a fuse to protect each circuit; can be reset.

Civil Rights Act of 1968 and 1988 Amendments Laws stating that within constitutional limits, fair housing should prevail throughout the United States.

Clapboard Boards, usually thicker at one edge, used for siding.

Clean Air Act Requires businesses (including real estate developers) to meet air quality standards.

Closing Costs Expenses paid by the buyer and the seller upon the sale of the property.

Closing Statement An accounting of funds made to the buyer and seller separately. Required by law to be made at the completion of every real estate transaction.

Cloud on the Title Any conditions revealed by a title search that affect the title to property; these are usually relatively unimportant items, but cannot be removed without a quitclaim deed or court action.

Code of Ethics (See Ethics.)

Collar Beam A beam that connects the pairs of opposite roof rafters above the attic floor.

Collateral The property subject to the security interest. (See Security Interest.)

Collateral Security A separate obligation attached to a contract to guarantee its performance; the transfer of property or of other contracts or valuables to ensure the performance of a principal agreement.

Collusion An agreement between two or more persons to defraud another's rights by the forms of law or to obtain an object forbidden by law.

Color of Title That which appears to be good title but which is not title in fact.

Commercial Acre A term applied to the remainder of an acre of newly subdivided land after the area devoted to streets, sidewalks and curbs, and so on has been deducted from the acre.

Commercial Banks Operate under license or charter from the state of federal government.

Commercial Paper Bills of exchange used in commercial trade.

Commingling A broker has mixed the funds of his or her principal with the broker's own money.

Commission An agent's compensation for performing agency duties; in real estate practice, a percentage of the selling price of property, percentage of rentals, and so on.

Commitment A pledge or a promise or firm agreement.

Common Interest Developments Projects with individual ownership of buildings and common ownership of land; for example, condominiums and planned unit developments.

Common Law The body of law that grew from customs and practices developed and used in England "since the memory of man runneth not to the contrary."

Community A part of a metropolitan area that has a number of neighborhoods that have a tendency toward common interests and problems.

Community Property Property accumulated through joint efforts of a married couple or registered domestic partners.

Compaction Whenever extra soil is added to a lot to fill in low places or to raise the level of the lot, the added soil is often too loose and soft to sustain the weight of the buildings. Therefore, it is necessary to compact the added soil so it can carry the weight of buildings without the danger of their tilting, settling, or cracking.

Comparable Sales Sales that have similar characteristics as the subject property and are used for analysis in the appraisal process.

Competent Legally qualified.

Competition, Principle of Holds that profits tend to breed competition and that excess profits tend to breed ruinous competition.

Component One of the features making up the whole property.

Compound Interest Interest paid on original principal and on the accrued and unpaid interest that has accumulated.

Conclusion The final estimate of value realized from facts, data, experience, and judgment.

Condemnation The act of taking private property for public use by a political subdivision; declaration that a structure is unfit for use.

Condition A qualification of an estate granted that can be imposed only in conveyances. They are classified as conditions precedent and conditions subsequent.

Condition Precedent A condition that requires a certain action or the happening of a specified event before the estate granted can take effect; for example, most installment real estate sales contracts, which state that before the buyer can demand transfer of title, all payments shall be made at the time specified.

Condition Subsequent When there is a condition subsequent in a deed, the title vests immediately in the grantee. But upon breach of the condition, the grantor has the power to terminate the estate; for example, a condition in the deed prohibiting the grantee from using the premises as a liquor store.

Conditional Commitment A commitment of a definite loan amount for some future unknown purchaser of satisfactory credit standing.

Conditional Sales Contract A contract for the sale of property stating that delivery is to be made to the buyer but title is to remain vested in the seller until the conditions of the contract have been fulfilled. (See Security Interest.)

Condominium A system of individual fee ownership of units in a multifamily structure combined with joint ownership of common areas of the structure and the land. (Sometimes referred to as a vertical subdivision.)

Conduit Usually, a metal pipe in which electrical wiring is installed.

Confession of Judgment An entry of judgment upon the debtor's voluntary admission or confession.

Confirmation of Sale A court approval of the sale of property by an executor, an administrator, a guardian, or a conservator.

Confiscation The seizing of property without compensation.

Conformity, Principle of Holds that the maximum of value is realized when a reasonable degree of homogeneity of improvements is present.

Conservation The process of utilizing resources in such a manner that minimizes their depletion.

Consideration Anything of value given to induce one entering into a contract; it may be money, personal services, or even love and affection.

Constant The percentage that, when applied directly to the face value of a debt, develops the annual amount of money necessary to pay a specified net rate of interest on the reducing balance and to liquidate the debt in a specified time period. For example, a 6% loan with a 20-year amortization has a constant of approximately 8½%. Thus, a $10,000 loan amortized over 20 years requires an annual payment of approximately $850.

Construction Loans Loans made for the construction of homes or commercial buildings. Usually, funds are disbursed to the contractor-builder during construction and after periodic inspections. Disbursements are based on an agreement between borrower and lender.

Constructive Eviction Breach of a covenant of warranty or quiet enjoyment; for example the inability of a lessee to obtain possession because of a paramount defect in title or a condition making occupancy hazardous.

Constructive Notice Notice given by the public records.

Consumer Goods Used or bought for use primarily for personal, family, or household purposes.

Contour The surface configuration of land.

Contract An agreement, either written or oral, to do or not to do certain things.

Contribution, Principle of Holds that maximum real property values are achieved when the improvements on the site produce the highest (net) return, commensurate with the investment.

Conventional Mortgage A mortgage securing a loan made by investors without governmental underwriting; that is, not FHA insured or VA guaranteed.

Conversion Change from one character or use to another.

Conveyance As a verb, refers to the process of transferring title to property from one person to another. As a noun, refers to the document used to effect the transfer of title (usually some kind of deed).

Cooperative Ownership A form of apartment ownership. Ownership of shares in a cooperative venture that entitles the owner to use, rent, or sell a specific apartment unit. The corporation usually reserves the right to approve certain actions, such as a sale or an improvement.

Corner Influence Table A statistical table used to estimate the added value of a corner lot.

Corporation A group or body of persons established and treated by law as an individual or unit with rights and liabilities or both, distinct and apart from those of the persons composing it. A corporation is a creature of law having certain powers and duties of a natural person. Being created by law, it can continue for any length of time the law prescribes.

Corporeal Rights Possessory rights in real property.

Correction Lines A system of compensating for inaccuracies in the government rectangular survey system due to the curvature of the earth. Every fourth township line, 24-mile intervals, is used as a correction line on which the intervals between the north and south range lines are remeasured and corrected to a full six miles.

Correlate the Findings To interpret the data and value estimates to bring them together to a final conclusion of appraised value.

Correlation The result of bringing the indicated values developed by the three appraisal approaches into mutual relationship with each other.

Cost A historical record of past expenditures or an amount given in exchange for other things.

Cost Approach One of three methods in the appraisal process. An analysis in which a value estimate of a property is derived by estimating the replacement cost of the improvements, deducting therefrom the estimated accrued depreciation, then adding the market value of the land.

Counterflashing Flashing used on chimneys at roofline to cover shingle flashing and to prevent moisture entry.

Counteroffer Automatically does away with the buyer's original offer; in effect, is merely an offer made by the seller to the buyer.

Covenant Agreements written into deeds and other instruments promising performance or nonperformance of certain acts or stipulating certain uses or nonuses of the property.

CPM Certified property manager; a designation of the Institute of Real Estate Management.

Crawl Space An exterior or interior opening permitting access underneath a building, as required by building codes.

CRB Certified residential broker.

Credit Unions Mutual, voluntary-membership, cooperative organization of people who agree to save their money together to provide money for loans to each other.

Cubage The number or product resulting from the multiplication of the width of a thing by its height and by its depth and length.

Curable Depreciation Items of physical deterioration and functional obsolescence that are customarily repaired or replaced by a prudent property owner.

Curtail Schedule A listing of the amounts by which the principal sum of an obligation is to be reduced by partial payments and of the dates when each payment will become payable.

Curtesy The right that a husband has in his wife's estate at her death.

D

Damages The indemnity recoverable by a person who has sustained an injury, in his or her person, property, or relative rights, through the act or default of another.

Data Plant An appraiser's file of information on real estate.

Debenture Bonds issued without security.

Debtor The party who "owns" the property that is subject to the security interest—previously known as the mortgagor or the pledgor.

Deciduous Trees Trees that lose their leaves in the autumn and winter.

Deck Usually, an open porch on the roof of a ground or lower floor, porch, or wing.

Decree of Foreclosure Decree by a court in the completion of foreclosure of a mortgage, contract, or lien.

Dedication An appropriation of land by its owner for some public use accepted for such use by authorized public officials on behalf of the public.

Deed Written instrument that, when properly executed and delivered, conveys title.

Deed Restriction A limitation in the deed to a property that dictates certain uses that may or may not be made of the property.

Default Failure to fulfill a duty or promise or to discharge an obligation; omission or failure to perform any act.

Defeasance Clause The clause in a mortgage that gives the mortgagor the right to redeem his or her property upon the payment of obligations to the mortgagee.

Defeasible Fee Sometimes called a base fee or qualified fee; a fee-simple absolute interest in land that is capable of being defeated or terminated upon the happening of a specified event.

Deferred Maintenance Existing but unfulfilled requirements for repairs and rehabilitation.

Deficiency Judgment A judgment given when the security pledge for a loan does not satisfy the debt upon its default.

Depreciation Loss of value in real property brought about by age, physical deterioration, or functional or economic obsolescence. Broadly, a loss in value from any cause.

Depth Table A statistical table used to estimate the value of the added depth of a lot.

Desist and Refrain Order An order directing a person to desist and refrain from committing an act in violation of the real estate law.

Deterioration Impairment of condition. One of the causes of depreciation and reflecting the loss in value brought about by wear and tear, disintegration, use in service, and the action of the elements.

Devisee One who receives a bequest made by will.

Devisor One who bequeaths by will.

Directional Growth The location or direction toward which the residential sections of a city are destined or determined to grow.

Discount An amount deducted in advance from the principal before the borrower is given the use of the principal. (See Point[s].)

Disintermediation The relatively sudden withdrawal of substantial sums of money that savers have deposited with savings banks, commercial banks, and mutual savings banks. This term also includes life insurance policy purchasers borrowing against the value of their policies. The essence of this phenomenon is that within a short period of time, financial intermediaries lose billions of dollars as owners of funds held by those institutional lenders exercise their prerogative of withdrawing their money from these financial institutions.

Disposable Income The after-tax income a household receives to spend on personal consumption.

Dispossess To deprive one of the use of real estate.

Documentary Transfer Tax A state-enabling act that allows a county to adopt a documentary transfer tax to apply on all transfers of real property located in the county. Notice of payment is entered on the face of the deed or on a separate paper filed with the deed.

Dominant Tenement Term used in connection with right-of-way rights and is the property that benefits from the use of the easement.

Donee A person to whom a gift is made.

Donor A person who makes a gift.

Dower The right that a wife has in her husband's estate at his death.

Dual Agency Where a broker represents the buyer and the seller in a real estate transaction.

Duress Unlawful constraint exercised upon a person whereby the person is forced to do some act unwillingly.

E

Earnest Money The down payment made by a purchaser of real estate as evidence of good faith.

Easement Created by grant or agreement for a specific purpose, an easement is the right, privilege, or interest one party has in the land of another; for example, right of way.

Easement in Gross An easement that does not have a dominant tenement.

Eaves The lower part of a roof projecting over the wall.

Ecology The relationship between organisms and their environment.

Economic Life The period over which a property will yield a return on the investment, over and above the economic or ground rent due to land.

Economic Obsolescence A loss in value caused by factors away from the subject property but adversely affecting the value of the subject property.

Economic Rent The reasonable rental expectancy if the property were available for renting at the time of its valuation.

Effective Age of Improvement The number of years of age that is indicated by the condition of the structure.

Effective Interest Rate The percentage of interest that is actually being paid by a borrower for the use of money.

Emblements Growing vegetable crops.

Eminent Domain The right of the government to acquire property for necessary public or quasi-public use by condemnation; the owner must be fairly compensated. The right of the government to do this and the right of the private citizen to get paid is spelled out in the Fifth Amendment to the U.S. Constitution.

Encroachment Trespass The building of a structure or construction of any improvements partly or wholly on the property of another.

Encumbrance Anything that affects or limits the fee simple title to property, such as mortgages, easements, or restrictions of any kind. Liens are special encumbrances that make the property security for the payment of a debt or an obligation, such as mortgages and taxes.

Endorsement The act of signing one's name on the back of a check or note, with or without further qualification.

Equal Credit Opportunity Act Federal law that prohibits lenders, when granting a loan, from discriminating based on a borrower's sex, race, color, religion, age, marital status, or handicap, in addition to other items.

Equity The interest or value an owner has in real estate over and above the liens against it; branch of remedial justice by and through which relief is afforded to suitors in courts of equity.

Equity of Redemption The right to redeem property during the foreclosure period, such as a mortgagor's right to redeem.

Equity Sharing Where an owner-occupant and a non-owner investor pool their money to buy a home. A contract sets out the arrangements between the occupying owner and the non-occupying investor.

Erosion The wearing a way of land by the action of water, wind, rain, or glacial ice.

Escalation The right reserved by the lender to increase the amount of the payments and/or interest upon the happening of a certain event.

Escalator Clause A clause in a contract providing for the upward or downward adjustment of certain items to cover specified contingencies.

Escheat The reverting of property to the state when heirs capable of inheriting are lacking.

Escrow The deposit of instruments and funds with instructions to a third neutral party to carry out the provisions of an agreement or a contract; when everything is deposited to enable carrying out the instructions, it is called a complete or perfect escrow.

Estate As applied to the real estate practice, signifies the quantity of interest, share, right, or equity of which riches or fortune may consist in real property. The degree, quantity, nature, and extent of interest that a person has in real property.

Estate of Inheritance An estate that descends to heirs. All freehold estates are estates of inheritance, except estates for life.

Estate for Life A freehold estate; not an estate of inheritance, but one that is held by the life tenant for his or her own life or the life or lives of one or more other persons.

Estate from Period to Period An interest in land where there is no definite termination date but the rental period is fixed at a certain sum per week, month, or year. Also called a periodic tenancy.

Estate at Sufferance An estate arising when the tenant wrongfully holds over after the expiration of his or her term. The landlord has the choice of evicting the tenant as a trespasser or accepting such tenant for a similar term under the conditions of the tenant's previous holding. Also called a tenancy at sufferance.

Estate of Will The occupation of lands and tenements by a tenant for an indefinite period, terminable by one or both parties without notice. Estates of will are not recognized in California.

Estate for Years An interest in lands by virtue of a contract for the possession of them for a definite and limited period of time. A lease may be said to be an estate for years.

Estimated Remaining Life The period of time (years) it takes for improvements to become valueless.

Estoppel A doctrine that bars one from asserting rights that are inconsistent with a previous position or representation.

Ethics The branch of moral science, idealism, justness, and fairness dealing with the duties that a member of a profession or craft owes to the public, to clients or patrons, and to other professional members. Various real estate trade associations have codes of ethics that govern their members.

Eviction Dispossession by process of law. The act of depriving a person of the possession of lands in pursuance of the judgment of a court.

Exchange Officially called an Internal Revenue Code 1031exchange that allows an owner to trade one property for another and to defer the income tax.

Exclusive Agency Listing A written instrument giving one agent the right to sell property for a specified time but reserving the right of the owner to sell the property without the payment of a commission.

Exclusive Right-to-Sell Listing A written agreement between the owner and agent giving the agent the right to collect a commission if the property is sold by anyone during the term of the agreement.

Execute To complete, to make, to perform, to do, to follow out; to execute a deed; to make a deed, including especially signing, sealing, and delivering; to execute a contract is to perform the contract, to follow out to the end, to complete.

Executor/Executrix A person named in a will to carry out its provisions as to the disposition of the estate of a deceased person.

Expansible House A home designed for further expansion and additions in the future.

Expansion Joint A bituminous fiber strip used to separate units of concrete to prevent cracking caused by expansion as a result of temperature changes.

Expenses Certain items that appear on a closing statement in connection with a real estate sale.

Expressed Contract Contract wherein the parties have agreed to perform an act or acts verbally or under a written agreement.

Extended Coverage Originally established for real estate lenders, this policy requires the title company to make a physical inspection of the property and insures against certain unrecorded title risks excluded under the standard policy.

F

Facade Front of a building.

Fair Market Value The amount of money that would be paid for a property offered on the open market for a reasonable period of time with the buyer and the seller knowing all the uses to which the property could be put and with neither party being under pressure to buy or sell.

Fair Housing (See Open Housing Law.)

False Promise False statement about what the promise is going to do in the future.

Farmers Home Administration An agency of the Department of Agriculture. Its primary responsibility is to provide financial assistance for farmers and others living in rural areas where financing is not available on reasonable terms from private sources.

Federal Deposit Insurance Corporation (FDIC) An agency of the federal government that insures deposits at commercial banks and savings banks.

Federal Housing Administration (FHA) An agency of the federal government that insures mortgage loans.

Federal National Mortgage Association (FNMA) "Fannie Mae" A private corporation whose primary function is to buy and sell existing mortgages in the secondary market.

Fee An estate of inheritance in real property.

Fee Simple In modern estates, the terms fee and fee simple are substantially synonymous. The term "fee" is of Old English derivation. Fee-simple absolute is an estate in real property by which the owner has the greatest power over the title that it is possible to have, being an absolute estate. In modern use, it expressly establishes the title of real property in the owner, without limitation or end. The owner can dispose of it by sale, trade, or will.

FHA 203b Program The most important section for the average home buyer or real estate agent. Under this program anyone who is financially qualified is eligible. Their credit history is important but need not be perfect. The buyer must have a minimum cash investment but it can come from an approved gift from family members and certain non-profits. The borrower is allowed to carry more debt than most conventional lenders allow. The Mortgage Insurance Premium (MIP) must be obtained and can be either purchased up front or financed as part of the loan. The MIP added to the loan is allowed to exceed maximum FHA loan limits. Loans are available up to four units. The maximum FHA loan amounts vary from region to region.

Fidelity Bond A security posted for the discharge of an obligation of personal services.

Fiduciary A person in a position of trust and confidence, as between principal and broker; the broker as fiduciary owes certain loyalty that cannot be breached under the rules of agency.

Filtering Down The process of making housing available to successively lower-income groups.

Financial Intermediary Financial institutions such as commercial banks, savings banks, mutual savings banks, and life insurance companies that receive relatively small sums of money from the public and invest them in the form of large sums. A considerable portion of these funds are loaned on real estate.

Financing Statement An instrument filed to give public notice of the security interest and thereby protect the interest of the secured parties in the collateral. (See Security Interest and Secured Party.)

Finish Floor Finish floor strips are applied over wood joists, deadening felt, and diagonal sub-flooring before finish floor is installed; finish floor is the final covering on the floor: wood, linoleum, cork, tile, or carpet.

Fire Stop A solid, tight closure of a concealed space that is placed to prevent the spread of fire and smoke through such a space.

Fiscal Controls Federal tax revenue and expenditure policies used to control the level of economic activity.

Fixity of Location The physical characteristic of real estate that subjects it to the influence of its surroundings.

Fixtures Appurtenances attached to the land or improvements, which usually cannot be removed without agreement, as they become real property; for example, plumbing fixtures or store fixtures built into the property.

Flashing Sheet metal or other material used to protect a building from seepage of water.

Footing The base or bottom of a foundation wall, pier, or column.

Foreclosure Procedure whereby property pledged as security for a debt is sold to pay the debt in the event of default in payments or terms.

Forfeiture Loss of money or anything of value resulting from failure to perform.

Foundation The supporting portion of a structure below the first-floor construction or below grade, including the footings.

Franchise A specified privilege awarded by a government or business firm that awards an exclusive dealership.

Fraud The intentional and successful employment of any cunning, deception, collusion, or artifice used to circumvent, cheat, or deceive another person, whereby that person acts upon it to the loss of his or her property and legal injury.

Freehold An estate of indeterminable duration, such as fee simple or life estate.

Frontage Land bordering a street.

Front Foot Property measurement for sale or valuation purposes; the property measures by the front foot on its street line each front foot extending the depth of the lot.

Front Money The minimum amount of money necessary to initiate a real estate venture.

Frostline The depth of frost penetration in the soil. Varies in different parts of the country. Footings should be placed below this depth to prevent movement.

Full Performance All parties to the contract accomplish what they set out to do in the contract.

Functional Obsolescence A loss of value caused by adverse factors from within the structure that affect the utility of the structure.

Furring Strips of wood or metal applied to a wall or another surface to even it, to form airspace, or to give the wall an appearance of greater thickness.

Future Benefits The anticipated benefits the present owner will receive from property in the future.

G

Gable Roof A pitched roof with sloping sides.

Gambrel Roof A curb roof, having a steep lower slope with a flatter upper slope above.

General Lien A lien on all property of a debtor.

Gift Deed A deed for which the consideration is love and affection and where there is not material consideration.

Girder A large beam used to support beams, joists, and partitions.

Government National Mortgage Association (Ginnie Mae) Wholly owned corporation of the U.S. government, created in 1968 when Fannie Mae became a private corporation.

Grade Ground level at the foundation.

Graduated Lease A lease that provides for a varying rental rate, often based on future determination; sometimes rent is based on the result of periodical appraisals; used largely in long-term leases.

Grant A technical term used in deeds of conveyance of lands to signify an intent to transfer title.

Grant Deed A deed in which "grant" is used as the word of conveyance. The grantor implicitly warrants that he or she has not already conveyed to any other person and that the estate conveyed is free from encumbrances done, made, or suffered by the grantor or any person claiming under him or her, including taxes, assessments, and other liens.

Grantee The purchaser; a person to whom a grant is made.

Grantor Seller of property; one who signs a deed.

GRI Graduate, Realtors Institute.

Grid A chart used in rating borrower risk, property, and the neighborhood.

Gross Domestic Product (GDP) The total value of all goods and services produced in an economy during a given period of time using resources located in the country.

Gross Income Total income from property before any expenses are deducted.

Gross Lease Lease where the tenant pays a flat rental amount and the landlord is responsible for property taxes, hazard insurance, and maintenance.

Gross Rate A method of collecting interest by adding total interest to the principal of the loan at the outset of the term.

Gross Rent Multiplier A figure that, when multiplied by the gross income of a property, produces an estimate of value of the property.

Ground Lease An agreement for use of the land only; sometimes secured by improvements placed on the land by the user.

Ground Rent Earnings of improved property credited to earnings of the ground itself after allowance is made for earnings of improvements; often termed economic rent.

H

Habendum Clause The "to have and to hold" clause in a deed.

Header A beam placed perpendicular to joists and to which joists are nailed in framing for a chimney, a stairway, or another opening.

Highest and Best Use An appraisal phrase meaning that use which, at the time of an appraisal, is most likely to produce the greatest net return to the land and/or buildings over a given period of time; that use which will produce the greatest amount of amenities or profit. This is the starting point for appraisal.

Hip Roof A pitched roof with sloping sides and ends.

Holder in Due Course One who has taken a note, check, or bill of exchange in due course (1) before it was overdue, (2) in good faith and for value, and (3) without knowledge that it was previously dishonored and without notice of any defect at the time it was negotiated to him or her.

Holdover Tenant A tenant who remains in possession of leased property after the expiration of the lease term.

Holographic Will Document written, dated, and signed in its entirety in the handwriting of the maker. It requires no witnesses.

Homestead Law Designed to protect a homeowner's equity in a personal residence from forced sale by certain types of creditors.

Hundred Percent Location A city retail business location that is considered the best available for attracting business.

Hypothecate To give a thing as security without the necessity of giving up possession of it.

I

Implied Contract Contract wherein the parties have not formally agreed verbally or through a written agreement to perform an act.

Impounds A trust type of account established by lenders for the accumulation of funds to meet taxes, FHA mortgage insurance premiums, and/or future insurance policy premiums required to protect their security. Impounds are usually collected with the note payment.

Inclusionary Zoning An ordinance that requires a builder of new housing to set aside a designated number of units for low- and moderate-income people.

Income Approach One of the three methods in the appraisal process; an analysis in which the estimated gross income from the subject residence is used as a basis for estimating value along with gross rent multipliers derived.

Incompetent One who is mentally incompetent, incapable; any person who, though not insane, is, by reason of old age, disease, weakness of mind, or any other cause, unable, unassisted, to properly manage and take care of him or herself or property and, by reason thereof, is likely to be deceived or imposed upon by artful or designing persons.

Incorporeal Rights Nonpossessory rights in real estate.

Increment An increase. Most frequently used to refer to the increase of value of land that accompanies population growth and increasing wealth in the community. The term unearned increment is used in this connection since values are supposed to have increased without effort on the part of the owner.

Incurable Depreciation When the cost of the repair or remodel exceeds the value added to the property.

Independent Contractor An individual who is hired to accomplish results and little or no supervision is required.

Indirect Lighting Reflected from the ceiling or another object external to the fixture.

Injunction A writ or an order issued under the seal of a court to restrain one or more parties to a suit or proceeding from doing an act that is deemed to be inequitable or unjust in regard to the rights of some other party or parties in the suit or proceeding.

Input Data, information, and so on that is fed into a computer or another system.

Installment Contract Purchase of real estate wherein the purchase price is paid in installments over a long period of time; title is retained by seller, and upon default, the payments are forfeited. Also known as a land contract.

Installment Note A note that provides that payments of a certain sum or amount be paid on the dates specified in the instrument.

Installment Reporting A method of reporting capital gains by installments for successive tax years to minimize the impact of the totality of the capital gains tax in the year of the sale.

Institutional Lender A financial depository that gathers deposits from the general public and then invests these funds.

Instrument A written legal document created to effect the rights of the parties.

Interest The charge, in dollars, for the use of money for a period of time. In a sense, the "rent" paid for the use of money.

Interest Rate The percentage of a sum of money charged for its use.

Intestate A person who dies having made no will or a will that is defective in form, in which case the estate descends to the heirs at law or next of kin.

Involuntary Lien A lien imposed against property without consent of an owner; for example, taxes, special assessments, and federal income tax liens.

Irrevocable Incapable of being recalled or revoked; unchangeable.

Irrigation Districts Quasi-political districts created under special laws to provide for water services to property owners in the district; an operation governed to a great extent by law.

J

Jalousie A slatted blind or shutter like a Venetian blind, but used on the exterior to protect against rain as well as to control sunlight.

Jamb The side post or lining of a doorway, a window, or another opening.

Joint The space between the adjacent surfaces of two components joined and held together by nails, glue, cement, or mortar.

Joint Note A note signed by two or more persons who have equal liability for payment.

Joint Tenancy Joint ownership by two or more persons with right of survivorship; all joint tenants own equal interest and have equal rights in the property.

Joint Venture Two or more individuals or firms joining together on a single project as partners.

Joist One of a series of parallel beams to which the boards of a floor and ceiling laths are nailed; supported, in turn, by larger beams, girders, or bearing walls.

Judgment The final determination of a court of competent jurisdiction of a matter presented to it; money judgments provide for the payment of claims presented to the court or are awarded as damages.

Judgment Lien A legal claim on all property of a judgment debtor that enables the judgment creditor to have the property sold for payment of the amount of the judgment.

Junior Mortgage A mortgage second in lien to a previous mortgage.

Jurisdiction The authority by which judicial officers take cognizance of and decide causes; the power to hear and determine a cause; the right and power a judicial officer has to enter upon the inquiry.

L

Laches Delay or negligence in asserting one's legal rights.

Land Contract A contract ordinarily used in connection with the sale of property in cases where the seller does not wish to convey title until all or a certain part of the purchase price is paid by the buyer; often used when property is sold on a small down payment. (See Installment Contract and Installment Reporting.)

Land and Improvement Loan A loan obtained by the builder-developer for the purchase of land and to cover expenses for subdividing.

Landlord One who rents property to another.

Later Date Order The commitment for an owner's title insurance policy issued by a title insurance company that covers the seller's title as of the date of the contract. When the sale closes, the purchaser orders the title company to record the deed to purchaser and show that the examination covers this later date so as to establish the purchaser as owner of the property.

Lateral Support The support that the soil of an adjoining owner gives to a neighbor's land.

Lath A building material of wood, metal, gypsum, or insulating board fastened to the frame of a building to act as a plaster base.

Lease A contract between owner and tenant setting forth conditions upon which the tenant can occupy and use the property and the term of the occupancy.

Lease with Option to Buy Under this type of contract the property is rented for a period of time, at the end which the lessee is given the right to purchase per a set of agreed terms.

Leasehold Estate A tenant's right to occupy real estate during the term of the lease. This is a personal property interest.

Legal Description A description recognized by law; a description by which property can be definitely located by reference to government surveys or approved recorded maps; for example, Lot, Block, and Tract; U.S. Government Survey; and Metes and Bounds.

Less-Than-Freehold Estate An interest held by tenants who rent or lease property.

Lessee One who contracts to rent property under a lease contract.

Lessor An owner who enters into a lease with a tenant.

Level-Payment Mortgage A loan on real estate that is paid off by making a series of equal (or nearly equal) regular payments. Part of the payment is usually interest on the loan, and part of it reduces the amount of the unpaid balance of the loan. Also sometimes called an amortized mortgage.

Leverage The use of borrowed funds to obtain an asset.

Lien A form of encumbrance that usually makes property security for the payment of a debt or discharge of an obligation; for example, judgments, taxes, mortgages, and deeds of trust.

Life Estate An estate or interest in real property that is held for the duration of the life of some certain person.

Life Insurance Companies Can be a source for real estate financing, particularly for large commercial and industrial properties such as shopping centers, office buildings, and warehouses. Life insurance companies also provide a significant amount of money for new housing subdivisions.

Limited Partnership A partnership composed of some partners whose contribution and liability are limited.

Lintel A horizontal board that supports the load over an opening such as a door or window.

Liquidated Damages A sum agreed upon by the parties to be full damages if a certain event occurs.

Liquidity The ability to convert your investment to cash quickly.

Lis Pendens Suit pending, usually recorded so as to give constructive notice of pending litigation.

Listing An employment contract between principal and agent authorizing the agent to perform services for the principal involving the latter's property; listing contracts are entered into for the purpose of securing persons to buy, lease, or rent property. Employment of an agent by a prospective purchaser or lessee to locate property for purchase or lease may be considered a listing.

Living Trust Created during a person's lifetime to avoid probate proceedings.

Loan Administration Mortgage bankers not only originate loans, but also "service" them from origination to maturity of the loan. Also called loan servicing.

Loan Application A source of information on which the lender decides whether to make the loan; defines the terms of the loan contract; gives the name of the borrower, place of employment, salary, bank accounts, and credit references; and describes the real estate that is to be mortgaged. It also stipulates the amount of the loan being applied for and repayment terms.

Loan Closing When all conditions have been met, the loan officer authorizes the recording of the trust deed or mortgage. The disbursal procedure of funds is similar to the closing of a real estate sales escrow. The borrower can expect to receive less than the amount of the loan (as title, recording, service, and other fees may be withheld), or he or she can expect to deposit the cost of these items into the loan escrow. This process is sometimes called funding the loan.

Loan Commitment Lender's contractual commitment to a loan based on the appraisal and underwriting.

Loan Qualification Ratios One of the methods a lender uses to qualify a borrower.

Louver An opening with a series of horizontal slats set at an angle to permit ventilation without admitting rain or sunlight.

M

MAI Member of the Appraisal Institute. Designates a person who is a member of the American Institute of Real Estate Appraisers.

Margin of Security The difference between the amount of the mortgage loan(s) and the appraised value of the property.

Marginal Land Land that barely pays the cost of working or using.

Market Data Approach One of the three methods in the appraisal process. A means of comparing similar types of residential properties that have recently sold to the subject property.

Market Price The price paid regardless of pressures, motives, or intelligence.

Market Value The price at which a willing seller would sell and a willing buyer would buy, neither being under abnormal pressure. As defined by the courts, the highest price estimated in terms of money that a property will bring if exposed for sale in the open market, allowing a reasonable time to find a purchaser with knowledge of the property's use and capabilities for use.

Marketable Title Merchantable title; title free and clear of objectionable liens or encumbrances.

Material Fact One the agent should realize will likely affect the judgment of the principal in giving consent to the agent to enter into the particular transaction on the specified terms.

Mechanic's Lien A lien created by statute that exists against real property in favor of persons who have performed work or furnished materials for the improvement of the real estate.

Metes and Bounds A term used in describing the boundary lines of land, setting forth all the boundary lines together with their terminal points and angles.

Minor Any person under 18 years of age.

Misplaced Improvements Improvements on land that do not conform to the most profitable use of the site.

Mobile Home Defined by California health and safety code as "a vehicle designed and equipped to contain no more than two dwelling units, to be used without a permanent foundation."

Modular A building composed of modules constructed on an assembly line in a factory. Usually, the modules are self-contained.

Moldings Usually, patterned strips used to provide ornamental variation of outline or contour, such as cornices, bases, and window and door jambs.

Monetary Controls Federal Reserve tools for regulating the availability of money and credit to influence the level of economic activity.

Monument A fixed object and point established by surveyors to establish land locations.

Moratorium The temporary suspension, usually by statute, of the enforcement of liability for debt.

Mortgage An instrument recognized by law by which property is hypothecated to secure the payment of a debt or an obligation; the procedure for foreclosure in the event default is established by statute.

Mortgage Bankers Lend their own money and then either resell the loan to another lender or keep the loan for an investment.

Mortgage Brokers Do not lend their own money. Instead, they find a lender and a borrower and get a fee for bringing them together.

Mortgage Companies Place more home loans than do institutional lenders.

Mortgage Contracts with Warrants Warrants make the mortgage more attractive to the lender by providing the greater security that goes with a mortgage and a greater return through the right to buy stock in the borrower's company or a portion of the income property itself.

Mortgage Insurance Insurance against financial loss available to mortgage lenders to protect against loss resulting from default by borrowers.

Mortgagee One to whom a mortgagor gives a mortgage to secure a loan or performance of an obligation; a lender. (See Secured Party.)

Mortgagor One who gives a mortgage on his or her property to secure a loan or assure performance of an obligation; a borrower. (See Debtor.)

Multiple Listing A listing, usually an exclusive right to sell, taken by a member of an organization composed of real estate brokers with the provision that all members will have the opportunity to find an interested client; a cooperative listing.

Mutual Water Company A water company organized by or for water users in a given district with the goal of securing an ample water supply at a reasonable rate; stock is issued to users.

N

NAR National Association of REALTORS®.

NAREB National Association of Real Estate Brokers.

Narrative Appraisal An extensive written report of all factual materials, techniques, and appraisal methods used by an appraiser to determine value.

National Environmental Policy Act requiring an environmental impact report on all projects using federal funding.

Negative Amortized Note The loan payment does not cover even the monthly interest. Each month this shortage is added to the principal owed, resulting in an increased loan balance, which in turn, incurs additional interest.

Negotiable Capable of being negotiated; assignable or transferable in the ordinary course of business.

Net Lease Sometimes referred as a triple net lease. The tenant pays rent along with the landlord's property taxes, hazard insurance, and maintenance.

Net Listing A listing with the provision that the agent retains as compensation all sums received over and above a net price to the owner.

Nominal Interest Rates The percentage of interest stated in loan documents.

Non-Institutional Lenders Do not accept deposits from the general public and are not as strictly regulated as institutional lenders.

Notary Public An appointed officer with authority to take the acknowledgment of persons executing documents, to sign the certificate, and to affix a seal.

Note A signed written instrument acknowledging a debt and promising payment.

Notice Actual knowledge acquired by being present at the occurrence.

Notice of Completion Document that an owner of real property files at the County Recorder's office once construction work on the property is completed.

Notice of Nonresponsibility A notice provided by law designed to relieve a property owner from responsibility for the cost of work done by a tenant on the property or materials furnished therefore notice must be verified, recorded, and posted.

Notice to Quit A notice to a tenant to vacate rented property.

O

Offset Statement Statement by owner of property or owner of lien against property, setting forth the present status of liens against said property.

Open-End Mortgage A mortgage containing a clause that permits the mortgagor to borrow additional money after the loan has been reduced without rewriting the mortgage.

Open Housing LAW Passed by Congress in 1968 and 1988 to prohibit discrimination in the sale of real estate because of race, color, religion, sex, or handicap of buyers.

Open Listing An authorization given by a property owner to a real estate agent wherein said agent is given the nonexclusive right to secure a purchaser; open listings may be given to any number of agents without liability to compensate any except the one who first secures a buyer ready, willing, and able to meet the terms of the listing or who first secures acceptance by the seller of a satisfactory offer.

Opinion of Title An attorney's evaluation of the condition of the title to a parcel of land after examination of the abstract of title to the land.

Option A right given for a consideration to purchase or lease a property upon specified terms within a specified time.

Oral Contract A verbal agreement; one that is not reduced to writing.

Orientation Placing a house on its lot with regard to its exposure to the rays of the sun, prevailing winds, privacy from the street, and protection from outside noises.

Overhang The part of the roof extending beyond the walls to shade buildings and to cover walks.

Overimprovement An improvement that is not the highest and best use for the site on which it is placed by reason of excess size or cost.

Ownership in Severalty When a person acquires real property and holds title solely in his or her own name.

P

Participation In addition to base interest on mortgage loans on income properties, a small percentage of gross income is required, sometimes predicated on the fulfillment of certain conditions, such as minimum occupancy or a percentage of net income after expenses, debt service, and taxes.

Partition Action Court proceedings by which co-owners seek to sever their joint ownership.

Partnership A decision of the California Supreme Court has defined a partnership in the following terms: "A partnership as between partners themselves may be defined to be a contract of two or more persons to unite their property, labor or skill, or some of them, in prosecution of some joint or lawful business, and to share the profits in certain proportions."

Party Wall A wall erected on the line between two adjoining properties, which are under different ownership, for the use of both properties.

Par Value Market value, nominal value.

Patent Conveyance of title to government land.

Penalty An extra payment or charge required of the borrower for deviating from the terms of the original loan agreement. Usually levied for being late in making regular payment or for paying off the loan before it is due.

Penny The term, as applied to nails, serves as a measure of nail length and is abbreviated by the letter d.

Percentage Lease Lease on the property, the rental for which is determined by the amount of business done by the lessee; usually, a percentage of gross receipts from the business with provision for a minimum rental.

Perimeter Heating Baseboard heating, or any system in which the heat registers are located along the outside walls of a room, especially under the windows.

Personal Property Any property that is not real property.

Physical Deterioration Impairment of condition. Loss in value brought about by wear and tear, disintegration, use, and actions of the elements.

Pier A column of masonry, usually rectangular in horizontal cross section, used to support other structural members.

Pitch The incline or rise of a roof.

Planned Unit Development (PUD) A land-use design that provides intensive utilization of the land through a combination of private and common areas with prearranged sharing of responsibilities for the common areas.

Planning Commission An appointed body of citizens charged with the responsibility of advising the elected board of supervisors or city council members in matters of land use.

Planning Departments Agencies within city and county government, staffed with professionally trained planners. The planning department employees provide technical services for planning commissions, elected officials, and citizens.

Plate A horizontal board placed on a wall or supported on posts or studs to carry the trusses of a roof or rafters directly; a shoe, or base member as of a partition or other frame; a small flat board placed on or in a wall to support girders, rafters, and so on.

Pledge The depositing of personal property by a debtor with a creditor as security for a debt or engagement.

Pledgee One who is given a pledge or a security. (See Secured Party.)

Pledgor One who offers a pledge or gives security. (See Debtor.)

Plottage Increment The appreciation in unit value created by joining smaller ownerships into one large single ownership.

Plywood Laminated wood made up in panels; several thicknesses of wood glued together with grain at different angles for strength.

Points Under certain loans, discounts, or points, paid to lenders are, in effect, prepaid interest and are used by lenders to adjust the effective interest rate so it is equal to or nearly equal to the prevailing market rate (the rate charged on conventional loans).

Police Power The right of the state to enact laws and enforce them for the order, safety, health, morals, and general welfare of the public.

Prefabricated House A house manufactured and sometimes partly assembled before delivery to the building site.

Prepaid Items of Expense Prorations of prepaid items of expense that are credited to the seller in the closing statement.

Prepayment Provision made for loan payments to be larger than those specified in the note.

Prepayment Penalty Penalty for the payment of a mortgage or trust deed note before it actually becomes due if the note does not provide for prepayment.

Present Value The lump-sum value today of an annuity. A $100 bill to be paid to someone in one year is worth less than if it were a $100 bill to be paid to someone today—for several reasons, one of which is that the money has time value. How much the $100 bill to be paid in one year is worth today will depend on the interest rate that seems proper for the particular circumstances. For example, if 6% is the appropriate rate, the $100 to be paid one year from now would be worth $94.34 today.

Presumption A rule of law that courts and judges shall draw a particular inference from a particular fact or from particular evidence unless and until the truth of such inference is disproved.

Prima Facie Presumptive on its face.

Principal The employer of an agent or the amount of money borrowed or the amount of a loan.

Principal Note The promissory note that is secured by the mortgage or trust deed.

Private Grant An owner voluntarily conveys his or her ownership rights to another.

Private Lenders Individuals who invest their savings in real estate loans either by directly granting loans to borrowers or by turning to mortgage brokers who find borrowers for the private lender.

Private Mortgage Insurance (PMI) Insurance used to guarantee lenders the payment of the upper portion of a conventional loan if a borrower defaults and a deficiency occurs at the foreclosure sale.

Privity Mutual relationship to the same rights of property; contractual relationship.

Probate An action that takes place in superior court, and the estate property may be sold during the probate period for the benefit of the heirs or to cover court costs.

Procuring Cause That cause originating from a series of events that, without break in continuity, results in the prime object of an agent's employment producing a final buyer.

Progression, Principle of The worth of a lesser valued residence tends to be enhanced by association with many higher-valued residences in the same area.

Promissory Note Following a loan commitment from the lender, the borrower signs a note, promising to repay the loan under stipulated terms. The promissory note establishes personal liability for its repayment.

Property The rights of ownership. The right to use, possess, enjoy, and dispose of a thing in every legal way and to exclude everyone else from interfering with these rights. Property is generally classified into two groups: personal property and real property.

Proposition 13 Limits real property taxes to one percent of the full cash value of the real property, plus an amount for local assessments and bonds.

Proration Adjustments of interest, taxes, and insurance on a pro rata basis as of the closing date. Fire insurance is normally paid for three years in advance. When a property is sold during this time, the seller wants a refund on that portion of the advance payment that has not been used at the time the title to the property is transferred. For example, when the property is sold two years later, the original buyer wants to receive one-third of the advance premium that was paid.

Proration of Taxes To divide or prorate taxes equally or proportionately to time of use.

Proximate Cause That cause of an event which, in a natural and continuous sequence unbroken by any new cause, produced that event and without which the event would not have happened. Also, the procuring cause.

Public Grant A governmental agency deeds property to an individual or an institution.

Public Report Report issued by the real estate commissioner which merely states that the subdivider has conformed to all laws and regulations.

Purchase and Installment Saleback Involves purchase of the property upon completion of construction and immediate saleback on a long-term installment contract.

Purchase of Land, Leaseback, and Leasehold Mortgages An arrangement whereby land is purchased by the lender and leased back to the developer with a mortgage negotiated on the resulting leasehold of the income property constructed. The lender receives an annual ground rent, plus a percentage of income from the property.

Purchase and Leaseback Involves the purchase of property subject to an existing mortgage and immediate leaseback.

Purchase Money Mortgage or Trust Deed A trust deed or mortgage given as part or all of the purchase consideration for property. In some states, the purchase money mortgage or trust deed loan can be made by a seller who extends credit to the buyer of property or by a third-party lender (typically a financial institution) that makes a loan to the buyer of real property for a portion of the purchase price to be paid for the property. (In many states, there are legal limitations upon mortgagees and trust deed beneficiaries collecting deficiency judgments against the purchase money borrower after the collateral hypothecated under such security instruments has been sold through the foreclosure process. Generally, no deficiency judgment is allowed if the collateral property under the mortgage or trust deed is residential property of four units or less with the debtor occupying the property as a place of residence.)

Q

Quantity Survey A highly technical process in arriving at a cost estimate of new construction, sometimes referred to in the building trade as the price take-off method. It involves a detailed estimate of the quantities of raw material (lumber, plaster, brick, cement) used, as well as the current price of the material and installation costs. These factors are added together to arrive at the cost of a structure. It is usually used by contractors and experienced estimators.

Quiet Title A court action brought to establish title; to remove a cloud on the title.

Quitclaim Deed A deed to relinquish any interest in property the grantor may have.

R

Radiant Heating A method of heating, usually consisting of coils or pipes placed in the floor, wall, or ceiling.

Rafter One of a series of boards of a roof designed to support roof loads. The rafters of a flat roof are sometimes called roof joists.

Range A strip of land six miles wide determined by a government survey, running in a north-to-south direction.

Ratification The adoption or approval of an act performed on behalf of a person without previous authorization.

Real Estate Association or Board An organization whose members consist primarily of real estate brokers and salespersons.

Real Estate Settlement Procedures Act A federal disclosure law effective June 20, 1975, requiring new procedures and forms for settlements (closing costs) involving federally related loans.

Real Estate Trust A special arrangement under federal and state law whereby investors pool funds for investments in real estate and mortgages and yet escape corporation taxes.

Realtist A real estate broker holding active membership in a real estate board affiliated with the National Association of Real Estate Brokers.

Realtor A real estate broker holding active membership in a real estate board affiliated with the National Association of REALTORS®.

Recapture The rate of interest necessary to provide for the return of an investment. Not to be confused with interest rate, which is a rate of interest on an investment.

Reconciliation (See Correlation.)

Recording The process of placing a document on file with a designated public official for everyone to see. This public official is usually a county officer known as the county recorder. The recorder designates the fact that a document has been given to him or her by stamping it and indicating the time of day and the date when it was officially placed on file. Documents filed with the recorder are considered to be placed on open notice to the general public of that county. Claims against property usually are given a priority on the basis of the time and the date they are recorded, with the most preferred claim status going to the earliest one recorded, the next claim going to the next earliest one recorded, and so on. This type of notice is called constructive notice or legal notice.

Recovery Fund Fund established by the state of California whereby the public can recover money when there are certain uncollectable court judgments obtained against a real estate licensee on the basis of fraud, misrepresentation, deceit, or conversion of trust funds in a transaction.

Redemption Buying back one's property after a judicial sale.

Refinancing The paying off of an existing obligation and assuming a new obligation in its place.

Reformation An action to correct a mistake in a deed or another document.

Registered Domestic Partnership Established when persons meeting the criteria specified by Family Code section 297 file a Declaration of Domestic Partnership with the Secretary of State of California.

Rehabilitation The restoration of a property to satisfactory condition without drastically changing the plan, form, or style of architecture.

Release Clause This is a stipulation that upon the payment of a specific sum of money to the holder of a trust deed or mortgage, the lien of the instrument as to a specific described lot or area shall be removed from the blanket lien on the whole area involved.

Release Deed An instrument executed by the mortgagee or the trustee reconveying to the mortgagor the real estate that secured the mortgage loan after the debt has been paid in full. Upon recording, it cancels the mortgage lien created when the mortgage or trust deed was recorded.

Remainder An estate that takes effect after the termination of the prior estate, such as a life estate.

Remainder Depreciation The possible loss in value of an improvement that will occur in the future.

Rental Offset Section 1942 of the Civil Code allows a tenant to spend up to one month's rent to make repairs. The repair bill can then be used to offset the next month's rent as long as some basic rules are followed.

Replacement Cost The cost to replace a structure with another having utility equivalent to that being appraised, but constructed with modern materials and according to current standards, design, and layout.

Reproduction Cost The cost of replacing the subject improvement with one that is the exact replica, having the same quality of workmanship, design, and layout.

Rescission of Contract The abrogation or annulling of contract; the revocation or repealing of contract by mutual consent by parties to the contract or for cause by either party to the contract.

Reservation A right retained by a grantor in conveying property.

RESPA Real Estate Settlement Procedures Act.

Restriction Relating to real property, the owner of real property is restricted or prohibited from doing certain things relating to the property or from using the property for certain purposes. Property restrictions fall into two general classifications—public and private. Zoning ordinances are examples of the former type. Restrictions can be created by private owners, typically by appropriate clauses in deeds or in agreements, or in the general plans of entire subdivisions. Usually, they assume the form of a covenant or promise to do or not to do a certain thing. They cover a multitude of matters, including use for residential or business purposes; for example, houses in tract must cost more than $100,000.

Reversion The right to future possession or enjoyment by the person or heirs creating the preceding estate.

Reversionary Interest The interest a person has in lands or other property upon the termination of the preceding estate.

Ridge The horizontal line at the junction of the top edges of two sloping roof surfaces. The rafters at both slopes are nailed at the ridge.

Ridge Board The board placed on edge at the ridge of the roof to support the upper ends of the rafters; also called roof tree, ridge piece, ridge plate, or ridgepole.

Right of Survivorship The right to acquire the interest of a deceased joint owner; a distinguishing feature of a joint tenancy.

Right of Way A privilege operating as an easement upon land, whereby the owner does by grant or by agreement give to another the right to pass over the land, construct a roadway, or use as a roadway; the right to a specific part of the land; the right to construct through and over the land telephone, telegraph, or electric power lines; or the right to place underground water mains, gas mains, or sewer mains.

Riparian Rights The right of a landowner to the water on, under, or adjacent to his or her land.

Riser The upright board at the back of each step of a stairway. In heating, a riser is a duct slanted upward to carry hot air from the furnace to the room above.

Risk Analysis A study made, usually by a lender, of the various factors that might affect the repayment of a loan.

Risk Rating A process used by a lender to decide on the soundness of making a loan and to reduce all the various factors affecting the repayment of the loan to a qualified rating of some kind.

S

Sale-Leaseback A situation where the owner of a piece of property wishes to sell the property and retain occupancy by leasing it from the buyer.

Sales Contract A contract by which buyer and seller agree to terms of a sale.

Sandwich Lease A leasehold interest that lies between the primary lease and the operating lease.

Sash Wood or metal frames containing one or more window panes.

Satisfaction The discharge of mortgage or trust deed lien from the records upon payment of the evidenced debt.

Satisfaction Piece An instrument for recording and acknowledging payment of an indebtedness secured by a mortgage.

Savings Bank (Savings and Loan) Financial institution that accepts savings from the public and invests these savings mainly in real estate trust deeds and mortgages.

Seal An impression made to attest the execution of an instrument; for example, a notary public's seal.

Secondary Financing A loan secured by a second mortgage or trust deed on real property. These can be third, fourth, fifth, sixth, and so on, ad infinitum.

Secondary Mortgage Market A market where existing real estate loans are bought and sold.

Secret Profit If the real estate agent derives any profit other than the agreed commission without disclosing the nature of the profits to the principal.

Section Section of land is established by government survey and contains 640 acres.

Secured Party The party having the security interest. Thus, the mortgagee, the conditional seller, the pledgee, and so on are all referred to as the secured party.

Security Agreement An agreement between the secured party and the debtor that creates the security interest.

Security Interest Designating the interest of the creditor in the property of the debtor in all types of credit transactions. It replaces such terms as the following: chattel mortgage, pledge, trust receipt, chattel trust, equipment trust, conditional sale, and inventory lien.

Seizin Possession of real estate by one entitled thereto.

Self-Contained Appraisal Report (See Narrative Report.)

Seller's Agent The seller appoints a real estate broker to find a buyer for the seller's property.

Separate Property Property owned by a husband or wife or registered domestic partners that is not community property; property acquired by either spouse or registered domestic partners prior to marriage or registered domestic partnership or by gift or device after marriage or registered domestic partnership.

Septic Tank An underground tank in which sewage from a house is reduced to liquid by bacterial action and drained off.

Servicing Supervising and administering a loan after it has been made. This involves such things as collecting payments, keeping accounting records, computing interest and principal, foreclosing on defaulted loans, and so on.

Servient Tenement Property that is subject to an easement or upon which the easement is imposed.

Severalty Ownership Owned by one person only; sole ownership.

Shake A hand-split shingle, usually edge grained.

Sheathing A structural covering, usually boards, plywood, or wallboards, placed over exterior studding or rafters of a house.

Sheriff 's Deed A deed given by court order in connection with sale of property to satisfy a judgment.

Shopping Center, Regional A large shopping center with 250,000 to 1,000,000 square feet of store area, serving 200,000 people or more.

Sill The lowest part of the frame of a house, resting on the foundation and supporting the uprights of the frame; the board or metal forming the lower side of an opening, as a door sill or windowsill.

Single Agency Where a broker represents either the buyer or the seller, not both, in a real estate transaction.

Sinking Fund A fund set aside from the income of property that, with accrued interest, will eventually pay for replacement of the improvements.

Six-Month Rule A homeowner with a valid formal declaration of homestead has six-months in which to invest his or her equity money into the purchase of another home, thereby continuing to protect the equity against creditors up to the exemption amount.

Soil Pipe A pipe carrying waste out off a house to the main sewer line.

Sole or Sole Plate A member, usually a two-by-four, on which wall and partition studs rest.

Span The distance between structural supports such as walls, columns, piers, beams, girders, and trusses.

Special Agency An agent has limited or well-defined powers, perhaps confined to a single transaction.

Special Assessment A legal charge against real estate by a public authority to pay the cost of public improvements such as streetlights, sidewalks, and street improvements.

Specific Liens Liens that attach to only a certain, specific parcel of land or piece of property.

Specific Performance An action to compel performance of an agreement; for example, the sale of land.

Standard Depth Generally, the most typical lot depth in a neighborhood.

Standard Policy The assurance that title is free and clear of all encumbrances of public record, other than the items revealed in the title examination and listed exceptions in the title policy.

Standby Commitment The mortgage banker frequently protects a builder by a "standby" agreement, under which the banker agrees to make mortgage loans at an agreed price for many months in the future. The builder deposits a "standby fee" with the mortgage banker for this service. Frequently, the mortgage banker secures a "standby" from a long-term investor for the same period of time, who pays a fee for this privilege.

Statute of Frauds State law that provides that certain contracts must be in writing in order to be enforceable; for example, a real property lease for more than one year and an agent's authorization to sell real estate.

Statute of Limitations States that you must begin the lawsuit within a legally prescribed time period.

Statutory Will A preprinted form approved by the state in which a person merely fills in the blanks, usually without formal legal assistance. This statutory will requires at least two witnesses.

Steering The unlawful directing of a perspective buyer or tenant to certain neighborhoods or the refusal to tell about the availability of housing in another neighborhood.

Stock Cooperative Corporation formed for the purpose of holding title to a building.

Straight-Line Depreciation A definite sum set aside annually from income to pay the cost of replacing improvements, without reference to interest it earns.

String, Stringer A timber or another support for cross members. In stairs, the support on which the stair treads rest.

Straight Note Commonly referred to as an "interest only" note. Under the straight note, the borrower agrees to pay the interest, usually monthly, and to pay the entire principal in a lump sum on the due date.

Studs or Studding Vertical supporting timbers in walls and partitions.

Subdivided Lands Act Defines a subdivision as the division of land into five or more lots for the purpose of sale, lease or financing, whether now or in the future.

Subdivision Map Act Covers the division of land into two or more lots for the purpose of sale, lease or financing, whether now or in the future.

Subject to Mortgage When a grantee takes a title to real property subject to mortgage, he or she is not responsible to the holder of the promissory note for the payment of any portion of the amount due. The most the grantee can lose in the event of a foreclosure is equity in the property. (See Assumption of Mortgage.) In neither case is the original maker of the note released from his or her responsibility.

Sublease A lease given by a lessee.

Subordinate To make subject to or junior to.

Subordination Clause A clause in a junior or a second lien permitting retention of priority for prior liens. A subordination clause is also used in a first deed of trust, permitting it to be subordinated to subsequent liens as, for example, the liens of construction loans.

Subpoena A process to cause a witness to appear and give testimony.

Subrogation The substitution of another person in place of the creditor, to whose rights the former succeeds in relation to the debt. The doctrine is often used when one person agrees to stand surety for the performance of a contract by another person.

Substitution, Principle of Affirms that the maximum value of a property tends to be set by the cost of acquiring an equally desirable and valuable substitute property, assuming no costly delay is encountered in making the substitution.

Succession The handing down of property to another person.

Sum of the Years Digits An accelerated depreciation method.

Summary Appraisal Report A uniform short-form appraisal frequently used for loan purposes.

Supply and Demand, Principle of Affirms that price or value varies directly, but not necessarily proportionally, with demand and inversely, but not necessarily proportionally, with supply.

Surety One who guarantees the performance of another; a guarantor.

Surplus Productivity, Principle of Affirms the net income that remains after the proper costs of labor, organization, and capital have been paid, which is imputable to the land and tends to fix the value thereof.

Survey The process by which a parcel of land is measured and its area is ascertained.

Syndicate A partnership organized for participation in a real estate venture. Partners may be limited or unlimited in their liability.

T

Take-Out Loan The loan arranged by the owner or builder-developer for a buyer. The construction loan made for construction of the improvements is usually paid from the proceeds of this loan.

Tax Sale Sale of property after a period of non-payment of taxes.

Tenancy in Common Ownership by two or more persons who hold undivided interest, without right of survivorship; interests need not be equal.

Tenancy in Partnership Exists when two or more persons, as partners, pool their interests, assets, and efforts in a business venture, with each to share in the profits or the losses.

Tentative Map The Subdivision Map Act requires subdividers to submit initially a tentative map of their tract to the local planning commission for study. The approval or disapproval of the planning commission is noted on the map. Thereafter a final map of the tract embodying any changes requested by the planning commission is required to be filed with the planning commission.

Tenure in Land The mode or manner by which an estate in lands is held.

Termite Shield A shield, usually of noncorrodible metal, placed on top of the foundation wall or around pipes to prevent passage of termites.

Termites Antlike insects that feed on wood.

Testator One who leaves a will in force upon death.

Threshold A strip of wood or metal beveled on each edge and used above the finished floor under outside doors.

Title Insurance Insurance written by a title company to protect property owner against loss if title is imperfect.

Title Report A report that discloses the condition of the title, made by a title company preliminary to issuance of title insurance.

Title Theory Mortgage arrangement whereby title to mortgaged real property vests in the lender.

Topography Nature of the surface of land; topography may be level, rolling, or mountainous.

Tort A wrongful act; wrong, injury; violation of a legal right.

Township A territorial subdivision six miles long and six miles wide containing 36 sections, each one mile square.

Trade Fixtures Articles of personal property annexed to real property, but which are necessary to the carrying on of a trade and are removable by the owner.

Trade-In An increasingly popular method of guaranteeing an owner a minimum amount of cash upon sale of present property to permit the purchase of another. If the property is not sold within a specified time at the listed price, the broker agrees to arrange financing to purchase the property at an agreed-upon discount.

Treads Horizontal boards of a stairway.

Treaty of Guadalupe Hidalgo Ended the war with Mexico and whereby California became a territory of the United States.

Trim The finish materials in a building, such as moldings, applied around openings (window trim, door trim) or at the floor and ceiling (baseboard, cornice, picture molding).

Trust Account An account separate and apart and physically segregated from broker's own funds in which a broker deposits funds collected for clients.

Trust Deed Just as with a mortgage, this is a legal document by which a borrower pledges certain real property or collateral as guarantee for the repayment of a loan. However, it differs from a mortgage in a number of important respects. For example, instead of having two parties to the transaction, there are three. There is the borrower, who gives the trust deed and who is called the trustor. There is the third neutral party (just as there is with an escrow), who receives the trust deed and who is called the trustee. And, finally, there is the lender, who is called the beneficiary because the lender benefits from the pledge arrangement. In the event of a default, the trustee can sell the property and transfer the money obtained at the sale to the lender as payment of the debt.

Trustee One who holds property in trust for another to secure the performance of an obligation.

Trust Funds Money or other items of value that an agent receives on behalf of a principal in the course of a real estate transaction that requires a license.

Trustor One who deeds property to a trustee to be held as security until the trustor has performed any obligations to a lender under terms of a deed of trust.

Truth-in-Lending Law Law with the purpose of helping borrowers understand how much it costs to borrow money.

U

Underimprovement An improvement that, because of its deficiency in size or cost, is not the highest and best use of the site.

Underwriting The technical analysis by a lender to determine the borrower's ability to repay a contemplated loan.

Undue Influence Taking any fraudulent or unfair advantage of another's weakness of mind or distress or necessity.

Unearned Increment An increase in value of real estate resulting from no effort on the part of the owner; often caused by an increase in population.

Unenforceable Contract A contract that appears to be valid, but it cannot be sued upon.

Uniform Commercial Code Establishes a unified and comprehensive scheme for the regulation of security transactions in personal property, superseding the existing statutes on chattel mortgages, conditional sales, trust receipts, assignment of accounts receivable, and others in this field.

Unilateral Contract Created by only one party extending a promise without a reciprocal promise by another party.

Unit-in-Place Method The cost of erecting a building by estimating the cost of each component part; that is, foundations, floors, walls, windows, ceilings, and roofs (including labor and overhead).

Unlawful Detainer Action Process of legally removing a tenant from possession which involves a series of steps.

Unruh Civil Rights Act State law that makes it unlawful for people engaging in business in California, including real estate agents, to discriminate when providing business products and services.

Usury On a loan, claiming a rate of interest greater than that permitted by law.

Utilities Refers to services rendered by public utility companies, such as water, gas, electricity, and telephone.

Utility The ability to give satisfaction and/or excite desire for possession.

V

VA Loans Department of Veteran's Affairs guarantees a portion of a loan.

Valid Having force or binding force; legally sufficient and authorized by law.

Valley The internal angle formed by the junction of two sloping sides of a roof.

Valuation Estimated worth or price; estimation: the act of valuing by appraisal.

Vendee A purchaser; buyer.

Vendor A seller; one who disposes of a thing in consideration of money.

Veneer Thin sheets of wood.

Vent A pipe installed to provide a flow of air to or from a drainage system or to provide a circulation of air within such system to protect trap seals from siphonage and back pressure.

Verification Sworn statement before a duly qualified officer to the correctness of contents of an instrument.

Vested Bestowed upon someone; secured by someone, such as a title to property.

Void To have no force or effect; that which is unenforceable.

Voidable That which is capable of being adjudged void, but is not void unless action is taken to make it so.

Voluntary Lien Any lien placed on property with consent of or as a result of the voluntary act of the owner.

W

Wainscoting Wood lining of an interior wall; lower section of a wall when finished differently from the upper part.

Waive To relinquish or abandon; to forego a right to enforce or require anything.

Warranty Deed A deed used to convey real property that contains warranties of title and quiet possession, and the grantor thus agrees to defend the premises against the lawful claims of third persons. It is commonly used in many states, but in others, the grant deed has supplanted it because of the modern practice of securing title insurance policies that have reduced the importance of express and implied warranty in deeds.

Waste The destruction of, or material alteration of, or injury to premises by a tenant for life or years.

Water Table The distance from surface of ground to a depth at which natural groundwater is found.

Will An instrument that leaves real estate of a decedent to an heir(s); for example, witnessed will, holographic will, and statutory will.

Witnessed Will A formal typewritten document signed by the individual who is making it, wherein he or she declares in the presence of at least two witnesses that it is his or her own will.

Writ of Execution An order from the court allowing the judgment holder to attach or seize real or personal property belonging to the judgment debtor.

Y

Yield The interest earned by an investor on his or her investment (or bank, on the money it has lent). Also called return.

Yield Rate The yield expressed as a percentage of the total investment. Also called rate of return.

Z

Zone The area set off by the proper authorities for specific use, subject to certain restrictions or restraints.

Zoning The act of city or county authorities specifying type of use to which property may be put in specific areas.

INDEX